CHURCHILL'S ARMY

1939–1945

CHURCHILL'S ARMY

1939–1945

Conway
BLOOMSBURY
LONDON · OXFORD · NEW YORK · NEW DELHI · SYDNEY

Conway
An imprint of Bloomsbury Publishing Plc

50 Bedford Square   1385 Broadway
London   New York
WC1B 3DP   NY 10018
UK   USA

www.bloomsbury.com
CONWAY and the 'C' logo are trademarks of Bloomsbury Publishing Plc

First published 2016
Text © Stephen Bull
Illustrations © see credits on individual images for detail of copyright holders.

British Library Cataloguing-in-Publication Data
A catalogue record for this book is available from the British Library.
Library of Congress Cataloguing-in-Publication data has been applied for.

ISBN: HB: 978-1-8448-6400-3
ePDF: 978-1-8448-6398-3
ePub: 978-1-8448-6399-0

2 4 6 8 10 9 7 5 3 1

Page design by CE Marketing
Printed and bound in China by C&C Offset Printing Co.

Bloomsbury Publishing Plc makes every effort to ensure that the papers used in the manufacture of our books are natural, recyclable products made from wood grown in well-managed forests. Our manufacturing processes conform to the environmental regulations of the country of origin.

To find out more about our authors and books visit www.bloomsbury.com. Here you will find extracts, author interviews, details of forthcoming events and the option to sign up for our newsletters.

Contents

Following Allied
invasion a Sherman
tank of a British
armoured unit moves
up to a new position
north of Ramacca,
Sicily, at sunset.
(Official/author)

Acknowledgements

ANY VOLUME THAT IS ENCYCLOPEDIC IN NATURE and claims any sort of thoroughness will inevitably draw upon a wide variety of people, books and collections. This study of Churchill's Army in the Second World War is no exception. A large number of works have been consulted, with the aim of bringing together knowledge accumulated over the years since 1945 by many of the leading lights in their specialist areas to create a work that is as comprehensive as possible in the limited space available. Nevertheless it has to be admitted that the key focus here is the fighting soldier and his weapons, dress and equipment for battle, rather than, say, an exhaustive study of engineering stores or soldiers' welfare. This is, indeed, also reflective of Churchill's own interests in 'his' army. The major sources consulted are listed in the bibliography and notes. The astute observer will note that whilst some of the leading secondary works are referred to, use has also been made of primary material – in the shape of manuals and instructions – and objects in museum collections.

Particular thanks are due to my many former colleagues at the National Army Museum, especially Michael Ball; to the staff of the Imperial War Museum, London, Salford Quays and Duxford; the Firepower Museum of the Royal Artillery; and to the staff of the Royal Armouries, Leeds. Likewise, I should like to highlight the long-term co-operation and assistance of Ian Hook, Curator of the Essex Regiment Museum; Andrew Robertshaw, Royal Logistics Corps; Jane Davies, Lancashire Infantry Museum; Colonel Mike Glover, Fusiliers Museum; Brigadier Colin Sibun, Army Museums Ogilby Trust; Colonel Martin Steiger, Duke of Lancaster's Own Yeomanry; Captain John Cornish, 14th/20th King's Hussars and King's Royal Hussars. Warm thanks are also due to Brigadier Ken Timbers; Colonel John Downham; Colonel John Tustin; Colonel Frank Hewitt; Colonel John Pharo-Tomlin; Captain Teddy Dickson; David Rogan; Ian Maine; John Anderson; Simon Jones, Ian Skennerton and Ray Westlake. Sadly, acknowledgment is made posthumously of Herbert Woodend, Anthony Carter and Peter Hayes, who were all experts in their respective fields and have had a very significant formative influence on the work that follows.

Introduction

OUR VIEW OF WINSTON S. CHURCHILL as pugnacious warrior, making morale-raising appeals for armed resistance to Nazism, or pictured clutching a Tommy gun or inspecting troops, alone make the title *Churchill's Army* highly apposite. Indeed, it will always be difficult to imagine Britain's wartime Prime Minister without at the same time calling to mind the ultimately victorious British Army of 1939 to 1945. Yet hindsight, propaganda and the imperative of the defeat of Hitler and Imperial Japan have led to a tendency to oversimplify the image of Churchill the war leader and 'his' Army in the popular mind. For whilst Churchill was undeniably a towering statesman – dynamic, mercurial and an inspiration in the way that most politicians of his era, indeed any era, were not – his relations with both the Army and the War Office were often ambiguous and altered considerably, and not only with the progress of the Second World War but over decades.[1]

Intriguingly, the young Winston was a soldier first and a politician a slightly belated second. Indeed, up until well after the point at which the Nazi Party came to power in 1933, Churchill had far more military experience than Hitler. Whilst the latter had served as a junior NCO and regimental runner in the First World War Churchill had an officer's experience of various conflicts stretching back into the nineteenth century, had commanded a battalion and been Secretary of State for War. As early as 1888, the year before the birth of Hitler, Winston joined the Rifle Corps at Harrow. On leaving school he required three attempts to pass the Sandhurst entrance exam, before what turned out to be a very successful period at the Royal Military Academy. From thence he was commissioned into the 4th Queen's Own Hussars. As a young subaltern in a cavalry regiment his pay was only £120, which was merely a fraction of what was needed to pay for his equipment and expenses. Winston appears to have been happy during his time with the unit, and in 1920 agreed to write a foreword to the regimental history. In the dark days of July 1940 he even found time to inspect the regiment, and the following year was made its colonel-in-chief.

Nevertheless, promotion to high command does not seem to have been the energetic young Winston's driving

ambition. Instead he looked for the most dangerous and challenging assignments, and sought to record them, as author or war correspondent. Family wealth and influence were not impediments to the fulfillment of this desire. In Cuba in 1895 he covered the War of Independence for the *Daily Graphic*, and it was not without some satisfaction that he was able to report coming under fire for the first time on his twenty-first birthday. It was also in Cuba that he acquired a taste for the local cigars. The following year he accompanied his regiment to India and fought in Malakand. In 1898 he transferred to Egypt, and in September of that year was on attachment to the 21st Lancers in the Sudan when they made their charge at the Battle of Omdurman.

His developing career of soldier–writer–adventurer was interrupted but briefly by the Oldham by-election, in which he was defeated, before departing for South Africa as a war correspondent for the *Morning Post*. Here occurred the celebrated incident in which Winston was captured when the armoured train in which he was travelling was ambushed. Though taken by the Boers to Pretoria as a prisoner of war he escaped and rejoined British forces, being amongst the first into the newly

Churchill in khaki and slouch hat during his service with the South African Light Horse, c.1899. (Hulton Archive/Getty Images)

Below right: Winston Churchill among a group of officers observing British Army manoeuvres on Salisbury Plain, 1910. (Hulton Archive/Getty Images)

Far right: On the quayside Churchill wears naval uniform as First Lord of the Admiralty, on the occasion of the return of the King and Queen from India, February 1912. (Topical Press Agency/Getty Images

relieved town of Ladysmith. Churchill finally entered Parliament in 1900: but this did not spell the end of his military connections, because two years later he joined the Yeomanry as an officer of the Queen's Own Oxfordshire Hussars, reaching the rank of major by 1905. Nevertheless, political concerns were now very much to the forefront and Churchill's rise to the top was brisk. He entered the Cabinet in 1908 and was Home Secretary by 1910.

Before the end of the following year Winston was First Lord of the Admiralty, and his sojourn there was arguably a particularly formative experience – and of great relevance to his later conduct as Prime Minister. Characteristically 'hands on', he took himself out to Antwerp soon after the outbreak of the First World War in 1914, and was also involved in many novel developments and schemes. One of the most successful of these was the invention and deployment of the 'Landship' – for, extraordinary as it may seem now, the Admiralty was a partner in the birth of the tank. Churchill's first intervention in this sphere came, arguably, as early as September 1914, when in a memorandum to Colonel Ollivant and Captain Sueter he asked for work to begin on a trench-spanning 'car'. Later, he thought about a 'collective shield' on caterpillar tracks. This was Churchill at his most imaginative, and unlike some of his efforts this was a sustained interest with subsequent sponsorship in the form of the 'Landship Committee'. Conversely, it was the lateral and impulsive element in Churchill's thinking that led to some of his worst decisions during the First World War, in particular the enthusiastic backing he gave to the disastrous Dardanelles Campaign of 1915, which soon turned into one of his darkest episodes. Forced out of the Cabinet, he immediately sought both atonement, for the 'legitimate gamble' of Gallipoli, and a new adventure, rejoining the Army and forcing himself to the Western Front, regardless of the personal danger. He became, as his biographer put it, 'the escaped scapegoat'.[2]

Upon his arrival in France in November 1915, Churchill intended to rejoin the Queen's Own Oxfordshire Hussars, but Sir John French, commander of the British Expeditionary Force (BEF), had other plans, suggesting that Churchill could

soon command a brigade. In preparation, Winston was attached briefly to the Guards with whom he was to learn the rudiments of trench warfare before assuming greater responsibility. The 2nd Battalion Grenadier Guards were as surprised as their new major to discover a former senior Cabinet member in their midst, and for his first night parked him in a signaller's dugout somewhat out of direct harm's way: but Churchill was intent on doing things properly, and by the next evening was in the front line. Here he discovered his colleagues in a ramshackle German trench, 'filth and rubbish everywhere' and 'graves built into the defences and scattered about promiscuously, feet and clothing breaking through the soil, water and muck on all sides; and about this scene in the moonlight troops of enormous rats creep and glide, to the unceasing accompaniment of rifle and machine guns'. As Captain Grigg recorded: 'It was very cold and very wet – first a bitter frost, and then rain, sleet and thaw, which put us up to the calf in mud and slime. That part of the line is in bad order, too, and we had nothing but a small dug out about 2 feet 6 high with a wet mud floor to live and sleep in, and we all got kinks in our spines getting in and out of the beastly thing. But Winston accepted the situation with great cheerfulness and we had quite a good time.'[3]

Though Churchill had 're-become' a soldier, as his wife Clementine put it, aspirations to major generalship came to nought. Field Marshal French was displaced in favour of Sir Douglas Haig, and rumour of Churchill's impending elevation to lead 56th Brigade in 19th Division gave rise to critical comment at home. One MP referred to the possible promotion over the heads of others as a 'grave scandal'. Prime Minister Asquith vetoed the appointment, and Winston duly cancelled the order for his new uniform. Churchill was clearly extremely upset at this turn of events and vented his feelings in letters so outspoken and depressed that he later thought better of his actions and asked his wife to burn them. This she did. As a sop, Winston was handed command of 6th Battalion Royal Scots Fusiliers on New Year's Day 1916.

With the Royal Scots Fusiliers he at least achieved his wish of commanding troops at the front. The 6th Battalion had been badly mauled at Loos, and was now slated to return to the line after replacements and recuperation. Not all of the officers were looking forward to the arrival of the new commander, who joined them in billets at Moolenacker Farm near Meteren on 5 January 1916. Lunch was followed by a battalion inspection in which Churchill revealed his relative inexperience by giving

the wrong drill orders. In his turn he looked on his officers as 'young boys' – plucky and intelligent, but many of them new and untried. On 13 January Winston tried his hand at grenade-throwing, a task, he observed, that needed to be 'approached gingerly', so he was impressed by one of the junior officers who interposed when men dropped live bombs by accident and threw them away in the nick of time. The next day Churchill was with the Canadians, learning about raids, and this was soon followed by a session at the machine gun school.

Next the battalion moved into the line at Ploegsteert Wood. At this time 'Plug Street' was a relatively quiet sector, and Lieutenant Colonel Churchill's headquarters was at Laurence Farm, about 500 yards (457m) behind. For the next few weeks 6th Royal Scots Fusiliers held the line: sometimes in the front trenches, sometimes rotated to the rear. Despite being in a quiet area, 6th Royal Scots Fusiliers still suffered fifteen killed and twenty-three wounded during this period. Winston's approach to war was unsubtle, but it inspired his men with confidence. Often he was right out at the front, gruff-voiced and moving like a 'baby elephant' at night in no man's land when silence would have been far more appropriate. On one occasion he actually sat on his torch and illuminated everything – much to the consternation of those accompanying him. At other times he got up on the fire step and showed his head in plain view of the enemy in order to encourage his sentries to be alert. He was also on the receiving end of shelling, and had one especially near miss that struck his HQ whilst he was in residence and destroyed some of his belongings. He exuded an all-round unflappability and confidence, on at least one occasion even producing his paints and sketching Laurence Farm in broad daylight, though it was in range of enemy batteries. Very

Major Churchill, wearing a French steel helmet, pictured with General Fayolle, at French XXXIII Corps HQ, Camblain L'Abbé, December 1915. Third from left is liaison officer Captain Edward Spears, in the Second World War not only an MP but also a Major General and confidant of Churchill. (Hulton Archive/Getty Images)

Winston as commanding officer 6th Battalion Royal Scots Fusiliers, pictured at Armentières, 11 February 1916. The officer in the cap is Archibald Sinclair who served with the Life Guards before becoming second in command of Winston's battalion. Sinclair later served as military secretary to Churchill, became leader of the Liberal Party in 1935, and was Secretary of State for Air in Churchill's government in 1940. (Keystone/Getty Images)

briefly Winston also got his wish to take charge of the brigade – whilst Brigadier Walsh was away. Even so it is difficult to avoid the impression that Winston was often frustrated by the Army, and what he perceived as a lack of movement and 'drive'. He was also concerned about technical matters – for example, the imperfection of communications and the slowness of the new 'tanks' to materialise. Whether any of this was discussed when Churchill met with Lloyd George, Bonar Law and F.E. Smith behind the front is unrecorded.

On 2 March Churchill's battalion was relieved and he took the opportunity to return to London. Here he made an impassioned speech in the Commons, criticised the government and called for the return of Admiral Fisher to the Admiralty, meeting with opposition, derision and sad resignation from his listeners. Winston soon returned to the front, temporarily beaten, but now more determined than ever to go back to full-time politics at the next decent opportunity. It was, he informed his mother, only a question of 'how and when'. He was equally convinced that there should be no big offensive on the Western Front for the rest of the year. For the time being, Britain should improve her armies, pile up munitions and send arms to Russia. Verdun was to be regarded as an abject lesson – Britain should not repeat the mistake. When a plan was put forwards to merge

the 6th and 7th battalions of the Royal Scots Fusiliers, Churchill appealed to Haig to be released, and to be able to use this freedom to promote the cause of conscription. Haig agreed, and in May Churchill left his men for the last time. Back in the UK he would argue various causes, ranging from those of manpower and the underemployment of Imperial forces, to the desirability of an Air Ministry, the publication of papers about Gallipoli and the paucity of awards of the Military Medal – but even under Lloyd George he was not immediately called to join the Cabinet. Only in July 1917 was his political rehabilitation at least partially completed when he took up the post of Minister of Munitions, a position Lloyd George himself had occupied before becoming Prime Minister.[4]

It is difficult to imagine that Churchill's attitudes to strategy, to technology and to the Army were other than very deeply impressed by his experiences of 1914–1918. He certainly professed himself horrified at the 'complete callousness and indifference to human life' that had been displayed in the First World War, as well as the resultant misery throughout Europe. After the Armistice, from January 1919, Churchill served as Secretary of State for War and as head of the fledgling Air Ministry, which had been established as recently as 1917. One of the themes of his work would be to ensure that all methods of fighting and winning war, other than putting masses of troops on the ground, were thoroughly investigated. It was in this spirit he sought to ensure that the RAF, founded as an arm separate from the Army in April 1918, became a permanent fixture, and he appointed Hugh Trenchard as Chief of Air Staff. The efforts of both the Army and the Royal Navy to subordinate the air service to their command were resisted. The RAF was developed along strategic lines with an emphasis on bombing targets well beyond the battlefield. Though the rationale may be criticised or supported, it is beyond doubt that in a period of retrenchment the overall effect on the Army of losing control of the 'Flying Corps', and becoming one of three rather than two services, was to lose a slice of potential funding. Less obviously, land-to-air co-ordination over the battlefield remained relatively undeveloped. Moreover, the strategic direction of travel of the RAF – in favour of the 'heavy bomber' – would also have unforeseen consequences later on, for when it was realised shortly before the Second World War that the air force lacked modern fighters with which to counter the enemy, these in their turn took priority over the equipping of the Army. As Secretary of State for War, Churchill has been described, with some justice, as a 'grave disappointment to the Army'.[5]

Churchill's lack of championing of the Army from high places would continue. After serving as Secretary for the Colonies from 1921, and a temporary loss of his parliamentary seat the following year, he became Chancellor of the Exchequer from 1924. Whilst it is generally remembered that he oversaw the disastrous return to the Gold Standard, which ushered in the economic instability leading up to the General Strike of 1926, he also had a more direct impact on the military. Army budget estimates were cut. Also, for all of his railings and magnificent bellicosity later on, it has to be remembered that he became intimately identified with what was later recognised as a millstone around the neck of any who wished to undertake the revision or expansion of British forces. This impediment was the so-called Ten-Year Rule. The rationale for the idea, first introduced in August 1919, was that for the purposes of planning it was assumed that Britain would not be participating in any major war for ten years. This thinking was designed both to save money in the short term, and to allow equipment programmes to be smoothed out financially in the medium. In 1928, as Chancellor, Winston made the ten-year period permanent, so that with every passing year it was still reckoned that a significant conflict lay ten years hence.

Such provisions certainly hampered research and development, and contributed to a climate of complacency in which politicians and administrators put off for tomorrow pretty much anything they were not minded to fund today. It may also be questioned from the macro-economic point of view whether an attempt to squeeze military spending at this juncture actually encouraged or discouraged the worldwide economic depression, through which Britain would wallow into the beginning of the new decade. From another perspective, however, revisionists now point out that in 1919 the Ten-Year Rule was realistic,

and indeed freed the country from investing in hardware or training that would have been all but useless by the mid-1930s. Moreover, funding was not pushed directly and ever downwards, but in fact fluctuated from year to year – rule or no rule. Such a stance also chimed rather well politically in an environment of disarmament and renunciation of war. Interestingly, the ten-year assumption was finally and formally jettisoned in 1933. Yet it does not take a mathematician to calculate that the rule was already wrong by the latter part of 1929, and the idea that Hitler conceived of the British Empire as having grown flabby and unwilling to protect the status quo by force can only have been fuelled by such a formal and long-standing statement of lack of intent. More than one British general concluded from this period that the Cabinet had neither the will nor the desire to find the wherewithal to fight.

Though it might have appeared that Churchill had definitively rejoined the mainstream, he would actually spend much of the next decade as an outsider: what he himself was pleased to call 'in the wilderness'. Progressively estranged from the Conservative Party leadership, he was omitted from the Cabinet of Labour Party leader Ramsay MacDonald's 'National Government' in 1931. Churchill opposed Indian independence and swam against the tide with loyal support for King Edward VIII during the abdication crisis. Remarkably, for such a long-term opponent of communism, he would eventually attempt – though unsuccessfully – to encourage the government to enter into an understanding with Russia in April 1939. If any proof were needed of his maverick nature, this provided it in spades. Without the responsibility of office and the financial restraints of government, Winston was entirely, if only progressively, converted to the camp of those advocating a robust foreign policy towards the nascent threat of fascism in Europe. So it was that just as others moved further towards appeasement he took an unfashionable and increasingly trenchant position against German rearmament. He was dubbed a 'warmonger' by the Labour Left, though during the early 1930s this was hardly a fair charge. Indeed, his initial objective of the period was not to go to war with the new dictators, but rather to ensure that there was no war.

By the middle of the 1930s, however, it was clear to Churchill, if not to many others, that the writing was on the wall. He became an avid consumer of military intelligence, and was soon regarded as the nexus of a sort of Shadow Cabinet in waiting. Interestingly, Stanley Baldwin, thrice Prime Minister between

Minister of Munitions Winston Churchill watches the march past of 47th (London) Division from the grandstand in the Grande Place, Lille, October 1918. Only in his middle forties he now had a variety of military experience from the perspectives of an officer, politician, and journalist. Within three months Churchill was Secretary of State for War: but presiding over plans for demobilisation. (Hulton Archive/ Getty Images)

Neville Chamberlain at Heston Airport on his return from Munich after meeting with Hitler, making his 'peace in our time' address. (Central Press/Getty Images)

of Czechoslovakia, the population of which was mainly ethnic Germans, be ceded. Some sort of line in the sand was expected but all Prime Minister Chamberlain got from negotiations was his 'piece of paper', promising much and delivering nothing. The Sudetenland was annexed and early the next year, following a Slovakian declaration of independence, the remainder of Bohemia and Moravia was occupied. Italy signed its 'Pact of Steel' with the ascendant Germany soon afterwards. Hitler regarded the upshot of his strong-arm diplomacy as an 'undreamt of triumph' – the 'flower wars' that yielded territories without a shot. Winston was unimpressed to say the least: this was a 'disaster of the first magnitude'. As he put it to the government in one speech in the House of Commons, 'You were given a choice between war and dishonour. You chose dishonour, and you will have war.' Already, many of the more military minded were gravitating towards Churchill, and around him was beginning to gather a circle of support – declared and undeclared. These figures included Admiral Keyes, Lord Beaverbrook, Professor Lindemann and Major General Spears, now a Tory MP; but from the Army perspective the most significant confidant was General 'Tiny' Ironside.

At the heart of Churchill's concerns of the period was that Britain should be properly equipped. Yet again, however, this was not – and perhaps could not be – anything that translated into the preparedness of the Army. His main arguments focused on the RAF, and bombing, and on this point there was already some response from those in power. Though the threat was so far mainly theoretical, and perhaps exaggerated by being viewed through reports from Guernica in the Spanish Civil War, the possibility of catastrophic casualties from the air – followed by civil breakdown – was taken very seriously in Britain. The only answer to strategic bombers, which would 'always get through', appeared to be a like force of equal power, and belatedly a properly organised civil defence. As far as the Army was concerned, all this amounted to nothing until long after it was too late. Already at a low ebb, projected Army funding for the second half of the 1930s was cut from £40 million to just £19 million.[6]

Rearmament finally began in earnest from 1937, and whilst this offered opportunities a good slice of the Army's share of the action went into mechanisation of a particular and limited sort. For the most part this did not mean the rapid production of new tanks and guns but a general introduction of wheeled motor transport for existing formations. In tune with concerns over bombing, another significant part of new Army investment

the wars and no great friend of Churchill, recognised that in the event that the political majority was proved wrong and Britain did go to war Winston would make an ideal 'War Prime Minister'. Developments such as the German reoccupation of the Rhineland by military force in 1936 served only to stimulate Churchill into more speech making and dire warnings. However, to his critics Winston's stance bore all the hallmarks of the relative luxury of parliamentary opposition and of freedom from genuine responsibility. As Neville Chamberlain admitted to his sister in 1938, he himself had little confidence in France, was worried that the Russians were angling for the Western powers to fall out with Germany, and feared that to come out with a 'bold' and 'courageous' lead against Hitler at this stage would be premature and totally counter-productive.

Though anti-war sentiment and appeasement remained strong, even as an outsider Winston was now iterating in new guise what was actually an ancient and traditional version of British foreign policy and grand strategy that had for centuries served the nation well: domination of the Continent by any one foreign power was dangerous, and in the longer context of history it mattered little whether that power was Spanish, French, or German, king or dictator. The Munich Crisis would later be recognised as a watershed. Germany entered Austria in March 1938 and now demanded that the Sudetenland region went into searchlights and other anti-aircraft measures. On the grounds that Britain might be able to undertake a 'limited liability' war, the overall size of the Army still remained small – tiny compared to those of Germany and Russia. As late as mid-1938 General Ironside was moved to remark that Britain could never 'even contemplate' a force for use in a foreign country, her only possible contribution being naval and air forces. In early 1939 the 'Regular' Army of full-time professional soldiers numbered but six divisions with a somewhat larger 'Territorial' Army of part-timers. Only in March of that year was it decided to increase the Territorials to twenty-six divisions, bringing the total number of divisions to a more respectable thirty-two. Actual mobilisation of the Territorials, pulling them away from their civilian employment, would not occur until the autumn. Not until May 1939 did conscription reappear in the guise of a new Training Act, but even then new 'Militiamen' were initially called up only for six months. Significantly, 'rearmament' had as yet taken little account even of this limited new manpower. Left-over rifles from the First World War existed in tolerable numbers,

but mortars and machine guns were short. The Regulars were still inadequate in tanks and heavy artillery, and the Territorials were much worse. Part of the Yeomanry were still riding horses, and only the Regulars – and not all of these – had received something as basic as the latest 'Battle Dress' uniform.

Hitler, buoyed by the outcome in Austria and the Czech lands, was minded to seek new conquests sooner rather than later. This was both the beginnings of an active armed aggression and the result of cool calculation: for if things were left too long his enemies might grow stronger, or more unified. He was also aware that his own rearmament and preparation so far was in breadth rather than depth. German efforts had gone mainly into battlefield strike power, not into those things that might sustain a long war, or indeed a war economy. Another significant factor in his cogitations was the Molotov–Ribbentrop Pact lending a window of opportunity in which to deal with Poland, in cahoots with the Russian dictatorship. Accordingly, Poland, though guaranteed by the Western powers, was swiftly swallowed from both west and east in the first of what would be dubbed the 'lightning wars' – the Blitzkrieg. Even Britain's counter-declaration of war had something feeble and resigned about it. A 'final note' requested that Germany should withdraw, and a state of conflict was assumed when that did not happen. The word was not accompanied by action. Moreover, it has been argued, probably correctly, that the British Army was actually less well prepared at the outbreak of the Second World War than it had been in 1914.

In many ways the crisis of 1939 and 1940 was the part for which the 64-year-old Winston Churchill had been practising all his life, and it was one he embraced with a gusto that would have been remarkable in a much younger man. In August 1939 he flew across the Channel to talk directly to the French, only to fume inwardly at their 'Maginot mentality' and general defensive posture. At Strasbourg he glowered across the Rhine, musing that it could be mined. Then, on the morning of 1 September, even as the Panzers were advancing into Poland, Chamberlain telephoned Churchill to ask him to meet him at 10 Downing Street. That same afternoon, even before the formal declaration of hostilities, he was invited to join a compact six-man War Cabinet. With the outbreak of war he was duly reinstalled at the Admiralty. Because western Europe remained quiet during the 'Phoney War', and Britain was reluctant to unleash a full-blown air war that could have invited the destruction of her own cities, the major focus of attention for Winston Churchill was the sea war of the Senior Service. At the same time, he agitated for a swifter and more ambitious build-up of the Army in France, hoping that it would be possible to find at least half the strength that the French themselves put into the field. As he put it, it was to be doubted that the French would acquiesce in a situation in which they were left to pay 'the whole blood tax on land'. Any such French reluctance might also result in Britain having 'to continue the war singlehanded'.

A posed image of men looking at recruiting posters under the watchful eye of a scarlet-coated soldier, 1938. The posters carry two key messages, the 'modernity' of the British Army, and the traditional local nature of its regiments: Scottish; Welsh; Lancastrian, and Yorkshire. Most regiments had a regional background, but given equipment shortages 'modernity' was a more debatable claim at this date. (Science & Society Picture Library/Getty Images)

Though technically responsible only for naval matters, and the Admiralty rightly occupied much of his enormous energy, Churchill was not slow to offer Chamberlain the benefit of his previous experience relating to both the Army and the Royal Air Force. With Lord Gort moving to lead the British Expeditionary Force in France, a new Chief of the Imperial General Staff was needed, and perhaps predictably Churchill threw his weight behind Ironside, who was soon installed. On 10 September Winston wrote to the Prime Minister, beginning, 'I hope that you will not mind my sending you a few points privately'…

'1. I am still inclined to think that we should not take the initiative in bombing, except in the immediate zone in which the French armies are operating, where we must of course help. It is in our interest that the war should be conducted in accordance with the more humane conceptions of war, and that we should follow and not precede the Germans in the process, no doubt inevitable, of deepening severity and violence. Every day that passes gives more shelter to the population of London and the big cities, and in a fortnight or so there will be far more comparatively safe refuges than now.

'2. You ought to know what we were told about the condition of our small Expeditionary Force and their deficiencies in tanks, in trained trench mortar detachments, and above all in heavy artillery. There will be a just criticism if it is found that heavy batteries are lacking… In 1919 after the war when I was Secretary of State for War, I ordered a mass of heavy cannon to be stored, oiled and carefully kept; and I also remember making in 1918 two 12" howitzers at the request of GHQ to support their advance into Germany in 1919. These were never used but they were the last word at the time. They are not easy things to lose… It seems to me most vitally urgent, first to see what there is in the cupboard, secondly to recondition it at once and make the ammunition of a modern character. Where this heavy stuff is concerned I may be able to help at the Admiralty, because of course we are very comfortable in respect of everything big…

'3. You may like to know the principles I am following in recasting the Naval programme of new construction. I propose to suspend work upon all except the first three or perhaps four of the new battleships, and not to worry at present about vessels that cannot come into action until 1942. This decision must be reviewed in six months. It is by this change that I get the spare capacity to help the Army. On the other hand I must make great effort to bring forward the smaller anti-U-boat fleet. Numbers are vital in this sphere. A good many are coming forward in 1940,

but not nearly enough considering that we may have to face an attack by 200 or 300 U-boats in the summer of 1940…

'4. With regard to the supply of the Army and its relation to the Air Force, pardon me if I put my experience and knowledge, which were bought, not taught, at your disposal. The making by the Ministry of Supply of a lay-out on the basis of 55 Divisions at the present time would not prejudice Air or Admiralty, because (a) the preliminary work of securing sites and building factories will not for many months require skilled labour; here are months of digging foundations, laying concrete, bricks and mortar, drainage etc. for which ordinary building trade labourers suffice; and (b) even if you could not realise a 55 division front by the twenty-fourth month because of other claims, you could alter the time to the thirty-sixth month or even later without affecting the scale. On the other hand, if he does not make a big lay-out at the beginning, there will be vexatious delays when existing factories have to be enlarged. Let him make his lay-out on the large scale, and protect the needs of the Air Force and Army by varying the time factor. A factory once set up need not be used until it is necessary, but if it is not in existence, you may be helpless if you need a further effort. It is only when these big plants get into work that you can achieve adequate results.'[7]

Similar concerns regarding the guns were expressed direct to Dr Burgin, the Minister of Supply, who hurried to assure Churchill that the heavy guns had indeed been stored and were already undergoing refurbishment. So it was that the Royal Artillery soon had an adequate number of heavy pieces, albeit of an elderly type, unlike the enemy who had been denied heavy guns in 1919 but had now made up the deficiency by the manufacture of newer types during the later 1930s. A few days later new Churchillian exhortations were aimed at convincing his colleagues that Belgium needed to be persuaded to strengthen its frontier with Germany with 'deep defences' and physical obstacles; particularly against tanks, because an attack by three or four armoured divisions, 'so effective in Poland, can only be stopped by physical obstacles defended by resolute troops and a powerful artillery'.

All this was admirable, and it distanced him from those politicians on both sides of the Channel who were being criticised as half-hearted and vacillating: but one cannot help but observe that Churchill, like many of his colleagues – and even more so the French – was viewing the military situation of 1939 as a repeat of 1917. The vision in which heavy artillery and deep static lines were capable of stopping modern balanced formations of mobile armour, artillery and infantry was commonplace, but it soon proved to be painfully wrongheaded. Churchill had not been serving at the front in 1918 when the war of movement had begun again, and his outlook in 1939 does not yet appear to have absorbed the possibility of increased mobility that he had helped to encourage with his endorsement of tanks and other trench-breaking technologies. As he freely admitted after the event, 'I did not dissent from the general view that anti-tank obstacles and field guns, cleverly posted and with suitable ammunition, could frustrate or break up tanks'. As to counter-attacking what was assumed to be the solid enemy 'front', Churchill also imagined that new trench-digging machines could be used to burrow their way towards and into the enemy trenches, and troops rushed forwards under cover to attack the enemy. Chamberlain was eventually bombarded with so many ideas and memos that he asked Churchill to desist and save the gist of his output for the many times that they met in person.

Winston was one of those most keen to send British troops to Norway. Remarkably, as early as the last days of 1939, he had even submitted to the Prime Minister a timetable of proposed action in which, over the course of a single week, Sweden and Norway would be promised British and French assistance, followed swiftly by the launching of a flotilla for Norway. The main object of this enterprise would be the arrest of German vessels in Norwegian waters and the interruption of the trade in iron ore with Germany. An initially reluctant Chamberlain was first placated by the king of Norway, then forced into action by the *Altmark* incident, when, on Churchill's direct order, this German supply vessel carrying British prisoners was seized in the Jösing Fjord by Royal Navy destroyers. This little triumph was followed by a scheme to lay mines in Norwegian waters and the preparation of a more major land-based 'project'. Churchill had even, like French commander-in-chief General Gamelin and Chamberlain, nurtured visions of aiding Finland against the communist Soviet Union – thereby 'getting a foothold in Scandinavia'. Had this surreal adventure succeeded in full the result could easily have been catastrophic, driving Russia yet further away whilst at the same time, and at great expense, aiding what would soon be one of Germany's partners. Perhaps luckily, peace was concluded between Finland and Russia, which removed this dangerous possibility. Yet, paradoxically, it was action in Norway – one leading to fiasco – that nevertheless helped to precipitate the crisis that led ultimately to the fall of Chamberlain and his government.

In a northern English port British soldiers load a ship for the expedition to Norway, 28 April 1940. Some of the men wear gas capes against the weather, others leather jerkins. The original caption speaks of 'sheepskin coats, blankets and equipment' being stowed, but these parcels are relatively small, and specialised kit for cold weather warfare was as yet a rarity in the British Army. (Reg Speller/ Fox Photos/Getty Images)

On 9 April 1940 Denmark was seized by Germany and airborne troops landed in Oslo. Hitler had thus removed any doubt by striking first. The following day, the Royal Navy scored a success, sinking five enemy destroyers at Narvik. A few days later, British troops formed part of a joint expeditionary force with the French, strongly supported by the Royal Navy, to Namsos and Åndalsnes in the Trondheim area. Yet the venture was poorly planned and two of its commanders were incapacitated even before they left the British Isles. The British and French were at first hamstrung by their desire not to be seen as the aggressors. Moreover, as General Ironside later complained, Winston seems to have believed that he could run the whole show, by committee, from London. On 21 April he first suggested the sending of troops to Narvik, then changed his mind and wanted Namsos reinforced. Yet whatever the Army did was unlikely to bear fruit in the long run because there were no RAF bases in Norway and the enemy, having already arrived, was free to observe or bomb virtually at will.

The advance to Norway rapidly became a retreat. Åndalsnes was evacuated on 1 May and Namsos a couple of days later. There remained only the most tenuous of holds on Narvik,

Winston Churchill
in defiant pose
with a Thompson
submachine gun
during a visit to
coast defences
near Hartlepool,
1940. This image
was used both to
raise British morale,
and by the enemy
to suggest Churchill
was a 'gangster'.
(Official/author)

which was occupied by a very unprepared brigade of Guards. These could not be supported and were finally withdrawn early in June. Churchill's conceit that the British Army could be supplied from the UK across the sea more easily than the enemy could be across the Continent by air and land was proved sadly wrong. As Winston himself remarked shortly after the war: 'Considering the prominent part I played in these events and the impossibility of explaining the difficulties by which we had been overcome, or the defects of our staff and governmental organisation and our methods of conducting war, it was a marvel that I survived and maintained my position in public esteem and Parliamentary confidence.'[8]

The apparent final nail in the coffin of Chamberlain's administration was the news on 10 May that the enemy had fallen upon the Low Countries. Interestingly, however, and as a result of Norway, Prime Minister Chamberlain had already decided to leave of his own volition and was that very morning hosting a meeting at Downing Street at which the Conservative Chief Whip, Lord Halifax, and Churchill were present. Halifax was, on the face of it, the favoured successor, but he had no stomach for the job, seeing his membership of the House of Lords as a potential impediment to the popular support needed for the task. The mantle duly fell to Churchill, which could very quickly have proved to be a poisoned chalice. A swift and concentrated German blow through the French line effectively outflanked the British Expeditionary Force now advancing into Belgium.

The Anglo-French defence reacted in confusion and with feet of clay. The Panzers were near Gravelines on the Channel coast by 22 May. As Churchill himself put it, 'apparently the Germans can go anywhere and do anything'. Belgium capitulated on 28 May as the British Expeditionary Force fell back on Dunkirk, already under aerial attack. A largely successful withdrawal across the Channel, in ships little and large, was a result of luck as much as judgement, for whilst everything possible was done to get the troops away their escape depended at least partly on Hitler's decision that his tanks were best conserved to finish off the French.

Churchill's ensuing war leadership was by turns energetic, industrious, personalised and indomitable: but perforce of a very different nature to that of the enemy. Hitler, as a dictator and head of an army that swore its personal allegiance to him man by man, could simply issue 'War Directives'. Churchill, as Prime Minister of a National Government in a democracy, and whose hold on power was more tenuous than historical perspective might lead us to believe, had to use subtler means when dealing with ministries and the armed forces. Moreover, the Nazi leader tended to refer to his subordinates only within their very specific professional ambits: military, civil and economic, reserving to himself the grand overview. He would thus tell a general that something was impossible, or conversely imperative, due to political or economic considerations and expect no contradiction. Churchill, by contrast, was often faced by a debating society in which there was more cross-fertilisation of knowledge, something that could open the door to both greater frustration and greater realism. In practice, however, the War Cabinet and Defence Committee exercised less real influence as time went on, and often the Prime Minister worked essentially in direct collaboration with the Chiefs of Staff with Ministers only involved when directly affected by the point at hand. Churchill referred to such gatherings as 'staff conferences'.

There were, of course, many Cabinet and other formal meetings that operated in the normal way, but in addition to these Churchill favoured 'Minutes'. These were dictated notes sent to individuals or groups several times a day, thousands per year, containing questions, exhortations or demanding facts. Some Minutes were to encourage and others to rebuke, though frequently they were intended merely to initiate dialogue or produce the information upon which informed decisions could be made. The most commanding documents were marked 'Action This Day'. The key strength of such interventions was also their weakest feature: by speeding up actions of government and command, Churchill lent urgency where haste was needed but he also tended to cut across lines of control and communication, and on occasion he set in train initiatives without resources or quickly contradicted previous decisions. At their best Minutes could hit a nail on the head at a crucial moment; at their worst Minutes might be perceived as threatening or ill-advised meddling. An impatient Churchill saw failure to respond immediately as unimaginative obstructionism or hidebound conservatism, traits which were all too easily believable of the traditionally minded Admiralty and War Office. Some subordinates observed that at times of crisis, and these were frequent, there were so many things demanding 'Action This Day' that any sense of priority was lost. Others reflected from experience that though Churchill's efforts were prodigious, he took a rest in the middle of the day in order to continue at night. Those around him were not afforded such luxury and could easily find themselves working around the clock to keep up – much to the detriment of their own efficiency.

Where Churchill certainly scored decisively over the Nazi style of direction was in his empathy and directness of approach, striking a chord with both civilians and military personnel, in dark times and the moments of triumph, though the latter were all too rare early in the war. His speeches delivered good news well and, arguably, bad news better. Certainly, part of his power of persuasion was in making the many see the war as he saw it. So it was, for example, that in February 1944 he outlined an official terminology to the Foreign Secretary in which enemy countries were to be 'invaded' and occupied countries 'entered' then 'liberated'. Moreover, like the Royal Family, Churchill was to be seen amongst bomb damage, and was so keen to take personal risks that he had sometimes to be forcefully dissuaded by his advisors. In the celebrated instance of D-Day, his enthusiasm to get amongst the troops at the front on the first day was quelled only by a conversation with the king. Nevertheless, he made it to France soon afterwards, and was a repeat visitor thereafter. Indeed, during the war Churchill travelled very widely, most tellingly to the USA where he acted to cement the 'special relationship' and encourage American participation – and in this he was materially aided by the fact that his own mother was American. He would also venture to the Wartime conferences at Cairo, Teheran, Yalta and Potsdam. The Prime Minister's modes of transport ranged from trains and cars to battleships, but his swiftest were aircraft. One was the specially converted B-24 Liberator bomber, named *Commando*,

on which Churchill warranted a sleeping berth but his aides, doctor and detective made do with seats. Later, a larger four-engined York aircraft was used.

Churchill, like Hitler, operated from a bunker whilst conducting the war. Though 10 Downing Street had an Annex with steel shutters and reinforced walls it was nothing like strong enough to withstand bombing; indeed, one incendiary bomb did crash through the roof and into a secretary's bedroom. So it was that other arrangements were resorted to. The Cabinet War Rooms in the converted basement of the Office of Works' building that faced St James's Park were selected no doubt because they were the strongest in the Whitehall government complex and were conveniently located between 10 Downing Street and Parliament. The building of this citadel had commenced as early as 1938 under the auspices of General Sir Hastings Ismay, later to be Churchill's chief staff officer and representative on the Chiefs of Staff Committee, and Major Sir Leslie Hollis. Work began in June 1938, accelerated during the Munich Crisis and was completed just before the outbreak of war. In 1941, further development of the Courtyard Rooms created a suite of nine rooms with a dining area for the Prime Minister and his wife Clementine, staff accommodation for aides and a meeting room for the Chiefs of Staff. Though contingency plans were drawn up to move Churchill and his War Cabinet to a command

Churchill inspecting bomb damage in Battersea, south London, 10 December 1940. Unlike Hitler Churchill was keen to visit the scenes of enemy destruction, and scored uplifting propaganda coups in this way. He was often very well received – but this was by no means guaranteed. (Reg Speller/Fox Photos/ Getty Images) centre near Worcester in the event of an emergency, his entourage remained utterly convinced that Winston would not in fact have moved from the capital. As Halifax later reported, Churchill said that he would have manned a pillbox and died at the end of Downing Street. That this was not mere bravado is strongly suggested by Churchill's infuriating conduct during the Blitz, when neither his aides nor his police minder, Walter H. Thompson, succeeded in convincing him to look to his personal safety. He frequently ignored Clementine's advice to sleep in the shelter, spurned the steel helmet thrust upon him and sometimes insisted on watching a raid from the rooftop. He also took shooting lessons and began carrying a revolver.

This carefree sort of attitude was summed up by a Minute of June 1941:

> *'We have to contemplate the descent from the air of perhaps a quarter of a million parachutists, glider borne and crash landed aeroplane troops. Everyone in uniform, and anyone else who likes, must fall upon these wherever they find them and attack them with the utmost alacrity – "Let everyone Kill a Hun" – This spirit must be inculcated ceaselessly into all ranks of HM forces*

– in particular in military schools, training establishments and depots. All the rearward services must develop a quality of stern, individual resistance. No building occupied by troops should be surrendered without having to be stormed. Every man must have a weapon of some kind, be it only a mace or pike. The spirit of intense individual resistance to this new form of sporadic invasion is a fundamental necessity.'[9]

What Churchill undoubtedly did best was to articulate the defiance of his people, and as an orator and master of the *bon mot* he was without equal. Yet perhaps it was Winston's romanticism and pigheaded unreasonableness that were simultaneously his greatest qualities and greatest curses as war leader. Cool objectivity told many politicians that 1940 was the time to give up and seek an accommodation with the enemy. In Churchill the challenge of the hour aroused huge determination to resist and persist, whatever the odds. At the same time, such contrarianism often caused him to latch, limpet like, onto unlikely courses of action and attempt to push through their prosecution in the face of both good advice and repeated disappointment. Examples include an enduring desire to re-enter the Continent through Norway, thereby 'unrolling the map of Europe' in much the same way that Hitler had begun to roll it up early in the war; the obsession with seizing part of Sumatra to form a forward airbase against the Japanese; and the fixations with first Italy and then the Balkans. In these last he ran counter to the wishes of his American allies, and sought to form his own hedges against the advance of communism.

Churchill's strategic view of the Second World War was undoubtedly overshadowed by both positive and negative experiences in the First World War. One of his most important considerations was to avoid repeating the battles of attrition in the west exemplified by the Somme and Passchendaele. A reprise of 1914 to 1918 would not only be inhumane and wasteful, but might also be politically damaging to Churchill. Chamberlain had been unceremoniously dumped over a relatively small campaign, and there was no guarantee that Winston would not himself suffer a similar fate. Churchill's desire to avoid a major conflagration in France was manifested as early as March 1940, when in consideration of the landings at Narvik he observed that though such a course of action was difficult, 'it had to be balanced against the much worse prospect of very costly fighting on the Western Front later on'. Such considerations, his knowledge of the earlier history of his island nation and extensive experience at the Admiralty all gave Winston a strong impression of Britain's

Highlanders digging in under a camouflage net, 'somewhere in France', c.1939. There was a widespread expectation that the conflict, like the First World War, would be heavily dependent on trenches and field fortifications. Churchill was one of many convinced that there would be long periods of stasis. (Author)

military strength as being at heart naval. Early worries about strategic bombing, the Battle of Britain and actual nightmares occasioned by the loss of the *Prince of Wales* and *Repulse* in December 1941 gave an aerial perspective to this naval outlook.

In this picture the Army was usually something that had to be landed by the Royal Navy. For though Churchill had himself been an Army officer and appears to have had genuine empathy for the fighting soldier, his overriding view of the Army, like many of his peers, was as a projection of Imperial influence.

Therefore, like it as not, land force was seen primarily as the spearpoint of the navy, which, naturally for an island nation, was the Senior Service. Combined with the understandable phobia against creating a new and bloody 'Western Front', what has been dubbed an overarching 'strategy of evasion' – striking anywhere but against the main enemy force – became the signature of Winston's policy. Nevertheless, his style as warlord was one of constant action and aggression. As John Keegan has put it:

> 'His heart was fired by daring lunges at the enemy weak points: by O'Connor's offensive into Italian Libya, by the expedition to Greece, by the torpedo attack on the Italian fleet at Taranto, by Wingate's penetration of the Japanese position in Burma, by the idea of a drive towards Vienna through the river valleys of Yugoslavia. His head told him that the power of the German Reich had to be broken by other means: the defeat of the U boats, the strategic bombing of German cities, and the invasion of north west Europe. Throughout the war his conduct of

Tank crew briefing beside a Mk VI light tank, Iraq April 1942. Both the officer and other ranks wear 'Combination Overalls' and Field Service caps, and carry goggles. Older models of tank were deemed adequate for theatres where the enemy also lacked modern equipment. (Official/ author)

operations was to oscillate between the romantic and the realistic; he could rarely resist an adventure but was consistently drawn back to the mainstream of strategy by his own commonsense'.[10]

Sir John Dill regarded Winston's ideas as a potential 'menace' when combined with a personality nobody could possibly tame, and became frustrated that so much of his own time was spent trying 'to prevent stupid things being done rather than in doing clever things'. General Ismay, so often an emollient between Churchill and others, lived in fear of Norway becoming a new 'Arctic Gallipoli'. As Chief of the Imperial General Staff from Christmas 1941 Alan Brooke came to see one of the most important parts of his job as being to restrain Churchill's new strategic interventions and dramatic flourishes:

'Whether I exercised any control or not, I knew by now the dangers to guard against. I had discovered the perils of his imperious nature. I was now familiar with his method of suddenly arriving at a decision as it were by intuition, without any kind of logical examination of the problem. I had, after many failures, discovered the best way to approach him… I would not suggest that I could exercise any real control over him. I never met anybody that could, but he had grown to have confidence in me, and I had found that he was listening more and more to any advice that I gave him.'[11]

In his diaries General Pownall likewise talked of keeping Churchill 'on the rails'. So it was that the British war effort was both sustained yet also sometimes threatened by Winston's own mercurial genius.

There were certainly occasions when Churchill's rhetoric and thrusting desire for action became flights of fantasy, or objects with which to goad his generals. One especially nauseating piece of grandstanding came in March 1941 in the wake of Exercise Victor. The staff planned a simulated invasion of Norfolk by the enemy, during which the Germans were assumed, for the sake of stimulating suitable responses from the defenders, to have landed five divisions. Winston's reaction was not to praise or criticise

Bayonets fixed, Eighth Army infantry bring in an injured German during the desert war: an official image passed by the publicity censor. The fighting in North Africa contributed to the Allied cause, but without risking premature confrontation in Europe. (Official/author)

the actions of the defenders, or the exercise, but to demand to know how the Germans succeeded in their imagined invasion, and that this plan should be presented to him immediately:

> 'All of this data would be most valuable for our future offensive operations. I should be glad if the same officers would work out a scheme for our landing an exactly similar force on the French coast at the same extreme range of their fighter protection, and assuming that the Germans have naval superiority in the Channel. Such an enterprise as this accomplished in 48 hours would make history, and if the staffs will commit themselves finitely to the adventure and can show how it is worked out in detail I should very much like to bring it before the Defence Committee for action at the earliest moment.'

It is difficult in hindsight to determine whether Winston was motivated by a misguided idea that this would somehow raise morale, or was merely treating his underlings to a sarcastic browbeating for having the temerity to lay plans to fight back in response to an eventuality that he regarded as totally unthinkable.[12]

Much remains controversial about the Desert War in North Africa, which would soon became a surrogate stage on which the British Army could first engage the Italians and then the Germans, and eventually inflict upon them one of the first defeats of note. In his more fanciful moments, of which there were a few, Churchill would see North Africa as not only the key to the Middle East and Mediterranean, and the protection of the Suez Canal, but also a lever with which to bring Turkey into the war. Yet even in early 1941 Sir John Dill was aware that it was the defence of the United Kingdom that was paramount – 'Egypt is not even second in order of priority'. Moreover, the situation was further muddied when the North African theatre of war was denuded of resources in the ill-fated attempt to protect Greece and Crete.

Arguably Churchill's clearest strategic insight was his perception that if the USA was at Britain's side, and Germany was at war with Russia, the end would inevitably be an Allied victory. So it was that he laboured first, and untiringly, to bring Britain and the USA together. Second, he temporarily

'Battleship row' during the surprise Japanese attack on Pearl Harbor, 7 December 1941. From left to right the USS *West Virginia*, USS *Tennessee* and USS *Arizona*. The Japanese and Hitler completed Churchill's key objective of bringing the USA into the war. (US Navy/Interim Archives/Getty Images)

swallowed both his natural antipathy for communism, and his distaste for Stalin's brutality, just long enough to make sure of the result. With Japan's invasion of Malaya and its attack on Pearl Harbor, Churchill appeared to be facing a severe regional reverse – however, rather than seeing this as heralding a defeat, he had the statesmanlike realisation that this marked the beginning of the end for the Axis Powers. So it was that en route to America to meet Roosevelt, Churchill set out his strategic vision. This argued first for a clearing of North Africa in 1942, improving the security of passage through the Mediterranean, a securing of sea lanes and the commencement of a maritime campaign in the Far East. This phase would end with the defeat of Italy, and the war in the west could then be concluded by means of an attack into northern mainland Europe after the Germans had been weakened, both by the Soviets and by various indirect approaches from the Western Allies. All this was realised in the end, as eventually would be Churchill's desire to contribute to the victory against Japan by attacking from India, through Burma,

and ultimately recapturing Singapore. Winston was shunted into many byways by his impetuous imagination – for example, his recurring wish for a new campaign in Norway; his fixation with beating what appeared to be an indestructible Rommel; or the circuitous advance on Vienna. Nevertheless, the bones of what he conceived at the end of 1941 and the beginning of 1942 did in fact come to pass. The best of his subordinates laboured hard to keep him focused on this path and ultimately it was the Army that carried out much of this plan.

Though Churchill was not a general, and never commanded in the field during the Second World War, his impact upon the Army was surprisingly significant and direct. As we shall see, he intervened positively – or meddled, depending upon one's perspective – at virtually every level, sometimes taking detailed interest in particular equipment or personnel at a micro level, but more often acting as a modern-day 'warlord', taking a direct part in the formation of strategy and campaigns. Perhaps

most obviously he insisted on approving the selection of the senior generals. In this way his influence was bound to be felt, as commanders were very conscious that the most important promotions depended on his favour, and that keeping such appointments entailed the maintenance of at least a basic level of his confidence. Winston made quite a few good decisions, but his criteria were more often based on gut feeling than analysis. Sometimes his choices were essentially down to recognition of personal bravery and thrusting spirit. It pained him to remove Auchinleck for just these reasons, and he admired Gort and Freyberg for their personal valour even when their shortcomings as commanders were exposed. Wavell he found difficult to tolerate due to what Churchill saw as excessive caution and pessimism. There is more than a kernel of truth in Keegan's assertion that Churchill would really have preferred to exercise command himself, everywhere and all the time. He was a sort of 'frustrated Malborough, who itched to be both the general on the field and the presiding genius of the alliance'.[13]

One point that particularly exercised Churchill about the British Army was its 'teeth to tail' ratio. In wars of the past, and in quite a number of foreign armies of the Second World War, a large proportion of the troops were in the front-line combat arms – the infantry, tanks and artillery. Yet, as battle had become more technical, machines more complicated, supplies more diverse and troops gradually became better looked after, in terms of medical and other care, the service and support arms had grown. Bodies such as the Royal Army Service Corps, Ordnance Corps, Royal Army Medical Corps, and various rear-area and line-of-communications formations, had swelled to the point where they cumulatively greatly outnumbered the front-line infantry, which traditionally had made up more than half of the entire Army.

After much muttering, and some indirect action, Winston attempted a personal intervention regarding the forces earmarked for the invasion of Europe in 1944. Seizing on the statistics that 2,000 clerks and officers were required for records and that it was planned that there would be one vehicle for every 4.84 men on the ground in France before the end of June, he scheduled a meeting with Montgomery and his staff to investigate 'the British tail'. In the event, however, Monty buttonholed the Prime Minister personally, telling him that it was unacceptable for Churchill to address his staff directly on this point, as the staff were merely there to give their commander advice and it was the job of the commander

to take the decisions. Moreover, with arrangements made and troops already gathering, to attempt to rebalance the Army at the eleventh hour courted disaster. Churchill was visibly moved and backed down, and when introduced to Montgomery's staff did not raise any criticism.

To be fair to both parties, the argument as to whether the 'tail' should outnumber the 'teeth' was never entirely cut and dried. More men facing the enemy with bullet and bayonet undoubtedly increased the chances of local success on a given day, but in the bigger picture men who were poorly fed, had poor communications, insufficient ammunition and unmaintained vehicles were not likely to have long-term staying power, high morale or good mobility. Yet whether an Army dentist was 'worth' a soldier with a submachine gun, or whether regular accurate pay was more useful than receiving mail from home on time, was extremely difficult, if not impossible, to judge or strictly quantify. Whether a 'correct' balance actually existed, or whether some solutions were merely better than others, remains open to question. Suffice it to say that in the end, and despite some very serious defeats, the British Army neither collapsed nor suffered casualties on the scale of those suffered by the major Continental powers.

Montgomery at a press conference in Normandy, June 1944. Ultimately the D-Day landings were hugely successful, but the final drive to victory was not achieved without significant casualties, or friction between big personalities. (Official/author)

Opposite: German prisoners gathered on a Normandy beach. Often topped with wire and protected by belts of mines, sea walls presented a considerable obstacle. Scaling ladders were one way to cross, but specialised armoured vehicles worked much better. (Official/author)

The leaders of the Big Three meeting at Potsdam, (from left) British Prime Minister Winston Churchill, American President Harry S. Truman and Soviet leader Joseph Stalin, Germany, 2 August 1945. (Imagno/Getty Images)

Many accused Churchill, in private at least, of micro-managing to a counter-productive degree, and sometimes to the detriment of the bigger picture. As General Ironside put it, Churchill often tried to run the war by a series of meetings and then attempted 'to supervise all military arrangements as if he were a company commander running a small operation to cross a bridge'. Winston also demanded a direct input into matters of production and organisation at the most trivial level – which, in retrospect, somewhat eerily parallels Hitler. So it was that he argued with the President of the Board of Trade about the 'twenty workers' and additional paper required to make playing cards for Army and civilian markets; discussed the state of readiness of the Dover garrison to withstand a 'Storm Troop' raid; worried Brooke for an exact list of tanks held by each unit in Africa, and then the strength of every division in the UK; and quizzed the Minister of Aircraft Production whether a six-

engined plane with a 4,600-mile (750km) range and an all-up weight of 250,000lb (113,400kg) should be considered.

In perhaps his most miniscule interventions Winston spoke up for his old regiments, the Queen's Own Oxfordshire Hussars and 4th Queen's Own Hussars. In the case of the former, he supported their request to keep their old buttons rather than take those of the artillery when they became gunners. In the case of the latter, he wrote at some length to the Secretary of State for War in December 1943 regarding Army Council Instructions and their applicability to 'unauthorised head dress'. As Colonel of the regiment he asked that the 4th should be assured that the black beret was 'only a war time measure', and that afterwards they should be 'allowed to purchase and wear service dress caps'.

Perhaps more constructively, Churchill sought to show himself and to inspect and encourage the troops whenever and wherever he could: reviewing his beloved Commandos here, visiting an anti-aircraft battery there and, on several occasions, going as close to the front line as his minders would allow, as in Normandy in 1944. All too often visits were fleeting, but that was not the point, as the history of the King's Dragoon Guards recorded of a morale-raising Churchill visit: 'The whole Brigade was on parade together, mounted in tanks, and Mr Churchill walked quickly round, as it was a wet and unpleasant day, only talking to one or two of the regiment. He gave a short address, which unfortunately was only heard by a small section of the parade, but despite all these drawbacks his visit, as always, had an inspiring effect.'

By January 1945 the war was moving into its final stages, and the political coalition that had held together since the dark days was wearing thin. Moreover, though he was as yet only dimly aware of it, the public's tolerance of Churchill, and the traditional and stoic values for which he stood, was also corroding slowly away. In May the Labour Party decided to end its role in the coalition. Rather than be pushed into an election at a time not of his choosing, Winston chose to go to the country on 5 July 1945. As servicemen could not return their votes so easily, and the disruptions of war interrupted normal procedure, it would be some time before the result of the ballot would be known. So it was that in mid-July, and with Germany defeated, Churchill set out for the Potsdam Conference to meet Stalin and the new US President, Harry Truman. He took with him the Labour Party leader, Clement Atlee. By the time they came home again, Atlee would be Prime Minister and Churchill's wartime premiership had ended. For Winston it was a cruel twist of fate that he was no longer Prime Minister when, on Hirohito's personal order, Japan laid down its arms, and the biggest conflict in world history finally ended.

Service personnel and civilians celebrate the end of hostilities in London's Piccadilly Circus, August 1945. Though Churchill would serve a second term as Prime Minister from 1951 to 1955, nothing would ever equal his performance in the Second World War. (Ministry of Information Photo Division/IWM/via Getty Images)

CHAPTER ONE
The Generals

MOST MODERN ARMIES have a considerable number of generals, and the British Army of the Second World War was no exception. Many generals were required for the divisions and corps of the active Army, and the hierarchical nature of command meant that the regimental officer and common soldier rarely served under one general, but perhaps under a brigadier, who served under a major general, who answered to a lieutenant general. Yet there were other general officers in staff and specialist positions, and quite a few who were essentially ceremonial or semi-retired. The vast majority of the senior generals of the Second World War had seen service in the First World War, were public school educated, and quite a few had had experience in India. As might be expected, having cut their teeth in 1914 to 1918, the majority were scions of the infantry or artillery, the arms that had dominated the war, particularly on the Western Front. Some were of Anglo-Irish extraction, and a number were drawn from the titled aristocracy. Overwhelmingly, they had attended the military colleges of Sandhurst or Woolwich and Staff College, Camberley, but few had a university education. This much might, perhaps, be expected: but it may come as

Left to right: Lieutenant General Miles Dempsey, Field Marshall Lord Alanbrooke, Winston Churchill and Field Marshal Bernard Montgomery at Château de Creully on 12 June 1944 (Galerie Bilderwell/ Hulton Archive/Getty Images).

something of a surprise that, as Correlli Barnett has observed, in the mid-1930s the average age of the higher commanders was seven years older than it had been in 1914. The number of generals would increase as the war progressed, not least because of the raising of new units and forces.[2] Against these figures of the old school would soon be contrasted a growing minority of younger men, and others like Slim and Harding, of relatively humble origins.

As head of state King George VI was titular head of the Army, also acting in a ceremonial capacity as colonel-in-chief of approximately thirty regiments. These naturally included the Foot Guards and Household Cavalry, but also several line infantry regiments, the 11th Hussars and the Royal Army Ordnance Corps. As the king was also Duke of Lancaster, he was similarly colonel-in-chief of the Duke of Lancaster's Own Yeomanry. For the Honourable Artillery Company, which had pretensions as the oldest military unit in the land, he took the

suitably ancient title of 'Captain General'. King George VI was created field marshal in December 1936, but was not regarded as 'active'. Indeed, no reigning British monarch had led his troops in battle since Dettingen in 1743.

However, the supposedly 'active' clutch of eleven field marshals in the Army List of August 1939 was also virtually moribund in terms of command. It was headed by the name of Prince Arthur Duke of Connaught. This son of Queen Victoria was in his late eighties at the outbreak of war, and was dead by 1942. Also on the list were King Alfonso XIII of Spain – given the title of British field marshal in 1928 – and Emperor Hirohito of Japan. Already a general, Hirohito was created field marshal in 1930, probably in the forlorn hope of improving Anglo-Japanese relations. Were it not for the First World War Kaiser Wilhelm II of Germany would probably have still been on the list also, for he had been made a British field marshal in January 1901, and lived until 1941. Field Marshals Birdwood,

Staff officers meet at Camberley, Surrey, 1946. Left to right: General Sir Richard O'Connor; General Sir Alfred Godwin-Austen; Lieutenant General Sir Brian Horrocks; General Sir Miles Dempsey, and Lieutenant General Sir Allan Harding. (Topical Press Agency/Getty Images)

Cavan, Jacob, Milne, Chetwode, Montgomery-Massingberd and Deverell had at least all been genuine field commanders in their earlier years, but the first four were now well into their seventies. Sir Philip Chetwode was seventy and had been appointed field marshal shortly before he stepped down as Commander-in-Chief India in 1934. Montgomery-Massingberd and Deverell had both been retired from the post of Chief of the Imperial General Staff in recent years, in 1936 and 1937 respectively. Some of those on the list would still be field marshals at the end of the Second World War, but it is difficult to escape the conclusion that by 1939 'field marshal' had effectively become a courtesy title rather than a job description.

There were nine full generals in August 1939, and of these Lord Gort, the current Chief of the Imperial General Staff, was the most important of the active generals. Others included Sir Walter Kirke, Inspector of Home Forces; Sir William Bartholomew, to whom soon fell the duty of chairing the committee on the sorry events of the Dunkirk campaign; Sir Edmund Ironside; and Sir Henry Jackson. Interestingly, the Army List also included five further generals – four for the Indian Army and Sir William Godfrey of the Royal Marines, though of course Royal Marines were not soldiers, and came under the purview of the Admiralty. There were no less than eighteen lieutenant generals, each ranking highly enough to take command of an entire army or theatre of war. Amongst these were names soon to be familiar, Sir John Dill, Sir Archibald Wavell and Michael Barker being only the most obvious. Sir Ronald Adam is less well known, but significant since he was Deputy Chief of the Imperial General Staff, and in early 1939 had been one of those pushing for the establishment of 'tactical schools' for officers: too little too late, but of importance for the future. There were four more lieutenant generals for the Indian Army and Royal Marines. There were ninety-three substantive major generals in 1939, plus a further twenty-eight amongst the Royal Marines and Indian Army.

To command at general officer level was a complicated business, and highly demanding when done well. Thousands of men had to be directed through sometimes convoluted chains of command, and whilst chiefs of staff and staff officers in general were supposed to cope with the minutiae it was a poor general who did not have a grasp of strategy, tactics, communications and logistics – and a realistic idea of what his men and machines might be capable. Moreover, the Second World War marked something of a watershed in terms of man management and public relations. The British public were no longer likely to accept casualties on the scale of 1914–1918 without adverse comment, and personality and public recognition were becoming more important than in the last war due to the increasing reach of new media, including radio and film. Generals who were unaware of this could be every bit as hamstrung in their leadership and aspirations for promotion as those who had limited comprehension of new military hardware and tactics.

In truth, Britain's generals of 1939–1945 showed the full gamut of abilities from brilliance to incompetence, and a commander who had been good one day might be bad the next through damaged nerve or body, or changing circumstance. Yet it may also be argued that because there had been no war against a modern enemy for years, and the Army had become shrunken and underfunded in the inter-war years, the talent pool of command was actually less deep in 1939 than it had been in 1914. Importantly, the British Army had very little recent experience of acting under service conditions in large formations – such as divisions and corps. It was therefore perhaps not unexpected that many British generals of the Second World War, at least to begin with, shone in tasks that were best suited to battalions and brigades, but often found themselves sadly out of their depth when called upon to advance in strength or inspire whole armies and fronts.

Though many generals were thrust aside through the vexations of war and advancing age, complete dismissal was vanishingly rare. Most were pushed sideways or upwards into desk jobs, ceremonial positions or quiet theatres. Perhaps most bizarrely, some unsuccessful combat generals were put into posts training others. Moreover, a 'demotion' did not usually appear precisely as such. On taking up new commands, most generals, and many more junior officers, did so in 'acting' or 'temporary' capacities, only a 'substantive' rank being a position as of right. So it was that if a general proved unsuitable at a new level it was possible for them to 'revert' to their substantive level. Though we read in campaign histories about generals being 'dismissed', this was rarely strictly true, nor expressed in such terms. By the time the British Army was back on the continent of Europe, and the Japanese advance in the East was stemmed, much had changed: and whilst there were still many familiar old names on the roll of senior British generalship, there were also many new ones. As of July 1944 the most senior commanders on the active list were as follows:

Churchill visits US 9th Army and inspects the concrete 'tank traps' of the 'Siegfried Line', or 'West Wall', near Aachen, February 1945. US General Simpson stands foreground right, Montgomery and Alan Brooke are to the left of the picture. (Fred Ramage/Keystone/Getty Images)

Field Marshals

Lord Birdwood
Sir Claude Jacob
Lord Milne
Earl of Cavan
Sir Philip W. Chetwode
Sir Archibald Montgomery-Massingberd
The Duke of Windsor
Sir Cyril Deverell
Lord Ironside
Rt Hon J.C. Smuts
Sir John G. Dill
Viscount Gort
Viscount Wavell
Sir Alan Brooke

Generals

Sir H. Maitland Wilson
Sir George J. Giffard
Sir Frederick A. Pile
Sir Harold R.L.G. Alexander
Sir Ronald F. Adam
Sir Thomas S. Riddle Webster
Sir Bernard L. Montgomery
Sir William Platt
Sir Bernard C.T. Paget
Sir Harold Franklyn

Generals, Indian Army

Sir Claude J.E. Auchinleck
Sir Hastings Ismay

Lieutenant Generals

W.G. Holmes
Sir A.F. Andrew Thorne
L. Carr
Sir Alexander Hood
Sir Clarence A. Bird
Sir Richard N. O'Connor
Sir H. Colville Wemyss
Sir Wilfrid G. Lindsell
HRH Duke of Gloucester
Sir T. Ralph Eastwood
T.J. Hutton
Sir Henry Pownall
Sir Giffard Martel
Sir Alan G. Cunningham
Sir H. Charles Loyd
Sir Noel M.P. Beresford-Peirse
Sir Edwin L. Morris
Sir Kenneth Anderson
Sir F. Noel Mason MacFarlane
A.E. Percival (Acting)
A.E. Grassett (Temporary)
A.E. Nye (Temporary)
G.N. Macready (Temporary)
J.A.H. Gammell (Temporary)
R.G.W.H. Stone (Temporary)
Sir Bernard C. Freyberg (Temporary)
J.G.R. Swayne (Temporary)
C.W. Allfrey (Temporary)
Lord Louis F.A.V.N. Mountbatten
(Honorary)

F.E. Morgan   (Temporary)
H.B.D. Willcox (Temporary)
E.C.A. Schreiber (Temporary)
Sir Oliver W.H. Leese (Temporary)
M.G.N. Stopford (Temporary)
A.F.P. Christison (Temporary)
M.C. Dempsey (Temporary)
H. Lumsden (Temporary)
H.M. Scoobie (Temporary)
H.E.R. Wetherall (Temporary)
G. Wilson (Temporary)
Sir Richard MacCreery (Temporary)
J.T. Crocker (Temporary)
Sir Humfrey M. Gale (Acting)
A.F. Harding (Acting)
N.M. Ritchie (Temporary)
F.A.M. Browning (Acting)
B.O. Hutchinson (Acting)
S.C. Kirkman (Acting)
J.G.W. Clark (Acting)
G.C. Bucknall (Temporary)
M.B. Burrows (Acting)
Sir Arthur F. Smith (Acting)
W.D. Morgan (Temporary)
D.G. Watson (Acting)

Lieutenant General, Royal Marines (Naval)

Sir Thomas L. Hunton

Lieutenant Generals, Indian Army

Sir Lewis M. Heath
G.N. Molesworth
W.J. Slim (Temporary)
G.A.P. Scoones (Temporary)
A.B. Blaxland (Local)
R.B. Deedes (Acting)
J.B. Hance (Local)

Lieutenant General, Territorial Army

Sir Ronald M. Weeks (Temporary)

The following brief biographies cover some of the most significant British generals of the war.

SIR HAROLD R.L.G. ALEXANDER, EARL ALEXANDER OF TUNIS (1891–1969)

Born in London and educated at Harrow, Harold Leofric George Alexander entered Sandhurst in 1910. The following year he was commissioned into the Irish Guards, and was a platoon commander on the retreat from Mons in 1914. Thereafter he was present at most of the major engagements of the First World War on the Western Front, including Ypres, Loos, the Somme, Bourlon Wood and Cambrai. He was wounded, repeatedly promoted and awarded the Military Cross (MC) and Distinguished Service Order (DSO). During the German Spring Offensive of 1918 he was an acting brigade commander. In 1919 'Alex' was sent to Poland, and then on to Latvia as part of the Allied Mission to secure its independence. This could not be done without military action, and he was soon employed leading a force of ethnic Germans – the Baltic Landwehr. He

returned to the UK in May 1920 and now commanded 1st Irish Guards; periods at the defence college and various staff appointments followed. In 1935, and now ranking as a temporary brigadier, Alexander led an expedition to Malakand against the Pathans. As usual, he was noted for his personal toughness and willingness to share the privations of his troops. By 1937 he was Major General Aldershot Command.

With the outbreak of war Alexander was appointed to lead 1st Division in France. During the retreat he landed up commanding the whole of I Corps, and distinguished himself in persisting in the attempt to extricate every last man from the beaches. He returned to the UK on the last destroyer to leave Dunkirk. His personal conduct under fire, previous war record, immaculate dress, calm gentlemanly manners, personal confidence, solid public school background and good looks harkened back to an earlier age, which impressed many, not least Churchill. It is often said that Alexander lacked an intellect that, when combined with his list of genuine qualities, could have made him a modern-day Wellington. If this was so, Alexander had wit enough to know it, and the common sense to leave management details to staff officers better qualified than himself to manage and focus on being the sort of leader that men might emulate.

Promoted to general and awarded the KCB in 1942 he was despatched to Burma in the hope of holding Rangoon (Yangon). This he failed to do, yet maintained his cool, as well as the confidence of Churchill, and later the same year was made Commander-in-Chief Middle East. He was thus Montgomery's commanding officer during the victories in North Africa. Whether happy accident or conscious decision on the part of the Chief of the Imperial General Staff, Brooke, with matters thus arranged the unflappable, tried-and-tested Alexander stood between the Prime Minister and the thrusting and bumptious Montgomery. Alexander largely left Montgomery to do things his own way, and translated Churchill's precipitous interventions into something more

palatable. At the same time, Alexander looked and acted much better than he spoke, and was content to let Monty have his theatricals and speeches so long as they achieved the desired result.

In 1943 Alexander was made leader of the 18th Army Group, and commanded the invasions of both Sicily and Italy. However, it was clear that Alexander, a genteel diplomat in public, had severe reservations about relatively inexperienced Americans. As he had been appointed Deputy Supreme Commander in the Mediterranean, and was now simultaneously grappling with the difficulties of Italy, whilst Britain's US allies were quickly becoming the senior partner, Alexander's position was viewed as untenable. So it was that 'Alex' was shuffled sideways as Commander of the Allied Armies in Italy, where he was faced with a series of fortified enemy lines across the country. Alexander was left to front such difficult and close-run affairs as Anzio and Cassino, and doomed to be the chief of a theatre that, after June 1944, would become a relative sideshow. So whilst Churchill continued in his fanciful ideas of pushing right out of Italy into Yugoslavia, and even as far as Vienna, this was never really practical. Terrain was one serious issue, another was resources, because until very late in the day Alexander was never able to deploy the sort of odds that were enjoyed by both the Soviets in eastern Europe and by the Overlord planners. As Eisenhower wished, the biggest western reserves were kept for France, and Operation Anvil, later renamed Dragoon, pushed even more men into the South of France.

Alexander's men continued to fight their way painfully northwards through Italy, a relatively thankless and low-profile task compared to that of Montgomery in France. Even so he was rewarded by being made a field marshal in 1944 and by the surrender of enemy forces in northern Italy on 29 April 1945. Raised to the peerage, Alexander later served as Governor General of Canada (1946–1952) and then as Minister of Defence. He retired in 1954, and died in 1969.

Sir Charles W. Allfrey (1895–1964)

Born in Northamptonshire, the son of a British Army officer, Charles Walter Allfrey was commissioned into the Royal Artillery in 1914. Twice wounded during the First World War he won the MC in 1918. After the end of the war in Europe he won the DSO with the Iraqi Army and was an instructor at the Staff College. Though he was in France as a staff officer early in the Second

World War, ranking as colonel, he returned to the UK in February 1940 to become commander of II Corps artillery.

By 1942 he had risen as far as lieutenant general and went to North Africa to lead V Corps. This he would do throughout the remainder of the war in Tunisia and then in Italy, until August 1944 when he was given the important, but less demanding, task of General Officer Commanding (GOC) British troops in Egypt. He was confirmed as permanent lieutenant general and knighted. In many ways Allfrey was lucky to survive as a combat commander as long as he did, Montgomery's scathing initial opinion being that he was not yet up to the standards of his other corps commanders and 'inclined to fiddle about with details, is very slow, and inclined to bellyache'. To Leese, Montgomery described Allfrey as 'amateur'. Nevertheless matters improved, and Monty subsequently claimed to have educated Allfrey into adopting more active methods.

Sir Kenneth A.N. Anderson (1891–1959)

Born in India, Kenneth Arthur Noel Anderson was educated at Charterhouse and Sandhurst and was commissioned into the Seaforths in 1911. He was wounded and won the MC on the

first day of the Battle of the Somme in 1916. After a protracted recovery he went to Palestine, where he was an acting major at the end of the First World War. Thereafter he attended the Indian Staff College, Quetta, where he did not sparkle. However, he held various staff postings and became commanding officer of 2nd Seaforths on the North West Frontier, and was made temporary brigadier in January 1933.

Anderson commanded 11th Brigade in France in 1940, and after Dunkirk he was given 1st Division, advancing from major general to lieutenant general in 1941. Though not greatly experienced, other than in the brief French campaign, he commanded the First Army during Operation Torch in 1942. Here there were difficulties in integrating the Allied command structure, and a number of muddles in battle, variously ascribed to Anderson or his even less experienced US opposite numbers. Nevertheless, with the build-up of forces and the arrival of Alexander, Anderson won through, and following the final Axis surrender was confirmed as a substantive lieutenant general in July 1943. Eisenhower's analysis was interesting, for whilst he found Anderson shy and fixated on written orders he was also felt to be honest, blunt, selfless and 'devoted to duty'. In late 1943 Anderson commanded Second Army in the UK, which would have meant that he held a key position in the command of the D-Day invasion forces. Montgomery found Anderson capable enough under the right circumstances but not the right material for Army level command, particularly at such a critical juncture. Anderson was therefore moved on to the Eastern Command whilst Dempsey got the crucial invasion job. In 1945 Anderson was given East Africa Command. He was promoted to general in 1949, retired in 1952 and died in Gibraltar in 1959.

SIR DESMOND F. ANDERSON (1885–1967)

Desmond Francis Anderson was commissioned into the Devonshires in 1905. He fought with distinction in the First World War, being repeatedly Mentioned in Despatches, and was awarded the DSO. After the war he attended the Staff College and reached the rank of major general in 1937. The last of a variety of staff postings before the war was as major general in charge of administration in Eastern Command, under Lieutenant General Guy Williams. After the outbreak of the Second World War Anderson was quickly advanced to divisional commands, but was briefly an assistant to the Chief of the Imperial General Staff, and by December 1940 was leading III Corps. In 1942 III Corps was part of the Tenth Army in Persia and Iraq, but in 1943 he moved on to command II Corps. Ranking as lieutenant general, he retired in 1944.

SIR CLAUDE J.E. AUCHINLECK (1884–1981)

Claude John Eyre Auchinleck was born at Aldershot into an Anglo-Irish military family, and after the early death of his father he entered Wellington College on a scholarship. He then

'The Auk' in his field marshal's uniform and medal ribbons c.1946. Arguably a soldier's soldier with many good qualities and huge potential, his career was often shaped by Churchill, and factors beyond his control. (Baron/ Getty Images)

Far left: Allied vessels approaching the Normandy coast covered by barrage balloons. On 6 June 1944 the British first wave comprised 6th Airborne on the eastern flank of the invasion, 3rd Infantry Division at Sword beach and 50th Infantry Division at Gold. Armour supported and Commandos followed hard on their heels. (Official/ author) went on to Sandhurst and gained experience with the King's Own Shropshire Light Infantry prior to joining the Indian Army in 1904. In 1914 he was machine gun officer with the 62nd Punjabis in Egypt, and subsequently fought the Turks in Mesopotamia, where he was present at many of the chief actions. By the time of the entry into Baghdad, Auchinleck was commanding the battalion, had been Mentioned in Despatches and awarded the DSO. After the First World War he attended the Indian Staff College at Quetta, held various staff appointments and then attended the Imperial Defence College in the UK. Back in India, and promoted to temporary brigadier, he led two punitive expeditions against rebellious tribes during the mid-1930s. In late 1937 he was made Deputy Chief of the Indian General Staff, and chaired the India Modernisation Committee.

After the outbreak of the Second World War, Auchinleck was recalled to the UK, taking command of IV Corps. Now ranking as lieutenant general he was soon appointed to lead the Anglo-French land force in Norway, on the grounds of his skill in mountain warfare. He entered the Scandinavian fiasco on 13 May 1940, and in less than a month had completed an evacuation on the orders of the Cabinet. Thereafter he returned to the UK, soon taking over the post that Alan Brooke vacated as GOC Southern Command. Very quickly he ran up against Montgomery, with whom he had a number of disagreements, but Auchinleck was also instrumental in the organisation of the Home Guard at this vital juncture.

In November 1940 Auchinleck became Commander-in-Chief India and was promoted to full general. Whether this was, as some have said, a mark of the significance placed on India, or whether Churchill preferred Auchinleck out of the way, remains to be argued. Nevertheless Auchinleck was a popular figure, and his swift action in crushing a rebellion in Iraq met with Churchill's definite approbation. In June 1941 Auchinleck was appointed Commander-in-Chief Middle East, and on the advice of Dill he resisted premature pressure for an offensive until November. In the event the attack was a failure and British forces were pushed as far back as Gazala and further efforts were pre-empted by the enemy. Though the 'Auk' took personal charge of the Eighth Army, Churchill decided he should be relieved and replaced with Alexander.

Auchinleck may not have been the most dynamic or successful of commanders, but part of his misfortune was to be prominent on the scene more than once when Britain's fortunes were at a very low ebb, and part to be in the way of Montgomery's ambitions. His peers regarded him as professional, honourable and able to get along with most people, though distrustful of politics. Eventually, in June 1943, Auchinleck succeeded Wavell as Commander-in-Chief India, though after November his post was subordinated to Mountbatten's South East Asia Command. Auchinleck was involved in the post-war reorganisation of the Indian Army, being created field marshal in May 1946. Bizarrely, he was nominally commander of both the Indian and Pakistan forces, having to stand down when they came into conflict – and for Auchinleck this tragedy was piled on top of a divorce. Having lived in Suffolk for some time, in his last days Auchinleck settled in Morocco, where he died in 1981 and was buried in the military cemetery in Casablanca.

Merton Beckwith-Smith (1890–1942)

Educated at Eton and Oxford Merton Beckwith-Smith was commissioned into the Coldstream Guards and fought in the First World War. The British *Official History* of the war claims that the then Second Lieutenant Beckwith-Smith of 1st Coldstreams actually led the first 'trench raid' on 14 October 1914, and in doing so was wounded and won the DSO. He stayed with the Army after 1918 and in the early 1930s transferred to the Welsh Guards, commanding the 1st Battalion until 1937.

He had ranked as temporary brigadier from January 1933, and was therefore prime candidate to command 1st Guards Brigade in the Second World War. He led this formation in France in 1940, and after Dunkirk was given command of 18th (East Anglian) Division. With the crisis of the outbreak of war in the Far East, this division was hurriedly sent out to Singapore, but arrived too late to have any significant impact. Instead, it arrived just in time to be captured by the Japanese in Percival's surrender of February 1942. On 11 November that same year Major General Beckwith-Smith died of disease in captivity.

Sir Alan F. Brooke, Viscount Alanbrooke (1883–1963)

Born in France of an Ulster family, Alan Francis Brooke attended Sandhurst and was commissioned into the Royal Artillery in 1902. He was subsequently stationed in India, where he suffered hearing damage brought on by gunfire. In 1914 he commanded an ammunition column in France, and during the First World

War was quickly promoted, seeing artillery combat commands. He was credited with introducing the 'creeping barrage' to the British Army in 1916, a concept that he said was inspired by the French. He was awarded the DSO in 1917, and posted to the Canadian Corps during their attack on Vimy. Repeatedly Mentioned in Despatches, he ended the war a lieutenant colonel. In the inter-war period he attended both the Staff College and became an instructor at the Imperial Defence College. Ranking as brigadier he commanded 8th Infantry Brigade in 1934, and the following year was promoted to major general. By 1936 he was Director of Military Training, and by July 1939 was GOC Southern Command, and had been made a KCB.

With the outbreak of war Sir Alan Brooke took command of II Corps, and was instrumental in extracting his men through Dunkirk. Brooke then took charge of the military defence of the southern portion of the UK. When Churchill grew tired of Sir John Dill in 1941, Brooke replaced him as Chief of the Imperial General Staff. Brooke was now head of the Army. He would remain so for the rest of the war, and it is said that under the weight of such heavy responsibility he survived on four or five hours of sleep each night. On many occasions he steered Churchill away from flights of fancy, and the result was an ongoing relationship of mutual exasperation and admiration.

Brooke attended the major Allied conferences, selected generals and advised the Prime Minister on virtually all aspects of operations and strategy. Arguably the long, and often grudging, relationship of Churchill and Brooke was the pivotal one for Britain's military performance during most of the war. From the Chief of the Imperial General Staff's perspective, Churchill's behaviour could be infuriating, as he examined minute detail, changed strategic direction or apparently sought argument for its own sake. Yet whilst the Prime Minister finally tired of so many and cast them aside, his sometimes stormy association with Brooke proved enduring, and arguably their very different characters were complementary.

Brooke was made a field marshal in 1944, and was created Baron Alanbrooke of Brookborough in September 1945 and Viscount Alanbrooke in 1946. Amongst various post-war appointments he was Master Gunner of England. Eventually he obtained greater leisure to pursue his hobby of ornithology and he died in 1963.

Sir Frederick A.M. Browning (1896–1965)

Browning takes leave of men of 1st Airborne Division prior to his move to South East Asia, December 1944. (Universal History Archive/ Getty Images.)

Far left: From gunner officer to Chief of the Imperial General Staff and field marshal, Alan Brooke rose to the pinnacle of the British Army. More remarkably he stayed put and forged an immensely constructive relationship with Churchill. (Getty Images.)

Frederick Arthur Montague Browning was born in London and served in France during the First World War, winning the DSO and Croix de Guerre. In the inter-war period he was adjutant at Sandhurst, and a keen sportsman, competing in the 1928 Winter Olympics as a member of the British bobsleigh team, as well as enjoying riding and boating. By the mid-1930s he ranked as lieutenant colonel, was commanding officer of the 2nd Grenadier Guards and married to the novelist Daphne du Maurier. At the outbreak of the Second World War, Browning was promoted to brigadier and made commandant of the Small Arms School, but in 1940 was given command of 24th Guards Brigade.

In 1941, with the formation of the new airborne forces, he was again promoted: to lead 1st Airborne Division. In December 1943 'Boy' Browning was made lieutenant general, and early in 1944 he became commander of I Airborne Corps, in which role he would later serve – somewhat uncomfortably – under US direction. Browning's command during Operation Market Garden in the Netherlands brought him dramatically to the fore, and though he has been widely criticised for communication issues and other problems Montgomery did not blame him for the ultimate failure of the operation. The 1st Airborne Division held on for longer than expected, and Browning was liked and respected by his troops, but Arnhem was famously a 'bridge too far' for speedy relief by ground forces. Browning later served as Mountbatten's chief of staff in India, was knighted, and was Military Secretary at the War Office from 1946 to 1948. He subsequently became Comptroller of the Household at Buckingham Palace, a position sadly terminated by a nervous breakdown. He died of a heart attack in 1965.

A 25 pdr field gun stands sentry at the Arnhem bridge over the Lower Rhine. Badly damaged during Operation Market Garden, the bridge was rebuilt and reopened in 1948. In the 1970s the Arnhem road bridge was officially renamed the John Frostbrug, or 'John Frost Bridge', in honour of Lieutenant Colonel, later Major General, Frost who held the crossing with 2nd battalion of the Parachute Regiment in September 1944. (Author)

GERARD C. BUCKNALL (1894–1980)

Gerard Corfield Bucknall was commissioned into the Middlesex Regiment in 1914 and fought on the Western Front. After the First World War he served with the Egyptian Army and attended the Staff College. He commanded 2nd Middlesex in 1939, but quickly advanced to general and by 1941 was leading 53rd Division. In the run-up to D-Day he was given charge of XXX Corps, which he led in Normandy,

but Montgomery removed him in August because, so he said, he 'could not manage a Corps once the battle became mobile'. Horrocks replaced Bucknall, who thereafter was made GOC Northern Ireland, a post he held until retirement in 1947. In the mid-1960s he was the last Lord Lieutenant of Middlesex, before the position was abolished in 1965.

SIR ARCHIBALD J.H. CASSELS (1907–1996)

Born in Quetta, India, Archibald James Halkett Cassels was educated at Rugby School and Sandhurst, where he won the Sword of Honour. He was commissioned into the Seaforth Highlanders in 1926. For the next twelve years he saw service in India, including operations against the Afridis, then Palestine and the UK, and was a substantive captain by 1938. He was a brigade major in France in 1940, and following training at the Staff College he rejoined the 52nd Division as a staff officer. Various postings followed, but by early 1944 he was a brigadier on the Imperial General Staff and one of the planners for D-Day. From July he commanded 51st Highland Division in Normandy, narrowly escaping death in a friendly fire incident and winning the DSO. He fought throughout the campaign in northwest Europe, including the Battle of the Reichswald and the advance into Germany. In May 1945 he was made acting major general.

In 1946 he commanded 6th Airborne Division in Palestine, and was later Director of Land Warfare at the War Office. He commanded the 1st Commonwealth Division in Korea, and was a temporary lieutenant general by 1953. He went on to serve in Malaya, then as Commander-in-Chief British Army of the Rhine and as Chief of the Imperial General Staff. He was also an important figure in the reorganisation of the Territorial Army. He was made a field marshal in 1968 and following his retirement lived in Scotland until his death in 1996.

SIR MICHAEL O'MOORE CREAGH (1892–1970)

The son of a general who had won the VC, Michael O'Moore Creagh, known sometimes as 'Dickie', fought in the First World War and won the MC, rising to brigade major by 1918. He attended the Staff College, ranking as colonel by 1934 and was commanding officer of the 15th/19th Hussars. In December 1939 Creagh was in Egypt commanding the mobile force that a few months later was given the name of the 7th Armoured Division. The unit inflicted a serious defeat on the Italians at Sidi Barrani and then drove forwards in the victorious Operation Compass counter-attack. Further success was scored when Creagh sent forwards Lieutenant Colonel Combe and his 'Combe Force' cut off the enemy at Beda Fomm. However, Creagh was dropped with the failure of Operation Battleaxe in September. He retired in 1944.

SIR JOHN T. CROCKER (1896–1963)

Nicknamed 'Honest John' and described not unfairly as a 'quiet man of influence', John Tredinnick Crocker joined the Artist's Rifles as a private in the First World War and was later commissioned into the Machine Gun Corps. He was awarded both the MC and DSO. Between the wars Crocker first went into the law, but then returned to the Army with the Middlesex Regiment before a transfer to the Tank Corps. He attended the Staff College and went on to hold staff posts under Hobart and Brooke. By February 1937 he ranked as a substantive colonel. In France in 1940 he was a brigade commander in 1st Armoured Division, later being promoted to lead 6th Armoured Division and then IX Corps. He fought in Tunisia in 1943 and was wounded during the abortive offensive of Operation Vulcan.

Later that year Crocker took command of I Corps, and on D-Day had responsibility for a significant section of the landing grounds and the taking of Caen. Though the invasion was carried

off successfully in the face of stiff resistance, Caen held out for two months. Crocker then had to battle more than one difficulty as his formation was placed, not entirely smoothly, under the First Canadian Army and in October 1944 his only son was killed. After the war Crocker's posts included General Officer Commanding (GOC) Southern Command; Commander Middle East Land Forces; and Adjutant General. Though considered for Chief of the Imperial General Staff, this appointment went to Slim. After the Army, General Crocker was Vice-Chairman of the Commonwealth War Graves Commission.

SIR ALAN G. CUNNINGHAM (1887–1983)

Alan Gordon Cunningham was born in Dublin and was commissioned in 1906. In the First World War he was awarded both the MC and DSO. Between the wars he spent time in Malaya and rose to major general of the 5th Anti-Aircraft Division. Early in the war he was moved to Kenya and promoted to lieutenant general, and in 1941 he was directed to launch an offensive into Ethiopia. In less than two months Cunningham's forces, acting in concert with those of General William Platt, had crushed the Italians. For Cunningham this signal success led to a knighthood and in August 1941 his appointment to lead the new Eighth Army. However, the advance in North Africa faltered and Auchinleck relieved Cunningham, who returned to the UK to become commandant of the Staff College. Later, he was GOC Eastern Command. After the war Cunningham was High Commissioner in Palestine and colonel commandant of the Royal Artillery. He died in Tunbridge Wells in 1983.

Sir Miles C. Dempsey (1896–1969)

Dempsey with Montgomery, pictured in Normandy, 16 July 1944. (IWM/Getty Images)

Born in Cheshire, though claiming a somewhat fanciful Irish pedigree, Miles Christopher Dempsey graduated from Sandhurst in 1915 and was commissioned into the Berkshire Regiment. He served on the Western Front and was awarded the MC. 'Lucky' remained as a career officer with the Army after the First World War and by the mid-1930s had reached the level of brigade commander. He returned to France with the British Expeditionary Force (BEF), leading 13th Infantry Brigade, and retired via Dunkirk in 1940. Raised to divisional status he then commanded, successively, 46th and 42nd Divisions. He fought in North Africa, and by 1942 was a lieutenant general commanding XIII Corps of the Eighth Army. Dempsey helped to plan the invasion of Sicily, and then led the invasion of Italy – fighting his way up the peninsula to Salerno. Thereafter he was selected to lead Second Army, and withdrawn to the UK to prepare for the D-Day landings. On 6 June 1944 it was troops under his command who made the crucial assaults at Gold, Juno and Sword beaches. Following tough fighting in Normandy, Dempsey eventually led them to Brussels and Antwerp. He was the first British Army commander across the Rhine, and his troops had seized much of northern Germany, including Hamburg, by May 1945.

After the war he was appointed commander of Middle East Land Forces, and retired in 1947, though he retained several significant honorary posts including colonel commandant of the SAS. A director of a number of businesses in later life, he died in Berkshire in 1972. Never a particularly high-profile figure, he is however usually regarded as a highly competent general and a very safe pair of hands in commanding both combat troops and combined operations.

Commonwealth troops dash ashore from an American type LCVP, or 'Landing Craft Vehicle Personnel'. This vessel and its British-built cousin the LCA or 'Landing Craft Assault' were capable of carrying a platoon of troops. Generals and politicians shaped strategy, but execution depended on availability of key equipment. (Official/author)

Sir John Greer Dill (1881–1944)

The son of an Ulster bank manager, Dill was commissioned into the Leinsters on leaving Sandhurst in 1901 and quickly proceeded to South Africa for the Boer War. Back in Ireland he served as battalion adjutant, then attended the Staff College just before the outbreak of the First World War. In 1914 he was brigade major to 25th Infantry Brigade in France; he was at the Battle of Neuve Chapelle and awarded the DSO in 1915. Thereafter he had different staff appointments of increasing responsibility and was repeatedly Mentioned in Despatches. Despite his relatively junior rank at the time, he has since been referred to as the 'operations brain' of Haig's headquarters, but whether this is complimentary or not depends entirely on one's view of Haig's command. At the end of the war Dill ranked as brigadier. In the inter-war period he commanded a brigade of the Territorials, and in 1926 joined the staff of the Imperial Defence College. After a time in India he was promoted to major general, and in 1934 became Director of Military Operations. Two years later he was promoted again, this time to lieutenant general, and went to command British forces in Palestine.

By 1939 Dill was GOC Aldershot Command and a holder of the KCB. Some thought that he would succeed Sir Cyril Deverell as Chief of the Imperial General Staff, but in the event he briefly commanded I Corps before being recalled to the UK in April 1940 to become Vice Chief to Sir Edmund Ironside. However, within a few weeks Ironside was dropped and Dill gained the prize. Dill lasted as Chief of the Imperial General Staff for just over eighteen months, from May 1940 to December 1941. Tellingly, he quickly recognised that in terms of strategic priorities holding the UK had to come first; also that Singapore was poorly defended and might be threatened with catastrophe. Much to the Prime Minister's displeasure, he regarded Egypt as less of an issue, and whilst it has often been said that he failed to stand up to Churchill, he was very clear on this important matter. He also defended Wavell when the latter was exhorted to take to the offensive without the preparations he deemed vital. When Wavell was replaced by Auchinleck, Dill was not slow to warn the latter that he would likewise come under huge pressure to achieve swift results.

Churchill, who nicknamed Sir John 'Dilly-Dally', regarded him as overcautious, if not actually obstructive, and was pleased to see him retire at sixty. However, common sense suggests that during late 1940 and early 1941 Britain was neither ready nor equipped to undertake some of the more dramatic ventures that the Prime Minister had in mind, and Dill's hesitancy at the time may have turned out to be wise. Alan Brooke suggested his predecessor for a peerage, but this was refused. Dill was subsequently shipped off to serve as head of the British 'Joint Staff Mission' to Washington, DC, but if the Prime Minister ever regarded this as a convenient way to sideline his old chief of staff it was singularly unsuccessful. The Americans were keen to know that Dill was no mere functionary, and Churchill reassured them that Dill would speak not merely as head of the mission but as representing the Prime Minister in his capacity as Minister of Defence.

Dill attended the major Allied conferences and cultivated very useful contacts with the US establishment. He was part of the committee dealing with the atomic bomb, and formed a remarkable rapprochement with US Army Chief of Staff General George C. Marshall, in whom he encouraged the 'Germany first' policy – and therefore perhaps achieved more on the diplomatic front than he ever did on the military. In private, however, Dill was disappointed that no matter how significant a 'go-between' he might now be, he was no longer 'one of the principals'. Dill died in Washington, DC, in November 1944, was given a state funeral and buried at Arlington National Cemetery, Virginia. The American chiefs of staff eulogised him for his 'selfless devotion to the Allied cause' and as a personal friend.

Sir Geoffrey C. Evans (1901–1987)

Geoffrey Charles Evans was commissioned into the Royal Warwickshires in 1920, and within two years was adjutant of his battalion. He attended the Staff College in 1937, and ranking as major was seconded to the Indian Army in 1939. The following year he was in the Western Desert and took part in the successful Operation Compass against the Italians before moving on to the Sudan. By early 1941 he was in command of 1st Royal Sussex, and in November fought in Operation Crusader. In 1942 he was put in charge of Silver Group during the breakout from Benghazi. Soon afterwards, and now brigadier, Evans was transferred to the Far East, becoming successively a staff officer and commander of 9th Indian Brigade in the Arakan, Burma. In the Battle of the Admin Box, Evans led a desperate defence when cut off behind enemy lines. Thereafter he fought at Imphal and was promoted to acting major general. In 1945 Evans led 7th Indian Division in the crossing of the Irrawaddy.

At the end of hostilities Evans was made commander of Allied land forces in Siam (Thailand). For his various campaigns he was awarded the DSO three times. Later, Evans became commander of British forces in Hong Kong, a lieutenant general and was knighted KBE. He retired in 1957.

Sir Francis W. Festing (1902–1976)

Francis Wogan Festing was born in Dublin and educated at Winchester College and Sandhurst, before being commissioned into the Rifle Brigade in 1921. He served in India and the UK, going to the Staff College at Camberley in 1934 – whence he would return a few years later as an instructor. By early 1940 he was a temporary lieutenant colonel: in April he was air liaison officer for the Norway expedition, but later in the year was appointed commanding officer of 2nd East Lancashires. In 1942, as acting brigadier, he led 29th Infantry Brigade to Madagascar: thereafter he led 36th Division in India and Burma. He won the DSO, and by dint of his proclivity to lead from the front earned the nickname 'Front Line Frankie'. He was indeed lucky to survive the war unscathed, once narrowly escaping a Japanese ambush, and on another occasion leading a platoon in combat. Official communications would have us believe that the personal motto of Festing was 'a Jap before breakfast'. He was finally made substantive major general in November 1944, and at the end of the war was made General Officer Commanding (GOC) Land Forces, Hong Kong.

Despite a serious illness in 1949, reductions to the Army and controversy over his command in Egypt in the early 1950s, his career prospered. He was made Chief of the Imperial General Staff in 1958 and promoted to field marshal in 1960. As he himself noted, he was thereby the first Roman Catholic to lead the British Army since 1688. In later life he devoted time to his collections of firearms and Japanese swords. He died at Hexham, Northumberland, in 1976.

Prince Henry W.F.A., Duke of Gloucester (1900–1974)

Henry William Frederick Albert was the third son of the Duke of York, the future King George V, and was born at Sandringham and educated at Eton. He was commissioned into the Rifle Brigade in 1919. In 1921 he joined the 10th Royal Hussars. He reached the rank of captain in 1927, and

was created Duke of Gloucester the following year. Though he entered the Staff College in 1936, and was promoted to major general in 1937, this was no sign of a developing military career because he now stood third in line to the throne. He therefore retired from the Army.

This status was dramatically reversed in 1939 when Gloucester was appointed chief liaison officer on the staff of Lord Gort. He proceeded to France and on 15 May 1940 he was slightly wounded in an air attack and was ordered home. Thereafter much of his work was morale-raising and ceremonial, and he appeared on visits as far apart as the Mediterranean and India. He was made a field marshal in 1955 and later became Governor-General of Australia (1945–1947). He died in 1974.

Sir Francis W. de Guingand (1900–1979)

Francis Wilfred de Guingand was educated at Ampleforth and commissioned into the Middlesex Regiment, serving in Africa in the late 1920s. He failed to gain entry to the Staff College at the first attempt, but was nominated by his friend and mentor Montgomery in 1935. In 1939 he was Military Secretary to the

Secretary of State for War. After short periods as an instructor and as commandant of the new School of Combined Operations he was posted to headquarters in Cairo, where he was instrumental in laying plans for the evacuation of Greece. By February 1942 he was Director of Military intelligence, Middle East, and when Montgomery was appointed to lead the Eighth Army he called on de Guingand to become his chief of staff. He fitted quickly into his new role and was important to Montgomery, both for his meticulous staff work and his diplomatic handling of both British and American colleagues, many of whom were affronted in one way or another by Montgomery.

He was promoted to major general in 1943, after the successful conclusion of the campaign in North Africa, and knighted in 1944. The following year he was awarded the American Legion of Merit by the USA. He accompanied Montgomery to northwest Europe, and was appointed Director of Military Intelligence at the end of the war. In 1946 he left the Army to pursue business interests in Rhodesia, and wrote an autobiography and other books about the war.

Sir Allan F. Harding, 1st Baron Harding of Petherton (1896–1989)

Usually known as 'John', Allan Francis Harding was the son of a solicitor's clerk, and himself an employee of the Post Office Savings Bank, but was commissioned into the Territorials and went to Gallipoli in 1915, where he was wounded. Upon recovery he continued to serve in the Middle East, winning the MC at the fourth Battle of Gaza in 1917. After the war he was posted to India, and despite a reasonably successful time he failed the Indian Staff College course and returned to the UK to enter the Staff College at Camberley in 1928. Only in 1938 did he reach the rank of lieutenant colonel, and at the outbreak of the Second World War was commanding officer of the 1st Somerset Light Infantry on the North West Frontier, where in 1940 he was Mentioned in Despatches during operations against the Fakir of Ipi.

However, Harding's biggest opportunity came with his transfer to the Western Desert as a staff officer. When O'Connor was captured, Harding assumed temporary command and was instrumental in holding Tobruk. In the campaigns that followed he was awarded the DSO twice. In 1942 he was promoted to major general, and that September was given command of 7th Armoured Division and fought at El Alamein. He narrowly escaped death more than once, and was badly wounded in January 1943 when a shell peppered him with fragments and took off three fingers. He was invalided back to the UK with a third DSO. He was subsequently promoted acting lieutenant general, and in December 1943 was appointed chief of staff to Alexander in Italy. He was knighted in the field by King George VI. By March 1945 he was commanding XIII Corps, with whom he reached Trieste on 3 May.

Opposite: The Duke of Gloucester in the uniform of the 10th Royal Hussars. The cap and collar badges are Prince of Wales plumes. (The Print Collector/ Getty Images)

Eighth Army mine-clearance school in the desert. Men worked in pairs when using detectors to locate and mark mines, which were lifted by a third man working a safe distance behind, clearing marked lanes. Mine fields were an important feature of defended areas particularly in the desert war. (Official/ author)

A succession of important posts followed the conclusion of hostilities, and by 1951 Harding was Commander-in-Chief British Army of the Rhine. The next year he succeeded Slim as Chief of the Imperial General Staff, and was made field marshal in 1953. From 1955 he was Governor of Cyprus for a difficult two years. In 1958 he was ennobled as Baron Harding of Petherton and Nether Common. He lived well into his nineties and died at Sherborne in 1989.

Sir Percy C.S. Hobart (1885–1957)

Percy Hobart: tank innovator and divisional commander, in battle dress and beret. (IWM/Getty Images)

Born in India of Irish parentage, Percy Cleghorn Stanley Hobart – nicknamed 'Patrick' – graduated from the Royal Military Academy Woolwich in 1904 and was commissioned into the Royal Engineers. During the First World War he served in both France and Mesopotamia, being present at several significant engagements, including the battles of Loos and Kut. He was Mentioned in Despatches and awarded both the MC and DSO, and attended the Staff College after the war. Hobart was described by a contemporary as having a fascinating and forceful mind, interested in many things both within and outside the Army.

Convinced of the worth of tanks, and influenced by the works of Basil Liddell Hart, he transferred to the Tank Corps in 1923. Four years later, Hobart's sister married Montgomery, with whom Hobart had a highly competitive relationship. After a period as an instructor at the Indian Staff College in Quetta, Hobart became the commander of the first permanent armoured brigade and by 1937 ranked as major general. The following year he formed and trained the 'Mobile Force' in Egypt – precursor to the famous 'Desert Rats' 7th Armoured Division. He was ushered into retirement in 1940 by, so it was said, a War Office concerned at his 'unconventional' ideas. He then passed into the Home Guard, initially ranking as lance corporal.

On the advice of influential friends Churchill brought Hobart out of retirement in 1941, whereupon his first task was the training of 11th Armoured Division. Despite illness he went on to raise a new unit, the 79th Armoured Division. In 1943 this unit was converted into a specialised formation with vehicles dedicated to the battlefield tasks of overcoming the sorts of fixed defences that had bedevilled the Dieppe raid. These 'Hobart's Funnies' did sterling work on D-Day, as well as in northwest Europe, and many of the ideas introduced continue to have relevance to the present day. Hobart finally retired in 1946, and died in 1957. His honours included Knight Commander of the Order of the British Empire (KBE), Companion of the Order of the Bath (CB) and the American Legion of Merit from the USA.

Sir Brian G. Horrocks (1895–1985)

The son of an army doctor, Brian Gwynne Horrocks was born in India in 1895. He was academically undistinguished, being, by his own admission, an 'idle' student at Sandhurst. War in 1914 proved a rude awakening as he was rapidly commissioned into the Middlesex Regiment, caught up with his regiment on the retreat from Mons, and was wounded and captured at Ypres on 21 October. Despite repeated escape attempts he remained a prisoner until the end of the war. In 1919 he applied to serve against the Bolsheviks and was promptly despatched to Siberia, where he was again captured, as well as contracting typhus. He was eventually repatriated via Finland in 1920. On rejoining his regiment he served successively in the army of occupation in Germany, the war in Ireland, and in Silesia. In 1924 he competed in the pentathlon at the Olympic games in Paris. He attended the Staff College in 1931 and by 1936 was brigade major to 5th Infantry Brigade.

On the outbreak of the Second World War Horrocks was an instructor at the Staff College ranking as lieutenant colonel, but was sent to France to command 2nd Middlesex. After Dunkirk he was appointed to lead 9th Brigade, and by mid-1941 he was an acting major general commanding 44th Division. Following a time leading 9th Armoured Division he took charge of XIII Corps under Montgomery in Egypt. At Alam el Halfa Ridge Horrocks fought a good defensive battle – as he later remarked, it was 'one of the few battles in which I fought that went exactly according to plan'. In December 1942 Horrocks was given command of X Corps and awarded the DSO. Early the next year he again distinguished himself at the Mareth Line. Finally leading IX Corps during the offensive into Tunisia, he accepted the surrender of the remains of Rommel's Army Group Africa. He was made Companion of the Order of the Bath (CB), and temporary lieutenant general.

Badly injured by a ground-attack fighter in June 1943, Horrocks was fortunate to survive, but by the breakout after D-Day he was sufficiently recovered to be given XXX Corps to lead in northwest Europe. He forged as far forwards as Antwerp before being halted on the Scheldt. Soon afterwards XXX Corps was directed to link up with the 1st Airborne Division at Arnhem. The degree to which Horrocks contributed to the failure of Operation Market Garden is debatable – some commentators assert that XXX Corps lacked urgency, others that faulty intelligence resulted in a highly unrealistic timetable on narrow roads against stiffening resistance. Horrocks's own memoirs refer to extended lines of communication and the quick arrival of enemy units. In 1945 XXX Corps crossed the Rhine and by late April had captured Bremen. At the end of hostilities Horrocks received a shower of awards from Britain, Belgium, France, the Netherlands and the USA, being generally

Victory parade in Tunis, 20 May 1943: British troops march past the Allied commanders and a crowd. The Tunisia campaign of November 1942 to May 1943 cost the Axis about 300,000 men, many of them taken prisoner. (Official/author)

recognised as one of the most successful British generals. US commander J.M. Gavin dubbed him the 'finest corps commander' of the war.

Horrocks commanded the British Army of the Rhine in the late 1940s but was invalided out of the Army and in 1952 appointed to the position of Black Rod in Parliament. In later life he maintained a high profile, wrote widely, appeared on television, was a film consultant and even sponsored a board game. He died in 1985.

Sir Richard A. Hull (1907–1989)

Richard Amayatt Hull was born at Cosham, Hampshire, into an Army family and was educated at Charterhouse and Trinity College, Cambridge. He joined the 17th/21st Lancers in 1928, and served with them in India. Upon mechanisation, Hull, now the adjutant, drove the regiment's first tank in 1938. Following the Indian Staff College at Quetta he returned to the UK. In 1942 he led Blade Force in Algeria and was awarded the DSO for his actions at Teboura Gap. Thereafter he led a number of different brigades in North Africa, until December 1943 when he was made Deputy Director of Staff Studies. He fought in Italy in late 1944, now commanding 1st Armoured Division as an acting major general, his rank being made temporary just before the Japanese capitulation.

This was, however, but halfway in a very successful career. By 1954 Hull was a lieutenant general, and in 1961 Chief of the Imperial General Staff. He was created field marshal in 1965, retiring from active service two years later. He died at Pinhoe, Exeter, in 1989 and was given a state funeral at Windsor.

Sir William Edmund Ironside, 1st Baron Archangel and Ironside (1880–1959)

Born in Edinburgh, Edmund Ironside was the son of a military surgeon. He was educated at Tonbridge School, Kent, and on leaving the Royal Military Academy Woolwich was commissioned into the Royal Artillery in 1899. He served extensively in the Boer War and afterwards remained in German South West Africa, using his vast linguistic skills to good effect in military espionage, becoming, it is said, the model for the character Richard Hannay in John Buchan's *The Thirty-Nine Steps*. After this interlude Ironside returned to more normal

duties and by 1908 was ranking as brigade major, going on to the Staff College in 1913. Through much of the First World War he was a staff officer behind the Western Front, and also commandant of the machine gun school at Camiers, but in early 1918 took command of a fighting brigade. Now a major general he was redeployed to northern Russia in late 1918, quickly becoming Commander-in-Chief of Allied forces there. In 1920 he was moved to Hungary, then to the Black Sea theatre and, finally, to Mesopotamia to command the North Persian Force.

Ironside's career thereafter settled down somewhat into a series of increasingly senior staff appointments and commands in the UK, Gibraltar, the Middle East and India, though his time was hardly unexciting because he was involved in two air crashes. These accidents shortened his legs, reducing 'Tiny' Ironside to 'only' about 6 feet-4 inches in height. Nevertheless he retained what Brian Bond has noted as a 'commanding presence and a popular reputation', and was one of those who clearly saw the folly of allowing the Army to be feeble and under-resourced at such a critical juncture. Perhaps even more importantly, he was strongly supported by Churchill and on mobilisation in 1939 Ironside replaced Lord Gort as Chief of the Imperial General Staff. This was a job for which, even he was prepared to admit, he lacked the right temperament. So it was that his new position quickly turned into frustration.

At first he backed to the hilt the dubious intervention in Norway, but later, realising that Churchill was keen to go ahead with entirely inadequate preparation and resources, sought to hold it off until the chances of success were vastly improved. The mission quickly dissolved in failure. Ironside was thus badly wrongfooted. Next, he was one of those presiding over the serious reverse in France. However, on visiting Gort on the battlefront in May 1940 Ironside quickly, and wisely, came to the conclusion that withdrawal was the only practical option. His timely support of evacuation, though entirely contrary to his nature, and in some ways an accident of history, was one of the things that helped Britain to survive.

Ironside was prompted into resignation by Churchill, but was not immediately abandoned, becoming GOC Home Forces instead. His defence plan for the UK, which involved a series of 'stop lines', was roundly criticised by ambitious rivals – but in the absence of tanks, or a significant mobile reserve, it is difficult to see what other strategy could have been adopted at that time. Nevertheless beach defences and static lines could only ever be a stopgap measure, even Churchill himself quickly realised that the battle would not really be 'won or lost' on the beaches but by the reserves available. Ironside was replaced as Home Forces' commander by Sir Alan Brooke in late July, but he went with dignity, receiving the consolation of a field marshal's baton. In 1941 he was granted a peerage. He quickly retired from public life, but survived the war and died in London in 1959.

HASTINGS L. ISMAY, 1ST BARON ISMAY (1887–1965)

Though born in India, Hastings Lionel Ismay was educated at Charterhouse and entered Sandhurst in 1904, doing well in the examinations. On returning to India he served briefly with the Gloucestershire Regiment and other units before finding a permanent place in the cavalry of the Indian Army in 1907. The following year he served in Afghanistan. In 1914 he was appointed second in command of the Somaliland Camel Corps and moved on to Africa to fight the uprising of the 'Mad Mullah', a campaign not successfully concluded until 1920. Ismay received the DSO for his part. Thereafter he attended the Staff College and was appointed Deputy Assistant Quartermaster General of the Indian Army. He sat on various committees, and served at the War Office as an intelligence officer, and by 1936 was Deputy Secretary of the Committee of Imperial Defence – two years later he became the Secretary.

On the outbreak of war 'Pug' Ismay was promoted to major general and began working with Neville Chamberlain. He was subsequently retained by Churchill when he became prime minister eight months later, becoming Secretary of the Imperial Defence Chief of Staffs Committee, and essentially a key link between the military and civilian leaderships. Here Ismay displayed both tact and patience. He also attended the Allied conferences with both Churchill and Eden and was reportedly well liked by Eisenhower. Ismay was an integral part of the planning for the Normandy landings and was promoted to full general in May 1944. He accompanied King George VI to France after the invasion, and went with Churchill to Potsdam after VE Day.

After the war he remained on good terms with Churchill and received various honours, including the Knight Grand Cross of the Order of the Bath (GCB) and the title Baron Ismay of Wormington. In 1947 he went to India with Mountbatten as his chief of staff, drawing up plans for partition and not very successfully attempting to persuade interested parties to accept a peaceful solution. Back

in the UK he became Chairman of the Council of the Festival of Britain, and from 1951 Secretary of State for Commonwealth Relations. Finally, in March 1952, he was made Secretary General of NATO. Prophetically, Ismay expressed the hope that one day the whole free world would be able to shelter under the 'NATO umbrella'. He retired in 1957 and died in 1965.

SIR ROBERT E. LAYCOCK (1907–1968)

Laycock pictured at his desk in 1943, an image that belies his reputation as man of action. (Popperphoto/Getty Images.)

The Eton-educated son of a brigadier, Robert Edward Laycock attended Sandhurst, followed by a commission into the Royal Horse Guards in 1927. Despite being on the Continent prior to May 1940 he missed the French campaign due to being recalled for a staff appointment in the UK. David Niven later claimed that he was instrumental in introducing Laycock to Dudley Clarke, founding father of the Commandos, and soon Laycock was charged with raising No. 8 (Guards) Commando.

Early the next year, Laycock, now ranking as colonel, led a Commando group the size of a small brigade to the eastern Mediterranean. Drawn mainly from No. 7, No. 8, and No. 11 Commando and the Middle East Commando, this group was known as 'Layforce'. Though a raid was mounted on Bardia, its biggest action was in covering the retreat from Crete in April 1941, a mission in which it suffered very heavy casualties. Later, Laycock personally led the unsuccessful raid attempting to assassinate Erwin Rommel, and in its aftermath he escaped only by spending a prolonged period evading the enemy behind their own lines. In 1942 Laycock was redeployed to lead a brigade in the attack on Sicily, and was awarded the DSO. If not always successful, his courageous and wide-ranging service was certainly well acknowledged in October 1943, when, as major general, Laycock was promoted to Chief of Combined Operations as replacement for Lord Louis Mountbatten. In that role he was instrumental in the remoulding of the Commando force prior to D-Day. He remained in his post until 1947. From 1954 to 1957 Sir Robert Laycock was Governor of Malta. He died suddenly of a heart attack in 1968.

Sir William O.H. Leese, 3rd Baronet of Send Holme (1894–1978)

William Oliver Hargreaves Leese was the Eton-educated son of a barrister and was commissioned into the Coldstream Guards in 1915. He fought on the Somme, was wounded three times, Mentioned in Despatches and awarded the DSO. He attended the Staff College in 1927 and reached the rank of lieutenant colonel in the mid-1930s. Following several staff appointments, he proceeded to India in 1938 as an instructor at the the Indian Staff College, Quetta.

Early in the Second World War he was chief of staff to Gort in France, and after Dunkirk was appointed to form 29th Infantry Brigade. In December 1940 Leese ranked as major general and he led, successively, the Wessex Division, 15th Scottish Division and Guards Armoured Division. In late 1942 he went to North Africa with the rank of acting lieutenant general to command XXX Corps. He proved successful during the advance on Tunis, and was again Mentioned in Despatches. His corps then took part in the invasion of Sicily, before Leese was withdrawn to the UK for D-Day preparations. However, as matters worked out he did not campaign in northwest Europe, for when his mentor Montgomery was withdrawn from Italy Leese was designated to succeed as commander there. So it was that he commanded the Eighth Army at Cassino in May 1944. Later that year he moved to command Allied Land Forces South East Asia – a not entirely unsuccessful interlude, but one that was marred by his inability to read either the local conditions or Mountbatten's whim, and it ended with his

premature removal. He retired from the Army in 1947, and later became known as a horticulturist and President of the MCC.

Herbert Lumsden (1897–1945)

Educated at Eton, Herbert Lumsden served with the Territorials before entering Sandhurst. He was commissioned into the Royal Artillery in 1916 and won the MC in 1918. In the inter-war period he was a keen competitive rider, but in 1929 went to the Staff College. Ranking as major he held several staff appointments with the cavalry, becoming commanding officer of 12th Royal Lancers in 1938. He served in the French campaign of 1940, won the DSO and was later given command of 6th Armoured Division in the UK.

In North Africa he commanded 1st Armoured Division and during the campaigns of 1942 was twice wounded, winning a second DSO. At El Alamein he commanded X Corps, but failed to sparkle and was removed by Montgomery. After a spell in the UK commanding VIII Corps he went on to the Pacific theatre as Churchill's representative to MacArthur. On 6 January 1945 Lieutenant General Lumsden was killed instantly when a kamikaze struck the USS *New Mexico* from which he had been watching a bombardment.

Sir Richard L. McCreery (1898–1967)

Born in Rugby, Richard Loudon McCreery was educated at Eton and Sandhurst, joining the 12th Royal Lancers in 1915. He was wounded and won the MC. Despite his injury, he continued to be a keen horseman and by 1935 was commanding officer of his regiment. He fought in France in 1940 and ended the campaign leading 2nd Armoured Brigade. Posted to the Middle East, he became chief of staff in that theatre and an advisor to Auchinleck on armour. Later, he was chief of staff to Alexander and had a hand in planning El Alamein. In 1943 'Dick' McCreery took command of X Corps in Italy, becoming temporary lieutenant general on 30 July. He fought at Salerno and Monte Cassino and was knighted in the field by the king. At the end of 1944 he took command of the Eighth Army and led it in the battles on the Po.

After the war McCreery commanded the British occupation army in Austria, and from 1946 he succeeded Montgomery as commander of the British Army of the Rhine. From 1948 he was on the Military Staff Committee of the United Nations and in 1949 was promoted to full general. Critical of Montgomery in later life, he died in October 1967.

SIR FRANK W. MESSERVY (1893–1974)

Frank Walter Messervy was commissioned into the Indian Army in 1913 and saw action in both France and the Middle East during the First World War. In the early 1930s he was an instructor at the Indian Staff College, Quetta, and from 1938 commanding officer of the 13th Duke of Connaught's Own Lancers. At the outbreak of war Colonel Messervy was a staff officer with the new 5th Indian Division, which moved to the Sudan in 1940 to counter the Italian threat. Messervy was then appointed to lead the mobile 'Gazelle Force', which he did with success. Thereafter he commanded 9th Brigade with the rank of acting brigadier, but was soon promoted to lead 4th Indian Division, helping to bring the East Africa campaign to a satisfactory conclusion.

Through the rest of 1941 Messervy's 4th Indian Division fought in North Africa, in Operations Battleaxe and Crusader, but early in 1942 Messervy replaced the wounded commander of 1st Armoured Division, which suffered badly during Rommel's offensive. When Herbert Lumsden returned to lead 1st Armoured Division, Messervy was given charge of 7th Armoured Division. Again worsted by the enemy at Gazala, and with his HQ overrun, Messervy was lucky to escape. In 1943 he was moved to the Far East theatre as Director of Armoured Fighting Vehicles, and later he became commander of 7th Indian Division. At Kohima and Ukhrul he was instrumental in stemming the Japanese advance and then inflicting defeat. From the end of 1944 he led IV Corps during the attack on Meiktila and the advance to Rangoon.

After the enemy's surrender he became Commander-in-Chief Malaya Command and, with the partition of India, Commander-in-Chief Northern India Command. From 1947 to 1948 Messervy was Commander-in-Chief of the Pakistan Army, but was quickly retired due to disagreements with Jinnah. He died in the UK in 1974.

SIR BERNARD L. MONTGOMERY, 1ST VISCOUNT MONTGOMERY OF ALAMEIN (1887–1976)

Montgomery, centre, with Lieutenant General Lumsden, left, and Lieutenant General Oliver Leese, right, in Egypt, 1942. Leese proved more successful than Lumsden in North Africa. Lumsden was killed in action in the Far East in 1945, the British Army's most senior combat fatality of the Second World War. He is remembered on the Brookwood Memorial. (Popperfoto/Getty Images)

Men of the Scots Guards at Alamein. Famously Churchill's 'end of the beginning' of the war, the battle of El Alamein was also a major milestone in Montgomery's successful career. The troops shown are armed with SMLE rifles, and right, a Bren gun. (Official/author)

Opposite: 'Monty' in characteristic pose in the turret of his Grant tank, North Africa, November 1942. (IWM/Getty Images)

The rodent-like demeanour, showmanship, conceit and double-badged beret of 'Monty' are all now so iconic that it is difficult to separate the soldier and his image. Equally complex is any dispassionate evaluation of his leadership, given that he is one of relatively few commanders to have been so thoroughly studied, yet so often observed through the medium of his own writings. Monty had Churchill's support, but the Prime Minister also had a clear view of the field marshal's vainglorious nature. Of his habit of inviting defeated German generals to dinner, Churchill remarked that, 'No worse fate could befall an enemy officer'. Nevertheless, whatever the opinion of Montgomery the man, it must be conceded that he was one of the most significant generals of the war, of any nation.

Bernard Law Montgomery was the son of a churchman, born in Kennington, London. St Paul's School was followed by Sandhurst and a commission into the Royal Warwickshires in 1908. He served in India, but was deployed to France at the beginning of the First World War and took part in the retreat from Mons. In October 1914 he was critically wounded during an attack and awarded the DSO. After recovering at home he was made brigade major and he trained men of the 'New Armies' in Lancashire. Back at the Western Front he was a staff officer during many of the major engagements, including the Somme and Passchendaele.

After the First World War Montgomery commanded 17th Royal Fusiliers in Germany, but returned to the UK to enter the Staff College for a one-year course in 1920. In 1921 he went to the war in Ireland where he served in the same brigade as Percival: here one of his subordinates would memorably describe Montgomery as a 'tiger for work' and a 'martinet for punctuality'. Having already begun correspondence with Liddell Hart and developed an interest in tanks, Montgomery was appointed to the Staff College as instructor in 1927. In 1931 he became commanding officer of 1st Royal Warwickshires, ranking as lieutenant colonel. He then served in the Middle East and India, before another period as instructor, this time at the Indian Staff College. In 1937 he was promoted to temporary brigadier commanding 9th Infantry Brigade, but also suffered tragedy with the early death of his wife. On 21 May 1938 he was promoted to major general and took charge of 8th Infantry Division in Palestine, where he was instrumental in quelling the revolt. Despite a lung infection, Montgomery was back in the UK in 1939, now in charge of 3rd Infantry Division.

In France his abrasive attitude, demands to have colleagues sacked and bold issuance of a very modern-sounding directive concerning venereal disease rapidly made him unpopular with his superiors. Before too long, perhaps fortunately for him, the Germans intervened and Monty was able to demonstrate that his inconvenient opinions were coupled with an ability to control his division in battle. When Brooke eventually assumed acting command of the British Expeditionary Force, Monty took charge of Brooke's II Corps. Back in the UK he received the Companion of the Order of the Bath and was made acting lieutenant general. In 1942 the chance death of General Gott in an air crash presented the opportunity to lead the Eighth Army in North Africa – and it was at a vital time, when Rommel might break into Egypt, but also when British strength was increasing. Montgomery declared, with some theatricality, that any plans for a retreat were to be destroyed and he at first parried the enemy at Alam Halfa, then, in late October and early November, inflicted a serious reverse on them at El Alamein. Monty was knighted and promoted to full general. It was telling that whilst Auchinleck decreed that Rommel, the legendary 'Desert Fox' and 'Wizard of Oz', was to be studiously ignored, Monty deliberately established a rival personality cult of his own. This was successful to such an extent that Montgomery eclipsed Alexander, his superior in theatre. Gradually, the Axis troops were forced back towards final defeat in Africa, and in 1943 Monty went on to command the Eighth Army in Sicily and Italy.

At the end of the year Montgomery was withdrawn to the UK to lead 21st Army Group in the lead-up to D-Day. The landings succeeded, but fighting stalled in Normandy and gradually tensions, hitherto mainly latent, between Montgomery and his American opposite numbers began to emerge. Though eventually won, Caen turned into an attritional battle. With the breakout, Eisenhower took over command of forces on the ground, but Monty had the significant consolation of promotion to field marshal. Nevertheless, further setbacks were experienced with Operation Market Garden and the enemy's offensive in the Ardennes – the first backed by Monty, the latter missed initially by Eisenhower. Despite these episodes the Germans were being overwhelmed and Montgomery's part in the Allies' final victory involved the encirclement of Army Group B in the Ruhr. He accepted the surrender of German forces at Lüneburg Heath in northern Germany on 4 May 1945.

Honours and senior appointments flowed. Monty was created a viscount and Chief of the Imperial General Staff in 1946, and

Eisenhower's deputy in NATO in 1951. He also wrote widely, including memoirs, campaign narrations, and a general history of warfare. Whilst a grand figure, he was also a lonely one, and his self-righteous outspokenness could make him a loose cannon politically. Possibly this was aggravated, as during the 'Phoney War', by the dearth of active military operations to absorb his still-significant energy. However, in the early 1970s his health declined, and by 1974 his mind had grown feeble. Montgomery died on 24 March 1976 at his home at Islington Mill, Hampshire. Eisenhower's tribute was very much to the point: 'Whatever they say about him, he got us there.'

Sir Philip Neame (1888–1978)

Born at Faversham, Kent, Neame served in the Royal Engineers, ranking as lieutenant at the outbreak of the First World War. On 19 December 1914 on the Western Front he won the Victoria Cross (VC) by holding up the enemy single-handed with grenades. Ten years later at the Olympic games he won a gold medal in one of the shooting events. Neame stayed with the Army as a career officer, and by the early part of the Second World War had reached the rank of major general. However, he was taken prisoner in North Africa in 1941, later escaping from captivity with O'Connor. After the war he was Lieutenant Governor of Guernsey. He is remarkable as the only person ever to win both the VC and Olympic gold.

Sir Archibald Wavell, Commander-in-Chief Middle East Command, right, confers with O'Connor, commander of the Western Desert Force, outside Bardia, 4 January 1941. That Libya was not always hot is attested by the 'British warm' coats, and scarves, worn by both generals. (Fotosearch/Getty Images)

Far right: General Sir Bernard Paget talks to American soldiers during an inspection, 29 May 1943. (Fred Ramage/Getty Images)

SIR RICHARD N. O'CONNOR (1889–1981)

Richard Nugent O'Connor was born, in India, into an Army family, but schooled in England, where he attended Sandhurst in 1908. He served in France in the First World War, winning the MC and rising to command a battalion of the Honourable Artillery Company. Transferred to the Italian front in 1917, by the end of the war he had been awarded the DSO and bar. Following the Staff College, he served as adjutant of a battalion of the Cameronians, and was later made brigade major of the mechanised 'Experimental Brigade'. He was a full colonel by 1936, and later served as a major general in India.

In 1939 he was in Egypt, where a small British and Empire contingent found itself threatened by a massing of Italian force in Libya. O'Connor was appointed to command the 'Western Desert Force' and soon promoted to lieutenant general. During Operation Compass O'Connor's little army, less than 36,000 strong, advanced and broke the defences of Sidi Barrani, attacking the Italians in the flank and rear. For the cost of just 600 casualties, 38,000 of the enemy were captured and the threat to the Suez Canal lifted. In January 1941 O'Connor took Tobruk, and in February he finally defeated the enemy at Beda Fomm, where 7th Armoured Division and the Australians captured

another 20,000 men for even fewer losses. In all, O'Connor's attack advanced 800 miles and accounted for approximately 130,000 of the enemy. With the Italians hovering on the brink of total defeat in North Africa, Germany was forced to commit the Afrika Korps under Rommel.

In April 1941, at his moment of triumph; the newly knighted O'Connor was captured by a German patrol. He spent two years in Italian POW camps, but eventually escaped. After returning to Europe he commanded VIII Corps and fought in Normandy and the attempted relief of airborne forces during Operation Market Garden in the Netherlands. In 1945 he was appointed GOC Eastern Command, in India.

SIR BERNARD C.T. PAGET (1887–1961)

Bernard Charles Tolver Paget was the son of a clergyman and educated at Shrewsbury School and Sandhurst. He was commissioned into the Oxfordshire and Buckinghamshire Light Infantry and fought in France during the First World War, being repeatedly Mentioned in Despatches and awarded both the MC and DSO. A full colonel by 1929, he was later chief instructor at the Indian Staff College. Paget commanded a brigade from 1936, and was promoted to major general in 1937.

Soon after the outbreak of war Paget was given command of an infantry division and fought in the Norwegian campaign of 1940. The following year he was knighted, promoted to lieutenant general and was later made GOC Home Forces. In 1943 he was promoted to full general and appointed commander of 21st Army Group. In this capacity he was charged with joint leadership, along with Air Marshal Leigh Mallory, of the British invasion force for D-Day.

Their first formal meeting about this great matter took place on 7 December. Paget thought that the blow should fall on the Pas de Calais, hitting the toughest German defences, but taking the shortest sea crossing. His staff was of the opinion that Caen in Normandy could be attacked, but would not be taken for at least three days, or more. They would be proved more than correct in this particular. However, Brooke and Churchill were already looking for a replacement commander, and Montgomery made it abundantly clear that he would be more than willing to take Paget's job. Paget was duly shuffled out, becoming Commander-in-Chief Middle East Command. He retired from the Army in 1946 and from 1949 was Governor of the Royal Hospital Chelsea. He died in Hampshire in 1961.

ARTHUR E. PERCIVAL (1887–1966)

Arthur Ernest Percival was born at Aspden, Hertfordshire, and educated at Rugby School where he proved a good sportsman but was academically undistinguished. Becoming an officer with the Bedfordshire Regiment, he served in the First World War was wounded and won the MC on the Somme, and in 1917 was promoted temporary lieutenant colonel. Before the end of hostilities he briefly commanded a brigade, and was awarded a DSO. In 1919 in northern Russia he fought against the Bolsheviks, and was subsequently in Ireland during the civil war, during which the IRA accused him of brutality, a claim subsequently disputed. Two assassination attempts were made against him, which he survived, then he led a raid against his would-be killers in which they themselves died. Following the Staff College in 1923, he went to West Africa with the Nigeria Regiment and then commanded the 2nd Cheshires in Malta. His next appointment was as chief of staff to General Dobbie in Malaya. Percival considered the possibility that the Japanese might one day attack from the north, and he submitted a report to the War Office about this possibility. Transferred back to Europe, he was promoted to acting major general, but in early 1941 was back in Malaya again, this time as General Officer Commanding. The Japanese did indeed attack from the north through Siam, and by sea, just as he had hypothesised.

Though Percival proved mediocre at best in senior command, it may be argued that his task in defending Malaya and Singapore was virtually impossible because there was little air cover and the naval 'Force Z' sent to the theatre in support was attacked by Japanese aircraft and destroyed. Moreover, though Percival had adequate numbers of men, they were a mixed bag of Indian, Australian and British troops, plus local volunteers. His strategy was hamstrung by a requirement to guard the exposed airfields of northern Malaya, not to disrupt the local economy and to preserve a force to advance into the Kra Isthmus, whilst at the same time having to wait for the Japanese to attack, thus giving the enemy the initiative. His relations with others were complicated by Churchill's demand that immediately after any Japanese attack a civil and military war council should be formed in Singapore.

Interestingly, a number of contemporaries formed the opinion that Percival, whilst intelligent and personally brave, simply lacked the drive, decisiveness and character necessary for senior command. As Ian Morrison, a journalist in Malaya, explained, Percival was: '...a man of considerable personal charm, if one met him socially. He was an able staff officer with a penetrating mind, although a mind that saw the difficulties to any scheme before it saw the possibilities. But he was a completely negative person, with no vigour, no colour, and no conviction. His personality was not strong, and as a leader he did not appeal either to the troops (to whom he was unknown except by name) or to the general public.'

Acting Lieutenant General Percival, centre, in conference with Air Vice Marshal Conway Pulford, left, and Air Chief Marshal Sir Robert Brooke-Popham, Commander-in-Chief Far East Command, in Malaya 1941. The campaign that led to Percival's capture, the death of Pulford, and the surrender of Singapore, was, as Percival himself put it, 'a pretty sticky business'. (Carl Mydans/The Life Picture Collection/ Getty Images)

In three months the Japanese advance reached Singapore, where Percival surrendered on 15 February 1942. The image of the lanky, buck-toothed general advancing under a white flag to capitulate doubtless grated with Churchill, but the decision to defend in the Far East with minimum resources, then to call for a fight to the finish, lay ultimately with the Prime Minister himself. It was a calculated gamble that failed. Following what was arguably Britain's worst defeat of the war, and certainly its largest single surrender, Percival would spend the remainder of hostilities in captivity. After the war he was president of FEPOW, the association for Far East Prisoners of War. He died in 1966.

SIR FREDERICK A. PILE, 2ND BARONET (1884–1976)

Born in Dublin, Frederick Alfred Pile, nicknamed 'Tim', was commissioned into the Royal Artillery in 1904 and saw service in India. During the First World War he was in France from 1914, and was brigade major by 1916. In 1923 he transferred to the Tank Corps and went to the Staff College, Camberley. Thereafter he was an important figure in the mechanisation of the Army, commanding the first Experimental Mechanised Force, becoming Assistant Director of Mechanisation, and in 1932 commander of the Canal Brigade Experimental Mechanised Force in Egypt. Going back to gunnery in the later 1930s, he was GOC 1st Anti-Aircraft Division, later becoming head of Anti-Aircraft Command. He held this position right through the war, afterwards becoming Director General of Housing with the Ministry of Works. His awards and decorations included the MC, DSO and the Knight Grand Cross of the Order of the Bath (GCB). A dispatch of his, number 38149, about the anti-aircraft defence of the UK, appeared in the *London Gazette*. His collected papers are preserved in the Liddell Hart Centre for Military Archives at King's College in London.

SIR HENRY R. POWNALL (1887–1961)

Educated at Rugby School, Henry Royds Pownall attended the Royal Military Academy at Woolwich and was commissioned into the Royal Artillery. He served in both the UK and India prior to the First World War and was promoted to captain in 1914. He fought on the Western Front and was awarded the DSO. In the early 1920s he was brigade major at the School of Artillery, Larkhill, and subsequently attended the Staff College. By the early 1930s he ranked as lieutenant colonel and was

serving on the North West Frontier of India. Thereafter came a series of staff appointments, culminating in his becoming Director of Military Operations at the War Office.

In the French campaign of 1940 Pownall was chief of staff to the British Expeditionary Force under Gort – a position pre-emptively ended by the evacuation from Dunkirk. Back in the UK he gained some public prominence, first as Inspector General of the new Home Guard, then GOC Northern Ireland and, finally, Vice Chief of the Imperial General Staff. Thereafter he moved to take up a series of senior appointments in the Middle and Far East, including that of chief of staff to Mountbatten in South East Asia Command from 1943 to 1944. In retirement he occupied a number of business and honorary positions, but is perhaps best remembered as the military consultant to Churchill when the latter was writing his six-volume history *The Second World War*. He died in 1961 and his diaries were published posthumously.

SIR NEIL M. RITCHIE (1897–1983)

Neil Methuen Ritchie was born in British Guiana and commissioned into the Black Watch in 1914. He served in both the Middle Eastern and Western theatres during the First World War, winning the MC. He served extensively as a staff officer, including periods under Brooke and Montgomery during the French campaign of 1940, and took part in the Dunkirk evacuation. Following the removal of Cunningham, Ritchie, still aged only forty-four, was appointed as a stopgap to lead the Eighth Army in North Africa. In the event, inexperience showed and he was swiftly worsted by Rommel. Auchinleck took charge of the Eighth Army himself.

enough by mid-1916 to become a draft conducting officer and he took reinforcements out to France and the Middle East. Promoted to captain in September 1916 he then rejoined his regiment, but in March 1917 he was again wounded, this time at Marl Plain, where he won the MC. After the First World War Slim transferred to the Indian Army, spending the early 1920s with 6th Gurkha Rifles and seeing various actions on the North West Frontier. He entered the Indian Staff College, Quetta, in 1925, and after various staff postings became an instructor at the UK Staff College. By 1938 he was a lieutenant colonel commanding 7th Gurkha Rifles back in India, and was given 10th Indian Infantry Brigade the following year.

Remarkably, Ritchie retained the confidence of Brooke, who appears to have understood that he had been out of his depth – with both an awkward command situation and pitted against Rommel at the height of his powers. As Brooke put it, 'Ritchie had done me so wonderfully well in France… and I had grown so fond of him, that I hated seeing him subjected to this serious reverse'. Ritchie was given command of 52nd Division in the UK and rose up the ladder again to take charge of XII Corps in northwest Europe. He remained in the Army after the end of the war, eventually becoming Commander-in-Chief Far East Land Forces in 1947. He lived to eighty-six, and died in Canada.

SIR WILLIAM J. SLIM, 1ST VISCOUNT SLIM (1891–1970)

The background of William Joseph Slim was quite unlike that of most other senior generals. Born near Bristol into the Catholic family of a wholesale ironmonger, he moved to Birmingham as a child. His first jobs were as an assistant teacher and as a clerk in a factory, though by 1912 he was a member of the Birmingham University Officer Training Corps. In 1914 he obtained a temporary commission with the Royal Warwickshires. The next year he was severely wounded at Gallipoli, but had recovered

He led his brigade in Eritrea, but in January 1941 received his third battle wound when strafed by an Italian aircraft. Nevertheless, he recovered and within six months was leading 10th Indian Division against the Vichy French in Syria as an acting major general. Identified as a promising commander, he was moved on to Burma in March 1942 and put in charge of I Burma Corps, then XV Corps, reaching the rank of temporary lieutenant general in March 1943. Though forced to retreat from the Arakan, it was a skilful withdrawal and in October Mountbatten chose Slim to lead Fourteenth Army. In early 1944 he parried the Japanese advance at Imphal and Kohima, and from then on he forced the enemy steadily backwards through Burma, reaching Rangoon in May 1945. At this moment of triumph General Leese decided to relieve Slim – the reaction of both 'Uncle Bill' and many of his comrades being anger and incredulity. Mountbatten then dismissed Leese. Slim was created a full general in August 1945, and in 1946 commandant of the Imperial Defence College. He retired in 1948.

Slim then became Deputy Chairman of British Rail, but Prime Minister Clement Atlee decided – against the advice of Montgomery – to have Slim as Chief of the Imperial General Staff, so he was brought back and duly promoted to field marshal. After his term of office Slim became Governor-General of Australia (1953–1960), and in 1960 was ennobled as Viscount Slim of Yarralumla and Bishopston. Described as inspirational and one of the greatest commanders of the Second World War, he died in Chelsea in December 1970.

SIR MONTAGU G.N. STOPFORD (1892–1971)

Born into an Army family, Montagu George North Stopford attended Wellington College and Sandhurst and was commissioned into the Rifle Brigade in 1911. He served in India and won the MC during the First World War. He went to the Staff College between the wars and was a divisional commander in the French campaign of 1940. He commanded XII Corps from 1942, and Indian XXXIII Corps in Burma from 1943. His finest hour was at the Battle of Kohima in 1944, where he was instrumental in opening the road to Imphal and inflicting serious damage on the enemy. Arguably this was a turning point in Slim's campaign; as Stopford himself put it, 'our superiority in strength (particularly reserves) material and morale is so great that we can use our initiative to the full'. He was prominent during the advance on Mandalay, and in May 1945 he took command of Twelfth Army. After the war he held a number of senior positions, including Commander-in-Chief of South East Asia Command in 1946–1947, finally ranking as a full general. He retired in 1949 and died in 1971.

SIR GERALD W. TEMPLER (1898–1979)

Gerald Walter Templer was born in Colchester of an Army family and educated at Wellington College, proceeding to Sandhurst in 1916. He was commissioned into the Royal Irish Fusiliers and

after a period in Ireland went to the Western Front, where he saw action in 1918. From 1919 he served in various parts of the Middle East and in 1928 entered the Staff College. Serving with the Loyal Regiment in Palestine in 1936 he was awarded the DSO for anti-terrorist operations.

Gerald Templer fought in both World Wars, finally advancing to Chief of the Imperial General Staff and field marshal in the 1950s. He is commemorated by the Templer Medal, awarded by the Society of Army Historical Research for works on the British Army. (Keystone/Getty Images)

In the early part of the Second World War Templer ranked as lieutenant colonel and was an intelligence officer with the BEF in France. After Dunkirk he briefly commanded 9th Royal Sussex, prior to assuming a brigade command in November 1940. By April 1942 he was a major general commanding 47th (London) Division, but was wounded by friendly fire from an aircraft during a ground-attack demonstration: nevertheless he recovered well enough to be again promoted to acting lieutenant general before the end of the year, assuming command first of II Corps and then of 1st Division in Tunisia. In the Italian campaign Templer was fed in as a replacement for the commander of 56th (London) Division during the battles on the Volturno. In 1944 he led the division during actions around Anzio, and after it was withdrawn he went on to command 6th Armoured Division. He had been in this post less than two weeks before he was injured by a landmine that blew up a lorry in his convoy, showering him with debris. After recuperating he was posted to the Special Operations Executive (SOE) in London. Later, he was Director of Civil Affairs and Military Government in Brussels and then executive head of the British zone in Germany.

After returning to the UK in 1946, Templer served as Director of Military Intelligence; Vice Chief of the Imperial General Staff; and then as High Commissioner during the insurgency in Malaya, where he was credited with coining the phrase 'hearts and minds'. In 1955 he became Chief of the Imperial General Staff and was instrumental in preparing the armed forces for Suez the following year – the military operations of which were successful, despite the highly embarrassing political repercussions. Field Marshal Sir Gerald Templer died in London in 1979.

JOHN VEREKER, VISCOUNT GORT (1886–1946)

John Standish Surtees Prendergast Vereker, son of the 5th Viscount Gort, was born in London to an Anglo-Irish family and attended Harrow school. Following Sandhurst, he was commissioned into the Grenadier Guards in 1905, first coming to prominence in 1910 when he commanded the bearer party at the funeral of King Edward VII. Despite a highly unfortunate hunting accident in Canada, in which he shot and killed his local guide, he was promoted to captain and accompanied the British Expeditionary Force to France in 1914. He soon proved himself a fearless warrior – Mentioned in Despatches eight times, winning the MC and awarded the DSO twice. He was wounded, but was back in the front line commanding 1st Grenadier Guards by the time of the German Spring Offensive of 1918. Wounded twice more, he also won the Victoria Cross. As the *Dictionary of National Biography* put it, and with little exaggeration, Gort was an officer of the 'rarest gallantry' who disregarded personal danger and kept alive the spirit of his troops through virtually any loss or strain. Having become one of Britain's most highly decorated soldiers, he went to the Staff College in 1919, subsequently became an instructor and established a friendship with tactician Basil Liddell Hart. Various staff postings and promotions followed, including a stint in Shanghai, before he became Director of Military Training, India.

Personally fearless, Lord Gort was not an outstanding battlefield general. Nevertheless he made an important contribution to the defence of Malta. (Planet News Archive/Getty Images)

By December 1937 Gort was a full general and Military Secretary to the Army Council. Indeed, his final rise to the pinnacle was so meteoric that he became Britain's youngest ever Chief of the Imperial General Staff, and jumped ahead of men like Dill and Brooke who had been longer-serving and were therefore technically senior to him. Gort was without doubt an extremely brave commander, and an early supporter of mechanisation, but his relationship with British Secretary of State for War Leslie Hore-Belisha was an uneasy one, and in many matters Gort displayed an intensely conservative streak. Some of his contemporaries even attributed the break-up of his marriage to the single-minded way he pursued his profession. Another matter, no flaw in a battalion commander but a serious drawback in a leader of armies, was Gort's obsession with detail. More than once his immediate subordinates looked to him for an important decision, only to find themselves sidetracked into minutiae. On the outbreak of war Gort was appointed commander of the British Expeditionary Force in France.

During the frustrating winter of 1939 to 1940 his relationship with his political master Hore-Belisha reached its nadir over the matter of pillbox building along the French border with Belgium. For example, the regimental history of 2nd Dorsets records that on arrival in their sector, the French concrete blockhouses were a kilometre apart and weakly manned. When the Dorsets dug trenches these filled with water, and only by 'herculean' effort were breastworks erected. Completed works stood out on the flat terrain 'like sore thumbs'. Nevertheless, Gort regarded any overt criticism from home, even before serious action had commenced, as 'a knife in the back'. Yet, remarkably, it was not the Secretary of State for War who came out on top, but the commander of the British Expeditionary Force. Gort retained the confidence of both the Prime Minister and the king, and in January 1940 Hore-Belisha resigned.

In the event the nature of the defences proved irrelevant, because, in accordance with the plan developed with his French allies, Gort advanced his army into Belgium in May 1940 but had to retreat back towards the Channel coast because of the collapse of French forces further to the south. With his force decisively outflanked, Gort was forced into a series of defensive stopgaps, detaching elements to cover the holes that were appearing along the flank of his positions. Whilst he appears to have done his best to encourage his allies, and indeed lingered longer in an attempt to mount counter-attacks than some of his subordinates would have wished, he realised that without support there were few options remaining. On the advice of Ironside, Churchill ordered Gort's return to the UK, and most of the BEF subsequently escaped through Dunkirk.

No further battlefield command was forthcoming; instead, Gort was made Inspector General of Training, though Churchill did consider bringing him back to the forefront later on. In the event, Gort was made Governor of Gibraltar in 1941 and then Governor of Malta in 1942. In defending, with great courage, a relatively small island, where he was not called upon to deliver any great strategic feats but to hold out at all costs and encourage

British troops entrenched on the Elbe near to the end of the war in Europe. The men foreground are armed with a Bren gun and No. 4 rifles. In the distance are a camouflaged 6pdr anti-tank gun and a carrier. (Official/author)

through his own confidence his command to stay the distance, Gort finally showed his best qualities to full effect. He did sterling work in maintaining Maltese resistance under air attack, and was himself injured in 1942 whilst helping at a fuel dump set alight by enemy bombers. In a remarkable departure, the entire island was awarded the George Cross for its fortitude. In 1944 Gort became High Commissioner in Palestine. However, his health gradually declined, and, though he survived the war and was granted a viscountcy, he died in 1946.

SIR ARCHIBALD P. WAVELL, 1ST EARL WAVELL (1880–1950)

Born at Colchester into an Army family, Archibald Percival Wavell attended Winchester College on a scholarship and entered Sandhurst in 1900. In May 1901 he joined the Black Watch during the Boer War. Injured in a football match in October 1902, he returned to the UK before being sent out to the Punjab. From 1903 to 1909 he served in India, including active service in the Bazar Valley campaign. After Staff College and learning Russian, he was sent to Russia as

a military observer. In 1914 he served on the Western Front and was appointed brigade major of 9th Brigade. He was wounded in 1915, losing an eye, and won the MC. Following convalescence, he returned to France for a period before going out to the Middle East as a liaison officer, working with the Russians again, as well as Sir Edmund Allenby – of whom Wavell later wrote an approving biography. Following a time with the army of occupation in Germany, other staff duties and a quiet period of writing whilst on half pay, he was appointed acting brigadier in 1930. In 1937 he took command of British troops in Palestine and Transjordan, where he was Wingate's commanding officer.

Always something of an intellectual, and with his considerable reserves of self-sufficiency, the stocky Wavell was often regarded as taciturn – even unfriendly. These were qualities that failed to appeal to Churchill, who frequently regarded him as lacking in drive. Nevertheless, it would be grossly unfair to say that Wavell lacked imagination, for he had taken an early interest in armoured mobility, from the point of view of infantry as well as tanks, and would later support the development of raiding forces. Perhaps paradoxically, Wavell had actually delivered a Lees Knowles Lecture on the relationship of soldiers to politicians. Promoted to general in 1939, Wavell was Commander-in-Chief Middle East by that July. Following setbacks in Somaliland Wavell succeeded in foiling an Italian attack on Egypt and then went onto the offensive. However, whilst Somaliland was recovered, the Germans took Greece and Crete, beating forces that Wavell sent there under pressure from Churchill. Mid-1941 also saw very mixed results, for though Wavell was instrumental in the successful Syria campaign, offensives in the Western Desert failed. Churchill's loss of confidence was signalled when Wavell was ordered to take up the post of Commander-in-Chief India, whilst Auchinleck was brought to the Middle East.

At first Wavell fared well in his new post, but in December 1941 the Japanese launched their Pacific War against the USA and UK. Even as he was promoted to field marshal, Wavell's new 'South West Pacific' command almost collapsed as Malaya and Singapore fell, and the enemy made advances on every front. Wavell's sphere was therefore circumscribed to India and Burma only, but a counter-offensive in the Arakan ground to a halt in May 1943. The following month he was finally removed from operational responsibility, but was made Viceroy and Governor-General of India, and subsequently created Viscount Wavell of Cyrenaica and Winchester.

Sir Archibald Wavell pictured on 1 February 1945 when Viceroy of India. His chest full of medal ribbons eventually included no less than thirty-one orders, decorations, and awards: more surprisingly he published a dozen books including translations from Russian and an anthology of poetry. (Popperphoto/Getty Images)

Very quickly, new crises arose with famine in Bengal and demands for independence: Wavell did his best, introducing food rationing and releasing the Congress Party leader Mahatma Gandhi from prison. Nevertheless, the new British government was set on ending British rule in India and serious inter-religious and political violence spread during 1946. Wavell's advice was that either a date should be set for independence or more troops should be sent to provide long-term security. Neither was done, and Wavell was retired in early 1947. He died in May 1950 and was buried at Winchester. As a commander Wavell fought many campaigns and endured many failures, but as his apologists note he was often up against superior odds and goaded from behind.

RONALD M. WEEKS, 1ST BARON WEEKS (1890–1960)

The son of a mining engineer, Ronald Morce Weeks was educated at Charterhouse and Cambridge. As a Territorial during the First World War he was called to the front in 1915, winning the MC twice as well as a DSO. He went back into business after 1918 but remained with the Territorial Army, becoming a substantive colonel by 1938, and in 1939 he was a staff officer with 66th Infantry Division. By 1941 he was Director General of Army Equipment, and the following year Deputy Chief of the Imperial General Staff, now ranking as lieutenant general. Weeks remained in this appointment until 1945 when he became a senior figure in the Allied Control Council in Germany under Montgomery. He retired from the Army in 1946, and became Chairman of Vickers. He was created Baron Weeks of Ryton in 1956. Though never a senior battlefield commander, he has been justly described as 'industrious and decisive', and appears to have had a better grasp of technology and production than many of his contemporaries.

SIR HENRY C.B. WEMYSS (1891–1959)

Henry Colville Barclay Wemyss was commissioned into the Royal Engineers in 1910 and fought in the First World War, winning the MC and DSO. During the inter-war period he transferred to the new Royal Corps of Signals and attended the Imperial Defence College. By early 1939 he had reached the rank of major general and was appointed Director of Mobilisation at the War Office. The following year he was promoted to acting lieutenant general and then became the Army's Adjutant General. With the establishment of the Military Mission to Washington, DC, Wemyss was made head of the Army component. He held this appointment until early 1942, when replaced by Dill. Wemyss was then made Military Secretary to the Secretary of State for War. He was promoted to full general in 1945 and retired the following year.

SIR HENRY M. WILSON, 1ST BARON WILSON OF LIBYA (1881–1964)

Born in Suffolk, Henry Maitland Wilson attended Eton and Sandhurst and was commissioned into the Rifle Brigade in 1900. Tall and bulky, he was predictably nicknamed 'Jumbo'. He campaigned in South Africa and then served with his regiment in Egypt and India. In 1914 he was the brigade major of 48th Brigade. He served on the Western Front during the First World War, gaining three Mentions in Despatches, fighting on the Somme and winning the DSO in 1917. He attended the Staff College Camberley in 1919 and was commanding officer of 2nd Rifle Brigade by 1923. Following various staff appointments, and a period on the North West Frontier, by 1935 he had reached the rank of major general.

In 1939 Wilson was General Officer Commanding British Troops in Egypt, and in 1941 became the governor of the captured Italian colony of Cyrenaica. His expedition to support the Greeks was not a success, but the withdrawal was skilfully executed. Wilson was soon made General Officer Commanding Palestine and Transjordan, and forces under his direction entered Baghdad and also took control in Syria and the Lebanon. In 1943 Wilson returned to Egypt as Commander-in-Chief Middle East. Though he successfully supported the efforts of the Eighth Army, an expedition to the Dodecanese failed. From January 1944 Lieutenant General Wilson was Supreme Allied Commander in the Mediterranean, eventually returning in triumph to Athens. Following the death of Dill he joined the British Military Mission to Washington, DC, and was promoted to field marshal in December 1944. After the war he was created Baron Wilson of Libya and Stowlangtoft. He died in 1964 and was buried in the village where he was born.

ORDE C. WINGATE (1903–1944)

Wingate lived to only forty-one, never reached the highest levels of command and died on active service, yet he is remembered as one of the most innovative – and eccentric – British generals of the Second World War. He was described by Churchill as 'a man of genius who might have been a man of destiny'. Orde Charles Wingate was born in India of a Plymouth Brethren family, his father being a retired Army officer. Strictly parented and educated at Charterhouse, he entered the Royal Military Academy at Woolwich in 1921 and was then commissioned into the 5th Medium Brigade of the Royal Artillery at Larkhill. He gained a reputation amongst his colleagues as a penurious but keen horseman of great determination and rebellious temperament. He learned Arabic, and in 1927 was seconded to the Sudan Defence Force. Characteristically, he cycled most of the way from England to Khartoum. In 1928 he achieved the local rank of major and worked on the borders of Ethiopia against poachers and slave traders. Thereafter he tested his own mettle and powers of endurance on an expedition to the Libyan desert, sponsored by the Royal Geographical Society. On the way home in 1933 he met a sixteen-year-old girl whom he later married. Posted to Palestine as an intelligence officer, he worked against the Arab Revolt in 1936–1939, and in the process became a committed Zionist and founder of the so-called 'Special Night Squads' to spring pre-emptive attacks on the rebels. His tough, no-nonsense tactics made him a hero of the Jewish community and earned him a DSO.

Wingate started the Second World War as commander of an anti-aircraft unit in the UK, but Wavell had him posted to Africa where he led the mixed Gideon Force in guerilla actions against Italian forces in Ethiopia. Still only a temporary lieutenant colonel, he was instrumental in the capture of 20,000 Italians and at the end of the campaign he was dropped back to major, having been awarded a second DSO. Depressed and suffering from malaria, Wingate attempted suicide. After recovering, his fortunes also rose. He captured the imagination of Churchill, who regarded him as having the potential to become a new 'Lawrence of Arabia', as well as the support of Wavell, and in 1942 he was sent to the Far East where it was hoped his amazing determination and unorthodox tactics might work their magic against the Japanese.

He took command of 77th Infantry Brigade, soon to be known as Chindits, and trained them ruthlessly, almost to destruction, in the jungle near Gwalior. Whilst Wingate disdained the Indian Army, which he referred to as a system of 'outdoor relief', he made extensive use of Gurkhas. In Operation Longcloth in Burma in early 1943 Wingate led his columns in 'deep penetration' raids behind enemy lines and severed a main

rail line, but they found themselves out of supplies and pursued by three divisions of the enemy. Though ruinously damaged, the Chindits were proclaimed as heroes and the first real sign that the Japanese could be beaten. Though Wingate caught typhoid, a new Chindit mission was prepared, this time with adequate air cover and supply, and by early March 1944 fortified bases had been set up and successes achieved.

On 24 March, at what was arguably the peak of his career, Major General Wingate was killed in an air crash. His remains were eventually interred at Arlington National Cemetery in the USA, and he is commemorated in London by a monument on Victoria Embankment, Though many today regard him as a visionary who was ahead of his time, his contemporaries were divided. Major General Symes, a commander who was sidelined in order to accommodate Wingate's plans, described him as fanatical, ruthless, arrogant, untidy, unorthodox, lacking in technical knowledge, impatient, demanding, but a 'doer'. A junior officer, after seeing Wingate lecture for the first time, regarded him as the 'worst dressed officer' he had ever seen, but with eyes and voice of steel, and complete confidence in his own opinion.

The controversial and strong-willed prophet of unconventional strategy and tactics Orde Wingate, pictured in 1943. His positive attitude and aggression appealed hugely to Churchill but his career was cut tragically short. He was buried in the USA with nine other victims of the B-25 bomber crash in which he died. (William Vandivert/ Getty Images)

CHAPTER TWO
The Regiments and Corps

Cadets march through an English town early in the war. Both the other ranks, and the officer, right, wear Service Dress. The other ranks, leather belts date back to the First World War; the officer wears the 'Sam Browne' with waist belt and shoulder strap. (Keystone-France/ Gamma-Keystone via Getty Images)

The British Army was made up of historic regiments, and, arguably, rested on regimental tradition more than any other national force. Except in major wars, the Army relied mainly on professional soldiers, and conscription was resorted to only in the most dire emergencies – the last time before the eve of the Second World War being 1916. Lack of conscription was both a blessing and a curse. On the positive side, a small, all-volunteer professional army made for high standards of training; close-knit loyalty, in what were effectively 'regimental families'; and limited cost. Long-term 'career' soldiers understandably had significantly more experience than could be expected of a short-term conscript. On the negative side, a professional army meant that military training was limited to only part of society; the army was often too small to take on major commitments; and the relatively narrow scope of society's investment in its military could lead to a lack of understanding on both sides. There was also a tendency to pronounced social stratification, with officers drawn predominantly from the upper and upper-middle classes, and 'other ranks' from the lower end of the social spectrum, topped up with men who might otherwise be unemployed. The limited reintroduction of conscription in May 1939 was far too close to the outbreak of war to change this general picture very dramatically by the time of the invasion of Poland in September. Indeed, the expansion of the Army, from less than a million at the outbreak of war to a zenith of nearly three million, would not be achieved for several years, with the two and a half million mark reached only in late 1942.[1]

The British Army also contained a class of soldier that was neither professional nor conscript, in the shape of the part-time Territorial. As Lord Haldane had explained in 1907, henceforth the Army would consist of a Field Force and a Home Force:

'The Field Force is to be so completely organised as to be ready in all respects for mobilisation on the outbreak of a great war. In that event the Territorial or

Band of the Queen's Own Cameron Highlanders, Aldershot, 1934. Bands retained full dress after it had been withdrawn from the rank and file, in this instance full Highland attire with kilt and doublet. (Author)

THE BAND, 2nd BATTALION THE QUEEN'S OWN CAMERON HIGHLANDERS

ALDERSHOT, 1934

Home Force would be mobilised also, but mobilised with a view to its undertaking, in the first instance, systematic training for war. The effect of such training, given a period of six months, would be, in the opinion of all military experts, to add materially to the efficiency of the force. The Territorial Force will, therefore, be one of support and expansion…'

In point of fact the Territorials were not genuinely new, but had been created mainly by renaming and reorganising the part-time 'Volunteer' battalions that had come into existence in 1859 during the scare of war with France. The ancient and well-nigh universal Militia had already declined into a species of reserve. The Yeomanry, effectively the mounted version of the Militia, became part of the Territorial Force but maintained their old name. In 1914 the Haldane reforms were found somewhat wanting when, with an immediate need for more men on the Western Front, the Territorials were asked to volunteer anew, this time to undertake 'Imperial' or 'Foreign' service alongside the Regulars. The picture was then further complicated with the creation of 'New Armies' of volunteers raised at the behest of Lord Kitchener, working outside the established Territorial system. Interestingly, Territorials

could be either particular battalions of the line regiments or Territorial-only regiments, though the latter were affiliated to a line regiment. For example, in 1939 the South Wales Borderers technically had no Territorial battalions, but the Territorial Monmouthshire Regiment formed 'part of the Corps of the South Wales Borderers'.

Broadly speaking, the 'teeth' arms of the British Army were the regiments of the cavalry, artillery and infantry, and the supporting units were the 'corps' of engineers, supply, transport, medics and chaplains. Quite a few of the regiments of the line – both cavalry and infantry – had been raised originally by individual noblemen to serve the Crown and many traced their lineage back to the seventeenth century, some even to the army of George Monk that had helped to restore the monarchy in 1660. The brigade of Guards and Household Cavalry formed almost an army within the Army, born out of the personal guard of the sovereign, and it could be argued that this lineage stretched back to before the English Civil War. The guns of what was once described as the 'train of artillery' had become the Royal Regiment of Artillery as early as 1716. Eighteenth-century reforms gradually eroded the proprietary rights of colonels and marked regiments as Crown property by the granting of numbers. The infantry regiments were reformed again in the 1870s by Lord Cardwell, as a result of which they were linked in pairs, becoming battalions of new regiments with county or other fixed geographic associations. These reforms did not impact so directly upon the cavalry, which remained essentially peripatetic for some time.

Following the First World War, in 1922 the Army's mounted arm was reduced in numbers and some regiments were amalgamated in pairs, resulting in, for example, the 4th/7th Dragoon Guards, the 17th/21st Lancers and the 14th/20th King's Hussars. These Churchill dubbed, with scarcely concealed contempt, the 'vulgar fractions'. The Yeomanry had already undergone a major reorganisation in 1920, when some of its regiments were disbanded, and many others began to convert into units of other arms of

43 DIV. FOOTBALL COMPETITION, CLASS "A" 1942. WINNERS, 4TH BN. THE DORSETSHIRE REGT.

service such as artillery, tanks or signals. During the 1930s the majority of the Regular cavalry were dismounted and, together with the Royal Tank Regiment, became part of the new Royal Armoured Corps in April 1939. Whilst military engineers had long existed to deal with the planning and building of fortifications and the use of 'fireworks', in the nineteenth century the permanent establishment of various specialist Corps was recognition that warfare had become increasingly technical and industrialised.

A further round of reorganisation of the infantry in the 1930s saw an increase in the number of Territorial battalions, some of which were only listed as 'provisional titles' as late as August 1939. Others were converted to searchlight or tank units. A number of Regular infantry battalions were converted to machine gun battalions. The result of these many, and ongoing, changes – one overlying another – was an organisation steeped in worthy traditions that most of its members revered and strived to uphold, but that even experts could find difficult to fully understand. The outbreak of war undeniably found the Army at an awkward moment of transition between old and new. Many Territorial battalions were not yet filled, others were undergoing the process of conversion and some were, as yet, just names on paper. The Royal Armoured Corps was particularly poorly and patchily equipped.

The following list and order of precedence is taken from the official Army List of August 1939. Where given, the location of the unit is also included. It was usual for one Regular battalion of each infantry regiment to be garrisoning some part of the Empire, whilst the other was in the UK. However, in some regiments both were overseas. The colours mentioned are those of the dress uniform and facing, and the numbers of battalions are as in the 1939 Army List. The Militia battalions, in 'suspended animation' since the 1920s, have not been included; also not shown are the Malta, Palestine, Cyprus and Bermuda units. Regiments created after September 1939 are appended at the end.[2]

The winners of the 43rd Division 'Class A' football trophy, 1942: 4th Battalion The Dorsetshire Regiment. (Author)

Far left: Other ranks of the Duke of Lancaster's Own Yeomanry, seen mounted, 1938. They are armed with rifles carried in leather 'buckets' on the saddle, ammunition being held in 1903-type bandoliers over the shoulder. The unit remained on horseback until conversion to artillery in 1940. (DLOY collection)

CAVALRY (HORSED)

The Life Guards	Hyde Park Barracks	
		scarlet – blue
The Royal Horse Guards	Windsor	blue – scarlet
1st King's Dragoon Guards	Palestine	scarlet – blue
The Royal Scots Greys	Palestine	scarlet – blue
Remount Service		

YEOMANRY

Royal Wiltshire (hussars)	Trowbridge	blue – scarlet
Warwickshire (hussars)	Warwick	dark blue – white
Yorkshire Hussars	York	blue – scarlet
Nottinghamshire (hussars)	Newark	green – green
Staffordshire (hussars)	Wolverhampton	blue – scarlet
Shropshire (dragoons)	Shrewsbury	blue – scarlet
Ayrshire (hussars)	Ayr	blue – scarlet
Cheshire (hussars)	Chester	blue – scarlet
Yorkshire Dragoons	Doncaster	blue – white
Leicestershire (hussars)	Leicester	blue – scarlet
North Somerset (dragoons)	Bath	blue – white
Duke of Lancaster's Own (dragoons)		
	Manchester	scarlet – blue
Lanarkshire (lancers)	Lanark	blue – scarlet
Northumberland Hussars	Newcastle upon Tyne	
		blue – scarlet

Nottinghamshire
(South Notts hussars, converted to artillery)
Denbighshire (hussars, converted to artillery)
Westmoreland and Cumberland
(hussars, converted to artillery)
Pembroke (hussars, converted to artillery)
Royal East Kent (hussars, converted to artillery)
Hampshire (dragoons, converted to artillery)
Buckinghamshire (hussars, converted to artillery)
Derbyshire (dragoons, converted to Royal Tank Regiment)
Dorset (hussars, converted to artillery)
Gloucestershire
(hussars, converted to Royal Tank Regiment)
Hertfordshire (dragoons, converted to artillery)
Berkshire (dragoons, converted to artillery)
1st County of London (hussars, converted to signals)
Royal 1st Devon (hussars, converted to artillery)
Suffolk (hussars, converted to artillery)
Royal North Devon (hussars, converted to artillery)
Worcestershire (hussars, converted to artillery)

West Kent (hussars, converted to artillery)
West Somerset (hussars, converted to artillery)
Oxfordshire (hussars, converted to artillery)
Montgomeryshire
(dragoons, converted to part of 7th Battalion Royal Welch Fusiliers)
Lothians and Border Horse
(dragoons, converted to Royal Tank Regiment)
Queen's Own Royal Glasgow
(dragoons, converted to artillery)
Lancashire Hussars (converted to artillery)
Surrey (lancers, converted to artillery)
Fife and Forfar
(dragoons, converted to Royal Tank Regiment)
Norfolk (dragoons, converted to artillery)
Sussex (dragoons, converted to artillery)
Glamorgan (dragoons, converted to artillery)
City of London 'Rough Riders'
(lancers, converted to Royal Tank Regiment)
2nd County of London Westminster Dragoons
(converted to Royal Tank Regiment)
3rd County of London 'Sharpshooters'
(hussars, converted to Royal Tank Regiment)
Bedfordshire (lancers, converted to artillery)
Essex (dragoons, converted to artillery)
Northamptonshire
(dragoons, converted to Royal Tank Regiment)
East Riding of Yorkshire
(lancers, converted to Royal Tank Regiment)

SCOUTS (formerly Yeomanry)

Lovat Scouts	Inverness		blue – blue
Scottish Horse	Dunkeld	Atholl grey – yellow

CAVALRY, TERRITORIAL ARMY

Inns of Court Regiment	Lincoln's Inn	blue – green

ROYAL ARMOURED CORPS / MECHANISED CAVALRY

1st King's Dragoon Guards		
	Aldershot	scarlet – blue
The Queen's Bays	Tidworth	scarlet – white
3rd Carabiniers	Sialkot	scarlet – yellow
4th/7th Royal Dragoon Guards		
	Aldershot	scarlet – royal blue
5th Royal Inniskilling Dragoon Guards		
	Colchester	scarlet – royal blue

3rd The King's Own Hussars

	Tidworth	blue – scarlet

4th Queen's Own Hussars

	Tidworth	blue

7th Queen's Own Hussars

	Egypt	blue

8th King's Royal Irish Hussars

	Egypt	blue

9th Queen's Royal Lancers

	Tidworth	blue – scarlet

10th Royal Hussars	Tidworth	blue
11th Hussars	Palestine	blue
12th Royal Lancers	Aldershot	blue – scarlet
13th/18th Royal Hussars	Shorncliffe	blue – buff
14th/20th King's Hussars	Secunderabad	blue

15th/19th The King's Royal Hussars

	York	blue

16th/5th Lancers	Risalpur	scarlet – blue
17th/21st Lancers	Colchester	blue – white
Royal Tank Regiment		blue – black

ROYAL REGIMENT OF ARTILLERY   blue – scarlet

(Field Medium, Heavy, Coast and Anti-Aircraft Branch)
Also including the Honourable Artillery Company since 1920

CORPS OF ROYAL ENGINEERS   scarlet – blue

ROYAL CORPS OF SIGNALS   scarlet – black

FOOT GUARDS

Grenadier Guards (3 battalions)

	London, Aldershot	scarlet – blue

Coldstream Guards (3 battalions)

	London, Aldershot, Egypt	
		scarlet – blue

| **Scots Guards** (2 battalions) | Windsor, Egypt | scarlet – blue |
| **Irish Guards** (2 battalions) | London | scarlet – blue |

Welsh Guards (2 battalions)

	Gibraltar, London	scarlet – blue

INFANTRY

The Royal Scots (The Royal Regiment)

	Aldershot, Hong Kong	
		scarlet – blue

(2 Regular, 3 Territorial battalions of which one converted to a searchlights)

The Queen's Royal Regiment (West Surrey)

	Surrey, Palestine, India	
		scarlet – blue

(2 Regular, 6 Territorial battalions of which one converted to searchlights)

The Buffs (Royal East Kent)

	Pembroke Dock, Palestine	
		scarlet – buff

(2 Regular, 2 Territorial battalions)

The King's Own Royal Regiment (Lancaster)

	Madras, Palestine	scarlet – blue

(2 Regular, 2 Territorial battalions)

The Royal Northumberland Fusiliers

	Egypt, Dover	
		scarlet – gosling green

(2 Regular, 6 Territorial battalions of which two converted to searchlights and Royal Tank Regiment)

The Royal Warwickshire Regiment

	Fyzabad, Aldershot	scarlet – blue

(2 Regular, 4 Territorial battalions)

Royal Engineers tighten the linkage of an 'Inglis Bridge'. According to the 1936 *Manual of Field Engineering* bridges were divided into six categories according to load. These were, in ascending order, assault; pack; light; medium; heavy and super heavy. An 'assault bridge' was defined as being able to take assault troops on foot, whilst at the other end of the scale a heavy bridge could take 'all loads normally with the army in the field'. 'Super heavy' bridges accommodated abnormal loads. (PNA Rota/ Getty Images)

The Royal Fusiliers (City of London Regiment)
Jhansi, Dover   scarlet – blue
(2 Regular, 5 Territorial battalions of which one converted to searchlights)

The King's Regiment (Liverpool)
Peshawar, Gibraltar   scarlet – blue
(2 Regular, 4 Territorial battalions of which one converted to Royal Tank Regiment)

The Royal Norfolk Regiment
Delhi, Bordon   scarlet – yellow
(2 Regular, 4 Territorial battalions)

The Lincolnshire Regiment
Nasirbad, Portland scarlet – white
(2 Regular, 1 Territorial battalion)

The Devonshire Regiment Rawalpindi, Malta
scarlet – lincoln green
(2 Regular, 6 Territorial battalions)

The Suffolk Regiment   Devonport, Mhow scarlet – yellow
(2 Regular, 2 Territorial battalions)

The Somerset Light Infantry
Poona, Gibraltar   scarlet – blue
(2 Regular, 4 Territorial battalions)

The West Yorkshire Regiment Secunderabad, Palestine
scarlet – buff
(2 Regular, 2 Territorial battalions of which one converted to Royal Tank Regiment)

The East Yorkshire Regiment Jullundur, Plymouth
scarlet – white
(2 Regular, 2 Territorial battalions)

The Bedfordshire and Hertfordshire Regiment
Palestine, Gravesend
scarlet – white
(2 Regular, 2 Territorial battalions)

The Leicestershire Regiment Razmak, Palestine
scarlet – pearl grey
(2 Regular, 2 Territorial battalions)

The Green Howards   Catterick, Ferozepore
scarlet – grass green
(2 Regular, 4 Territorial battalions)

The Lancashire Fusiliers Quetta, Colchester
scarlet – white
(2 Regular, 6 Territorial battalions)

The Royal Scots Fusiliers Karachi, Edinburgh scarlet – blue
(2 Regular, 2 Territorial battalions)

The Cheshire Regiment   Sudan, Aldershot   scarlet – buff
(2 Regular, 4 Territorial battalions)

The Royal Welch Fusiliers Blackdown, Lucknow
scarlet – blue
(2 Regular, 6 Territorial battalions)

The South Wales Borderers Landi Kotal, Londonderry
scarlet – blue
(2 Regular battalions)

The King's Own Scottish Borderers
Portsmouth, Jubbulpore
scarlet – blue
(2 Regular, 4 Territorial battalions)

The Cameronians (Scottish Rifles)
Barrackpore, Catterick
green – dark green
(2 Regular, 4 Territorial battalions)

The Royal Inniskilling Fusiliers Wellington, Catterick
scarlet – blue
(2 Regular battalions)

The Gloucestershire Regiment Mingaladon, Plymouth
scarlet – primrose yellow
(2 Regular, 4 Territorial battalions of which one converted to searchlights and one to Royal Tank Regiment)

The Worcestershire Regiment Palestine, Sialkot
scarlet – grass green
(2 Regular, 4 Territorial battalions)

The East Lancashire Regiment Holywood, Ambala

scarlet – white

(2 Regular, 2 Territorial battalions)

The East Surrey Regiment Colchester, Shanghai

scarlet – white

(2 Regular, 4 Territorial battalions of which one converted to artillery and one to Royal Tank Regiment)

The Duke of Cornwall's Light Infantry

Lahore, Shorncliffe scarlet – white

(2 Regular, 2 Territorial battalions)

The Duke of Wellington's Regiment Bordon, Multan

scarlet – scarlet

(2 Regular, 5 Territorial battalions of which one converted to artillery)

The Border Regiment Aldershot, Calcutta

scarlet – yellow

(2 Regular, 4 Territorial battalions)

Royal Sussex Regiment Egypt, Belfast scarlet – blue

(2 Regular, 4 Territorial battalions)

The Hampshire Regiment Palestine, Aldershot

scarlet – yellow

(2 Regular, 4 Territorial battalions)

The South Staffordshire Regiment Palestine, Cawnpore

scarlet – yellow

(2 Regular, 4 Territorial battalions)

The Dorsetshire Regiment Malta, Aldershot

scarlet – grass green

(2 Regular, 2 Territorial battalions)

The South Lancashire Regiment Dover, Bombay

scarlet – buff

(2 Regular, 3 Territorial battalions)

The Welch Regiment Palestine, Agra scarlet – white

(2 Regular, 3 Territorial battalions of which one converted to searchlights)

The Black Watch (Royal Highland Regiment)

Dover, Palestine scarlet – blue

(2 Regular, 4 Territorial battalions)

The Oxfordshire and Buckinghamshire Light Infantry

Colchester, Bareilly

scarlet – white

(2 Regular, 4 Territorial battalions)

The Essex Regiment Egypt, Warley scarlet – purple

(2 Regular, 5 Territorial battalions of which two converted to searchlights)

The Sherwood Foresters Palestine, Bordon

scarlet – lincoln green

(2 Regular, 4 Territorial battalions)

The Loyal Regiment (North Lancashire)

Aldershot, Malaya scarlet – white

(2 Regular, 3 Territorial battalions)

The Northamptonshire Regiment Dinnapore, Ballykinler

scarlet – buff

(2 Regular, 2 Territorial battalions)

The Royal Berkshire Regiment Blackdown, Lucknow

scarlet – blue

(2 Regular, 4 Territorial battalions)

The Queen's Own Royal West Kent Regiment

Shorncliffe, Malta scarlet – blue

(2 Regular, 4 Territorial battalions)

The King's Own Yorkshire Light Infantry

Strensall, Maymyo scarlet – blue

(2 Regular, 3 Territorial battalions of which one converted to artillery)

The King's Shropshire Light Infantry Bordon, Jamaica

scarlet – blue

(2 Regular, 1 Territorial battalions)

The Middlesex Regiment Hong Kong, Gosport

scarlet – lemon yellow

(2 Regular, 7 Territorial battalions of which one converted to searchlights)

The King's Royal Rifle Corps

Egypt, Tidworth   green – scarlet

(2 Regular, 6 Territorial battalions)

The Wiltshire Regiment (Duke of Edinburgh's)

Bangalore, Catterick

scarlet – buff

(2 Regular, 2 Territorial battalions)

The Manchester Regiment Malaya, Aldershot

scarlet – deep green

(2 Regular, 7 Territorial battalions of which one converted to Royal Tank Regiment)

The North Staffordshire Regiment Poona, Aldershot

scarlet – black

(2 Regular, 2 Territorial battalions)

The York and Lancaster Regiment York, Sudan

scarlet – white

(2 Regular, 1 Territorial battalion)

The Durham light Infantry Tientsin, Woking

scarlet – dark green

(2 Regular, 8 Territorial battalions of which two converted to searchlights)

The Highland Light Infantry Fort George, Palestine

scarlet – buff

(2 Regular, 4 Territorial battalions)

The Seaforth Highlanders Shanghai, Glasgow

scarlet – buff

(2 Regular, 4 Territorial battalions)

The Gordon Highlanders Aldershot, Malaya scarlet – yellow

(2 Regular, 8 Territorial battalions)

The Queen's Own Cameron Highlanders

Aldershot, Ahmednagar

scarlet – blue

(2 Regular, 4 Territorial battalions)

The Royal Ulster Rifles Rawlpindi, Parkhurst

green – dark green

(2 Regular, 2 Territorial battalions)

The Royal Irish Fusiliers Guernsey, Malta   scarlet – blue

(2 Regular battalions)

The Argyll and Sutherland Highlanders

Palestine, Secunderabad

scarlet – yellow

(2 Regular, 7 Territorial battalions)

The Rifle Brigade   Tidworth, Palestine green – black

(2 Regular, 4 Territorial battalions)

INFANTRY – TERRITORIAL ARMY

The Monmouthshire Regiment

(4 Territorial battalions of which one converted to searchlights)

The Cambridgeshire Regiment

(2 Territorial battalions)

The London Regiment

(25 Territorial battalions of which one converted to searchlights, one to signals, three to Engineers, one to artillery, also includes Artists Rifles)

The Hertfordshire Regiment

(2 Territorial battalions)

The Herefordshire Regiment

(2 Territorial battalions)

ROYAL ARMY CHAPLAINS DEPARTMENT	black – purple
ROYAL ARMY SERVICE CORPS	blue – white
ROYAL ARMY MEDICAL CORPS	blue – dull cherry
ROYAL ARMY ORDNANCE CORPS	blue – scarlet
ROYAL ARMY PAY CORPS	blue – primrose yellow
ROYAL ARMY VETERINARY CORPS	blue – maroon
ARMY EDUCATIONAL CORPS	blue – Cambridge blue
THE ARMY DENTAL CORPS	blue – emerald green
QUEEN ALEXANDRA'S IMPERIAL MILITARY NURSING SERVICE	grey – scarlet
TERRITORIAL ARMY NURSING SERVICE	blue grey – scarlet
AUXILIARY TERRITORIAL SERVICE	
CORPS OF MILITARY POLICE	blue – scarlet
OFFICER TRAINING CORPS	

(Senior Division, Universities; Junior Division, Schools)

Regiments and Corps Created, or Revived, after 3 September 1939

NORTH IRISH HORSE
Raised in 1900, this was revived as a Territorial regiment of the Royal Armoured Corps in late September 1939.

THE PIONEER CORPS
A Labour Corps had existed in the First World War and a new Auxiliary Military Pioneer Corps was formed in October 1939. This became the Pioneer Corps in November 1940.

THE INTELLIGENCE CORPS
A form of Intelligence Corps was formally accepted by the War Office in 1913, albeit consisting of personnel who continued to wear the cap badges of their own parent units. The new Intelligence Corps was approved in July 1940.

ARMY PHYSICAL TRAINING CORPS
Though Army Physical Training Staffs had existed for some time the Army School of Physical Training was not formed until 1940, and that same year the corps was formally recognised.

ANTRIM MILITIA
Already existing as a battery the unit was expanded to a regiment of the Royal Artillery in 1940.

ARMY CATERING CORPS
Existing cooks were transferred to create the new corps in March 1941.

RECONNAISSANCE CORPS
Brigade Reconnaissance Groups were formed in 1940, the corps being created from these in January 1941.

ARMY COMMANDOS
First formed in June 1940, drawing both on new volunteers for Special Service and the Independent Companies that were formed earlier in the year for the Norwegian campaign.

THE HOME GUARD
Raised as the Local Defence Volunteers in May 1940 on a zone basis, but soon reorganised as part-time Auxiliaries to the Regulars on a part-time home defence basis as the Home Guard. Accepted as a part of the military forces of the Crown and almost entirely cap badged to existing regiments of the line. Stood down in late 1944 and disbanded on 31 December 1945.

THE PARACHUTE REGIMENT
Originally conceived as a part of the Commandos, troops were quickly separated off to gain parachute training at Ringway, Manchester, subsequently becoming a Parachute Corps of Parachute Battalions, which were eventually formalised as the Parachute Regiment in 1942.

Captain Cook of the Intelligence Corps, wearing leather jerkin and holstered pistol, examines a German prisoner towards the end of the war in Western Europe. (Official/ Author)

Far left: A member of the ATS gives instructions to a driver of the First Aid Nursing Yeomanry, at the Motor Transport Training Centre, Camberley, 1941. (Ministry of Information/IWM via Getty Images)

22nd Dragoons, 23rd Hussars, 24th Lancers, 25th Dragoons, 26th Hussars and 27th Lancers

These new cavalry regiments, mainly operating tanks, were raised around cadres from existing units between December 1940 and February 1941.

Army Air Corps

Authorised in August 1941 as Air Observation Post Squadron, Royal Artillery but enlarged and formalised as a corps in February 1942. Acted as an umbrella formation for the Parachute and Glider Pilot regiments. The Special Air Service was added to the Army Air Corps in April 1944.

Glider Pilot Regiment

Formed in 1941 and also capable of fighting on the ground as part of larger airborne operations.

Women's Army Corps

Women's services granted full military staus, 1941.

Special Air Service

No. 11 Special Air Service Battalion was originally created in late 1940 as part of the development of the parachute arm. The tiny 'L' Detachment, 1st Special Air Service Brigade, later formed separately in North Africa under David Stirling, was misleadingly named in order to deceive the enemy. Its first date of action, 17 November 1941, is usually regarded as the birthday of the unit. Following expansion, the SAS was formally recognised as a regiment of the Army Air Corps in 1944.

The Highland Regiment and the Lowland Regiment

Created in 1942 from young recruits to other Scottish regiments, these were disbanded in late 1943.

Corps of Royal Electrical and Mechanical Engineers

Formed in May 1942 from Royal Army Ordnance Corps and Royal Army Service Corps personnel.

'Home Defence Battalions' of older men were attached to regular regiments, but intended to guard vulnerable points in the UK. Later in the war some were also sent abroad. (Official/ Author)

Battalions, Squadrons and Batteries

Infantry regiments were divided into battalions, each battalion in its turn being made up of companies. Each company was made up of platoons supported by its own 2-inch mortar. The platoon was the lowest level of command where there might be an officer as leader and men with a dedicated HQ function. Each platoon was made up of sections – the smallest combat unit, commanded by a junior NCO. As of 1939 there were four 'rifle' companies to the battalion, and each company totalled one hundred all ranks, being three officers and ninety-seven other ranks. Half of the platoons were commanded by warrant officers (class III). Somewhat questionable anti-tank defence was provided by Boys anti-

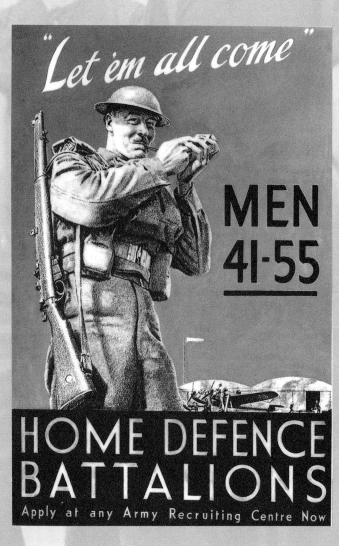

tank rifles, and the 'headquarters' company included ten Bren gun carriers and the heavy weapons, namely six 3-inch mortars, and four anti-aircraft Brens. All of the infantry battalion transport was now mechanical. At the outbreak of war, battalion strength was therefore 670 all ranks, a considerable number of men, but really not enough when it was considered that crew served weapons, various 'detached duties' and casualties ate into 'bayonet strength' on the battlefield. There were often as few as twenty-two officers. Battalion establishments were thus significantly increased and altered during the course of the war.

As the history of the King's Own Yorkshire Light Infantry explained:

'By May 1941, the battalion strength had been increased to 807. Every platoon was commanded by an officer, 24 men were added to each rifle company, and the carrier platoon received an extra section of four carriers. By the spring of 1943 a major change had taken place. Rifle companies remained the same

as before save for the addition of three men apiece, but a new Support Company was formed by detaching the carriers, mortars and pioneers from Headquarter Company. The AA Brens were abolished. The Support Company consisted of a mortar platoon (six 3-inch mortars), a carrier platoon (13 carriers including a flamethrower section), an anti-tank platoon of six 6-pounder guns, and an assault pioneer platoon. The battalion now had 36 officers and 809 other ranks. This remained the basic organisation until the end of the war.'[5]

Nevertheless, there were many variations to the constitution of a battalion, official and otherwise. In the Western Desert large infantry anti-tank companies were formed before the general appearance of the 6-pounder anti-tank platoons, and 'battle patrols' and 'tank hunting platoons' were also created. In Italy some battalions also formed ad hoc Vickers machine gun platoons. As manpower shortages and the demands of the Italian terrain bit home in the autumn of 1944, battalions were reduced from four to three rifle companies. Transport was shaped to need by the addition of horses and mules.

British paratroopers in training pass a Wellington bomber on an RAF station. The men wear early type large shock-absorbing helmets and several carry Thompson submachine guns. (Popperfoto/Getty Images)

The Loyal Regiment (North Lancashire) 1939–1945

AN EXAMPLE OF THE EXPANSION AND DEVELOPMENT OF A LINE INFANTRY REGIMENT[4]

1938: Two Regular battalions (**1st** and **2nd**)
Militia battalion (**3rd** – on paper only, not recruited)
Two Territorial battalions (**4th** Preston, **5th** Bolton)

1939: As above, but a duplicate battalion in process of formation at Bolton (becoming **6th** Battalion)

1940: Two Regular battalions (**1st** and **2nd**)
4th Territorial Battalion (converted to become 62nd Searchlight Regiment)
5th Territorial Battalion
6th Territorial Battalion
7th Battalion (formed Preston 4 July 1940)
8th Battalion (formed Ashton-under-Lyne 4 July 1940)
9th Battalion (formed Lancaster 4 July 1940)
50th (Holding) Battalion (formed Bolton 5 June 1940 but converted to **10th** Infantry battalion 9 October 1940)
Eight battalions of the Lancashire Home Guard badged to the Loyal Regiment:
5th Preston (County)
6th Kirkham
8th Preston
12th Leyland
13th Croston
14th Bolton (County)
15th Bolton
24th Wigan (County)

1941: Two Regular battalions (**1st** and **2nd**)
62nd (**4th** The Loyal Regiment) Searchlight Regiment RA TA [Royal Artillery Territorial Army]
5th and **6th** Territorials (converted respectively to 18th and 2nd battalions the Reconnaissance Corps)
7th Battalion (converted to 92nd Light Anti-Aircraft Regiment Royal Artillery 15 November 1941)
8th Battalion (converted to 93nd Light Anti-Aircraft Regiment Royal Artillery 15 November 1941)
9th Battalion (converted to 148th Regiment Royal Armoured Corps 22 November 1941)
10th Battalion
Eight Home Guard battalions

1942: **1st** Battalion
2nd Battalion and 18th Battalion Reconnaissance Corps (both captured by Japanese at fall of Singapore, February 1942)
4th, **6th**, **7th**, **8th** and **9th** converted and redesignated as above
10th Battalion disbanded and personnel used to reconstruct **2nd** Battalion
Eight Home Guard battalions

1943: Two Regular battalions (**1st** and **2nd**)
4th, **6th**, **7th**, **8th** and **9th** converted and redesignated as above
Eight Home Guard battalions

1944: Two Regular battalions (**1st** and **2nd**)
4th, **6th**, **7th** and **8th** converted and redesignated as above
148th Regiment Royal Armoured Corps disbanded in Normandy 27 August 1944
Home Guard 'stood down' 1 November 1944

1945: Two Regular battalions (**1st** and **2nd**)
4th, **6th**, **7th** and **8th** converted and redesignated as above
30th Battalion (formed Penrith 12 February 1945) as a garrison battalion
31st Battalion (formed Penrith 12 February 1945) as a garrison battalion

Changes to armoured establishments were even more marked over the course of the war. Tanks were organised both into small formations to support the infantry and larger armoured divisions, but the basic units were regiments, divided into squadrons, which were themselves divided into troops. As of 1944 the usual arrangement was either five troops of three tanks, or four troops of four tanks making up a squadron. Three such squadrons were combined with an HQ squadron containing miscellaneous elements such as reconnaissance and anti-aircraft troops and a light aid detachment to complete the regiment under direction of regimental HQ (RHQ). However, in practice, and over time, nothing was quite so simple because there were five major reorganisations of the armoured divisons during the war, and many other minor changes. In many cases the task, the available equipment and the demands of service determined the detail.

For example, the King's Dragoon Guards began the war as a regiment equipped with fifty-three light tanks and one Militia squadron formed of the new class of Militia conscript. Later, personnel strength fluctuated violently as, over a period of just ten days, 1,400 reservists took their place on the strength, and many were posted back out again, with quite a few officers going to help form 51, 53 and 55 Training Regiments. Following this upheaval strength was again reduced, to twenty-five officers and 480 other ranks. In the winter of the 'Phoney War', change continued at Wimborne with more postings and 'the weeding out of unsuitable personnel'. As of May 1940 it was recorded that the unit had only twenty-seven tanks, or about half its proper establishment. After the fall of France the regiment was hastily divided into 'penny packets' for the defence of airfields, each squadron providing two troops, three tanks per troop, to form ad hoc formations with thirty riflemen and Local Defence Volunteers. Moved to the Midlands, the RHQ and three squadrons were still spread out, over three stately homes and billets, with 'A' Squadron sleeping in stables. In North Africa in 1941 it was decided that the unit should become a 'temporary armoured car regiment', and it duly received South African-made Marmon Harringtons. These were found reliable but underarmed, and therefore they were mounted with 'various captured enemy weapons', including 20mm and 37mm guns. 'Temporary' turned into years as the King's Dragoon Guards received, successively, AEC, Humber, Daimler and – finally, in 1943 – American-made Staghounds, which were described as 'heavy, but very fast with

numerous refinements'. The Staghounds were mounted with 37mm guns and three machine guns, and for a bigger punch were supplemented by eight 75mm self-propelled guns that October. All the while the actual numbers of vehicles, and even squadrons, varied. Normally there were five troops per squadron and three 'sabre' squadrons, plus the HQ, but a fourth squadron was added in March 1944. Troops might consist of anywhere between two and five armoured fighting vehicles, depending on the time and numbers of vehicle casualties. Sometimes a new machine came in before the last was phased out, so that at one point in 1942 most troops consisted of a Daimler and two Marmon Harringtons. Later, the notional troop establishment was four Daimler armoured cars plus a White Scout Car acting as an armoured troop carrier for an NCO and seven men for dismounted patrols.[5]

Unsurprisingly, Winston joined in the tinkering of armoured unit establishments with enthusiasm. The 11th Armoured Division in Tunisia was a particular case in point: Churchill decided that given the special role he expected it to play, it should be given 'an altogether special outfit' with the freedom to call temporarily upon units in the UK. Amongst other things he recommended that the anti-tank gun quotient should be 'at

A bicycle patrol of the Black Watch on the south coast of England c. 1941: their rifles are old P14 Enfields. Loss of equipment and danger of invasion in the months after the retreat from Dunkirk led to many units of infantry and artillery being re-equipped from old stocks and positioned on vulnerable parts of the coast. (FPG/ Hulton Archive/ Getty)

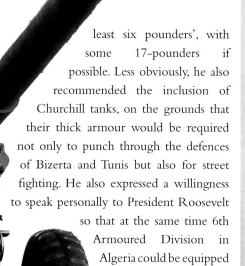

least six pounders', with some 17-pounders if possible. Less obviously, he also recommended the inclusion of Churchill tanks, on the grounds that their thick armour would be required not only to punch through the defences of Bizerta and Tunis but also for street fighting. He also expressed a willingness to speak personally to President Roosevelt so that at the same time 6th Armoured Division in Algeria could be equipped with Shermans.

Artillery organisation varied over time and with the class of ordnance – and there were many unit types, which made the Royal Artillery easily the biggest single regiment in the army. Artillery brigades were formed of regiments and batteries, and guns grouped into troops and sections. There were both Regular and Territorial formations, and later some classes of artillery were manned by the Home Guard. At the beginning of the war the basic unit supporting the infantry was the Royal Artillery 'Field Regiment', comprising two batteries of relatively light ordnance. Each field gun battery consisted of twelve pieces, each of three four-gun troops. Within each troop the guns were paired as sections. The two-battery regiments were found difficult to divide satisfactorily to support the three battalions of an infantry brigade, and accordingly the field regiments were reorganised on a three-battery basis in 1941, with eight guns to each battery. The Royal Artillery Mountain Batteries equipped with light pieces could trace a lineage from India in 1889, though they underwent various amalgamations and disbandments and redefinition as 'Pack Artillery' and field batteries. Many others formed part of the Indian Army establishment.

The Royal Artillery's so-called medium regiments were descended from the First World War's Royal Garrison Artillery units, and as of 1920 had been defined as those with 60-pounder guns and 6-inch howitzers. During the Second World War the medium regiments would field weapons of similar size, including the new 5.5-inch guns. Their longer range guns

The 5.5-inch Medium gun was under design at the outbreak of war, and suffered various teething troubles that delayed its appearance on the battlefield in North Africa until 1942. Thereafter it served in most theatres of war. After D-Day in particular it was a mainstay of the Royal Artillery, firing more than two and a half million shells in North Western Europe by May 1945. (Author)

were particularly suitable for counter-battery work, and their fire could also be superimposed upon that of the field guns to created concentrated fireplans. As of early 1939 a medium regiment contained two batteries, each of four guns, and was usually considered as a corps asset. Heavy and super heavy artillery was similarly organised at corps and Army level. Many heavy batteries were reorganised in 1940 as the nucleus of the coast batteries and regiments formed in expectation of invasion. Interestingly, the heavy regiments of 21st Army Group in the field in northwest Europe from 1944 had four batteries of four guns. Half the batteries were equipped with 7.2-inch howitzers, half of them with US 155mm weapons.

Regular anti-aircraft 'machine gun batteries' were formed from 1935, but the terminology changed to 'light anti-aircraft battery' from 1937, probably to reflect the deployment of light

artillery other than machine guns in this role. More than 500 such batteries were formed at various times, and over 150 'light anti-aircraft regiments' were also created, though not all were in existence simultaneously. Small 'light anti-aircraft troops' were created from Territorial Army Reserve personnel to cover vital points in the UK from 1938, though manning arrangements were changed in 1940 to use Territorials rather than the Reserves who were still required to maintain other employment. Anti-aircraft batteries using larger weapons were redefined as 'heavy' from 1940, thus making sense of existing nomenclature. More than 600 of these were formed in total, the main armaments being 3.7-inch calibre and larger, though some also doubled as coast defence. AA batteries of different calibres formed part of field units, and were also used within the static defensive 'commands'. Whole AA brigades were formed to cover 21st Army Group in Europe from 1944. A new generation of searchlight units was also formed from the late 1930s.

Anti-tank artillery units included not only light and later heavier weapons on ground mountings and wheeled carriages, but also self-propelled anti-tank guns, which were also manned by the Royal Artillery. The first anti-tank regiments were converted from other units in 1938. Initially, the main armament was 2-pounder anti-tank guns, later giving way to 6-pounders. In the later part of the war, in the infantry divisions the anti-tank element was usually an anti-tank regiment in which there were four batteries, each battery comprising a four-gun, 6-pounder troop and two four-gun, 17-pounder troops. Airlanding anti-tank batteries were also formed from 1942, initially by conversion of existing anti-tank units, and much of the old Royal Horse Artillery was itself converted to an anti-tank role.

A remarkable aberration, particularly in evidence in the period 1940 to 1942, were the many, often ad hoc, 'defence' and 'coast' batteries and regiments then mounted on UK shores. Some were created from existing home units, others from personnel evacuated from Dunkirk, or scraped together

A 3-inch gun of 303rd Battery 99th AA Regiment at Hayes Common, Kent, May 1940. This model of gun was produced in numbers in the First World War, and being relatively light and swift to operate was used extensively early in the Second World War. Many different types of ammunition were devised for its use. However, improvement in aircraft performance quickly rendered the 3-inch piece obsolete. Some were deployed in other roles, but by 1942 it was no longer classed as a front-line AA gun. (Official/IWM/via Getty Images)

from other sources. Their armaments included 9.2-inch, 6-inch and 4-inch guns, 12-pounders and 6-pounder twins. Examples of the diversity at that time of emergency include a large number of redesignated heavy batteries: coast batteries 301 to 347 were formed in great haste in June 1940 and another group came together in August; and coast batteries 424 to 431 were created from various command cadres in 1941. Some units were shoehorned into existing fortifications, others into new concrete works or field defences. Amongst the many other miscellaneous Royal Artillery units were a variety of 'training regiments', most of them UK based, and 'survey and observation units', both ground and air. Counter-mortar batteries were formed at Sennybridge in January 1945. Field radar groups and 51 (Mixed) Radar Anti-Aircraft Battery were created in March 1945.[6]

The Royal Engineers (RE) had crucial expertise in a diverse range of roles. Their most obvious tasks included construction of defence works, minelaying and clearing, bridging, demolitions, bomb disposal, the skilled work needed to build camps, and the operation and maintenance of specialised equipment. The corps was 90,000 strong at the outbreak of war, and by 1945 it numbered 280,000. The three major types of RE unit were the field units, which conducted most of the battlefield tasks; the line of communication units and transport units, which constructed, maintained and operated facilities such as railways, docks and inland waterways. There were also fortress units for specific overseas garrisons. At the sharp end of the war the Royal Engineers were organised as field companies and field park companies. In 1944 the Royal Engineers also manned the armoured AVREs (Assault Vehicle Royal Engineers) and provided obstacle clearance units. Originally, vehicle recovery and repair was split between the Royal Army Service Corps and the Royal Army Ordnance Corps, each of which had other major functions in terms of vehicle driving and munitions. This arrangement proved clumsy and as a result it was decided to form a new corps during 1942. Thus was created the Royal Electrical and Mechanical Engineers (REME) the main body of which was formed by transferring RASC heavy repair workshops and RAOC workshop units into the new corps. Later, the REME would also take on maintenance of other technical equipment, perhaps most importantly radar.

A photo from the early part of the war showing evacuated young Channel Islanders in training for British regiments. The islands were 'demilitarised' when threatened, but promptly occupied by the enemy, a loss much bemoaned by Churchill. Raids on the islands were a propaganda coup, and led to a waste of enemy resources, but also proved problematic. (Popperfoto/Getty Images).

Recruitment and Conscription

Though conscription existed in the latter part of the First World War it ended with hostilities and was not revived until the eve of the Second World War. By 1938 the size of the Army had risen from its nadir in the 1920s to about 381,000, but it was still tiny by Continental standards and barely commensurate with what was then a colonial world power. In August 1938 a new Emergency Powers (Defence) Act was passed empowering the government to take provisions in defence of the nation, and amongst these were powers to call up reservists. Thought was also given as to what should constitute 'reserved occupations', but conscription was still avoided. The British Army was thus an all-volunteer professional force until well into 1939. Early that year the government issued a booklet entitled *National Service*, with a foreword by Neville Chamberlain, containing an application form to encourage 'voluntary service'. Yet as the Prime Minister explained the 'call is to peace and not to war', peace only being maintained if Britain were strong enough to deter thoughts of aggression. The voluntary service drive encompassed civilian services such as Air Raid Precautions

(ARP) and the police as well as the armed forces. Just six pages of *National Service* were devoted to the Army, and according to the 48-page guide there were no less than nine routes into its various parts.[7]

The first of these was recruitment into Regular Service. Officer candidates were expected to be unmarried and 'approved as suitable by the Army Council'. The 'channels of admission' for officers were through the College Cadets by competitive examination, through a university after graduation, through the Supplementary Reserve or Territorial Army, or up through the ranks. Other ranks were to be aged between eighteen and thirty, of good health and 'fit for service in any part of the world'. Virtually every branch and regiment of the Army would take recruits but there were particular vacancies for skilled men in all the technical corps, who would be entitled to special 'tradesmen's rates' after passing a test to become skilled men at 'special schools' in which they would also receive general education. The courses lasted from three to five years. Boy entrants were also taken as trumpeters, drummers, musicians and 'general duties', though in the event underage soldiers were not allowed to go overseas. Prospective recruits for the other ranks were directed to recruiting offices, TA drill halls, post offices or employment exchanges for details of terms of service, pay and allowances.

The Supplementary Reserve provided three pools of men already trained in one sphere or another who 'would be required immediately on mobilisation'. Category 'A' was to provide transportation and dock units; 'B' to complete units of Royal Engineers and Royal Corps of Signals, and 'certain personnel not in other units'; and 'C' was men who would 'undertake duties sufficiently similar to their civil occupations for peace time training to be unnecessary'. Tradesmen in the Supplementary Reserve were aged nineteen to forty-two, non-tradesmen were nineteen to thirty-eight, while thirty to forty-five was allowed for the Royal Army Pay Corps. The reservists were held on retainers of anything from £6 to £15 per annum, and had to undertake set numbers of training days to remain eligible. Category 'A' reservists were required to do fifteen days of training, while category 'B' usually had to do the same plus twenty drills similar to those of the Territorials. Category 'C' simply continued to do similar work in their civilian occupation. The Infantry Supplementary Reserve was intended to provide an additional reserve of trained men specifically for the infantry of the line, and took men aged from seventeen to thirty. On enlistment such reservists did six months training in a depot or

with a Regular infantry battalion. During training pay was the same as for the Regulars, after which a man was maintained on his retainer.

The Supplementary Reserve of Officers covered all branches of the Army and it was open to men aged eighteen to thirty who had passed an Army entrance examination or the matriculation of a recognised university. They might also be accepted on production of a relevant certificate from other educational establishments; officers aspiring to the technical corps required a technical qualification. Supplementary Reserve officers undertook preliminary training of different lengths depending on the branch of service and types of certificate they already held. This ranged from no mandatory training at all for well-qualified people going into certain parts of the Royal Army Medical Corps and Royal Army Ordnance Corps who were to do similar work to their civil occupations, to four weeks for an officer who had an Officer Training Corps certificate 'B' going into the infantry or the Guards, or eight weeks for an officer who had an Officer Training Corps certificate 'B' going into the tanks, cavalry or artillery. Up to as much as seventeen weeks was needed for a candidate who had the necessary level of general education but held nothing specific to his proposed service. Officers in these reserves were given a £20 annual retainer and an 'outfit allowance' of £40 upon commissioning. Cavalrymen received £50 for their outfit.

Demonstration of army mobility, February 1939: a tracked Light Dragon Mk IIC towing a 2pdr anti-tank gun. Vickers Armstrong Dragons accommodated a gun crew and were capable of towing light pieces over rough terrain. They were thus precursors of the many different models of tracked carrier used by the British Army for a variety of purposes during the war. (Keystone-France/ Gamma-Keystone via Getty Images)

Other types of officer reserve included the Emergency Reserve and the Cadet Reserve. Emergency Reservists were allowed to join aged between thirty-one and fifty-five, and were intended to be specialists, with or without experience, who might be needed as commissioned officers in war. To qualify, an officer needed only to be sufficiently fit for home service. Cadet Reservists were those trained in the Officer Training Corps or 'officer producing units', possessing a certificate, who registered in peacetime to be considered for commissioning. They had to be aged between eighteen and thirty-one but simply registering did not denote a legal commitment.

National Service described the specific responsibilities of the Territorial Army as: the gun and searchlight defence of the country against hostile air attack; the defence of the ports; and 'the provision of a field force to supplement the Regular Army either in the defence of this country or the defence of British interests abroad'. Candidates for commissions could also go into the 'officer producing group of the Territorial Army which consists of the Honourable Artillery Company, the Inns of Court Regiment, the Artists Rifles and the 22nd Battalion (Westminster Dragoons) Royal Tank Corps'. Ordinary age limits for the Territorials were seventeen to thirty-eight, but men up to forty-five were allowed as tradesmen and as much as fifty for the Home Service Anti-Aircraft and Coast Defence. Candidates for Territorial Army commission were aged between eighteen and thirty-one. Normal training requirements for a Territorial officer were a camp of fifteen days and twenty drills per year, each drill being a minimum of one hour. Men doing shorter camps could do increased drills, and new recruits were expected to undertake an additional twenty drills in the first year. Army rates of pay applied during camp. There were also annual 'proficiency grants' of £3, a weapons training grant of 10 shillings and an extra 1 shilling per drill over the minimum twenty up to a maximum of thirty. If mobilised, pay and conditions changed to those of the Regulars.

'National Defence Companies' get little mention in the histories but according to *National Service* in 1939 they consisted of: 'Ex soldiers who are prepared to give an honourable undertaking that in time of emergency they will come up to defend important points; the companies are affiliated to units of the Territorial Army. The minimum age for enrolment is 45.' In peacetime there was no training requirement. Had not the notion of Local Defence Volunteers, later the Home Guard, so

gripped the imagination of Churchill and public alike in 1940, the National Defence Companies might have assumed far greater importance. As it was, the job that they were intended to do was very much like the one actually assumed by others during the war. The women's Auxiliary Territorial Service (ATS) was formed to undertake specific non-combatant duties in the event of war, namely driving, clerical, and 'general' duties. Counted under this last heading were cooking, orderly and storekeeping functions. Both married and single women, aged from eighteen to forty-three, were eligible for general duties and, up to the age of fifty, for 'local'. Officers enrolled indefinitely, others for an initial period of four years. On appointment the officers received a uniform grant of £16 while other ranks received a free-issue uniform.

Potential recruits were graded according to fitness, and many with disabilities, or the very unfit, were not required to serve. John Atkinson faced his medical board in Preston in August 1940, and was immediately passed as 'Grade I'. (Author)

The push towards voluntary enlistment had some impact, but nothing like enough, so in April 1939 the Military Training Act was passed. Under this first wave of conscription all fit and able British men aged twenty and twenty-one were liable for six months military training. Yet at the outbreak of war the Army was still well under a million men and more legislation was required for a proper war footing. So it was that in October 1939 all men not in reserved occupations and aged between eighteen and forty-one became liable for service in the armed forces. This sounds simple, but in practice recruits were called up in waves according to age, and there were many different exceptions and types of reserved occupation ranging from train drivers to farmers. Most men in engineering work were exempted on the grounds that they would be needed for war production, but other categories had exemption at different ages. For example, a trade union official could be called up at twenty-nine but not at thirty. Moreover, employers could ask for deferments. Conscientious objection was also permitted, and early on about twenty-two in every thousand men refused to join up. Objectors went before tribunals, which accepted or rejected them.

With the general call-up commencing from October 1939 the first focus was on fit men in the twenty to twenty-three age range, but as the war progressed the age band caught in the conscription net gradually widened. By May 1940 men up to the age of twenty-seven had been registered, and ever-older men were taken in. Not long afterwards the Army's 'approved strength' was at fifty-five divisions, of which eleven were to be armoured, but this was not easy to attain or maintain. As a tetchy Churchill observed in March 1941, at the outbreak of war the government had not really taken into account how many men the corps, line of communications troops and others would actually absorb. There were now fifty-seven divisions in existence under British control, but in fact only thirty-six were genuinely 'British', the remainder being 'overseas troops'. Even at this date, four of the British Army divisions were abroad – three in the Middle East and one in Iceland. The remaining thirty-two were committed to the Home Forces. Taking into account wastage, and the flow of eighteen- and nineteen-year olds, Churchill's advisors could encourage him only to the extent of being able to maintain an army of two million.[8]

By mid-1941 it was clear that the numbers being recruited had reached a plateau because the bulk of the remaining fit men under forty-one were in reserved occupations. In November 1941 Churchill himself recommended a drastic expansion of conscription. In a memo to colleagues he proposed that the age for compulsory male military service be raised to fifty-one, and lowered to eighteen and a half – possibly even eighteen. For women he suggested that it might not yet be necessary to introduce compulsory service in the ATS, but that should the Cabinet decide in favour it might be worthwhile addressing

women on an individual basis rather than by age. Though neither older men nor women would add very much to actual fighting capacity, he imagined that their presence would free up more young men for the front line, and that women in particular could be directed into industry. Moreover, Winston was already alive to the burden on the 'fighting units', calling for the reduction of 'rearward services and non fighting troops' by a quarter.[9]

These cogitations formed the basis of another act of Parliament surprisingly quickly, being announced by Churchill in the Commons on 2 December 1941 and widely reported the following day. In the event, the age range for male conscription was extended from eighteen and a half to fifty, and single women were made liable for conscription between the ages of twenty and thirty. In practice this meant that the class of men born in 1923 would be registered immediately, with their call-up beginning in the New Year of 1942. Furthermore, registration of all young people now began at sixteen, with a view to smoothing the process and determining what deferments might be required. Technical and medical students were to be allowed to complete degrees, others could be registered as reservists and remain at university for a year. About 1,700,000 women were affected by the change in the law, though in point of fact relatively few of these actually served in the ATS, which reached its peak strength of 212,500 in September 1943.[10]

By mid-1942 the total strength of ground forces was well over four million, 2.5 million in the Army proper, 1.6 million in the Home Guard and 150,000 in the ATS. The 4.5-million barrier was exceeded the following year, yet there were still problems of manpower and achieving the right flow of people

Women of the ATS at the Royal Artillery Experimental Unit, Shoeburyness, using the glass screen of a 'Window Position Finder' for sighting the burst of shells in the air or water, *c.* 1943. Their coloured 'Field Service' caps are in red over blue artillery colours: Churchill encouraged the use of such distinctions for women. (Official/ IWM/ via Getty Images)

to where they were needed most. Juggling the requirements of industry and services involved some complex advanced planning and negotiation. Each fighting service submitted its estimate of requirements six months ahead, taking into account probable operations, and the Manpower Committee balanced these against the needs of the home front and made a recommendation to the government, which took the final decision. The General Staff of the War Office cut and trimmed accordingly, creating orders of battle and bringing into existence new units or disbanding them to meet needs. So it was, for example, that the war began with about half the Army's manpower in the infantry, a figure that climbed to 60 per cent in 1940 after the loss of heavy equipment at Dunkirk and the requirement to put boots on the ground in defence of the UK. Thereafter there was a progressive rebalancing as guns and tanks were produced and brought into service, so that eventually the infantry and artillery were each about one-fifth of the Army. With the ceiling of Army manpower

set by government, increases in one branch usually required reductions in another. This was also mirrored in industry, where even civilians in reserved occupations could be obliged to move from one area of the country to another, and in December 1943 Ernest Bevin, Minister for Labour, selected one in ten of the call-up for the mines. Nearly 22,000 'Bevin Boys' were siphoned off in this way, together with another 16,000 who volunteered to go to the mines.

Yet despite massive expansion, and the orchestrated direction of labour, the Army faced a growing crisis of manpower. The need to find enough troops, for the forthcoming invasion of Europe, the Far East, Italy and many far-flung garrisons set up tensions that showed at home during 1943. Several 'lower establishment' divisions in the UK were reduced to cadres. Churchill was particularly shocked by the impact on the infantry. On 3 May 1943 he wrote to the Chief of the Imperial General Staff:

A Sergeant of the Army Film and Photographic unit contemplates the danger of German snipers. The AFPU was set up in late 1941 and disbanded in 1946. Shooting pictures proved as dangerous as shooting the enemy and the unit suffered a similar level of casualties to the front-line infantry. (Official/Author)

'You should notice that 75 percent of the latest losses fall on the Foot Guards and the rifle armed infantry, while practically no loss is inflicted on the administrative services. Taking the longer period, there are nearly 64 percent in the Foot Guards and rifle armed infantry. All the other categories together make up 1,443,000 officers and men. If you contrast these figures

and proportions with the reinforcements by units which have been sent up during April and are to be sent during May, the extraordinary disparity becomes manifest. Who is responsible for these drafts, and what instructions have been given to him? The picture unfolded at present is that the fighting troops are not being replaced effectively, although masses of drafts are sent to the technical and administrative services, who were originally on the most lavish scale, and who have since hardly suffered at all by the fire of the enemy. The first duty of the War Office is to keep the rifle infantry up to strength.'[11]

In the effort to find enough infantry, men were transferred from the RAF Regiment and the Royal Artillery. A few hundred officers were 'loaned' from Canada. Such measures helped, but from mid-1944, as fighting in Normandy put a huge strain on a diminishing pool of trained infantry recruits, the implications became serious. To some extent this had been foreseeable because projections had been based on sixteen British and Canadian

Far left: Men of the East Yorkshires under fire near Caen, Normandy, 1944. (Official/ Author)

Infantry advance through fog to the Wessen Canal, Netherlands, September 1944. (George Silk/Life Picture Collection/ Getty Images)

In 1944 mounting casualties were a serious cause of concern for the Prime Minister. This is the Arnhem Oosterbeek War Cemetery where 1,438 identified British war dead are interred. A further 246 are unidentified or commemorated. The majority here are Airborne troops or infantry: the graves foreground are of men of the East Yorkshire Regiment. (Author)

infantry divisions for the invasion force, with relatively little scope for reinforcement. Though losses were indeed anticipated, and a shortfall of about 35,000 men was predicted at an early stage, it was not fully appreciated how high a proportion of losses would fall upon the infantry, particularly as fighting moved inland. The very day the Allies landed in Normandy, Churchill was fuming that the Cabinet had just been told that the Army manpower shortage could reach 90,000 – a figure that might lead to the reduction of anything up to five divisions. His suggestions included retraining other men for the infantry role, and looking again at troops in the UK, whom he calculated numbered about 1.6 million, to find the shortfall.

Early relief at the relatively modest British death tolls during the landings on 6 June quickly turned to consternation as fighting in the Bocage and repeated attempts to capture Caen began to resemble some of the battles of the First World War. By the end of June, 21st Army Group total casualties had reached about 30,000, whilst the pool of trained infantry remaining uncommitted was barely one-tenth of this figure. In early July General Adam went to Normandy to meet with Montgomery, warning him that should infantry losses continue at this rate the only option would be to disband units, using the troops thus freed up to build up the remainder. Montgomery's problem was further complicated by the fact that the US Army in theatre was growing larger and the US casualty rate was running even higher, leading to criticism from his Allies.

Churchill was certainly concerned, partly about the fact of the losses and partly about the way they would be perceived. On 16 July he wrote to General Ismay:

> *'I wish the British casualties, dating from the outset of the operations [in Normandy], to be issued, subject to military considerations, at regular monthly intervals, covering the same period as the fortnightly Allied casualties. I am particularly concerned that the Canadian casualties, although stated separately, should be included in the British publication of casualties; otherwise they will very readily be assumed to be part of the American casualties… The matter should be put to the Dominion Office. It is a great mistake to whittle away the British share in these battles by a form of presentation…'[12]*

Eventually, in mid-August, Montgomery had to bite the bullet. He sought and obtained permission to disband 59th Division. The 50th Division went the same way in November 1944. Though kept in being, 1st Airborne Division never really recovered following heavy casualties at Arnhem. Various brigades, including several armoured formations, were also disbanded or reduced in size. Churchill was peeved, writing to ministers and staff:

> *'I am much distressed by the impending cannibalisation of the 50th Division. We cannot afford at this stage to reduce our stake in the Western line of battle. We must examine all possibilities which are open. For instance there are nearly 80,000 Royal Marines… The 50th Division might close its three brigades to two and add a third Royal Marine brigade… The Staffs should be combed for able bodied fighting officers and men… Every training or exceptional establishment in the Army should be examined, not only from the point of view of reducing its size, but also of substituting elderly men or recovered wounded. It is a painful reflection that probably not one in four or five men who wear the King's uniform ever hears a bullet whistle, or is likely to hear one. The vast majority run no more risk than the civil population of Southern England. It is my unpleasant duty to dwell on these facts. One set of men are sent back again and again to the front, while the great majority are kept out of all the fighting, to their regret.'[13]*

Winston's angry response achieved not very much. Little extra was, in fact, done and the Prime Minister was reminded that the manner in which manpower was distributed at source, and the length of time required in training, set finite limits as to what could be achieved. It is still a matter for debate whether units in the UK could, or should, have been reduced still further to squeeze out more able-bodied men for the front-line infantry. This controversy does, however, serve to remind us of just one of the pressures to husband resources, and highlights the very real need to maximise the use of equipment, guns, shells and tanks, rather than waste troops. Winston remained unperturbed by opposition to what he saw as an attempt to prune the fat from rear areas. In December 1944 his new target was the Middle East. In addition to spending cuts in this now dormant theatre, he proposed that manpower in general should be reduced by one-quarter, and that specifically 50,000 men

should be given up for active areas of operations. Winston's point about the relative sacrifice of Britain in the war would be further elaborated after the conflict when he calculated that one person in 165 from the UK had died whereas just one in 775 had from the United States.[14]

Celebration in Cherbourg on Bastille Day, 14 July 1944. British troops armed with No. 4 rifles and a Sten gun march under British and French flags, marking the recent liberation of the city. (FPG/Hulton Archive/ Getty Images)

CHAPTER THREE
Uniforms and Personal Equipment

Ceremonial

Traditional full dress parade ground scarlets disappeared from the rank and file of the line units of Britain's armies in 1914 never to return. Nevertheless, the Guards, bands and officers still continued to wear the full panoply of bearskins, Victorian-style blue cloth helmets and scarlet tunics when occasion demanded. Full dress officers' uniforms of the inter-

war were described at length in the official *Dress Regulations for the Army* in 1934. Officers of the Foot Guards wore dress similar to that introduced in the early nineteenth century. Their 'cap' was the famous black bearskin with a 'plain taper chain' and a lining of black leather. Interestingly, the taller the officer the higher his bearskin was supposed to be; officers greater than 6 feet (0.8m) in height wore a bearskin 10 inches (25cm) tall, whilst the shortest had a cap no more than 8.5 inches (21.6cm) in height. A Foot Guards regiment could be

French postcards depicting the ceremonial uniforms of the Household Cavalry, Life Guards (left) and Royal Horse Guards (right), 1940. The oldest and most senior regiments of the regular Army, the Household Cavalry had their origins in the personal mounted guards of the sovereign, dating from at least 1660, and arguably even earlier. Only the Territorial Honourable Artillery Company claimed an even older lineage, back to 1537 and the reign of Henry VIII. The Household Cavalry uniforms with helmet with falling plume, 'jacked boots', and cuirass consisting of a breast and back of polished steel worn over scarlet or blue woollen jackets, were essentially nineteenth century in style. (Author)

Armée Britannique
Life Guard

Armée Britannique
Horse Guard

determined by its plume: the Grenadiers wore a white goat hair type on the left, the Coldstreams a scarlet cut-feather on the right; though the Scots Guards wore no plume, the Irish Guards took a blue cut-feather on the right, and the Welsh Guards a longer plume in green and white on the left. The Foot Guards' scarlet cloth tunic with blue collar and cuffs was also distinguished regimentally: the Grenadiers wore nine buttons, equally spaced, and four bars of embroidery at equal distances on each skirt and sleeve flap; the Coldstreams had ten buttons in pairs and four bars of embroidery, again in pairs; the Scots Guards had nine buttons, in threes, and three bars of embroidery; the Irish Guards ten buttons – arranged four, four and two – and four bars of embroidery grouped towards the centre. The ten buttons of a Welsh Guards officer were in groups of five, and he had five bars of lace. The double-breasted Guards officer's great coat was of 'milled Atholl grey cloth' lined with 'Wellington red'. There was also an 'undress' uniform with a blue frock coat and forage cap, and at dinner mess dress was worn that consisted of a short scarlet 'mess jacket' worn over a 'mess vest' of 'garter blue' cloth with blue cloth 'overalls'.

In full dress line infantry officers wore the 'blue cloth' helmet, a piece of headgear dating back to the 1870s, constructed of cork and covered in a fabric so dark that it appeared almost black. At the crown was a spike and at the front a regimental badge, with the other fittings being of gilt metal. In Fusilier regiments a short bearskin, or black racoon skin, known as a 'fusilier cap' was worn. Tunics were scarlet and had eight buttons with collar and cuffs of the regimental facing colour. In most units the facing material was described simply as 'cloth' but the Royal West Kents were entitled to velvet. Lace patterns varied depending on the national origin of the regiment, with the Welsh and English using a rose, and the Irish a shamrock. In the Norfolks, Somerset Light Infantry, North Lancashires, East Yorkshires, Leicestershires, East Surreys and the York and Lancasters there was a black line at the top and bottom of the lace and in the shoulder cords. Overalls were of dark blue cloth, and blue frock coats and forage caps were worn in 'undress'. Scarlet mess jackets were short with a roll collar. Officers of rifle regiments continued to wear tunics of rifle green with regimental facings and a busby of black persian lambskin. Most regiments also had rifle green overalls or pantaloons, but the King's Royal Rifle Corps wore black. Rifles mess dress was also rifle green.

Highland officers wore a distinctive full dress with a black ostrich feather 'bonnet' having a diced border of regimental pattern and vulture feather plume. For most the plume was white, but for the Black Watch it was red. The scarlet 'doublet' had collar and cuffs of regimental facing colour, gauntlet cuffs and 'Inverness' skirts. Regimental pattern kilts, trews or pantaloons were all permitted, and with the kilt came a distinctive regimental pattern sporran, gaiters, hose tops, garters and shoes. Into the hose tops could be tucked the knife known as a skean dhu. Highland officers wore a basket hilted sword, officially, if technically erroneously, referred to as a 'Claymore'. Whilst regulation stipulated hilt and scabbard some variety of blade was permitted, and in fact quite a few Highland officers carried old, remounted, family blades. In levee dress buckled shoes were worn, and the Black Watch and the Argyll and Sutherland Highlanders added an even more decorative sporran. Glengarry caps of similar appearance to those used by other ranks were worn by officers in 'undress' together with trews and a serge frock coat. Trews were also worn with Highland officers' mess dress, together with some particularly decorative scarlet mess jackets, incorporating regimental linings, and a variety of regimental mess vests. Other Scottish regiments also had distinctive full dress with, for example, green cloth shakos being worn by Highland Light Infantry officers, and rifle green shakos worn by those of the Cameronians with a doublet of similar hue. Officers in the Lowland regiments wore blue 'Kilmarnock bonnets', though the Royal Scots Fusiliers took the fusilier cap.

A collection of Player's cigarette cards showing a range of territorial British Army uniforms from the late 1930s, including dress, ceremonial and battledress. (Author)

56TH (CORNWALL) A/A. REGT. R.A., 1939

4TH/5TH BN. THE BUFFS (ROYAL EAST KENT REGT), 1939

THE NORTH MIDLAND CORPS SIGNALS, 1939

3RD COUNTY OF LONDON YEOMANRY (SHARPSHOOTERS), 1939

INFANTRY, T.A., 1939

58TH (SUFFOLK) MEDIUM REGIMENT, R.A., 1939

ROYAL ARMY ORDNANCE CORPS, 1939

8TH (1ST CITY OF LONDON) BN., THE ROYAL FUSILIERS, 1937

7TH/9TH (HIGHLANDERS) BN., THE ROYAL SCOTS, 1939

LONDON IRISH RIFLES, 1939

The Grenadier Guards rehearse for the trooping of the colour on Horse Guards Parade, London, June 1938. The historic ceremony, held on the sovereign's official birthday but suspended after the outbreak of war, was revived in 1947. Curiously a police horse, Winston (1937–1957), named in honour of Churchill, carried King George VI on this occasion. (Planet News Archive/SSPL/Getty Images)

officers of the Royal Engineers and Royal Corps of Signals wore a scarlet full dress complete with busby, the full dress of the Royal Tank Corps was drab by comparison – tank officers wore the black beret and a blue cloth tunic enlivened only by black facings and gold lace.

Had the 1930s not commenced with a worldwide economic depression it is possible that full dress might ultimately have made a general comeback for all ranks in all regiments: as it was an interesting halfway step was taken and, in 1936 it was announced that a smartly cut blue uniform would be adopted for the Coronation. This outfit, of cap, jacket and trousers, or overalls, and commonly known as 'Coronation Blues', was presented to the king at Buckingham Palace in 1937, and duly approved. In this attire, seen on the parade grounds of the late 1930s, infantry, cavalry and artillery all wore a dark blue patrol jacket with regimental collar badges, whilst rifles wore green. The peaked cap was usually of dark blue with a coloured band; red for the majority of the infantry and artillery, and of regimental colour for the cavalry. Many of the hussars were an exception in that they wore red or crimson caps, and the caps of the lancers had 'quarter welts', symbolically continuing the tradition of square-topped lance caps. According to instructions issued in May 1940, neither full dress nor mess dress were to be worn for the duration of the war.[1]

Cavalry officers' full dress was, if anything, an even more splendid affair, with a positive riot of different colours and patterns which told the historic story of the many different types of horsemen who had made up the mounted arm. The Household Cavalry wore a helmet of German silver, with nine-buttoned scarlet cloth tunics for the Life Guards and blue tunics for the Royal Horse Guards. Gauntlet cuffs were worn and facings were blue for the Life Guards and scarlet for the Royal Horse Guards. Officers of Dragoon Guards and Dragoons wore a helmet but variously in gilt or gilding metal, or white metal for the 1st Royal Dragoons and 5th Inniskilling Dragoon Guards. Hussar officers wore short busbys of black sable fur, together with ostrich feather plumes and busby bags in regimental colours. Hussar officer tunics were close fitting, and of blue cloth with loops of gold chain gimp and Austrian knots. Most of these tunics had blue collars, but the 3rd Hussars wore scarlet and the 13th/18th Royal Hussars, buff. Royal Horse Artillery full dress was also in the hussar style, with a scarlet busby bag and a blue cloth jacket with scarlet collar. Lancers officers' full dress headgear was the black patent leather lance cap with a cloth top in facing colour, and their tunic was blue cloth, double-breasted with pointed cuffs and regimental facings. Interestingly, whilst

Service Dress 1918–1945

Britain had emerged from the Great War with her fighting troops clad in 'service dress' – a loose-fitting suit made of drab khaki woollen mixture cloth, comprising a jacket with four pockets and metal shoulder titles, trousers and cap, worn with boots and puttees. For active service the cap was substituted with a steel helmet, and mounted men wore breeches and tied their puttees at the ankle rather than the knee. Highland troops wore a similar jacket, but with rounded skirt fronts, kilts and kilt aprons, and the loose tam o'shanter headgear. The outfit was worn with regulation shirt and underwear. The impression of drabness was, if anything, increased with the first years of peace: massive demobilisations saw the disappearance of many famous battalions, and the colourful formation signs, which had relieved the muddy tedium of serge, were discontinued.

In 1922 the British Army faced further drastic reductions. The cavalry units were cut severely, bringing into being the hybrid units, which Churchill is said to have dubbed 'vulgar fractions'. At the same time, infantry regiments whose recruiting areas now lay within the boundaries of the new Irish Free State ceased to exist, and units such as the Royal Irish Regiment and Royal Munster Fusiliers disbanded. The result was the loss of many cap badges and traditions. By the mid-1920s, however, new elements of smartness and formality were creeping back into peacetime soldiering. Perhaps most significantly, an Army Council Instruction of 1924 saw the introduction of a new service dress jacket, similar to the old, but tighter fitting, and usually worn with collar badges. This new-style garment was intended for use on parade and 'walking out', whilst the old-type baggy jackets were retained as a 'second' for training. Soon afterwards service dress trousers, which had hitherto been close fitting around the lower leg and habitually worn with puttees or leggings, were now altered to a slightly fuller style.[2]

The usual headgear for wear with service dress was the matching peaked SD cap. This had a brown leather chinstrap secured by two small brass buttons, and the outline of the hat was maintained by an internal support in the shape of a wire-former. The precise shape, and whether it was more or less 'set up' at the front, was dictated as much by regimental fashion as by regulation. Since Battle Dress ('BD', or battle dress) was not immediately issued to all troops at its time of introduction, service dress continued to be used in tandem for some time. Thus it was that whilst the infantry of the BEF were largely supplied with the latest clothing by 1940, many mounted troops and rear-echelon units were still to be seen in 'SD', or service dress. In a few instances the old service dress actually survived throughout the whole war, with bandsmen on parades being a particularly good example. Officers were supposed to visit specified commercial 'regimental tailors' for their kit, but with economies and transfers between units and theatres this was not always possible in wartime. Other ranks' service dress was issued ready to wear, in coarser cloth, unlined and with maker's details and sizes on interior labels. If one was lucky it fitted, but often issue garments required the attentions of the unit tailor. Issue items were marked with the soldier's name and an abbreviation of the name of his regiment or corps, but were not supposed to have battalion or company numbers.

Privately purchased officer's service dress was discussed in detail in the *Dress Regulations* of 1934, in which the jacket was described as:

'Drab material of sealed pattern cut and shade, single breasted cut as a lounge coat to the waist with a back seam, loose at the chest and shoulders but fitted at the waist; military skirt to the bottom edge, opening at the back from the bottom of the garment to the waist line; length of skirt 13 inches for an officer 5 feet 9 inches in height, with a proportionate variation for any difference in height; step collar... two cross patch breast pockets... two expanding pockets below the waist at the side... inside watch pocket... Four large regimental buttons down the front... Badges of rank in metal on the shoulder straps. Shoulder straps of the same material as the jacket, fastened with a small regimental button.'

The open collar was worn with shirt and tie, theoretically of Army-wide regulation hue, but in practice lighter and darker shirts and ties were sometimes adopted as unofficial regimental distinctions.

Interestingly, there were jacket variations for Guards, whose officers had their jacket buttons grouped according to

Rifle inspection for men of 2nd Cameronians (Scottish Rifles) at the Tower of London. On parade the Scottish Service Dress jacket with 'rounded off' skirt fronts is worn with Glengarry cap and regimental Douglas tartan trews. Belts and officers' gloves were of black leather according to the style of 'rifle' regiments. (Official/ author)

Male and female officer Service Dress worn to an open air investiture at Buckingham Palace. The female uniform is that of the First Aid Nursing Yeomanry. The male officer ranks as a Brigadier, or Substantive Colonel, as denoted by his Royal Crest cap badge. His Service Dress jacket has gorget patches on the collar. In accordance with convention gloves are carried. (Planet News Archive/SBBL/Getty Images)

'regimental arrangement'. So there were three sets of two for the Coldstreams, two sets of three for the Scots Guards, two sets of four for the Irish Guards, and evenly spaced buttons for the Grenadiers and Welsh. The jacket for officers of Scottish regiments retained rounded skirt fronts, though with no skirt vent for the Cameronians whilst the Argyll and Sutherland Highlanders boasted two. Buttons for service dress, both for officers and other ranks, were usually of regimental pattern, whilst battle dress buttons were plain khaki. However, there also existed a 'general service' button bearing the royal arms. Hussars were something of an exception, having mainly the plain buttons that harked back to the plain 'ball' buttons worn by their regiments with the hussar dress of yesteryear.[3]

Officers wore service dress with the famous 'Sam Browne' leather belt, which usually consisted of a waist-belt with a strap running around the body and over the right shoulder to the left hip (there was a variation with a vertical strap running up over each shoulder and crossing at the rear). On the waist-belt were 'D' rings and studs allowing for the attachment of a sword frog, pistol holster, ammunition pouch or other items. Most belts were brown, but black ones could be worn by rifle units.

Officers' service dress caps were of two possible forms: a stiff variety for formal occasions and a 'soft pattern' with no stiffener around the crown and a flexible peak. In most instances the chinstrap was brown and the buttons bronze, but in the case of rifle officers the strap and buttons were black. Likewise, the usual gloves worn by officers were to be of 'brown dogskin or buckskin', but rifle regiments wore black. Boots for officers were generally brown with 'plain toe caps' unless otherwise specified. Breeches were worn in the field or on formal occasions but trousers were permitted in barracks and offices. Out of the front line officers continued to wear pre-war style service dress quite widely throughout the war, but in 1942 an 'austerity' type jacket was introduced with the objective of saving on materials and labour. This simplified version of the jacket, which never became universal and was in use alongside the normal garment, lacked pocket pleats on the breast and had slit pockets without flaps or buttons in the skirts. Wartime regulations also allowed for a variety of material to be used, including barathea, whipcord or serge, provided it was of the correct drab shade. Furthermore, officers who transferred from one unit to another were allowed to continue to use boots of the 'wrong' colour, or jackets of the wrong configuration, until they wore out, thus saving scarce resources.

Women's ATS Service Dress[4]

The all-female Auxiliary Territorial Service (ATS) was officially brought into existence as part of the Territorial Army in September 1938. Though the ATS would also wear battle dress the corps was entitled to its own distinctive service dress, comprising a khaki drab jacket and skirt in 'Saxony' serge, worn with cap, drab shirt and tie, thick stockings and brown shoes. As first issued in 1938 the ATS service dress jacket was open collared, tailored to the female form and closed down the front with four brass buttons. It was fitted with four flapped pockets closed with smaller buttons, the breast pockets being patch pockets with pleats. Perhaps surprisingly, it buttoned on the same side as a male garment. It was said that this feature was specifically required by the head of the ATS, Chief Controller Helen Gwynne-Vaughan, a veteran of the First World War, on the grounds that decorations could still be worn on the uppermost side of the jacket. In 1941 a much younger replacement, Chief Controller Jean Knox, oversaw a revision of

King George VI performs an inspection during a visit to Eastern Command, October 1939. The women wear the early version of the ATS Service Dress, buttoning in the male fashion and without the integral front fastening belt introduced later. Everyone, including His Majesty, wears a respirator, hung in its bag over the right shoulder. (Fox photos/Getty Images)

many aspects of the ATS, including its uniform. A new version of the jacket appeared that incorporated a neat integral belt, and some early jackets were also fitted retrospectively with this distinctive feature. As the war progressed, the pleats were deleted from the jacket pockets, brass buttons were replaced by plastic and fastenings were deleted entirely from the lower pockets, producing a 'simplified' or 'economy' version of the original jacket.

The service dress shirt was in khaki cotton poplin, and unlike the jacket it usually fastened right over left in civilian female style. The skirt was known officially as the 'Skirt, Serge, ATS'. It was 'A' line in shape, reached to just below the knee and had a pocket on the left hip. The soft peaked cap was of a distinctive style with a small flap, which could be turned down around the back and sides to provide the neck with a modicum of weather protection. Early caps had the peak and band reinforced with rows of stitching, a feaure later deleted. An optional headgear for 'walking out' was a coloured field service cap in brown with light green piping, though it would also appear that on occasion the caps of other corps were also worn when personnel from the ATS were attached. For the information of the prurient, official ATS underwear featured a rather ghastly broad pink suspender belt and large woollen, later cotton, panties. The first type of stockings were in khaki Lisle, later replaced by ones

made of khaki rayon. An alternative type, for cold weather, were made of wool.

Greatcoat, and 'Coat, British Warm'

Before 1939 the other ranks' greatcoat was a long, single-breasted garment of khaki drab serge, with button-down shoulder straps and side pockets, closed to the neck with five brass buttons. That year, however, a new pattern of greatcoat was introduced, which was double-breasted and intended to be worn with the collar open. Because the greatcoat was a robust garment, and old coats were supposed to be retained for fatigue and maintenance duties, it was not surprising that both single- and double-breasted greatcoats were worn for a long time afterwards. Various modifications to the double-breasted coat including a 'jigger button' inside to prevent the front sagging. A reduction in overall length came in 1941. A distinctive blue-grey other ranks' greatcoat was retained by the Foot Guards for formal wear.

Officers' greatcoats, as described by the 1934 *Dress Regulations*, were of a 'Universal Pattern', double-breasted and made of drab

Winter 1939–1940: a Driver of the Royal Army Service Corps at Ramsgate prior to shipment overseas. Cold-weather kit includes double-breasted greatcoat, scarf, balaclava, and leather gauntlets. The respirator case is worn on the chest for quick access. (Fox photos/Getty Images)

Far right: Battle Dress as wedding suit, Aberdare, 1943. Ostensibly 'combat' clothing the 'BD' has been smartened here with sharp trouser creases and is worn open at the collar over shirt and tie. By 1944 other ranks were officially allowed shirt and tie with battle dress on appropriate occasions. (Author)

that it could be of varying shades of drab so long as all the officers of a unit wore the same colour. The result was that this coat was seen in a range of colours, from a fairly dark drab khaki through to a fashionably light 'camel', approximating the hue of the mounted type breeches. Some officers also wore the 'trench coat' on informal occasions; though not mentioned in the 1934 regulations, this was a double-breasted gaberdine waterproof for use in inclement weather. First seen in the Boer War, it had become popular because it was so practical during service in the trenches in 1914–1918.

'Battle Dress'

By the early 1930s experiments had begun to find a more modern, practical and comfortable fighting uniform than the old service dress. An early contender, announced in 1932, was an outfit consisting of a four-pocket, open-necked serge jacket, trousers with gaiters, a pullover and a rather shapeless gaberdine hat, which

cloth reaching to within a foot of the ground. The sleeves were unlike that of the other ranks' coat in that they had deep turn-back cuffs: the shoulder rank insignia and buttons were usually of gilt metal, though those of rifle units were black. During the war a slightly modified 'alternative' pattern coat was also approved for wear by officers, which was fractionally shorter and lacked the cuff turn-back detail. Guards and senior officers were entitled to use an 'Atholl grey' greatcoat for parades.

Another approved overcoat for officers was the 'British Warm', which had already seen service in the First World War. Knee-length and double-breasted, with two rows of three large leather buttons down the front, the overcoat had a collar that was usually worn open, and pressed flat accordingly, but on at least some examples was capable of being closed across the throat by means of a small button concealed under the lapel. Metal rank badges were worn on the shoulder straps. The British Warm varied in other minor details, and it was accepted

could be folded away when not in use. A few years later, a set of experimental 'overalls' made their debut. The jacket, or 'blouse', portion of these overalls was novel, if not revolutionary, in that it was very short-waisted and made of khaki denim. It closed to the neck, had plastic buttons and no collar badges. The overall trousers were equipped with a huge pocket on the left leg, and the ensemble was completed by the newly introduced 'fore and aft' field service cap. By 1937 the experimental overall jacket was being referred to as 'Battle Dress', and the decision had been taken to replicate the style of the overalls in woollen serge to create a new fighting uniform. Thus the '1937 Pattern Battle Dress' was born, but it would be at least another year until all the details of the clothing were finalised.

In October 1938 a 'Provisional Specification' was issued to describe the uniform, which was now being issued to new recruits.

The new battle dress blouse was loosely cut, but terminated at the waist, and could be joined to the trousers by means of buttons. It had box-pleated patch pockets, measuring approximately 6 inches by 7 inches, (15cm by 17.5cm) closed with flaps, and two internal pockets. The buttons fastening the front of the blouse were concealed by a flap, there were buttons at the cuffs, and two hooks and eyes closed the collar. The waist of the garment was gathered in and secured by means of a cloth strap and buckle. The blouse had shoulder straps, which in the case of officers bore rank badges, usually embroidered, but occasionally of brass.[5]

The battle dress trousers were moderately wide with a strap and button at the bottom of each leg, which allowed the trouser to be narrowed before web anklets were put on. The trousers had no less than five pockets: the large pocket on the left leg, closed by a flap and concealed button, was sometimes

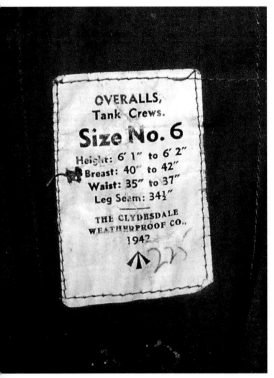

A typical clothing label, similar examples being sewn into greatcoats, Battle Dress, and other issue garments. This one is in a set of tank crew overalls from 1942. The 'broad arrow' device denotes government ownership, and was also stamped into weapons, onto webbing, and elsewhere. Clydesdale Weatherproof was just one of a multitude of contractors, and supplied a variety of garments including shorts, and skirts for the ATS. (Author)

called a 'map pocket' and it measured 11 inches by 7 inches (27.5cm by 17.5cm). The much smaller right leg pocket, which was fitted rather higher up, was pleated, and had a button but no flap. This pocket was sometimes referred to as the 'field dressing pocket'. The other three pockets were ordinary slit-type trouser pockets on either side, and a flapped back pocket. As issue garments neither the trousers nor the blouse were lined, but most of the pocket interiors, collar and belt backings were of a yellowish khaki material.

The war had been in progress no more than a few months when modifications began to simplify battle dress and economise on materials. In June 1940, for example, a new specification was issued for slimmer-fitting blouses and trousers, and cheap-looking 'revolving shank' buttons to be used on field dressing pockets. Buttons and straps on the trouser legs were deleted not long afterwards, and in 1942 more patterns appeared in which pocket pleats, belt loops and flaps concealing buttons were all deleted. By the middle of the war, battle dress blouses of simplified form were actually being marked on the label as 'Blouse 1940 Pattern', and those garments lacking pocket pleats and concealed buttons are now commonly referred to as such.

A strict definition of 'Blouse 1940 Pattern' is, however, hard to give, and the reasons for this ambiguity are not difficult to guess. It is very likely, for example, that the designation 'Blouse 1940 Pattern' was actually applied retrospectively to some of the earliest modifications, and that some of the specifications merely tidied up things that already existed in practice. In the UK there were a mass of different contractors, and battle dress was made for British forces in New Zealand, the USA, Canada, and possibly elsewhere, thus the number of minute variations is legion. New Zealand battle dress, for example, is seen as late as 1943, and possibly later, complete with pleated pockets and concealed buttons.

The material and colour of battle dress is particularly prone to variation. Some of the finest garments – lined, neatly tailored, and of quality material – are obviously bespoke

items made for officers, but even amongst issue pieces there is considerable scope for possibilities. The British specification of 1938 dictated 'Serge S.D. No 1. 55" Pattern No T 90', but batch variations and wartime exigencies meant that the precise weight and shade were difficult to control. Even so, it is noticeable that British-made battle dress is often browner and coarser than other types; the author's father was just one young recruit who did his best to avoid being shovelled into scratchy British garments and sought out the relative comfort of colonial cloth instead. An examination of a number of New Zealand- and American-made battle dresses tends to confirm that they were not only of finer material but also greener in colour than British 'B.D.' blouses.

Officers wore battle dress open at the neck with shirt and tie from an early date, and indeed privately purchased blouses were soon made with collars pressed so as to lay neatly open and flat. Before long this open-necked style was also being aped by other ranks when 'walking out' or at civilian functions. According to one regulation, soldiers with sensitive skin were allowed to have their collars lined with soft cloth to avoid chaffing, and so for medical or sartorial reasons many neck closures were soon being lined or altered. In 1944 officialdom bowed to the inevitable and the issue began of a new shirt, with collar attached, and a khaki tie. Ties were to be allowed in barracks, on leave, or walking out, though tiepins and non-regulation ties were forbidden. After the war, 1949 Pattern BD blouses featured open necks as a matter of course.

There were also some less obvious modifications applied to battle dress both by individuals and by unit tailors. Sometimes darts were put in to produce a closer fit; pleats were removed, added, or pressed flat. Sometimes the hairy nap of the cloth was pressed down or even shaved, and occasionally weights were worn in the leg of the trouser on parade to produce a definite overhang over the top of the web anklets. Battle dress was warm and fairly practical, but not without drawbacks. Perhaps the worst feature was the abutment of the trousers and blouse with precious little overlap, the buttoned closure of which was soon parted by strenuous exercise. In retrospect it is also possible to see the shape of the battle dress as a not strictly practical expression of the fashion of the 1930s – short jacket and high-waisted trousers – when a jacket with a skirt offers both better coverage of the body and the possibility of larger and more convenient pockets.[6]

The 'Universal' and 'Coloured' Field Service Caps

The 'Universal Pattern Field Service Cap' of khaki drab serge, commonly worn with the battle dress during the early war period, was not a terribly practical head covering but at least it had the advantage that it stowed away neatly, folded completely flat and was easy to carry. On the head it assumed a distinctive 'fore and aft' impression, totally unlike that of the SD cap. When properly worn it inclined slightly to the right of the skull, with the small brass buttons to the front and the regimental badge over the left eye. It could be unfolded over the head and neck to provide some cover for the neck and ears, but in practice was rarely worn in this manner. The officer's 'Universal Pattern Cap' was similar but made of better-quality materials.

An optional variant was the 'Coloured Field Service Cap' which was similar in shape, but of cloth coloured according to regiment. Similar caps had been worn in the nineteenth

A Royal Artillery Coloured Field Service Cap, worn at a rakish non-regulation angle. Other ranks usually wore metal badges with this headgear, as shown here. (Author)

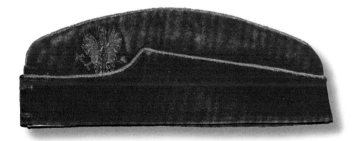

Far left top: Officer's Coloured Field Service Cap 14th/20th King's Hussars: red with gold piping and embroidered eagle. (Author)

Middle: Officer's Coloured Field Service Cap 26th Hussars. Scarlet body; primrose peak; blue curtain and embroidered eagle with 'XXVI'. (Author)

century, but the type worn in the Second World War was formally introduced in 1937 by way of an amendment to the *Dress Regulations*. It was described as 'similar in shape to the Glengarry', and the colour or colours chosen were picked at the behest of the 'colonels commandant' or 'colonels of regiments or corps', the badge being of 'authorised regimental pattern'. For the most senior officers, generals and substantive colonels not attached to a corps or department, there was also a special blue cloth version with scarlet top and gold French braid. The coloured caps, which were to be maintained in addition to a forage cap, were officially described as 'entirely optional' but authorised for use with mess dress or other informal occasions, but not 'parade or duty'.

Though the following table shows many of the main variations it should be noted that about 140 types have been identified, and that in addition to the main coloured panels most units also had various distinctive pipings around the crown, peak and curtain of the cap. Fuller details are contained in both the June 1937 amendment to the *Dress Regulations* and the reference work *British Army Uniforms and Insignia*.[7] (7)

Bottom: Other ranks Coloured Field Service Cap, Royal Engineers: dark blue with yellow piping and metal badge. (Author)

Unit	Crown	Body	Peak	Curtain
Queen's Royal Regiment	Light green	Dark blue	Dark blue	Dark blue
Buffs	Dark blue overall			
King's Own	Red	Dark blue	Dark blue	Dark blue
Royal Warwickshires	Dark blue overall			
Royal Fusiliers	Cambridge blue overall			
King's (Liverpool)	Dark blue overall			
Royal Norfolks	Yellow	Dark blue	Dark blue	Dark blue
Lincolnshires	Dark blue	Red	Dark blue	Dark blue
Devonshires	Dark green	Dark green	Black	Black
Suffolk Regiment	Dark blue	Dark blue	Yellow	Dark blue
Somerset Light Infantry	Rifle green overall			
West Yorkshires	Buff	Dark blue	Buff	Dark blue
East Yorkshires	Dark red	Dark red	Black	Black
Beds and Herts	Dark blue overall			
Leicestershires	Grey	Black	Grey	Black
Green Howards	Green	Green	Black	Black
Lancashire Fusiliers	Primrose yellow	Cherry	Cherry	Cherry
Cheshire Regiment	Dark yellow	Dark blue	Dark blue	Dark blue
Royal Welsh Fusiliers	Dark blue overall			
South Wales Borderers	Light green overall			
R. Inniskilling Fusiliers	Buff	Cambridge blue	Cambridge blue	Cambridge blue
Gloucestershires	Pale yellow	Dark blue	Dark blue	Dark blue
Worcestershires	Light green	Light green	Dark blue	Dark blue
East Lancashires	White	Dark blue	Dark blue	Dark blue
East Surrey Regiment	Black	Black	Brown	Black

A soldier of one of the fusilier regiments wearing the issue Field Service Cap at Leytonstone, London, early in the war. (Author)

Far right: Scottish troops wearing life jackets prior to the Rhine crossing 1945. The headgear is the Balmoral Bonnet. (Official/author)

Glengarry Caps and Bonnets

Scottish regiments were entitled to a 'Glengarry Pattern' field service cap. The Royal Scots, Royal Scots Fusiliers, King's Own Scottish Borderers, Seaforth Highlanders, Gordon Highlanders, Argyll and Sutherland Highlanders, Black Watch and Queen's Own Cameron Highlanders all had a dark blue glengarry with a red 'toori' or pompon. All but the last three had diced bands in varying configurations of red, white and green. The Highland Light Infantry glengarry was in rifle green, and that of the London Scottish was dark blue with a royal blue toori, but no diced band. Other exceptions to the general rule were the Lovat Scouts and the Scottish Horse, which wore a dark blue 'Atholl bonnet', and the London Irish Rifles, which sported a 'caubeen', a traditional voluminous Irish headgear not unlike a very loose

beret in configuration. Many Scottish troops also sported the 'Balmoral bonnet', which was worn by both officers and other ranks and produced both as a service wear and a dress item. Also referred to as a tam o'shanter, the Balmoral was made in khaki drab, had a matching toori and looked not unlike a large beret with a soft crown that was pulled forwards and displayed the regimental badge on the left side. The badge was usually worn on a backing patch of the regimental tartan.

Other Caps and Berets

Berets had been worn in some armies prior to the Second World War, most notably by the French Chasseurs Alpins. A similar beret, also in black, but somewhat smaller in outline was adopted by the Royal Tank Corps – royal approval for this embellishment being accorded in 1924. The 11th Hussars adopted a beret of brown, with a special regimental band in cherry red in 1928. Grey berets were used by the Royal Dragoons from about Christmas 1939, though these had to be paid for out of regimental funds. As more units mechanised or were converted, use of the black beret spread, being formally adopted by units of the Royal Armoured Corps and the Guards Armoured Division (which habitually referred to berets as 'caps') in 1941.

'Browning was determined that the parachute soldier should wear a distinctive head dress of which he should feel proud. A number of berets in various shades of red, blue, and green were placed one by one on the head of an orderly paraded for the purpose before Sir Alan Brooke. Chief of the Imperial General Staff. His choice hovered between a maroon red and blue. Unable to make up his mind, he asked the opinion of the orderly, who replied: "Well, sir, I really like the red beret as the blue reminds me of some labour corps". This settled the matter and the red was chosen.'

With several other colours already earmarked, the green beret was approved for the Special Service Brigade, or Commandos, in October 1942. Like the red beret it was soon used as a mark of special distinction, Commando troops not receiving it until they completed training. The same month a rather less exciting but thoroughly practical khaki beret was likewise approved for the Reconnaissance Corps and motorised battalions of the infantry.

Berets were cheap, easy to produce and presented little obvious outline to an enemy rifleman. For anyone operating in vehicles, berets also had the considerable advantages that they were peakless and easy to stow away. Thus, from 1942 the beret was also taken up, in various colours, by other units. The famous red beret of the airborne forces was formally introduced in July 1942. Various stories surround its selection, including the idea that the precise shade of maroon was chosen by Daphne du Maurier, wife of Major General 'Boy' Browning. It was certainly the case that his pre-war racing colours were light blue and claret. Yet the story given in the history of the Parachute Regiment is as follows:

Later, the Special Air Service (SAS) adopted beige berets, and some wore this headgear in a bleached, almost off-white or sand colour. Photos from 1944 show the SAS beret being worn on the parade ground with the large shield-shaped cloth 'winged dagger' badge.

Similar to the beret, but not identical, was the khaki cloth 'general service' (GS) cap. This was approved for universal use and therefore lacked the exclusivity of the coloured berets, and was not particularly well received. The prime intention was to find something simpler and more practical to replace the old field service caps, and in this at least the GS cap succeeded. First

Kilted Scottish soldiers march through a London Park wearing the Balmoral Bonnet, September, 1939. (Popperfoto/Getty Images)

Royal Armoured Corps personnel in black berets in the latter part of the war. Garments worn here include the leather jerkin and, centre, the oversuit for tank crew. (Author)

Opposite top left: A privately made version of the knitted 'Cap, Comforter'. This pattern for this particular version was promoted by a magazine entitled *Knitted Comforts for Servicemen*. (Author)

Top right: A fleece cap worn by an officer of the Pioneer Corps in Iceland. Similar headgear, of a type also worn in the Royal Navy, was used by some troops in Norway in 1940. (Author)

Middle: A Royal Engineer serving with the Guards Armoured Division wearing the khaki 'Cap, General Service'. Similar to a beret, but fuller in style, the 'GS' headgear was widely used but never replaced the soft headgear already in service. (Author)

introduced in late 1943, it was issued gradually – first to front-line units, then behind the lines and at home. As late as mid-1944 there were still training formations who had not been issued with GS caps, and others who attempted to avoid it by clinging on to other more cherished headgear. As was so often the case, officers, particularly of Guards regiments, sported variations on standard patterns. As the history of the Scots Guards relates:

> 'When the 2nd Battalion reformed in Scotland in 1944 they were issued with GS caps for all other ranks, and in order that the officers should be able to appear on parade dressed similarly to their men, special "Caps GS" of a fine khaki cloth were made for them. These hats which were known as "Killwhillies", had a patch of Royal Stuart tartan as a backing to the cap star but they were not worn for very long and replaced by khaki berets. This practice of wearing a patch of tartan backing on officers' berets found favour in all battalions except the 3rd, and in many cases the metal cap star was replaced by an embroidered star taken from the shoulder strap of the then unwanted "jumper".'[8]

Nevertheless, the GS cap was common currency, particularly after D-Day in Europe.

Two forms of knitted headgear also saw widespread use. The ubiquitous woollen 'cap comforter' was khaki in colour and somewhat shapeless but it served to keep the head warm, and was favoured as an alternative to the steel helmet by raiders. It was also versatile: when pulled out to full length it could also be pressed into service as a short scarf. A general issue early in the war, it was also produced at home by relatives and made in rather more elegant non-standard versions for officers. Its use was somewhat restricted later on when it was limited to field units and those deployed in cold climates. The balaclava helmet was also knitted wool, covered most of the face save for an aperture in the middle, and was so named after a battle in the Crimean War where it probably first saw significant use with British troops. Though the balaclava was not as widely seen as the cap comforter, and does not appear to have been a universal issue, it was also privately produced and particularly useful in circumstances where wind-chill or the need for facial concealment were important factors.

Just how many types of headgear might co-exist in one unit at any one time was difficult to judge, particularly during the latter part of the war. An officer of the Scots Guards who

counted the different sorts to be found in the 2nd Battalion of his regiment on 3 February 1944 discovered no less than eleven distinct varieties. These included steel helmets, with and without the regimental diced band and camouflage net; officers' service dress caps, usually threadbare and dirty, and with various sorts of badge; other ranks' service dress caps, some of the old soft pattern; cap comforters, with and without badges; old khaki 'fore and aft' field service caps; blue fatigue caps; American woollen peaked 'stocking caps'; balaclavas; glengarry caps and Balmoral bonnets amongst the pipers. Berets were apparent in no less than four major sub-species: small black types with tartan flashes; large black *chasseur* types; and small brown ones, with or without flashes and badges. One man who had been in the Commandos refused to give up his green beret.[9]

Helmets and Armour

As early as July 1915 the British Army obtained some French steel helmets for examination by the 'Inventions Committee' in the hope that something could be found to combat the large numbers of head injuries, sustained by troops in the trenches, caused by small fragments and shrapnel. A French-style helmet was later worn by Churchill himself. Soon after the appearance of the French headgear, John L. Brody patented a shallow steel bowl with liner and chinstrap that would become the model for all British steel helmets until the latter part of the Second World

War. Brody's original helmet was supplemented by an improved type from May 1916, subsequently to be known as the 'Mark I'. Not long afterwards all British troops on the Western Front had a steel helmet, and by the end of the First World War the 'tin hat' was accepted as a general part of the equipment of a soldier. It is worth noting that, though very tough, British steel helmets, like those of other nations, were not capable of preventing penetration from a direct hit by a rifle or machine gun bullet at close ranges. What they were able to do was stop smaller and slower-moving fragments of munitions, and specifically shrapnel balls from shells, and to cushion blows from other debris thrown around in battle. The shallow-bowl shape with brim was consciously selected for maximum protection from objects falling from above – and during the First World War the headgear had sometimes been referred to as a 'shrapnel helmet'. The shallow design made for easy manufacture without overstressing the steel and creating weakness, but, as has often been remarked, it gave little protection from any horizontal missile or blow.[10]

By the early 1920s helmet stocks were reduced, in keeping with a smaller Army, and from the mid-1930s various minor modifications were approved, initially with a view to the long periods of storage likely during peacetime, and to improve the old chinstrap. During 1936 a completely new liner was devised using vulcanised fibre, leather oilcloth and a system of four riveted rubber buffers to reduce shocks to the skull. In its later configuration, just

The steel helmet Mk II, exterior and interior views. (Author)

before the outbreak of war, the liner was a clever shock absorber capable of being set up with the buffers in different positions, or even omitted, during assembly, to cater for different sizes of head, from 6.25 to 7.75 inches. Finally, in 1938, a 'Mk II' helmet was introduced. Though visually similar to its immediate predecessor it was always made with the latest lining and was completely non-magnetic. Helmet shells were tested by shooting them with a specially modified rifle that consisted of a short smoothbore barrel converted to fire a half-inch spherical lead ball using a less powerful charge.

The rarely seen 'aero patent' visor fitted to a steel helmet. Proved unsuccessful in trials, only small numbers were given to the Home Guard. (Author)

The 'Steel Hemet, Despatch Riders, Mark I'. (Author)

ATS despatch riders of Eastern Command wearing coats and the early 'pulp' helmet. (Fox photos/Getty Images)

Understandably, with war looming, new production contracts were placed with both the shell and liner manufacturers, with final assembly undertaken by P.B. Cow Limited of Slough. With the crisis of Dunkirk two years later came a fresh production impetus, after many helmets were lost and it was realised that further expansion of all the fighting forces was inevitable. The position was worsened during late 1940 by enemy air attacks on steel facilities, and in particular by a raid that hit Briggs Motor Bodies and destroyed helmet presses as well as stock. Such was the

demand, from the Home Guard as well as civil defence units, that it was decided that non front-line organisations could make use of slight 'seconds' rejected for minor faults during manufacture. Such minor defects included small deviations from the standard weight or specification. Some helmets were now also produced in mild steel, which was less ballistically resistant, but deemed good enough for home service in an emergency. Substandard helmets were identified by the drilling of holes in the brim next to one of the strap-securing lugs. There were from one to four holes, and broadly speaking the more holes the worse the helmet. Work was further speeded by the main contractors subcontracting tasks to many smaller firms. Eventually, twelve million steel helmets would be made in the UK between 1938 and 1943, with at least an additional five million of similar designs being made in Commonwealth countries.[11]

Whilst the 'Mark I*' and 'Mark II' supplied the needs of most regiments and corps throughout the war the familiar 'soup bowl' helmet was not the only one used by the British Army. As early as 1941 a realisation that the shallow helmet provided less than optimal protection led to the Medical Research Council (MRC) examining a new and deeper shell design to match up with the latest model of liner. Before the end of that year samples of the new shell – shaped very much like a tortoise, and offering about a third better coverage – were under way. The new headgear, soon designated 'Mark III', was found to provide better protection, and though it weighed a little more was actually slightly more comfortable owing to its shape. There was some hesitation over the production of the 'Mark III' for a number of reasons. The first was a concern that it was not distinctively British enough in outline – and whilst at first glance this seems ridiculous, and being mistaken for American or Russian was not necessarily a problem, once fully camouflaged it was also vaguely like some enemy helmets. The second objection was on the grounds of pure practicality: the deeper helmet required a good grade of manganese steel to press it without problems, and a modest improvement in performance was not really a good enough reason to justify the replacement of the millions of helmets already in use. However, by 1943 the objections, both practical and theoretical, had been overcome and a partial issue was begun before the end of the year. In particular it was decided to give priority to the assault waves first in on D-Day.

Finally, in early 1944 it was decided to modify the basic helmet lining again, this time to make it possible to detach the

inner easily, so that the shell could do duty as a basin or bucket, and to make the issue of a new liner or shell for a defective helmet much easier. The design of the new liner, with its 'lift the dot' device to separate it from the shell, was completed in September 1944, and helmets so equipped were designated as the 'Mark IV'. Again it was not thought possible to replace all the helmets in use, so a decision was taken to replace Mark IIIs as required on a maintenance basis, and to give new helmets en masse to troops who were sent from Europe to the Far East after the German surrender.

Certain specialist troops also used distinctive protective helmets. On the outbreak of war, those worn by motorcyclists, such as despatch riders and military police, were not made of steel but of a toughened lightweight papier-mâché. This material was often described as 'pulp'. It was brimless and when properly fitted rode quite high on the head because its impact resistance depended on an inner sling keeping the skull clear of the outer, thus creating a gap between helmet and head. A leather neckflap also carried the chinstrap. This antique-looking 'pulp helmet' with its distinctive row of lacing around the base finally began to be replaced in 1943 by the despatch riders Mark I steel helmet. This was similar in general outline but fitted closer to the head, and it lacked the lacing. Its use was made compulsory for motorcyclists and passengers under most circumstances.

In about 1936 a helmet made of composite materials, and with a padded band around the brow, was introduced to protect tank crews from banging against the inside of their vehicles. At first glance this had the same general appearance as a miner's helmet of the period. Examples of an improved type from about 1939 show a multipiece construction and the use of rubber grommets in the ventilation holes. By 1941 the pattern was updated by the use of a hard-fibre shell and the inclusion of a curtain around the

sides and rear into which earphones for radio communication could be fitted. Finally, the fibre helmet was replaced by a rather more soldierly looking, and more effective, brimless steel helmet not unlike the despatch rider's in outline. This Royal Armoured Corps pattern steel helmet had a lining like the one used in the ordinary Mark II and Mark III steel helmet used by the infantry. It also had a simple, flat, elasticated chinstrap.[12]

The helmets of the paratroops went through an almost equally significant metamorphosis. The first 'training' helmets were monstrosities of sorbo rubber, with a thick ring of the material around the brow and pads coming down over the ears. The thick band and smaller skull lent a strangely alien-like appearance to the wearer. This type was later replaced by a rather more fitted pattern, which was linen covered but again was padded with sorbo rubber. Happily a steel helmet of less ludicrous appearance was soon introduced for combat. This had a similar shell to those used finally by the Royal Armoured Corps, and differed mainly in the types of liner and fittings used. In an early version a narrow rim of hard rubber ran around the lower outside edge. In a second type there was also a rubber band around the outside, though it was wider and flatter than that on the first helmet. Finally, the rubber was omitted altogether in what became the commonest type. All three variations had chinstraps and cups, and an arrangement of straps anchored at different positions inside the helmet so that one strap passed in front of each ear, and one behind, to create a firm cradle on the head. These straps were originally of leather, but finally they were also made of webbing.

Though the drilling of holes and fitting of metal badges to helmets was actively discouraged, painted and stencilled

Tankers of the 26th Hussars in training in the Far East wear personalised US tank crew helmets and goggles with a mixture of Khaki Drill uniform and overalls. (King's Royal Hussars Museum/)

Men of 3rd Infantry Division during the bloody fight for Caen, Normandy, 1944. The machine gun is not British issue, but a French 8mm Hotchkiss type. Some of the men, including the figure holding the strips of ammunition, right, wear the Mark III steel helmet, which was deeper and offered better protection than its predecessor. (Official/author)

a 'dark hessian cover' with additional 'hessian knots and string laced round in two-inch loops'; and draping a garnished net over the entire helmet and head when taking part in observation. Never the less, there were quite a few other variations to be seen, and one of the more fanciful Home Guard options for camouflage during streetfighting was the attachment of odd bits of rubbish.

Though body armour had been fairly widespread during the First World War it was something of a rarity during the Second World War. There seem to have been a number of reasons for this, not least of which was the more mobile nature of many of the campaigns; another was the weight of armour required to stop projectiles. Nevertheless, there were a number of British experiments, a plan to make body armour a general issue, and a limited distribution of an official MRC type. As early as October 1939 some simple armour plates were offered up for testing by the company of Thomas Firth and John Brown, and these prompted the Ministry of Supply and Assistant Chief of the Imperial General Staff to consider body armour, and if manganese steel plates of a similar quality to the steel helmet were useful. Thereafter a number of other issues were also investigated – for example, the area of the body it was desirable to protect, and whether it might in fact be better to insert a plate inside the respirator case which usually hung over the chest in battle. Others suggested that layers of materials other than steel might give better protection for less weight.

By late 1940 the MRC had formed a Body Protection Committee under Lord Falmouth to come to an authoritative opinion on behalf of the Army. The War Office now asked specifically for feedback on two possibilities: a lightweight option of up to 4lb (1.8kg) for troops expected to retain a high degree of mobility and a heavier set for those manning static positions. In an extensive report issued in January 1941 a body protection subcommittee advised that armour could be a practical possibility, but in order to remain sufficiently light it would need to be restricted to the chest to protect the heart, major blood vessels and lungs; the upper part of the belly; and a relatively small area of the lower back. Never the less, even

Parachutists wearing the final form of the rubber padded training helmet check their kit prior to an exercise. Their parachutes are worn over smocks of two different patterns, and respirator bags are carried. (Central Press/Getty Images)

insignia were used with some frequency. Before the war it was quite common for regimental badges to be painted on the left side. The Gloucestershire Regiment had a special small silver transfer to apply to the rear of the helmet, replicating the traditional 'back badge' worn on caps. There was also some use of flashes, similar to those used on tropical headgear, but in paint, applied to the side of the helmet – for example, the red and blue colours of the Royal Artillery. An official decision of 1940 confirmed the painting of Military Police helmets with 'MP' on a blue background. Late in the war this marking was joined by coloured bands, red for the provost wing, white for traffic control and Oxford blue for those deployed to 'vulnerable points'.

In combat, widespread use was made of helmet camouflage. Early in the war sacking covers, not unlike those used in the latter part of the First World War, were not uncommon, but nets and painting soon predominated. Different styles of painting included bands of contrasting colour to disrupt the obvious disk shape of the helmet, and the application of various roughened textures. The 1944 publication *Infantry Training* prescribed a number of possibilities for helmet camouflage. These included netting with short lengths of sacking material or 'scrim' and 'natural garnish' to 'break the dome and shadow under the rim';

with this limited coverage a fully bulletproof design was not practicable, and so a 1mm plate was settled on that was able to stop revolver bullets at 5 yards (4.6m) and rifle bullets at 700 yards (640m), plus lower-velocity splinters and shrapnel.

Three prototypes were duly produced, and of these the third was chosen for troop trials. It consisted of three parts: a small breastplate; a backplate, shaped like an inverted 'T', which hugged the kidneys and lower spine; and a semi-circular abdominal plate suspended below the breast plate. The parts were articulated on webbing straps, and sponge rubber edging around the reverse helped absorb impacts and reduced wear and tear on the user. In February 1941 a decision was made to manufacture 5,000 sets, and later that year this armour went into use with various home commands and in the Middle East. Reports were sought on whether it was comfortable; if it impeded efficiency; and if those testing it believed it should become a general issue to all ranks and arms, or whether it should only be used by certain troops. On the strength of these trials it was eventually recommended that one million sets should be manufactured. However, in early 1942, about the time of the fall of Malaya to the Japanese, it was realised that the amount of rubber required for this new commitment was prohibitive and a new design was produced that substituted rubber with a thick felt backing. Further trials were embarked upon, including the use of the body armour by tank crews. In the final full production model of the armour, the plates and pads of felt were encased in a canvas cover.

By 1943 the War Office was working on the supposition that almost seven million sets of armour should be produced, not just for British troops but also those from the Dominions and other Allied powers. Of these, 2.5 million were to go to the British Army in the field. This ambitious target was never achieved, and even orders of 500,000 placed in the latter part of that year were scaled back. In the end, production appears to have been relatively limited, with a total of about 79,000 sets being made. A significant portion of these went to the RAF, Canadians and French SAS, leaving about 15,000 actually distributed to the British Army during 1944. Some went to the Royal Engineers, in both northwest Europe and Italy, and some to the British SAS. However, some 12,000 sets were given to the Airborne forces, half each to the 1st and 6th Airborne Divisions. This was perhaps a strange decision, for though the airborne forces were always likely to be in the thick of close-quarter fighting, the armour could not stop rifle bullets at close range, nor did transport aircraft and gliders have limitless load-carrying capability.[13]

Khaki Drill and Jungle Green Uniform

Infantry test the MRC body armour: this weighed 3½lbs (1.6kg), protecting parts of the chest and abdomen, and the kidney area at the back. Despite grand plans to equip much of the Army only the Airborne would receive significant issues. (Official/author)

Lieutenant W.K. Fussell, Royal Corps of Signals, clad in 'Jungle Green' uniform during the latter part of the war in the Far East. His accoutrements include the modern-looking jungle service hat and a pattern of spectacles specially designed to be slim-fitting enough to work under a gas mask. (Author)

During the inter-war period and up until 1942, Khaki Drill (KD) clothing was regulation for British troops in all warm climates. During the 1930s there had in fact been not one but two slightly differing shades of Khaki Drill in use, the 'No. 2 Green' and the 'No. 4 Brown', the latter being gradually phased out in favour of the greener type cloth. Usually troops serving on stations abroad were entitled to three suits of Khaki Drill uniform, each of which comprised a jacket and long trousers; however, there was an option available to unit commanders to substitute one or two pairs of Khaki Drill shorts for the third pair of trousers, and photographs suggest that this was a choice frequently exercised. The 'KD' shorts, which had been an official issue since 1935, were of slightly varying patterns and in practice were seen worn at knee length, as well as slightly above and even slightly below. However, the vast majority featured an integral, small, double-belt closure buckled with two single-pronged buckles at the front, so arranged to take account of slightly stouter or thinner wearers.[14]

Tropical shirts with both long and short sleeves were also worn. The issue 1938 type shirt was a 'pullover' type, with integral collar and a four-button half-front opening only. Some had no top button, but did have buttons under the wings of the collar to secure it down. Some additional KD was locally made, more or less officially worn, and exhibited minor variations from sealed patterns. These included features lifted from American garments, non-standard buttons, different or omitted pleats and full front opening. Given the cheapness of labour and abundance of material in parts of India, North Africa and Hong Kong, some garments were privately purchased by other ranks in both the Middle and the Far East, an option that was usually only open to officers in the UK.

In 1941 a decision was taken to run down stocks of old-type KD trousers and to make further issues of shorts or 'Bombay bloomers'. The Bombay bloomer was effectively a hybrid of shorts and trousers, having deep turn-ups, which could be

The Union flag is raised at Fort Dufferin, Mandalay, after its recapture by 19th Indian Division. Indian divisions included a proportion of British battalions, the 19th having one British battalion per brigade in 1945. (Popperfoto/Getty Images)

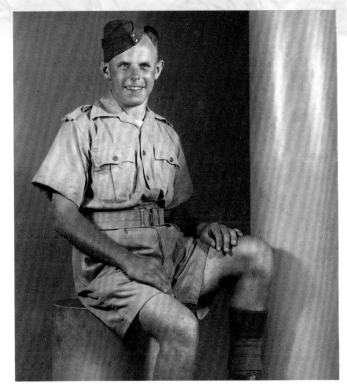

folded down into long-leg trousers. These had existed since before 1939, but never seem to have been that popular with soldiers, who regarded them as neither particularly comfortable or smart. When knees wore out, or soldiers required shorts, they were frequently cut down by regimental or local tailors. A multitude of slightly varying KD trousers were seen throughout the duration of the war, including a number of new types: an Indian-made version featured the double-belt closure common to the old shorts; another, manufactured in the UK late in the war, had a wraparound belt that fastened above the left hip, again with a degree of adjustment for fit. One other unusual KD garment sometimes seen was the 'Tropical Combination Suit', a strange one-piece item that combined shorts and short-sleeved shirt. This was gathered at the waist and was fastened down the front with brass buttons. It was worn as an informal working outfit.

Officers' KD uniform, as noted in the 1934 Dress Regulations, was essentially a copy of service dress in lighter material, worn with a shirt of 'drab material' and matching tie. One oddity seen occasionally early in the war were privately purchased shirts for officers that incorporated buttoned-on removable 'spine pads'. It was traditionally thought that these offered protection against heatstroke, as Lieutenant Colonel E.T. Burke explained in his privately produced manual *Tropical Tips for Troops*:

> *'In the very hot weather a spine pad is advisable if you have to be out during the day, This consists of a fairly thick piece of khaki material which is worn down the middle of the back. The shirt and tunic must be provided with buttons to which it can be attached.'*

Another unusual item, once common and still endorsed by Burke in 1941, was the 'cholera belt':

> *'You must have two medium weight pull on woollen body belts – sometimes referred to as "cholera belts". Always wear one of these on going to bed at night or on taking a siesta during the day. If by chance these belts become mislaid, extemporise by wrapping a puttee round your waist and abdomen'.* [15]

Belief in such Victoriana was soon proved fallacious, but practical experience of modern war in the Middle East quickly showed what garments were really necessary, and indeed in what quantity. The result was that officers were soon notified of 'Scales of Tropical Clothing' with which they were to provide themselves for service in warm climates. The normal scale pertaining in 1943 included six 'Bush Shirts', three pairs of KD shorts, and three pairs of KD trousers to be worn over six 'vests, thin' and 'drawers, thin'. British officers also wore Khaki Drill during the summer months in the USA and Canada.

At the outbreak of war the normal tropical headgear for all ranks was the old 'Wolseley Pattern' helmet – a rigid hat with a deep brim, covered with six panels of Khaki Drill cloth and wound with a folded decorative cloth band or 'pagri'. Officers' helmets were privately purchased, other ranks were issued. The design of the helmet dated back to before the First World War, but other than a modicum of sun protection it was not very useful. Troops in India and Burma were

A postcard from 'Basil', wearing KD uniform in Cairo, September 1941: *'what do you think of your husband?'* (Author)

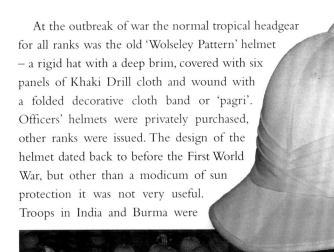

The Wolseley Pattern helmet (Author), and stocks of the headgear ready for shipment overseas. (George W Hales/Getty Images)

The Wolseley, the solar pith hat and some slouch hats were seen with unit distinctions. Some of these were divisional, but many were regimental. At the outbreak of war some of the most important of these were as follows:

Wolseley Pattern Helmet	
Unit	**Distinction**
Guards	Regimental plume and pagri badge
Royal Fusiliers	White plume
Black Watch	Red hackle
Duke of Cornwall's Light Infantry	Red feathers
Lancashire Fusiliers	Yellow hackle
Royal Berkshires	Red strip, right side
Durham Light Infantry	'DLI' on patch
Solar Pith Hat	
Unit	**Distinction**
Royal Scots; Highland Light Infantry	Tartan patch
Cameron Highlanders	Cameronians
Queen's Royal (West Surrey)	Blue patch with red top, 'QUEEN'S' in white. Grey and blue ribbon above pagri
Royal Warwickshires	Blue patch with orange stripe
King's (Liverpool)	Red patch with 'KING'S' in white
Royal Norfolks	Yellow patch with narrow vertical black stripe through centre
Lincolnshires	Blue patch with red sphinx
Suffolks	Yellow patch in shape of castle
Somerset Light Infantry	Top fold of pagri in rifle green
West Yorkshires	Red patch with white horse
Lancashire Fusiliers	Scarlet patch with 'L' and 'F' in white either side of a grenade
Cheshires	Diamond shaped patch vertically bisected buff and cherry red (cerise)
South Wales Borderers	Fourth fold of pagri green; fifth fold white
Worcestershires	Diamond shaped patch in green
East Surreys	Red patch on black ground. 'EAST SURREY' in white
Duke of Cornwall's Light Infantry	Patch with horizontal stripes of green, red and white and a red feather at front of helmet
Duke of Wellington's	First fold of pagri scarlet
Royal Sussex	Red patch with 'ROYAL SUSSEX' in white
Hampshires	Narrow patch vertically divided yellow and black

Mounted officer and dismounted other rank, 14th/20th (King's) Hussars, at Lucknow before the war. The regimental flash worn on the 'Solar' pith hat, or 'topee' is dark blue over primrose yellow, diagonally divided by a crimson line. (KRH Museum)

the exception in that from 1938 they were expected to wear a slightly different sun helmet of a rather more solid appearance, called the 'Khaki Solar Pith Hat'. Not surprisingly, battle experience in the Middle East and North Africa demonstrated the dubious utility of sun helmets, and fairly quickly unit commanders, as well as individual troops, quietly dispensed with them. This was later formalised by orders issued in late 1942 limiting the use of the 'Universal' type Wolseley to the Sudan, Transjordan and the Lebanon, whilst only small stocks were kept in active theatres of war where they were presumably intended for sentries and semi-formal wear.

With the gradual demise of the sun helmet as practical combat wear, the 'bush' or 'slouch' hat was seen more and more often in tropical areas. Made of felt with a cloth *puggaree* winding around the crown, slouch hats were constructed with a press stud so that the left side of the brim could be worn folded up, and out of combat this was the general rule. The original purpose of this arrangement was so that the hat did not obstruct the rifle when brought to a 'slope arms' position during drill. Interestingly, the slouch hat was by no means a new design, even in 1939, having been worn by the Yeomanry, and in the Boer War, as well as by the Australians and other colonial forces.

KD uniform was less than suitable for the wide range of duties and climatic conditions in which it was expected to serve. Shorts were not practical anywhere that malaria was a problem, as mosquitos could easily attack an exposed leg. In the jungle, likewise, shorts offered no protection against thorns. Perhaps less obviously, even in its greener shades, KD was not particularly good camouflage against the deep green of jungle in the wetter seasons. As early as 1942 these issues were partially addressed by dying existing patterns to darker shades, and in 1943 the Indian Army produced a 'jungle green' clothing that was effectively a replica of battle dress in aertex and cotton. This was widely used, particularly in Burma in 1944.

The Lethbridge Mission, which made a fact-finding tour of the Far East in late 1943, also had comments to make, with the result that a whole new line of British 'jungle green' uniform was designed. This 1944 Pattern uniform included a new jungle shirt, trousers and neck cloth, and a modern-looking 'V'-necked pullover with reinforced elbows and shoulders, and slots to allow the epaulettes of the shirt to be buttoned through. Officers could then show their rank distinctions over the pullover. A new, rubberised green poncho doubled as a bad-weather garment and a gas cape. The simple jungle service hat, with vents and brim, was flexible – and unlike the slouch hats hitherto widely worn, it could be easily rolled and stowed.

Protective Clothing, Coats and Camouflage Smocks

Apart from the woollen greatcoat, one of the earliest concessions to fighting in cold climates was the 'Coat, Sheepskin Lined', also known as the 'Tropal' coat. This tan-coloured, heavy-duty canvas garment was similar to the Army Service Corps' full-length driver's coat of the First World War, and fastened with metal clasps that were easy to manipulate with cold or gloved hands. It was certainly warm yet it was unsuitable for any energetic movement, and so best suited to sentries or other fairly static duties. By 1939 such coats were also being lined with kapok, thus becoming the 'Coat, Kapok Lined'. Seen in action in Norway in 1940 this coat continued to be used throughout the war; later examples sometimes had toggles and cord loops rather than clasps. It was frequently worn with a balaclava and

the sheepskin winter cap with side flaps that could be brought down to fasten under the chin.

Duffle coats were also issued for cold-weather static duties, perhaps most widely in western Europe in the winter of 1944–1945. Macintoshes and privately purchased trenchcoats often formed part of the officer's wardrobe. Later in the war these coats were also produced to a standardised design by the Army, obviating the need to go to commercial tailors and retailers.

Characteristically eccentric officers clothing in the desert. These unofficial coats were dubbed the 'Hebron' type. (Author)

Patrol wearing two-piece snow camouflage suits and helmet covers. The leader carries a Sten gun covered in white cloth, and is followed by a radio operator. Germany, 1945. (Official/author)

Far right: Wartime instructions for Home Guards and regulars on making a sniper suit. (Author)

was just one of many jerkins in use, quite a few of which were either run up by unit tailors or entirely unofficial. Fleece jerkins were especially popular with officers during cool nights in the desert, and were also used in Italy and western Europe.

Snow camouflage garments were in existence prior to 1939, and the basic suit consisted of a white smock and overtrousers. The smock had a hood that could be pulled up, but white helmet covers were also used. The simplest type of snow smock was made out of lightweight cotton, lacked pockets and gave little or no additional warmth to the wearer. In other versions, apparently mainly manufactured later, the smock was windproof and featured four pockets. The unsuccessful Norway campaign highlighted many failings in clothing and equipment, and as a result a new range of specialist garments was developed. One of the most important pieces, introduced in 1942, was the windproof smock. This hooded garment in lightweight, tan-coloured cotton fabric pulled over the wearer's head and

For other ranks, whose duties involved standing around in the rain for long periods, such as Military Police or traffic control, a 'Coat 1A' could be issued. This was single-breasted, fly-fronted and of a khaki-coloured rubberised cotton with large hip pockets. Early in the war despatch riders wore a mid-thigh-length rubberised double-breasted coat with a hat and goggles, fashioned not unlike those of early fliers. From the middle of the war, however, a large rubberised tan coat with a large collar, flap-over front and large pocket was issued for motorcyclists. This could be buttoned around the legs for added protection and to prevent the coat flapping into the wheels. Early cloth helmets, which provided no protection other than against the elements, were generally abandoned and replaced by the pulp and metal despatch rider's helmet.

Very widely seen, and in general use by the infantry and many services, was the sleeveless leather jerkin, which again had been used as early as the First World War. In its Second World War incarnation the jerkin was sleeveless, collarless and made of stout brown leather, closing at the front with four large buttons. It was blanket-lined for warmth and proved very popular and durable. It is, however, worth noting that this basic official type

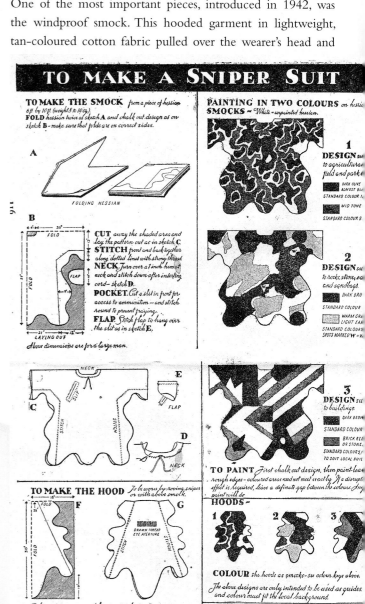

closed to the neck with a short zipper. The hood incorporated a drawstring, and the smock featured four flapped pockets, closed with buttons like those found on the battle dress. The smock also had a drawstring at the base, and it was teamed with simple trousers of a like material, without a front opening. The trousers had three pockets, consisting of slit pockets at the hip and a large one above the left knee. The bottoms of the trousers fitted snugly to the leg using buttoned tabs. A second version of this suit was also produced in a printed camouflage material, of chocolate and mid-brown and khaki green on a light brown base. Popular with specialist troops, the suit was also issued to some infantry and other troops in the latter part of the war in Europe.[16]

With the greatcoat relegated largely to formal occasions and rear areas, the soldier was now expected to keep himself warm essentially by layering the clothing he had. Depending on the season, location and generosity of the supply chain, these layers could number anything up to eight on the body and four on the legs. On the body, if all garments were available, they were donned in the following order: string vest, wool vest, angola shirt, wool jersey, battle dress, duffle coat, windproof smock and snow camouflage smock. On the legs, woollen drawers (long or short), battle dress trousers, windproof trousers and snow camouflage trousers. In practice, of course, it was much more usual for perhaps

1st Mountain Artillery Regiment training with a 3.7in 'pack' Howitzer in Wales, 1942. The crew wear hooded windproof smocks in pale tan cotton and mountaineering breeches with long socks and ankle puttees. They carry rucksacks, which were also used by the Commandos. The gun broke down into smaller loads for movement across mountain terrain. (Official)

Grimy crewmen on a Wolverine self-propelled gun in a variety of clothing, France, 1944. The headgear includes the GS cap; American type tank helmet; and, top, the Royal Armoured Corps steel helmet. (Mansell/Life Picture Collection/Getty Images)

three to five layers to be worn on the body, and two or three layers on the legs.

The 'Denison Smock, Airborne Troops' was one of the most advanced and flexible pieces of clothing issued during the war, being a printed camouflage garment designed to be worn over the battle dress. Opening only part-way down the front by means of a concealed zipper, it had four voluminous external patch pockets, two internal pockets and a wide crutch piece that prevented it riding up when crawling or parachuting. In its original 1941 version it had knitted cuffs, later replaced by buttoned straps. The printed pattern had a light green base, over which were patches of dark green and brown. As first designed, the smock had to be pulled on over the head, but was occasionally modified by means of a full-

length zipper allowing it to be put on like a jacket. Though intended specifically for airborne forces, the Denison also saw use with some ground troops, such as snipers. The Denison was windproof and showerproof but not waterproof.[17]

Tank crew had worn distinctive protective clothing before the war in the form of a two-piece working dress in black drill material. The suit had a small standing collar, and trousers that fastened tight around the ankle with a cloth strap and had a large patch pocket on the left thigh. Black looked smart, but very probably was selected initially as the colour for working dress due to the amount of oil and other dirt in which tank crew had to operate in both action and maintenance situations. Some of these black suits survived into the war, but by then both serge and denim battle dress in khaki was being issued to tank crew. Not long afterwards one-piece oversuits were also issued. These

were advantageous not only in that they protected whatever was worn underneath, but being made in one piece were less liable to snagging on the internal fixtures of the tank. These oversuits were issued in a variety of patterns at different times, made in denim, jungle green cloth and light khaki fabrics. Photographs exist of this general type of garment being worn in 1941, and a surviving suit from 1942 has the specially reinforced shoulder straps that also featured later on. The purpose of these straps was that if a man was injured or stuck in his vehicle, rescuers had only to heave on them to pull him free. In perhaps the most common version of the oversuit, or 'pixie suit', the garment had a total of thirteen pockets, including two pockets on the front of each leg, places to put pens and pencils over the left breast, and reinforcement at the seat, elbows and knees. It also had a detachable hood.

Home Guard Uniform

In the beginning the 'uniform' of the Local Defence Volunteers was a simple khaki armband with the letters 'LDV', usually in black; as soon as it became available, volunteers were issued with a denim version of the normal battle dress. Whilst not as warm as the serge version it had a number of advantages, including being easier to clean, and garments in this fabric were also used by the Regulars as a fatigue dress.

As of July 1941 Army Form H 1158 'Receipt for Clothing and Equipment' was used to sign out to Home Guards the items supplied by, or at the expense of, the War Office that were in their care. As such it is a good guide as to the possible scope of the uniform and personal equipment. The basic uniform was the battle dress ('B.D.') blouse and trousers, though denim blouse and trousers are still given as an option. This was worn with black ankle boots and leather anklets, though gumboots are listed as an additional possibility. The belt was also leather, rather than the web of the Regulars. Shoulder titles, regimental flashes, chevrons and other rank badges could also be issued for the battle dress. The headgear was the 'Cap, FS', fore and aft field cap, and, whilst it did not appear on the printed receipt, a regimental cap badge was normally also issued and signed for. A field dressing and steel helmet were general, and for cold weather gloves and a Home Guard cape, though a greatcoat could be provided in lieu. The personal equipment on the standard 1941 form comprised a haversack, water bottle with carrier, mess tins, blanket, groundsheet and respirator. Those equipped with

rifles would also expect a bayonet with scabbard and frog, a 'pullthrough' for cleaning and an oil bottle. Commonly, a few rounds of ammunition were also signed out. Usually stowed with the respirator were eyeshields, anti-gas ointment and gas detectors. A torch was also an optional extra.

Personal Equipment

In the nineteenth century, Britain's soldiers, like those of most powers, used personal equipment that was made out of leather. However, by the beginning of the next century there were indications that 'webbing', of woven cotton, might be the thing of the future – it spread weight better and was less prone to the stiffness and deterioration of hide in the wet. In the USA, Captain

Rear view of Tom Payne, a typical Fusilier of 6th Royal Welsh Fusiliers, in Normandy, August 1944, using the 1937 Pattern web equipment. Items shown include the small pack, with gas cape folded under the closure; the light model respirator on the left hip; the 'GS' shovel; entrenching tool packed with its cover; and a water bottle. (Author)

Anson Mills had patented a machine for making webbing as early as 1877, and in 1899 his company established a plant in the UK for the production of belts. Though the company made strenuous attempts to market its wares, and some items of webbing found their way to the Boer War, it was not generally adopted by the British Army – nor for that matter did it find a ready market with major nations such as France or Germany. Only after 1906 was the matter taken really seriously, and one of the motivating factors appears to have been a realisation that a rifle with a rate of fire as high as that promised by the Short Magazine Lee Enfield was likely to require a larger and more rapid supply of cartridges. It would be most convenient if the ammunition was already in chargers, distributed so as to spread the weight and to make a loss of the load unlikely. Mills's company had already worked with the Royal Navy, and now entered into partnership with Major A.R. Burrowes of the

Royal Irish Fusiliers to create a new set of equipment. The basics of this were supporting straps over the shoulders, a removable backpack, a haversack, water bottle and two sets of five smaller cartridge carriers. The whole equipment could be removed as one after the waist-belt had been unfastened.[18]

Trials with various units followed, as did approval from Lord Kitchener, and so was born the web equipment' Pattern 1908. In the First World War the web equipment served its purpose well, but even though production reached a peak of 20,000 sets a week it still proved necessary to use as a stopgap 1914 leather type equipment as well. In 1918 huge amounts of the web equipment, which had also been purchased in several sub-variants by the Dominions, remained on hand. Mills attempted to improve upon the 1908 type to stimulate new business, but little was forthcoming. Thus it was that the old webbing

Ski kit in use during training. It took time for effective equipment to be developed for winter and mountain conditions. The men here wear windproof smocks, gauntlets, and a ski caps, a new model of which was introduced in 1943. Practical military skiing was essentially of the cross-country variety. (Author)

remained standard Army issue until the late 1930s, some even surviving to see action in the Second World War.

However, by this time new trends were apparent that the 1908 equipment seemed ill-fitted to meet. Importantly, there was a growing realisation that mechanisation would entail more soldiers travelling in vehicles, and probably less entrenchment. To these ends any new equipment had to be easy to sit down in. From 1932 Mills therefore offered four new possibilities to the Braithwaite Committee, one of which was approved in 1934 but not immediately adopted, as there was a probability that the Lewis gun would be replaced. Troops would now need to be able to carry not only chargers for their own rifles but also magazines for a new gun. A somewhat bulky harness for Lewis gun magazines had in fact been used in 1914–1918, but the prospect of the adoption of a modern light machine gun (LMG), or even some form of automatic rifle, promised that a less cumbersome solution might be possible. The choice of the Bren gun with its distinctive, slightly curved, thirty-two-round box magazine finally confirmed the direction of travel. Mills modified the equipment that he had offered in 1932, adding a large oblong pouch capable of holding both rifle ammunition and Bren magazines either side of the belt.

The new webbing was adopted as the 'Equipment, Web, 1937', with notification appearing in the *List of Changes* in June 1938. A detailed manual was issued the following year, which explained:

'The Pattern 1937 Equipment has been designed to meet modern conditions of warfare. Mechanisation, the introduction of the Bren gun and Anti-Tank rifle necessitate changes in the personal equipment of the soldier to aid mobility as well as facilitate the carriage of ammunition, grenades, food and water, and other items necessary in the field. The equipment is actually a development of the 1908 Pattern Web Equipment. It is considerably lighter in weight than the 1908, and has a basic principle which enables it to be adapted to suit all Arms. It is easy to assemble and adjust; and possesses the important feature that no articles are suspended below the waist line (except the bayonet and officer's haversack) to impede the wearer.

Although the 1908 Pattern Pack and Supporting Straps are included in and are attachable to the 1937 equipment for the purpose of changing stations, normally there is no pack in the 1937 equipment, as the kit accommodated in that article is carried in regimental transport. A large haversack is therefore carried on the back and contains rations, water bottle and other necessaries. The principle of carrying the haversack "rucksack fashion" allows this article to be easily discarded for access to its contents, without disturbing the remainder of the equipment. As is well known, the rucksack method is comfortable and self-balancing. The shoulder straps used for carriage of the haversack are provided with hooks for attachment to the equipment in front, to prevent pressure at the armpits. These same shoulder straps are also used for carrying the 1908 Pack when desired – the haversack then being transferred to the left side of the equipment attached to the ends of the braces. The water bottle in carrier is then taken out of the haversack and attached to the ends of the braces at the right side of the equipment.'[19]

The equipment was described as being made of 'strong and durable webbing', waterproofed and dyed in the yarn before being woven, and waterproof treated 'so as to render the fabric practically impervious to the weather'. The material was pre-shrunk before being cut, and where possible pieces were woven to correct widths rather than to one size and cut afterwards. Pouches were woven as separate items, with a minimum of additional sewing to add to its strength and durability. All the various buckles were stamped from sheet brass and of a 'tongueless or self-locking' variety. Altogether the manual mentioned nineteen different elements, including the 1908 type pack and supporting straps that were reused as part of the system. The key to all this was the new waist-belt, 2.25 inches (5.6cm) wide and thus somewhat narrower than the 1908 original, which came in three sizes and closed with a plain 'clasp buckle'.

The 'basic pouches' were interchangeable and each could carry two Bren magazines. Optional loads included fifty rounds of .303 ammunition (a total of a hundred in the two-pouch set) with chargers and cotton bandoliers, hand grenades or mortar rounds – or very often a mixture to take account of the widest range of combat possibilities. Larger 'utility pouches', designed to be worn with a supporting 'yoke', were to take three Bren magazines or two anti-tank rifle magazines, grenades, or three 2-inch mortar bombs, or a water bottle or small arms ammunition. A pair of fully laden utility pouches with six Bren magazines weighed just over 16lb (7.3kg). The 'haversack' complete with mess tin, full water bottle, cardigan, groundsheet, eating utensils and emergency ration was over 21lb (9.5kg). Other web items mentioned in the original list included shoulder straps, 'brace attachments', bayonet frog, the water bottle carrier, pistol cases and pistol ammunition pouch,

Compasses were of several varieties, the issue Mark III being liquid damped with blackened case, and having luminous markings for night use. However a good compass was a durable item and officers could obtain their own, so different models were pressed into service. The pouch on the left matched the 1937 webbing, the leather example was of an earlier type also in widespread use. (Author)

cartridge carriers, officer's haversack, binocular case, compass case and compass 'pocket'.

So it was that different parts of a company could carry the munitions they needed, all drawing on the basic repertoire of elements of the 37 Pattern equipment. For example, the 1942 manual *Light Machine Gun* mentions an eight-man infantry section carrying a 'normal' 350 rounds of rifle ammunition, twenty-four Bren magazines (containing up to 768 rounds), six Thompson magazines (containing 180 rounds) and eight assorted grenades. The section's fighting equipment was distributed thus, with the weights shown including clothing:

Section commander: Thompson with six magazines, two LMG magazines, wirecutters, matchet, whistle (weight 65lb/29kg).

No. 1 rifleman: Rifle No. 3 (suitable for sniping), bayonet, fifty rounds, four LMG magazines (weight 61lb/28kg).

No. 1 bomber: Rifle, bayonet, fifty rounds; two No. 36 grenades, two smoke grenades, one LMG magazine (60lb/27kg).

No. 2 rifleman: Rifle, bayonet, fifty rounds, four LMG magazines (weight 61lb/28kg).

No. 2 bomber: Rifle, bayonet, fifty rounds, two No. 36 grenades, three LMG magazines (weight 60lb/27kg).

Second in command: Rifle, bayonet, fifty rounds, two LMG magazines, two smoke grenades (weight 61lb/28kg).

No. 1 Bren: LMG, fifty rounds, four LMG magazines in basic pouches, spare parts wallet (weight 75lb/34kg).

No. 2 Bren: Rifle, bayonet, fifty rounds, four LMG magazines in basic pouches, two utility pouches (weight 63lb/29kg).

The manual states that, during movement, 'the immediate small arms supply is limited to that carried by the section. Normally an individual should not carry more than four magazines, except for short distances. In addition, the 350 rounds for rifles can, in an emergency, be filled into the magazines'. This arrangement was to be 'a guide', but it depended on the situation – patrol work and other special duties were obvious examples where different loads might be needed.[20]

The real beauty of the system was that the 1937 webbing's range of pieces meant that it was not just for the infantryman but could be assembled in different ways to suit all arms. Five different 'sets' were recommended by the manual *Pattern 1937 Web Equipment*:

For infantry: Waist-belt, braces, basic pouches, bayonet frog, water bottle carrier, haversack and shoulder straps.

Men not in an infantry battalion: Waist-belt, braces, cartridge carriers, bayonet frog, water bottle carrier, haversack and shoulder straps.

Officers, WOs [Warrant Officers]: Waist-belt, braces, brace attachments, pistol case, ammunition pouch, binocular case, compass pocket, water bottle carrier, haversack, shoulder straps and officer's haversack.

Personnel with pistol: Waist-belt, braces, brace attachments, pistol case, ammunition pouch, water bottle carrier, haversack and shoulder straps.

Royal Armoured Corps: Waist-belt, pistol case with cartridge loops, haversack, pack and supporting straps.

Taking together the various pieces of webbing, equipment and clothing, the manual concluded that when 'changing stations' the weight carried by each of the main types of differently equipped personnel would be as follows, rounded to the nearest pound: infantryman 56lb (25kg), rifle-armed but not in an infantry battalion 47lb, (21kg) officers 42lb (19kg) and men armed with pistol only 37lb (17kg). This did not count steel helmets, anti-gas capes and some other possible sundries, or the extra load represented by a Bren gun rather than a rifle, so in reality another 5–20lb (2–9kg) had to be added, bringing the real total weights to between about 42lb (19kg) and a hefty 76lb (34kg). 'Large packs' could also be carried on the man to create a 'full marching order' if they were not stowed in vehicles or dumped prior to action. The weight borne by a soldier with a PIAT or an anti-tank rifle, who did not have the benefit of platoon transport, is difficult to calculate exactly but it was clearly excessive. Commandos, who did not get any transport as a matter of course in the middle period of the war but were expected to deal with other types of equipment, certainly carried more than 80lb (36kg) on occasion.

Though officers were theoretically less burdened than their men, the list of things they did carry was often substantial. According to *Army Training Memorandum* No.26, from November 1939, the 'kit required by an officer on overseas service', not counting 'items of dress on the person', was as follows:

Army Book 153	Technical books and
Binoculars	instruments according to
Box of matches	arm of service
Cardigan (in haversack if	Pay advance book AFW 3241
not worn)	Pistol and ammunition
Compass	Pocket knife
Emergency ration (as issued)	Protractor
Field Service Pocket Book	Ration bag
Field dressing	Steel helmet
Gloves	Set of web equipment
Identity disks	Torch
Knife, fork, spoon	Wrist watch
Map case	Whistle and lanyard
Mess tin and cover	Waterbottle

Anti-gas equipment: Cape, cotton waste, personal gas detector, ground detector and eye shields.

Carried in the pack or haversack: Cap comforter, field service cap, greatcoat, housewife, mug, spare socks, scarf, spare laces and buttons, washing and shaving kit.

Baggage, valise containing a selection of the following, not exceeding a total weight of 50lb (23kg) for a commanding officer and 30lb (14kg) for other officers:

Bedding (sleeping bag	Small mirror (may be in
recommended)	pack)
Ground sheet	Shoes or slippers
Canvas bucket	Spare clothing and boots
Gum boots	(one set)
Air or cork mattress	Towels (two)
Mackintosh	Writing materials

The onset of war meant that it became necessary to take on new contractors to produce the webbing needed to supply an expanded Army, to replace sets lost and to create new bags, pouches and other items not part of the original kit but required for new weapons, tools and other items. Obvious examples included ammunition pouches for submachine gun magazines, new pistol holsters and map cases. It would appear that at least some of the new contactors lacked the special machinery needed for 'reduction weaving', resulting in some expedients in production.

Though the web equipment was pretty good, the glowing description presented in manuals did overlook certain inconveniences. Perhaps the most obvious was that it was possible for the inexperienced soldier to assemble the kit incorrectly. Some veterans have also made it clear that their particular unit actually wore the kit slightly differently to the 'proper' ways described, this being recognised as correct for their own battalion or company. One very different way to wear the web equipment received official sanction at the highest level: the 'Brooksbank' method, as described in *Army Training Memorandum* No. 45 of May 1943. The aim of the method was to lighten the load, while at the same time facilitating energetic crouching and crawling in action. The gas mask satchel was slung on the back, whilst the haversack was slung diagonally round the body by means of a brace and a pack strap around the waist. The haversack was also worn towards the back most of the time, but could be pulled round to the left hip in order to access the ammunition; the pouches and waist-belt were omitted.

Strong fingers, or some effort, were required to force the 1937 webbing into its brass clips and buckles – much more, for example, than is needed to assemble a German leather equipment set after it has 'worn in'. Though the web equipment was versatile, and ultimately it was possible to provide a range of additional pouches and items, not every new gadget or requirement could be accommodated within the system without more or less clumsy modifications. Also, whilst the webbing could be left alone for months or years without any serious deleterious effects, generations of regimental tradition and NCOs looking for tasks to shower on their hapless recruits were not to be thwarted. The equipment could be taken apart, washed in warm water and have cleaner applied – and therefore this was done. Many sets of equipment were camouflaged or darkened for the battlefield, then cleaned and blancoed for the sake of parade ground appearance. Five standard blanco colours have been noted in Army use: a light khaki, khaki, dark green, black and white. In some instances sets of webbing were even painted white to provide an ultra-smart ceremonial look, though this rendered them stiff and useless for any practical purpose. Finally, though the manual was clear in stating that 'metal work will not be polished, but allowed to get dull, so as to avoid catching the rays of the sun', some units had their men polish every buckle and fitting so that they shone.

Whilst the 1937 web equipment was standard issue in tropical areas as well as temperate until almost the end of the war, obsolete types persisted in outpost garrisons of India and the further flung corners of the British Empire for some time. Some soldiers early in the war fought in the 1908 webbing that had been used in the trenches of the First World War. However, neither type was perfect in jungle conditions, where the thick web got damp and eventually became prone to rot. Local modifications were often made to adapt the equipment to conditions: for example, some Chindits added basic pouches to either side of the 1908 Pattern large pack to create something more akin to a rucksack; others added straps and buckles to belts so that equipment could be stowed at the waist without the need to wear the standard shoulder braces. Less drastic minor conversions were also carried out so that items of American equipment could be used with British belts.

One outcome of a mission by Major General J.S. Lethbridge to the Far East in 1943–1944 was a recommendation that a new type of equipment – lighter and of a pre-dyed green, rot-

Far right: Front view of Fusilier Payne wearing 1937 Pattern webbing. His steel helmet, ammunition pouches, belt and shoulder braces are obvious. Less apparent are a jack knife, spike bayonet, and signal pistol, attached to the belt under his arm. His right hand holds the web sling of the No. 4 Rifle. (Author)

The contents of Fusilier Payne's small pack. Items include, foreground, washing, shaving and cleaning kit, cutlery and balaclava. In the background are rations, socks, gas cape, camouflage face net and mess tins. (Author)

resistant material with corrosion-resistant fasteners – should be introduced. The result, first demonstrated in the UK early in 1945, was a new webbing known as the 1944 Pattern. The key manual describing the new equipment appears not to have circulated until 1946, but it explains some of the thinking involved:

> 'The equipment incorporates a new principle of design to enable the load to be evenly carried and distributed and well balanced. It was first used in the tropics but has proved equally suitable for all conditions of modern warfare. The main object is to reduce the weight of the equipment and to maintain adequate strength in its construction to carry everything needed. This has been achieved by using fine yarn to reduce the thickness of the various types of webbing, and the light alloy fittings which have been darkened.'

Three main positive features were identified: the large basic pouches were supported like a sling by braces crossed and joined at the back; the haversack and pouches increased capacity; and the waist-belt could be worn loose for comfort 'in tropical areas' without affecting the carriage of the equipment.

Just nine basic components were listed for the 'rank and file' in the 1946 manual, and these included a modern-looking rucksack as well as the haversack. A further nine pieces were included as 'additional items', amongst them were pistol pouches and a sheath for a machete. Waistbelts, which now featured distinctive grommets, came in two sizes, 'large' and 'normal', and the manual helpfully observed that 'normal' would fit 95 per cent of the troops. A 'quick release' feature was used on the basic pouches rather than the old snap fasteners, and loops on the side formed an alternative frog for the bayonet. When fully stowed a soldier could wind his bedding roll around the outer edge of the haversack and carry a 'lightened' shovel on its back. Though it was not as tough as the old 1937 Pattern equipment, the new type did find favour with the troops. Its water bottle, for example, was of a much more practical design, with a 'bag type' carrier; also the web could not be blancoed and there was no brass to polish. 'Scrubbing, bleaching, and the use of Blanco on the equipment is forbidden' read one sentence in the new manual, which must have been welcome indeed.[21]

Though the 1937 and 1944 webbing accounted for the vast majority of equipment worn during the war, a number of other items saw service. One of the most interesting was the 'battle', or 'assault', jerkin – arguably a forerunner of modern, personal load-carrying equipment. Devised by Colonel Rivers-MacPherson in 1943, the jerkin was made of canvas and worn like a waistcoat. To the front it incorporated two ammunition pouches, and on the back a small pack. Further pouches and a method of attaching a pistol holster were below the waist. This equipment saw some limited use in Europe from 1944. A lighter, simplified form had only two magazine pockets, one on either side of the chest. Another pack with a brilliant future ahead of it was the Bergen rucksack. Already widely used in Norway, and by walkers and mountaineers in Europe, the Bergen was a capacious framed canvas bag with shoulder straps. It scored significantly over conventional packs in that it could take not only heavier loads but also odd-shaped items, and it distributed the weight with greater comfort. Though it saw some use earlier on, the Bergen was most widely seen with the Commandos and other forces from 1943 onwards.

For even heavier and more awkward loads there was the Yukon pack, which had been in use for many years and had seen service in the First World War. Inspired by an old North American design, it consisted of a simple wooden frame to which could be roped various items, such as grenade boxes. In another version, familiar to the Indian Army, and later used in the Far East, this became known as the Everest pack. By late 1944 there were determined attempts to supplement, if not replace, these museum pieces with a universal 'General Service Manpack Carrier'. This had a modern, lightweight alloy frame, quick-release webbing straps and, like some of its predecessors, it also featured a 'tump line' that could be worn around the head. Formally accepted the following year, it became the 'Carrier, Manpack, GS, 1945'.

Sundry Equipment

The list of items a soldier could carry was virtually limitless, from clinometers and maps to cleaning equipment and whistles, but certain items were carried by most troops much of the time. Perhaps most obvious amongst these were identity discs, a 'housewife', mess tin, clasp knife, wash kit, gas mask, pay book and field dressing. Though some men added personal identification in the form of a privately purchased metal bracelet or tag, all ranks were issued with official identification in the form of a pair of fibre tags to wear around the neck on cotton string. These were intended mainly for the purpose of identification in case of death or severe injury. When a man was killed the green tag remained with the body and the red was removed as evidence. Both tags gave the soldier's number, surname and initials, and his religious denomination: CE for Church of England, RC for Roman Catholic, Meth for Methodist, Pres for Church of Scotland or Presbyterian, J for Jewish and Q for Quaker.[22]

The 'housewife' was an old piece of kit. Some versions unrolled, but the latest issue was of the 'holdall' type, like a small bag. In either instance, the items inside were intended for immediate repairs to clothing. During the war common contents included grey wool for sock darning, needle, fawn-coloured linen thread, thimble, and buttons for the shirt and the battle dress. The wash kit was held in an issue white cotton roll that tied with a tape. Typical contents included a razor, a toothbrush, a comb and a shaving brush.

The mess tin set was vital because even when food came from a field kitchen something was required to carry the meal from the cauldrons. In the front line, food was actually heated in the mess tins. The standard issue set was a pair of oblong aluminium tins with folding metal handles, and with one tin a little larger it was possible to stow one inside the other. Though enamel mugs were also issued, it was perfectly possible to carry liquid, such as tea or soup, in one tin and food, such as a stew, in the other. There was also issue cutlery, but a spoon was the irreducible minimum. As with so much equipment there were also quite a few privately purchased variations, mainly used by officers. These included better-quality pieces with their own covers, and even a variation in which a whole set of pieces with metal plates, cutlery and condiment set were contained in a small pack virtually identical to the ordinary soldier's small haversack.[23]

The clasp knife, also referred to as a 'Jack knife' was like an overgrown penknife – immensely robust, suitable for a number of tasks and carried by British soldiers for many years before 1939. It was, however, useless as a weapon, and its chunky ugliness was probably as much a defence against theft as it was an increase to its durability. The type current at the outbreak of war had hard, black, chequered grips, a steel blade, a marlin spike and a combined tin opener and bottle opener. When the blades were closed, a short protrusion at the fore end made a rudimentary screwdriver. The knife could be suspended by its ring from a lanyard, or from a clip and belt loop. A cheaper version in stainless steel and without the textured grips was introduced later in the war.

Given the widespread use of poison gas in the First World War, anti-gas precautions were taken extremely seriously during the late 1930s and into the early years of the Second World War. In 1939 the soldier's first line of defence was the service respirator, a form of gas mask superior to the types in use in the civilian world, and developed from the 'small box respirator' (SBR) design that had been standard issue at the end of the First World War. Like the old SBR, the new mask had a separate facepiece and 'box' joined by a pipe. The facepiece was secured to the head by an arrangement of elasticated strapping, and the box rested in a small haversack. In the 'alert' position the haversack was worn high on the chest ready for the soldier to pull on his mask swiftly. When breathed through, the respirator air entered through a slot in the box where it was filtered and neutralised, then passed up the tube. Having been exhaled again, the air came out through an outlet valve

on the front of the facepiece. This arrangement had a number of advantages, not least of which was that the weight of the box did not have to dangle from the soldier's face, and that the box could be redesigned or improved in the light of new types of gas without rendering the facepieces, tube and valve arrangements redundant. Snagging of the rubber tube was a danger, but this was partly obviated by its flexibility and corrugated form, making it more flexible whilst remaining relatively strong. Early models of the gas mask had a khaki fabric exterior covering the facepiece and tube, but this was later dispensed with and later marks of the equipment had an exposed black rubber face and tube.

In 1942 it was ordered that the mask and its haversack should be worn inside a hessian sandbag cover. This appears to have had two main purposes: the prevention of wear and tear to the equipment, and a modicum of camouflage – the rough and rather shapeless locally made hessian covers being less obvious than the neatly stitched and squared-off haversacks. In 1943 a smaller, lighter and cheaper mask made its appearance. This was the 'light pattern' respirator, and it represented a total departure in that the filter container screwed directly into the side of

the facepiece and the mask was held in a small, oblong, canvas container, usually held on the soldier's belt. On the face of it the 'light pattern' had a number of disadvantages because a left-handed soldier had difficulty using a weapon with it on and the head took all of the weight. However, it was a significant advance in that it was distinctly lighter overall and much less bulky. These two factors may well have encouraged units to carry the 'light pattern' respirator that would otherwise have dispensed with their earlier equipment given the absence of gas warfare. The first to be issued with the new gas mask were those ready to go overseas, with the result that it was the main type of mask used by the British Army in northwest Europe after D-Day.

The mask was only one part of the full anti-gas equipment, which included an anti-gas cape, curtain and eyeshields, as well as anti-gas ointments and an anti-dim kit to prevent fogging of the lenses of the facepiece. Gas capes came in various types and were particularly intended to prevent droplets of gas reaching the skin or contaminating the uniform. Though the earliest versions were indeed capes, by 1938 the basic Army model was in fact a sleeved, lightweight, oilskin coat with a collar. It was to be worn on the march when under threat of a gas attack, or rolled on top of the equipment. In practice, it got worn mainly as a form of impromptu rainwear. Later, many capes were provided with a 'quick release cord' that allowed the garment to unfurl down the back when the cord was pulled, and from 1940 capes were produced with camouflage patterns. Variants of the cape were also made for both stretcher-bearers and mountain warfare operations.

Royal Engineers bridge building in full anti-gas kit. This includes a respirator, an anti-gas suit, hood, overboots and gloves. The debilitating effect and the delay of taking such precautions in war can be imagined. (Fox Photos/Getty Images)

Gas mask assembly in a depot of Western Command, September 1942. Pipes and masks are joined by an airtight seal. By now the face pieces were of black rubber rather than having a khaki covering. (George W. Hales/Fox Photos/Getty Images)

The 'curtain' was an attachment for the helmet, which, in conjunction with the mask and cape, completely protected the head and neck. The anti-gas eyeshields came in brown card wallets and were effectively flimsy goggles, to be worn when no mask was in place. The primary intention was to prevent small droplets of gas or spray from getting into the eyes, but they were equally useful to keep out dust and sand; indeed, later in the war they were actually designated as 'anti-dust' as well as 'anti-gas' and were produced in a tinted form as well as plain. Remarkably, many photographs of Erwin Rommel show British anti-gas eyeshields being worn on his peaked cap. Whilst this was the limit of what most infantrymen and vehicle crews received, some specialist troops had much more. Full gas suits – like boilersuits with gloves, overshoes and hoods – were issued in particular to those taking part in decontamination. Generally, anti-gas precautions became less strict as the war progressed, but one not very popular innovation (appearing from 1942) was the 'anti-vesicant' (AV) version of the battle dress. These were standard garments which had been impregnated with anti-gas chemicals, to prevent penetration by mustard gas vapour. The cloth of these 'AV' uniforms often appeared to be powdery white, and all smelled very unpleasant. If any other identification was needed they were stamped inside with the letters 'AV' in black ink.[24]

The 'Army Book 64' carried by all British soldiers. This example belonged to Sapper John Atkinson who was born in 1908 and enlisted at Clitheroe, Lancashire, in December 1940, and served with 751 Field Company, Royal Engineers. His records show that he was entitled to the Africa Star and service chevrons. (Author)

The *Soldier's Service and Pay Book*, also described as 'Army Book 64' was supposed to be carried by the soldier at all times. It had a brick red, or reddish brown cover, and was small enough to slip into the breast pocket of the uniform. Pay book was something of a misnomer because, like as not, it would record reasons for stoppages. On its second page the book recorded the soldier's regimental number, name, date of birth, place of birth, religious denomination, any approved society to which the soldier belonged, and his place and date of enlistment. The form of enlistment – Regular, Territorial, Reserve or Supplementary Reserve – was also included. This information was signed and dated by the soldier. On the third page were measurements, distinctive marks and a fitness category as determined by a medical officer. Later in the volume were noted postings, inoculations and wounds, and the address of the next of kin. On security grounds, the precise unit was never mentioned in additions and amendments to the booklet during service, though it might be added on discharge.

The 'first field dressing' was intended to be used for immediate first aid, even prior to the arrival of a medic or a stretcher-bearer, and was effectively a pad in a sealed packet. Whilst many men carried them in their trousers, battle dress or equipment, later in the war photographs also show them attached to the steel helmet in battle. This may have kept them

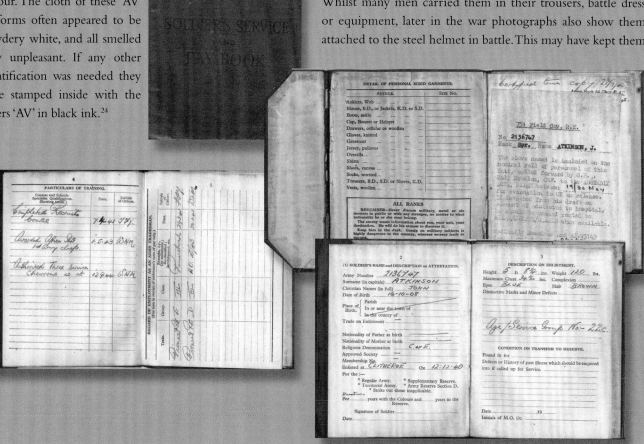

out of the way and broken up the helmet outline, but the most important factor was that here in this way it was easily seen by one's comrades. The drill was either for the casualty to apply his own dressing, or for the nearest man to apply it for him. Using one's own dressing on another was frowned upon because the casualty would then be evacuated with his own unused dressing, leaving his helper with nothing.

Though binoculars were not issued to everybody, they were widely used by officers, observers and other specialists, who had dedicated web pouches for use with standard equipment and binoculars were also seen being used with commercial and older patterns of leather case. Unfortunately, much of the existing store of optical equipment had been sold off at the end of the First World War, but some of the No. 2 type binocular, first introduced in 1909, and the No. 3 type, from 1911, manufactured by the companies of Zeiss and Ross, were retained. Both were fairly compact, had a six times magnification and weighed in at just over 2lb (900g) including their cases. More stock would later be obtained in various matt and crackle finishes, and indeed the No. 2 type would still be going strong in 1947, when it was ordered that they should now be finished in olive drab. New official models, in the form of the No. 4 Mark I and No. 5 Mark I types, were introduced in 1927 and 1935, respectively. The former was originally intended for Royal Engineer and anti-aircraft units but was officially listed as obsolescent in 1936; the No. 5 type, in various marks, would remain current throughout the war. These No. 5 binoculars were powerful 7x50 types, suitable for coast watching and various artillery observer tasks.

As in 1914, it was suddenly discovered that there were not enough binoculars to hand, nor could enough be manufactured in time to meet the burgeoning demand. By late 1940 matters were so desperate that a campaign to acquire binoculars from the public was commenced with a broadcast by Lord Derby. Ideally, these binoculars were to be donated, but collection centres were authorised to pay anything up to £17 for the No. 2 type and £27 for the No. 5 type if they were offered for sale. A survey of January 1941 noted that the retail trade had responded in a patchy way to such patriotic efforts, with some hoarding supplies to sell to their normal customers, while others, like Selfridges, had made their stock available to the government. It should be noted that the biggest private customers were officers, who were themselves buying them for military use, though doubtless at a great profit to the sellers. Never the less, by April 1941 the Binocular Office in Regent Street, London, had collected almost 71,000 pairs. Remarkably, 1,561 were loans for the duration and each was engraved with the owner's details for later return. Efforts were now stepped up again with an order that officers who had been issued with binoculars since 1919 should now return them to store, and an invitation was given to other ex-service personnel to 'present' binoculars for current service.

By the middle period of the war, supply was catching up with demand and the early, desperate efforts to acquire binoculars had ceased. After the victory in North Africa, and particularly the subsequent invasions of Europe, large quantities of enemy equipment began to fall into British hands and these items were quite widely used by troops in the field. In January 1945 another official pattern of binoculars was added to the list in the shape of a special type for airborne forces. These were stubby, made of brass, and had originally been intended as an Air Ministry store. They were Galilean rather than prismatic, and 2.5x50 magnification. Whilst they were undoubtedly tough enough for the shock of air landing, they were of antiquated design and low magnification, looking rather more like opera glasses than a precision military instrument.[25]

An officer with covered steel helmet observing in France, October 1939. He wears Service Dress, gas mask case, and an unofficial identification tag at his wrist. (Hulton Archive / Getty Images)

CHAPTER FOUR
Badges and Medals
Cap Badges[1]

The cap badge was arguably the most important of all British Army insignia, being a historic repository of martial pride and regimental tradition. The notion of the headdress insignia as representing a party in battle appears to have begun with sprigs of foliage or flowers worn as 'field signs' to distinguish friend from foe on the medieval battlefield, but by the end of the seventeenth century devices were also embroidered onto headgear such as the grenadier cap. The cap badge evolved its recognisably modern form during the nineteenth century as both technology to stamp them out of metal, and suitable types of headgear to which such badges could be affixed made their appearance. Cap badges were avidly collected and 'souvenired' t.he symbols could be read by the initiated as a synopsis of identity: some emblems or words appeared over and over, and were held in common by several different units, or a general type of unit. No attempt will be made here to describe every cap badge, which has been done very well elsewhere[1] but it is worth noting the history of some of the major devices that saw repeated use in the Second World War.

The crown was arguably the earliest regimental symbol, and indeed crowns, like lions, had been used on royal liveries even before the existence of regiments. On cap badges crowns could be used in various ways, either as the mark of a current monarch – as a 'King's crown' or 'Queen's crown', or they could symbolise a particular ruler. In a number of instances the crown appeared incidentally as part of the 'Royal Crest' as was the case with the badges of the Royal Dragoons; Loyal North Lancashires and Royal Army Pay Corps. Sometimes what appeared to be crowns were not in fact so as for example the ducal 'coronet' appearing on the badges of the Duke of Lancaster's Own Yeomanry. The monarch was also Duke of Lancaster, so this Lancashire regiment wore a coronet rather than the crown. Grenades or 'granadoes' were another early symbol, being first used by engineers as early as the sixteenth century: but thereafter they spread to other types of troops, including the artillery in general, and the various regiments of Fusiliers. The Grenadier Guards adopted the flaming grenade as a device following the grant of the title 'Grenadier' to mark their victory over the Imperial Guard at Waterloo.

Field Marshall Montgomery presenting medals to British officers in Normandy, on 16 July 1944 (Roger Viollet/Getty Images).

Men of the Manchester Regiment with their .303" Vickers machine guns set up with the gun 'No. 1' ready to fire, and the loader prone with the ammunition belt box. Though no arm insignia are worn the regimental fleur de lys badge is painted onto the side of the steel helmet. (Author)

Similarly an eagle was adopted by the Scots Greys to commemorate the capture of a French Eagle, but in other regiments such as the King's Dragoon Guards, 14th/20th King's Hussars, and Lanarkshire Yeomanry eagles were adopted in honour of foreign royal patrons. In the instance of the King's Dragoon Guards the bird was the double-headed Hapsburg eagle, first adopted when Franz Joseph became colonel of the regiment in 1896. It had been discontinued during the First World War, but reinstated in 1937. Prince of Wales 'plumes', or triple feathers, were used by numerous regiments to denote the title, or patronage of, the Prince of Wales, or connections with Wales. These included the 3rd Carabiniers; 10th Royal Hussars; 12th Royal Lancers; Royal Wiltshire Yeomanry; South Lancashires; Middlesex; Welsh Regiment and North Staffordshires. Apart from the grenade, depictions of other weapons of various types also formed part of the device of other regiments. So it was that the field gun was the badge of the Royal Artillery, and guns

also featured on the badge of the Royal Army Ordnance Corps, and crossed lances were shown on the badges of the 9th; 12th; 16th and 24th Lancers, plus the Army Education Corps. Crossed swords were used by the 25th Dragoons, and crossed carbines by the Carabiniers and County of London Yeomanry.

Stars featured on a large number of badges, and might symbolise the Bath Star, Star of the Garter, the Thistle, or St Patrick of the old knightly orders, or the old star-shaped helmet plates worn on the headgear of yesteryear. So it was that stars were integrated into the cap badges of the 4th/7th Royal Dragoon Guards; Coldstreams, Scots and Irish Guards; Devonshires; Cheshires; Worcesters; East Surreys and Highland Light Infantry. A five-pointed star formed the central feature of the badge of the Cameronians, and a Jewish six-pointed star was also used to distinguish chaplains of that faith.

Many Scottish regimental devices featured St Andrew's crosses or 'saltires'. These included the badges of the Royal Scots; Gordon Highlanders; Black Watch; King's Own Scottish Borderers; Scottish Horse and Tyneside Scottish. For Irish and Irish-related units, harps fulfilled a similar national function, being worn by several regiments including the King's Royal Irish Hussars, and on the grenade of the Royal Irish Fusiliers. Lions were used on both English and Scottish cap badges, as for example the King's Own; the Hampshire Regiment; Herefordshires; Duke of Wellington's; London Scottish; Ayrshire Yeomanry; and the Glasgow Yeomanry. Lions also featured as part of Royal Crests. By contrast, tigers usually symbolised previous connections with the Indian subcontinent, as for example on the devices of the Leicesters; Hampshires; and York and Lancaster Regiment. Horses were generally symbolic of the royal house of Hanover, and the running horse was still to be seen on the badges of the 3rd Hussars; Northamptonshire Yeomanry; King's Liverpools and West Yorkshires. An exception to the general rule were the Queen's Own Royal West Kent, whose rampant horse badge represented 'Invicta', the unconquered white horse of Kent.

Bugles and hunting horns were another common device denoting historic 'light infantry' and 'rifle' units. The connection arose initially due to the fact that the invention of rifles was closely associated with hunting, and moreover drums were highly unsuitable for use with any fast-moving units operating in broken country. 'Rifle' units often wore black, or darkened badges – these having been deemed more suitable for troops attempting to camouflage themselves on the battlefield. Bugles or horns were used by many units including the Somerset; Oxfordshire and Buckinghamshire; King's Own Yorkshire; King's Shropshire; Durham; Duke of Cornwall's, and Highland Light Infantry regiments as well as the Cameronians. Crosses also featured not only on some rifle unit badges such as that of the King's Royal Rifle Corps, but on the badges of the Sherwood Foresters, Wiltshire Regiment and Border Regiment.

Another mythical beast was the sphinx, bestowed to regiments for service in Egypt against the armies of the French at the beginning of the nineteenth century. It remained on the cap

Universal 'Field Service' caps bearing the badges of, top, the Loyal Regiment (North Lancashire), and, bottom, the Royal Engineers. (Both author)

Right: Cap badge of the South Wales Borderers.
Far right: Cap badge of the Essex Regiment. (Both author)

badges of the Lincolnshires; Lancashire Fusiliers; South Wales Borderers; East Lancashires; South Lancashires and Essex. In the unique instance of the Glosters a sphinx badge was worn on both the front and, rather smaller on the back, of the cap, commemorating the fortitude of the regiment when its men turned back to back to fight off the enemy at Alexandria in 1801. Mythological human figures featured only twice on British Army cap badges; Mercury, the wing-footed messenger on the device of the Royal Corps of Signals; and Britannia, complete with union flag shield, on the badge of the Royal Norfolks. Perhaps more expectedly dragons featured on the badges of the Monmouths; Buffs; and Berkshires; a fox on the badges of the East Riding Yeomanry, and stags' heads on those of the Seaforth Highlanders. The serpent appeared on the badge of the Royal Army Medical Corps as part of the traditional Rod of Ascèlepius device.

A thistle, another Scottish emblem, was seen for example on the star of the Scots Guards. Various other flora, and even vegetables, created another sizeable category of cap badge device. Harking back to the royal houses of those counties, roses, naturally enough, occurred on many Yorkshire and Lancashire cap badges. These included those of the East Yorkshires; King's Own Yorkshire Light Infantry; York and Lancasters; Loyal North Lancashires; Lancashire Hussars; and Duke of Lancaster's Own Yeomanry. The acorn was used by the Cheshire Regiment and the South Nottinghamshire Yeomanry. However, the leek of the Welsh Guards, and the sheaf of corn of the Lothians and Border Horse, were unique to those regiments. Castles were used on a number of badges to symbolise real fortresses, most notably that of Gibraltar, which was successfully defended during the great siege that ended in 1783. Two-tiered triple-towered castles

and keys, symbolic of Gibraltar, were prominent on the devices of the Northamptonshires; Devonshires; Dorsets; Suffolks and Essex. Castles of other designs were used by the East Surreys, Inniskillings and King's Own Scottish Borderers, the latter being a particularly splendid-looking example in a sort of north British Gothic style.

Whilst the vast majority of regimental cap badges either dated back to the nineteenth century, or were based on even older designs, several regiments and corps now came into existence and some radical new designs were applied. Obvious examples include the spear and lightning of the Reconnaissance Corps, and the somewhat art deco wings of the Parachute Regiment. The scorpion badge of the Long Range Desert Group was said not merely to denote the dangers of the desert, but to be a reference to a specific incident in which a New Zealander, Gunner Grimsey, was stung three times by such a creature in 1941.

Other ranks' cap badges were often slightly different to those of officers in that whilst other ranks' pieces were usually made in brass and/or white metal, more expensive materials such as gilding metal and enamel saw more widespread use on officer

examples. Some regiments also used woven or embroidered cap badges, especially for berets and soft headgear, as for example the 'winged dagger' of the SAS. As early as December 1940 a suggestion was made that badges could be made in plastic, an idea which gained ground the following year after tests with various possible materials and the production of samples. Eventually cellulose acetate, a thermoplastic supplied in powder form, was settled upon, at least in part because it was particularly suitable for injection moulding. In an *Army Council Instruction* of June 1942 an announcement was made that in future all cap badges would be made from plastic, exceptions only being made in cases where the fragility of a particular design rendered production impractical. To avoid any waste the new badges were to be introduced on a 'maintenance' basis, that is supplied as other stocks ran out, with plastic and metal being worn simultaneously within units.[2]

In the event it appears that plastic cap badges were manufactured for the Corps first, with particularly large batches produced for the Royal Engineers, Royal Army Service Corps and Pioneer Corps. Other regiments followed, but a recent study suggests that at least one or two units never in fact had a plastic badge, even in the unlikely event that they would have wanted to wear it. It is known for example that a badge for the Army Dental Corps was never manufactured in plastic owing to the very small number required, and whilst plastic badges were produced for the Army Physical Training Corps the total run was only 3,830, and these did not even enter production until November 1944. The appearance of the plastic cap badge was greeted with horror in many regiments, and not only by martinets who liked to see the things shine. Some units, and many individuals, therefore managed to avoid them entirely. As the Scots Guards history recorded:

The Guardsman's cap star remained the same throughout the war. In 1943 an attempt was made by Ordnance, no doubt with the laudable intention of saving metal, to foist on all regiments a plastic substitute for the normal brass. The plastic star was very ugly and extremely unpopular and it was worn only at the last resort when no brass ones were available.[3]

Metal regimental collar badges, consisting of either a small simplified variation of the cap badge, or another secondary symbol drawn from the history of the unit, were worn on service dress and Khaki Drill uniforms in 1939. Depending on each precise model they were made in either matching or mirror image types. In theory they were not required for either the new battledress, or for units newly raised after the outbreak of war – but both of these strictures were sometimes broken in practice.

Cap badge of the York and Lancaster Regiment. (Author)

Rank Badges

Badges of rank evolved from early, and rather minor, variations in dress and equipment, over a very long period of time. It is believed, for example, that the origin of the NCOs' stripes was the carrying of white match cord for firearms around the shoulders of 'file leaders' in the armies of the seventeenth century. Since file leaders were the junior leaders of small groups of men, white cord on the upper arm became the distinction of the 'non-commissioned' officer. However, chevrons in their modern form were not adopted until about 1800. 'Gorget patches' on the collars of some officer uniforms are the skeuomorphic descendants of the 'gorgets' worn by officers in the seventeenth century, themselves a symbolic vestige of the neck armour worn by knights and gentlemen in earlier eras. Lace variations were hangovers from times in which officers wore their own expensively decorated dress, whilst common soldiers wore either plain civilian clothes or were issued 'uniform'. By the twentieth century, warfare and military formations had become complex indeed and required many different gradations in rank, and many types of unit required various types of leader.[4]

Far left: A Staff Sergeant of the Duke of Lancaster's Own Yeomanry in Service Dress, *c.*1939. Rank is denoted by the chevrons and small king's crown: the ducal coronet between the two is a regimental distinction for NCOs. Also worn are shoulder chains, 'DLO' metal titles, metal rose collar badges, and cap badge featuring the rose, coronet, and oak and laurel leaves. (DLOY Museum)

Non-commissioned badges of rank of the Second World War were based on chevrons in white, off white, buff or black. On service dress and battledress and khaki greatcoat the chevrons were of worsted yarn and generally off white with detail picked out in drab fabric. One-, two- and three-bar chevrons were worn point downwards on the upper arm, under the shoulder title and any formation badges, with four-point chevrons being worn point upwards on the forearms. The meanings of the NCO chevron rank badges for the line infantry regiments were:

One chevron	Lance Corporal
Two chevrons	Corporal
Three chevrons	Lance Sergeant or Sergeant
Three chevrons, with crown above	Staff Sergeant
Four chevrons, with drum above, forearm	Drum Major

The title drum major had been revived as recently as 1928. The three-stripe lance sergeant appointment ranked between corporal and full sergeant, an appointment which was discontinued in 1946.[5]

A Bombardier of the Royal Artillery in Battle Dress with Field Service cap. Bombardier, like the equivalent infantry Corporal, was a two-stripe rank. Above the chevrons are worn an arm of service strip and the proficiency badge of a fitter, armourer, or mechanic. (Author)

Nevertheless, in different types of unit, and in certain specific regiments, titles of different ranks varied. 'Private' was the lowest rank in the infantry and parachutists, but in the Foot Guards it was 'guardsman', and in Rifle and Fusilier regiments 'rifleman' and 'fusilier' respectively. 'Kingsman' was the name for the ordinary soldier in the King's Liverpool Regiment. In cavalry and armoured units the correct title was 'trooper'. In the Artillery the lowest rank was 'gunner' or 'driver'; in the Engineers 'sapper'; in the Signals 'signalman', and in the Royal Army Service Corps 'driver'. One-chevron artillery NCOs were known as 'lance bombardier', and those with two chevrons as 'bombardier'. Three-chevron NCOs of the Household Cavalry regiments were entitled 'corporal of horse'. Customarily, but confusingly, Grenadier Guards one-chevron NCOs and two-chevron NCOs were dubbed 'corporal' and 'sergeant' respectively, but these 'local' ranks were unpaid, though they might for example be expected to command a guard. Other ranks and appointments not following the basic rules of one to four chevrons, as given above, included drum and pipe majors of the Foot Guards, who wore their four chevrons point downwards on the upper arm; and trumpet majors of the Household Cavalry, who had crossed trumpets over their four-bar chevrons worn point uppermost on the forearm. Artillery sergeants wore a gun badge, and Grenadier Guards and Royal Engineer sergeants a grenade over their chevrons. Grenadier Guards Colour sergeants wore a grenade, over crossed swords, over the chevrons.

An interesting distinction of cavalry NCO rank badges was the addition of a special regimental device, positioned over, or upon, the arm chevrons of the right arm. Warrant officers wore them below the rank badge on the right forearm. These traditional embellishments were formally approved by a 1930 *Army Council Instruction* and mentioned in the 1936 *Clothing Regulations*. This latter document stipulated that they were to be of metal and 'authorised regimental design' worn on the right arm 'at the discretion of commanding officers'. They were used generally on service dress, and very often on battledress. According to the strict letter of regulation, NCOs cavalry arm badges were for 'full ranks' only, and should not have been worn by lance corporals, but it would seem that this stricture was ignored in a number of regiments. Some latitude appears to have been inevitable as usually the badges were purchased directly by regiments. During the inter-war period these badges cost anything from less than a shilling up to 25s 6d for the 17th/21st type cast in silver. Devices used during the 1939 to 1945 period included:

Life Guards	Crown
Royal Horse Guards	Crown
1st King's Dragoon Guards	Monogram 'KDG' and crown
The Queen's Bays (2nd Dragoon Guards)	Wreath with 'Bays' and scroll
3rd Carabiniers	Crossed carbines, plumes, 'Ich Dien'
4th/7th Royal Dragoon Guards	St Patrick star, motto, coronet 'IV–VII'
5th Royal Inniskilling Dragoon Guards	Horse of Hanover on green
1st Royal Dragoons	Royal Crest on black
Royal Scots Greys	French Napoleonic eagle on black
3rd The King's Own Hussars	Horse of Hanover
4th Queen's Own Hussars	Monogram QOH, crown, motto, 'IV'
7th Queen's Own Hussars	Monogram QO, crown, red backing
8th King's Royal Irish Hussars	Crown, harp, green backing
9th Queen's Royal Lancers	Crown 'AR' entwined and reversed
10th Royal Hussars	Prince of Wales crest, red backing
11th Hussars	Prince consort's crest and motto
12th Royal Lancers	Prince of Wales crest, blue backing
13th/18th Royal Hussars	Monogram QMO
14th/20th King's Hussars	Prussian eagle in oval
15th/19th The King's Royal Hussars	Royal Crest, scarlet backing
16th/5th Lancers	Crowned Harp
17th/21st Lancers	Death's head, bones, and 'Or Glory'
22nd Dragoons	Castle 'XXII' on star
24th Lancers	'XXIV', crossed lances, and 'Lancers'
25th Dragoons	'XXV', crown, swords, and scroll
26th Hussars	Prussian eagle, 'XXVI'
27th Lancers	Elephant and 'Hindoostan'
Staffordshire Yeomanry	Crown, motto, Staffordshire knot
North Somerset Yeomanry	Star, crown, royal cypher
Duke of Lancaster's Own Yeomanry	Ducal coronet

NCO's Royal Crest arm badge 15th/19th The King's Royal Hussars. (Author)

NCO's Prussian eagle arm badge 14th/20th King's Hussars. The regimental eagle or 'hawk' was adopted because Princess Frederica of Prussia was the 'Royal Patroness' of the unit from 1798. (Author)

In the case of the 5th Royal Inniskillings, 8th King's Royal Irish Hussars, 13th/18th Royal Hussars, 16th/5th Lancers, 17th/21st Lancers and 25th Dragoons, the NCO badge was actually positioned on the chevrons, whilst in other regiments the badge was just above. It is known that the Bays, Scots Greys, and possibly others occasionally used a cap badge or collar badge as an arm badge when the correct piece was unavailable. The 14th/20th King's Hussars Prussian eagle was originally produced in silver, later in a blackened version, and was also improvised from cap badges mounted on ovals. The 22nd and 25th Dragoons,

The shoulder of
a Battle Dress,
manufactured in
1945, and worn by
a Sergeant of the
14th/20th King's
Hussars. Reading
from the top are the
brass shoulder title;
53rd Welsh Division
badge; NCO's
regimental eagle;
and sergeant's
chevrons. Having
fought in Italy in
1945, the regiment
took part in the
occupation of
Germany from 1946
where they were
attached to 53rd
Welsh Division.
(Author)

Far right: The
shoulder of a
parachutist's Battle
Dress, c.1944.
Reading from the
top: cloth shoulder
title of the Parachute
Regiment; qualified
parachutist's
proficiency wings;
the Airborne
'Pegasus' badge;
corporal's chevrons.
The image of
Bellerophon hero of
Greek mythology,
riding Pegasus, was
designed by artist
Edward Seago. The
badge was worn
by all the Airborne
divisions. (Author)

23rd and 26th Hussars, and 24th and 27th Lancers were all raised during the war, and whilst no 23rd Hussars arm badge has been identified, and the 27th Elephant was inspired by an earlier regiment of the same number, the others were influenced by their parent regiments. So it was that the similarity between the 14th/20th and 26th Hussar devices was due to the fact that the former was instrumental in the raising of the latter in 1941; however, the 26th Hussar eagle has outstretched wings. The badge of the 22nd Dragoons drew on both the 4th/7th and 5th Royal Inniskilling Dragoon Guards. Confusingly the death's head badge of the 17th/21st is often referred to as a 'motto', as taken together the skull and wording can be read as 'Death or Glory'.[6]

'Warrant officers' were different to 'commissioned officers' in that they held their rank by virtue of a warrant rather than a commission, and had not passed through an officers' training college or military academy. They thus fitted into the rank structure above the basic grades of 'non-commissioned' officer, but below the 'commissioned officer' ranks that commenced at

second lieutenant or 'subaltern'. At least in the regular peacetime Army, there was usually a clear social divide between the officer and the warrant officer. Many of the former were ex-public, or at least Grammar, school-educated, and entered the Royal Military Academy at Sandhurst, or the Artillery equivalent at Woolwich at the end of, or soon after, their school education. They thus commonly began their Army careers as officer cadets. Those undergoing instruction at an officer cadet training unit wore white cap bands, and from 1940 strips of white tape at the base of their shoulder straps. Those cadets who 'passed out' successfully were commissioned as 'subalterns'. Those who showed promise would be full lieutenants or captains within a few years. A few officers were commissioned from the ranks, but this was relatively uncommon until after 1939 and with extensive expansion of the forces.

Warrant officers by contrast usually rose through the 'other ranks' and were experienced NCOs by the time they received their warrants. They might remain warrant officers for a long

period of time, perhaps gaining eventually the coveted position of regimental sergeant major, or after another interval, being promoted to full officer status as battalion quartermaster. In the perhaps extreme case of 2nd Battalion, the Dorsetshire Regiment, J.R.H. Bolingbroke served as RSM, before eighteen years as quartermaster. At the beginning of the Second World War he was succeeded by 'Chippy' Edwards, who had been made warrant officer in 1916, and had himself been RSM. However, warrant officers generally did enjoy a few of the trappings of commissioned officers, as for example the wearing of Sam Browne shoulder belts with service dress and better quality clothing.

As of 1938 there were three 'classes' of warrant officer, with 'I' being the highest. Interestingly the new 'class III' was introduced specifically to undertake the work of a platoon commander, and to serve as an orderly officer. Officially the explanation of this departure was that it was necessary to accommodate new terms and conditions being introduced for commissioned officers: however, in practical terms it made junior commanders available both more quickly and more cheaply. That the invention of the 'class III' was not a huge success may be judged by the fact that in 1940 it was decided that no further promotions would be made to this class. Those 'class III' warrant officers still in post would remain only until they were promoted or left, the class being allowed to wither thereafter. The warrant officers 'I' and 'II' were older classes, and would survive the war. 'Class II' covered quartermaster sergeants, junior master gunners, various instructors, and certain types of orderly room sergeant and foreman. The warrant officer (class III) rank badge was a crown on the lower sleeve; class II had the crown in a wreath.

Regimental sergeant major was the most senior rank of 'class I' warrant officers, and just under him within this class came bandmasters; superintendents of various types; garrison sergeant majors; conductors of the Royal Army Ordnance Corps; and the senior grades of farrier and master gunner. The basic badge of the warrant officer (class I) was the Royal Arms in a wreath worn on the forearms: however, there were significant variations. Master gunners wore a gun over the Royal Arms, and bandmasters a crown over a lyre on a wreath. The RSMs of the Foot Guards had a very large version of the Royal Arms worn on the upper arms of battledress, though technically this was unofficial, being paid for by regimental funds, and the Honourable Artillery Company followed the same tradition.

Rank badges for the regimental officers were based on a system of stars (commonly known as 'pips') and crowns displayed on both shoulder straps of the uniform. The common type of star was struck in gilding or similar metal and was enamelled with a design incorporating the motto of the Order of the Bath *Tira Juncta in Uno*, or 'three joined in one' on red enamel, surrounded by a green wreath. In the centre were depicted three small crowns representing England, Scotland, and Ireland as united under George I. Variations on the normal design of star, inspired by other orders of chivalry, were worn by a number of regiments. The Grenadier, Coldstream, Welsh Guards and Household Cavalry all wore a design incorporating a central cross rather than crowns; the Scots and Irish Guards insignia bore thistle and shamrock respectively. Bronzed or blackened pips were worn by rifle regiments and battalions as well as chaplains. Rank stars were also woven in a somewhat simplified form for use with battledress, and produced in plastic during the latter part of the war. The stars came in different sizes to suit jackets and greatcoats, and were also produced smaller to fit, for example, onto the otherwise very crowded shoulder straps of brigadiers. The officers' crown rank device was of the King's 'Imperial Crown' design as introduced in the reign of Edward VII, and was also made in darkened versions as well as cloth and plastic.

Fabric rank insignia were sewn to the shoulder strap, metal devices being attached by loops underneath the piece held in place by a pin. Interestingly officers' cloth rank insignia were made both on a subdued khaki backing, and, from 1940, on colour-coded backings to denote arm of service. These colours were red for staff and military police; scarlet for infantry and those on the 'general' list; blue for signals and engineers; yellow for service and pay corps; 'rifle' green for rifles; black for chaplains and physical training; cherry for medical; green for intelligence, reconnaissance and dentists.

Company and Regimental Officer Rank Badges	
Second Lieutenant	One star
Lieutenant	Two stars
Captain	Three stars
Major	A crown
Lieutenant Colonel	A crown over a star
Colonel	A crown over two stars

'Field' officers were regarded as over and above the regimental system and, as well as pips and crowns, incorporated swords and batons, symbolic of command, into their rank badges. The sword depicted was the general officer's slightly curved 'mamluke' type, the baton was a short, classically inspired double-ended bar as carried by many senior commanders of the past.

Field Officer Rank Badges	
Brigadier	A crown over three stars arranged in a triangle
Major General	One star over crossed sword and baton
Lieutenant General	A crown over crossed sword and baton
General	A crown over a star, over crossed sword and baton
Field Marshal	A crown over crossed batons within a laurel wreath

Field officers were not supposed to wear a regimental cap badge and so brigadiers wore the Royal Crest of a lion on a crown; generals the crossed sword and baton within a wreath topped with the Royal Crest; and field marshals a similar device but with crossed batons. Montgomery's famous 'double-

badged' beret eccentricity combined a Royal Tank Regiment badge and a general's rank badge, contrary to all regulations. Additionally, field and staff officers wore a number of other distinctions. Those with honorary Royal appointments, or acting as aides-de-camp to the King, also wore his 'GR' cypher on the shoulder straps.

Coloured 'gorget patches' were worn on the collars of Staff and Field officers as well as 'substantive colonels', and consisted of a patch of coloured material with a button at the top and cord running vertically through the centre. These made their appearance in the late nineteenth century, and as of the 1934 *Dress Regulations* were coded in the following manner: red for generals; purple for senior chaplains; dull cherry for Royal Army Medical Corps; maroon red for Royal Army Veterinary Corps; dark blue for Royal Army Ordnance Corps; Cambridge blue for Army Education Corps; emerald green for Army Dental Corps; and primrose yellow for Royal Army Pay Corps. Beech brown

Shoulder of a sergeant's Battle Dress, 1st Battalion Loyal Regiment. Reading from the top: regimental cloth shoulder title; 1st Division white triangle; arm of service and brigade indicator strips; signaller proficiency badge; rank chevrons. The 1st Loyals were part of 2nd Infantry Brigade, 1st Infantry Division during the Operation Shingle landings at Anzio in 1944. The indicator strips are thus red for infantry, and there are two, to show 2nd Brigade. (Author)

and scarlet were added to these hues during the war to take account of the new Auxiliary Territorial Service and Royal Electrical and Mechanical Engineers respectively. Up until mid-1940 it was assumed that no gorget patches would be worn on battledress, but as of May it

was ordered that in lieu of their use a scarlet cord boss would be worn on the points of the BD collar. These were indeed manufactured and worn in some instances, but within months there was a complete change of heart to the effect that miniature gorget patches of the type used on service dress would now be worn on battledress. Interestingly, photographs demonstrate that gorget patches were sometimes also worn on shirts.

Whilst the Home Guard eventually adopted exactly the same ranks and badges as the rest of the Army, the new force maintained – at least in theory – up to as late April 1941, an entirely separate structure of ranks and appointments, and some very different badges. As of August 1940 these were, in ascending order:

Volunteer	No rank badge
Squad commander	Two chevrons on upper sleeve
Section commander	Three chevrons on upper sleeve
Platoon commander	One dark blue stripe on shoulder straps
Company commander	Two dark blue stripes on shoulder straps
Battalion commander	Three dark blue stripes on shoulder straps
Group commander	Four dark blue stripes on shoulder straps
Zone commander	Dark blue solid bands on shoulder straps

To old soldiers in particular this was a weird system, and many simply adopted old rank badges and traditional names. Others used a mixture of old and new. However, in February 1941 Home Guard officers were granted the right to hold the King's Commission, and about the same time warrant and non-commissioned officers were formally recognised as such, and terms like 'corporal', 'colour sergeant' and 'warrant officer' were also being used in the official documentation. As of April, the Home Guard was formally permitted the same ranks as the Regular Army, though curiously Home Guard officers were then supposed to buy their own badges. This was not as trivial

Home Guard shoulder title and battalion insignia, 12th Lancashire (Leyland) Battalion. The 'EL' stood for East Lancashire, though the battalion was actually cap badged to the Loyal Regiment. (Author)

Far left: The cap badge of the Highland Light Infantry incorporates a light infantry bugle and the elephant commemorating the battle of Assaye, 1803. (Author)

as it might seem, as at the time a single rank pip cost about a shilling, and the complete set of rank insignia for a brigadier cost the better part of a pound. However, the name 'volunteer' continued to have some currency until service in the Home Guard was made compulsory, by which date all conscripted soldiers were known as 'private'.

Shoulder Titles and Arm of Service Strip

Regimental and Corps 'shoulder titles' were introduced during the 1880s, and were traditionally worn in brass on top of the shoulder on khaki uniforms, on both shoulder straps or epaulettes. However, on ceremonial dress and the 1902 type service dress they were also seen in the form of a curved strip of embroidered cloth running around the apex of the sleeve, where there was more space for lettering and they could more easily be read when viewed from the sides. Though the *Priced Vocabulary of Clothing and Necessaries* of 1907 pronounced the metal type as universal from that date henceforth, embroidered types were in fact worn by the Guards from 1914 onwards, and were later adopted for the new battledress. Embroidered shoulder titles were therefore by far the most common type during the Second World War, but there were quite a few exceptions, most notably the cavalry who mainly used metal. Moreover, *Army Orders*

Cloth shoulder titles of the Royal Artillery, Royal Army Medical Corps and Royal Army Service Corps. (Author)

at all during the conflict and in place of these or the metal titles, simple shoulder slides, embroidered with the unit name in black on khaki worsted, were issued to be slipped over the shoulder straps. Never the less many infantry regiments took to wearing coloured cloth shoulder titles on their battledress unofficially, and often the title was in the facing colour of the regiment. So it was, for example, that the Durham Light Infantry wore a green title with red lettering, but there were many oddities and exceptions. For the Border Regiment examples of titles with the word 'Border' survive in yellow, on green, with a purple edging.

Such titles continued to be worn for some time, though it would appear that only the Guards, Airborne, Army Physical Training Corps and a few other specialists actually received official sanction for their use. Indeed, the Guards had long-standing permission for titles which were white on red for the

made clear that old patterns of title were supposed to be used up before new stocks were introduced. Early in the war shoulder titles were often omitted entirely as a nod to security. Never the less some infantry units were seen with old-style metal titles on the shoulder straps of their battledress, and this was actually recommended by Lord Gort in late October 1939, as the metal titles were easy to remove and might support *esprit de corps*.

Metal cavalry shoulder titles of the period were an abbreviation of the regimental title, usually cast in one piece horizontally, positioned to be read right way up by a viewer standing beside the wearer. In the yeomanry a 'Y' was usually positioned above the name. The cavalry and yeomanry lettering and numerals as approved in the 1936 *Clothing Regulations* were as opposite.

It should be noted that the metal titles were not worn in all orders of dress: moreover, the household cavalry also had cloth titles 'Life Guards', blue on red, and 'Royal Horse Guards' reversing these colours.

If cavalry shoulder titles sometimes neglected the letter of the law, those of the infantry and corps were downright confusing, and indeed many changed as the war progressed. In theory coloured shoulder titles should not have been worn

Life Guards	LG
Royal Horse Guards	RHG
1st King's Dragoon Guards	KDG
The Queen's Bays (2nd Dragoon Guards)	BAYS in gothic lettering
3rd Carabiniers	3DG
4th/7th Royal Dragoon Guards	4/7 DG
5th Royal Inniskilling Dragoon Guards	(Image of castle) over DG
1st Royal Dragoons	ROYALS
Royal Scots Greys	GREYS
3rd The King's Own Hussars	3KOH
4th Queen's Own Hussars	4H
7th Queen's Own Hussars	7H
8th King's Royal Irish Hussars	8H
9th Queen's Royal Lancers	IXL
10th Royal Hussars	10H
11th Hussars	11H
12th Royal Lancers	12L
13th/18th Royal Hussars	13/18H
14th/20th King's Hussars	XIV/XX KH
15th/19th The King's Royal Hussars	15/19H
16th/5th Lancers	16/5L
17th/21st Lancers	17/21L
Derbyshire Yeomanry	Y/DERBYSHIRE
Royal Gloucestershire Hussars	Y/RGH

Lothians and Border Horse	Y/L&B HORSE
Fife and Forfar Yeomanry	Y/FIFE & FORFAR
Westminster Dragoons	WD
Sharpshooters	SHARPSHOOTERS
Northamptonshire Yeomanry	Y/NORTHAMPTON
East Riding Yeomanry	Y/E RIDING
Northamptonshire Yeomanry	Y/NORTHAMPTON
East Riding Yeomanry	Y/E RIDING

Grenadiers and Coldstreams; yellow on royal blue for the Scots; white on emerald green for the Irish; and white on black for the Welsh. According to the history of the Scots Guards, different shoulder titles came and went quite quickly:

'Cloth shoulder titles, which had been worn during the First World War and which had been authorised for wear with service dress in 1936, but never used, gradually made their appearance in 1939. On mobilisation however, these blue and gold shoulder titles were scarce and for some time the white metal thistles and brass "SG" which had been worn between the wars on other ranks service dress were used on battledress. At one time pieces of khaki cloth designed to slip over the shoulder straps, embroidered with the letters "SG" in black, were issued but were most unpopular and seldom worn'.[8]

Naturally Churchill had his own opinion on shoulder titles, wading into the debate to the Secretary of State with a note in November 1942:

'I was shocked to hear yesterday, when visiting the 53rd Division that an Army Council Instruction had been issued three days ago ordering the immediate removal of all regimental shoulder badges. Both the general commanding the division and the Commander-in-Chief Home Forces expressed to me their surprise and regret. There is no doubt that it will be extremely unpopular and tend to destroy the regimental esprit de corps upon which all armies worthy of the name are founded. I was also told that the Army Council Instruction was accompanied by a notification that no discussion of it was to be allowed. Who is responsible for this? I hope you will give directions to cancel the instruction before great harm is done.'

Further controversy followed with other aggrieved parties remarking to the prime minister that some of the offending badges had been paid for, not by the Ministry, but out of regimental or personal funds.

In 1943, therefore, officialdom finally bowed to what was already a *fait accompli* in many quarters, and to Churchillian ire, and recognised coloured cloth shoulder titles throughout the Army. Simultaneously, concerted effort was made to regularise gaudy individualism by creating uniformity of hue. From henceforth the colours of cloth shoulder titles would be white on scarlet for the infantry; black on green for rifles; red on blue for the artillery and Commandos; and blue on red for engineers. Most of the other corps took a shoulder title in the colour of

A selection of 1940 type Battle Dress with special forces insignia. Left to right, Colonel, Airborne; Warrant Officer Special Air Service; and Sergeant, Airborne Artillery. Note the distinctive 'red beret' of the parachutist tucked under the shoulder strap of the Sergeant's uniform. (Author)

their original uniform facings. For units with short names the name of the county or part of county could be fitted onto the title, and for those with longer names just the initials appeared. So it was that the Suffolk Regiment was rendered 'Suffolk' in white capital letters on scarlet, whilst the King's Own Yorkshire Light Infantry was 'K.O.Y.L.I.'

This seemed to settle the matter, but it was not to be. Changes and exceptions quickly began to erode what had begun as a neat new plan. The Oxfordshire and Buckinghamshire Light Infantry had an ampersand in their title, 'Oxf.&Bucks.', but everybody else got 'and' if they required articulation. The Cameronians and King's Own Scottish Borderers, like their Highland comrades, opted to wear tartan patches instead of the titles and this was formally accepted in *Army Council Instructions* of October 1943. The South Wales Borderers may have objected to the apparent anonymity of 'SWB' and their name was soon approved in full. The 'Glosters' likewise changed to a more formal 'Gloucestershire'. Whilst the 'Royal Corps of Signals' went to 'Royal Signals' in 1944, the 'R.A.P.C.' expanded their shoulder title to 'Royal Army Pay Corps' a few days before the end of the European war. Territorials mainly followed the basic colour rules but whilst the Tyneside and Liverpool Scottish were given tartan patches, the London Scottish received white on scarlet, as did the Lovat Scouts. The 'Brecknockshire' territorials titles were changed to the name of their parent unit 'South Wales Borderers'.

'Arm of Service' strips for wear on battledress were introduced in September 1940. These consisted of a strip of coloured material 2 inches by 1/4 inch (5cm by 0.6cm), and were for the most part in the same hues as the backings of officers' rank badges already noted. However, the arm of service strip for Royal Artillery was red and blue, reversed blue and red for Royal Engineers. The Royal Army Service Corps was yellow and green, and the Royal Army Ordnance Corps red, blue and red. Additional strips were also introduced in 1941, in green and yellow for the Reconnaissance Corps; black, red and black for the Army Physical Training Corps; red and green for the Pioneer Corps; and grey and yellow for the Army Catering Corps. The Air Corps strips in Cambridge blue and dark blue were introduced in 1942. All strips were positioned horizontally on the arms of the battledress blouse immediately below corps or divisional signs, and on the upper sleeves of the greatcoat. The Arm of Service strips would remain current for the duration of the war and beyond, with a full list being published in mid-1943.

From April 1941 the Home Guard also adopted 'regimental distinctions' sewn on the upper arm: these were effectively small oblong shoulder titles printed in very dark blue on khaki denim backing. They were manufactured in two parts, the County or City abbreviation, and the number of the battalion. Usually, but not invariably, the letters appeared above the numerals. Important exceptions to the general rule included Somerset, where the numbers were worn above the letters, and Suffolk, where the letters were mounted in line with the numbers. Yet there were also many other battalions that defied obvious convention. For example, many Lancashire units administered by the East Lancashire Territorial Association adopted regimental titles: 'MAN', for Manchester Regiment; 'EL' for East Lancashire; 'LF' for Lancashire Fusiliers; or 'LR' for Loyal Regiment. Some 'Motor Transport' units also added 'MT' as an additional row of letters between their county abbreviation and the number. Lincolnshire had four different letterings – one for Lincoln, and three others for different divisions of the county. Peebles used 'TWD', Tweedale being the old name for the county. Bizarrely the City of London (Press) Battalion wore their '5' over 'COL', an arrangement that was soon ridiculed as standing for 'the fifth column'. Later in the war higher numbers were also introduced to identify the Home Guard rocket batteries. No attempt can be made to list all of the more than 1,300 Home Guard battalion and battery distinctions, but the list opposite gives some idea of the possible wide variety

It is interesting to note that initially the ATS were not allowed to wear the distinctions of the units of the Royal Artillery, Royal Army Service Corps, or other formations to which they might be attached. This caused some resentment, and some local breaches of the letter of the law. Again this was one of the matters in which Churchill would make personal intervention, writing in October 1941 that:

'Women should be enlisted in the ATS and should always wear that badge. This ensures their special needs in treatment, accommodation etc. are kept up to a minimum standard wherever they may be by the women organising the ATS. However, when they are posted to a combatant unit and share in practice with the men the unavoidable dangers and hardships of that unit they should become in every respect members of it. They should wear in addition to the ATS badge, all regimental insignia appropriate to their rank. Although their well being is still supervised by ATS authorities, they should be considered as detached from the ATS and incorporated into the combatant unit. This does not

A 1	1st Anglesey (Holyhead) Battalion
BDF 4	4th Bedfordshire (Luton) Battalion
BHM 22	22nd Warwickshire (Birmingham Handsworth) Battalion
CAM 5	5th Cambridgeshire (Cambridge) Battalion
EL 28	28th [East] Lancashire (Nelson) Battalion
ESX 14	14th Essex (West Thurrock) Battalion
F&D 7	Denbighshire (Denbighshire and Flint) Battalion
GLS 5	5th Gloucestershire (Gloucester) Battalion
IOM 2	2nd Manx (Douglas) Battalion
G 2	2nd City of Glasgow Battalion
KT 3	3rd Kent (Canterbury) Battalion
L 10	10th Lincolnshire (Skegness) Battalion
LF 21	21st Lancashire [Fusiliers] (Bury) Battalion
LON MT 2	London (2nd Motor Transport) Battalion
MRY 1	1st Moray (Elgin) Battalion
NTS 6	6th Nottinghamshire (Mansfield) Battalion
SY 2	2nd Surrey (Farnham) Battalion
SY 4	4th Surrey (Guildford) Battalion
TWD 1	Peebleshire (Peebles) Battalion
WR 101	West Riding Rocket Battery 101

imply any alteration in their legal status, nor need it involve any Parliamentary discussion…'[9]

Proficiency Badges[10]

Proficiency badges of various descriptions had been worn by other ranks and junior NCOs in the British Army since the nineteenth century. As a group they encompassed trade and qualifications, skill at arms, and badges of appointment and instructors badges. For the most part they were worn on the arms. Usually prize and skill at arms badges were applied to the lower left arm, and trade and appointment to the upper right. By 1914 proficiency badges were made in either brass or cloth, were worn on both full dress and service dress, and existed in a wide variety. Prior to the war a few regiments also took to wearing skill at arms and instructors badges on coloured backings, as for example the East Surry and Royal Berkshires who used red cloth, or the Durham Light Infantry and Royal Northumberland Fusiliers who took different shades of green. Never the less, during the Second World War all these types of badge were to be seen on khaki service dress and battledress,

and were usually woven, cotton on worsted, for the most part in subdued colours and white on a khaki background. Most badges were officially recognised types, as announced in *Army Orders* or *Army Council Instructions*, and like other badges were manufactured according to 'sealed pattern' designs, but some unofficial badges did get made and worn.

Many proficiency badges had existed in 1939, but the system was overhauled, regularised and changed during the course of the war. Some badges such as the 'Hotchkiss Gunner' died a natural death as the equipment to which they referred was phased out, and others came in. Significant milestones of 1940 included the introduction of the parachutists qualification badge and the bomb disposal badge. The latter was designed

Left: Radio operator badge. (Author)

Centre: Hammer and pincers proficiency badge: used at different times to denote various trades and proficiencies including; armament technician, armourer, fitter, blacksmith and metal worker. (Author)

Bottom: Despatch rider badge: seen in several different patterns, with and without a wheel, and the wings horizontal, as here, or raised. (Author)

Badge for a qualified parachutist. (Author)

Group 'B' tradesman badge. This encompassed a very wide range of possible proficiencies. The 1944 regulations allowed its use for not only clerical skills, but bricklaying, mining, photography, electrician and even massage and watch making. (Author)

by Queen Mary of Teck, the queen mother, in recognition of the dangerous work of bomb disposal units. Detailed regulations for the award of the internal combustion engine vehicle drivers' badges came in 1942, and a table of recognised proficiency badges was issued in 1943.

In September 1944 a detailed policy for the wearing of 'tradesmen's badges, instructors badges and badges for skill at arms' appeared. According to this document no one ranking as sergeant or above should wear any skill at arms or tradesmen's badges, and the number of badges worn by others was limited to a total of two, no more than one in any particular category. Badges were to be approved by the soldier's commanding officer. Tradesmen were listed in four groups lettered 'A', 'B', 'C' and 'D', to be signified by the letter in Gothic script over a wreath, the badge being worn only by those qualified as 'class I' or 'II' in their trade. Certain other already exisiting trade badges were also authorised again. Skill at arms and instructors badges were also retained. The following list of badges does not claim to be exhaustive, but does encompass the major types and meanings.

Royal Armoured Corps recruits receiving wireless instruction. Fitting wireless to tanks became standard practice during the Second World War, considerably improving tactical usefulness. It also required more technically minded troops. (Hulton Archive/Getty Images)

Description	Position on arm(s)	Meaning
'A' in wreath	upper right	electrician; draughtsman; surveyor etc.
'B' in wreath	upper right	bricklayer; clerk; miner; mason etc.
'C' in wreath	upper right	baker; butcher; clerk; cook; printer etc.
'D' in wreath	upper right	crane driver; sawyer; waterman etc.
'H' in wreath	upper right	height taker, AA guns
'L' in wreath	upper right	gun layer
'P' in wreath	upper right	artillery plotter or predictor
'R' in wreath	upper right	range taker instructor
'S' in wreath	upper right	surveyor
'AE' in wreath	upper right	ammunition examiner
Bugle	upper right	bugler
Circle with lightning flashes	upper right	radio mechanic
Crossed axes	upper right	pioneer
Crossed cannon	upper right	gunnery instructor
Crossed flags	upper right	signal instructor
Crossed rifles	upper right	musketry instructor
Crossed swords	upper right	physical training instructor
Drum	upper right	drummer
Hammer and pincers	upper right	fitter; armourer; mechanic etc.
Parachute wings	upper right	qualified parachutist, operational
Spur	upper right	riding instructor
'BC' in wreath	lower left	Bren carrier diver
'BG' in wreath	lower left	Bren gunner
Bomb	lower left	bomb disposal personnel
Crossed rifles	lower left	marksman
Crossed rifles and 'S'	lower left	sniper
'DR' winged wheel	lower left	despatch rider
'EAG' in wreath	lower left	ATS experimental gunnery assistant
'HG' in wreath	lower left	Hotchkiss gunner
Glider	lower left	glider trained personnel
'LG' in wreath	lower left	Lewis, or light machine gunner
'LMG' in wreath	lower left	light machine gunner
'M' in wreath	lower left	mortar man
'MG' in wreath	lower left	machine gun marksman
Parachute	lower left or right	parachute trained
'QI' in wreath	lower left	qualified instructor, Royal Engineers
'R' in wreath	lower left	range taker or position finder
Rifle and star	lower left	best shot in company or first class shot
'SB' in wreath	lower left	stretcher bearer
Steering wheel	lower left	motor vehicle driver
'SP' in wreath	lower left	special proficiency
'Army Fire Service'	both upper	Army fireman
Royal Crest on wings	left breast	Army flying badge
Bagpipes	various	piper or pipe major

Divisional Signs[11]

The 'charging bull' badge of 11th Armoured Division. Formed in Yorkshire in March 1941, the division fought extensively in Northern Europe after D-Day, crossing France, Belgium and the Netherlands before crossing the Rhine at Wesel on 28 March 1945. (Author)

For much of its existence the British Army was small enough and wore such distinctive uniforms that it required no specific devices to indicate different divisions. It was the mass conflict of the First World War, conducted in a universal khaki service dress, that produced a colourful new heraldry of war, with divisional signs sprouting on signposts, uniforms and even vehicles. Most of these insignia disappeared between the wars, and in the interests of security such displays were actively discouraged after the Second World War began, an *Army Council Instruction* of May 1940 declaring that, 'divisional signs will not be worn by British divisions during the war'. Whilst signs were relatively little seen in the early part of the war, it would never the less appear that the edict was unpopular, sometimes counterproductive, and occasionally ignored. Indeed, by that autumn there was a softening of approach such that not only divisional, but brigade, corps, command headquarters and other devices were all accepted provided that those used on clothing did not exceed a cost of one and a half pence to the public purse. They were to be in cloth and worn on both upper arms of the uniform. The new designs were to be decided by commanding officers and reported to the War Office. Perhaps perversely a few divisions do not appear to have worn signs even when they were expected to do so, and others applied them only to their best battledress worn for parades.

The crossed keys badge of 2nd Infantry Division. After retiring from Dunkirk in 1940 the division was later deployed to India and Burma to fight the Japanese. (Author)

Some signs were simple, while others were witty. Many of the tank division signs were plays on knightly armour or similarly tough animals. The 'panda' of the 9th was said to be a play on 'panzer' but was in fact the badge of a polo team

of another brigade. The crossed keys of 2nd Infantry Division were the subject of much conjecture, with some speculating that they represented the historic arms of the Archbishop of York: however, General Loyd explained that his last command had been a Guards brigade with a single key as its sign, so on coming to his new command he doubled it. Other signs were regional, as for example the Scottish thistle and Yorkshire and Lancashire roses. The 'Y' of 5th Infantry also stood for 'Yorkshire'. The horseshoe of the 13th was to counteract any superstitious suggestion of bad luck. A few signs took inspiration from similar devices used in the First World War.

Divisional signs were as follows:[12]

Division	Badge
Guards Armoured	Ever open eye: white, on blue shield, red border
1st Armoured	White rhino on black oval
2nd Armoured	Knight's helmet, in white on red backing
6th Armoured	Clenched white mailed gauntlet on black square
7th Armoured	Jerboa (desert rat), on red, later black
8th Armoured	'GO' on green traffic light within black square
9th Armoured	Face of giant panda, black and white
10th Armoured	Fox's mask, red on black or yellow circle
11th Armoured	Black bull with red detail on yellow oblong
42nd Armoured	White diamond within red diamond
79th Armoured	Bull's head on inverted yellow triangle, black border
1st Infantry	White triangle
2nd Infantry	White crossed keys on black square

Division	Badge
3rd Infantry	Inverted red triangle surrounded by three black triangles
4th Infantry	Fourth quadrant of red circle
5th Infantry	'Y' in white on khaki or black
6th Infantry (later 70th)	Four pointed red stars on white square
8th Infantry	Red cross on blue shield
9th (Scottish)	Silver or white thistle on dark blue circle
12th (Eastern)	White diamond
13th Infantry	Black horseshoe on red square
15th (Scottish)	Lion rampant in yellow circle, white border on black
18th Infantry	Stylised black windmill on orange–yellow background
23rd (Northumbrian)	White Tudor rose on green square
36th Infantry	Red and white interlocking circles on black background
38th (Welsh)	Yellow (St David's) cross on black shield
40th Infantry	Brown acorn on white square
42nd Infantry	White diamond within red diamond
43rd (Wessex)	Wessex wyvern in gold or yellow on blue square
44th (Home Counties)	Red oval
45th (West Country)	Yellow drum with red, white and blue detail, on khaki
46th (N. Midland and W. Riding)	Oak tree in green and brown with white outline
47th (London)	Two red 'bow' bells and ribbon on dark blue
48th (South Midland)	Blue macaw, on red diamond within blue oval
49th (West Riding)	White polar bear on black oblong
50th (Northumbrian)	'TT' red letters inter-linked on black square
51st (Highland)	'HD' joined within red circle on blue square
52nd (Lowland)	White St Andrew's cross on blue, 'MOUNTAIN'
53rd (Welsh)	Red 'W' resting on horizontal bar, on khaki
54th (East Anglian)	'JP' joined in blue, on red circle
55th (West Lancashire)	Red rose with green stem and leaves, five each side

Division	Badge
56th (London)	Black cat on red background
57th (dummy formation)	'D'
59th (Staffordshire)	Pit headgear in red, against black triangle, on blue
61st Infantry	Red diamond on blue square
66th (Lancashire and Border)	Light blue triangle with horizontal yellow stripe
70th Infantry	Four-pointed red star on white square
77th Infantry	Red sword raised by white arm from water on black
78th Infantry	Yellow battle axe on black
80th Infantry	Red liner on yellow background within light blue border
Airborne Divisions	Pegasus in pale blue on dark maroon square
1st Anti-Aircraft	Black dornier pierced by red sword on light blue
2nd Anti-Aircraft	Flying witch on broomstick in red on dark blue
3rd Anti-Aircraft	'AA' and white thistle on blue square
4th Anti-Aircraft	One or three buckles
5th Anti-Aircraft	Dornier coming nose down in red flames on khaki
6th Anti-Aircraft	Black and white target pierced with red arrow
7th Anti-Aircraft	Sword point down and scales in red on blue
8th Anti-Aircraft	Red star on black bomber nose down, on blue
9th Anti-Aircraft	Black cat, tail-shaped '9' looped around red aircraft
10th Anti-Aircraft	Black profile lion's head outlined white, on khaki
11th Anti-Aircraft	Black Prussian eagle pierced with red arrow on khaki
12th Anti-Aircraft	'Double six' domino on red horizontal diamond

SOME COMMAND AND OTHER FORMATION SIGNS

Far right top: Rhino badge of one of the East African formations deployed to Burma as part of 14th Army, and the 14th Army badge showing its number in Roman numerals 'XIV'. The 14th, comprising almost a million men at its peak, was a composite of Indian and British troops, and other colonial formations, and existed from 1943 to the end of 1945. (Author)

Far right bottom: The archer badge of Anti-Aircraft Command. Initially adopted by General Pile's headquarters only, the use of this device was eventually extended to all parts of the Army air defence of Great Britain. (Author)

Command or Formation	Description
11th Army Group	Yellow sampan on dark blue sea with red sky
HQ 15th Army Group	White shield with blue wavy lines on red square
HQ 21st Army Group	Crossed swords on blue cross on red shield
First Army	Sword, point down, on red cross on white shield
Second Army	Sword, point down, on blue cross on white shield
Eighth Army	Gold cross on white shield on dark blue oblong
Ninth Army	Elephant and castle in red on a black circle
Tenth Army	Golden Assyrian winged lion on black background
Twelfth Army	Burmese chinthe on red, black, red bars, and 'XII'
Fourteenth Army	Red shield, with horizontal band over sword, 'XIV'
I Corps	White spearhead on scarlet diamond
II Corps	Blue wavy bands on white oblong, red salmon
III Corps	Green fig leaf on white background
IV Corps	Black elephant on red background
V Corps	White Viking ship, red cross on sail, all on black
VIII Corps (1944)	Horsed white knight charging, on scarlet square
IX Corps	Originally a black cat, later a trumpet
X Corps	White circle over white bar on green or red backing
XI Corps	Black and white chequered Martello tower
XII Corps	Three trees in white oval on black background
XXV Corps	Cyprus lion (or leopard) in red on yellow background
XXX Corps	Black charging boar in white circle on black square

Command or Formation	Description
Anti-Aircraft Command	Black bow, arrow and archer's arms on red square
I AA Corps	Red eagle in flight struck by arrow, sky blue background
II AA Corps	Blue mailed arm holding dagger on red background
Combined Operations	Red albatross, Tommy gun and anchor on dark blue
Commando Brigades	Upward pointed red dagger on black

Armlets[13]

'Armlets' or armbands were worn in considerable profusion during the First World War as a quick, easy, but impermanent way to mark out the wearer as assigned to some special duty or appointment. They were reduced in scope and more rigidly controlled during the inter-war period. So it was that those seen with any great frequency prior to 1939 were those of senior officers commanding formations or with War Office duties, liaison officers, officers in command headquarters, and those of other ranks on duty with the Military or Regimental police. After the outbreak of war the number of duties requiring the wearing of armlets increased. Literally dozens were formally approved, and unofficial examples also crept in, with both the regular and auxiliary forces. The following list is not exhaustive, covering only the most significant types:

Officers' Armlets	
Description	**Meaning**
Red over blue 'MS'	Military Secretary's branch
Red over blue 'G'	Chief Imperial General Staff branches
Red over blue 'DGMP'	Director of Munition Production branch
Red over blue 'TA'	Territorial Army directorate
Red over blue 'PR'	Public Relations
Red over blue 'P'	Pay Corps
Red over blue 'A'	Provost Marshal
Red over blue 'DJA'	Deputy Judge Advocate's department
Red, black, red horizontally 'ADS'	*Aides-de-camp*
Red, black, red horizontally 'G'	General Staff branch
Red, black, red horizontally 'A'	Adjutant General's branch
Red, black, red horizontally 'A' and gun	Royal Artillery
Red, black, red horizontally 'Q'	Quarter Master General's branch
Red, black, red horizontally 'E'	Royal Engineers
Red, black, red horizontally 'S'	Signal service
Red, black, red horizontally 'M'	Medical services
Red, black, red horizontally 'O'	Ordnance services
Red, black, red horizontally 'V'	Veterinary services
Red, black, red horizontally 'PM'	Provost Marshal's officers
Red, black, red horizontally 'C'	Assistant Chaplain General
Blue, black letters 'BM'	Brigade Major
Blue, black letters 'SC'	Staff Captain
Green, black letters 'GA'	Garrison Adjutant
White over blue	Army signal service
Khaki with 'FIRE' in blue	Fire superintendent
Black, orange, black horizontally with 'C'	Motor contact officer
Red with 'CRO'	Chief Recruiting Officer
Black and white vertical stripes 'PRESS'	War correspondent
Narrow green armlet	Intelligence
Green lettered 'FSP'	Field Security Police
Blue over yellow	Field survey

A second lieutenant of the Gloucester Regiment. His badges include an embroidered version of the regimental sphinx worn on his beret; cloth rank star on his shoulder strap; cloth shoulder title; the polar bear badge of 49th Division; and an arm of service strip. On his forearms are overseas service stripes and a wound stripe: both of these types of badge had been worn in the First World War and revived following Churchill's personal intervention. Note also this officer's holstered revolver retained by a lanyard around the neck. (Ray Westlake/Author)

Officers' Armlets	
Description	Meaning
White with various wording	Officers with special duties on troopships
'ALO'	Air Liaison Officer
Black	Private purchase: allowed to signify mourning
Other Ranks' Armlets	
Black, red letters 'MP'	Military Police (on duty)
Black, red letters 'MPSC'	Military Provost Staff Corps
Green lettered 'FSP'	Field Security Police
Blue, black, red letters 'GMP'	Garrison Military Police
Black, red letters 'RP'	Regimental Police
Red Cross on white	Medical or dental Corps
White, red letters 'SB'	Stretcher bearer
Yellow	Sanitary service
White, black word 'REMOUNT'	Remount service
White over blue	Signaller, despatch rider on duty
Blue over yellow	Field survey
Green	Intelligence personnel
Blue	Hospital patient or convalescent

Good Conduct, Service and Wound Stripes

Worn as a chevron point upwards on the left forearm, a single good conduct badge represented two years of unblemished service. More were added as the period of good conduct extended, though with very long periods of service stripes represented different time periods – five years being required for two stripes, and twelve for three. Worn in worsted on service dress and battledress, good conduct stripes were also made in cotton for Khaki Drill clothing. Strictly speaking they were to be worn only by soldiers ranking as corporal or below. According to the *Vocabulary of Clothing* as amended in 1939, the stripes were manufactured as single items, or as blocks of up to five. Whilst it was highly unusual to see personnel sporting more than this number, there were a few men in the ranks who eventually carried anything up to ten, with Private A. Carter of the King's Shropshire Light Infantry for example clocking up half a century of good conduct between the last year of Queen

Victoria's reign in 1901 and January 1951. The full list of time qualification periods was as follows:

Number of Years	Number of Stripes
2	1
5	2
12	3
16	4
21	5
26	6
32	7
38	8
43	9
48	10

In the First World War 'wound stripes' consisting of thin vertical gold-coloured bars to be worn on the lower sleeve had been given to injured servicemen. Chevrons for service overseas were also worn. Both these practices had been discontinued in the inter-war period, and matters would remain this way until after the entry of America into the Second World War, when the idea was revived. Interestingly it was Churchill himself who finally pressed the issue, writing to General Ismay on 17 June 1943:

'I am strongly of the opinion that wound stripes should be issued as in the last war. Pray bring this to the notice of the three departments. The War Office are of course the principle party concerned. Let me have any papers on the subject. There must be no further delay in this, on account of the 'Purple Hearts' which the Americans are giving to their own soldiers and are distressed not to give to ours. The second question is the issue of chevrons for every year of service abroad, which I think would also be greatly appreciated by the soldiers.'[14]

Despite this plea for swiftness, reinstatement of wound stripes was not announced in an Army Council Instruction until 16 February 1944. Troops were then instructed to put in a claim to their commanding officers for a gold wound stripe for each wounding in the current conflict, and a red one for those sustained in previous wars. In case of doubt the final proof of a wound was an entry in the records of the War Office Casualty Branch. Qualifying wounds or injuries were those 'due to enemy action', or friendly fire during combat, including those sustained in the Home Guard, but accidental injury 'not directly attributable to enemy action' and self-inflicted wounds were not counted. Service chevrons were also reintroduced, commanding officers awarding one per year on the basis of the entries in the pay book. The chevrons themselves were red, small, and worn point upwards on the lower right sleeve. They were manufactured individually, and in blocks of two, three and four, making them easy to sew neatly to the uniform.

Medals

Unlike some armies, British troops did not wear medals with combat dress, but awards were symbolised on battledress and service dress by a short length of the ribbon on the left breast above the pocket of the uniform. Where a recipient had a large number of awards, these might run to more than one row of ribbons. On battledress and service dress the ribbons were often sewn direct to the cloth, but might also be mounted on a ribbon bar that looked neater and could easily be detached during cleaning of a uniform, or for transfer to another jacket. Additionally, France had awarded two whole battalions the *Croix de Guerre* in 1918. So it was that the 2nd Devonshires and 4th King's Own Shropshire Light Infantry were entitled to wear the ribbon of this medal. However, it was not worn on the breast, but rather on the shoulder of the jacket. All actual orders, decorations and medals were worn only during ceremonial parades or other specified events. They were then either suspended simply from a bar to which they were sewn and then secured to the uniform by means of a long pin, or could be 'court mounted' *en bloc* with stiffening holding the medals rigidly together. Both actual medals and ribbons were arranged in order of precedence, with the most important closest to the centre of the chest and the least significant closest to the left arm.

The order of precedence began with the Victoria Cross, followed by the George Cross; then, British orders of knighthood and other distinctions; decorations; medals for gallantry and distinguished conduct; campaign medals; police medals; coronation and jubilee medals; and long service and efficiency; and any other British medals. At the end were placed authorised foreign awards, orders being followed by decorations and medals. So it was, for example, that a winner of the Victoria Cross who was a veteran of the First World War would wear his VC closest to the centre, followed by his campaign medals, and the Victory Medal for 1914–1919, ending perhaps with a French or Belgian *Croix de Guerre*. Never the less, it was not entirely unknown for recipients to put up their medals out of order, and there are groups to very highly decorated soldiers in collections today where this occurs.

Medal ribbon bar on an officer's Service Dress, showing the ribbons of, left to right, the Military Cross; 1939–1945 Star; Africa Star and Italy Star. (Author)

It should be remembered that many of the medals of the Second World War were not actually produced or awarded until hostilities had ended. So it was that the medals most commonly seen worn during 1939 to 1945 were those of 1914 to 1918 and the inter-war period. Moreover, medal winners sometimes received a ribbon long before the actual medal. In all instances gallantry medals had to be mentioned in the *London Gazette*, hence the common reference to awards being 'gazetted'. The key decorations awarded to British Army personnel during the Second World War were the Victoria and George crosses; Distinguished Service Order; Military Cross; Distinguished Conduct Medal; Distinguished Service Medal and Military Medal. Never the less, there were others that could be won under specific circumstances. For example, Army officers could be awarded the Distinguished Flying Cross, and the George Medal was available for decorating Army personnel where purely military awards would not normally be granted.

The 'court mounted' medals of Lance Bombardier R. Stansfield 88th Field Regiment, RA TA. These are, left to right, the 1939–1945 Star; the Pacific Star; the 1939–1945 War Medal, and the Territorial Efficiency Medal with its distinctive green and yellow ribbon. Stansfield was captured at Singapore in 1942. (Author)

Some decorations awarded to army personnel. Left to right: Distinguished Service Order; Military Cross; Victoria Cross; Distinguished Conduct Medal; French *Croix de Guerre*.

The simple bronze Victoria Cross with its distinctive dark patina was introduced in 1856 and has remained the pre-eminent British decoration ever since. Suggestions were put forward for a new 'order of merit', open to all ranks, by Captain G. T. Scobell MP as early as 1854. This was taken up by the Duke of Newcastle, who recommended a new 'cross' to Prince Albert with the further idea that the new award should bear the name of Victoria. Yet the name of the cross is not just a dutiful nod to the monarch, for the Queen took a direct and personal interest in its institution and design. For one thing the proposed motto on its face was 'For the Brave': Victoria rejected this on the grounds that it would suggest that those who did not win the new award would thereby be traduced as not being brave, and so instead substituted the wording 'For Valour'. Furthermore, on being presented with a copper proof of the medal, she dictated a letter to Lord Panmure:

> *'The cross looks very well in form, but the metal is ugly; it is copper and not bronze and will look very heavy on a red coat with the Crimean ribbon. Bronze is, properly speaking, gun metal; this has a rich colour and is very hard; copper would wear very ill and would soon look like an old penny. Lord Panmure should have one prepared in real bronze, and the Queen is inclined to think that it ought to have a greenish varnish to protect it; the burnished parts would then show up very bright and show the design and inscription. The reverse ought not to be quite flat, but should be finished much as the front.'*[15]

Though the award was usually recommended by a commanding officer up the chain of command all the way to the monarch for approval, at an early stage in its history it was established that under certain circumstances the medal could be awarded for an action, and a specific individual then chosen by his peers whose selection was then referred back. It was also allowed that the medal could be awarded posthumously. Traditionally it has been asserted that all Victoria Crosses were cast from the metal of a Russian cannon captured in the Crimea, and a large ingot of this material was indeed retained at Woolwich Arsenal, and later the Central Ordnance Depot at Donnington, for such purpose. Never the less, recent analytical work suggests that other guns have also been used in the same way. The medal has been used increasingly sparingly with the progression of time, at least in part because other awards for less than the most exceptional valour have been gradually introduced. Though it was originally awarded with a blue ribbon for the Navy, after 1918 all were hung from a crimson ribbon. The date of the act of gallantry and the recipient's name are engraved on the reverse, the name being on the suspension bar and the date on the cross.

It is interesting to note that the original Royal Warrant under which the cross is awarded has been updated a number of times, under the hand of successive monarchs. So it was that in the inter-war period, for example, no less than four new warrants were issued. That of 1920, heralded as a 'general revision and recodification', also bears the name of Churchill by virtue of his ministerial position, as well as that of King George V. The warrants of 1931, 1938 and 1939 respectively revised the conditions of the award, and extended it to Burmese forces and warrant officers. Even while the Second World War was underway, two more warrants were made out. That of 1941 extended eligibility to the Indian Air Force, whilst the warrant of December 1942 also covered the Home Guard. The specific wording here mentioned both 'the Home Guard and any lawfully constituted force corresponding thereto', and the 'Women's Auxiliary Services'. It is also worth noting that the warrant of 1961 extended the provision of a pension of £100 retrospectively to officers who had won the cross, a benefit hitherto reserved to non-commissioned officers and other ranks. The same document also introduced formally a sealed pattern for a miniature version of the cross for use on 'certain occasions' when the actual cross was not worn. In the event just 182 Victoria Crosses were awarded to all services during the war, and of these sixty-one went to the Army – ten being awarded to officers and men serving with the Commandos. Whilst the warrants for the award were detailed in their provision, it was never the less the case that 'irregular submissions' received consideration, and in at least one Second World War Army instance was actually approved. The Victoria Cross of New Zealand Sergeant J.D.

Hinton for his bravery in Greece in 1941 was recommended in the first instance by the commander of the British Prisoner of War Hospital at Kalamai.[16]

Interestingly the George Cross, ranking just below Queen Victoria's more famous cross, is actually even rarer, with only 106 given between 1940 and 1947. The blue-ribboned George Cross is struck in silver and was first instituted in September 1940, being awarded to both civilians and members of the armed forces for acts of the greatest heroism or courage. In January 1941 it also replaced the existing Empire Gallantry Medal. Famously, the George Cross was also awarded to the Island of Malta for its collective resistance to the enemy.

The various orders of knighthood were open only to officers. On service uniforms, orders were represented by ribbons, for example that of Order of the Bath being red, and that of the Order of St Michael and St George being red and blue. The cross-shaped enamel and silver gilt Distinguished Service Order, with crown and wreath on its centre, was first instituted in 1886, and also awarded only to officers. It was issued unnamed, though during the Second World War the year of award was inscribed on the back of the suspension bar. Though still not a common medal, provision was made to mount a silver gilt bar with a crown on its crimson and blue ribbon for repeat awards. In the event a little under 5,000 were awarded during the Second World War, with 500 first bars and fifty-nine second bars. Eight recipients won three bars to the DSO.[17]

The Military Cross, struck in silver, was instituted in late December 1914, and was available to officers and warrant officers only. Though not officially named, Second World War Military Crosses have the year on the reverse. Bars could be given for repeat awards. About 11,000 were awarded from 1939 to 1945, with 480 double and twenty-four triple recipients. One of the best known of these last was Brigadier Peter Young, originally of the Bedfordshire and Hertfordshire Regiment, but later a leader of the Army Commandos. His first was won in the raid on Vaagso, Norway, in street fighting; the second in Sicily, and the third in Italy. The Distinguished Conduct and Military medals were reserved for warrant officers and other ranks, with the former medal coming into existence in the Crimea, and the latter being instituted in 1916. Arguably the DCM is of particularly special significance as it was, next to the Victoria Cross, the highest medal for valour for a British Army other rank. Approximately 1,900 were awarded during the Second

World War. The DCM ribbon is red and blue, the MM ribbon red, white and blue. Though the Military Medal was the junior award for bravery in the field, the First and Second World Wars demonstrated just how necessary its introduction had been. During the First World War more than 115,000 were awarded, with a further 15,000 during the Second World War.

Unlike most other classes of medal, gallantry and distinguished conduct medals were given for a very specific reason, such as an act of valour, or distinguished service during a sequence of events – not for simply being present in a theatre of war or meeting a general criteria. The reason for the award of such a special medal was spelt out in a citation. The exact rules for the making of an award and the issue of the citation varied from medal to medal, but generally required that the deed or deeds be witnessed by specified parties, and that the unit commanding officer refer a recommendation up the chain of command. Whilst the pre-eminent awards commanded considerable respect, the process was often regarded as fallible and long-winded. Remarkably, however, it continued to operate even in Singapore after the

Campaign Stars, Clasps and Medals
instituted in recognition of service
in the war of 1939-45

NUMBER OF STARS, MEDALS, CLASPS or EMBLEMS ENCLOSED [   ]

Order of Wearing	Description of Ribbon	Clasp or Emblem (if awarded)
1 1939-45 Star	Dark blue, red and light blue in three equal vertical stripes. This ribbon is worn with the dark blue stripe furthest from the left shoulder.	Battle of Britain
2 Atlantic Star	Blue, white and sea green shaded and watered. This ribbon is worn with the blue edge furthest from the left shoulder.	Air Crew Europe or France and Germany
3 Air Crew Europe Star	Light blue with black edges and in addition a narrow yellow stripe on either side.	Atlantic or France and Germany
4 Africa Star	Pale buff, with a central vertical red stripe and two narrower stripes, one dark blue, and the other light blue. This ribbon is worn with the dark blue stripe furthest from the left shoulder.	8th Army or 1st Army or North Africa 1942-43
5 Pacific Star	Dark green with red edges, a central yellow stripe, and two narrow stripes, one dark blue and the other light blue. This ribbon is worn with the dark blue stripe furthest from the left shoulder.	Burma
6 Burma Star	Dark blue with a central red stripe and in addition two orange stripes.	Pacific
7 Italy Star	Five vertical stripes of equal width, one in red at either edge and one in green at the centre, the two intervening stripes being in white.	
8 France and Germany Star	Five vertical stripes of equal width, one in blue at either edge and one in red at the centre, the two intervening stripes being in white.	Atlantic
9 Defence Medal	Flame coloured with green edges, upon each of which is a narrow black stripe.	Silver laurel leaves (King's Commendation for brave conduct. Civil)
10 War Medal 1939-45	A narrow central red stripe with a narrow white stripe on either side. A broad red stripe at either edge, and two intervening stripes in blue.	Oak leaf

The leaflet sent out with campaign medals specified the number enclosed and listed order of wear, the colours of the ribbons, and what clasps or emblems might be affixed to the ribbons. So it was that the Africa Star might have an 8th or 1st Army clasp, or the endorsement 'North Africa 1942–43. The 'Oak Leaf' applied to the War Medal denoted a 'Mention in Despatches'. (Author)

British capitulation of 1942, with commanding officers keeping lists of those they wished to put forward for decoration through the years of captivity. Many of these recommendations were later confirmed. In some instances, however, rules allowed for 'immediate' awards, short circuiting the process, though these were still announced in the *London Gazette*.

Written citations vary in length and detail according to the proposer, type of award, and the substance and complexity of the report. However, it is worth repeating just three examples of the many that recorded unique acts of bravery. The first relates the deeds of Private George Sands, 5th Cameron Highlanders, fighting in France after D-Day:

> '*On 13th June, after the attack and capture of St. Honorine-La-Chardonnerette, Private Sands was Bren gunner of a section of D Company which had consolidated in some enemy trenches. About 0915 hours a heavy counter attack developed and Private Sands' section was attacked by about 20 Germans and a tank. Private Sands was wounded in both legs but continued to operate his Bren gun until the attack on his front had been repulsed. He refused to be evacuated and crawled to a position from which he could engage another expected counter attack. He did this, continuing to operate his gun until the enemy withdrew. Only then was he evacuated.'*

Sands' later recollections were that his determination was borne of adrenaline and anger from having seen comrades killed and wounded. One enemy bullet had in fact torn into the barrel of his Bren gun, causing a further injury to his cheek. The wounded private was recommended for a Military Medal by battalion commander Lieutenant Colonel Monro. This being duly endorsed by the commanders of both the Brigade and 51st Highland Division, Sands soon received his medal.

The citation of Trooper Leonard Acaster, 4th Royal Tank Regiment, was printed in the *London Gazette* in February 1942, and recorded his remarkable escape whilst fighting in North Africa:

> '*On the night of 30th November 1941, Trooper Acaster was driver of an 'I' (infantry) tank which went into action when the squadron counter attacked on El Duda. A shell penetrated the tank, killing the gunner and wounding Trooper Acaster in the face. The tank halted and being close to the enemy was quickly invested by them in the darkness. Trooper Acaster, with great presence of mind feigned death, and the remainder of the crew were taken*

> *prisoner. As soon as the enemy moved off Trooper Acaster started up his tank again and drove it back in the direction of our lines where he met other soldiers who helped him out and led him to a regimental aid post. Trooper Acaster was badly wounded in the face and his eyes were filled with blood, rendering him half blind, while the pain was intense. His courage and presence of mind was most conspicuous and his devotion to duty in thus saving his tank from capture under the most trying conditions sets an example that has rarely been equalled in the service.'*

Acaster received an 'immediate' award of the Distinguished Conduct Medal.

Some Victoria cross awards were posthumous. This is the grave of Captain Lionel E. Queripel (1920–1944), Royal Sussex and 10th Parachute Regiment. Queripel fell at Arnhem having shown repeated gallantry attacking a strongpoint and being wounded in both arms and the face. In a final act of courage he protected the withdrawal of his comrades with pistol and grenades. An image of the medal was inscribed on the gravestone of a recipient. (Author)

Originally of the Royal Norfolk Regiment, Lieutenant George A. Knowland was with No. 1 Commando when he died a hero's death fighting the Japanese:

> '*In Burma on 31st January, 1945, near Kangaw, Lieutenant Rowland was commanding the forward platoon of a troop positioned on the extreme north of a hill which was subjected*

to very heavy and repeated enemy attacks throughout the whole day. Before the first attack started, Lieutenant Knowland's platoon was heavily mortared and machine gunned, yet he moved about among his men keeping them alert and encouraging them, though under fire himself at the time. When the enemy, some 300 strong in all, made their first assault they concentrated all their efforts on his platoon of 24 men, but, in spite of the ferocity of the attack, he moved about from trench to trench, distributing ammunition, and firing his rifle and throwing grenades at the enemy, often from completely exposed positions.

Later, when the crew of one of his forward Bren guns had all been wounded, he sent back to Troop headquarters for another crew and ran forward to man the gun himself until they arrived. The enemy was less than ten yards from him in dead ground down the hill, so, in order to get a better field of fire, he stood on top of the trench, firing the light machine gun from his hip, and successfully keeping them at a distance until a Medical Orderly had dressed and evacuated the wounded men behind him. The new Bren team also became casualties on the way up, and Lieutenant Knowland continued to fire the gun until another team took over.

Later, when a fresh attack came in, he took over a 2-inch mortar and in spite of heavy fire and the closeness of the enemy; he stood up in the open to face them, firing the mortar from his hip and killing six of them with his first bomb. When all the bombs were expended he went back through heavy grenade, mortar and machine gun fire to get more, which he fired in the same way from the open in front of his platoon positions. When those bombs were finished, he went back to his own trench, and still standing up fired his rifle at them. Being hard-pressed and with enemy closing in on him from only ten yards away, he had no time to recharge his magazine. Snatching up the Tommy gun of a casualty, he sprayed the enemy and was mortally wounded stemming this assault, though not before he had killed and wounded many of the enemy.

Such was the inspiration of his magnificent heroism, that, though fourteen of the twenty-four of his platoon became casualties at an early stage, and six of his positions were overrun by the enemy, his men held on through twelve hours of fierce and continuous fighting until reinforcements arrived. If this northern end of the hill had fallen, the rest of the hill would have been endangered, the beach head dominated by the enemy, and other

The reverse of the Defence Medal, showing the oak tree and lions. (Author)

The obverse of the War Medal showing the head of King George VI. (Author)

units farther inland cut off from their source of supplies. As it was, the final successful counter attack was later launched from the vital ground which Lieutenant Knowland had taken such a gallant part in holding.'

Remarkably George Knowland had joined the Army only in 1941, as a private, and had been commissioned within a year. His sacrificial action was marked with the award of the Victoria Cross.

On the eve of war the key Army service and campaign medals were the General Service Medal and India General Service Medal, awarded for a number of relatively small campaigns around the world prior to September 1939. Yet the Second World War was so exceptional that an entirely new set of medals was introduced. These comprised of two rather conventional-looking general medals, and the very distinctive run of campaign 'stars' for service in various parts of the globe.[18]

The two general medals were the Defence and War medals. The cupronickel Defence Medal showed the uncrowned head of the King on the obverse, and on the reverse a design with a crown resting on the stump of an oak tree flanked by lions. It bore the dates '1939' and '1945' and the legend 'The Defence Medal'. Its ribbon was flame-coloured with green edges and thin black stripes. This somewhat gaudy arrangement denoted enemy attacks on England's green and pleasant land, whilst the black stood for the 'black out'. It could be awarded to a wide range of different people including not only personnel of the armed services and Home Guard, but Civil Defence, and persons serving in non-operational areas outside the UK. Anyone who had received a civil 'King's Commendation' was to mark this by wearing silver laurel leaves on the ribbon of the Defence Medal. The War Medal, also in cupronickel, bore the crowned head of the King, and on the reverse a lion standing in triumph on a two-headed dragon and the dates '1939' and '1945'. Its ribbon was a patriotic red, white and blue. The award went to armed forces personnel with twenty-eight days' service, operational and non-operational, or less if one was killed or wounded sooner. It also went to merchant seamen with similar time at sea. Any serviceman with a Mention in Despatches was to place a small oak leaf on the ribbon of the War medal. The Defence and War medals were both issued unnamed.

The six-pointed polished bronze stars designed by the Royal Mint engravers had a circlet in the middle at the centre of which was the Royal Cypher, and on which was marked in block capitals the title of the medal. Perhaps because so many were made, the relevant government committee decided that they too would not be issued named, but that individuals could add their own details to the reverse if they so wished. The ribbons for the campaign stars, said to have been designed by the King himself, arguably showed greater creativity than the medals which were identical apart from the lettering. These ribbons were a blaze of colour, and each had symbolic meaning. The 1939–1945 Star, awarded to Army personnel for six months' service in an operational command, or two months if this included an airborne operation, was suspended from a ribbon of dark blue, red and light blue. These stripes represented the Navy, Army and Air Force respectively. The ribbon first appeared in August 1943, long before the actual medal.

Fusilier F. Jefferson (1921–1982) 2nd Lancashire Fusiliers, standing in front of a German StuG III assault gun which he knocked out with his PIAT when his company was counterattacked at Monte Cassino, Italy, 16 May 1944. Jefferson was awarded the Victoria Cross. (Sgt Menzies/ IWM via Getty Images)

Rarely the Atlantic Star could be granted to Army personnel if they had qualifying service on, or over, the Atlantic. Its ribbon was dark blue, white and sea green. Similarly enough prior air service led to the award of the Air Crew Europe with its light blue, black and yellow ribbon representing continuous service night and day. By contrast the Africa Star was worn most by Army personnel. The qualification was simple: entry into North Africa on the establishment of an operational unit. For these purposes any country along the North African coast counted, as did Abyssinia, Somalia, Eritrea, Sudan and even Malta, though not West Africa. The pale buff ribbon of the Africa Star, with its broad stripe of red and thinner stripes of light and dark blue, represented the desert and the fighting services. The medal ribbon could also be mounted with any one of three different bars, '8th Army; '1st Army'; or 'North Africa 1942–43'. When only the ribbon was worn it was fitted with an emblem to symbolise the bars, an '8', a '1', or a small silver rose. Anyone who qualified for more than one bar or emblem was to show only the one to which he or she had first qualified.

The ribbon to the Pacific Star was dark green with red edges, a central yellow stripe, and thin stripes of dark and light blue. These colours represented the beaches and forests as well as the fighting services. The award was interesting in that whilst many Navy and RAF personnel obviously qualified, so did quite a few from the Army. The reason for this was that countries in the area invaded either by the enemy, or the Allies, also counted as 'Pacific'. So it was that those fighting in Malaya or China with the Army, up to 15 February 1942, were eligible. The major exception was Burma, which did not count, since there was also a Burma Star. The Burma Star ribbon was blue with a wide red stripe in the centre. Thin orange stripes also ran down the blue. The red symbolised the Commonwealth forces, and the orange the sun. Qualification was service in Burma between December 1941 and September 1945. Curiously one could never get both a Burma Star and a Pacific Star, instead a doubly entitled recipient wore the medal for which he qualified first, and a bar for the other. A small rose denoting this qualification could also be worn on the ribbon when the medal itself was not worn.

The Italy Star was particularly appropriate in that its ribbon was stripes of the red, white and green of the Italian flag. It was awarded not only for service in Italy but various islands, the Aegean, Greece and Yugoslavia. Similarly personnel entering Austria in the last days of the war were eligible. The France and Germany Star related to service in those countries, and indeed

anywhere in Europe, or the Channel, south of a line from the Firth of Forth, or east of the Bay of Biscay from D-Day to victory in Europe. One could therefore become eligible without setting foot in either country, though obviously the vast majority of British soldiers fighting in the final European campaigns did so. The ribbon of this star was red, white and blue, being by a happy coincidence not only the colours of the British flag, but also that of France and the Netherlands. One could not receive this medal as well as either the Atlantic or Air Crew Europe stars.

Other general conditions pertaining to the campaign stars included a requirement to complete qualification for the 1939–1945 Star before beginning to earn certain of the other awards; no more than one bar was to be awarded for any one star; and it was a rule that in general time served did not count towards more than one star at a time. With several of the awards a Mention in Despatches or Commendation could trigger an automatic granting of the relevant star, even if a time qualification was yet to be reached. Interestingly, time spent as a prisoner of war did count towards qualifying for the 1939–1945 Star, but only if this was already earned by the date of capture could time in captivity begin to account towards another award.

Campaign medals were mailed to their recipients in little buff cardboard boxes, with medals unmounted in translucent packets, and ribbons neatly folded rather than already attached to the award. For this reason the accompanying leaflet gave a full description of each ribbon, and the 'order of wearing'. This was the 1939–1945 Star; Atlantic; Air Crew Europe; Africa Star; Pacific Star; Burma Star; Italy Star; France and Germany Star; Defence Medal and finally War Medal. Given that the awarding of certain of the medals was mutually exclusive, the maximum number of campaign stars that it was possible to win was five, and to do this the recipient had to have served in both Europe and the Far East. Adding these to the two general medals took the total of campaign medals for any one soldier to possibly have to seven.

The Italy Star was awarded for the Italian campaign of 1943–1945. The medal was instituted at the end of the war in Europe, and included service in Sicily, and other areas of this theatre as well as the Italian mainland. The basic design of the Italy Star was similar to the other campaign stars. (Author)

CHAPTER FIVE
Small Arms and Infantry Support Weapons

Rifle and Bayonet

Historically the British Army prided itself on the standard of its 'musketry' – or use of shoulder arms. For much of its recent history this conceit was justified, for more often than not British troops shot more often, and more accurately, than their opponents. It may be claimed that at least occasionally this saved disastrous situations, when generalship, tactics, or other arms of service failed. The reasons for this area of success appear to have been several. Significantly, in a traditional professional Army soldiers stayed soldiers longer than in conscript armies, and were therefore likely to get more practice. By the second half of the nineteenth century, great store was put on marksmanship,

and there were distinctive badges, and often financial incentives, for soldiers to become good shots. There was little civilian gun control in the UK, and from 1859 – at the beginning of the Victorian volunteer movement   civilian rifle clubs formed the nucleus of what would become the 'Volunteer Battalions' of the regular regiments. Officers who hunted or shot were often prepared to lavish time on what they regarded as sport, even when other training was neglected. Moreover, the way that the British Army was deployed around the world meant that whilst it was very difficult to bring large bodies of troops together for full manoeuvres, 'personal training' and range practice was possible almost everywhere. Britain, as the first industrial nation, also had a long history of small arms, production, supported by an ability to export its wares. From the early nineteenth century

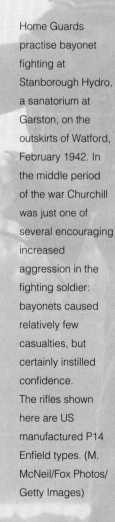

Home Guards practise bayonet fighting at Stanborough Hydro, a sanatorium at Garston, on the outskirts of Watford, February 1942. In the middle period of the war Churchill was just one of several encouraging increased aggression in the fighting soldier: bayonets caused relatively few casualties, but certainly instilled confidence. The rifles shown here are US manufactured P14 Enfield types. (M. McNeil/Fox Photos/ Getty Images)

An image from the official rifle manual showing how to load the SMLE under cover. (Author)

Far right: The long First World War vintage 'sword' bayonet used with the SMLE, and one of the models of 'spike' bayonet used with the No.4. (Author)

The SMLE was usually loaded from the top, but the ten-round box magazine was also detachable. (Author)

necessary. Lord Kitchener supported the firepower lobby with the observation that open movement against modern weapons might be impossible without darkness and the spade.

These home truths were reinforced by Major N.R. McMahon, Chief Instructor at the Hythe School of Musketry, at the General Staff Conference of 1910. His conviction that winning the firefight was crucial to winning the battle was backed by the historical argument that the long bow was less accurate than a crossbow, yet English archers with enough swift arrows had come to dominate the medieval battlefield. Though there was contrary argument that movement was key, good firepower was not incompatible with swift movement – if only that firepower came from a handy rifle in the hands of trained infantry. The new .303-inch Short Magazine Lee–Enfield, adopted in the aftershock of the South African experience,

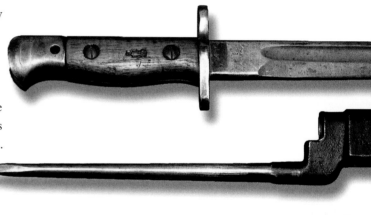

until 1900, a case can certainly be made that British military rifles were better than many round the world.

However, in the early twentieth century came worrying recognition that the British Army was in danger of falling behind in its firepower. Boer farmers with Mausers came close to defeating the British, and often inflicted heavy casualties with their long-range accuracy, fieldcraft, and sniping skills. Moreover, accuracy was only half of the story as any enemy that learned to fire two or three quick shots, in approximately the right direction, might overwhelm slow but accurate British troops outnumbered on colonial battlefields, or facing a larger conscript army. Worse still, there was the dawning realisation that machine guns were serious weapons of war, and the War Office was showing slowness in acquiring the numbers of automatic arms that experts believed

was just such an arm. It was a compromise, being a universal arm for infantry, cavalry, and just about everybody else: but for a bolt action – one that loaded one round at a time from its magazine by movement of a bolt – it was relatively swift and reliable. It had a ten-round box magazine under the action loaded using two five-round chargers, and a sufficiently short bolt pull that the firer did not have to take his eye from the target until his gun was empty. Its range and accuracy were also scarcely less than those of slightly slower, longer, and heavier Continental infantry arms. It was powerful enough to shoot through a brick at short distances, and to drop a man at a mile away – if he was unlucky enough to be struck at that range. So it was that 'rapid fire' and McMahon's 'mad minute' became features of training. 'Bursts' of fire and the shooting of '12 to 15 rounds per minute without serious loss of accuracy' became part of the rubric of the *Musketry*

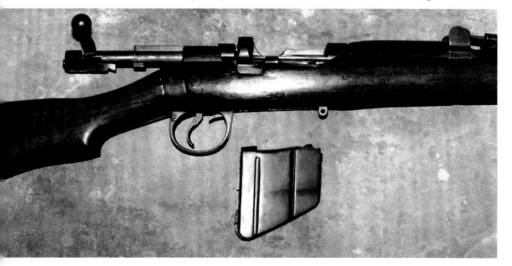

Regulations. The wisdom of this preparation was dramatically proven on the field on Mons in 1914.[1]

This was all most gratifying, but angst re-emerged after 1918, and with good reason. Now there were new fears that Britain was falling behind in the development of semi-automatic arms. In November 1926, the issue of a specification for a semi-automatic service rifle came to nothing, frustrated by lack of both funds and an entirely suitable candidate for the job. Whilst the USA went on to find a very satisfactory semi-automatic in the shape of the Garand rifle in the late 1930s, the British Army had to fall back on its substantial stocks of old SMLE Mark III rifles. Having been the mainstay of the First World War, this was now expected to do similar duty in another global conflict. Indeed, more SMLEs were now produced by Birmingham Small Arms at a unit cost of just over £6 apiece, whilst the government operation at Enfield Lock focused on parts manufacturing, repairing and assembly tasks. During the Second World War, the SMLE would be known officially as the 'No. 1', thus distinguishing it from other issue types.

Training was outlined by the manual *Rifle*, of 1937. This aimed to make the soldier 'a steady and accurate shot', 'a quick shot at targets appearing at short and indefinite intervals', and a 'handyman' with the rifle, able to 'fire bursts of 5 to 10 rounds at rapid rate'. It began in a thoroughly traditional manner with the 'naming of the parts' by the instructor, and the injunction that each man should be able to recognise his own piece, by 'peculiarities of colour and marking', if not by its serial numbers, which should match on weapon and bolt. The basics of mechanism, cocking, magazine, and trigger pressure were then explained. So ended lesson one. In lesson two the recruit got down to cleaning, using the 'pull through' and little brass bottle of oil kept in the butt trap of the SMLE. In the third lesson came loading, using chargers, pressing the rounds down with the thumb, and the identification of jams. Such stoppages were not common, but where they did occur were usually the result of damage to lips of the magazine, a faulty cartridge, or dirt. All of these the soldier could remedy, but a worn or broken part needed expert assistance. More cleaning, and what to do with the rifle if it came into contact with gas, formed lesson four, with officers and NCOs learning how to make competent inspections in lesson five.[2]

The science of aiming filled all the lessons from six to twelve, starting with pointing at a simple circular 'grouping target' fixed at 100 yards (91m), and working up in difficulty by stages. This naturally included accurate observation, setting the sights and adjustment for wind and distance, but also covered the greater complexities of 'aiming off' – that is aiming ahead of – moving targets, including infantry, cavalry and vehicles. Interestingly vehicles were taken to include tanks, since:

'Although .303-inch ammunition will not penetrate armour, fire against armoured vehicles causes the visors of turrets to be closed and hinders the crew. Further, a bullet hitting armour breaks up into small molten fragments which can enter slots and

crevices and may injure the crew. A chance bullet may enter a gun embrasure. Armoured vehicles will therefore be engaged by .303 fire and assistance thereby given to anti-tank weapons.'

Actual firing instruction filled lessons thirteen to twenty-two, with the object of teaching the soldier 'to handle his rifle so that in war correct action will be instinctive'. Despite the butt of the rifle being made in short, medium, and long sizes to accommodate tall and short men, left-handed soldiers were taught to shoot right-handed, and any inclination to use the left shoulder 'discouraged'. Four firing positions were taught. These were prone, in practice the normal firing position, especially useful 'for firing in the open or from low continuous cover such as a bank or fold in the ground, and from isolated cover'; kneeling, as when shooting over a low wall, or crops, or to improve line of sight; standing, to engage aircraft, fire over high cover, or take a 'snapshot' on the advance; and sitting. This last was useful when firing from a steep slope, or perhaps down or across a valley, but could also be used in instances where cover height precluded kneeling or lying. Once the basics had been learned, and aim checked by instructors or other pupils,

Troops undergoing tactical training. The soldier on the left is armed with the No. 4 rifle and has an extra bandolier of ammunition. The man on the right has a broad bladed 'Smatchet' on his belt, a weapon intended to intimidate in close combat. (Author)

the trainees moved on to the use of cover. Ideal cover permitted 'free use of weapons', gave a good field of fire, was bulletproof, inconspicuous, and easy to advance from. In taking cover for fire, troops were warned not to use 'precise drill movements', and instructors were told not to insist on 'exact similarity' from their students. Where possible it was better to fire around cover, and in such a way as to ensure that the legs were concealed as well as the main mass of the body and part of the head.

Under the heading of 'fire discipline', troops were taught to respond to the commands 'load', 'stop', 'unload', and 'fire', and set sights at given distances. Fire was to be delivered as slow, rapid, and 'snapshooting'. Rapid fire was defined as the 'maximum effort of the rifleman, and is only required for short but critical periods'. Whilst being delivered, the butt was kept into the shoulder, except during recharging of the magazine. Troops were gradually worked up to a general rate of ten rounds in forty seconds, though it was possible to go faster still. Some sources state that twenty-five rounds a minute was obtainable in extremis, and records even higher than this were in fact set. On courses such as those given to Commandos, from mid-

1940 special rapid fire methods were taught. For example, in the unofficial manual *All in Fighting* Captain P.N. Walbridge outlined a method in which the bolt and trigger were operated simultaneously, and with which he himself claimed to have achieved four rounds in five seconds. This was hardly typical, but fifteen rounds a minute from well-trained men certainly was, and had been routinely achieved since the First World War.[2]

The SMLE Mark III was fitted with the Model 1907 'sword' bayonet, a fearsome-looking implement with a 17-inch (43cm) blade. It had originally been designed with a view to giving the soldier sufficient 'reach' in bayonet fighting, all the more necessary, apparently, because the rifle itself was shorter than many of its contemporaries. Whilst the First World War had demonstrated that bayonets were unlikely to cause many casualties, they were carried throughout the Second World War; and, initially at least, were still regarded as significant. As the manual *Bayonet* of 1937 explained:

> 'The bayonet is the weapon of attack for hand to hand and night fighting; full effect will be gained only by the collective efforts

Men of the Territorial Kensington Regiment, which formed part of the Middlesex, with their SMLE rifles on the eve of war. Like the First World War vintage rifles the Kensingtons would be back in France. (Felix Man/Picture Post/Getty Images)

of platoons or sections. The use of the bayonet, or the threat of it, will often enable infantry to drive the enemy from his position or cause him to surrender. Under such conditions the use of the bullet must not be forgotten… In an infantry assault, the greatest moral effect will be attained by a steady advance in formation. But, once hand to hand fighting begins, it is unlikely that any regular formation can be maintained. Such conditions will often occur during the looser fighting when the enemy's foremost line of defended localities has been penetrated, in unexpected encounters by small bodies of men in woods or confined places, or at night.'

The real object of bayonet training was to instil confidence and to fit the soldier to play his part as one of a team. Never the less, it was recognised that as troops varied significantly in physique and ability they should be encouraged to develop their own bayonet fighting style, and words of command should be reduced to a minimum. However, once close combat had been joined it should be the 'instinctive action' of the man to either 'go straight for an opponent' or to 'parry an opponent's attack and then immediately to counter-attack'. Whilst moving with a fixed bayonet, troops were taught to adopt the 'high port' position, with point skywards, dropping the muzzle down to the 'on guard' stance once within about 20 yards (18m) of an opponent. The two basic strokes, both ideally to be actioned on the move, were the 'parry' – straightening the left arm vigourously and beating off the opponent's weapon, and the 'thrust' – making 'a point' and pushing with the body inclined forward, putting its weight behind the stroke. As the manual observed, 2 or 3 inches (5–7.5cm) penetration was adequate to be effective, and withdrawal was possible simply by drawing straight back. Where the blade was deeply wedged it could be achieved by slipping the left hand forwards, and placing the foot on a prostrate opponent before pulling out.[3]

These were the minimum requirements: but instructors were also encouraged to teach the 'butt stroke', swinging the rifle round horizontally to bring the butt into the opponent's chin – preferably with the weight of the body behind the stroke – and 'other methods of attack'. These other methods might be particularly needed if protagonists got so close that it was no longer possible to thrust with the bayonet. In such an eventuality the instructors were to 'suggest' strangling, punching,

Sniper training with the P14, officially dubbed the 'Rifle No. 3' in the Second World War. The P14 was arguably even more accurate than the SMLE, but had a five-round magazine. For these reasons sniping was its usual combat role. As was often the case two men act as a team here, one fires, the second (wearing a beret with the Norfolks cap badge and holding binoculars), acts as observer. (Official/ author)

kicking and kneeing. Perhaps fearing that orderly training might get out of hand, the manual specified that 'these measures will not be practised'. If anything the unofficial ninepenny Gale and Polden manual published after the outbreak of war was even more gung-ho. For according to this document, which appears to have been widely used by the Home Guard and anybody not given the official manual, bayonet fighting was all about killing, and that could only be achieved with fighting spirit; good direction; strength and quickness. Above all it was the 'fighting spirit' that gave the 'great moral superiority, which enables a dwarf to kill a giant'. Here the butt stroke became a furious flurry of blows, 'Swing the toe of the butt to your opponent's jaw while advancing the rear foot. If your opponent jumps back and you miss, then step in with the rear foot and bash the butt into his face… If he again jumps back, close up, and slash the bayonet across his face or neck'. The Gale and Polden manual also maintained that even when the bayonet fighter was without his weapon he could continue, fending off the opponent's bayonet with his left hand and then grabbing his rifle.[4]

However, the Second World War was not a war of 'steady advance' in formation, and bayonet charges by British units were almost vanishingly rare. Where some armies, notably the Japanese, persisted in using them outside the confines of jungle or the obscurity of night, they were usually spectacular failures.[5] Moreover, the whole tactical way rifles were used had to change radically: for now most sections had their own automatic weapon, and most soldiers of 1940 were

not the highly drilled professionals of August 1914. In 1938, *Infantry Section Leading* characterised the rifle as 'the personal protective weapon of the individual': in 1939 the new *Light Machine Gun* manual qualified this statement with the words that, 'the rifle may be needed, in an emergency, to augment the fire of the section, or for local protection'. By 1942 it was clear that the rifle was regarded essentially as an adjunct to the automatic weapon. As *Light Machine Gun* explained, 'The Bren LMG is the principle weapon of the infantry and every man will, therefore, be trained to use it… The rifle is the personal weapon of the individual. It will be needed to augment the fire of the LMG when required in an emergency, for local protection, and especially for "sniping" a single enemy.' A new edition of the *Rifle* manual also appeared in 1942. Though much of the content was familiar, it was clear that the tone had changed, and the nature of the business was made crystal clear with the insertion of the objective, 'maximum efficiency for killing the enemy'. There was less talk about the niceties of shooting at targets and more about the practicalities.

Whilst the SMLE was the main rifle in use early in the Second World War it was not the only one, for a plan had existed just before the First World War to replace the SMLE with a new rifle with a Mauser type action. By 1913 this was well advanced, and a rifle of a .276-inch calibre with a five-round integral magazine had not only been designed and built, but reached the stage of approval for issue on a trial basis. The outbreak of war in 1914 derailed this project entirely. To have rifles of different calibres would not have been sensible, so the plans for the new weapon were passed to the USA. Here the rifle was made in .303-inch calibre and supplied back to the UK as the 'Pattern 1914' or 'P14', and later in .30-inch calibre for the US Army as the 'Pattern 1917', 'P17' or 'US Enfield'. In British service the P14 served as a training rifle, but towards the end of the First World War was adopted as a sniper arm in which role its great accuracy was an advantage, but its small magazine no great handicap. Between the wars, the British P14 was stored away. In 1924 a major stocktaking revealed that there were approximately 1.5 million SMLEs on hand, in addition to three-quarters of a million P14s, plus smaller numbers of a few other types. In May 1926 an effort was therefore made to rationalise the situation, by renaming the various weapons into a logical sequence. The SMLE became officially known as the 'Rifle No. 1'; the .22-inch training rifle became the 'Rifle No. 2'; and the P14 became 'Rifle No. 3'.

Patrolling in the snow of the Italian hills. The two-man team includes an observer with an M1 Thompson of the type used later in the war, and a marksman with a No. 4 rifle. Both have snow shoes and white coats and gloves, and the rifleman wears goggles. (Author)

The outbreak of war, followed by the disaster of Dunkirk, made any and every rifle a candidate for immediate use. The 'Rifle No. 3' was of course used as a sniper rifle, whilst the American P17 was soon imported for the Home Guard. As this took a different cartridge to British-made arms, it was marked with a broad red band around the fore-end to warn the unwary. A new rifle, to be known, not entirely unexpectedly, as the 'No. 4', also made its appearance. Like the 'No. 3', this had started out as a replacement project for the old SMLE, and again the development of this rifle went back some years, with trials in 1930. However, the 'No. 4' was very much an old Lee-Enfield at heart, modified mainly with a view to simplification, replacing the old-fashioned bayonet and improving the sights. This weapon was approved on 15 November 1939, but the first wartime production rifles were not completed until 1941, with the 'No. 4' eventually being made in the USA and Canada as well as the UK. Apart from the differently shaped fore-end, the most obvious difference between the 'No. 1' and the 'No. 4' was the curiously shaped bayonet of the latter – so radically dissimilar in fact as to require some explanation. Various tests had shown that in reality the length of the bayonet made little difference, moreover the old 'sword' was heavy and affected aim if left attached. The new bayonet was an exercise in minimalism: it

had no handle, and was in essence nothing but a steel 'spike' – an 8-inch (20cm) stiletto blade – calculated to be the best thing to pass through clothing and the human body with least resistance and cost. It was useless for anything else, and unimpressive for ceremonial use or as a psychological prop for its user.

Though bayonets were of marginal use, and new machine guns and tactics tended to reduce the general combat importance of the British rifle, sniping continued to develop during the course of the war. In addition to the 'No. 3' Mark I (T) rifles, No. 4s were also fitted with telescopes. The methods of 1940 as summarised in the unofficial manual *Fieldcraft, Sniping and Intelligence* by Major Nevill Armstrong were a marginally updated compendium of knowledge from the First World War. Many of its diagrams, showing dummy heads to be raised from trenches, or sniping camouflage, and remarks on sniping in trench warfare, were actually lifted from the instructions of 1914–1918. A new official resume entitled *Notes on the Training of Snipers*, also appeared in 1940, and this was updated in 1941. The objective of sniper training was defined as being to 'assist in securing and maintaining the initiative across the whole battle front', and specifically:

'i. *To anticipate enemy movement by observation properly related to intelligence.*

ii. *To deny enemy intelligence by sniping his observers, harassing his patrols and forestalling his raids.*

iii. *To establish a complete moral and physical domination of no man's land if static war develops.'*[6]

Snipers were to be organised under the battalion intelligence officer, whose duty it was to report to the commanding officer on all matters of observation, sniping and intelligence. Each company in the battalion was to supply two snipers – one of whom was an NCO – to create the intelligence section, and companies were to be ready to supply more in the event of loss. For the individual sniper the primary object was 'to kill'. Apart from being an expert shot, he was expected to be trained in observation and fieldcraft; use and care of equipment such as telescopes, binoculars and sniper scopes; map reading and compass work; reporting; judging distances; camouflage and the use of hides. His craft was to be practised in all possible light conditions and at night. Interestingly snipers were expected to operate at ranges up to about 400 yards (366m) , beyond this sniping being 'rarely effective'. For as was explained, a man able to make a 3-inch (7.5cm) target group at 100 yards could expect a spread of shot of about 12 inches (30cm) at 400 yards (366m), and this would be insufficient to be sure of hitting a moving head, or loopholes and vision slits.

In open or semi-open warfare it was expected that snipers would work alone, but from fixed positions a two-man sniper and observer team would be the norm. Their services were particularly valuable in covering retreats and road blocks, blind spots not overlooked by other units, and in combating enemy snipers and discovering likely lairs amongst fallen trees, sunken roads, and other positions of cover. *Notes on the Training of Snipers* recommended use not only of camouflage and stealth but 'a home-made sniper suit'. This consisted of a smock and hood cut from rough hessian canvas, 'latrine canvas', sacking, or sandbags sewn together. The whole set was matt painted in standard camouflage colours to match the local environment, with gaps and irregularities in the paintwork to create disruptive effects. Two particular patterns were offered to suit 'hedge field and parkland', and 'rocks, stone, earth or sandbags'.

The importance of sniping in its broadest sense was perhaps underlined by the fact that the general manual *Rifle* of 1942 also contained sections on sniper rifles; the use of the telescopic sight; and the 'sniper sling', which provided a firm support in shooting. Following experiences in North Africa and Sicily, it was decided to have a sniper instructor with each battalion, and a sniper school was set up at Llanberis in North Wales in September 1943. A similar facility was established in the Middle East, and another with 21st Army Group near Coursalles in 1944, though this was later moved to Zon in the Netherlands. By the latter part of the war the degree to which a significant proportion of fire on the battlefield resembled sniping was recognised by the fact that each section in the infantry battalion was expected to have a man designated as a sniper or sharpshooter. Instructions at the end of the war saw the men of the battalion sniper section operating mainly in pairs, one with the sniper rifle, the other providing observation and close range cover with a sub-machine gun. Both were provided with Denison smocks; a few rounds of tracer ammunition as well as standard 'ball'; emergency rations and water; plus a telescope and pair of binoculars – the former being more powerful and steadier for long-distance observation, the latter quicker and with a wider field of view.[7]

By far the most common sniper arm was now the No. 4 (T). As Captain Clifford Shore explained:

Paratrooper of the First Airborne Task force stands watch over resting comrades in woodland with slung No. 4 MK I (T) sniper rifle. (Past Pix/SSPL/Getty Images)

> 'This sniper rifle, the standard sniping weapon of the British Army, was a selected No. 4 rifle of above average accuracy on factory test, fitted with two metal plates to take the telescopic sight – No. 32 TS – a cheek rest and special sling. The '32' telescopic sights were paired with rifles and not interchangeable. The focus could not be altered, and the power of the scope was

three [times]. The elevation drum mounted on top of the TS was graduated from 0 to 1000 yards and adjusted in 50 yard clicks in the case of the Mark I sight, and in one minute clicks with the Mark II and III. Lateral adjustment was obtained by turning the deflection drum situated on the left side of the scope. Provided careful maintenance was observed the TS could be removed from a sniper's rifle and afterwards replaced without alteration to the zero being greater than one minute of angle'.[8]

As of the middle period of the war, it was realised that not only was the old Enfield design falling behind the latest generation of military firearms in terms of technology, but also that it was not ideal for every battlefield circumstance. However, given the massive numbers of 'No. 1' and 'No. 4'

rifles now in use, the difficulties of changing from the existing .303-inch cartridge, and the daunting prospect of completely retraining the entire infantry arm, it was ultimately decided impractical to change the basic characteristics of the service rifle. So it was that despite some experimentation with radical new designs the Short Magazine Lee–Enfield and its No. 4 reworking remained for the duration. However, this did not prevent the introduction of one further version. For in the jungles of South East Asia specific complaints were being raised that could be addressed without altering the basics of the bolt action mechanism or the cartridge.

The factors that were different about combat in forests and other very close terrain were the normally limited range of

Men of 5th (Scottish) Parachute Battalion in Athens fighting the communist resistance movement, December 1944. The soldier foreground is using the M1A1 variant of the US .30 calibre carbine with folding stock for airborne use. The basic M1 was also used by the British Army, particularly in the Far East. (Lt Morris/IWM via Getty Images)

engagement; the need for the soldier to carry all his arms and ammunition and supplies without resorting to engined transport; and the cramped conditions that made carrying anything long or clumsy doubly difficult. Specifically it was contended that the standard service rifle was really too heavy to be carried for long periods at full alertness, and so long, particularly with bayonet attached, that it tended to catch in vegetation and was difficult to point and shoot quickly when trees were apt to get in the way. Conversely, the fact that fields of view were very short and targets not usually fired upon outside close ranges made the ability of the Enfield to engage at upwards of a thousand yards an attribute of limited utility. Jungle patrols and later the experiences of the Chindits behind enemy lines would underline the point that, in this theatre of war, short-range but powerful weapons were the ideal.

So it was that along with the extensive use of sub-machine guns, and sometimes even shotguns, there were odd ad hoc attempts to reduce the weight, and even the length, of the service rifle. Such potentially dangerous unauthorised tinkering was unacceptable, but the idea itself was formally taken on board in June 1943 when a proposal for a lighter rifle was forwarded to the Infantry Weapons Development Committee. Shortly afterwards some shortened No. 4 rifles with sporting type half-stocked fore-ends were tested on the range at Bisley. Initial results were disappointing as the original designers of the Lee–Enfield had been careful to match the length of the barrel and weight of the arm to the power of the round. The lightened rifles bucked and kicked horribly, whilst short barrels failed to conceal in any way the great gout of flame accompanying the ignition of a powerful cartridge. However, the designers refused to be defeated. A small batch of 'No. 4 Lightened Rifles' was ordered and completed by September 1943, these being fitted with a simple 'flash eliminator' at the end of the barrel. This by no means eliminated all the unpleasant characteristics, but lightness and shortness were achieved after a fashion, and loss of muzzle velocity was only marginal. Another order for 1,000 weapons was placed. A revised design received official approval in March 1944, and in the meantime a much bigger order was placed with the Fazakerley factory.

In its final production form the new weapon became the 'No. 5' rifle, popularly known as the 'Jungle Carbine'. Its barrel was 20.5 inches (52cm) long against the 25.2 inches (64cm) of the No. 4, and its weight a little over 7lbs (3.8kg), a saving of nearly 2lbs (907g) over the full-length piece. In addition to the provision of a flash eliminator, the butt was fitted with a rubber pad as a sop against the mighty kick. The sights were similar to those on the No. 4, but could only be set at up to 800 yards (732m), against the hitherto normal 1,400 yards (1,280m). A new knife type bayonet with a blade of just 8 inches, (20cm) mounted on a short bar, replaced the full-length sword bayonet on the No. 5. The opinion of the troops varied. Those who simply had to carry it were much impressed by its light and handy configuration, and there were even suggestions that it should eventually replace the No. 4. Those who had to fire it were less convinced, complaining that it was less accurate and led to bruising of the firer. Though large numbers of No. 5 rifles were made, their use never became universal, even in the Far East where the No. 1 and No. 4 were still to be seen in widespread use.

The Enfield family of rifles, supplemented by the P14 and P17, accounted for the vast majority of long shoulder arms used by the British Army during the war. However, there were a few other more specialised pieces that saw some service. The US Garand M1 rifle first introduced in the mid-1930s became general issue for American front-line combat infantry, and was the first semi-automatic to be used so. It was speedy in operation, yet retained the power and range associated with the previous generation of bolt actions. In the British Army it was much admired by aficionados, a few of whom managed to acquire one unofficially in combat zones shared with US troops. The usefulness of the Garand was also appreciated in official circles, but any large-scale adoption was discouraged by the fact that the US Army itself needed massive numbers, and in its current form the weapon used a different cartridge. However, Garands were issued to British personnel in at least a few instances, notably to some Commandos fighting in the Far East at the end of the war.

Another American small arm, used on a somewhat larger scale, was the M1 Carbine. Interestingly, the carbine had never been conceived as a front-line combat arm, but as a handy weapon for specialist troops – drivers, cooks, heavy weapons teams and the like. In such a role it would replace pistols and other weapons with something quick, light, and handy, but requiring no great range, power, or exhaustive training on the part of the user. What the winning designers at Winchester came up with at the end of 1940 more than fulfilled the brief, for the M1 was a gas-operated semi-automatic, weighing just 5lb (227g) and loading from a fifteen-round box magazine. Anybody who could shoot a rifle could fire the M1, and many preferred to as it was so light. It could fire very swiftly – and the ammunition was easy to carry. Indeed, the most controversial part was the short .30 cartridge, which made accurate fire tricky at anything more than a couple of hundred yards, by which time it was running out of stopping power. However, this was not the point, as users of the M1 were not intended to be long-range sharpshooters. Moreover, speed of operation at close range was exactly what was required in such close terrain as jungle. The British Army was fortunate that US factories turned out more than six million of the little carbines, and so some of these were made available, notably to Chindit patrols in Burma.[9]

One interesting shoulder arm that only ever saw action on a micro scale was the unusual De Lisle Carbine. This curiosity looked like a short, fat Enfield rifle, and the bolt action mechanism was indeed of the Lee type, drawn from the SMLE. There all similarity ended, for the broad girth of the de Lisle fore-end hid a very effective sound moderator, and the barrel and magazine were of .45 calibre, to accommodate the same rounds used by the Colt Model 1911 semi-automatic pistol. The meaning of this strange configuration was simple, for the .45 ACP round was of subsonic velocity, yet, due to its weight and calibre, very effective. This enabled the de Lisle to be almost silent, but useful up to a couple of hundred yards, just the characteristics required by clandestine forces.

The Sub-Machine Gun – 'SMG'

The sub-machine gun, a handy short automatic weapon firing a pistol type cartridge, and light enough for one man to carry and fire on the move, was invented in the First World War. Though powerful at close range and excellent for use in confined spaces, such as trenches and built-up areas, it was not effective over longer ranges. Since then many new models were developed by a number of nations – notably the Americans, Germans, and Italians, but also the Austrians, Czechs, Hungarians and Finns. A number of different models were tested in the UK despite sneers about them being 'gangster' weapons. The Birmingham Small Arms Company (BSA) investigated the manufacture of the Thompson in Britain, most notably in 1938, and were even instrumental in efforts to get a Hungarian type made under license in early 1939, but failed to get any orders. So it was, shamefully, that the British Army went to war without an 'SMG' of any description.

Any illusions that they were dispensable were quickly shattered. Early preparation for a conflict that might include trench warfare in the West, and did eventually feature street fighting in Calais, evacuation from Dunkirk, and the sudden need for arms of all and any description, quickly produced panic demand for a sub-machine gun that would be available in the shortest possible time. There appeared to be three possible routes to a rapid solution: copying something with a proven track record; importation; and an entirely new design that would be as easy as possible to manufacture at low cost. In the event

British infantry with the 1928 type Thompson with drum magazine. Initial orders for the British Army specified 474,100 drum magazines, 870,040 box magazines, and millions of rounds of ammunition. (Fox Photos/Getty Images)

all three options were followed, and sooner or later all three bore fruit to a greater or lesser extent. Importation sounded quickest and easiest, but with much of Europe occupied, and sea lanes under threat, this was easier said than done. Never the less, 100,000 Thompsons were ordered from the USA in early 1940, and the first arrived by the summer of 1940, a few being on active service with the Commandos by the end of June: many more would follow. The belated effort to copy the German MP 28 Bergmann design led to the production of the Lanchester model adopted by the Navy in 1941. The new design direction led to the bizarre and downright ugly Sten gun – which proved easy to produce, and was eventually made everywhere from BSA to the workshops of toy manufacturers.

The ideal role for the sub-machine gun: winkling the enemy from confined spaces. The 'SMG' was originally conceived as a trench sweeper, but eventually every British infantry section, and quite a few others, were to have one. (Author)

The Thompson was named after General John T. Thompson, design director of the Auto-Ordnance Corporation. This had been founded as early as 1916, and had experimented with sub-machine gun ideas during the latter part of the First World War, though it was 1919 before successful working prototypes of the Thompson appeared, and 1921 before production commenced. In 1927 some went to the US Marines, the 1928 model being later adopted by the US Army. However, numbers with the

military remained quite small until the later 1930s. In many ways the .45-inch calibre 'Tommy gun' was a Rolls-Royce amongst sub-machine guns, solidly well made, properly finished, powerful, reliable, but extremely heavy and expensive. Even unloaded it weighed just under 11lb (5kg) against the less than 9lb (4kg) of the SMLE rifle. Its price was almost £50 ($225) – when a grenade could be had for a few shillings, and a decent house cost only £250 ($1,125).

The 1928 Model Thompson, the first type to find its way to the British Army, was capable of being fitted with a range of magazines, eighteen-, twenty-, or thirty-round box magazines, or fifty or one hundred drums. The official British manual *Thompson Submachine Gun* of 3 July 1940 refers to two types of magazine then in service, the fifty-round drum, and the twenty-round box. Fifty-round drums were supplied early on, looked very impressive, and needed changing less often – but were costly to produce, added weight, and rattled on the move. The drum also required some effort to load: first the winding key and cover had to be removed, then the rounds were put in one at a time in an anti-clockwise spiral working from the outer edge, bullets pointing upward. The cover was then replaced and the key inserted, being used to tension the mechanism by a set number of 'clicks'. This performance made the various types of box magazine the more practical option. These had adequate capacity, yet were relatively easy to load and carry. To fill one, you simply pushed rounds into them one at a time from the top, pressing firmly downwards and backwards, and provided they were not overloaded, and the cartridges were kept clean, there were few problems.[10]

The cyclic rate of fire from the Thompson was a rapid 800 rounds per minute, so the user was advised to use very short bursts, or the single round option setting. In theory the rate might have been even higher still, the manufacturers claiming that optimum speed was achieved by the 'John B. Blish' system of the mechanism using an 'H'-shaped component and friction – though the effect in practice was probably minimal and the idea would later be dispensed with. Surprisingly, the recoil of the Thompson was quite modest, the British manual actually stating there was 'no shock' whatever, though the firer had to make sure that the gun continued to be pointed at the target and exert downward pressure as the muzzle would 'climb' during bursts. This controllability was perhaps the one useful aspect of the heavy weight, lighter arms being much more prone to heavier kick and reduced accuracy. For a firearm of the period the muzzle velocity of discharge was actually relatively low at 909 feet (277m) per second, making the flight of the bullets slightly subsonic: but this did not detract from the effect, a rapid succession of soft-nosed rounds .45 inches in diameter, imparting what the manual rightly described as very great 'moral effect' as well as physical impact. There was a very optimistic aperture leaf back sight on the early gun, graduated to 600 yards (549m), the battle sight – set to a permanent 50 yards (45.8m) – being a much more practical position. In most circumstances the battle sight was used, with the firer aiming slightly high at anything over 100 yards (91m), and slightly low at close targets.

Trainees were taught to fire the Thompson from two basic positions, shoulder – much like the rifle – or from the waist. This was much less accurate and useless for anything but close range, but could be done on the move, or quickly in case of surprise. The waist firing position was described thus:

> '*The left foot is advanced with the knee bent, the weight of the body being balanced on the left leg, rear leg braced. The right hand is on the pistol grip with the forefinger on the trigger, the left hand on the foregrip. Muzzle directed towards the target and slightly below the horizontal. The whole attitude must be one of aggression and determination.*'

One useful trick in the shoulder position in order to achieve rapid aim at near targets was to align roughly the cut-out in the cocking handle and the foresight, squeezing the trigger immediately. In this way sudden targets of opportunity were less likely to be missed. However, the 1940 manual considered bursts as essentially an 'emergency' measure, single shots – repeated as necessary – being the norm.

Even the highly finished Thompson with its wooden stock and quality engineering was gradually forced to give ground to the demands of mass production. In 1942 a number of simplifications were imposed producing the M1, and M1A1, models. A slightly heavier bolt made any fancy delay system obsolete, the bolt handle was moved to a more convenient position on the right hand side, and the drum magazines were dropped with twenty- and thirty-round boxes becoming standard. About 500,000 Thompsons were eventually ordered from the USA, of which the largest portion went to the Army and Home Guard, though some were also used by Empire and Dominion forces, RAF, and Special Operations.

Though the Thompson fulfilled a vital role at a moment of crisis, it was never a complete solution to the need for a mass issue sub-machine gun. For apart from being expensive it was heavy, an unnecessarily elaborate design now twenty years old, produced overseas, and using a cartridge not readily compatible with anything else to be found in Europe. So it was that the search for a truly British SMG continued in parallel with orders from the US. The Lanchester, which we have observed was basically a copy of a German design, was developed during the later part of 1940 and put through acceptance trials in November. However, just as production was about to commence, a new possibility was put forward by Major R.V. Shepherd and H.J. Turpin of the Chief Superintendent of Design's department.

At first known by the unprepossessing acronym 'N.O.T. 40/1', this weapon bore every resemblance to a piece of cheap plumbing equipment, and unusually the magazine struck straight out on the left-hand side. It was accurately described, even in a highly plauditary contemporary publication, as 'an ugly brute'. Never the less, during extensive testing at Enfield in January 1941 it succeeded in firing 5,400 rounds without breakage or malfunction and was declared 'fundamentally sound'. It was soon christened 'Sten' gun – by dint of the makers' initials joined with the first two letters of Enfield. The first major order of 100,000 guns was placed with Singer Manufacturing in March 1941. The

Winston's finest hour: with 'his' Army, making a point about trenchant resistance for the camera whilst raising morale. Here he inspects a Thompson SMG during a visit to coastal defences in the North East of England. Interestingly the soldier's equipment includes a rifle bayonet, suggesting that the Tommy gun is probably not his usual arm. (Popperfoto/Getty Images)

Sten Mark I featured a large flash hider and a folding wooden fore grip like a short piece of broom handle: but both these refinements were quickly discarded on the Mark I*. By the latter part of the year the Mark II was in production with major orders in hand at BSA and the Fazakerley ordnance plant. With production lines set up, and orders for parts farmed out to sub contractors, the price dropped to less than £3 per gun – meaning that approximately fifteen could be had for the price of each Thompson. Many firms were brought in to help, both large and small, many of whom had not been in armaments before. These included concerns as diverse as Tri-ang, the toy makers; British Vacuum Cleaners; Flexa Lawn Mowers; Philco Radio; and Oxo Limited.

Gurkha Havildar (Sergeant) Kul Bahadur Gurung, 23rd Indian Division, holding the Mark II Sten gun. (Popperfoto/Getty Images)

As the volume *British War Production* explained:

'The Sten consists of only 51 parts in all, and most of these parts could be made in any factory in Britain. In two or three factories it was produced "on the line". There were not enough factories of that kind, however, and any factory that could do even one operation on one component of the gun was brought into a production scheme. In London there were scores of such factories, ranging from garages employing 20 people to one production unit established in a disused chicken-house where three people were employed. The "belt" between these tiny production units was a truck which made a daily tour of all of them. It set out with a load of raw material, left it at the first factory, picked up the components that had been completed there, took them on to the next workshop where another operation was performed, collected the previous day's work from there, and so on all round greater London.'

The Mark II was in many ways the quintessential Sten, a weapon of extreme simplicity of manufacture and crude lines. Production of this model alone would exceed two million. The Mark II weighed under 7lb (3.18kg) and was of all metal construction. The key elements were a simple trigger mechanism with a change lever allowing single or automatic fire; the barrel; breech block and return spring; and the 32-round magazine. The cartridge used was a 9mm, a common type in European pistols and sub-machine guns, allowing a measure of interchangeability, though results varied with different production. The stock of the Mark II was a basic tubular strut with a shoulder piece at the end, or a tubular skeleton. One interesting feature of this model was the magazine housing which was capable of being swung through 90 degrees on pressing a catch, so allowing the gun to be stored flat whilst the breech was closed against dirt.

Technically the Sten was a 'blow back' weapon, meaning that it needed no complex locking mechanism or gas-trapping devices, but relied on the power of the cartridge, weight of the breech block, and the action of the return spring to create a balanced system that continued to fire as long as the trigger was depressed in the automatic mode. The first shot blew back the block, ejecting the spent cartridge on one stroke, and chambering another as it was pushed back by the return spring. The 'striker' to hit and ignite the cartridge was simply part of the block, not a separate component. The cyclic rate of fire was about 550 rounds per minute, but firing was practically limited by the need to change magazines, and the desirability of using very short bursts which were more accurate and less prone to malfunction than continuous spray. Despite this, about

100 rounds in a minute was possible from a trained man in an emergency, and half this presented no difficulty. Moreover, the few parts and simplicity of construction meant that the Sten could be field stripped quickly even by a comparative novice. All this made the gun highly practical for mass issue, and suitable to air drop to partisans in the field. The main drawbacks were really only two: the weapon could go off accidentally if loaded and dropped on a hard surface, and there were some stoppages due to feed problems, particularly if the magazine suffered much rough handling. Compared to the Thompson the Sten was light, but this was both an advantage and disadvantage according to circumstance. Its lightness made it easy to carry, but lack of weight also entailed lack of accuracy: whether this mattered significantly with short-range bursts is open to debate. Sten magazines could be loaded manually, but unless the soldier had iron fingers this was 'a very slow process' and much easier to accomplish with the aid of a loading tool.

After the Mark II came the Mark III, which had a sheet steel exterior forming the barrel jacket with a central top rib that provided both strength and a rough yardstick for aim during hurried shooting. The Mark IV was a prototype parachutist's model, and the Mark V produced from the beginning of 1944 was a comparatively luxurious version that included a wooden stock and one, or two, pistol grips. The Mark V, which saw service with the Airborne and others, was also fitted to take a 'spike' bayonet. The Mark II(S) and Mark VI were both 'sound moderated' versions with screw fit silencers produced in relatively small numbers. Final production of all Sten models exceeded four million, the vast majority in the UK and some in Canada, and roughly ten magazines were made for every gun. Carrying magazines in any numbers in action was originally something of a problem as they did not fit the 'basic pouch' of the webbing. However, this was partly solved by field modifications, and later addressed by an official lengthening of new pouches. A 'Bandoleer, Magazine, Sten' was also introduced which had seven magazine pockets and could be worn slung around the body, giving the soldier ready access to over 200 rounds. This saw most widespread use with Airborne units.

The Sten was eventually covered in a multitude of different manuals and instructions in a variety of languages. The most significant included a simple folded sheet aimed at the Home Guard, privately produced and sold at 25 shillings for 100, 'postage paid' to anywhere in the UK, and a relatively finely printed Gale and Polden booklet costing 1s 6d, but including a colour cover

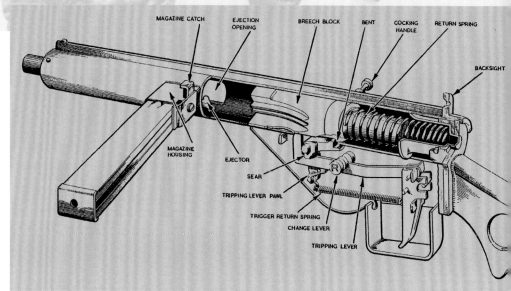

and photographs of different models and weapons instruction. However, the official Army manuals were those in the 'Small Arms Training' series, one in 1942 being entirely devoted to the Sten, and followed up with various amendments, another in 1944 superseding all the previous publications, but also including the Thompson. Interestingly the official literature usually speaks of the Sten and Thompsons as 'machine carbines' – the original English form of description of this class of weapon.[11]

According to the 1942 instructions, the entire teaching of the Sten gun could be achieved in a single period, though more was required to 'permit of sufficient practice to obtain proficiency'. Sensibly the lessons began with safety precautions, and a guide to identifying the Mks I to III of the Sten family, followed by the brief explanation:

> 'The machine carbine is a short-range weapon introduced for the purpose of engaging targets from 10 to 100 yards. At greater distances the speed of the bullet is so reduced that it has lost much of its penetrative power. The weapon is especially useful when on patrol or for fighting in close country such as woods or villages. Under these conditions the enemy may appear at close ranges and from different directions, and by firing from the waist such targets can be instantly engaged. Where time permits the weapon will always be fired from the shoulder. It is an automatic weapon, operated by the recoil of the spent case acting on the face of the breech block. The carbine will fire bursts or single shots, and it will fire most makes of 9mm ammunition, including the German and Italian.'[12]

Loading and unloading instruction was followed by holding and firing, the value of a correct grip being only really possible to demonstrate by means of firing. At the waist position the left foot was 'advanced with the knee bent', and the right hand was on the butt with the forefinger ready to squeeze the trigger.

Manual diagram of the mechanism of the Mark III Sten. Compared to many firearms there were few parts, and operation was simple. The most obviously different feature of the Mark III was the prominent top rib, intended to bestow strength without additional weight. Orders for the Mark III commenced in 1942 with Lines Brothers being the main contractors. Eventually about 876,000 of this model were made. (Author)

Importantly the left arm passed under the Sten so that the hand was on the barrel locking nut, and the left wrist was under the magazine: fingers were kept clear of the ejection port to avoid trapping them or impeding the flow of empty cartridges once firing commenced. The right arm helped to hold the gun into the firer's side. In the shoulder position the stance was similar, but the right elbow was raised with the shoulder into the butt for sighting along the barrel. In either instance grabbing the magazine – or using it as a handle – was not recommended as this was an easy way to interrupt, or actually damage, the feed, causing stoppages. For ranges under 25 yards (23m) firing the weapon from the waist by 'sense of direction' was deemed satisfactory; for anything over this, time permitting, aim was to be taken using the battle sight.

When the Sten ceased firing there were just three possibilities for action. If the working parts had stopped forward this was a signal the magazine was empty – the soldier was to change it, cock the weapon by pulling the bolt back, and continue firing. If the gun stopped in another position the firer re-cocked the weapon and examined the ejection port, anything there being 'vigorously' shaken out. If this failed, or a live round remained in the chamber, the magazine was taken off, any spent cases shaken free, the round fired, and the half-fired magazine, or a fresh one, put on. Out of action the gun could be easily stripped and cleaned. Pressing in the stud on the end of the recoil spring released the tension that effectively held the Sten locked together, and the butt could then be slid off. The cap or ring

around the stud was turned and the cap, spring and housing freed. With the major parts separated the bore was cleaned with pull through and flannelette, 'in the manner taught for the rifle', and the inside of the body, ejector and breech clock were cleaned and oiled. Magazines were wiped with an oily rag and checked to make sure that they had suffered no damage and fitted neatly into the housing. This was pretty much all the soldier was expected to do: the Sten was not entirely idiot proof but was certainly an uncomplicated and quick weapon to deal with compared to almost anything else.

The 1944 official Sten instructions added very little to those of 1942, considering how many guns of several different models had been taken into service in the meantime. Never the less, they did contain several useful photographs, and a note on how to carry the gun, slung over the shoulder, 'at the trail, like the rifle', or in front of the body with the sling around the neck. When the enemy was likely to be encountered, the Sten was brought to point forwards in the 'ready' position. The shoulder firing position was now also divided into two: the aimed version using the sights, and the swift pointing method aligning the barrel on the enemy without use of sights. Interestingly, though not mentioned in either of the official instruction manuals, the Sten was also practical to use prone, as its side magazine did not snag against the ground. Final production of the Sten ran to over four million units, of which a significant portion went to the British Army, but some went to Empire forces and Allies, and over a million were dropped by the Special Operations Executive to resistance organisations in Europe.[13]

The Light Machine Gun – 'LMG'

The widespread introduction of automatic rifles and light machine guns at platoon, and even section, level for the first time during the First World War helped to revolutionise infantry combat. By the latter part of the conflict even very small infantry units had their own machine weapon able to provide local light support, making meaningful 'fire and movement' fully practicable at the lowest tactical levels. One of the guns with which the British Army entered the Second World War was a weapon it used to great effect in the First – the Lewis gun.[14]

The original Lewis gun was designed by Americans, Colonel Isaac Lewis improving on the ideas of Samuel Maclean to come up with a weapon originally intended to be mounted on a tripod much like any other machine gun. However, the Lewis featured three attributes that would soon free it from the tyranny of a fixed mounting. It was air cooled, so needed no water jacket or pipes; it had a drum magazine, and therefore required no belts; and finally it was at least marginally lighter than traditional machine guns so it was possible to be carried by one man. In the standard unmodified Mark 1 infantry model, as formally introduced to the British Army in 1915, it was just over 50 inches (127cm) in length; weighed 26lb (11.8kg); and had a removable top-mounted 47-round magazine. Its outline was distinctive, with a thick cylindrical barrel jacket enclosing cooling fins and the flat-looking ammunition pannier above. The cyclic rate of fire was 550 rounds per minute, though the actual maximum practical was limited by the need to change drums, and to avoid overheating. Taking these factors, and the need to maintain aim, into account it was suggested that 'an average of 150 rounds per minute' could be maintained by a trained gunner. However, at least one source defined a slower, more careful, 'normal' rate of fire as five bursts (or about twenty-five rounds) per minute. The Lewis was reasonably accurate to a decent range, and for training purposes it was assumed that all trainees should initially be able to get all rounds of a burst within a 16-inch (40cm) diameter grouping at 100 yards (91m), before proceeding to longer range firing. Nor did it have a particularly heavy recoil. During the First World War, and some years afterwards, the Lewis was widely regarded as one of the best 'light automatics'. Indeed, when it first appeared it was both feared and envied by the enemy.

Home Guards with an American made 1918 model Lewis gun mounted for anti-aircraft fire. Unlike the basic British infantry weapon this piece has no cooling fin assembly around the barrel and is fitted with a 'spade' grip. The gunner wears a Middlesex Regiment cap badge. (Official/author)

As was remarked in *Small Arms Training*, 1931:

'The chief characteristic of this weapon is its power of delivering heavy bursts of fire with the employment of few men. Its effective range is the same as the rifle… It is a shoulder controlled weapon, air cooled and capable of a high rate of fire. To avoid overheating, strain, excessive expenditure of ammunition and, at the same time, to produce the necessary volume of fire, it is best to fire in bursts of four or five rounds. The accuracy of the gun permits of only a small margin of error in aiming, range estimation, or allowance for the effect of atmospheric conditions. Accurate observation of fire is therefore, essential; if less than four or five rounds are fired in a burst, observation will be possible only under the most favourable circumstances.'[15]

On the down side it was not without reason that trainers demanded that Lewis gunners develop 'mechanical aptitude'. For the Lewis gun was prone to an interesting range of stoppages that required the firer to be something of a mechanic as well as a soldier. The 1931 manual listed eight of the most obvious, which the 1939 edition expanded to ten – without counting running out of ammunition. Causes included damaged magazines; faulty extraction; poor feeding; broken striker, return spring, or extractor; and various types of wear. Thus it was that whilst the Lewis was quite light and reliable by the standards of 1915, the same could not really be claimed twenty years later. Never the less, the fact that many Lewis guns had been manufactured during the First World War, and the huge demand for machine weapons, meant that it was still quite widely seen during the Second World War, though not usually with front-line infantry.

In fact a number of slightly differing Lewis guns were used after 1939. In addition to the basic Mark 1 type these included the Mark 2; Mark 2★; the .300 'Savage Lewis'; and a lightened version of the Mark 1. The Mark 2 and Mark 2★ weapons were models originally intended for use on aircraft, but also seen on other vehicles and mountings, and were usually distinguishable by their more slender barrel arrangement and 97-round drum. The lightened Mark 1 Model lacked the cooling fin arrangement and had a wooden fore-end. The 'Savage Lewis' was made in the USA by Savage Arms, and was a simplified version of the original in the standard .300 US calibre. As supplied to the Home Guard they were fitted with either a wooden or a metal skeleton butt, and 'battle sights' set to a standard 400 yards (366m). The omission of more complex sighting arrangements mattered little in practice, and the different calibre was highlighted by a broad red band around the body in front of the magazine post.[16]

The reappearance of the Lewis gun in its various guises was accompanied by a rash of new manuals. These included the official *Small Arms Training* pamphlet number 20, *.303-inch Lewis Machine Gun*, that appeared on 6 December 1940 but gained wider circulation in 1941, and several unofficial or semi-official publications. The new official manual briefly repeated much that had already been said in 1931, but there were significant addenda. For example, the 'effective range' was now stated to be 1,000 yards (914m) and the maximum rate for accurate fire was set at 120 rounds per minute. The new publication also did its best to convey a sense of urgency: 'practice should be arranged in such a way as to ensure that no time is wasted. This can be done by each individual carrying out a cycle of action which leaves the gun ready for the next man. Those not actually handling the gun will be constantly questioned so that interest may be maintained.'[17]

The popular Gale and Polen instruction *The Complete Lewis Gunner* of 1941 was also largely a recycling of existing information, though in this instance the main source material was the publisher's own Lewis manual of 1918. Its tone was essentially upbeat and laudatory, stressing that the Lewis was worth fifty riflemen: it was a 'trump card' that could be operated like 'a submarine'. 'It does its work best by popping up when and where it is least expected and delivering a smashing blow in a trice. Before the enemy has time to recover from its surprise it escapes, by reason of its mobility and invisibility, to some other spot, from which it can repeat the dose.' A one-page addition pointed out the differences between the US .300 Lewis and the British model. Jacklin and Whipp's *Know Your Weapons: The .303 Lewis Gun* was also a commercial manual covering much the same ground, but more succinctly and, at one shilling, half the price of the Gale and Polden instruction. Perhaps most interesting of the private purchase manuals was Company Sergeant Major Bodman's *.300 Lewis Machine Gun for the Home Guard*. This was timely, being published in 1940, and had run to five editions by March 1942. It was particularly useful as one of the few attempts to specifically tackle the American-model Lewis.[18]

Though the Lewis had been a remarkable weapon in its youth, and was still a worthwhile stopgap, particularly for the Home Guard, its Second World War encore was entirely overshadowed by a newer and much better gun. This now famous 'LMG' was the Bren gun. By the beginning of the 1930s it had been noted that the Lewis was gradually being outclassed by a new generation of light support weapons, and, despite shortages of funds, it was appreciated that no modern army could expect to be successful without an efficient light machine weapon. So, thankfully, whilst much was left undone, time and trouble was devoted to this issue. Interestingly, British theorists were happy to accept that when it came to infantry combat, 'light' took precedence over 'machine' when it came to usefulness, and aimed for a weapon with easy to carry self-contained box magazines rather than the greater capacity of belts. It was certainly true that the German MG 34 was much better for sustained fire, and was also a genuine 'general purpose' weapon – but the Bren scored well in terms of getting from point to point rapidly, and in the conservation of ammunition. Perhaps more importantly it was popular with the troops, rugged, accurate, and durable. It became the tactical lynchpin of the section, and it is arguable that without it, British infantry would have been lost against the weaponry of the Germans.

Like many weapons, the Bren did not appear immaculate from the ether but descended from a distinguished lineage. A promising class of light machine guns was identified in the shape of the Czech 'ZB' family of arms, and these were thoroughly tested. The results were encouraging and so it was decided that a British version of the ZB-30 should be made at Enfield to accommodate existing .303-inch ammunition. The modifications required from the Czech original included reducing the cyclic rate of fire from 600 to a more manageable and economical 480; slightly shortening the barrel and removing its fins; a new ejector; and other minor changes. This achieved, the new weapon was put into full production in 1937. The name 'Bren' was a bolting together of the first two letters of the Czech armament facility at Bruno, and the first two letters of Enfield. As of September 1939 Enfield was turning out 400 guns a week, and by June 1940 more than 30,000 had been issued. In excess of a third of a million were made by 1945 – the majority at Enfield, and others in Canada, though interestingly

A slightly wounded Bren gunner turns his weapon skyward at Tobruk. The mount used is the 'tripod anti-aircraft', and the gunner adopts the textbook firing position described in the 1939 manual *Light Machine Gun* – with the left hand on the carrying handle, right on the pistol grip. A twelve magazine steel ammunition box stands to the left of the picture. (Official/author)

An early model Bren gun being used from its tripod in a support role. Good and reliable as it was the Bren was less effective for sustained fire than belt-fed weapons. There were four marks of Bren gun with production in Britain and Canada exceeding 337,000 by 1945. (Kenneth Rittener/Getty Images)

the Indian Army continued to use the Anglo–French–designed Vickers–Berthier due to insufficient supplies of the Bren.

The Bren was covered by the 1939 manual *Light Machine Gun*, which explained that the 'chief characteristic' of the gun was 'its power of delivering volume fire with the employment of few men'. Though it could shoot further, and was sighted up to 2,000 yards (1,839m), its 'effective range' was about 1,000 yards (914m). The weapon could be fired by one man, or more effectively by a team of two. In team operation the 'No. 2' carried spare magazines and a Bren barrel in addition to his own rifle, and adopted a position to the left of the gun. As a magazine was expended the No. 2 replaced it with a full one, then put his hand on the gunner's back with the word 'On' to let him know that fire could recommence. In order to improve accuracy, conserve ammunition, reduce strain on the weapon, and avoid overheating, it was recommended that the Bren be fired either by single rounds, or short bursts of four or five rounds. In the selective fire, single shot, mode about thirty rounds a minute was deemed ideal, particularly if these were delivered at irregular intervals, so deceiving the enemy that they faced only rifle fire. However, for 'rapid rate' a trained man was expected to be able to deliver 120 rounds per minute. This equated to four magazines, and up to ten magazines could be fired in quick succession, but after this the firer was instructed either to slow the rate of fire, or to change the barrel to avoid overheating. This could be accomplished in a few seconds by lifting the barrel latch and pulling forwards using the carrying handle, a job done by the 'No. 2' in a two-

man team. In engaging moving targets, the Bren gunner was directed to select a point ahead of the target and fire a long burst of eight to ten rounds as the enemy moved into the zone of fire, maintaining the necessary 'lead' to ensure a hit. This method minimised the amount of traversing needed, which in any case was practically limited by the bipod mount.[19]

Though frequently fired at point targets such as individuals, the Bren was also capable of creating 'beaten zones' of fire. From the bipod at 500 yards (475m) the zone was 175 yards (160m) long by 2 yards (1.8m) wide, and at 1,000 yards (914m), 115 yards (105m) long by four wide. Firing from a tripod 'tightened' and intensified the cone of the beaten zone of fire so that at 1,000 yards (914m) it was reduced to 100 yards (91m) in length and 3 (2.7m) wide. Interestingly there were some who thought that the Bren was actually too accurate, and that in failing to create a sufficient 'cone of fire' it was not performing as a machine gun should. However, this was to miss the point that it had never been designed as a fixed–position sustained fire weapon. Perhaps more telling was an official report of 1944 that criticised British small arms generally, on the grounds that the core notion of conserving ammunition was unsound on the modern European battlefield. It was then suggested, for example, that Bren gunners were much more likely to inflict serious damage on the enemy when firing at targets in the open if they ignored their training and simply fired complete magazines as quickly as possible.[20]

Compared to many machine guns the Bren was indeed light at about 23lb, (10.4kg) and was reasonably simple to operate. The tripod, when used, weighed a further 30lb (13.6kg). There were few problems with the new gun, which quickly proved reliable, but it had one minor weakness in common with many others that were fed from spring-loaded box magazines. For though the Bren magazine was made for thirty rounds, an instruction in *Army Training Memorandum No. 26*, of November 1939, recommended that it should only be filled to twenty-eight rounds as stoppages were more common when the magazine was filled to capacity. Moreover, when the Bren was to be left unfired for particularly long periods, a magazine with only twenty rounds was suggested: 'this prevents the spring becoming weak (and in extreme cases fracturing), owing to it being kept fully compressed'.

The Bren usually served as direct light support on its light bipod, and indeed provided the main firepower of infantry sections. In its

Private Doug Mason of Tonbridge posing with his Bren gun during the battle of Monte Cassino, Italy, 1944. Compared to many machine guns of the period the Bren was relatively light. When unarmed Mason bumped into German parachutists whilst picking up wounded on Castle Hill, and by bluff took six of them prisoner. (Bettman via Getty Images)

A King's Own Scottish Borderers infantry section doubling up on the town of Ulzen, April, 1945. Beyond the Bren gunner, foreground, can be seen riflemen and a PIAT operator. The men wear 37 Pattern web equipment and jerkins, and both Mark II and III steel helmets are worn. (Official/author)

infantry role the manual *Light Machine Gun*, 1942, explained that the 'fighting section' was eight men, with three additionals held in reserve. In combat the section was to operate with one Bren, with both its team and the riflemen carrying additional magazines for the Bren gun, allowing for rapid reloading. *Infantry Training* (1944) listed the infantry section as ten strong, again with one Bren, but sometimes sections acquired a second gun. Brens could be used in support from the tripod: this gave better long-range accuracy, but did not fully tackle the issues of sustained fire. The Bren could likewise be used in an AA role ideally from the 'Tripod, Anti Aircraft'. However, special 200-round drum magazines supplied for this role did not prove popular, and if pointed skyward in the latter part of the war the weapon was usually fitted with the normal curved box magazine.[21]

The Vickers and other Machine Guns

The Vickers .303-inch machine gun, first introduced in 1912, was still the main 'medium' machine gun of the British Army in 1939, and would be retained in service until long after the conflict was over. Its design was based on the original ideas of Hiram S. Maxim, and it was manufactured by Vickers, sons and Maxim, of Crayford, Kent. The Vickers therefore had much in common, not only with the German MG 08, but the Russian Maxim, and other guns of the era. The key modification from the original Maxim concept was that in the Vickers the lock

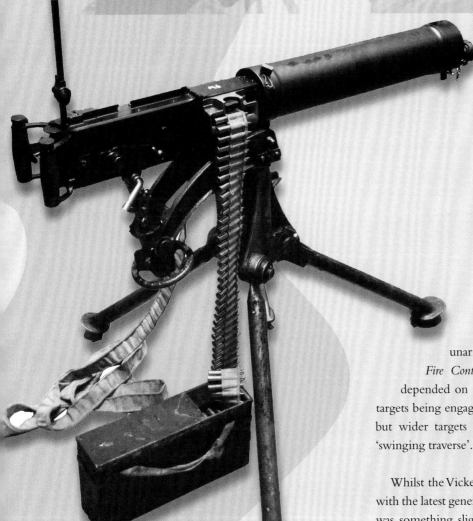

a metal can. The system both reduced the generation of visible steam, and allowed the collected water to be tipped back into the gun. Properly laid on its mounting the Vickers had a remarkable range, even being able to bring plunging fire on positions up to 4,500 yards (4,115m) away. Such set–piece 'barrages' were ideally created with a group of guns, with at least one per 30 yards (27m) of the front to be attacked. At closer ranges, where several guns formed interlocking zones of fire, it created large and fearsome 'beaten zones' well nigh impassable to any unarmoured target. As explained in the manual *Fire Control*, the precise method of delivery often depended on the width of the target: narrow or enfilade targets being engaged with little or no movement of the piece, but wider targets required 'tapping across' or even a steady 'swinging traverse'.

Whilst the Vickers was effective enough, it was not on a par with the latest general purpose German machine guns, and there was something slightly schizophrenic about the logic behind its deployment. Originally Vickers guns had been allotted on a scale of two per infantry battalion, but at the end of 1915 they had been gathered together into the companies of the Machine Gun Corps. With the disbandment of this formation in 1922, the Vickers had passed back to the infantry, but this was reversed again in 1936 with the decision to pool the guns into 'Machine Gun Battalions'. These MG battalions were created by the conversion of existing infantry battalions. One of these was 1st Battalion the Manchester Regiment, as was recorded in the regimental history:

'On May 24 notification was received to the effect that the reorganisation of the battalion on a machine gun basis would take place, probably in October 1937, and that the training of the battalion in that role was to commence forthwith. The battalion was made up to its full war establishment of machine guns (36) during May, in addition to 27 'D.P.' (Drill Purpose) guns. All Lewis guns with the exception of four for AA purposes were withdrawn, except in the case of B Company in Cyprus, which retained its Lewis guns.' [22]

A late model Vickers .303 machine gun and tripod. Early types had fluted water jackets, later examples plain cylinders. Various models were also produced for mounting in aircraft and vehicles over the long service life of the weapon, which was only officially terminated in 1968. The gun was reliable, and for 'area fire' could be used on unseen targets over 3,000 yards away. For direct close range fire its ability to shoot several rounds a second with good accuracy proved deadly. (Author)

mechanism broke upwards on firing. It was also a little lighter, though the unloaded weight was still 40lb (18kg) without the tripod. Being water-cooled, the weapon was ideal for sustained fire – particularly in defensive situations – and could plug away apparently endlessly, given brief pauses between bursts and to change the 250-round belt. There were some minor modifications during the production life of the Vickers, and some weapons lacked the distinctive fluted outer barrel casing of the original gun, but they required few substantive changes. So many had survived from the First World War period that relatively few new guns were required.

The Vickers was carried into action in two main loads, barrel and tripod, and the former clamped atop the latter on reaching the firing position. The gunner sat behind the weapon holding the spade grips and viewing through the sights, the loader sat or lay to his right feeding the cloth belts. With prolonged firing the water in the barrel jacket heated, and as it turned to steam this was directed away down a rubber pipe to be condensed in

Cavalrymen in training with the Hotchkiss light machine gun, 1940. A veteran of the First World War the Hotchkiss was loaded using metal strips holding the ammunition. According to the original caption the men seen here were jockeys in civilian life. (Reg Speller/ Fox Photos/Hulton Archive/Getty Images)

As of 1940 three 'Motor Machine Gun' Brigades were also formed as a mobile counter-invasion measure. Under the organisation pertaining in the latter part of the war, each infantry division had one Machine Gun Battalion. These contained three machine-gun companies, each of three platoons. The machine-gun platoon was four guns under command of an officer, divided into two sections. There was also a heavy mortar company with sixteen 4.2-inch mortars. However, lumping medium machine guns together never did work for Special Forces, and there were early complaints that the Commandos, for example, having no

Vickers guns, lacked sustained local fire support. As a result the Chindits, parachute units, and Commandos were all given their own Vickers guns attached at unit level. For example, as of 1943 the order of battle of a Commando of six Troops included its own Heavy Weapons Troop including mortars and machine-gun detachments.

Like many other machine guns the Vickers was used on a variety of mountings during the war, and though arguably a relatively heavy water-cooled gun with a modest cyclic rate of fire was less than ideal, it was sometimes used in an anti-aircraft role. So it was, for example, that a radial twin Vickers was used from the back of a Bedford 30cwt truck. As the manual of 1942 explained, two trucks comprised a section, the twin-gun mounting on one together with the section commander, driver and five crewmen, while the section corporal, driver and five men were on the other. The guns could be fired from the back of the trucks or dismounted from tripods, with the vehicles moved away into cover. Two vehicles allowed for carriage of a dozen belt and ammunition boxes, and enough men to prepare and defend a position. In addition to the two machine guns,

A Vickers machine gun team concealed inside a house during the Italian campaign: sandbags help hide the team and weight the front of the tripod. The gun is fitted with a large flash hider on the muzzle. (Author)

standard equipment for the section included at least five rifles and a sub-machine gun. A .50 calibre Vickers was also produced from 1933 through to 1939. This was used by both the Army and the Navy, and on land was used mainly as tank armament. As of 1940 over a thousand of these guns were in service.[23]

Though the Bren, Vickers, Lewis and Besa were the most significant machine guns in British Army service, there were a range of other weapons in use for various purposes, particularly with the Home Guard, whose rapid expansion from 1940 to 1941 could not be supplied through normal channels. Thus it was that weapons appeared from store, and guns both old and new came in from the USA. Many of the most useful were Browning designs. Two of these, the air-cooled .30 and .50, actually saw extensive use with the regular Army, mainly as vehicle-mounted pieces, and had been produced in the immediate post-First World War period. Similar in general design, they were both belt fed and recoil operated. The .30 Model 1919 was fed from a 250-round belt and capable of a cyclic rate of 500 rounds per minute, whilst its larger brother the .50 calibre Model 1921 had a similar rate of fire but owing to its much larger round was generally operated with shorter 110-round metallic link belts. Interestingly, though, the smaller weapon had always been envisaged as a weapon that could be used from a vehicle; the powerful .50 calibre had been designed with anti-tank and anti-aircraft work in mind. By the Second World War the .50 was not capable of dealing with armour, but remained a potent piece against soft-skinned targets, low-flying aircraft and personnel.

Two key Browning machine weapons also went to the Home Guard. The first of these was the .30 calibre Model 1917 machine gun. This weapon, similar in general outline to the Vickers and other Maxims of the First World War era, was water-cooled, and fired from 250-round belts. Also like the Vickers it was particularly useful as a defensive piece as it was heavy and required a tripod or similar mounting. As well as the calibre, another obvious difference between the two weapons was the Browning's pistol grip at the rear. The BAR was technically not a 'machine gun' as the acronym stood for 'Browning Automatic Rifle': however, in practice it was used in British service as something of a substitute for the Bren gun in a light support role. Though the BAR had seen war service in 1918, and was somewhat circumscribed by its twenty-round magazine, it remained a pretty effective weapon and was indeed also used by US troops throughout the Second

War. Two of its key attributes were its relatively lightweight, at 22lb (10kg), and proven track record. Like many other US-derived infantry weapons it was in .30 calibre.[24]

Another British machine gun to see service with the Home Guard was the Hotchkiss. Though based on a French design, the Hotchkiss for British service had been produced at Enfield in .303-inch calibre and supplied mainly to the cavalry and tank corps during the First World War. Quite a few survived in store, to be brought out and refurbished in time of need. Official statistics show 10,993 weapons being reconditioned at a cost of about £2 each. Whilst inferior even to the old Lewis, the Hotchkiss was a cost-effective stopgap, and clearly better than nothing. Ungainly in appearance, the Hotchkiss weighed 27lb (12kg) and was fitted with a little bipod and wooden butt. Its mechanism was a gas piston type, operating at a cyclic rate of up to 650 rounds per minute, but actual maximum performance was governed by the feed, which was from a rigid thirty-round strip or from a semi-flexible belt.

Mortars

Though mortars had been used in siege warfare for centuries, use of mortars as battlefield support weapons had been rare, and it was only in the First World War that recognisably modern lightweight pieces were developed. The most influential of these was arguably the 'Stokes' mortar devised by Sir William Stokes. This comprised a simple smooth bore barrel closed at the bottom, located on a base plate, and supported by a bipod. The bomb was slid into the barrel tail first, and when its propulsion unit was ignited at the bottom it shot back out of the barrel to land nose first and detonate. Such a mortar offered several advantages.

A carrier crew of 2nd Sherwood Foresters in the Anzio bridgehead, Italy 1944, demonstrating the use of a 2 inch mortar from the vehicle. Whilst the weapon could be used a low angles in an emergency high angle plunging fire was the norm, allowing the team to shower a target with bombs unexpectedly whilst remaining under cover and relatively safe from retaliation. (Sgt Loughin/IWM via Getty Images)

Two-inch mortar bombs as depicted in the manual *Handbook for the Ordnance, ML 2-inch Mortar*, 1939. The yellow paint denoted a high explosive round, the green was for smoke. Other markings showed the contractor, date of filling, and fuze details. Similar details were applied to other munitions. (Author)

Far right: A simplified 2-inch mortar of the mid- to late-war period: instead of a complex sight a white line is painted along the barrel for judging direction of fire. There were several different varieties of 2-inch with barrels of 24 inches (61cm) or 14 inches (36cm). (Author)

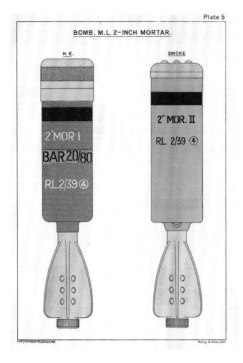

The first of these was that being mounted at a high angle, the projectiles dropped onto the enemy position, being thus able to hit places otherwise inaccessible behind hills or other cover. This also made it useful against field works and trenches. Worked with an observer, mortars could themselves be kept behind cover or concealed in a pit whilst in action. Another advantage was rapid fire, since simplicity meant that the mortar could operate almost as fast as the crew were able to put in the bombs. It was also the case that – being relatively low velocity weapons whose fire effect depended on the explosion of the bomb – the mortar itself could be light in proportion to its 'throw weight'.

While there had been something of a stagnation in mortar technology immediately after 1918, two new mortars based on the modern principles were devised for general issue to the British Army before 1939. The smallest of these was the 'Ordnance, M.L. 2-inch Mortar', usually known simply as the '2-inch Mortar'. During the 1930s, the Armament Research Department had examined foreign developments, and happened upon a promising Spanish 50mm weapon, and soon produced a similar design of their own. The new weapon had a percussion trip firing mechanism with a lever, and was just over 2 feet (61cm) in length with the base plate fitted, being so small that no bipod was required. Some stability was provided by teeth on the bottom of the base plate, and accuracy was aided by a lensatic sight with two bubbles similar to those found in spirit levels. The mortar had both a carrying handle and a sling fitting. The whole equipment weighed about 21lb (9.5kg), and had a maximum range of about 500 yards (457m), with approximately 100 yards (91m) being regarded as a practicable minimum.

This mortar was ordered into production in 1938, and issued during 1939 along with a dedicated *Handbook* and a new *Mortar (2-inch)* volume in the Small Arms Training Series. As these publications made clear, the 2-inch was essentially a platoon infantry weapon, and its key purposes were to engage targets with high-explosive rounds and to create smoke screens. This was very useful, but as *Mortar (2-inch)* explained:

'The number of bombs which can be carried into action is strictly limited owing to their weight. They should be used sparingly and only as part of a definite plan… Rates of fire depend on wind and circumstances. The maximum rate with accuracy is from three to four bombs a minute. The distance within which the H.E. bomb is practically certain to be effective against personnel in the open is about eight yards in all directions from the point of burst. Large fragments may, however, have sufficient velocity to inflict wounds up to 150 yards or more, particularly if the burst is on stony ground… The mortar can be fired either high angle or low angle. The former gives the bomb a steep angle of descent, but a considerable allowance must be made for any wind. The latter is much less affected by wind as the trajectory is comparatively flat.'[25]

The basic scale of issue as of 1939 was one mortar per platoon, with six containers of ammunition, each carrying six bombs, to be carried on the platoon truck. Other equipment for the mortar included a cleaning brush, a case for the sight, and a cover. Originally the mortar team was three, one to carry and fire the weapon, one to carry bombs, and a leader to direct the crew and spot the enemy. Everything could be done by one man in an emergency, though obviously he could not shift many of the 2lb (91g) bombs. The weapon was found very useful and widely used with virtually every type of troop throughout the war, and was also fitted to a number of different vehicles. The biggest single issue was that as first devised the 2-inch was heavier and more elaborate than necessary. The sight made little difference once a mortar team had practised with the weapon, and the base was larger than it needed to be. As a result, successive marks were made lighter and simpler as time progressed. The sight was deleted and replaced by a buff stripe up the khaki barrel as a rough guide to aiming, and the base plate was made smaller. In its simplest Mark VIII 'Airborne' form the

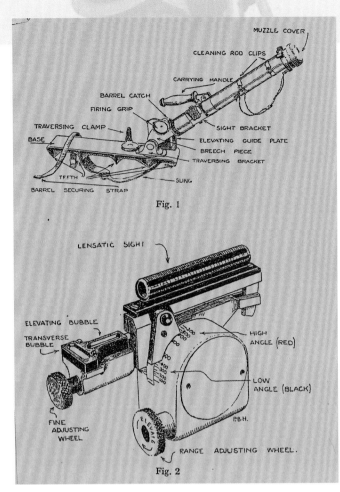

Fig. 1

Fig. 2

thing was little more than a 14-inch (36cm) tube with simple firing mechanism, though this limited the range to about 350 yards (320m). Conversely, maximum rates of fire were almost double to those originally envisaged as being possible.[26]

The other mortar developed immediately before the war was the 3-inch. Employed essentially as a battalion support weapon, this was a much more powerful prospect than its little brother, and indeed was closer in appearance to its ancestor the Stokes. The 3-inch could be dismantled into its major component parts – barrel, bipod and base – and carried around the battlefield, but as these weighed 44lb (20kg), 45lb (20.4kg) and 37lb (16.8kg) respectively, and bombs weighed 10lb (4.5kg) each, significant relocations were much better accomplished with transport. The upside was a range of 1,600 yards (1,463m), an ability to fire a wider range of projectiles, and rates of fire anything up to ten rounds a minute. Well handled, the weapon could be devastating, as a mortar platoon could put a number of bombs into the air simultaneously, arriving as a sudden rain on the target area. With multiple impacts the inaccuracy of any one bomb was relatively unimportant, whilst troops on the receiving end suffered considerable shock and had nowhere to run. In a Mark 2 Model with new bombs and a stronger barrel the range of the 3-inch would be pushed to 2,800 yards (2,560m). The typical equipment of an infantry 3-inch mortar platoon comprised two

mortars and an anti-tank rifle, plus two 30cwt trucks, seventy-five high-explosive and forty-five smoke rounds being kept with each mortar. A further reserve of forty-five high-explosive and twenty-seven smoke bombs were in reserve.

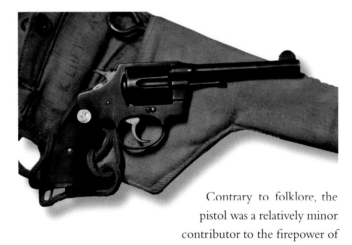

An issue Webley
.380 Mark IV
revolver with
its holster and
ammunition pouch
for use with the
37 Pattern web
equipment. (Author)

Later, a heavy mortar was added to the family. Entering service in 1942, the 4.2-inch was intended to equip chemical warfare companies of the Royal Engineers, but the punch it could deliver with high-explosive rounds to a range of 4,100 yards (3,750m) was too much of an opportunity to miss. The 4.2-inch mortar really ranked with the artillery, having a barrel over 5 feet (1.52m) in length that weighed 92lb and base plates and mobile mountings that ranged from 120lb (42kg) to 602lb (273kg). The normal detachment was six men, but given suitable initial deployment could be operated by two. Despite being comparatively clumsy, the 4.2-inch repaid the effort that had to be put in to move it, and at its debut at El Alamein succeeded in firing off all the ammunition supplied for it in that theatre of war. Never as numerous as the smaller types, 4.2-inch mortars were usually regarded as divisional assets.

Pistols

The Colt Police Positive: one of many different US-made revolvers and imported to the UK in 1940–1941 to help make up the shortage of arms. This example is shown with a holster and lanyard. Since officers often purchased their own pistols, and the Home Guard in particular had much freedom of choice there were a considerable variety of pistols in service. (Author)

Contrary to folklore, the pistol was a relatively minor contributor to the firepower of any army in the Second World War. Indeed, a soldier who could consistently hit a man-sized target at 20 to 30 yards (18–27m) without incident was doing well, and real effectiveness was limited to a few very particular circumstances. These included use in confined spaces and as a back-up arm for personnel such as drivers, and tank and heavy weapons crews. Officers also carried pistols, and originally many of these were private purchases rather than issue items, though they generally conformed to the standard calibre. After 1914 it had been increasingly realised that the pistol was of marginal effectiveness, and front-line infantry officers gradually began to carry long arms that gave them greater personal firepower and made them less obvious targets for snipers. Never the less, officers were still expected to possess a pistol or to have access to an issue piece.

Though the British Army had used a few semi-automatics in the First World War, notably the Webley and Scott .455, 'Pistol Self-Loading', and imported Colt types, it remained wedded to the revolver, even as nations such as the USA and Germany were changing to more modern weapons. Extraordinary as it may now seem, there were a number of genuine advantages to this conservatism. Most obviously revolvers were simple and robust with little to go wrong. A single misfire did not mean a revolver was out of action even temporarily: the user squeezed the trigger again, the cylinder went round, and a fresh cartridge was presented to the barrel and discharged. Conversely, automatics could be temperamental and prone to stoppages. If one round failed to fire, the action had to be cleared before it could be used again. Moreover, staying with revolvers meant continuity of training and use of a familiar domestic product.[27]

The biggest single change between the wars was a reduction in the standard calibre of Army pistols from .455- to .380-inch on the grounds of weight. The notion of a reduction had been decided as early as 1922, but the changeover would take years to achieve. A .380 round was introduced in 1929, but even as late as the Second World War emergency use was still made of old weapons in the .455 calibre. The change was also not without its critics, as the unjacketed .455 projectile was a real 'man stopper' calculated to deform on impact and incapacitate even the most determined of enemies with one shot. The .380 pistol was easier to carry and fire, but there remained doubt that it was effective enough for military purposes. Despite reservations, the new Enfield revolver was introduced in 1932 and by 1939 was the main sidearm. This weapon was officially described as the 'Pistol, Revolver, No. 2 Mark 1'. It broke open at the top to insert six cartridges into the cylinder, and could be operated as a single or double action, this meaning that one pull of the trigger both rotated the cylinder and discharged the round, but also that the hammer could be pulled back to rotate the cylinder before the trigger was squeezed. The single action facility gave marginally greater accuracy for deliberate single shots, but required a comb or spur on the back of the hammer. This was regarded as a menace by tank crews, given the possibility of accidents when worming in and out of confined spaces. As a result, a 'No. 2 Mark 1*' version was approved in 1938 that lacked the comb, and was thus double action only. A slightly simplified 'No. 2 Mark 1**' was also produced from 1942. Enfield revolvers were

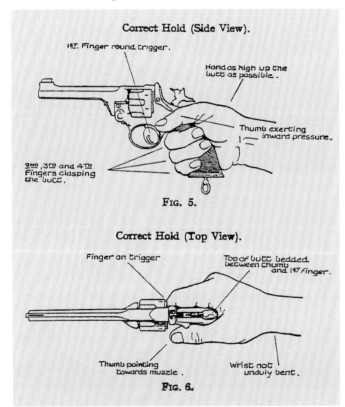

Correct Hold (Side View).

1ST. Finger round trigger.

Hand as high up the butt as possible.

Thumb exerting inward pressure.

2ND, 3RD and 4TH Fingers clasping the butt.

FIG. 5.

Correct Hold (Top View).

Finger on trigger

Top of butt bedded between thumb and 1ST finger.

Thumb pointing towards muzzle.

Wrist not unduly bent.

FIG. 6.

also produced by Albion Motors during the war, and shortages were further alleviated by contracts placed with Webley and Scott for a very similar weapon in the same calibre, the 'Webley Mark IV', 'Military' or 'War Service' model.

Pistol training was conducted according to instructions laid down in the pamphlet *Pistol .38 inch*, of 1937, a manual that was reprinted in 1940 and revised in 1941. Interestingly, this volume had already moved far beyond plodding target marksmanship, and it was accepted that really the pistol was 'unsuitable for firing by deliberate aim' but that it was useful for 'surprise and moving targets'. Whilst men were taught to fire at targets using the sights, 'service shooting' was to be instinctive, without deliberate aim,

shots being taken as soon as the gun was raised by a 'squeeze of the whole hand'. Trainees were taught to fire two quick shots at a time, preferably modifying their position to take advantage of cover. The expectation was only that shots would hit a head-sized target about 12 feet (3.7m) away. As the 1941 instructions explained, the basic tests of elementary training were threefold:

'No 1. General knowledge of the pistol. Men will be asked questions on safety precautions, care and cleaning. Standard – three out of four questions to be answered correctly.

No 2. Handling the pistol. Men will be tested in drawing and returning pistols, the "Ready" position, "Change hands" and "Loading and Unloading". Those who make serious faults will fail.

No 3. Firing. The test should be carried out at a distance of four yards between firer and instructor, the mark being the instructor's eye, the instructor being in a kneeling position. Firer in the 'Ready' position – using either hand – a latitude of aim will be allowed proportionate to the service standard, i.e. if the instructor considers the shot would have hit an area approximating to the size of his face, the shot will be considered correct. Two shots will be fired in quick succession on each of the three lifts of the pistol. Time, two seconds for each series of double shots. Standard – one shot of each series to be correct.'[28]

Though the biggest single bulk of British Army pistols were .380 Enfields even in 1945, there were many other types in use. Perhaps the most exotic of these were in the hands of the Home Guard, who used a bewildering variety of whatever was available. These encompassed civilian purchases, weapons captured in the First World War, and American imports mainly received in 1940 and 1941. Revolver types encountered included the old Webley .455, Smith & Wessons, and Colts, of various types, in both .38 and .455. In particular, the very well made 'S&W' .38 was manufactured in several barrel lengths and also proved popular with other officers, including those of the Commandos and Airborne. Semi-automatics were also seen in the Home Guard and these included the Colt models 1905 and 1911, the German P08 'Luger', and even the venerable Mauser C96 'Broomhandle'. Contract data also shows orders for a few .32 automatics, and even a handful of Colt 'New Service' revolvers in .357.[29]

Perhaps the most remarkable pistol used by the British Army during the Second World War was the highly successful Browning 9mm semi-automatic. Introduced by the Belgian FN

Instructions on the correct hold for the 'Pistol, Revolver, No. 2 MkI' from the standard Army manual. Since the ordinary pistol had a nasty habit of catching on things when tank crew were worming through hatches, a modified model of 'No.2' without a spur on the back of the hammer and a heavier trigger pull was approved in 1938, for issue to Royal Armoured Corps personnel. This was usually worn together with a holster that tied firmly to the leg. Later the modified pistol was also used by other troops. (Author)

Boys Anti-Tank Rifle

It is justly stated that the Boys Anti-Tank rifle was not a good anti-armour weapon. Never the less, it should be remembered that at the time it was designed, tanks were relatively flimsy, and the AT rifle was regarded as the state-of-the-art infantry answer to the problem of armour. Moreover, the Boys remained useful against soft-skinned targets, equipment, and personnel behind cover long after it ceased to be a viable proposition against the tank. It was named 'Boys' after Captain Boys, one of the designers, who died during its development. Following experimentation with the Oerlikon 20mm cannon and an overgrown .8-inch Elswick machine gun, Britain had followed the international trend set by Germany and Poland and set to work on a specification for a high-velocity, anti-tank rifle that could be operated by one man. With design work completed in 1936, contracts for 6,000 weapons were placed with BSA, who produced the Boys at Small Heath, Birmingham until production was halted by enemy bombing in late 1940. Thereafter, production was dispersed, both to other Midland factories and North America. By August 1943 and cessation of production, about 69,000 were made.

company as the 'High Power' or Model 1935, this weapon was a state-of-the-art pistol weighing just over 2lb (91g) with a then phenomenal thirteen-round magazine capacity. Apart from its reputation for reliability and ability to keep firing after other weapons had exhausted their magazines, the big advantage of the Browning was its round, as the 9mm was tried and tested. Moreover, whilst the cartridge was powerful enough for military purposes, it was not so powerful or bulky as to need either a massive weapon to fire it, or a strong and highly trained shooter to handle the gun. The biggest problem was that as the factory was in Belgium, after 1940 production went straight to the enemy. However, drawings enabled the establishment of new production facilities in Canada, and numbers were obtained in the latter part of the war for the British Commandos and Airborne, the troops most likely requiring the best possible pistol in close combat.[30]

In 1936 the bolt action .55-inch Boys was more than a match for the competition, having a five-round box magazine and an ability to penetrate 23mm of armour at close range. This performance dropped to 19mm at 500 yards (475m), but this was still very respectable given that the contemporary Panzer II had only 14mm of frontal armour as first designed. The Boys had a fearsome discharge and recoil, partially offset by a muzzle brake, sprung recoil mechanism, and rubber-padded butt. If there was a serious flaw in the idea, it was that the round had to hit something vital to actually halt a tank, and as a result early training emphasised aiming at crew compartments. One other drawback was that the Boys weighed 36lb (16kg), and whilst it could be operated by one man, it was better carried on the platoon truck, or between two men, over significant distances. AT rifle teams were therefore taught mainly to operate from static concealed positions – covering likely route ways – and to track their targets, ideally hitting them in the flank.

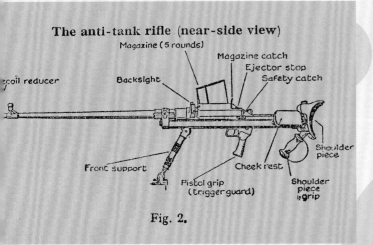

The anti-tank rifle (near-side view)

Magazine (5 rounds)
Magazine catch
Ejector stop
Safety catch
Backsight
ecoil reducer
Shoulder piece
Front support
Cheek rest
Pistol grip (trigger guard)
Shoulder piece & grip

Fig. 2.

Yet what was adequate in the mid-1930s was quickly outclassed in war, with even late models of the Panzer II carrying 30mm of armour. By 1940 it was being admitted that the Boys was only suitable against 'light armoured vehicles', which meant a serious gap in British infantry anti-tank capability, as until the PIAT made its appearance two years later, only mines and anti-tank grenades were of much use. Never the less, the Boys could still penetrate 14 inches (36cm) of brick, or 10 inches (25cm) of sand bags, and so continued to have some niche uses. In the establishments of 1941, the Boys was deployed twenty-five per infantry battalion, with three in each infantry company and thirteen distributed between the carrier platoon, headquarters and other sub units.[31]

Projector Infantry Anti-Tank 'PIAT'

Invented by Lieutenant Colonel Stewart Blacker of the Royal Artillery, the PIAT was an ingenious and powerful weapon that was arguably too long in gestation. Though far more effective than the anti-tank rifle it replaced, it was not as light or flexible as modern German anti-tank weapons of the middle war period such as the *Panzerfaust*. Blacker had begun his experimentations about a decade before the war, and by 1937 had come up with a weapon that he called 'Arbalest'. This was tested in 1939, but rejected on the grounds that the simple 2-inch mortar was a better bomb thrower.

However, from 1940 Blacker became involved in the invention and production of unusual weapons in an official capacity, and now put forward a modified version of his Arbalest. This was accepted as the 'Blacker Bombard' – a 29mm spigot

Boys Anti-Tank rifles carried during training in Northern Ireland; even over the shoulder, the Boys was a significant load. Contract records show orders from Enfield and BSA over the period 1935–1942, with only a handful of special experimental types produced between 1942 and 1945. (FPG/Hulton Archive/ Getty Images)

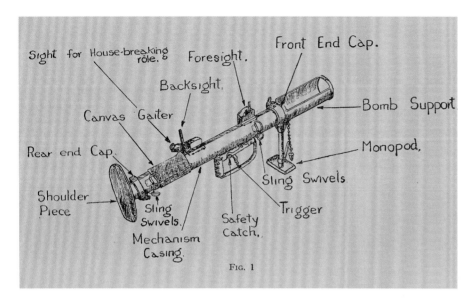

FIG. 1

The parts of the Projector Infantry Anti-Tank from the official manual of June 1943. The PIAT could knock out armoured vehicles, but to do so required both courage and skill, and preferably luck. A first-round hit was also a good idea. (Author)

mortar, of limited range but significant high explosive power – that could do double duty as a close range anti-tank piece or bombardment weapon. Though the Blacker Bombard was useful as an emergency Home Guard or airfield defence arm, it was heavy and not very mobile, being best deployed from a fixed position or pit. Blacker therefore set about designing something more handy that he christened 'Baby Bombard'. Though Blacker was soon called on for other tasks, this project was picked up by Major M.R. Jefferis. Initially he did not get very far, as lighter meant smaller, and the smaller the bomb became, the less useful was its anti-armour performance. It went to trials, but was initially declared ineffective. However, Jefferis now found an answer in the form of a 'hollow charge' projectile, a 3lb (1.4kg) bomb containing a shaped charge, the front end of which was in the shape of an inverted cone. Combining this with detonation on impact ensured that the full force of the explosive was focused on a tiny point on the armour of an enemy tank or fortification, making armour penetration of up to 75mm possible. Interestingly, Churchill was of the opinion that the weapon that became the PIAT was wrongly named, believing Jefferis' contribution significant enough to merit it bearing his name. Though Winston's opinion was ignored in this matter, Jefferis was at least eventually promoted to brigadier.

Official final approval for the Projector Infantry Anti-Tank was given on 31 August 1942, though a contract to ICI was dated as early as May. About 100,000 were produced by the end of the war. The PIAT manual of 1943 specified an issue of three weapons per infantry company, and these could be concentrated or distributed one to each platoon. The PIAT was essentially a

large hollow tube housing a massive spring, under which was the trigger mechanism. On the front was a trough to take the bomb. Though it was possible to operate with one man, a crew of two was recommended – one carrying the projector into action, and the other the bombs. 'No. 1' of the team was the firer, whilst 'No. 2' acted as loader. Given the short range of the PIAT, every effort was made to shoot it from cover. A slit trench was ideal, but the weapon could be used from almost anywhere, since unlike a bazooka there was no back blast to worry about.[32]

To cock the weapon for the first round the soldier was supposed to use both his feet and arms to 'overcome the resistance of the mainspring'. Having checked the dust and muzzle plugs had been removed, the loader then placed the bomb in the trough. He then prepared the next round as the first was being fired. The sighting system was approximate rather than exact, with settings provided for 70 and 100 yards (64 and 91m). When the 'No. 1' took aim against head-on (or retiring) tanks, he sighted at the centre of the vehicle, and for crossing targets a length in front from the centre of the tank. From these basics the PIAT operator had to apply his 'common sense', aiming a little up or down to compensate for range, or giving greater leads for fast vehicles. When the aim was correct the firer pressed the trigger, which had a long and heavy pressure. After a momentary hesitation, as the spring shot forwards and entered the tail of the bomb, the propelling cartridge exploded. This shot the bomb towards the enemy and simultaneously re-cocked the spring.

That the PIAT could do its primary job under the right circumstances was proven. It saw use from the invasion of Sicily, on D-Day, and was pretty crucial with the Airborne at Arnhem where lightly equipped Paratroops were confronted by armoured vehicles. No less than six men won the VC in action with the PIAT, commencing with Lancashire Fusilier F.S. Jefferson on the Gustav Line in Italy in May 1944. In Normandy it was estimated that about 7 per cent of all German tanks destroyed by British forces were knocked out by PIATs, slightly more than were accounted for by rocket-firing aircraft. The PIAT could also be used as a sort of heavy duty mortar or 'house breaker' in which role a range of 350 yards (320m) and both low- and high-angle fire were possible. Against pill boxes it was useful as a form of close-range portable artillery, acting in concert with Bren gunners and infantry to outflank and blast the target. On the downside it was cumbrous and took skill to use accurately. Trials determined that at 100 yards (91m) a hit rate of about

60 per cent was about what could be expected, and even then some fuses failed to detonate. With a weight of 32lb (14.5kg) the PIAT was double the weight of the US Bazooka, and 50 per cent heavier than the German 8.8cm Raketen *Panzerbüchse*. The PIAT was also a noisy beast, and though ear protection was not issued, firers were recommended to put cotton wool or a piece of rifle cleaning cloth into their ears.

Grenades

The story of British grenades during the Second World War is essentially simple. For there was one ubiquitous, old, but powerful, versatile, and trusted high-explosive fragmentation grenade in the shape of the 'Mills Bomb', which was familiar

Inserting fuzes into Mills bombs. The grenades were transported a dozen to a wooden box with a separate tub containing the detonator assemblies. With the components married up the weapon was 'primed' and ready for use. Keeping detonators and bombs apart, and using just one man for priming much improved safety. (Fox Photos/Getty Images)

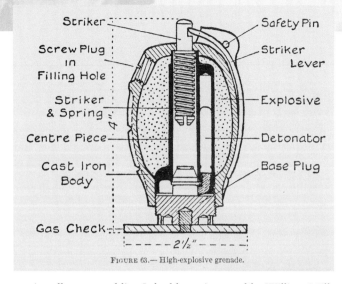

Striker
Screw Plug in Filling Hole
Striker & Spring
Centre Piece
Cast Iron Body
Gas Check
Safety Pin
Striker Lever
Explosive
Detonator
Base Plug
2½"

FIGURE 63.— High-explosive grenade.

The mechanism of the Mills bomb from the grenade manual. This example is shown with the 'gas check', a metal disk fitted when the bomb was used with a discharger. The disk contained the expanding gas from the discharge of the rifle, providing the motive force to launch the grenade. (Author)

Home Guards practise grenade throwing from a pit between rail lines. Training with live bombs was usually done with just one man in a pit, and an instructor on hand. A trench with a right angle was also favoured, since it made it possible to dive away around the corner in the event of a dropped grenade. (M.McNeil/Fox Photos/Getty)

to virtually every soldier. It had been invented by William Mills during the First World War, though his rights to this weapon were challenged by Belgian Captain Leon Roland, who had already produced a bomb using a similar mechanism. However, in addition to the Mills there was also a plethora of less familiar specialist models, some of which lasted only a short time in service as their perceived requirement came and went. Of

these some were significant, yet others hardly seen. Some were made with anti-tank use in mind, others for shock, practice, or incendiary purposes.

The main type of Mills Bomb current during the Second World War was the No. 36M, the 'M' standing strangely enough for 'Mesopotamia', where the particular type of waterproofing used with this bomb had first been put into practice. The No. 36 consisted of an iron body, externally marked into segments during casting. Contrary to popular opinion, these oblong divisions did relatively little to aid fragmentation, but did serve very well to give the soldier a good grip on the grenade whilst pulling the pin or throwing in wet weather. To avoid accidents, the Mills was usually transported long distances in a safe condition, and 'primed' near to the likely point of use by removal of the base plug and insertion of the igniter set, which comprised the cap, fuse and detonator. Once the pin was pulled the user held the bomb with its side lever still pressed against the

grenade body, but as soon as the missile left the hand the lever was released, allowing a spring-loaded striker to snap down onto a cap. When struck the cap immediately ignited a short length of fuse, giving four seconds before the detonator was reached, setting off the main charge.

Originally many grenades had been designed with either 'offensive' or 'defensive' purposes, the former usually having light-weight bodies and acting mainly by shock, the latter having heavier bodies or additional shrapnel for more destructive effect. By such yardsticks the Mills fell into the latter category, and whilst it could certainly be used on the move, the thrower was well advised to drop flat or lob it from cover, as it was extremely lethal at close range, and the largest pieces – such as the base plug – could whizz 100 yards (91m) from the point of the explosion. Having learned the basics of the mechanism, priming, and safety features, the trainee then moved on to practice throws with dummy bombs, perhaps over a wire, or out of a cage, or from a pit. Live bombs were generally used from one or other form of 'splinter proof' cover in training. How far the Mills could be hurled depended much upon circumstance, posture, and the individual, though from 25 to 35 yards (23 to 32m) was assumed to be the norm.

Actual grenade throwing was dealt with by the manual *Grenade*, 1937 (amended 1941), which offered the following advice:

'Grenades over 1lb in weight cannot be thrown – in the strict sense of the word – by the average man, whilst their characteristics require them to be thrown at a high angle. It will be found, therefore, that the best method of delivering the grenade by hand is by an overarm swing, similar to "bowling" in cricket. Accuracy is of more importance than the distance of a throw. Any tendency, therefore on the part of men to see how far they can throw the grenade, irrespective of accuracy will be checked at once... Distance mainly depends on a natural swing which is free and vigorous. Men will be allowed to throw in any way that is natural to them. Apart from the initial lesson anything that tends to drill movements in throwing will be avoided... During instruction the importance of observing the fall of the grenade will be emphasised.'

In addition to being hand thrown, the No 36M could also be projected from a rifle, using a 'discharger'. This cylindrical device was fixed to the barrel of the rifle by means of a 'locking base' and levers, and bombs for discharger firing were fitted with a 'gas check' disk and primed with seven second fuses. The rifle was charged with 'ballistite' cartridges having a special load and

no bullet. To use the discharger the user chose a position behind suitable cover, and rested the rifle on its butt at a 45-degree angle, trigger uppermost. To set range a shutter over a gas port on the discharger was adjusted. When the port was fully open this reduced pressure on firing, so limiting the range of the bomb to 80 yards (73m). Opening the port halfway gave 140 yards, (128m) and when completely shut resulted in the maximum 200-yard (183m) range. Intermediate positions, judged by eye, could be found for other distances. The bomb was then slid into the discharger, gas check first, and the pin was withdrawn. The discharger barrel now kept the side lever compressed, preventing the fuse from starting until the grenade had left the weapon.

The discharger could also be used for smoke and signal bombs. Another discharger-fired grenade, introduced in 1940, was the No. 68. This odd-looking beast combined fins similar to those found on the 2-inch mortar bomb with a gas check and stubby body: but the key to the bomb was its load. For the No. 68 contained a hollow charge intended to deal with enemy armoured vehicles. At a range of 100 yards (91m) it was claimed that this weapon could penetrate between 50 and 100mm of armour, but obtaining a good hit was easier

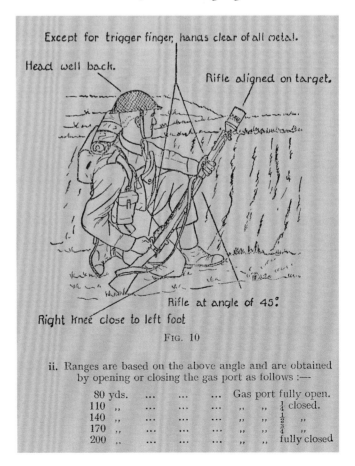

Except for trigger finger, hands clear of all metal.

Head well back.

Rifle aligned on target.

Rifle at angle of 45°.

Right knee close to left foot

FIG. 10

ii. Ranges are based on the above angle and are obtained by opening or closing the gas port as follows :—

80 yds.	...	...	...	Gas port fully open.
110 ,,	...	...	...	,, ,, ¼ closed.
140 ,,	...	...	...	,, ,, ½ ,,
170 ,,	...	...	...	,, ,, ¾ ,,
200 ,,	...	...	...	,, ,, fully closed

The correct use of the discharger with the firer behind cover and the rifle held against the ground trigger guard upwards. Though the rifle seen here is an SMLE, or 'No.1' rifle, dischargers were also made for other weapons. Technology for rifle projection had existed since the First World War and was widely used by the British Army. (Author)

The No. 69 Grenade was armed as the tape unwound and exploded on impact. The explosive filling was lyddite, baratol or amatol. (Author)

Workshop assembly of the No. 74 'Sticky Bomb'. Here metal outer casings and handles containing the mechanism are attached to the sticky glass flask. There was also a Mark II version of the bomb which used bakelite instead of glass. (Ministry of Information Photo Division/IWM via Getty Images.)

said than done. Unless shot from very close the bomb had to be aimed above, and forward of, any moving target. A small number were sent to France before its fall, and some to the Western Desert, although the largest issues were to the Home Guard in 1941–1942.

An anti-tank bomb that required the user to get even closer to the enemy was the 'ST' Grenade, or 'Sticky Bomb'. First developed in the desperate summer of 1940, but refused on grounds of danger and difficulty of manufacture, this grenade was eventually accepted as 'No. 74' in the official series. Alarmingly these bombs remained prone to leakage, and the nitroglycerin was not only an explosion risk but could also cause severe headaches if allowed contact with the skin. As described in the manual *Supplement* of August 1941:

'The body of the grenade consists of a glass flask filled with high explosive. To protect the grenade before use it is completely enclosed by a metal casing hinged at the bottom and held in position round the neck of the flask by a pin or clip. The glass flask is covered with a sticky envelope to cause it to stick inside the neck of the flask is a tube to hold it to the detonator assembly... The throwing handle is attached to the neck of the flask by a screwed ring. The handle contains the striker and the striker spring, held in position a lever fitting flush with the side of the handle and, in its turn, held securely in position by a safety pin... The detonator assembly consists of a percussion cap, 5 seconds fuze, detonator and a composition exploding pellet.'

The Sticky Bomb was delivered to the troops in metal cases of five bombs.

Actually using the No. 74 required extreme courage. The user first removed a pin allowing the outer metal casing to drop

free: a second pin, marked 'Danger', freed the mechanism so that now the thrower was preventing the bomb from activating only by keeping the lever depressed. According to the official leaflet the weapon could now be 'thrown overarm or lobbed', but if circumstances permitted it could be 'planted by hand on to the object, but this must be done with sufficient force to break the flask'. Naturally, getting close enough to smash a glass flask against the side of a Panzer was difficult enough, but getting back under cover within five seconds without being either shot or hoist with one's own petard was another matter entirely. Derek Whipp's unofficial manual, *Anti-Tank Weapons*, 1942, also suggested use from a slit trench, or dropping the bomb from a height. Both were probably reasonable alternatives, though dropping on the tank from above had the additional benefit of attacking the relatively thin top decking of an armoured vehicle.[33]

It was unsurprising that the indefatigable Churchill, who had already taken direct personal interest in rifles and sub-machine guns as well as other small arms, should also intervene personally in the matter of grenades. In the case of the Sticky Bomb he decided that in September 1941, given the lack of explosive for other more important munitions, filling should be paused, to give priority elsewhere. Given that no invasion of the UK had in fact occurred, and was unlikely to in winter, this was probably a fair decision.[34]

Another anti-tank bomb described in the 1941 *Supplement* was the 'hand percussion grenade' or No. 73. This powerful weapon weighed about 4lb (1.8kg), and was just over 11

inches (28cm) long, and as a result could only readily be tossed about 10 to 15 yards. As the instructions explained, it was therefore really limited to 'ambushes or road blocks'. It was kept relatively safe until thrown by a tape that pulled out a bolt in flight, and the bomb exploded on impact, the 'best effect being obtained when used against the track or suspension of a tank'. The No. 73 has aptly been described as looking like an old-fashioned thermos flask, and had a buff painted body. The 'Hand Incendiary Bomb', also included in the 1941 *Supplement*, was eventually given the designation 'No. 76', but this is somewhat misleading as it was actually in use quite early with the Home Guard, and earlier titles for it included the 'SIP' or 'Self-Igniting Phosphorus', and the 'AW' or 'Albright and Wilson'. This stubby but dangerous bottle, just over 6 inches (15cm) in length and weighing 1.5lb (680g), was really an improved version of the improvised 'Molotov Cocktail'. It contained a half pint of water, yellow phosphorus, benzene and rubber. It could be hurled against any solid target including vehicles and buildings, or shot from the Home Guard Northover Projector. It burned fiercely, and was very difficult to extinguish, reigniting spontaneously even if put out with water. As can be imagined it was not a wonderful weapon to transport, and had to be stored securely, and preferably separately to other supplies.

The manual *Grenade* was updated in 1942, and this general issue volume underwent reprinting until 1946, completely superseding the 1937 manual and its various supplements. Weapons noted in the latter part of the war included not only the No. 36 and its discharger, and the Nos 68 and 73 already mentioned, but also the Nos. 69, 75, 77, 82 and 83. The No. 69 was something of a departure in that, having a bakelite body, it was relatively lightweight at under 14oz (397g), and intended as an 'offensive' grenade. Additionally – and unlike the Mills – it was an explode on impact type, armed in flight by the unwinding of a tape. It relied on blast and shock, and was deemed particularly useful for assaults and house-to-house fighting. It could be bowled or lobbed in a variety of ways so long as the tape unwound and dropped free, allowing the bomb to detonate. It saw significant use after D-Day.[35]

The No. 75, or 'Hawkins', so named after its inventor, also saw considerable use, and was effectively an anti-tank mine, handy enough at 2.25lb (1.02kg) to toss at least short distances. It went off when compressed by something running over it. Thrown in front of a vehicle it might cause complete destruction, or blow a

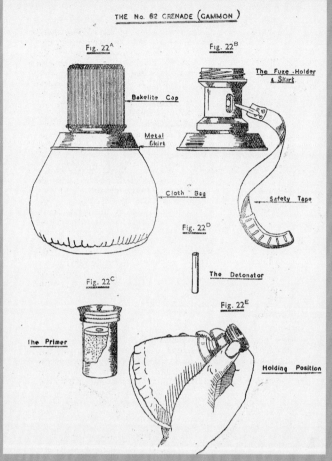

The Gammon bomb, or No. 82 grenade, designed by Captain Gammon of the Parachute Regiment. It could be used against armour, but was particularly effective against buildings. It was delivered to units as a kit of parts in a steel box from which fourty bombs could be assembled, with the explosive kept separate until required. (Author)

track from a tank. Usually, however, it was planted in various ways, or put on a rail track, or several were dragged across a road on a rope where they were collectively difficult to avoid. The manual described how they could be buried in staggered rows to form a minefield and used as demolition charges. The No. 77 smoke grenade actually came in two varieties, which it was as well not to confuse, as the Mark I contained white phosphorus and was highly incendiary, and the Mark II did not and was therefore relatively safe. Both were used to create instant smoke screens and were thus very useful on the battlefield. The No. 83 was also a smoke type, but was more practical for signal purposes as it produced coloured smoke and was available in red, yellow, green and blue.

The No. 82, also known as the 'Gammon Grenade', was a real novelty, being effectively a small stockinette bag with a percussion mechanism attached: plastic or other types of explosives were loaded into the bag. When plastic was used this was first gently formed into a pear shape. As the manual explained:

'It is of particular value against "soft-skinned" transport and light AFVs. It will penetrate about 1 inch of armour plate and

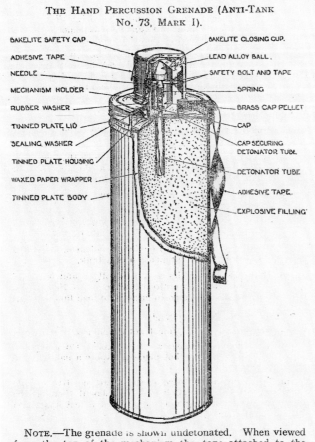

THE HAND PERCUSSION GRENADE (ANTI-TANK No. 73, MARK I).

BAKELITE SAFETY CAP
ADHESIVE TAPE
NEEDLE
MECHANISM HOLDER
RUBBER WASHER
TINNED PLATE LID
SEALING WASHER
TINNED PLATE HOUSING
WAXED PAPER WRAPPER
TINNED PLATE BODY

BAKELITE CLOSING CUP.
LEAD ALLOY BALL.
SAFETY BOLT AND TAPE
SPRING
BRASS CAP PELLET
CAP
CAP SECURING DETONATOR TUBE.
DETONATOR TUBE
ADHESIVE TAPE.
EXPLOSIVE FILLING

NOTE.—The grenade is shown undetonated. When viewed from the top of the mechanism the tape attached to the safety bolt is wound in a clockwise direction.

Printed under the Authority of HIS MAJESTY'S STATIONERY OFFICE by William Clowes & Sons, Ltd., London and Beccles.
G. 357—2234 2/41 140,000

will knock a sizeable scab of metal from the far side of a 1.5-inch plate. It will also penetrate 9-inch brick walls and pieces of wall will be thrown off with sufficient velocity to cause casualties. It can be used as an anti-personnel grenade, the effect in this role being considerably increased if pieces of stone or metal are embedded in the charge when it is moulded. The grenade can be used as a demolition charge with a detonator and a length of safety fuze. Weight up to 2lb according to the amount of explosive used. 1.5lb of explosive will normally be the most satisfactory amount.'

The Gammon Bomb was held in the palm of the hand whilst the safety cap was removed, holding the tape in place with thumb and forefinger. The tape unwound in flight, and the bomb exploded on impact. The device saw its most widespread use with Airborne forces where its lightness and versatility were a positive boon. One use, perhaps unforeseen at the time of introduction, was as a 'mouse-holing' charge in street fighting.[3]

Flame-Throwers

The modern flame-thrower was first used by the German Army in 1915, and though the British Army also created flame weapons in the First World War, the emphasis was on large positional weapons, and projectors throwing incendiary missiles. However, British interest in flame munitions was dramatically reawakened in the crisis of 1940, when there were plans to flood invasion beaches and routeways with flammable liquids, a revival of 'Molotov Cocktail' petrol bombs, and 'fougasse' weapons for projecting flame into roads. Soon, several portable or semi-portable flame weapons were in use.

The 'Harvey' flame-thrower consisted of a fuel cylinder and nitrogen bottle on a wheeled trolley, connected to 25 feet (7.6m) of reinforced canvas and rubber hose. Filled in the recommended manner with 22 gallons of creosote, the equipment weighed well over 500lb (727kg). Ideally, the Harvey was used as an ambush weapon and operated by two men, one of whom directed the hose. The range was up to 60 yards (55m) 'on a calm day', and the fuel was sufficient for about ten seconds' discharge. The flame-thrower team was best covered by riflemen or machine gunners to deal with vehicle crews or supporting infantry. In the slightly more handy 'Marsden' flame-thrower, the equipment consisted of a pack and hose arrangement weighing 82lb (37kg). Though only 4 gallons of fuel were contained, the flame was spark-ignited and the Marsden could deliver a jet short distances for a total of twelve seconds. Instructions recommended that the Marsden should be discharged in short spurts for maximum effect.

THE HARVEY FLAME-THROWER

The Northover Projector, or 'bottle mortar', on its little four-legged tubular stand, was soon something of a specialty of the Home Guard. The equipment weighed about 130lb (59kg) and was breech-loaded, being able to throw its incendiary bombs to about 300 yards (274m). Usually it was worked by a two-man crew, who were expected to be able to hit a target 4 foot square (0.37m square) with almost every round at 50 yards (45m), and a target the size of a tank 90 per cent of the time at 200 yards (183m). Presumably this dropped off markedly against moving targets, or those under cover.[36]

As the war moved on, new models of flame-thrower were developed, and the British Army became more concerned with offensive action, focusing on 'man pack' flame-throwers – to lead or accompany assaulting infantry – and vehicle mounted devices, mainly aboard tanks and armoured carriers. Troops were taught that flame had both physical and moral effects, and that with skilled use the enemy could not merely be burned but asphyxiated in confined spaces, smoked out, or simply intimidated into leaving a defensive position. Tactically it was best used by surprise, only

employed when essential, and immediately followed up by the infantry. Various tricks were possible, including bouncing squirts off walls to hit concealed targets, and 'wet' shots where the fuel was projected first and allowed to drain down before being ignited in a massive ball of flame. Foliage provided no protection against the flame-thrower unless extremely dense, and even then could be set alight if not very wet.

In the latter part of the war, the standard-model flame-thrower was the 'Lifebuoy', though as of 1945 a new type called the 'Ackpack' was imminently expected. The former weighed 64lb (29kg), the latter 48lb (22kg) when charged. Both types 'consist of a harness to which is attached a lifebuoy-shaped container of fuel, a sphere containing compressed gas, and the gun which is connected to the containers by flexible tubing. The containers are carried on the back and in both cases contain 4 gallons of fuel, giving ten to twelve one-second shots before refuelling.' The Lifebuoy had a range of about 40 yards (34.6m), the Ackpack 50 yards (45.7m).[37]

A demonstration of the 'Lifebuoy' flame-thrower in the Netherlands in the latter part of the war. The weapon was named after the shape of the fuel tank, and in its final version the squirts of inflammable liquid, propelled from the nozzle by compressed gas, were ignited by means of a battery system. (Pen & Sword/SSPL/Getty Images)

Swords and Knives

In 1939 swords were carried by the cavalry and yeomanry, and by officers and warrant officers on parades. They were also part of the ritual of commissioning. The 1908 Pattern cavalry trooper's sword had bowl guard, slightly inclined grip, and a straight 'T'-section blade of 35 inches (89cm). These factors made for an ideal thrusting weapon, but by the Second World War the chances of using it in such a fashion were minimal. It is said that when Edward VII was shown this sword for his approval, he declared it 'hideous'. Mounted officers carried the similar 1912 Pattern weapon, which was easily distinguished by its floral decoration to the guard, and ribbed shagreen (shark or ray-skin) grip. Though most cavalry officers followed the basic regulation pattern, there were regimental variations. Royal Artillery officers continued to use the old 'three-bar hilt' type sword, the first appearance of which dated back to the early nineteenth century.

The majority of dismounted officers used the 1897 Pattern Infantry officers' sword with a straight blade 32.5 inches (82.5cm) in length, and a half basket guard incorporating the monogram of the monarch. There were some regimental variations, most importantly to the guard, where other devices were incorporated. A slightly different pattern was carried by Rifles officers. Swords were purchased from various retailers, those by Wilkinson being marked with a unique serial number

a then substantial 13*s* 6*d*, were prepared by Wilkinson Sword and taken to the War Office for testing, and from January 1941 production commenced. Thereafter, new models with darkened blades and a variety of grips were made for British service, and very similar models were adopted by other nations. Techniques for use of the dagger were explained in the manual *All in Fighting* (1942).[39]

A Sergeant demonstrates the 'FS' knife to trainees. Stabs or cuts to arteries could render a man unconscious in seconds. (Express/ Getty Images)

recording the purchaser and date. Probably the most distinctive swords were those of the officers of the Highland regiments, being a full basket broadsword. These were referred to generally if strictly incorrectly as 'Claymores'. With huge expansion of the officer corps, economies, and widespread use of battle dress, even on parade, the ready availability of swords – and their subsequent use – declined markedly with time. Warrant officers' swords were often already unit or official property, and as the war progressed, previous insistence that every officer should have his own sword was not universally adhered to.[38]

Though swords can have seen virtually no use in anger in the British Army of the Second World War, there were some edged weapons that did. Bayonets have been mentioned in conjunction with rifles, but there were also at least a few fighting knives that saw action in raids and with special forces. The extraordinary broad-bladed 'Smatchet', designed as much to intimidate as to wound, enjoyed a brief vogue towards the middle of the war, particularly as a second weapon for men using the Thompson sub-machine gun. A brass-handled dagger incorporating a knuckleduster handle was also used, at least in small numbers, in the Middle East. Yet by far the most important was the Fairbairn–Sykes, or 'FS', knife. First proposed in November 1940 by W.E. Fairbairn and E.A. Sykes, what would become the quintessential 'Commando dagger' had a slender sharp blade and cross guard with checkered metal grip. Prototypes, costing

No. 29. The Smatchet (*contd.*)

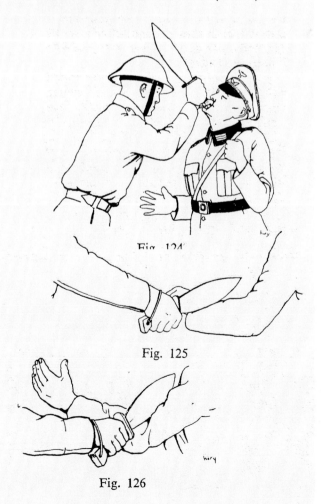

Fig. 124

Fig. 125

Fig. 126

The use of the smatchet against wrist or inner arm, or, with the pommel against the face. From the manual *All in Fighting*, 1942. (Author)

CHAPTER SIX

The Artillery

9.2-inch Mark 2 Howitzers in France, 1940. This model of ordnance could throw a 290lb (132kg) high explosive shell almost 14,000 yards (12.8km). Impressive as this was the 9.2-inch Mark 2 was a veteran of the First World War that was difficult to move and took hours to assemble and get ready for action. They were replaced by newer types as soon as possible. (Universal History Archive/UIG/Getty)

As the Royal Artillery motto 'Ubique' would suggest, the artillery went almost everywhere the Army campaigned. In the Second World War the artillery arm was both advanced and important, and it has been argued that this was perhaps disproportionately so – due to both suspect doctrine, and weaknesses in other arms.

Never the less, whilst the British Army has been criticised for its tendency to 'lean on the barrage' and its unwillingness to depart from ordered fire plans, there was also logic in this methodical approach. For if ordnance could be organised by industry and brought to the right place at the right time, expenditure of shells could sometimes be used as a substitute for human casualties. An army with fewer casualties would be likely to last longer, and maintain better morale, than one in which human strength was expended against technology. In this way efficient logistics

The First World War vintage 18pdr field gun. Quite a few survived after 1918, and on the outbreak of the Second World War various models of this ordnance were still to be found in colonial stations. Others reappeared as an emergency measure in defence of the UK in 1940. (Author)

could be made to play their part. From a Japanese point of view in particular this was not fighting in a 'manly' way: but it certainly helped defeat foes who were more willing to die for their countries, and played a particularly significant part in the latter period of the war when the onus was on Allied forces to advance, and once the British artillery arm had shed its antiques and was re-equipped with the latest generation of guns.

It has been argued with some cogency that a key feature, especially of Montgomery's battle plans, was the achievement of a concentration of artillery, thickening this with air power as necessary. Fire plans opened up the possibility of movement, and on occasion divisional concentrations were used to provide fire support on very narrow sectors of the enemy front. At its best and most flexible it proved possible to orchestrate the guns on a unit by unit basis, and at divisional, corps, or even Army level depending on the plan of operations. 'Army Groups Royal Artillery' – or 'AGRAs' – were first deployed from 1942. This being said, the very biggest and most concentrated barrages were not attained until 1944, when for example, during Operation Goodwood, an amazing 259 guns were in action per kilometre of the front. In Normandy it proved possible to dump, on

average, 20 tons of shells on each German battery in retaliatory 'counter battery' fire. Massed artillery was also a mainstay at Cassino and during the Rhine crossing.[1]

According to the *Operations* manual of 1942:

'Artillery is essentially an offensive arm, and no large-scale plan of attack can hope to succeed without full consideration being given to its best employment. In defence, artillery is also used offensively, to destroy enemy concentrations, batteries, etc., and in support of our own counter attacks… Artillery in the field is classified as mountain, field (including horse), anti-tank, medium, heavy, super heavy, and anti-aircraft. All except mountain are mechanically drawn. Artillery is normally allotted as follows: a proportion of the field, anti-tank, and light anti-aircraft artillery regiments form the divisional artillery; the remainder of the field artillery is organised into Army field regiments under higher command as a reserve, and allotted to formations as required; medium, heavy, super heavy, heavy anti-aircraft, and some light anti-aircraft are under corps or Army control, but a proportion of medium artillery and of heavy anti-aircraft artillery is sometimes decentralised to divisions.'

The signature characteristics of artillery were the ability to fire effectively at long ranges; flexibility to concentrate or disperse fire; and the ability to disengage from one target and engage another sector as required. In general, concentrating on targets for maximum effect was thought desirable. Artillery fulfilled its missions in three main ways: by 'interference', causing casualties, shaking morale, and impeding mobility; by 'neutralisation', and stopping the fire of enemy weapons; or by outright 'destruction' of defences, facilities, guns and the like.[2]

Field Guns

The 'field gun' was the original piece of artillery dedicated to the support of mobile forces in the field, and the basic ordnance of battle. The term 'field gun' was recognised from as early as the seventeenth century. So it was that the key subelement of the Royal Regiment of Artillery serving with the British Armies of the Second World War was the 'Field Regiment'. As general-purpose weapons, field guns had to be small enough to travel to most places troops could go, yet powerful enough and capable of sufficient range to strike the enemy at a distance. Though some were adaptable enough to confront armour, the main target of the field gun was enemy troops and batteries, in or out of field works or cover. Though field guns were occasionally used over 'open sights' and at relatively close-range targets, it was usual to employ 'forward observers', who relayed targets and corrections via telephones, cable lines and radio, back to the guns from a distance. This had the considerable advantage that guns were less liable to be overrun by the enemy, or successfully engaged by 'counter-battery' fire.

The two main weapons of the field artillery in the First World War had been the 18pdr field gun and the 4.5-inch howitzer. The 18pdr was made in large numbers from 1904 onwards, and the improved model of 1918 with Ashbury breech mechanism and new Mark 4 'box' carriage arguably marked perfection of the type. It threw a high-explosive round just over 11,000 yards (10.06km), was equipped with a hydropneumatic variable recoil system, and weighed 3,500lb (1,588kg) in action. It could also use a number of other types of round, including a slightly shorter-range shrapnel shell that ejected 375 lead-antimony shrapnel balls from its nose end in flight. Such shrapnel rounds were very effective against soft targets in the open, but as was discovered in the First World War, they were of limited usefulness against troops under cover. The 4.5-inch howitzer was a compact but relatively short-range gun that emerged from recommendations made in the Boer War, and was manufactured from about 1908. The 35lb (15.6kg) shell packed considerably more punch than the 18pdr, and the howitzer was capable of lobbing its rounds

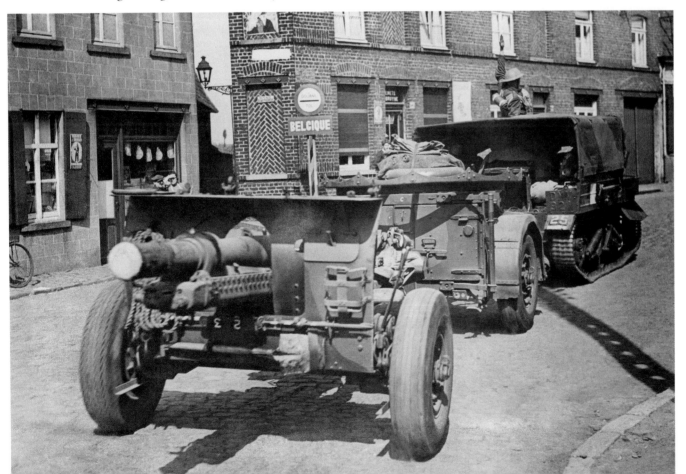

Towed behind a tracked 'Dragon' and limber full of shells an 18/25pdr crosses the Belgian border: this weapon was the basic field gun during the 1940 campaign. (Keystone-France/ Gamma-Keystone via Getty Images)

from the barrel at elevations up to 45 degrees. It was also good against light field fortifications, but its maximum range was only 7,000 yards (6.4km) with the most powerful type '5' charge. By 1939 there had been various minor improvements, most obviously the replacement of the original wheels with pneumatic rubber tyres.

Both the 18pdr and 4.5-inch howitzer would see use during the Second World War. The 18pdr was still in use in a number of colonial stations, and when the Royal Artillery returned from Dunkirk without many of its guns in 1940, old 18pdrs and other weapons were dug out of reserve as temporary stopgaps. Some were still in use in the early stages of the Burma Campaign. The 4.5-inch howitzer saw some use in France in 1940, and was also present in several other campaigns of the early part of the war, notably Eritrea and the Western Desert. It was not finally declared obsolete until September 1944.

Whilst both the 18pdr and 4.5-inch had been very good guns in 1914, by the inter-war period it was recognised they were showing their age, and to have two types was undesirable in terms of shell supply and training. Arguably the 18pdr shell was not large or effective enough, and the 4.5-inch could not be delivered far, or fast, enough from the present howitzer. From the mid-1920s there began a search for a form of universal gun and shell that could overcome all the possible objections and simplify supply. Several different types of small howitzer were devised and experiments made, until by the end of the decade a specification emerged for a weapon that was robust enough to be towed at 'high speed'; fire a 35lb (15.6kg) shell; muzzle velocity of 1,600 feet (488m) per second; range of over 12,000 yards (11km) ; a weight of no more than 30cwt; and a circular firing platform allowing the gun to be traversed all round. Such a beast was neither really gun nor howitzer, and so arose the term 'gun–howitzer'. Eventually, in 1933, a new proposal was put forward for a compact versatile gun–howitzer, firing a 25lb (11.3kg) shell intended to become the sole field artillery equipment. However, lack of funds precluded a complete new start, and as a result it was decided to proceed on the basis of a new barrel and mechanism reusing many of the existing 18pdr carriages. Quite what to call this hybrid at first nobody seemed quite sure. In 1936 the description 'Ordnance QF 3.45-inch Mark I' was applied, but soon '25pdr Mark I' was also used: but the popular term '18/25pdr' seems to have endured better because it appeared more descriptively accurate.[3]

Though many 18/25pdrs went to fight in France in 1939, and about 1,000 weapons were produced to this specification, by this time it was decided that a new gun carriage was not overindulgent in the face of another world war. So it was that the humped box trail and circular all-round traverse firing platform of the 4.1-inch howitzer of 1931 were picked up, dusted down, and revisited as suitable for the new 25pdr. A one-day trial and competition at Larkhill against a rival split-trailed design ended with a simple show of hands that the now-familiar

Detail of the 25pdr showing the traversing platform in its travelling position and the ammunition. (Author)

stumpy carriage and circular base plate won. Production of the complete new 25pdr equipment with new carriage was well under way in the winter of 1939, and the gun saw action in Norway early in the following year. The decision to adopt the 25pdr, in this form, and as a universal field gun, turned out to be a wise one, as this 'gun-howitzer' was not so much awkward compromise as a weapon that could indeed do most things well. Its range was 13,400 yards (12.25km), and its total weight just under 4,000lb. (1,814kg)

Whilst the 25pdr was no dedicated anti-tank gun, it did have the ability to penetrate up to 70mm of armour at close range, and thus means of self-defence when in danger of being overrun by anything short of a heavy tank. It could also deal pretty effectively with armoured cars or reconnaissance vehicles. In the earlier stages of the conflict in the Far East it did indeed discourage and occasionally destroy Japanese armour when British tanks were absent. Tactics for use of 25pdrs against armour were extensively tested in 1939, and the following instructions were published in *Army Training Memorandum No. 24* that September:

'1. All 25pdr guns must be sited in action that they can engage tanks from their positions, otherwise there will be unjustifiable waste of weapon power.

2. Reverse slope positions, where the advantage of grazing fire is obtained, should be sought. Forward slopes are to be avoided. 25pdr troops should be mutually supporting.

3. A long field of fire is not necessary. The temptation to open fire too soon should be avoided. A field of fire of over 800 yards is, for this reason, definitely dangerous. 500 yards is ample, and in many cases 200 yards will be sufficient. The object is to hit with the first round and with good drill, adequate warning arrangements and "tank preparation" this can be done.'

At various times the ammunition for the 25pdr included not only the ubiquitous high-explosive and armour-piercing, but smoke; coloured smoke; star shell; and chemical. A real oddity in the 25pdr arsenal was the 'propaganda shell'. Not an issue

The 25pdr in action in Tunisia. The gun was a versatile compromise of power to weight, and for cover could make do with a pit of modest dimensions. (Author)

as such, this was a converted smoke shell stuffed with leaflets. Usually 25pdr ammunition was carried in a small trailer for 32 rounds, and the main tractor was the Morris 4x4 'Quad'. The 25pdr gun was usually operated as a 'section' of two pieces, and each gun detachment was six men. The No. 1, or, detachment commander, was a sergeant; No. 2 operated the breech and rammed in the shell; No. 3 was the layer, aiming the gun; No. 4 the loader; and Nos 5 and 6 dealt with the ammunition supply, the latter also being second in command and setting the fuze indicators. The 25pdr was also adapted for many different tasks, being mounted in the Bishop and Sexton self-propelled guns; converted by the Australians into a 'baby' or short model suitable for the confines of jungle; and used as a test bed for many other projects. Total production of 25pdrs was about 12,000.

Arguably the 25pdr was at the height of its potency around 1940 to 1942, for, initially at least, it out-ranged the German 105mm howitzer, even though the latter threw a 32lb (14.5kg) shell. Whilst it can be imagined that the 25pdr was simply not a big enough weapon to winkle enemy troops from very deep cover, it was reasonably easy to deploy, rapid to traverse, not too bulky, and very good at preventing the enemy from showing his face whilst friendly troops were advancing or deploying. However, from about 1942 the 25pdr lost something of its edge; German tanks learned to stay back and use long-range weapons, and German howitzers were increased in range. Yet this is probably not a serious criticism, as Allied forces were themselves now beginning to deploy new weapons in greater quality and quantity by this time. Another point of interest regarding the 25pdr was that though compactness was of significant advantage in most circumstances, this set an effective limit to the amount of protection that the crew could glean from gun pits, yet still be able to engage close targets. According to *Construction of Gun Emplacements* (1940), digging or building up of breastworks around the gun had to be limited to 2 feet 6 inches (76cm), otherwise the barrel could not be levelled to horizontal. It is perhaps for this reason that the 25pdr was always used with the shield in place.[4]

The following tribute was paid by the US *Handbook of the British Army* early in 1943:

'The 25-pounder field gun-howitzer is the basic field piece of the British Army. It has been replacing both the 18 pounder and the 4.5-inch howitzer of the last war. The tube has a removable liner which can be changed in the field. The gun can be placed in firing order on its platform in one minute. From its steady

and easily worked mount it is capable of all round fire and of more effective close in defence and anti-mechanised action than any US field piece. The firing platform is in the form of a wheel which is carried either under the trail or on the back of the prime mover. To place the piece in action, the platform is lowered to the ground and the carriage is then manhandled or tractor drawn over it and coupled to its centre. To permit easy manoeuvring of the trail the spade has been embedded in a "box" commonly called a "banana" which functions very effectively and prevents the trail from digging in.'[5]

British War Production was even more upbeat: 'It is probably true to say that the 25pdr gun-howitzer is the finest gun of its type in the world today. It is relatively light, yet robust; it has a long range yet is extremely accurate; it is simple to build and maintain.'

Though the 25pdr effectively replaced the old 18pdr and 4.5-inch howitzer as workhorse of the field artillery, there were a few other small guns that survived from earlier times to see service after 1939. Amongst these were more than one type of 75mm, for though this calibre was not standard to Britain, some were acquired from other sources. Some 75mm small guns were French, others American, the former first obtained as anti-aircraft weapons as early as 1915, and the latter purchased in 1940, when Britain was in dire straights and lacking anything more modern.

Another old warrior was the 3.7-inch Mountain Howitzer. This was first designed at the behest of the Indian government in about 1910 to replace the old 'screw guns', and produced during the First World War. As well as being the first 'split trail' type used in British service it was also interesting in that its barrel was made in two parts, to be connected by a junction nut and sleeve when the piece was assembled for firing. The purpose of this ingenuity was to allow the howitzer to be taken into eight parts, or pack loads, for transport over mountainous terrain. These units were: the main carriage; wheels and axle; pivot; cradle; trail legs; shield and slipper; breech; and chase. Whilst it has been claimed that this multi-part 'pack howitzer' solution to difficult country originated in Russia in the nineteenth century, there had in fact been at least small-scale experiments with guns carried in parts as early as the year 1611. The 3.7-inch Mountain Howitzer saw service in the Far East and Italy, and was also adopted by the Airborne, and sometimes even carried on ships for use as a 'landing gun'. Though the range of the weapon was a fairly modest 6,000 yards (5.5km), it was compact at just under 47 inches (1.2m) long, and weighed less than 1,900lb (862kg) fully fitted for action. The 3.7-inch was still employed very profitably in the closing stages of the war, seeing action at Kohima in 1944 – where it was worked into places on steep slopes inaccessible to the 25pdr – and later in Burma.[6]

A much more modern small howitzer was the 95mm Infantry Howitzer, prototypes of which were first produced as early as 1942. This weapon was something of a compendium, drawing parts and inspiration from the 3.7-inch, the 25pdr, and the 6pdr anti-tank gun. The reason for its first existence was that the combination of small mounting and fairly large explosive shell was seen as a viable route to giving armoured vehicles more hitting power in a close support role. The 95mm was indeed used in such a way in versions of the Cromwell, Churchill and Centaur, and there was understandable hope that mounted on a small pneumatic-tyred carriage with a well-sloped shield it could do useful duty with the infantry. In fact – and despite its ability to be demounted into ten small loads – the 95mm Infantry Howitzer proved something of a 'White Elephant'. Tests with the gun on the carriage showed

it to be unstable when towed: moreover, it lacked elevation and its range was no better than the old Mountain Howitzer. It was declared obsolete in 1945.

A real oddity in the field of light artillery was the Smith Gun. This was demonstrated to Churchill, and in the face of a dubious Ordnance Board orders were placed in 1941. The first of 4,000 were with the Home Guard the following summer. Designed to provide a mobile support, the Smith Gun was a small smooth bore piece weighing 5cwt. The Smith and its trailer could be towed into action behind any small car, or the gun alone could even be pulled by a motorcycle. Without any mechanical traction the gun was light enough for man hauling with drag ropes. The wheel track of the piece was only 3 feet 6 inches. (1.07m) Though it was capable of greater ranges for bombardment, its flat trajectory fire was only about 200 yards (183m). The two main projectiles were an 8lb (3.63kg) anti-personnel round and a 6lb (2.72kg) anti-tank bomb: the former could knock a 3-foot (91cm) diameter hole in a 9-inch (22.5cm) thick brick wall, and the latter deal with 80mm of armour at

A demonstration of the Home Guard Smith gun, designed by Major Smith. It went into production after being seen personally by the Prime Minister. It was light and ingenious but of very limited performance. (Author)

50 yards (45.7m). However, the real novelty was in swiftness of deployment and mounting, as the gun travelled with both solid wheels on the ground, but for firing was upended so one wheel formed a revolving firing platform. The other wheel was now overhead and a small gun shield covered one of the crew.

The Smith Gun has been widely ridiculed as something of a hopeless peashooter, but the Home Guard envisioned it mainly as an urban ambush weapon, under which conditions its short range was no great handicap and its small size a great benefit. Instructions recommended that the piece could be trundled across rubble by the gun team, using planks or doors as simple ramps to clear obstructions, and might well be placed to fire through a loophole in a wall. The gun team was four: a commander; 'No. 1' to serve the breech and fire the gun; 'No. 2' who set the range and loaded; and 'No. 3' who doubled as ammunition carrier and vehicle driver. Ideally the gun team was supplemented by a Browning Automatic Rifle group to give covering fire and local protection. Perhaps the most justified criticism of the Smith Gun was not its range, but that by the time it was available in any numbers the need for it had disappeared.[7]

Medium Artillery

Next up the scale from the field guns, mountain guns, and small howitzers was the so-called 'Medium' artillery – a truly unimaginative description adopted essentially because these weapons were too bulky to be genuine field guns, yet too light to qualify as 'heavy'. The two original players in this range, the 60pdr and 6-inch 26cwt howitzer, were veterans – the former dating from 1904 and inspired by experience of the Boer War, the latter from 1915. Though the 60pdr looked like an antique, was 16 feet (4.9m) long, and weighed 12,000lb (5,443kg) when its carriage was taken into account, it had a decent range of 16,400 yards (15km) and its shell was not to be trifled with. By 1939 the 60pdr was scheduled for retirement, but enough suitable replacements were not yet to be had so it soldiered on. So it was that it continued to see front-line service until at least 1941, notably in the desert, and continued as a training piece for several years, not being formally retired until 1944.

The 6-inch 26cwt had been state-of-the-art when developed in 1915, and became the main medium weapon from the latter part of the First World War, right through to the beginning of the Second World War. It boasted the first hydropneumatic recoil system to be used on a British artillery piece in the field, a box trail, and was of wire-wound construction with an Asbury breech mechanism. By the late 1930s the standard model had rubber types. Though its 11,400-yard (10.4km) range was rather less than that of the 60pdr, it had the significant advantages of lighter weight, and a much shorter overall length, a considerable boon for being manoeuvred around bends or into cover. At the same time its shell was actually heavier than its older brother, and the barrel could be elevated right up to 45 degrees. The howitzer saw

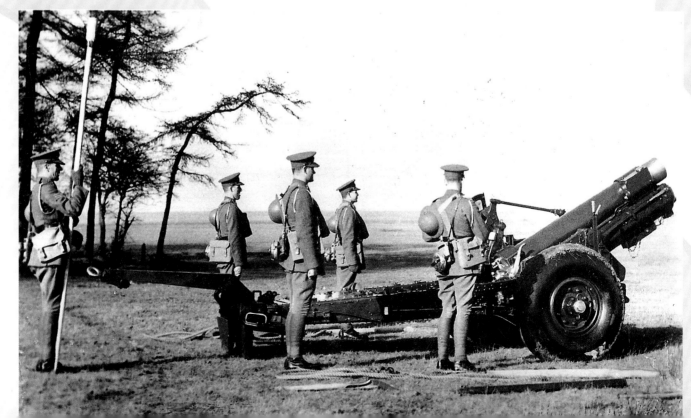

A 6-inch howitzer and crew. This gun was another veteran of the First World War, but a makeover between the wars saw the substitution of pneumatic rubber types for the original wooden wheels. It threw an 86lb shell six miles. (Author)

widespread use early in the conflict, but from the second half of the war was mainly confined to the Far East, as its place in the West was supplanted by more modern guns. Never the less, it remained current until the end, not being declared obsolete until October 1945, and for a veteran it performed well.

The first truly modern medium artillery piece to find its way into the arsenal was the 4.5-inch gun. The initial idea for development came in the early 1930s when it was finally appreciated that the venerable 60pdr needed replacement. At first it was thought that this could be done economically and simply by relining the barrel of the old guns to accept a new shell and so increase range. This worked up to a point, but there were not enough 60pdrs to convert for full re-equipment. So it was that in 1938 a fresh 'Mark 2' design was commenced, soon taking advantage of the new carriage being created for the 5.5-inch gun. It is therefore no surprise that the 4.5-inch and 5.5-inch would turn out looking similar, the most obvious point of difference being the longer barrel of the smaller-calibre weapon. Very often they were issued to regiments so that one battery was issued with each type of gun. The new 4.5-inch was approved on the eve of war, being issued from 1941. Firing a 55lb (25kg) high-explosive shell, the 4.5-inch had a range of 20,500 yards (18.75km), and like the 25pdr and many of the medium and heavy guns was loaded with a separate propellant charge behind the shell. A quick-release mechanism allowed the barrel to be levelled smartly for reloading and then re-elevated back into firing position without the need to turn a handwheel back and forth.

The 5.5-inch Medium was the answer to a new specification intended to replace both 6-inch gun and 6-inch 26cwt howitzer. The new weapon was to fire a shell of at least 90lb (40.8kg) to 16,000 yards (14.6km) and the whole equipment to weigh no more than 5.5 tons. In the event the original shell of the 5.5-inch weighed 100lb (45.4kg). Production difficulties and the incorporation of a number of up-to-date features slowed the arrival of this useful gun onto the battlefield, so it was 1942 before it reached the troops in the Western Desert. The weapon was immediately well liked, its reputation being only briefly sullied by some premature explosions in Italy. These were found to be the result of dirt and worn barrels.

In 1943 the range of the 5.5-inch was markedly increased by the introduction of a lighter-weight 80lb (36.3kg) shell. This was approximately the same size as the existing round, but more

tapered and made of a higher grade of steel with thinner walls. A super charge of 12lb 9oz (5.7kg) of cordite pushed this shell up to 18,100 yards – or just over 10 miles (16.5km). Other rounds produced for the 5.5-inch Medium included smoke, incendiary and chemical. In extremis the 5.5-inch could also be fired against tanks. In case of such an emergency the drill was to use the 100lb (45.4kg) shell, without its fuse, and the transit plug in the nose. A strike from this was said to be able to lift the turret from any tank if the crew were able to aim the gun in time.[8]

The 4.5-inch gun, seen here with its trail closed for towing. (Author)

The 4.5-inch gun in action at the Sangro River, Italy, late 1943. Arguably artillery superiority was one of the factors that made advance up the Italian peninsular possible in the face of a series of defensive lines and determined opposition. (Author)

Opposite: The 7.2-inch howitzer, ready for action. This was a powerful beast inclined to slide backwards on firing, a problem only really solved later in the war with the appearance of the new type Mark 6 with a more stable carriage. (Author)

Heavy, Super Heavy and Coast Guns

Arguably the heyday of the heavy artillery had been the First World War, when guns dominated position warfare and it had been possible to deploy long-range 'Siege Batteries' against static trenches and bunkers in the field. Deep bunkers placed a premium not only on big shells, but munitions capable of penetrating the ground before exploding. Until 1918 it mattered relatively little that the heavy ordnance was difficult to relocate and slow to load as usually the enemy was not going anywhere, and rail lines served to shift not only dedicated rail guns but much of the impedimenta of war.

For a number of reasons the development of heavy artillery stalled in the inter-war period. Perhaps the most obvious was that funds were generally short and the most significant demands upon

the Army were those of the colonial policeman. In such a role the biggest guns could play little part. A second reason was that if war came at all, most major powers were determined that it should be unlike the last. Again, in a war of movement, heavy artillery was not the ideal tool for the job. Perhaps less obviously the enthusiasts of air power were now also claiming that bombers, not guns, were the best way to reach out ahead of ground forces and strike at troop concentrations and communications. Therefore, a good deal of finance and research went into the material for both 'strategic' bombing and 'tactical' ground support. With the Royal Air Force established as an independent arm from April 1918, this work was divorced from the plans of the ground forces in a way that the work of the infant Royal Flying Corps – formally a branch of the Army – had never been. Not until the later 1930s and a gradual relaxation of tight purse strings was serious thought given to the matter of big guns, and even then new specifications for a 6.85-inch gun and a 7.85-inch howitzer were temporarily put on the back-burner so that the 25pdr and 3.7-inch anti-aircraft gun could take priority[9].

So it was that a veritable antique in the shape of the old '6-inch Field Gun' from the First World War was again trundled out from 1939 to do duty as a heavy piece on the new 'Western Front'. This beast, weighing nearly 23,000lb (1,043kg), and still mounted on traction engine wheels, was a modification of a coast defence gun. It was of a traditional wire-wound design, and featured the Asbury breech mechanism. A few were also seen in the Middle East, but later in the war they were relegated to training, being declared obsolete in January 1944. Another stopgap of the early war period was the first version of the 7.2-inch howitzer. Approved in 1941, this was a conversion of the old 8-inch howitzer, achieved by replacing the barrel liner and altering the breech mechanism to achieve greater range. Upon the acquisition of American 8-inch howitzers, a similar trick was performed, thus creating a 'Mark 2', 7.2-inch howitzer. Considering that these weapons were effectively cannibalisations of more First World War stock, the results were not unimpressive, as the early type 7.2-inch could throw a 200lb (91kg) shell almost 17,000 yards (15.5km). The loads behind the shell were four-part bagged charges, and major range adjustment was achieved by successively loading more of the numbered bags ahead of 'Charge 1' which contained the igniter.

As of 1943 the Royal Artillery began to receive supplies of the American M1 155mm gun, a useful weapon with a range of about 20,000 yards (18.3km) and a modern multi-wheeled split trail carriage. So finally it was decided that something other than converted elderly material should be fielded alongside the M1 and a project commenced to redesign the 7.2-inch. The new gun was formally adopted in December 1943 as the 7.2-inch howitzer, Mark 6. This modern-looking piece had many of the characteristics of the American M1, including a distinctive multi-wheeled carriage and greater range. Now a 200lb (91kg) shell could be thrown almost 20,000 yards (18.3km), though interestingly the same four-bagged charge system could be used for most of this distance. Only for extreme ranges was the four-bagged charge substituted with a 31lb (14kg) single-bag 'Charge 5'. The 'Mark 6' was now adopted as the standard equipment of the Heavy regiments. In 21st Army Group in North West Europe the usual equipment was four batteries in each Heavy regiment, two each of US 155mm and 7.2-inch Mark 6.[10]

Next up the scale was the 9.2-inch howitzer, and yet again the design originated in the First World War. Its shells were immensely powerful, but transport of this beast was painfully slow. For road transport it broke down into three major loads, one carriage for the barrel; one for the main mounting and cradle; one for the bed and 'earth box'. On arrival, assembly took much of the day, for apart from putting the gun together the earth box needed filling with 11 tons of soil to anchor the piece in place during firing. Yet the final results could be impressive as the 9.2-inch threw a 290lb (131.5kg) shell a reasonable 14,000 yards (12.8km), which was fair performance for an old weapon. Not surprisingly, however, radical redesign was called for, with no significant progress being made until

after the old 9.2-inch was deployed in France in 1940. Even then work was overtaken by events, as the US 240mm howitzer became available, and this was used rather than attempt to bring another heavy weapon into production at a critical time. The latest versions of the 240mm, which had been designed in the interwar period and the early part of the war, proved excellent and saw extensive use, particularly in the Italian campaign. Its performance was particularly impressive, being able to fire a 360lb (163kg) shell to a remarkable 25,000 yards (22.9km). Some use was also made of the old British 12-inch howitzer, though mainly in defence of the UK.

Anything much bigger, or requiring swift redeployment, began to go beyond what was practicable for easy road movement, and accordingly the real monster guns of the war were rail pieces.

Britain had used rail guns in the First World War, and some were brought out of store for the Second World War. The 9.2-inch Railway Gun, Mark 10 was a conversion of a coastal artillery type, almost 37 feet (11.3m) long, and its all up weight for action was no less than 202,000lb (91,626kg). The Mark 13 version was slightly more compact, and shaved a little off this weight to come in at 194,000lb (87,997kg). The ranges of these weapons were 21,000 yards (19.2km) and more than 22,000 yards (20.1km) respectively. The 12-inch Railway Howitzer was another First World War design, some of which were sent to France in 1940. Though the range of this piece was a relatively modest 14,000 yards (12.8km), its shell was a stunning 750lb (340kg).

At the most extreme end of the scale of super heavy artillery were a handful of rail guns usually identified by individual

A 6in Mark VII coast gun at Newhaven Fort: it replaces the one mounted in the same pit about 1941. As in many coastal batteries a small 'expense magazine' is close to the weapon, larger stocks being kept underground. (Author)

names, and their prodigious ranges. In the emergency of 1940 three 13.5-inch rail guns were created by using guns of the Iron Duke battleship class, mounted on old rail gun carriages. These became *Scene Shifter*, *Gladiator*, and *Piecemaker*. Originally the responsibility of the Marines, they were handed over to the Army in 1943, becoming a 'Super Heavy Railway Regiment' of the Royal Artillery. Throughout the war they remained in the UK, but did form a useful part of the defence of the South East, and indeed were powerful enough to lob 1,250lb (567kg) shells all the way across the Channel. However, this trio were not quite the biggest weapon to see British land service in the Second World War. For this beast, singular, was the 18-inch Railway Howitzer *Boche Buster*. This gun was in production at the end of the First World War and had been deployed to Salisbury Plain for training in the inter-war period. In 1940 it was shifted to the Dover to Canterbury rail line to bolster the anti-invasion defences. However, it did not have enough range for cross-Channel bombardment.[11]

It would be little exaggeration to say that anything and everything was, at one point during the Second World War,

used as a coast defence gun. The reasons for this were essentially twofold: for in the first place once a gun was put on coast defence duty it tended to stay there, and in the second the crisis of 1940 meant that many things hitherto despised found their way to an emplacement on the coast. So it was that the coasts of Britain were protected with everything from old machine guns, to First World War field guns, to Naval pieces and the latest heavy guns. At least eight types of Naval gun were used alongside US and other foreign pieces as well as ancient and modern Army ordnance. Many of these were classed as 'Emergency Batteries' and were perfectly adequate for taking on men running up a beach, or small vessels at close range, but the true 'Coast Artillery' was equipped with range-finding and position-finding equipment allowing it to track and engage warships at long range. Space therefore precludes description of every type of coastal defence piece, but some of the more important should be mentioned.

The twin-barrelled 6pdrs that were quite widely deployed might not sound particularly impressive, particularly when one

The massive 9.2-inch Mark 10 coast gun. The basic model 9.2 coast gun had existed for more than half a century by 1939, but a number of updates kept it relevant to modern war. With a maximum range of about 20 miles (32km) it remained capable of engaging ships out to sea as a 'counter bombardment gun'. (Keystone-France/Gamma-Keystone via Getty Images)

considers that they were first designed in the 1920s. Never the less, deployed in a pit on a traversing pedestal, and with a maximum rate of fire upwards of eighty rounds per minute, they were very useful for tracking and engaging small vessels. Each barrel had its own team of loaders, assisted by a semi-automatic breech system that meant that the shells were almost thrown into the gun and fired at the pull of a lever, laying and directing the fire being the duty of a different crewman who simply attempted to keep the guns on target. At Valletta, Malta, in July 1941 such twin 6pdrs managed to sink five small vessels in a couple of minutes.

Other guns of some antiquity, usually deployed individually – in a small turret or other traversing mountings – included the 12pdr, 4.7-inch Coast Gun and 6-inch Coast Gun. The 12pdr, which had been designed in the 1890s as a defence against torpedo boats, was usually on a small pedestal, later models

of which were fee swinging with the gun layer hooking his arm over an arm piece to traverse the weapon. Though pretty obsolescent by 1939, it was still capable of a range of 10,000 yards (9.1km) and fired anything up to fifteen rounds a minute in extremis. The 4.7-inch was a few years older and had been produced in many different models since 1890, and though slower to operate was rather more powerful, throwing a 45lb (20.4kg) shell to almost 12,000 yards (11km). The 6-inch Coast Gun had started life designated as an '80pdr' in 1882. Again there were a number of different models, and several different types of mounting. In some the crew was protected by a curved open-backed shield, in others a more angular set of plates was employed with shuttered oblong portholes to the front. An interesting variation on the theme was the Arrol-Withers platform with a slab-sided turret on a star-shaped platform that could be dismantled and moved as required. Though these had first been Royal Naval equipments, they were also adopted

Heavily camouflaged with scrim netting an old 60pdr gun awaits the enemy in the desert. Ready for action the 60pdr weight just over 12,000lb (5,443kg), not so different to the new 4.5-inch gun, but its range was inferior. After the desert campaign the 60pdr was largely relegated to training. (Official/author)

by the Army in 1942, and deployed to North Africa and Italy. The 6-inch Coast types current in the Second World War had a respectable range of over 24,000 yards (22km).

At the heavier end of the Coast Gun scale came the 8-inch, 9.2-inch, 14-inch and 15-inch pieces. The 8-inch had a long history as a coastal piece, and was originally deployed to outposts of Empire such as Hong Kong and Singapore. Early in the Second World War, the Army acquired some from the Navy for home defence. The 9.2-inch was used in significant numbers, becoming effectively thereby the standard heavy coast defence gun of the period. The unwieldiness of the 380lb (172kg) shells was offset by the use of barbette mountings with the barrel of the gun just clearing the parapet, the crew behind a shield, with the shells moved under power. The gun itself rested on a substantial steel plate platform underneath which was the shell pit. The shells entered the pit via lifts from underground magazines, and slid on a trolley into position. The gun captain then threw levers which opened a trap and hoisted the shell up to the gun on a hydraulic lift. Details of performance varied with the precise model, but the maximum range was over 36,000 yards (33km), and anything up to three rounds could be fired in a minute.[12]

There were only two 14-inch guns. These were sited near Dover in 1940 and 1941, and manned by Royal Marine gunners. 'Winnie' and 'Pooh', as they were called, were positioned at the personal instigation of Churchill. Remarkably their shells weighed over 1,500lb (680kg) apiece, and their 47,000-yard (43km) range enabled them to engage in long-range duels with the German battery at Cap Gris Nez. Though the total number of rounds fired was modest, they were still active as late as 1944. The 15-inch gun was designed for Naval use during the First World War, but during the 1920s this type was selected as a Coast piece for the defence of Singapore, and installed there in the 1930s. Five guns were emplaced there, being supplied by underground magazines with the shells moving under hydraulic power. Two more were installed at Dover in 1940. At the time of the fall of Singapore the pieces were disabled and later scrapped.

In a minute from November 1944, somewhat bizarrely, Churchill recommended that some of the super heavy artillery be relocated from the UK to the Western Front:

'General Eisenhower mentioned to me the possibility that should we reach the Rhine opposite the Ruhr in the course of the present operations the American long-range artillery would be able

The handy US 75mm Pack howitzer in British use in Italy late in the war. The piece broke down into four mule loads making it practical for rough terrain, and the range of the 14lb (6.4kg) high explosive shell was over 9,000 yards (8.2km). (Official/author)

to dominate and destroy at least half of that area. Cannot some of our heavy batteries erected in the Dover area be of use for this? A range of 30,000 yards is achieved by the medium American guns up to 240mm, but might not the intervention of our 12-inch and 13.5-inch and even 15-inch be accepted? What are the ranges of the principal guns that can be mounted on railway mountings? I am afraid that our 18-inch howitzers would be judged as too short-range. Anyhow, let the whole matter be examined with care, and a plan made out that can be offered to General Eisenhower for the transporting, probably through the port of Antwerp when it is open, of about twenty of these long-range, very heavy guns. Every dog has his day, and I have kept these for a quarter of a century in the hope they would have their chance.'[13]

Whether such a thing was examined very carefully is dubious, for even in the winter of 1944 the front was not static, and to have dismantled and then reassembled the biggest rail guns after transshipment was a mammoth undertaking that would probably not have repaid the efforts required.

Anti-Aircraft Guns

At the end of the First World War anti-aircraft guns had been relatively simple beasts, often 13pdrs, 75mm-, or 3-inch guns on high angle mounts, supplemented by Lewis guns on posts. With the development of strategic bombing there were significant advances in anti-aircraft gunnery. Various forms of power traverse were tried from about 1930. Later in the decade sound detection was supplemented by radar, and different forms of 'predictor' were used to help crews determine where the enemy aircraft might be by the time the shells their guns fired had reached the appropriate height. Anti-aircraft guns also became more specialised. Small types with rapid traverse and very high rates of fire were adopted as suitable for close-range, fast-moving targets, whilst much larger guns with great vertical range were used for striking at high-altitude heavy bomber formations. Rocket batteries were also developed. Though AA guns got very much better with time, aircraft also flew faster, and often higher, so the bringing down of aircraft with guns never became an easy business. Indeed, one-off aimed hits on planes were rare, major barrages with many tubes being the rule for serious interception, and generally vast numbers of shells were expended for the destruction of fairly modest numbers of planes. However, this was but part of the story, since to be effective anti-aircraft guns did not necessarily have to destroy,

20mm Quadruple Polsten guns. Manufactured in Canada to a joint British and Polish design the Polsten gun fired as fast as a machine gun to a range of up to 2,000 metres. At 1,000 metres it was an effective close defence against aircraft and could also be turned on ground targets. In different versions Polstens were towed, and truck or tank mounted. (Author)

or even damage, their targets. A spirited and reasonably accurate barrage might well force the enemy into evasive action, disturb the aim of his bombs or machine guns, or interfere with his navigation and ability to co-ordinate his formations. In all these instances the results of air attack could be mitigated.

During the course of the war, a variety of guns was used in the 'LAA' or 'Light Anti-Aircraft' role. These included the 20mm Polsten cannon, 20mm Hispano-Suiza, 2pdr AA and 40mm Vickers. Both the 20mm guns had rapid rates of fire – from 450 to 650 rounds per minute, and fired from sixty-round magazines. Useful against low-level attack, the effective ceiling of these guns was no more than 3,000 feet (914m). The 2pdr AA was a naval type 'pom-pom' weapon adopted for land use in 1936 for port and air facilities in a ground role. Often a pair was mounted on a Mark 1 pivot, with belt boxes and ejection chutes for spent cartridges off to either side. Each barrel could manage about sixty rounds per minute, giving the unit a maximum of 120 rounds per minute to an effective ceiling of 6,000 feet (1,825m). A degree of mobility was provided by a 'transporter' carriage that allowed the equipment to be relocated, though it could not be fired on the move. The 2pdr AA guns were declared obsolete as land weapons in 1943.

Far more successful and more widespread were the different models of 40mm Bofors gun. Developed by the Swedish Aktiebolaget Bofors company at the end of the 1920s, this weapon was marketed around the world during the 1930s. The Bofors product was first purchased by Britain in 1937 and some stocks were taken from Poland, which was also manufacturing the gun. Thereafter the UK obtained its own license to make the Bofors. The success of the weapon was down to three factors: it was flexible, being possible to fire from its wheeled carriage, a ground mount or other types of position and vehicle mount; it was large enough to inflict serious damage, yet small enough for mobility and swift aim; and it used an 'auto-loading' system. The gun was recoil operated, and had a vertically sliding breech block. In action one of the gun team fed in chargers of four shells from the top of the mechanism, and the rounds were automatically loaded by a spring rammer. The ejected cases were guided down a chute to the front.

The maximum ceiling for Bofors fire was 16,500 feet (5,029m)– at which height the shells automatically exploded even if no target was struck – and it was possible to harass enemy aircraft formations at such a range, but little accuracy could be expected beyond about 5,000 feet (1,524m), this being the effective limit of the predictor and sighting systems. At maximum speed the distinctive rhythmic fire of the Bofors was at a rate of sixty to ninety rounds per minute. A variety of sighting systems were used. In the early 'Polish' model the speed and distance of the target were set, allowing for enemy craft moving at up to 350mph (563kph) and a maximum range of 4,400 yards (4km). In others the gunner simply viewed through a large wheel type sight, and corrected visually to aim further forwards of faster-moving targets. With luck as well as judgement, plane and shell then coincided in time and space.

Though there were other heavy anti-aircraft weapons, it is the 3.7-inch that has attracted the most attention, as well as the most controversy. Following the issue of a specification in 1933 calling for a weapon that could be brought into action in fifteen minutes, yet trundled around at 25mph (40kph) under tow, the gun was designed by Vickers and entered production in 1937. The brute weighed 8 tons, could engage at anything up to 40,000 feet (12.2km), and with an auto-loader working at full speed could shoot anything up to twenty rounds per minute. Though it was true that the number of planes hit was small for the total number of shells fired, when deployed in batteries the 3.7-inch could put up a highly dramatic wall of fire. This was both off-putting and intimidating for enemy aircrews and a morale raiser for those on the ground.[14]

The powerful 3.7 AA gun, used in conjunction with equipment to determine the height and movement of aircraft. Hitting aircraft was extremely difficult, but with remote power control and radar later in the war performance improved. (Author)

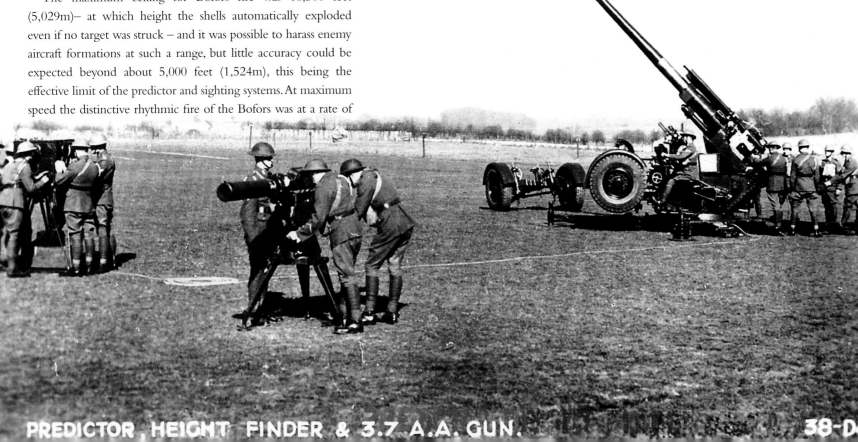

PREDICTOR, HEIGHT FINDER & 3.7 A.A. GUN.   38-D

A heavily camouflaged Bofors gun with crew scanning the sky through ring sights. (Author)

The speed of operation of the 3.7-inch was, it should be noted, as fast as the German 88mm, and this with a slightly larger shell. The 3.7-inch performed well, and also proved amenable to improvements with time. The two real points of controversy therefore were whether the time and resources devoted to this AA gun were effectively expended at a time of austerity; and secondly, whether there was a serious omission in not attempting to use it on the battlefield, and particularly as an anti-tank weapon, when with hindsight we are aware what was done with the '88'. The first question is down to simple choice, and in the event the decision was led in part by the widespread belief that airpower alone could cripple a nation, and partly by a desire to reassure the population that everything that could be done to protect them was being done. The answer to the second point is inevitably more complex, since contrary to popular opinion there were efforts to put the 3.7-inch on the battlefield.

This was actually done, for example in Italy in 1944, where the 3.7-inch was used, at least in small numbers, as a supplement to the field artillery, and the same year there were also attempts to convert the piece for anti-tank use. Furthermore, there were experiments with the 3.7-inch on a Canadian Ram tank chassis. That these improvisations and experiments were not more successful and widespread appears to be because efforts were not made soon enough, Western Allied armoured vehicles were generally smaller than the Tiger tank, and the 3.7-inch was physically so large and so heavy that it would have been simpler to design a tank around the gun.

Impressive as it was, the 3.7-inch was not the largest of the British AA guns, these being the 4.5-inch and 5.25-inch weapons. Interestingly the 4.5-inch was actually a modified Naval gun approved for land service in 1938. A serious downside was that it could manage only eight rounds per minute, but against this its ceiling was 44,000 feet (13.4km) with a 54lb (24.5kg) shell. It could also be deployed on the coast as a dual-purpose

anti-shipping and AA gun. It was largely superseded in 1944 by the 5.25-inch, which again was a naval type piece on a new mounting. Like the 4.5-inch, the 5.25-inch could be used as an AA or coast gun, and when emplaced on the coast was usually mounted in a huge armoured turret. As might be expected, the whole thing was engine-powered. As a result, the 5.25-inch could manage anything up to ten rounds per minute.[15]

It is interesting to note that Churchill attended a demonstration of the new anti-aircraft rockets at Shoeburyness as early as December 1941. He also maintained a long-term interest in conventional AA guns. Remarkably, as late as January 1945, he wrote to General Ismay:

'Arrangements should be made to leave a large number of static anti-aircraft guns which are not needed, in their positions for care and maintenance. I do not like breaking up batteries planted with so much care. The personnel can be removed and a few caretakers kept. Otherwise I am sure we shall find that in a few

The Red Sands 'Maunsell Fort' in the Thames estuary. Designed by Guy A. Maunsell these forts were designed to prevent enemy mine-laying here, and at various points around the coast. The main armament was 3.7-inch and Bofors AA guns. (Fred Morley/Fox Photos/Getty Images)

months we have simply stripped the western and northern parts of the country of every form of defence, and should the situation change we should have to begin almost from the beginning.'[16]

Anti-Tank Guns

The race to produce more powerful, better protected, and faster tanks – beginning in 1916, and continuing long after the Second World War – was just one part of the story of armoured warfare. Other arms sought to gain weapons with which they could combat the new menace of the tank, and one of the most important of these was the anti-tank artillery. As was explained by the operations manual *Defence*, of 1939:

'Anti-tank guns are direct-fire weapons, whose main object is the destruction of enemy tanks. They will be sited to cover the most important approaches which hostile tanks may use; and the fronts; and the flanks and rear of localities where the lie of the ground makes them vulnerable to tank attack. As anti-tank defence is only one aspect of the defence of an area it must be fully embodied into the general defensive system. Anti-tank guns

allotted to sectors will therefore be placed under the command of the brigade sector commanders concerned. It may be advisable to place anti-tank guns in the forward areas under the command of forward unit commanders.'

Anti-tank guns were special in that their key effectiveness in defeating armour depended on focusing the maximum kinetic energy on a small surface area. Commonly their shells were solid – though made of a variety of materials and shapes and hardened in different ways – and the gun that fired them used a powerful charge relative to the size of the shot. This combination gave high velocity, good accuracy, a flatter trajectory than ordinary guns or howitzers, and perhaps most importantly, good penetration. To be genuinely useful, anti-tank guns had to be powerful enough to cope with the latest armour and wreak sufficient damage on an enemy vehicle to put it out of commission, and also manoeuvrable enough to reach the point at which they were needed. They therefore needed to change as quickly as the armour they confronted, and indeed in many instances a gun was produced first, then modified for use in tanks themselves. Initially there was argument as to whether specific 'AT' artillery was really necessary, as ideally British tanks would fight enemy

A 2pdr anti-tank gun in firing position with kilted Argyll and Sutherland Highlanders crew, 1938. This same year the 2pdrs were taken from the infantry establishment and handed over to the Royal Artillery 'Anti-Tank Regiments'. Several hundred of these pieces were left behind in France in 1940, and some reused by the enemy. By 1942 there were more powerful weapons for the Anti-Tank Regiments and many of the remaining 2pdrs were passed on again to the Home Guard and infantry. (Author)

ANTI-TANK GUN.

tanks. Others wondered whether gun design should focus solely on small models, since it was likely that they would be needed to fit inside tank turrets or concealed on the battlefield and could be made more cheaply in numbers.

The 2pdr anti-tank gun approved on 1 January 1936 was very much a product of such lines of thought. It had a vertical sliding breech block, semi-automatic mechanism, and was percussion fired. It was light, at less than 300lb (136kg) for the basic gun and mechanism, and less than 82 inches (208cm) in total length. However, a three-legged all-round rapid traverse platform, telescopic sight, and shield, added more than another 1,000lb (454kg). Even so, the gun was perfectly adequate for the late 1930s, as at 1,000 yards (914m) it could penetrate 42mm of armour. The maximum range was 8,000 yards (7.3km) – though at such a distance targets were difficult to identify, let alone hit, and penetration was negligible. Slender as this performance may

now seem, it was in the realms of overkill when considered against the main pre-war German tanks, the Panzers I and II. A British report on a captured Panzer I determined that its maximum armour was 15mm, whilst the thickest turret-front armour of the Panzer II was 35mm. The original organisation saw the 2pdrs as part of the infantry, but in 1938 they were made part of the gunners, being formed into Anti-Tank Regiments of the Royal Artillery.[17]

Interestingly, whilst the 2pdr was fairly small, it was not that easy to protect – if the objective was use the standard shield, and allow for a significant degree of traverse. As the manual *Construction of Gun Emplacements* (1940) observed:

'Once the action has begun, there is no real hope of adequate protection unless the gun has a very limited arc of fire. The barrel being very low, the depth to which the tripod can be dug, even

The 6pdr anti-tank gun in action in the desert. The Sergeant, foreground, is the gun commander and in front of him is the gunner. On the right of the picture are the loader and an ammunition number with two more shells ready to fire. (Author)

The ungainly 17/25pdr at full recoil. It looked the ugly hybrid that it was, but the 17/25pdr was a big step in the right direction. While the pure-bred 17pdr on its own dedicated carriage was developed and produced the 'Pheasant' did duty in Tunisia and Italy. (Official/author)

if the ground is comparatively flat, will seldom exceed 1 foot. It follows that the results obtained, either from digging in or from the erection of breast works, will be almost entirely a moral sense of security, rather than any real protection. Furthermore, any considerable excavation or building up makes it very difficult to get the gun into the emplacement, and quite impossible to get it out quickly once the enemy has established contact. Although the above considerations necessarily limit the amount of protection that can be obtained in mobile operations, this must not be allowed to detract from the determination to do all that is possible. Even a moral sense of security is worth having.'

Indeed, the crux of the matter was that of finding a good position for the gun, and 'essential' all-round concealment. Probably the best course of action was to take a 'defiladed position', such as one with protection and concealment from one or both sides, and accept that traverse was going to be limited to a maximum of 200 degrees. This traverse could be much less still if the 2pdr was used to cover an anti-tank obstacle such as a ditch. The crew were provided with a slit trench, large enough to accommodate four men, and close to the gun emplacement. In cases where the position was held for a while it might prove possible to connect this crew cover trench to the actual gun emplacement. Likewise, the gun could be given overhead cover, protecting it from view, and thus the attention of dive bombers.

As in so many fields, the French campaign of 1940 proved a rude awakening from complacency. A large number of 2pdrs were destroyed or left behind on evacuation from Dunkirk, and the 6pdr gun which had been planned as a possible replacement for the little 2pdr as early as 1938 was not yet ready. The result was that the 2pdr was kept in production as a stopgap, and until 1942 remained on the battlefield, being increasingly reviled as a useless 'pea-shooter'. To his credit, Churchill was one of those growing increasingly impatient with this weapon. As he remarked to the Minister of Production and the Chief Imperial General Staff in July 1942:

'We have at present made or are completing about 20,000 2pdr tank and anti-tank guns. It is proposed in the next 12 months to make 20,000 more. This weapon is already out of date, and we shall be justly censured if we commit ourselves to a further enormous production of it. I understand that it is proposed to make a wide distribution to the infantry, so that every battalion may feel it can face enemy tanks. But the 2pdr is not the weapon we should make for this, as it cannot stop a tank except under the most favourable conditions.'[18]

The Panzer III, in use by 1939, and now commonplace, had a frontal armour of up to 57mm, and the Panzer IV upped this further still. The 2pdr could only stop its main enemy by luck, and could not even defend itself against infantry. In a number of instances enemy tanks simply 'stood off' to ranges over 1,000 yards (914m) and fired on the British anti-tank guns until they

were destroyed or displaced. According to an American estimate of early 1943, the 2pdr was now really only of use if enemy armour came with 500 yards (457m). Moreover, the 2pdr had no high-explosive capacity against infantry or fortifications – and was becoming less and less useful against tanks with each passing month.[19]

Early in the war, one of the upshots of this unhappy situation had been the adoption of some foreign guns to serve alongside the 2pdr. The Hotchkiss 25mm, also used in France, was respectable enough, though still incapable of dealing with newer German armour. The flexible Swedish Bofors, also produced in Poland and the UK, was much better. This saw action in the desert, and whilst serving with the Lancashire Hussars Yeomanry was mounted on 15cwt trucks. This 'Portee' arrangement provided some useful and fast-moving firepower against the Italian tanks, which were themselves quite poorly armoured. Interestingly 2pdrs and 6pdrs were also used in a similar way for a long time. Instructions on mounting the 6pdr Portee show that the usual method was to run the weapon up ramps into the back of the truck, pulling it in by means of a pair of hand-operated winches. The gun could be mounted to fire forwards or aft, or carried distances in travelling mode with its trail folded.

At Sidi Rezegh, George Ward Gunn posthumously won the VC for fighting German tanks at close range, in what was obviously a highly unequal battle, using 2pdr Bedford Portees:

'On the 21st of November, 1941, at Sidi Rezegh, Second Lieutenant Gunn was in command of a troop of four anti-tank guns which was part of a battery of twelve guns attached to the Rifle Brigade Column. At 10:00 hours a covering force of enemy tanks was engaged and driven off but an hour later the main attack developed by about 60 enemy tanks. Second Lieutenant Gunn drove from gun to gun during this period in an unarmoured vehicle encouraging his men and reorganising his dispositions as first one gun and then another were knocked out. Finally only two guns remained in action and were subjected to very heavy fire. Immediately afterwards one of these guns was destroyed and the portee was set on fire and all the crew was killed or wounded except the Sergeant, though the gun itself remained undamaged. The Battery Commander arrived and started to fight the flames. When he saw this, Gunn ran to his aid through intense fire and immediately got the one remaining anti-tank gun into action on the burning portee, himself sighting it while the Sergeant acted as loader. He continued to fight the gun, firing between 40 and 50 rounds regardless alike of enemy fire which was by then concentrated on this one vehicle, and of the flames which might at any moment have reached the ammunition with which the portee was loaded. In spite of this Second Lieutenant Gunn's shooting was so accurate at a range of about 800 yards that at least two enemy tanks were hit and set on fire and others were damaged before he fell dead, having been shot through the forehead.'

Whilst the 2pdr passed from being regarded as adequate to very poor during its front-line service life against the Germans from 1939 to 1942, this was not the entire story. After the summer of 1942, when the 6pdr replaced the 2pdr in the anti-tank artillery, many 2pdrs were reissued to the infantry, and some went to the Home Guard. In the Far East, against thin-skinned Japanese tanks, the 2pdr remained useful. Moreover, there were attempts to bring the weapon up to standard, mainly by means of increasing muzzle velocity. With the Littlejohn 'squeeze bore' muzzle adaptor for armoured cars and light tanks, a special skirted round was used. Reducing the diameter of the round increased its speed. In the experimental Canadian 'David' system the method was more radical, a 6pdr breech being used to fire a round having a 6pdr case and a 2pdr head. This was not put into production.

The 6pdr anti-tank gun was conceived prior to the outbreak of war, but with the 2pdr currently in production and the troops being trained in its use there appeared no immediate prospect of use. The year 1940 changed all this, but whilst an order for 400 was placed in June 1940, the 2pdrs still took priority. After what must have appeared an agonising delay, the first major production run of 6pdrs began to appear in November 1941. However, thereafter manufacture soon reached satisfactory proportions, with 1,500 being made in May 1942 alone. In the meantime the USA had come into the war, and her military had already reached similar conclusions about the needs for anti-tank guns, and so it was that the basic design was also produced in America, where it became the 57mm M1 anti-tank gun.

The 6pdr was impressive when set alongside its predecessor, having an armour penetration at 1,000 yards (914m) of 74mm, or almost double that of the 2pdr. This was improved later with uprated projectiles, as for example APBC, or APDS. The muzzle velocity was 2,693 feet per second (8.2m per second). In its basic Mark 2 towed format the gun and breech mechanism weighed 768lb (348kg), and was 101 inches (257cm) long overall. However, when gun, shield, and split-trail Mark 1 carriage

Opposite top: A battle-damaged 17pdr gun of one of the Air Landing Anti-Tank batteries supporting the Arnhem operation, displayed outside the Hartenstein Hotel. (Author)

were considered together the weight rose to 2,521lb (1,144kg), quite a burden, even when the entire crew pushed and shoved together. Though it was much larger, the 6pdr did have features in common with the 2pdr, being a conventional semi-automatic, vertical sliding block, percussion-fired type. In ideal conditions it could manage the better part of twenty rounds in a minute, though it was best used more deliberately from an ambush situation. Though the 6pdr was originally designed with both a traversing wheel and elevating wheel, the production version omitted the traversing wheel and featured a shoulder pad and freely swinging barrel, a system stolen from light Naval guns, allowing the gun layer to track targets quite rapidly with his full attention on the enemy. Maximum elevation and depression were 15 and 5 degrees respectively.

According to the new instructions *Gun Drill* and the manual *6pdr, 7cwt, Anti-Tank Gun*, appearing in 1944, the standard crew was five: commander; loader; layer; second in command (or 'link number'); with a Bren gunner serving as lookout and close defence. The commander was responsible for fire control, selection of position, and correction of fire. The loader operated the breech, always ensuring that there were half a dozen rounds ready to hand. The second in command relayed the orders of the commander, assisted in directing gun to target and helping to unload ammunition or cool the gun with water if required. In aiming, the layer was instructed to aim for the 'centre of mass' of a target unless ordered otherwise, or if the target was moving across the front. In which case he 'aimed off' to the fore, so correcting for movement. The gun was usually towed, as for example by a carrier when used by the infantry, but once uncoupled might

On the Senio river, Italy, 1945. The 6pdr was just small enough to work into ruined houses, carry in landing craft, or tow behind carriers. This gunner has stowed his field dressing under his helmet net. (Portfolio via Getty Images)

be shifted by drag ropes and bars. In choosing a place for the gun, concealment and positions at an angle to the front were recommended, these being best calculated to take enemy armour by surprise and preferably in flank or rear. Ideally the gun remained concealed until the enemy was within 800 yards (732m) and presented a good target, thus increasing the likelihood of a first round hit. Wherever possible, guns were positioned so that obstacles provided security from at least one side, and within the position of an infantry company giving additional protection against attack. Dedicated gun pits were ideal, but even a camouflage net thrown over the gun would help to break up its outline. The crew gained some protection from the gun shield which was made of four sections of bulletproof steel, the precise design of which was modified over the life of the weapon. Tools, drag rope, and spare parts were often stowed on the shield.[20]

As we noted, the 6pdr was sometimes used in a 'portee' role, but there were also other experiments with improved mobility. Two of these, the 'Deacon' and the '6pdr Firefly', reached limited scale production. In the Firefly the gun was mounted in the front of a Morris armoured car, and the weapon was fitted with the Molins auto-loading system. This allowed one-man operation in confined spaces. About 175 Deacons were made by mounting the 6pdr within a large shield on a turntable, on the back of an armoured AEC Matador lorry. These saw use in North Africa, though they were hampered by their disproportionate height and indifferent performance on sand.[21]

Though the 6pdr worked well enough there was consternation as early as 1941 when it was realised that the Germans were working on a new generation of heavy tanks, and that in all probability these would be too well armoured for it to cope with. As it was, even the 6pdr was not yet being made in numbers. A new specification was therefore quickly put forward. What was wanted now was an anti-tank gun that could penetrate up to 150mm of face-hardened plate at 800 yards (732m). Calculations suggested that the shot needed to achieve this would be 17lb (7.7kg) in weight and fly from the gun at 2700 feet (823m) per second. Nothing to hand could do this, and experiments confirmed that conversion of any existing piece would not be fruitful either. So it was that the 17pdr anti-tank gun was begun from scratch, though initially some pieces were mounted in the 25pdr field gun carriage, which, amazingly enough, was found tough enough to take this large and powerful weapon. This was all the more remarkable when one considered that the barrel recoiled 40 inches (40cm) on firing, and the

weight of the gun and breech mechanism was over 1,800lb (816kg) – or almost double the weight of the 25pdr barrel and mechanism. This apparently odd combination served with fair success in the Tunisian campaign, being sometimes known by the somewhat strange name 'Pheasant'.

There were two different barrel variations of the 17pdr as introduced in September 1942, the Mark II having lugs for tank mounting, and a muzzle cap rather than muzzle brake. Perhaps the most impressive thing about the weapon was that it eventually performed as well, if not better, than predicted. When using the APDS rounds with tungsten carbide core issued from August 1944, armour penetration was cited as anything up to 231mm at 1,000 yards (914m): moreover, this useful anti-tank gun was also able to fire a decent 15lb (6.8kg) high-explosive round to 10,000 yards (9.1km), giving anti-personnel capability. The original 25pdr type carriages soon gave way to the Marks I and II. The Mark I design was a simple split trail type with removable 'spades' at the ends, keeping the weapon from sliding or boring into the ground on

Breech detail of a 6pdr Anti-Tank gun. The piece was made in different barrel lengths and was manufactured in both Britain and the USA, and supplied to the Soviet Union. (Author)

recoil. Further improvements produced the Mark II carriage from mid-1943. Being of significant size, the 17pdr was best used with more substantial towing vehicles than its smaller cousins, and it was seen, for example, behind M3 half-tracks and Ford 8 trucks.

The 17pdr had a seven-man gun detachment, being commander; loader; layer; second in command; Bren gunner; and two ammunition numbers. To move the weapon without mechanical assistance was no easy matter, requiring the full effort of the team with the second in command and Bren gunner joining in to lift and turn the trail with trail spikes. Reasonably flat ground was required for accurate shooting, and the main method of sighting was with the integral direct-fire telescope. Though most effective as a surprise weapon, the 17pdr had enough power for some impressive long-range duels with armour, and knockout blows to Panzer IVs were recorded at over 1 mile (1.6km). By 1944 it was usual to have seventy-eight of the 6pdr, and thirty-two of the 17pdr anti-tank guns with each infantry division, armoured divisions having a mixture of self-propelled and towed 'AT' guns.

It was little surprise that there was more than one attempt to turn the 17pdr into a self-propelled gun. In the experimental 'Straussler conversion', the gun was given an auxiliary drive appended somewhat awkwardly to the side. This enabled the heavy gun to be shifted at modest speed, but also prevented 'digging in' unless the gun pit was huge. As a result, the contraption was not proceeded with, but variations on the theme were created post-1945. However, the Archer and Achilles self-propelled guns were used extensively in the latter part of the war; the former being based on the Valentine tank, the latter on the American M10 type.

Though the 17pdr was arguably the best British anti-tank weapon of the war, fear that development of even heavier and better-protected German tanks would render it obsolete remained constant. So it was that from 1942 there were experiments with even larger anti-tank guns. The target set was 25 per cent improvement on the performance of the 17pdr. Experts predicted that this would require a 55lb (25kg), round moving at about 2,600 feet (2.4km) per second – and a monstrous gun would be needed for such a shell. However, by 1943 it was concluded that similar performance could be squeezed from a somewhat smaller weapon, using discarding 'sabot' rounds to increase velocity and penetration. So it was that a conversion of the 3.7-inch anti-aircraft gun was attempted, initially to fire a 37lb (16.8kg)

round, and pilots were produced in early 1944. Eventually a 32pdr was settled upon, mounted on a two-wheeled split trail carriage. The appearance of the King Tiger after D-Day, with its sloped 150mm frontal plate, made it appear that the nightmare of a whole generation of German tanks resistant to the 17pdr would soon come true, but time was running out very quickly as the Allies pushed into Germany and the 32pdr never made it to full production. Whilst trials were completed in 1946, and half a dozen 32pdrs were later mounted into experimental 'Tortoise' self-propelled weapons, this was the end of the line for the type.[22]

The key elements of AT gunnery for the latter part of the war were explained in the manual *Artillery Training*, *pamphlet 9*, *Anti-Tank Gunnery* of June 1943. Basic principles remained unaltered. Crucial in all instances were points of aim, and the need to allow 'lead' for any moving target. According to standard procedure, the point of aim for an AT gunner was to be 'the centre of the visible mass' – though this would be adjusted for lead related to speed and approach angle, or on being ordered to do so for other reasons. Simplistically a target moving at 30mph (48kph) would be given twice the lead of one moving at 15mph (24kph). Crudely, gunners could think in terms of head-on targets, direct crossing targets and diagonal crossing targets. Provided relevant adjustments, or lack of them, were known for these, the gunner would be able to come to a swift approximate conclusion as to correct aim, for in practice it was 'impossible to judge the approach angle exactly'. Fire was not to be opened until there was a reasonable certainty of a hit, since the first round would probably disclose the gun's location to the enemy. Gunners were further taught that penetration of armour would depend not only on the nature of the armour and type of projectile, but angle of incidence, and 'striking velocity'. This would necessarily change with range and weight of projectile, though generally speaking the higher the velocity the better. Less comforting was the note that in certain instances, too high a velocity might cause a round to shatter against the armour.

At close ranges time of flight did not require any significant adjustment to aim, gunners of 6pdrs being informed that up to 1,200 yards (11km) 'time of flight' would have 'no appreciable effect on lead'. Likewise though it was desirable to lay an anti-tank gun on level ground, slopes of one in ten to one side or the other were perfectly acceptable. This was the case since although there was a slight tendency for the shot to be deflected towards the lower side, at up to 800 yards (732m) the effect would be less than one eighth of a 'unit of lead' on the 6pdr. Similarly a barrel had to be very worn before loss of muzzle velocity made an appreciable difference to aim, as a loss of 250 feet (76m) per second made only a 10 per cent difference in lead. Given time a gunner could correct aim for a second round, for example aiming on the right-hand edge of a target if his first shot had just missed to the left.

Such quick corrections might be ordered by the commander in terms of adjusting the lead, by 'right a quarter', for example. In some instances slight changes might be needed even after the first hit, perhaps in order to strike a more vulnerable part of the target. At longer ranges similar corrections might be required in terms of elevation as well as traverse, though the trajectory of the 17pdr was far flatter than that of the 6pdr, and fairly predictable at a mile, at which range targets were very unlikely to be easy to hit especially if moving or in any way concealed. Firing was usually conducted with the aimer observing his target through the gun telescope, but at night this might not be possible, and in such circumstances it was

recommended that crews fire over 'open sights'. This was obviously less accurate than using the optics, but might in fact be the only way the enemy could be seen.

In any event the window of time for tank engagement was usually seconds, and to this end all orders had to be given clearly, swiftly and simply according to a standard set of words. In changing targets, a gun commander was expected to preface his instructions with the words 'Fresh Target' and if necessary indicate its approximate direction using the clock system. For example, a tank appearing suddenly at about 20 degrees to the left of the position might be swiftly engaged with the command, 'Fresh Target 11 o'clock.' In the event of more than one target commanders were expected to engage the 'most dangerous tank first', though closest did not always mean most dangerous. Orders were expected to conclude with the word 'Fire', and in the event this was not required the commander would order 'Rest' for a temporary pause, or 'Cease Fire' for the weapon to be brought out of action.[23]

A 25pdr is slung aboard ship using a cargo net, June 1940. The official caption states that the gun is on its way to France to form a 'new British Expeditionary Force' – in the event a fairly hopeless aspiration. The 25pdr had a standard crew of six though operation with a reduced crew of four was also taught. (Official/author)

CHAPTER SEVEN

Armoured Fighting Vehicles

A Valentine tank emerges from a landing craft during an exercise in the run-up to D-Day. The landing craft is an LCM, or 'Landing Craft Mechanised' type, capable of transporting one medium tank or 60 troops. (Fox Photos/ Getty Images)

Britain had led the world in the invention, development, and deployment of the tank, and Winston Churchill was in the forefront of this epoch-making technology. In what was clearly one of his best military decisions, Churchill was one of the first to embrace the new idea, and tirelessly encouraged its development, even in the face of early doubt from Lord Kitchener. The tank was first used on the Somme on 15 July 1916, and by the end of the First World War he British Army had large numbers of machines, both of the familiar rhomboid designs, and the new 'Whippet' types with increased range and speed. For 1919 joint UK and US manufacture promised new 'Liberty' tanks, en masse, to sweep all before them. Yet between the Armistice of 1918 and September 1939 something went horribly wrong: for not only did the Germans steal a march in both tactics and technology, but Britain was also overtaken in sheer numbers of vehicles by several nations. During the war it proved difficult to catch up in this technological race, not least because the effective service life of the average tank design in midst of conflict was usually not more than about eighteen

months – unless a type was versatile enough to be up-gunned, up-armoured, or otherwise radically improved. Few tanks were so flexible. So it was that whilst machine guns, like the British Bren and German MG 34, both designed in the 1930s, were still perfectly effective in 1945, tanks of 1939 were but shadows of the beasts of 1945. It is frequently said that British tank design in the Second World War was inadequate, even that British tanks were 'death traps'. Though there were some good designs, as for example the tough Matilda II; the 'Firefly' that married an excellent British gun to an American Sherman; the Comet; and the genuinely remarkable Centurion – conceived too late to see action – there is more than a grain of truth in the negative generalisation.

German prisoners watch British armour advancing on the main road to Brussels. The tanks are, right, a US-made Stuart, and left, a Cromwell. (Official/author)

The problems from which most of the difficulties appear to have arisen were threefold. First, and arguably most important, was catastrophic under-investment in the period before 1938; second came the imperative of producing any design as quickly as possible following the loss of much of Britain's armour at Dunkirk. Third, an unnecessary diversification of effort brought about by the questionable doctrine that there had to be at least three entirely different types of tank – 'infantry' models requiring comparatively heavy armour but no speed; 'light' tanks; and 'Cruisers', taking a sort of modern cavalry role, needing speed but not much armour, nor a gun that could fire high-explosive rounds. Interestingly the idea that tanks might need more speed and firepower than armour

could be traced all the way back to the frustrations of 1916, but more recently to Staff College Conferences of the 1920s. Indeed, in 1929 no lesser figure than A. P. Wavell had suggested that ideally an armoured force's assets of mobility, firepower and armour should be in the proportion 3:2:1.

So it was that by mid-1939 there were ten different tank models in either production or development. These used six different types of suspension, seven different makes of engine, and four different transmissions. Yet there were no particularly large numbers of any model, good or bad. Perhaps paradoxically some of these technological issues also stemmed directly from the doctrinal: an exaggerated dual belief in the tank as both a battle-winning weapon – able to operate relatively unsupported – and also as an adjunct to the infantry in which it might be used as a sort of mobile pillbox. Yet these theories were also coupled with political unwillingness to buy tanks in numbers.[1]

'Uncle George' Milne, British Imperial Chief of the General Staff from 1926, had taken on tank guru Major General J.F.C. 'Boney' Fuller as Military Assistant, and was open to his new ideas. So it was that with the active support of Fuller and Colonel George Lindsay, Inspector Royal Tank Corps, an 'Experimental Mechanised Force' was formed as early as 1 May 1927. Never the less, corps and regimental rivalries, and general shortage of resources of all kinds, soon intervened. Lindsay wanted units of artillery, engineers, and a motor-cycle reconnaissance company added to the force, but unwisely was against the inclusion of infantry. Perhaps more understandably he also resisted any suggestion of the use of cavalry with tanks. Other arms were reluctant to part with units for the force, but equally Lindsay was set against the release of tanks for use in direct support of other types of unit. Eventually, however, some infantry and armoured carriers were injected into the experiment, and this turned out to be one of the most useful parts of this early exercise. A new 'tank brigade' was formed experimentally in 1931, and made a permanent feature under the new Chief of the Imperial General Staff, Sir Archibald Montgomery-Massingberd, in 1933. The following year a request was made for a general conversion of cavalry to armour, but with Army estimates at about four million pounds, only a derisory £207,000 was available for tracked vehicles.[2]

With a pro-tank culture developing, at least on paper, it was finally decided to begin large-scale mechanisation of regular cavalry regiments, a process announced in the press in February

1936. Initially it was proposed that under the new scheme the cavalry of the line would consist of twenty regiments, half horsed, and half mechanised. Eight specific units were now listed for conversion: 1st King's Dragoon Guards; The Queen's Bays; 3rd, 4th, 7th, 8th and 10th Hussars; and the 9th Queen's Royal Lancers. This would, it was thought, increase speed, range of action and striking power. In addition it was imagined that 'under certain conditions, the tank brigade would require the co-operation of equally mobile troops who can act in areas and under conditions suitable to tanks'. This would be accomplished in part by the conversion of fifteen infantry battalions to machine-gun battalions. In a climate of austerity, conversion to armour was simpler to announce than to achieve. In the case of the King's Dragoon Guards, for example, the regiment actually returned from India only in December 1937, and many of the men were promptly sent on leave or posted to the reserve. Moreover, there were not enough tanks to equip the whole unit in the new year, and 'as a result the year's training consisted almost entirely of individual instruction and courses in driving and maintenance, wireless, and gunnery; and a large number of recruits was taken on to replace those who had gone to the reserve'. Only in 1939 was the full strength of fifty-three machines to be achieved.[3]

Further down the line, it was intended to create a 'mechanised mobile division' of two mechanised cavalry brigades each consisting of two 'motor cavalry regiments and one light cavalry tank regiment', the tank brigade and divisional troops'. At the same

time it was proposed to convert the cavalry brigade in Egypt to a mechanised formation with one regiment each of armoured cars, 'motor cavalry' tanks, and light tanks. Moreover, under the scheme the mechanised cavalry as a whole would focus on these three types of unit. The 'motor cavalry' regiment itself would consist of a headquarters, headquarters squadron, and three mechanised squadrons each consisting of three troops of three sections. Following the big drive announced in 1936, other mechanisations followed with concomitant gradual reduction in horses: the 17th/21st Lancers, 14th/20th King's Hussars and others obtained tanks in 1938. In 1939 more regiments, including the 13th/18th, followed suit, and now most of the cavalry were 'mounted' with tanks or armoured cars. By the outbreak of war, just two regular cavalry regiments remained on horseback, the Royal Dragoon Guards and the Royal Scots Greys in Palestine. The Household Cavalry also retained horses for some time.

It is well known that the drive for mechanisation of the cavalry led to a backlash that has been widely interpreted as ultra-conservative, reactionary and counterproductive. Never the less, at least some of the opposition was not mindless nostalgia, but rooted in practical strategic requirements. In the mid-1930s Army commitments featured many colonial situations where horses were very useful for crossing inhospitable terrain, mounting small scouting patrols, or making deployments of what were now effectively 'mounted infantry'

A Churchill Crocodile flame-thrower tank viewed from the business end. A tank of the same registration, named 'Squirt', was presented to a fort in Brest, Brittany, half a century after the war. (Author)

Cruiser Mark IV, tanks being transported on the LNER rail network, without guns in place. The Mark IV had a battle weight of 33,000lb (14,970kg) and a maximum armour thickness of 60mm. A Vickers and a Besa machine gun plus a 2pdr was the usual armament. (Central Press/Getty Images)

– though the units concerned might retain cavalry titles. To keep mobile horses required fodder and other relatively simple supplies, but, other than horseshoes, few spare parts and certainly no tankers of fuel oil. Conversely the tank of the mid-1930s was far from ideal, being as yet imperfectly armoured, and prone to mechanical failure. Much depended on which enemy the British Army was expected to fight, where, and what resources could be devoted to a campaign. Such were the deficiencies of the British 'Mobile Force' in Egypt that wits referred to it as the 'Immobile Force'.

Arguably it was not until after German rearmament began in earnest that it became obvious that the main threat was European, and that armoured battle in a developed temperate theatre of war was very likely. Never the less, the parsimonious nature of British tank procurement prior to the Munich crisis of 1938 is difficult to exaggerate – total tank production of 1936 and 1937 being just seventy-four vehicles. As of 1936, the total tank strength was just 375 and of these more than half were designated as light tanks and most of the force was already obsolete even by pre-war standards. The few 'medium' tanks that did exist were Vickers types of riveted construction, with armour only 8mm thick, a puny air-cooled 90hp engine, and an old 3pdr 'Quick Firer' as the main armament. They have charitably been described as 'unsophisticated'. If the Army was then the 'Cinderella service', tanks enjoyed no priority within

this slender framework. Even so it was possible to create two 'mobile' divisions in 1938, and by 1939 these were being classed as 'armoured', though the majority of the actual tanks were light, and even then many of these were either out of date or lacking in some other way.

On the eve of war the British tanks embarked upon a significant organisational change that would remain relevant all the way through to and beyond 1945. For 4 April 1939 saw the creation of the Royal Armoured Corps – 'RAC'. This brought together both the Royal Tank Corps, which was re-christened the Royal Tank Regiment, and the 'Cavalry Wing' of recently mechanised cavalry regiments. Also included were seven regiments of the Yeomanry, as for example the County of London Yeomanry, the Westminster Dragoons and Royal Gloucestershire Hussars, already part of the Tank Corps with their armoured cars. Twelve infantry battalions of the Territorials were also converted in 1938 and 1939. So it was, for example, that 10th Battalion Manchesters – which had converted to tanks in 1938 as 41st Battalion Royal Tank Corps – now became 41st Royal Tank Regiment.

The RAC did not supersede the many units that it absorbed, but now acted as an umbrella formation for the armour, and over time the Royal Armoured Corps was massively expanded. Some new armoured 'cavalry' regiments were formed, namely those regiments numbered 22 to 27 in the order of battle, but the bulk of the new units were from other sources, converted Yeomanry, and new regiments of the Royal Tank Regiment converted from the infantry. The new 'regiments' of converted infantry took as their source material one existing battalion, in the process renumbering them in the range from '1' to '200'. Amongst many others, therefore 11th Battalion Duke of Wellington's Regiment became 114th Regiment RTR, whilst 8th Battalion of the Essex now became 153rd Regiment. In 1944 the Royal Armoured Corps also took in the Reconnaissance Corps.[4]

Armoured cars saw extensive service in the First World War, and cavalry regiments, reconnaissance units, and others, would use them in the Second World War. It was also the case that as the war progressed, armoured cars took over some duties traditionally performed by both cavalry and light tanks. Yet in the inter-war period there were no greater resources to devote to the armoured car than there were for the tank. Indeed, early armoured cars were often merely modifications of existing civilian designs. As the history of the 11th Hussars records, when the regiment swapped horses for wheels at the end of the 1920s, the vehicles then available were 'primitive in the extreme'. Two Lanchesters were received in 1929, soon to be followed by Rolls-Royce armoured cars, originally designed in 1917, but supposedly modernised since, becoming known in the regiment as the '1920–1924 Pattern'. As of the mid-1930s the squadrons of the regiment were organised into troops with three armoured cars, one wireless in each troop. The Rolls-Royce carried a crew of three, one of whom sat in the turret, operating a Vickers machine gun in a ball mounting. This vehicle would remain the main asset of the 11th Hussars until as late as 1941, albeit the turret was replaced with a two-man type and armament increased to a Boys Anti-Tank rifle and a Bren gun. Sufficient fuel for realistic exercises was hard to come by even though the 11th was something of a pioneer in the field, being the first cavalry armoured car regiment.

Building Matilda Tanks at Horwich : painting by poster and marine artist Norman Wilkinson (1878–1971). The London Midland and Scottish Railways was a wartime contractor on Cruiser, Centaur, and Matilda tank manufacture at their Horwich works near Bolton. (Science and Society Picture Library/SSPL/Getty Images)

Matters improved only marginally with deployment to the Middle East:

'In Egypt the regiment had 34 Rolls-Royces and five Crossley armoured cars – the Lanchesters, never really satisfactory, having been superseded. The Crossleys, which had wireless, were used as headquarters and command cars; they in turn were replaced in 1938 by Morris armoured cars. The latter had been designed to cope with soft sand, which they did well enough; they were very lightly armoured and had a two-man turret with the same armament as the later Rolls-Royces – which they were supposed to replace. But in 1938–1939 only 30 Morrises [were available], at a time when squadrons were being reorganised on a five-troop basis, so most of the old Rolls were kept and the Morrises were taken as replacements for the Crossleys. Thus when the regiment went to war in June 1940 each troop leader had one Morris, with wireless, and two Rolls.'[5]

The 12th Lancers, forming an armoured car regiment for the BEF in France and Belgium, appear to have fared only slightly better in having a few more of the Morris CS9 type vehicle – all of which were lost.

With the appearance of the Afrika Korps in the desert war, it soon became apparent that anti-tank rifles and machine guns were inadequate to face the latest generation of German armoured cars. Accordingly, progressively more powerful machines were introduced and more widely deployed. Distinction was drawn between 'Scout Cars', such as the Daimler 'Dingo' – that were often open-topped, lacked turrets, and intended for reconnaissance and liaison – and the armoured car proper. Marmon-Herrington armoured cars, using North American parts, but assembled in South Africa, were a stopgap that lasted until 1942. The fast 90hp Humber armoured cars produced by the Rootes Group from 1941 were at first armed only with Besa

machine guns, but these were successively upgraded with better armour and more capacious turrets, until the Mark IV type, which was fitted with a US 37mm gun. Daimler armoured cars, first produced in 1941, were fitted with 2pdr anti-tank guns. Heavy AEC armoured cars, at first mounted with 2pdr guns in the desert, were ultimately fitted with 6pdrs and 75mm guns during the fighting in Europe. With better armament and road speeds of 35 to 50mph, (56 to 80kph) the new generation of armoured car would eventually prove itself capable of taking over many of the tasks formerly entrusted to light tanks.

According to Churchill's own view in October 1940, Britain would never be able to compete with the enemy in numbers of men, and would therefore have to 'rely upon an exceptional proportion of armoured vehicles'. Though this was a reasonable suggestion before the entry of Russia and America into the war, it was clearly far out of date by the end of 1941, and it may be argued that focus on numbers over quality proved unhelpful in the long term. Moreover, early technical problems and failure to rationalise tank production in line with a coherent tactical armoured doctrine would cost dear. The early 'Cruisers' were a particular issue. As a regretful Wavell wrote to Churchill on the situation in North Africa in April 1941:

> 'I did not become aware till just before the German attack of the bad mechanical state of the cruiser [armoured] regiment on which we chiefly relied. A proportion of the tanks broke down before reaching the front, and many others became casualties from mechanical defects during the early fighting. The same seems to have occurred with the other cruiser regiment of 2nd Armoured Division, which went to Greece. Our light tank was powerless against German tanks, which were all armed with guns.' [6]

Just three months later Churchill himself was voicing his disapproval of the mechanical state of tanks in the UK, for of 1,441 infantry and Cruiser types with the troops at home he was informed that 391 were unfit for action. He would soon conclude that part of the reason for this level of inoperability was training, and would caution against too much running of large bodies of armour, even suggesting that for tactical exercises tank crews abandon their precious tanks altogether and exercise in carriers.

Another problematic issue was the pre-war assumption that tank-to-tank actions would be conducted at close range, whilst vehicles were in motion. To answer this scenario, early designs had emphasised guns that could be swung easily by the crew to engage on the move. As few tanks had significantly thick armour as yet, and range of engagement was not thought likely to much exceed about 500 yards (457m), the ideal gun was small, relatively light, and loaded with shells one man could swiftly manipulate into the breech. Such guns were to be found, or newly designed, in the 2 to 3pdr range, and naturally enough small guns operated by one, or at most two, crewmen required only small turret rings and modestly sized turrets. Fighting in both France and the Western Desert would gradually disabuse all these notions. German designers had already begun to think in the realms of tank main armaments of 50 or 75mm, and armour-piercing shells weighing 5lb (22kg) or more, and were perfectly happy that a tank stop to fire, or better still that part of a tank formation should stop to fire while the remainder advanced. Worse was quickly to follow since when British armour launched attacks of its own in North Africa they met, for the most part, not enemy tanks in the open, but entrenched and concealed enemy artillery including specialised anti-tank guns. By the Libyan campaign of 1941 to 1942 the enemy were also regularly using 88mm anti-aircraft guns in this role. Since the smaller British tank guns were incapable of firing high-explosive rounds this made the fight even less equal. British 'infantry' tanks might have been much

26 G.S. Publications 899

The tactical handling of the Armoured Division and its components

NOT TO BE PUBLISHED
The information given in this document is not to be communicated, either directly or indirectly, to the Press or to any person not holding an official position in His Majesty's Service.

Military Training Pamphlet No. 41

Part 2

The Armoured Regiment

1943—supersedes the 1940 edition
Crown Copyright Reserved
Prepared under the direction of the Chief of the Imperial General Staff

THE WAR OFFICE
FEBRUARY 1943

The official armoured regiment tactical manual of February 1943. Despite a vicious circle of tanks built to meet specifications based on dubious doctrinal conclusions there was incremental improvement with each campaign and new design. (Author)

tougher than their 'Cruiser' comrades, but being slow to match the pace of infantry, and not having heavy anti-tank guns, did not make for a comprehensive answer either.

Having started from such a low point, and having lost so much at Dunkirk, the period 1940 to 1942 remained bedevilled by inadequate designs and an emphasis was put on producing as much as possible as quickly as possible. For it had so far been felt, and reasonably enough at that moment, that no time could be lost in devising the perfect machine because it was probable that German invasion would catch the British Army without a sufficient amount of armour of any sort. Moreover, the doctrine that there were several different jobs for tanks to do, and therefore that there should be several significantly different types of tanks, was slow to die. Tough as the Matilda II and the steadily improved Churchill might be, these very useful machines were designed with infantry support firmly in mind. As such they were never fully effective in combating the latest enemy armour. Neither type could much exceed 15mph (24kph) even under ideal conditions. With its small turret the Matilda was incapable of taking more than a 2pdr, and not until 1942 were Churchills fitted with 6pdr anti-tank guns.

Arguably even when there was serious experimental thinking about armour, the tendency was to allow unfeasible or unsuitable projects to continue long after the supposed requirement that prompted them had disappeared. Such criticism could of course be levelled at both the mainstream 'Cruiser' fetish, and the albeit ultimately useful Churchill. The Valiant, another slow infantry tank, first conceived at the end of 1943, was produced as a pilot in 1944, and discontinued in 1945. However, there were worse examples, such as persistence with the later models of light tanks, out of date before they reached the battlefield, and the development of the Tortoise – a super heavy assault gun mounting a 32pdr, first suggested as early as 1942 and ordered in 1944 in answer to similar German weapons, before being dropped when pilot models were finally delivered long after the war had ended. Yet perhaps the most curious folly was the outlandish 'TOG'. Unlikely as it sounds, this was an acronym for 'The Old Gang', a committee of the old and bold including the First World War tank pioneer Major General Sir Ernest Dunlop Swinton, who began to design a heavy vehicle to a General Staff specification in 1939. Their inspiration was contemporary French armour, and the supposed need to cross the barren wilderness of 'no man's land' in safety. The first version of TOG

had side gun sponsons, a small turret, and a distinctly 1919 air. The second was a 179,000lb (81,193kg), 33 foot (10m) long, goliath with a crew of at least six but a maximum speed of under 9mph (14.5kph). Its most revolutionary aspect was that it was the first tank to carry a 17pdr gun. Work still continued in 1942, though the Churchill had by now been accepted as the standard heavy tank, and TOG was never adopted.

Only once it had become fully apparent that enemy machines such as the Panzers III and IV and the US Sherman were effective enough 'maids of all work' was it seriously considered that specialisation should be dropped in favour of genuinely mass production of a machine that balanced the 'armour triangle' of speed, armour and armament rather than sacrificing any one element for another. Just what could be done with the relatively humble, but mass-production, Sherman was proved when large numbers were first made available to Britain, and British amateurs took it upon themselves to attempt to fit it with the really effective 17pdr anti-tank gun. The idea would culminate in the remarkable Sherman Firefly at the end of 1943. Like the M3 series medium tanks before them, the American Sherman types had come just in time to provide both the bulk of equipment, and the breathing space of time, that hard-pressed British armoured regiments required in the middle of the war.

So from September 1942 it was belatedly concluded that there was a real need for a 'universal' British-made tank. However, this ran up against two further problems. The first was that both mainstream design and existing production models were geared to specialism: the second was the intention of the government that from 1943 no effort should be wasted on commencing any new tank that could not take the field in 1944. The logic to this notion was that since the war was now very likely to end by Christmas 1944, devoting significant resources to vehicles that would never fight would actually weaken the British Army in the field at the very time it needed maximum effort. Thus it was that the 'Cruiser' line was finally forced into giving birth to useful 'all rounders' in the shape of the Cromwell and the Comet. Given this background, it is perhaps surprising that the Cromwell with its 75mm gun was as good as it was, rather than that it was imperfect. The Comet may not have been perfect either – but with good speed, a gun derived from the 17pdr, space for a five-man crew, and armour of 101mm, it was streets ahead of any other British tank, and more than equal to all but the best of the German machines.

Though Churchill had the remarkable vision and foresight to back the tank in 1915, it is arguable that his interventions in the middle part of the Second World War were rather less helpful. For whilst experts had at last come to the conclusion that one good tank, able to do virtually anything, was far better than several that could only perform one significant task, Winston appears to have remained wedded to the notion that there should be fast tanks and slow, performing different tactical functions. In 1941 he had argued against attempting to create complete divisions of tanks of a similar type, suggesting instead what he called a 'mixed grill' approach. Moreover, like Hitler he seems to have been attracted to the idea of the super heavy tank, only a few of which would be produced, and being impervious to anything could smash their way forwards in the assault. So it was that he wrote to relevant committee members in April 1943:[7]

'We shall, I am sure, be exposed to criticism if we are found with a great mass of thin-skinned tanks of medium size, none of which can stand up to the German guns of 1943, still less to those of 1944. The idea of having a spear point or battering ram of heavily armoured vehicles to break the enemy's front and make a hole through which the lighter vehicles can be pushed has a very high military significance. A certain number of such vehicles should be attached to armies, and possibly even to corps, in each theatre. The warthog must play his part as well as the gazelle. The experimental development of a heavy tank – 60, 70, or 80 tons – cannot be laid aside. Occasions will almost certainly arise when it would be a solution of particular problems. We shall be much to blame if the necessity appears and we are found to have fallen behind the enemy. Pray let me have a report …'

Paradoxically the British tank industry uttered a genuine world-beater in May 1945, just as the war in Europe was ending. Yet even though it was heavier than what went before, it was not the one-trick monster of which Churchill dreamed. For the new A41 Centurion was a genuine product of the 'universal' tank theory. Its 600hp Meteor engine was powerful enough to shift a 25-foot-long (7.6m-long) tank weighing over 100,000lb (45,360kg) along at over 20mph (32kph); its 17pdr or 77mm gun was effective; and its armour was a massive 152mm. Interestingly early vehicles were fitted with not just the main armament anti-tank piece in the turret but a 20mm Polsten cannon, and the frontal armour of the hull bore something of a resemblance to that of the enemy King Tiger. The Centurion would go on to prove its worth with several armies: but not in the Second World War.

From puny beginnings, in 1939 British armour producers ended on a high note. Along the way they had manufactured much the same number of tanks as the Germans. To these had been added a large number of armoured vehicles produced in the USA and Canada. In June 1945 the Royal Armoured Corps directorate issued a summary of the totality of what had been achieved. As of that month there were 9,994 armoured cars; 5,443 light tanks; 13,667 Cruisers and 2,823 infantry tanks on the books. It was also estimated that during the course of the war to date, after the fall of Germany, and just a few weeks before the surrender of Japan, 15,844 tanks and 1,957 armoured cars had been lost.

The Light Tanks

A major strand of inter-war tank development was the series of small, fast – and relatively inexpensive – light tanks whose original tactical niche was envisioned as being not merely reconnaissance, but operations as part of a 'mobile division'. As outlined in the *Field Service Regulations* of 1935, such an outfit was intended to exploit gaps in the enemy line created by the infantry divisions and their slower supporting tanks. The mobile division would push its own tank brigade through, and Cruisers and light tanks, having   good speed and radius

of action, could 'strike a blow not only at the flanks of the enemy but also at his headquarters and rear services'. Mobile divisions might also be useful in parrying enemy armoured breakthroughs. Essentially machine-gun armed, British light tanks had historical precedent in the 'Whippet' tanks that had been a feature of the Tank Corps in the final stages of the First World War. The ambitious vision for the light tank was never fully achieved: but whilst they were essentially unable to take any punishment heavier than small arms fire, and were very quickly obsolete, it has to be remembered that they were adopted within the tightest of budgets, and that at their first inception similar concepts were afoot in several nations. Various light tanks were indeed produced in other countries, including Italy, Germany, France, Russia, and the USA. In terms of performance, the best of the British light tanks was not far removed from that of the German Panzer I, also still in use in the early part of the war. Moreover, light tanks were found perfectly adequate for policing duties in the colonies, where a smaller number of larger, more battle-worthy, machines would have been of no benefit.

A key figure in the early development of the British light tanks was Sir John Carden, and indeed some of them had components in common with the tracked carriers he was developing at the same period. Arguably the French First World War Renault FT17, also operated by US forces, was one of the important influences at this early stage. Carden Loyd Mark VII and VIII light tanks were supplied to the War Office from the end of the 1920s, and the Carden Loyd company itself was subsumed within Vickers in 1928. The Vickers-built Mark II, still in service in small numbers in the Second World War, grew out of these earlier designs, and had a similar hull shape, though it now featured a larger turret and Rolls-Royce engine. Small numbers of a Mark III, with a slightly roomier hull and improved suspension, were completed in

The Light Tank Mark II was a two-man tank with specifications not so very different to the German Panzer I. Both were machine-gun armed, had a maximum road speed of about 30mph (48kph), and modest armour protection resistant to small arms fire, but not much else. The Mark II was produced in several slightly differing types. (Author)

the mid-1930s. The British Army also took delivery of a few of a similar tank that Vickers had produced for the commercial market in 1939. The basic specification of all these vehicles was very much the same: they weighed about 10,000lb (4,536kg), were approximately 12 feet (3.7m) long and just over 6 feet (1.8m) wide, and had a maximum speed of 30mph (48kph). The maximum armour of the Mark II was 10mm, increasing to 12mm in the Mark III.[8]

Though the light tanks of the 1930s were fast for their time, they also had very significant handicaps that put a short and very finite limit to their usefulness. Perhaps most obvious was their tiny size, for whilst they were relatively easy to hide, both armament and crew were woefully inadequate. The single Vickers machine gun might have been enough to tackle enemy riflemen, but against any sort of anti-tank weapon – on the ground or in an enemy tank – it was virtually useless. The crew of two was also insurmountably restrictive, for if the driver was actually driving everything else fell to the commander who might be needed to shoot, command, reload, and attempt to communicate. On exercises, many light tank commanders actually chose to sit on top of the turret, with only their legs inside the tank, so as to be able to survey the battlefield and give useful information to the driver rather than man the gun. Engines which varied from as little as 66 to 88hp were also unsuited to the addition to armament or armour, since they soon become overloaded. Attempts were made to address the problems in the Marks IV, V and VI. In the Mark IV there was a little more internal space and speed, and some improvement to the suspension. The Mark V took the idea virtually as far

as it was possible to go, by enlarging the turret enough to accommodate a third crewmember, increasing the hull length to 12 feet 10 inches (3.9m), and mounting a second machine gun. This was a heavy-calibre .5-inch.

The key difference in the Mark VI was arguably the provision of a radio in the turret, though its machine guns were now usually Besa types. The first batch of fifty-one Mark VI tanks was delivered to the Mechanisation Experimental Establishment in January 1936, and further design tweaks led to the Mark VI 'A', 'B' and 'C'. Interestingly there were also experiments in which an open-topped turret with a 2pdr gun was mounted on the basic chassis. This created what was effectively a miniature prototype 'tank destroyer' and whilst sadly this was not put into production, it did point the way to what might be achieved later. So it was that the light tanks went to war still armed only with machine guns.

In May 1940 the weapons of the latest vehicles were the subject of the new instructional manual *Light Tanks, Mark VIC: Armament, 7.92mm and 15mm. Besa Machine Guns*. Though aiming telescopes

Mk VI Light Tanks training in the UK. These Vickers-made machines were still the commonest tanks in the British arsenal early in 1940, though the basic design was already a decade old. This picture was posted home by one of the crewmen in the first tank, delighted to have passed his 'third class tradesman's tests'. Black two-piece working dress was formally introduced for tankers in 1935. (Author)

WD ROAD
CAUTION
TANK DRIVING
GROUND

were provided, and the 15mm was sighted up to 1,800 yards, having heavy machine weapons as main armament in confined space was clearly not without problems:

> 'The crew commander must be trained to co-operate with the gunner in the general handling of the guns in the tank. This mainly applies to the 15mm MG. Loading, changing belt boxes and the rectification of stoppages single-handed by the gunner is in some cases a physical impossibility, and without the assistance of the crew commander the fire power of the tank would be considerably reduced... The crew commander's position in the tank is liable to interfere with the manipulation of the guns, especially when observing through the periscope to the right, but if the periscope is adjusted as when observing to the rear, the commander faces the right gun and will not interfere with the manipulation... Training in general handling should at all times be carried out with the crew commander (or man representing the crew commander) in the tank.'

Mark VI tank production continued into 1940, with about 1,000 being made, significant numbers going to the British Expeditionary Force in France, and the Middle East. Variants were also supplied to the Indian Army. In May 1940 in France the various subtypes of the Mark VI were still numerically the largest part of the tank force, even though it had recently been decided to abolish them and rearm the 1st (and only) Armoured Division (commanded by Major General R. Evans) with 'Cruisers'. In the Queen's Bays, one of the five tank regiments with 1st Armoured, there were twenty-nine 'Cruisers' and twenty-one light tanks. There were also notionally twenty-eight light tank machines for each of the seven Divisional Cavalry regiments attached to the infantry, though returns show some deviations from often under strength establishments. Tragically, and perhaps predictably, the light tanks suffered heavy loss, and the abandonment of the tank arm in France after Dunkirk meant that many fell into the hands of the enemy who made use of some of them, though many crews escaped back to the UK. Difficulty in producing enough better machines quickly meant that some of the early types of light tanks were still to be seen in British service as late as 1942.

Whilst it was now generally admitted that light tanks were unfit for the cutting edge of battle, a few British models were still developed for specialist roles. The most important by far were the Tetrarch and the Harry Hopkins. The Tetrarch name was actually adopted in 1943 when the Light Mark VII, first produced at the end of 1940, and which had seen service in Madagascar, was found a role with the Airborne. Limited though their impact would be, this was an interesting idea, since lightness was a prerequisite for air transport, and in the first flush of any drop the Airborne were otherwise bereft of anything even approximating to armoured support. The little Tetrarch carried a 2pdr or a 3-inch howitzer, and had only 14mm of armour maximum, but was capable of a remarkable 40mph (64kph) under ideal road conditions, and up to 28mph (45kph) even cross country. A mixed squadron of Tetrarch and Universal carriers would join 6th Airborne for the invasion of Europe in 1944, when they were carried in Hamilcar gliders. The odd little Harry Hopkins never did see service, though an order for ninety-nine vehicles was completed. The Hopkins, designed by Vickers in 1941, had been destined to become the Mark VIII light tank, but now lacked a suitable niche. This was made perhaps even more obvious by the attempt to carry a maximum 38mm of armour. Attempts were made to use the Harry Hopkins hull as a basis for a self-propelled howitzer and bulldozer.

Stuart M3

The US M3 'Honey' light tank, officially known in the UK as the General Stuart, was a successor to the M2. Devised at the Rock Island arsenal in the spring of 1940, it took advantage of experience from Europe, and latest US production techniques. It was of a compact conventional riveted design with fully rotating turret, mounting a 37mm main armament and, initially at least, three machine guns – one coaxially, and two in sponsons to either side at the front. It had a crew of four: commander; gunner; driver and co-driver. A fourth machine gun was often mounted atop the turret roof for use by the commander in an anti-aircraft or close defence capacity. It was fast at 36mph (58kph), but had a fairly limited road radius of action of 70 miles (113km), and was just under 15 feet (4.6m) in length and 7 feet 4 inches (224cm) wide. The main improvement over earlier models was an increase in the frontal armour, up to 51mm on the thickest part of the nose.[9]

With full production underway from early 1941, it was in immediate demand by Britain, the first eighty-four Stuarts reaching the Western Desert that summer, going to re-equip the King's Royal Irish Hussars. Stuarts were in action at Gabr Saleh in November during the Crusader offensive. Not long afterwards, Stuarts were also in action in the Far East, where they were used by both British and Indian Army units. Though it was unsophisticated, and the main armament was probably even less effective than the British 2pdr, the Stuart was soon popular, with crews remarking on its reliability and ease of driving. The modest range of action was addressed by the addition of two supplementary fuel tanks, each containing 25 gallons, mounted on the rear in such a way they could be jettisoned when no longer required. Minor headaches included an early lack of a turret 'basket' and an awkwardly placed propshaft that tended to impede the legs of the crew. Like a number of tanks of the early war period the small two-man turret arrangement was also limiting, partly because this led to overwork of the turret crew, and partly because it precluded any significant up-gunning of the Stuart at a later stage.

The turret traverse in early models was fully manual, and much of the work involved in turning the turret and aiming the gun fell to the gunner, who was presented with a series of handwheels. The elevating wheel was to his right and allowed 20 degrees up

and 10 degrees down, and incorporated the firing button, the turret traverse and fine traverse aiming wheels were to his left. A shoulder piece provided an alternative means of elevation, but was difficult to combine with the working of the wheels. The commander acted as loader and fired the top machine gun, as well as manning the radio in later models. The driver sat front left in the hull, controlling the tank by means of hand throttle, clutch and throttle pedals, and most importantly a pair of steering levers. These also doubled as brakes when pulled backwards. To hold the tank stationary, knobs on the tops of the levers were turned.

With time the Stuart was gradually improved through M3A1 and M3A2 types. The sponson machine-gun arrangement was dropped at an early stage as they were difficult to aim and quickly burned their way through the small arms ammunition supply, an otherwise quite healthy 6,000 to 8,000 rounds. A number of descriptions of drivers sitting under showers of hot brass, coming from various directions, give some indication of the problem. Other modifications included increased stowage, the fitting of a gyrostabiliser, and elimination of the turret

An M3 Stuart 'Honey' of the 8th King's Royal Irish Hussars in the desert during Operation Crusader. The regiment was reduced to just four Stuarts fit for action following night battle with 15th Panzer Division in November 1941, but was rapidly refitted with a further thirty-two machines. Recommitted to battle at Sidi Rezegh in December, the regiment fared better but the commanding officer Major PD Dundas was killed on 9 December. (Author)

cupola. A power traverse for the turret was also introduced with the M3A1. Many British Stuarts featured smoke dischargers on the turret sides, and sand shields for the desert. The smoke dischargers saw plenty of use in masking the Stuart when confronted by enemy armour with better guns. However, the most obvious improvement was the change over from rivet to welded construction. Direct hits on the riveted turrets of several models of tank, including the Stuart, had a nasty habit of popping out the plate fasteners which could fly around inside the tank causing death or injury. In the M3A3, with its fully welded

hull, the whole vehicle was made almost 1 foot (30cm) wider. Production continued into 1943, by which time about 10,000 M3 and M5 types had been built for both US and British forces. Though pretty much obsolete by 1944, it continued to be used in various places, particularly the Far East, where the Japanese had few tanks of any power.

Given its lightness and speed, the Stuart made a good reconnaissance vehicle, taking the lead during many an advance, then dropping back if challenged. The Stuart also served as

British Stuart Mark VI tanks (equivalent to the US M5 type) passing half tracks and other vehicles of 15th (Scottish) Division during the advance to the Elbe, April 1945. The M5 type was supplied to Britain in 1943 to 1944. (Sgt Laing/IWM via Getty Images)

platform for a number of conversions. Significant British types included the Stuart 'Kangaroo' late in the war, in which the turret was removed and seats added to create a small armoured personnel carrier, and dedicated reconnaissance vehicles in which the turret was also removed and various pintle-mounted machine guns were fitted. Self-propelled gun conversions appear to have been less successful, though there were a number of US experiments, and report of at least one British example in which an 18pdr took the place of the turret.

Matilda

The Matilda II was one of few British-made tanks capable of taking on the enemy on equal terms. It was better than anything fielded by the Japanese or Italians, and came as something of a shock when first encountered by the

Wehrmacht in France in 1940. It was tough, being found pretty much 'immune' to Italian guns in Libya, and, without too great hyperbole, enjoyed for a while the soubriquet 'Queen of the Battlefield'. Yet sadly its heyday was relatively short-lived, and its numbers often proved insufficient for the tasks at hand. Arguably its brief reign was but a year, from mid-1940 to 1941, at the end of which the Germans were able to deploy heavy anti-tank guns, such as the 88mm, to the desert. Never the less, the Matilda soldiered on thereafter, and was still seen in the front line at Alamein, but it proved an insufficiently flexible platform for any significant upgrade in its armament. Even so, the tank did have a somewhat less visible, but useful, 'second life' in the hands of the Australians in the Far East, where it remained adequate against the Japanese until the end of the war.

A German photograph showing a British Matilda II, damaged and abandoned in France. Up to 1942 the 7th Royal Tank Regiment took its tank names from the seventh letter of the alphabet 'G', hence the name 'Goat'. Others names used by the unit would include Grumble, Giggle, and Gnome, all of which had been used by 'G Battalion' of the Tank Corps in the First World War. The Matilda II was used in the desert, as a mine-clearing 'flail' tank, in Eritrea, and with the Australians in New Guinea. Almost 3,000 were produced. (Author)

The Matilda II in contemporary diagrams. Top: The exterior and stowage; bottom: The turret interior. (Author)

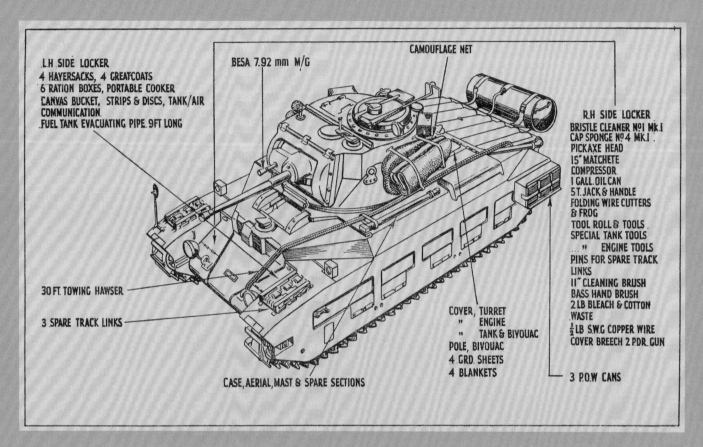

LH. SIDE LOCKER
4 HAVERSACKS, 4 GREATCOATS
6 RATION BOXES, PORTABLE COOKER
CANVAS BUCKET, STRIPS & DISCS, TANK/AIR
COMMUNICATION.
FUEL TANK EVACUATING PIPE. 9FT LONG

BESA 7.92 mm M/G

CAMOUFLAGE NET

R.H SIDE LOCKER
BRISTLE CLEANER Nº1 Mk.I
CAP SPONGE Nº 4 MK.I
PICKAXE HEAD
15" MATCHETE
COMPRESSOR
I GALL. OIL CAN
5 T. JACK & HANDLE
FOLDING WIRE CUTTERS
& FROG
TOOL ROLL & TOOLS
SPECIAL TANK TOOLS
... " ENGINE TOOLS
PINS FOR SPARE TRACK
LINKS
II" CLEANING BRUSH
BASS HAND BRUSH
2 LB BLEACH & COTTON
WASTE
$\frac{1}{2}$ LB S.W.G COPPER WIRE
COVER BREECH 2 PDR GUN

30 FT. TOWING HAWSER

3 SPARE TRACK LINKS

COVER, TURRET
  " ENGINE
  " TANK & BIVOUAC
POLE, BIVOUAC
4 GRD. SHEETS
4 BLANKETS

CASE, AERIAL, MAST & SPARE SECTIONS

3 P.O.W CANS

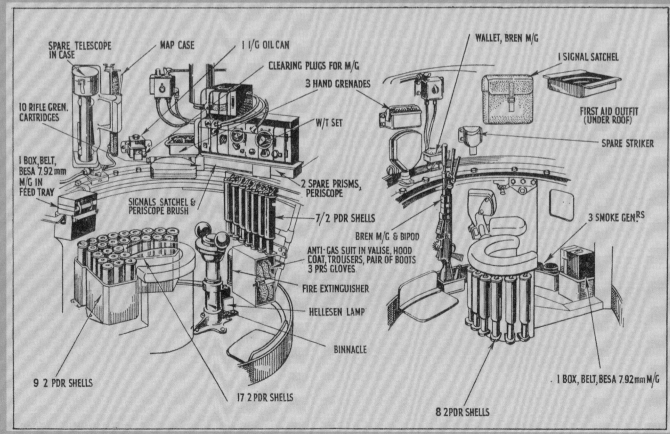

SPARE TELESCOPE
IN CASE

MAP CASE

I I/G OIL CAN

CLEARING PLUGS FOR M/G

3 HAND GRENADES

WALLET, BREN M/G

I SIGNAL SATCHEL

10 RIFLE GREN.
CARTRIDGES

W/T SET

FIRST AID OUTFIT
(UNDER ROOF)

SPARE STRIKER

I BOX, BELT,
BESA 7.92 mm
M/G IN
FEED TRAY

SIGNALS SATCHEL &
PERISCOPE BRUSH

2 SPARE PRISMS,
PERISCOPE

7/2 PDR SHELLS

BREN M/G & BIPOD

ANTI-GAS SUIT IN VALISE, HOOD
COAT, TROUSERS, PAIR OF BOOTS
3 PRS GLOVES

FIRE EXTINGUISHER

HELLESEN LAMP

BINNACLE

3 SMOKE GENRS

9 2 PDR SHELLS

17 2 PDR SHELLS

8 2 PDR SHELLS

I BOX, BELT, BESA 7.92 mm M/G

The story of this tank began as early as 1934 when outline specifications were put forward at the behest of Major General Percy Hobart for the possible development of two different 'infantry' tanks. Both were to have a speed of at least 10mph (16kph) – being, for that date, well-protected vehicles for infantry support capable of moving at least as fast as dismounted troops. The first of the infantry tanks was to be small and inconspicuous, machine-gun armed, and able to be produced in numbers: the second was to be larger, having a gun to engage enemy machines as well as machine guns. The following year, Sir John Carden met with Colonel Studd, the Assistant Director of Mechanisation, and during the course of their conversations produced a sketch and list of desirable attributes for the new machine-gun tank code named 'Matilda'. This was to be capable of 5–8mph (8–13kph), have a development cost of £15,000, and be ready for delivery in six months. No 'wireless' was deemed necessary. In the event a prototype, carrying the General Staff designation A11E1, was ready for trials in September 1936, though Carden himself was dead by this time.[10]

This simple, if slightly odd-looking, beast had a tiny turret with a single machine gun, but despite somewhat exposed tracks and running gear boasted an armour thickness of 60mm, making it better armoured than almost any tank of this period. It was 7 feet 6 inches (229cm) wide, and just under 16 feet (488cm) in length. It moved at about 8mph (13kph), and was hampered by its inadequate two-man crew, the driver, and a commander who had to double as gunner and loader. Though this would turn out to be an important consideration later, in the early design phase it had been anticipated that this would not matter – since it was intended that the Matilda tanks would operate in swarms, in close visual contact with the infantry, and would not be required to operate independently. The first Matilda did indeed look something like a mechanised duck, though the idea that the name was bestowed by veteran Tank Corps commander General Sir Hugh Elles during trials is apocryphal. About 140 of the Mark I Matilda were produced, and many of them went to the 1st Army Tank Brigade in France, where it proved fairly reliable and difficult to knock out – but not capable of inflicting

British Matilda II heavy infantry tanks moving across the desert near Tobruk. (British Official Photo/British Official Photo/The LIFE Picture Collection/Getty Images)

much damage on the enemy. However, that this might be the case had been realised long before the outbreak of war, and as early as 1936 plans for a 'scaled up' infantry tank – the 'A12' – were in the air with an intention to include an anti-tank gun and a larger crew.

However, it was not enough to build Matilda I larger, incorporate a gun, and give better protection to its tracks. Experiments determined that the increase in armour weight occasioned by making the tank bigger could not be borne by the little V-8 engine, that provided scarcely enough power as it was and quickly became overburdened. A more radical redesign solution was sought, taking inspiration from an earlier A7 medium tank and using twin-AEC diesel engines for motive power. As finally produced the new tank would weigh over 26 tons, having a crew of four, a maximum armour of 78mm, a 2pdr gun and machine gun, and a slightly more healthy 15mph (24kph) top speed. Pilot models were produced by the Vulcan Foundry at Warrington in 1937. Contracts with other companies followed, but largely due to its massive armour and one-piece side skirts, Matilda II was not an easy tank to make quickly, or in numbers. As the handbook observed, 'the construction of the hull of this tank is different from most other types, in that the use of a frame on to which the plates are built has been dispensed with. Instead, the hull is built up of specially shaped armour castings constructed so as to form a rigid structure'. Much of the strength came from the solid hull nose, and the way in which the top and bottom plates of the hull were rebated into the side plates. An internal bulkhead separated the 'fighting' and 'engine' compartments.[11]

In September 1939 only two of the new Matilda II type were actually with the Army. There were still very few in 1940 when the Germans invaded France and the Low Countries. Famously these were committed to the action at Arras on 21 May 1940, serving with 4th and 7th Battalions of the Royal Tank Regiment. As part of Major General Harold Franklyn's 'Frankforce', these sixteen Matildas counter-attacked in an attempt to close the gap that was opening in the Allied front, and protect the British line of supply. Whilst there were not enough Matildas to tip the battle, they did provide a brief check when Rommel discovered that his Panzer II and III tanks of 7th Panzer Division did not have sufficient firepower to overcome their thick armour. Elements of the SS motorised regiment *Totenkopf* were overrun, and only by concentrating superior forces, backed by anti-tank guns, were the British tanks halted.

The retirement of many British troops was then covered by French armour. 'Defence of Arras' was given as a battle honour to a number of units involved in this action. It has been suggested that it was this episode that engendered greater caution on the part of the German command and therefore made a significant contribution to the success of Operation Dynamo and the evacuation from Dunkirk. Conversely the capture of Matildas allowed the enemy an opportunity to examine them at close quarters, and to take them into account when designing the next generation of German tanks.

As noted, the Matilda was also deployed to the desert, where initially it gave good service. Later it was realised that the old 2pdr gun was not sufficient to cope with the latest enemy tanks and efforts were made to fit 6pdrs onto the Matilda. This proved fruitless, due to the small size of the turret ring. Never the less, the Matilda's heavy armour made it a suitable platform for experiments with new mine-clearance technology, and a few, fitted with flails to explode mines on the move, were actually used at Alamein in 1942.

Cruiser and Crusader

The story of the Crusader begins in the early 1930s, when British experts, including Lieutenant Colonel Giffard Le Quesne Martel, studied the work of the American designer W.J. Christie and the Russian tanks based on his ideas. Crucial to these was a new type of suspension in which large road wheels, capable of immediate reaction to the ground, were teamed with tracks. This arrangement made possible speeds hitherto unattainable in fully armoured tracked vehicles. The British A13, or Cruiser Mark III, was ready for trials by the autumn of 1937. However, early expectations of very high rates of movement were disappointed, and to reduce the chance of mechanical failure it proved necessary to govern the top speed down to 30mph (48kph), make changes to the clutch and transmission and shorten the track pitch. Despite such shortcomings a modest batch of sixty-five of the Cruiser Mark III was ordered. They were used in France in 1940, as well as in the desert in small numbers later on. The Cruiser Mark III was relatively lightly protected with a maximum of 14mm of armour, and armed with an initially adequate 2pdr gun and a machine gun.

Never the less, it was quickly realised that much better armour was required, and accordingly in 1939 a new standard of 30mm of protection was set for Cruisers. This was achieved essentially by uprating the existing A13 Mark III, adding new plates to its nose, glacis and turret. On the sides of the turret, distinctive 'V' sections were added, creating a spaced armour effect and a distinctive polygonal silhouette also apparent in the later Crusader. Whilst this feature did indeed give better protection and sloping facets were more likely to deflect projectiles, the overhanging turret sides also created a 'shot trap'. The 2pdr main armament remained unchanged, although a few of what would now be called the Cruiser Mark IV were fitted to take a 3.7-inch mortar. A total of 655 Mark IV types were built or converted from existing Mark III stock by companies including Nuffield, Leyland, LMS and English Electric. Whilst the Cruiser IV was a distinct improvement, its inability to fire high-explosives from its now obsolete 2pdr was found to be a distinct handicap in the Desert War, and like most Allied vehicles it was terribly vulnerable to the latest generation of German anti-tank gun. There were also complaints regarding cooling and steering.

Whilst the Cruiser IV was in the process of production, two further models were also created in parallel, building on the same general developmental tree. These were the Mark V Covenanter, and the A15 or Crusader. Like its predecessors, the Covenanter had a Christie type suspension with four road wheels either side, and on paper the tank looked fine, with a three-man turret, 2pdr main armament and coaxial Besa machine gun, and a Meadows twelve-cylinder 300hp engine. The silhouette appeared low and businesslike. However, the reality was tragically different: mechanical faults and cooling problems, combined with an armament that was now completely out of date, made for a vehicle that has been

described as 'one of the worst tanks ever produced'. Despite attempts to rectify problems, by the time it appeared, the Covenanter was clearly unfit to take the field head on against the latest enemy tanks, and was relegated mainly to training purposes, though some vehicles were used as bridge layers or were mounted with howitzers.

The Crusader A15 took the basic layout that had begun with the A13 and boosted it with the addition of a fifth wheel on either side. It was intended to offer the advantages of better trench-crossing ability, an additional machine gun mounted in a diminutive auxiliary turret, and better armour, whilst at the same time being relatively easy to produce as it used many of the components already being manufactured for the A13 series. Ultimately it was imagined that the basic design would prove sufficiently flexible and robust to allow for the addition of both better armour and armament than its predecessors. The initial order for the A15 was small, but as time passed and other models were proved inadequate, much more was expected of the new tank and the requirement was raised to a thousand by the end of 1940. Eventually seven companies would manufacture more than 5,000 Crusaders of several different models.

The Crusader I was first committed to the desert in the spring of 1941, seeing action at Capuzzo in June. Though a brave face was put upon the outcome, it was all too clear that the Crusader carried with it many of the faults of its lineage, lacking mechanical reliability, being not particularly suitable for the conditions of North Africa, and having insufficient punch in its 2pdr main armament. When it was working well it showed a good turn of speed at a maximum 27mph (43kph), but in most other

The Cruiser Mark III or 'A13', based on a Christie design, had a four-man crew, and was used in France and Libya. It carried eighty-seven rounds for its 2pdr gun and 3,750 for the machine gun. It was superseded by the Mark IV. (Author)

departments it was outclassed by the German Panzer III, which had better armour, armament, and serviceability. Looking at the problems of the Crusader gave rise to several reflections, perhaps the most significant of which was that its development cycle had been particularly unfortunate. Design had begun before May 1940, and so it had not been possible to commence from the knowledge soon to be derived from the French campaign, and the Crusader had been saddled with armament of limited usefulness. Moreover, it used a Liberty engine that dated back to the First World War.

Accordingly efforts were now made to uprate the Crusader to meet the challenges of the moment. One possibility examined was to fit it with a Rolls-Royce Merlin engine. The result in trials was spectacular, shooting the Crusader along a half-mile course at speeds of anything up to 50mph (80kph). Sadly it was clear, however, that the Crusader could never take the strain of being propelled in such a fashion, and the use of aero engines had to wait for the development of later models. It did

prove practical to improve both the gun and the armour. In the Crusader II, the difficult-to-operate additional front machine-gun turret was eliminated and extra armour was added to the turret and hull, bringing the thickness up from 40mm to 49mm. From May 1942, the Crusader III entered production. This further improved the maximum armour to 51mm, and more importantly changed the 2pdr for a much more effective 6pdr gun.[12]

However, the tank development race was not one that the Crusader could ever win. By 1942 the Germans had moved on much further again – to the development of monsters like the Tiger, and Britain was taking delivery of relatively reliable tanks like the Sherman that could be made in much greater numbers. Though the Crusader battled on in North Africa, it was eventually withdrawn from front-line tank duty in 1943. Even so, some Crusaders, in the form of specialist conversions such as AA mountings and gun tractors, would go on to see use in Western Europe up to the end of the war.[12]

The Cruiser Mark IVA on exercises in East Anglia, August 1940. The Mark IV and IVA were similar to the Cruiser Mark III, but with better armour. On this Mark IVA an extra armoured cover plate has been added to the gun mantlet. The Cruiser Mark IV was used by 1st Armoured Division in France, in the Western Desert, and as a training vehicle (Mr Puttnam/IWM via Getty Images)

Valentine

In early 1938 a consortium including the firm of Vickers gathered under Vulcan to plan and build an 'infantry tank' based on a further development of the old A10 specification. Vickers submitted its plans in February – and, according to some commentators, thus was born the idea of the 'Valentine' tank. Never the less, it has also been claimed that the title was drawn from the middle name of Sir John V. Carden, others arguing that it was simply a meaningless code word. In any case, more than a year passed as plans were considered, and it was noted, even at this early stage, that the small turret of the new vehicle might prove a handicap in service. Initial designs with a two-man turret were rejected, partly on this ground, and partly because 70mm of armour was required rather than the 60mm offered. A few months later, updated drawings were presented with a revision of the turret to accommodate a third crewman. Again there was equivocation: the War Office was still unhappy with the thickness of the armour; lack of protection for the suspension; the petrol engine, and lack of a cupola for the commander. However, by June 1939 it was becoming increasingly obvious that tanks might soon be required in volume, and an order was placed for 275

Valentines. By an unfortunate quirk of timing the Valentine – which was a reasonably reliable, if pretty unremarkable vehicle – was undergoing trials in May 1940 at just the time that most of the British tank arm was being destroyed or captured in France. As the trials were successful, and tanks were needed in numbers, and with the greatest urgency, the Valentine was rushed into production.

Though some early vehicles were completed with space for only three-man crews (Valentine II), the majority were of the improved four-man type (Valentine III). The Valentine III was 17 feet 9 inches (5.4m) long, and mounted a 2pdr main armament, and a coaxial machine gun. Its maximum armour was 65mm, and its radius of action about 90 miles (145km) on roads. However, its 'infantry tank' ancestry was apparent in its 15mph (24kph) top speed. By the beginning of 1942 it was pretty clear that the Valentine was outclassed in most departments, and from March of that year later marks were fitted with a 6pdr gun. Though this certainly helped, it was not a complete success, as the larger gun now necessitated reducing the turret crew back to two again. In Valentine IV, a 138hp GMC diesel engine replaced the original power unit. By early 1944, when Valentine production ceased, 8,275 vehicles had been made: this equated to about a quarter of British tank production in the Second

A slightly damaged Crusader III. As of the spring of 1941 the Crusader became a mainstay of the British tank force. Attempts to rectify disappointing performance included increased armour and a 6pdr main armament, seen here. Crusaders may be distinguished from earlier 'Cruiser' types by their fifth running wheel on either side. (Author)

World War. Valentines were also made in Canada from late 1941, though it would appear that the majority of these went to the Soviet Union, where they saw action on the Eastern Front.

The Valentine reached 8th Army formations in the desert in mid-1941, and, whilst there were many worse tanks in both British and foreign armies, it has to be said that it was verging on obsolescence within months, and struggled to keep pace in all senses. In some formations, as with the 17th/21st Lancers in 1942, it was teamed with Crusaders. These were 'Cruiser' tanks with a relatively fast top speed but little reliability, whilst the Valentines were not particularly well-protected infantry tanks, with fair reliability, but little speed. Moreover, the various models of Valentine were not always so neatly issued that those with the same engine and turret types were grouped together. Nevertheless, individual regiments often made those vehicles that had three-man turrets mounts for troop and squadron leaders, which did at least help with local command and control. None of this made the overall tasks of maintenance or co-ordination of larger formations any easier. A number of critics have suggested that the extended use of the Valentine was essentially a question of 'using up' an old design that might not have been volume produced at all were it not for the life-or-death crisis of 1940–1941.

In the same vein was the later use of many Valentine tank chassis for other tasks. One of the most unlikely yet most successful of these was the Archer self-propelled gun. Various other vehicles were considered as a mount for the 17pdr 'SP', including the Crusader, which was found too small, before the Valentine was settled upon. Yet the long and powerful 17pdr

gun did not really fit the Valentine either, until a novel solution was happened upon. By fitting the gun in an open-topped superstructure over the fighting compartment, but mounting it to fire backwards on a limited traverse, a compact and relatively low silhouetted 'tank destroyer' was created. Though the whole arrangement was distinctly weird, with the driver remaining in his original position, the result was more satisfactory in use than many vehicles that had been planned from scratch. Work started in 1942, with firing trials in the spring of 1943, and final issue to the anti-tank battalions of armoured units in Europe from October 1944. About 665 were built by Vickers, and the Archer remained in use well into the 1950s. The Archer had a crew of four, a maximum armour of 60mm, and a Bren gun as secondary armament. Almost 22 feet (6.7m) long, it had a maximum speed of 15mph (24kph), and a radius of road action of about 90 miles (145km).

The Valentine was also the basis for the Bishop self-propelled 25pdr. The idea that a field gun or small howitzer should be fitted to an armoured chassis was raised as early as the spring of 1941, when similar German machines were encountered in the Western Desert, and by August a Valentine prototype was produced. Whilst the project was overtaken by machines based on the US M3, the Bishop reached production and about eighty were made. The Bishop was tall in relation to the original Valentine, standing almost 2 feet (61cm) higher, and the square-looking gun position was open-topped. The Bishop had a maximum armour of 60mm. At thirty-two rounds its ammunition capacity was relatively slender, with the result that it was sometimes to be seen towing a limber of extra shells. It

The Valentine Infantry Tank Mark I, 1940, with the initial two-man turret. Despite being designated and designed as an 'infantry tank' Valentines were soon pressed into a 'Cruiser' role due to a general shortage of armour. (Fox Photos/Hulton Archive/Getty Images)

remained in front-line service until the end of the campaign in North Africa in 1943. Though small in numbers, and not the most successful SP gun, it had the distinction of being the first such British-designed weapon of the war.

The Valentine never achieved particular fame, and perhaps more importantly no great notoriety. Tributes are not that easy to find, but one did appear in *The Times* volume *British War Production*, 1945: 'The first tank to achieve real reliability was the Valentine. It was an unspectacular vehicle which performed consistently well, particularly in the Western desert. It was there that tanks of that type set up the astonishing record of running over 3,000 miles on their tracks without breakdown of any kind.' This was compared favourably even with the record of many of Rommel's tanks.[13]

Churchill

As early as the autumn of 1939 it was appreciated that both the Matilda and Valentine designs might have a relatively short useful service life. Moreover, it now appeared perfectly possible that a Second 'Great War' might follow the First in general outline with a period of relative immobility on a new Western Front between France and Germany, both of whom had invested considerable efforts in static defences; the Maginot Line and

the more recent Siegfried Line. Under these circumstances it seemed prudent that Britain should develop a new 'infantry tank' capable of negotiating shelled ground, at moderate speed, in support of dismounted troops. More precisely, the War Office had in mind something that could resist the fire of a 37mm anti-tank gun, and carry a pair of 2pdr guns backed up by three machine guns. It should be capable of being transported by rail, able to cross substantial trenches, and have a crew of seven. Perhaps predictably, early work on this A20 specification for a 'shelled area' tank soon produced a plan for what was effectively an updated First World War turretless 'landship'.

That this would not do under modern conditions was quickly comprehended by the Director of Mechanisation General A.E. Davidson, who insisted on the incorporation of a fully revolving turret. So it was that a prototype produced by Harland and Wolff in Belfast early in 1940 took the form of a long, flat-looking hull, with tracks running around and over the outside frame on no less than fourteen small bogies each side, atop which was perched a ridiculously small-looking turret filched from the Matilda II. An improved pilot A20E1, completed by Vauxhall in August 1940, proved both fuel- and oil-hungry. Again this was hardly satisfactory – some pointed out that the 2pdr would soon be out of date, or that it lacked a high-explosive capability, others complained that the wheels and suspension would be time-consuming and expensive to mass produce. At least one expert offered the opinion that now was not the time to add another tank type to already complicated production and that the whole idea should be dropped. But by now the BEF had been evacuated from France and the position was desperate. Even before their A20E1 had run, Vauxhall was asked to reduce the size of the new tank, which was to be powered by their Vauxhall-Bedford 350hp engine, and

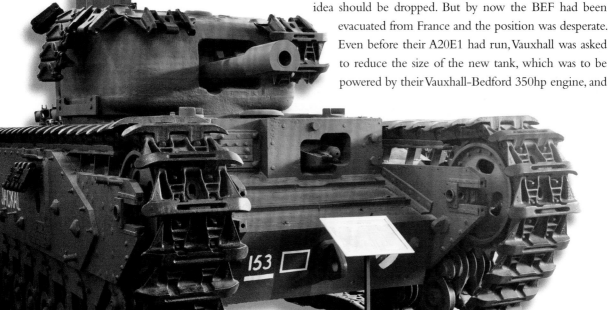

Churchill Mark V, 'Jackal', of 4th Coldstream Guards, damaged by a mine on 12 October 1944, during the battle for Overloon in the Netherlands. The Mark V was similar to the Mark IV, but carried a 95mm howitzer as main armament. (Author)

create a production vehicle to a revised A22 specification as soon as possible. The prime minister wanted a new simplified heavy tank in the field, in numbers, by the end of March 1941.[14]

So it was that new designs were pushed ahead, though still no better tank gun than the 2pdr was available. To give the new tank an anti-infantry and fortification capability, a 3-inch howitzer was therefore now incorporated into the hull. The very first production Tank, Infantry, Mark I (A22), rolled off the production line in May 1941 – its name came later in the year when Churchill himself suggested that all tanks, not just the Matilda and Valentine, should have names as well as numbers. The latest heavy tank, which had been thrust ahead at the prime minister's personal insistence, was duly given his name. What was retrospectively dubbed the Churchill I with its 3-inch howitzer was made in only relatively small numbers: it was 8 feet 2 inches (2.5m) wide, 10 feet 8 inches (3.3m) high, and had a maximum road speed of just over 15mph (24kph), though cross-country movement was about half of this. Though relatively slow, it had a very good armour thickness for its time of 100mm. Its radius

of action on roads was 90 miles, and it could cross a trench 10 feet (3m) wide. It could carry 150 rounds for its 2pdr and 58 rounds for the howitzer, as well as a coaxial machine gun. In the Churchill II, a second machine gun was mounted in place of the howitzer. With some difficulty the 6pdr anti-tank gun was fitted into the revised turret of the Churchill III, which began to enter service in the spring of 1942.

The first Churchills were definitely a rushed job, so much so that a note was included in the handbook to the effect that the makers knew there were faults but that these had been accepted on grounds of getting tanks to the troops as fast as possible. Teething problems included mud being sucked into air inlets; gearbox trouble; suspension and track issues; and very noisy running. Poor sealing meant that the vehicle leaked in heavy rain; moreover, the engine appeared underpowered. Whilst the howitzer made the Churchill I a heavily armed beast for its day, the cramming in of a large gun alongside the driver severely limited its traverse and elevation, so that it was effective to only a relatively short range.

A Churchill Mark IV, without armament, undergoing testing in a water tank. The Mark IV, first produced in mid-1942, was the most numerous model with a production of over 1,600 units. It featured a 6pdr gun in a cast turret, though some were subsequently retrofitted with a 75 mm. (Popperfoto/ Getty Images)

In 1942 the Churchill received its baptisms of fire – at Dieppe with the Canadians, and in the desert, but with very different results. At Dieppe the Churchills struggled in the teeth of fixed defences and heavy fire, slithering on the loose chert – a surface even more difficult than ordinary pebbles or shingle. Half the thirty tanks committed managed to make it over the sea wall and onto the promenade. They proved difficult to knock out, but some suffered from breaking tracks and turret failures and were impossible to retrieve when the overall plan – which was unrealistically ambitious – went badly awry. Many fell into German hands, and the enemy was thus given the opportunity to examine them at leisure. The resulting report dismissed the Churchill as generally uninspiring, the 3-inch howitzer and 2pdr as old-fashioned, and the 6pdr gun as inferior to Russian types of similar calibre. Perhaps more interestingly, some of the Dieppe Churchills were subjected to firing tests, where it was discovered that they were resistant to most of the smaller German anti-tank guns. However, the 75mm anti-tank gun could penetrate most places except the hull front. The 88mm could defeat the Churchill armour everywhere.

Never the less, the reports from the desert were far more encouraging. Following trials, six machines were formed into a Special Tank Squadron under Major King. This was committed to Operation Lightfoot, the opening phase of the Second Battle of El Alamein, where they confronted dug-in tanks and anti-tank guns – but advanced in a conventional manner following a barrage. The Churchills performed surprisingly well under desert conditions, and were very resilient to fire. The first to be knocked out was hit more than fifty times by anti-tank guns – both German and British – before it burst into flames, and the vast majority of the rounds failed to penetrate at all. Later on, another Churchill took thirty hits before the vehicle was stopped, and in this instance the crew managed to escape. Just how tough the Churchill could be when used in the way in which it was intended was similarly demonstrated by a test on Salisbury Plain in 1942, when sixteen tanks were driven in formation at 5mph (8kph) through two different air-bursting barrages of 25pdr gunfire, provided by three full regiments of the field artillery. From the several hundred rounds, fired by seventy-two guns, just two tanks were temporarily halted by track damage, but not a single tank crewman was injured.

Arguably it was these sorts of trial by fire that proved that the Churchill was well worth persisting with, and gradually many of the more minor faults were overcome. A plan to drop the Churchill from continued production and development was shelved. Now extensive 'reworking' schemes and belated intensive testing led first to more reliable vehicles, then to the improved Mark IV. This was the single most numerous Churchill model of the war, with a total production of

The Churchill Mark III appeared in March 1942, and was fitted with a distinctive welded turret to take a 6pdr gun. However it is not easy to distinguish the different models since there were programmes to update old tanks to the latest specification. It is thought that over 3,000 underwent retrospective modification. (Author)

over 1,600 vehicles. In the Mark V, a 95mm howitzer was used in the turret for the close support role. During 1943, many Churchills were deployed to Tunisia, where their reassuring bulk and resistance to being destroyed was warmly appreciated. Though not originally designed as a tank for dealing with other tanks, they also scored successes in this department, as for example at the celebrated action at Djebel Djaffa in April 1943, where Churchills faced a variety of German armour. Though the latest German Tigers knocked out two Churchills, the crews survived, and one of the enemy tanks was captured. Other Churchills suffered mine damage, but in most instances without injury to crews. An official study conducted in the UK that September showed that whilst 88mm projectiles were destroying Churchills with some regularity, only about half the hits from 75mm guns caused serious damage. As a later report put it, 'the Churchill stands up well to anti-tank fire. If set on fire it burns slowly and the crews have a good chance to bale out'. This was enough to make many forgiving of other shortcomings.

Churchill tanks of 21st Army Tank Brigade cross the river Reno close to a destroyed rail bridge near Bastia, April 1945. The brigade, which comprised Royal Tank Regiment units and the North Irish Horse, was equipped with several different models of Churchill. From early 1945 these included the Churchill Mark VII, thick armour, 'heavy' type. As with other Irish units of the RAC the tanks of the North Irish Horse were named after towns, counties and places of Ireland. (Sgt Wooldridge/ IWM via Getty Images)

Winston himself was delighted with the way that his namesake could absorb punishment, even writing to the various supply committee members that he thought that a proportion of Churchill tanks should be fitted with 'the heaviest armour possible' even if it meant creating crawlers that could not even manage 6mph (10kph). In the event, the Churchills Marks VI and VII produced in late 1943 and 1944 were further redesigned, the most obvious new feature being incorporation of a 75mm gun as main armament. In the Mark VII the armour was also much improved, leading some to call this tank the 'heavy Churchill'. With armour up to 152mm thick, the Mark VII was extremely tough, but the extra weight caused the top speed to drop to just over 12mph (19kph).[15]

The Churchill Mark VIII was much the same as the VII, except that its main armament was the 95mm close support howitzer. The essential similarity of these two vehicles allowed them to be covered together in a *Service Instruction Book* of June 1944. According to this document, the latest Churchills were approximately 41 tons in weight, 25 feet 2 inches (7.8m) long, and 10 feet 8 inches (6.3m) wide measured to the outermost edge of the air louvres. The engine was the horizontally opposed twelve-cylinder Bedford 'Twin-Six', and the petrol tank had a 150-gallon capacity. In addition to the main armament there were two 7.92mm Besa machine guns, one in the front hull, the other coaxial with the turret gun. Unlike some of the earlier types, the hull was of a fully welded construction:

'The hull is divided into four compartments. At the front is the driving compartment, which also houses the front gunner. Immediately behind is the fighting compartment containing the electrically-operated three-man turret. Behind this again is the engine compartment, and behind the engine compartment is the rear compartment, which houses the gearbox, the steering brakes and main brakes, the air compressor and the power traverse generator. The engine is designed to be as compact as possible, and particular care has been taken to ensure accessibility and provide long life of components such as valves, cylinder bores and bearings.'

The turret was electrically rotated, but had provision for manual cranking through a reduction gear, and revolved on 117 large steel ball bearings in a bronze cage. The turret had two double-top hatches, one almost circular in design, the other the shape of a playing card. The turret crew had four periscopes, two in the commander's cupola, and two more in the turret front. Commander and wireless operator used fold-up seats, whilst the gunner occupied the pedestal seat. The radio, a No. 38 type wireless set, was located in the upper rear portion of the turret with its batteries stowed underneath, and had three aerials atop the turret. A 'telephone installation' was provided for internal communication between the crew. Also mounted in the turret was a 2-inch 'bomb thrower' for smoke: the settings allowed bombs to be projected to 20, 70, or 110 yards (18, 64 or 100m), and the thrower was reloaded and operated entirely from within the vehicle.

The driver's main vision port was a circular door that could be closed from the inside, but he was also provided with two periscopes, a third serving the gunner sitting next to him. Both driver and gunner had double-hinged escape hatches overhead, normally operated from inside, but also provided with a locking system that could be opened from outside by a special key. The driver's main controls were a 'handlebar' for steering, and conventionally arranged clutch, brake and accelerator foot pedals. All three were hydraulically operated, and the clutch was also servo-assisted for lighter pedal action. The handbrake was on the driver's left, the gear lever with its gated arrangement for four forward and one reverse gear was to his right. When underway the driver exerted a 'firm steady movement' to the handlebar to effect a turn, but the tank could also be turned in neutral with the tracks rotating in opposite directions: the tank was therefore able to turn virtually on the spot.

Eventually total production of Churchills reached approximately 5,640, and the tank played an important part in post D-Day operations where eight regiments were deployed. Interestingly the Churchill was also platform for a wide variety of specialist vehicles. One of the most extraordinary was the 3-inch Gun Carrier, in effect a massive self-propelled gun with a slab-sided superstructure to house a 3-inch anti-aircraft gun, now intended as tank buster. This was powerful for its time when it appeared in 1942, but only fifty were made and evidence of service is lacking. The Churchill Crocodile flame-throwing tank, by contrast, certainly saw extensive battlefield use and about 800 were made. The fuel for the Crocodile was transported in an armoured two-wheeled trailer towed behind the tank, and was fed to the vehicle through a pipe. The flame-projector nozzle replaced the hull machine gun, and the weapon was capable of eighty one-second squirts to a range of about 100 yards (91m). If the trailer was damaged or fuel ran out it could be jettisoned, and the Churchill retained the use of its main armament throughout.

Another important Churchill variant was the AVRE, or 'Armoured Vehicle Royal Engineers'. Designed to carry and support assault engineers, these tanks were fitted with the Petard – a sort of 29cm-calibre spigot mortar. The 40lb (18kg) projectiles were short-range, but well adapted to bunker and building busting. AVREs could also carry fascines for filling up ditch obstacles, bridges, or mine clearance devices. They could also be used as a heavy duty, if slow, towing unit. Several hundred Churchills were converted to AVRE specification, and on D-Day they equipped 1st Assault Brigade of 79th Armoured Division. In the ARV and BARV the Churchill became a recovery vehicle with one or two jibs. In the 'Ark', the Churchill became a dedicated bridging tank. With the turret removed and ramps added over the top and at either end, an Ark could simply be driven into place, lower the end ramps, and allow other tanks and vehicles to drive over. In other variants, Churchills were fitted with ploughs; track or mat-laying devices; mine rollers or charge throwers for minefield clearance. Finally an attempt was made to make the Churchill platform for a new generation of

battle tanks mounting the powerful 17pdr anti-tank gun. These 'Super Churchills', developed to the A43 specification, took the overall weight of the vehicle to 50 tons, and the speed down to just 11mph (17.7kph). Known as the 'Black Prince' pilot model, half a dozen were delivered for trials in May 1945, but the type never reached full production.[16]

Lee and Grant M3

The US M3, known variously to the British as the 'Lee' or the 'Grant' depending on the precise model, evolved from the medium M2 of 1939. The basic M2 was armed with a 37mm gun in a small but conventional fully rotating turret, and machine guns firing front and rear lower down in the superstructure. Though the M2 was quite a promising tank for its day, US observers were shocked when, in May 1940, German machines with heavier armament cut their way through French and British machines. The US medium tank was therefore

Montgomery standing in front of an M3 Grant tank in the desert. The tank Christened 'Monty' used by Montgomery at El Alamein and in Italy, was returned from Austria to his old regiment in Warwick in 1948. Much restored, it is now part of the Imperial War Museum collections. (Hulton Archive/Getty Images)

immediately overhauled. The key issue was to somehow incorporate a 75mm gun, roughly equivalent to that mounted on the very latest German Panzers. Given the perceived urgency of the situation, and the apparent adequacy of the chassis of the M2, it was decided not to start again from a clean sheet but to integrate the new armament with as much of the old machine as was practicable. So it was that the M3 retained a small turret with a 37mm anti-tank gun, and much the same running gear. The result was an odd-looking animal in which the 75mm was carried in a limited traverse right sponson quite low in the vehicle, whilst the redesigned small turret for the 37mm was offset to the left, creating a non-symmetrical sort of overall balance. Between two and four machine guns completed a heavy armament. The basic M3 had a maximum armour thickness of 56mm and a nine-cylinder Wright Continental engine, giving a maximum speed of about 25mph. (40kph) The crew was no less than six, being the commander and driver, two gunners and two loaders.[17]

To smooth the manufacture of large numbers, and to secure the commercial future of the auto trade, the president of GMC, William Knudsen, ventured the suggestion that medium tanks, like cars, could be made in volume, on one production line. Automobile lines were duly converted, and in September 1940 began the building of the dedicated Detroit Tank Arsenal line. Members of the British Tank Commission were also able to make an input, designers being more than interested to have first-hand accounts of tank combat in France. By the summer of 1941 three plants were producing the M3, and by the end of 1942 made the better part of 7,000 units. The speed with which the M3 was designed, tested and put into production was remarkable indeed, being described by one commentator as 'probably unmatched in the history of armoured fighting vehicles'.

British orders were placed at an early stage, the model initially unique to British service being the Grant, though Lee types were soon also used, being supplied additionally under the 'Lend Lease' programmes. Both tank names came from generals of the

An M3 crosses
a river north of
Imphal to meet the
Japanese advance.
On 20 March 1944
six M3 Lee tanks
of 3rd Carabiniers
met and destroyed
an equal number
of Japanese
light tanks. (No.9
Army Film and
Photographic Unit/
IWM via Getty
Images)

American civil wars. First orders for the Grant were placed as early as October 1940, and the British specification omitted the cupola atop the turret, so reducing overall height, and elongated the turret itself. This modification allowed the radio gear to be carried in the rear of the turret, creating a little more room within the hull and putting the communications gear close to the commander. The first of the Grants were shipped to the 8th Army in North Africa early in 1942, and formed the bulk of 4th Armoured Brigade at Gazala in May. The Grants were a crucial and very welcome addition to the arsenal, for at that time they were the equal of many of the enemy machines.

Though the M3 was phased out as a first-line battle tank in the west with the advent of the Sherman and the advance of enemy technology, both Lee and Grant had quite long service

identical in their equipment. Records of 116th Royal Armoured Corps from April 1944 show seventeen Shermans, eighteen Lees and seventeen Grants, plus ten turretless Stuarts on the strength. 146th Royal Armoured Corps fielded mainly Valentines, but later topped up with Grants and finally Shermans. 149th Royal Armoured Corps similarly shed their Valentines sometime in 1943, getting one squadron of Shermans, the remainder being Grants. 150th Royal Armoured Corps got Lee tanks rather quicker, and other units also show mixtures of Grants and Stuarts. The 26th Hussars, formed in India, began with light tanks of various antiquity including the model IIB, and an old Crossley armoured car. It received five Lees and fifteen armoured cars in October 1942, then ten Grants in February 1943, and four Lynx armoured cars a few months later. The 3rd Carabiniers appear to have been equipped rather faster, shedding their Indian Pattern light tanks quite quickly for a mixture of Lees, Grants and Stuarts.[18]

Sherman M4

Though its contribution was not as dramatic as that of the Soviet T34, and it was less powerful, or advanced, than some of the latest enemy vehicles, it may reasonably be claimed that the Sherman tank was a timely miracle of production. It was also vastly superior to any tank fielded by the Japanese or Italians. Though not actually British, it has been claimed as 'the most important tank in British service'. Eleven plants in the USA eventually made 49,234 Shermans in different variants – a figure that equalled the wartime tank production of Britain

A Sherman in Normandy, June 1944. As Allied armour moved into the 'bocage' of sunken lanes, hedgerows and woodland, manoeuvre was more difficult and vehicles liable to attack with infantry anti-tank weapons. (Popperfoto/Getty Images)

lives in various guises. Some were converted for mine clearance, others were made into 'CDL' machines. In this variant the 75mm gun was retained, but the turret was replaced by an armoured searchlight mounting. In the Far East the Lee and Grant remained front-line battle tanks, where there were still some as late as the end of the war. Here, where the Japanese failed to develop any really modern machine, the M3 with its multiple armament remained a useful workhorse and infantry support.

Indeed, British armoured regiments in the Far East often sported rather odd mixtures of tanks, and frequently these were the cast-offs from the battlefields of Europe, or outdated models from the USA. Very probably no two units were absolutely

and Germany combined, and led some to dub it the 'tank that won the war'. It started life as the T6 medium tank project in 1941, part of the aims of which were to tackle the shortcomings already identified in the M3 Lee. Whilst it retained the basic engine chassis and suspension of its predecessor, significant advances were made with the armament, turret, silhouette and armour. Specifically the whole hull top was redesigned so that now there was a larger turret mounted in the centre to take a 75mm gun with a co-axial machine gun. Originally it was intended to include a commander's cupola atop the turret, but this was deleted during development, so reducing overall height. The drawings for the new tank were made in the spring of 1941, with a wooden mock-up appearing in May. Following approvals and detailed improvements, a prototype with a cast hull was produced at the Lima Automotive Works in September

1941. Another sample with a short-barrelled M2 gun was soon sent to the UK: this was emblazoned with the name *Michael*, in possible reference, it is said, to the head of the British 'Tank Mission' to the United States, Michael Dewar. This vehicle, a portent of thousands to follow, is still preserved at the Bovington Tank Museum.[19]

There were almost 7,000 of the M4 (known to the British Army as 'Sherman 1') constructed, with R-975 Continental nine-cylinder radial engine and welded hull. The M4 had a maximum speed of 24mph, (39kph) was 19 feet 4 inches (3.25m) in length, and weighed 66,900lb (30,345kg). The thickest armour on the turret was 75mm, that of the hull 50mm. At its weakest points the armour was 12mm. The crew was five. Three of these, the commander, gunner and loader/

M4 Shermans burst through smoke in a dramatic image of July 1942. Note the US .50 cal machine gun mounted atop the turret. Shermans reached North Africa in October 1942, and took part in the battle of El Alamein. (Camerique/Getty Images)

Top: A potentially hopeless task. A British Sherman recovery vehicle pulls up alongside two US servicemen sitting on an abandoned German Sturmtiger. The recovery vehicle weighs less than half the rocket-launching monster next to it. (Keystone/Getty Images)

Middle: A turretless Sherman BARV recovery vehicle tows away a crippled Sherman during the fighting in Normandy. (AFP/Getty Images)

Bottom: A Sherman 'Crab' in France, 1944. A whole brigade of 79th Armoured Division was equipped with these mine-clearing tanks whose rotors carried forty-three flailing chains to beat the ground, exploding the mines. (Pen & Sword/ SSPL/Getty Images)

or cranked round with a handwheel that also made possible the fine adjustments necessary for accurate firing, and in fact if the tank was pointed in approximately the right direction the power rotation got little use. From the British perspective the 75mm gun came as welcome revelation at the time of its introduction, for whilst its anti-armour performance was only marginally inferior to the 6pdr at longer ranges, it was capable of firing a very healthy high-explosive round. This made the Sherman at least the equal of the latest British armour in a straight tank-to-tank action, but more importantly gave it the capability to shell the enemy anti-tank guns that were such a threat to British tanks, and to offer far more useful support to infantry. In addition to the main armament there was a coaxial machine gun, a hull-mounted machine gun, and very often an anti-aircraft .50-calibre machine gun mounted atop the turret. Moreover, the whole package trundled along at a decent pace, and, unlike many tanks, was very reliable.[19]

In the M4A1 ('Sherman 2') the hull was cast and some early vehicles used up bogie units of the M3 type. About 6,500 of this model were built. Though the Sherman was a significant advance on what went before, and was indeed popular with most of its British crews, it soon acquired some unfortunate nicknames including the 'Ronson', or 'Tommy Cooker' – because it lit at first strike, and had a habit of incinerating its crews. This was addressed to some extent in the M4A2 type ('Sherman 3') of which there were over 8,000. This used a General Motors diesel engine, far less susceptible to fire. The M4A3 ('Sherman 4') used a Ford petrol engine, but most of these were retained by the US Army. The M4A4 ('Sherman 5') was slightly longer, slightly more powerful, and used a Chrysler 'Multibank' engine. This was in fact an expedient making use of five commercial automobile engines mounted on a common drive shaft. About 7,500 of this model were made, and some complained that British troops got more than their fair share of Shermans with this somewhat ad hoc arrangement.

The Sherman was very much an 'assembly line' tank, taking the production precepts of Henry Ford to even greater heights than had been achieved with the 'Model T' car. Several pre-existing works were reused for the Sherman, but presidential demands to increase medium tank production to 2,000 vehicles a month led to the introduction of a purpose-built plant at the Detroit Arsenal, and another at Grand Blanc, Michigan. So fast were the machines manufactured that in Sherman paint shops tanks were not simply painted and left to dry, but passed through

radio operator were in the turret; and two, the driver and bow machine gunner, were in the hull. There were two hatches in the hull and another in the turret. There was also an escape hatch under the tank, an exit especially useful if the Sherman turned over or the crew wanted to avoid enemy fire as they attempted to worm their way out. The turret could be power-rotated, a tunnel of infra-red lights that set the paint in under four minutes. The tank was also relatively easy to maintain.

The Sherman Firefly, also known as the 'Mayfly', was ultimately one of the most successful Allied tanks of the war. It was a British development based on the ubiquitous American Sherman hull that would see widespread use, particularly in northwest Europe, after D-Day. Yet it was a tank with a difficult birth that officialdom seemed hell-bent on preventing. As early as December 1941, the Tank Board had come to the conclusion that British tanks were seriously under-gunned for dealing with the latest German armour, and that existing designs were likely to be difficult, if not impossible, to uprate, with much bigger guns due mainly to relatively small turrets and turret rings. They had therefore recommended the development of a completely new tank, a 'large cruiser', and soon this would produce the A30 specification. Ultimately this train of thought led to the Comet and Centurion, but progress was painfully slow, and little of worth was achieved during 1942.[20]

By early 1943 the A30 Challenger had progressed as far as gunnery trials. The fact that it mounted the tried, tested and powerful 17pdr anti-tank gun boded well, but on arrival at Lulworth it was observed with more than a little disappointment by a number of Tank Corps officers. For essentially the Challenger was little more than a Cromwell, with the same Rolls-Royce Meteor engine, and an ungainly looking upright turret built by Stothert & Pitt, very similar to that used on TOG. Ammunition stowage was not great, and armour was to be reduced in thickness to reduce weight, but the suspension still complained about its new burden. Clearly the Challenger still had quite a bit of time-consuming development ahead, and even then there was no guarantee that the end result would be satisfactory. So it was that Major George Brighty put forward a new but very simple idea. The Sherman was reliable, reasonably up to date, and already available in quantity, and the 17pdr was proven as a weapon that could deal with enemy heavy armour: so he proposed that the two should be married together in the shortest possible time. In a fortunate coincidence Brighty was

A British Sherman, camouflaged and with extra track links applied to its frontal armour, during the fighting for Caen, July 1944. The city fell but by then the town was rubble and two-thirds of its population had fled. (Galerie Bilderwelt/ Getty Images)

soon joined at Lulworth by Major George Witheridge, a tank officer wounded in combat at the battle of Gazala recently attached to the Gunnery School in Egypt, and who had also gained experience in US methods at Fort Knox. At this point the new, and technically unofficial, Lulworth project – apparently winked at and quietly encouraged by Major General Raymond Briggs – met what was apparently a brick wall of official resistance. The policy was to develop an entirely new generation of superior British tanks – indeed a good all-round 'universal tank' – and the attempt to match Sherman and 17pdr was seen as a retrograde step that undermined the main effort, and might even deprive the new and supposedly better machines of the gun they really needed. Witheridge saw this long-winded route to theoretical perfection as wasting both time and lives, and Briggs, now Director Royal Armoured Corps, was convinced enough to argue the case with the Ministry of Supply.

As a result a professional designer, W.G.K. Kilbourne, was assigned to the project and gave new impetus to the difficult task of cramming the Tiger killing gun into the modest frame of the 'medium' Sherman. His efforts included shortening the recoil cylinders, redesigning the gun cradle, changing the breech to operate sideways, and even modifying the barrel of the weapon itself to save space. So it was that the mighty gun was shoe-horned into the rabbit hutch of the turret, but even this was not enough. For the gun breech now effectively divided the turret in two, leaving the loader effectively trapped on one side, and with no exit that did not require severe contortions. There was also nowhere left for the radio that the loader could comfortably reach. So it was that a hatch was added for the loader, and the radio was consigned to a distinctive, if square and ugly, bin on the back of the turret. The rounds for the 17pdr were large, and had to be pushed into every available space. About twenty-three could be reached quickly by the turret crew, a further forty were in two bins beneath the turret floor. Finally fifteen rounds took up the space previously occupied by the fifth crew member beside the driver, and the hull machine gun was deleted accordingly. The main armament and coaxial machine gun were fired electrically by the gunner's feet using two buttons; right for the 17pdr, left for the machine gun. The anti-armour performance of the Firefly was stunning – as good as, or even better than, the contemporaneous German 88mm tank guns depending on precise model and type of shot used. The vehicle was also reliable. However, in terms of protection the Firefly remained a Sherman: its main armament was slower to fire than the 75mm; and it lacked a hull machine gun. Never the less, most of these issues were subsequently dealt with by the simple expedient of integrating Fireflies into ordinary four-tank Sherman troops, in the proportion of three 75mm Shermans to one Firefly. This ensured that there were plenty of multi-machine-gun armed vehicles, and adequate capability to deal with other threats, whist the Firefly could focus on its main task of engaging enemy armour.

The Firefly conversion programme commenced in January 1944, with a set requirement for 2,100 machines – a figure which appears to have been met, and possibly slightly exceeded, by the end of the war. Though large numbers were converted, it was not simply a case of taking any Sherman and setting to work: some models were entirely unsuitable for conversion, others had traversing gear that was insufficient to the task. So it was that specific tanks had to be selected from the thousands that were imported from the USA. Even so, enough Fireflies

With skirts lowered and twin propellors disengaged for land action Sherman DD tanks of 'B' Squadron 13th/18th Royal Hussars support No. 4 Commando at Ouistreham on D-Day. The 13th/18th trained on DDs at Fritton Lake near Wickham Market, Orford Ness, and Woodbridge, Suffolk, as well as in Wales and Scotland. Subjects learned included moving from water to land mode with control of the vehicle changing from commander to driver as the tank came ashore; use of 'Davis Submerged Escape Apparatus'; and navigation. Five tanks sank, and one officer and one man were killed during training. Commonwealth War Graves records nineteen men of the regiment died on 6 June 1944. (Sgt Laing/IWM via Getty Images)

were on hand to deploy the desired proportion of 17pdrs on D-Day, and Fireflies fired their first shots in anger on 6 June 1944. Indeed, this actually happened before the tanks hit the beaches because a handful were mounted so as to be able to shoot over the bow ramps of landing craft on the run-in. Fireflies were used extensively during the advance through France and into Germany, and in the Italian theatre. As more became available, and Fireflies were used outside the confines of the close Normandy countryside, there were experiments with unit organisations, so that sometimes whole troops were equipped with the new tank, and sometimes more were deployed within specific tank troops.

Another British, or perhaps more exactly Anglo-Hungarian, Sherman innovation was the 'DD' tank used on, and after, D-Day. The problem that it set out to solve was simple – but apparently intractable. Tanks were armoured and heavy, yet often needed to cross rivers and seas to get at the enemy. Landing craft and ships

were the obvious answers, but very large and very expensive, as well as offering a massive sitting target until after they had hit the beach or docks and disgorged their loads. It would be much preferable if tanks could cross water obstacles under their own propulsion, or by being unloaded from landing craft long before they reached the beaches, creating only scattered targets, then appear immediately amongst the infantry that they were supposed to support. As early as 1941, there were experiments with various tanks involving both 'Lighters' and floatation devices. The former were effectively tiny tank-landing craft, since described, not inaccurately, as 'an enlarged shoe box fitted with an outboard motor'. These were to be carried in modified train ferries. The floatation experiments mainly involved putting tanks between huge floats or pontoons, though the bulk of the resultant equipment and the difficulty of powering it made progress slow. Another route was to make an entirely new light tank, with a sealed boat-like hull and propellor. This notion had some merit, but almost inevitably would take a long time to design and build, and the result was almost bound to be a compromise too far – being neither perfect boat, nor perfect tank.[21]

The answer to the problem came from British-resident Hungarian inventor Nicholas Straussler, whose basic idea was to use the displacement principle to give floatation to what were essentially standard models of tank. This was done by means of the simple expedient of canvas waterproof screens that, when erected, turned the tank into a form of temporary vessel, the screens forming lightweight sides, bow and stern, and the tank itself a heavy ballast and keel. Mobility came from the 'Duplex Drive' or 'DD' – a propellor powered from the tank's own gearbox and engine. In water the propellor was engaged, whilst on land, the tracks were used. Following early tests with a Tetrarch on Hendon Reservoir in June 1941, attention turned to the Valentine – which, being heavier, required bigger screens and tubular strengtheners as well as air-filled tubes to stay afloat. Quite a few Valentine DDs were made and extensively tested in Norfolk and Scotland and on the Solent. By 1943 development and deployment of 'swimming tanks' fell under the purview of Major General Hobart and 79th Armoured Division.

Never the less, though the Valentine DD later went to Italy, it would see relatively little operational use, and by the latter part of 1943 it was accepted that the more up-to-date Sherman would be modified for use in northwest Europe. Being heavier again, the screens for the DD Shermans were yet larger, extending 7 feet (2.1m) from deck to rim. Another issue was that on the Sherman the gearbox and final drive sprockets were located forward, and so a pair of propellors was driven from the tracks, rather than direct from the gearbox. This gave a maximum speed in water of about 5mph (8kph). By mid-1944 several regiments were equipped with DD Shermans, for both British and Canadian use. These saw mixed results on D-Day. Some were swamped, others fell foul of soft sand or enemy fire. Even so, those that got ashore did good work. Later, the Sherman DD was used in the landings in the South of France, and in the crossing of the Rhine and Scheldt. In Italy they were used in the crossing of the Po in April 1945, and finally a squadron of the Staffordshire Yeomanry took DDs across the Elbe.[22]

Cromwell and Comet

Remarkably enough the Cromwell, Centaur, Cavalier and Comet were all at least indirect descendants of the Crusader, and the Cromwell and Comet in particular were destined to become important tanks in the British order of battle in the latter part of the war. With these two models, many of the early faults of the Crusader would eventually be overcome, belatedly introducing some reasonably effective home-produced armoured fighting vehicles. Alongside the Sherman the Cromwell would form the main equipment of British armoured divisions in Western Europe after D-Day, whilst the Comet was the main tank of the 11th Armoured Division in the closing stages of the war.

By late 1940 some important lessons had been learned, prompting the Ministry of Supply to begin the search for a new 'Heavy Cruiser' of improved reliability, with better armour, armament, and a top speed of at least 24mph (39kph). Specifications for a new 'A23' model were issued by the Department of Tank Design to Vauxhall in January 1941, but already Nuffield was developing ideas of its own under the title 'A24'. The Nuffield tank appeared to offer greater promise and it was this that was worked up into several different designs over the next two years. The first of the pilot models appeared in January 1942 and would become known as the Cruiser Mark VII, or Cavalier. This tank was disappointing as its increased armour and weight was not offset by improvement to its engine, and an order for 500 machines was ultimately used to furnish training vehicles and mobile armoured observation posts for the artillery regiments of the armoured divisions. The A27L Centaur, the pilot for which was completed in June 1942, also retained the old Liberty engine pending the appearance of more powerful aircraft engines for use in tanks. Eventually 950 Centaurs were made. In some of these the original specification 6pdr gun was replaced by a 95mm support howitzer, and in this guise Centaurs served with the Royal Marines Armoured Support Group on D-Day.[23]

Meanwhile, experiments with fitting aero engines into a Cruiser type tank finally bore fruit at Leyland from 1942 with the production of the very similar-looking, but much improved, A27M Cromwell. Key to the success of the Cromwell was the perfection of the V-12 Meteor engine, a power plant redesigned for tanks but sharing most of its components with the existing Rolls-Royce Merlin. The new engine gave the Cromwell a 40mph (64kph) turn of speed, despite a 76mm armour which could be uprated to a maximum of 101mm with the addition of appliqué plates. Manufacture began in January 1943, and would run until 1945.

The Cromwell had a simple-looking box-like design with an improved Christie type suspension and live wheels either side running within 14-inch (35.6cm) tracks, later widened to 15.5 inches (39.4cm). The driver, located in the front right-hand portion of the hull, could drive whilst viewing through a front visor incorporating a 'wicket door' arrangement that allowed the aperture to be fully open, or partly shut with a 'very thick glass block' to observe through. When battened down for action the visor was completely closed and the driver was then limited to two periscopes, one either side of the visor and adjustable using handles. The co-driver, also acting as hull machine gunner, sat to the left of the driver, whilst the commander, gunner and loader were provided with seats in the turret turntable. The commander could only be seated when the cupola doors were open; when they were shut he stood upon the platform.

The original main armament of the Cromwell was the old 6pdr, supplemented by two 7.92mm Besa machine guns, a 2-inch (5cm) bomb thrower firing through the turret roof, and a Thompson SMG stowed inside. In extremis the crew could also fire their revolvers out through two small circular ports located in each rear side of the turret. However, from the Cromwell IV a 75mm gun was used as the main armament. This weapon has reasonably been described as being 'the first wartime British tank gun that could deal out a respectable high-explosive shell as well as an armour-piercing type'. In February 1943 it was decided that 10 per cent of Cromwells should be given a heavier weapon for close support purposes and so a 95mm howitzer was fitted in the Marks VI and VIII.[24]

The 1943 first edition of the *Cromwell Service and Instruction Manual* described the new 27-ton tank as a 'heavyweight fighting vehicle':

> 'The front part of the hull [and turret] accommodates the crew of five, while the rear part houses the engine and transmission. The front part is further subdivided into a fighting compartment, a driver's compartment and a forward gunner's compartment. A partition, with access holes cut in it, separates the personnel in the fighting compartment from the driver and front gunner, while a similar partition, also with an access hole, separates the driver from the front gunner. Single armour plate is used at the front and rear of the vehicle, but a double plate is placed at the sides, the outer plate of which affords protection to the suspension. The inner plate, on each side, carries five main suspension spring

housings… The turret consists of double-plated sides, the outer plates of which are bolted to the welded inner structure, and a single roof plate. It is rotated hydraulically… There are four external access doors, one to the driver's compartment, two in the turret roof and one to the front gunner's compartment, which can also be used as an emergency escape door.'[25]

Useful as the Cromwell was, it could still not take on the latest German tanks and hope to penetrate their frontal armour with a 75mm gun. The Comet, essentially a much re-engineered and improved version of the Cromwell, solved the problem by mounting a compact 17pdr, later also referred to as the 77mm. To accommodate the new weapon, an enlarged welded turret with a cast front and stronger suspension were required. The resulting tank was fast and reliable, and has been claimed as being not significantly inferior to the German Panther, though it came too late to have much impact until after the Rhine crossing of March 1945.[26]

A Comet tank and a Humber scout car of 11th Armoured Division pass transport on the way through Western Germany, 30 March 1945. According to after-action reports elements of the division had begun an attack on Gelnhausen early that morning, but despite artillery and fighter-bomber support the Germans had to be bypassed, other routes now being secured, the division completed the crossing of the river Main. The 11th Armoured claimed well over 20,000 enemy captured during March. (Sgt Laing/IWM via Getty Images)

Performance of Typical British Tank Armaments Against Armour

Type	Calibres in length	Type of round	Armour penetration at 1,000 yards (91m)
2pdr	50	AP	42mm
		APCBC	49mm
		SV	72mm
3pdr	40	APHE	25mm
6pdr	50	APCBC	80mm
75mm (Mark V)	36.5	APC	61mm
		APCBC	94mm
76.2mm (Mark II)	50	APCBC	110mm
		APDS	165mm
17pdr (Mark II)	55	APCBC	118mm
		APDS	230mm
95mm (Howitzer)	20	HEAT	110mm

These performances are those achieved against homogenous armour presented at 30 degrees to the gun. The round types are 'AP' – armour-piercing, introduced for tanks 1937 'APCBC' – armour-piercing capped shot, introduced for tanks 1942; 'SV' – Super Velocity, introduced for tanks 1943; 'APHE' – Armour-Piercing High-Explosive (multi-purpose), introduced for tanks 1928; 'APDS' – Armour-Piercing Discarding Shot ('Sabot'), introduced for tanks 1944; and HEAT – High-Explosive Anti-Tank.

Chapter Eight

Vehicles

Men of 11th Royal Horse Artillery (Honourable Artillery Company) Tunisia, April 1943. The open-topped truck is a 15cwt Canadian Military Pattern or 'CMP'. According to the 1944 manual these were made by Ford and General Motors, and used by 'all arms and services'. The rhino sign of 1st Armoured Division appears on the front bumper. (Sgt Loughlin/IWM via Getty Images)

In the early twentieth century, Britain was one of the world leaders in the motor trade, with numerous manufacturers and many international customers. As was explained in 1945:

> 'The British motor-car and commercial vehicle are products of an industry, which at the time war broke out, ranked among the premier industries of our country. It gave employment directly and indirectly to about 1,500,000 persons, and its products provided in taxation approximately one eleventh of the total revenue of the national exchequer. Its annual output in terms of chassis and vehicles was round about 500,000 vehicles, of which some three quarters were private cars and the remainder commercial vehicles.'[1]

Since before the First World War, various governments had appreciated the strategic potential of motorised transport and

had encouraged companies in the manufacture of suitable vehicles, and as early as the 1920s it was decided that a long-term goal should be total mechanisation of the Army. Achieving this required not only overcoming sceptics and the lobby in favour of the horse, but – probably more importantly – severe restraints on resources, and the practical issue of identifying viable vehicles to do the jobs required. Keeping up was made the more difficult by continual technical improvements within the industry, and fragmentation of the market. In spite of the problems a 'Mechanical Warfare Establishment' was set up in 1926, this being rechristened as the Mechanization Experimental Establishment (or 'MEE') in 1934. Located at Cove, near Farnborough, it was the job of MEE to test all forms of mechanical transport under consideration. Examinations included running vehicles for set numbers of miles, mechanical and performance tests, reports, and judgements as to suitability.

Army vehicles were somewhat arbitrarily divided into four categories: 'A' being armour, 'B' general transport, 'C' specialised vehicles such as cranes and earth movers. The fourth were broadly defined as 'Royal Army Service Corps' vehicles; this encompassed all 'second line' vehicles such as ambulances and fire engines. As the RASC also became responsible for some large-scale lorried troop movements and many other things, this somewhat antiquated definition was eventually dropped in 1942. Thereafter RASC vehicles were recategorised as 'B', whilst the Corps itself became the exclusive source of vehicle supply. Given that budgets entirely prevented the repeated

British vehicles and armour on the Wesel road out of Gelderen, just inside the German border. Carriers, a half track, and a jeep are all identifiable in the column. Tilts and tarpaulins protect against the rain and the armoured vehicle, foreground is littered with ammunition boxes, Jerry cans, and a kettle. (Official/author)

re-purchasing of the transport elements of the Army, still less acquiring fleets of vehicles large enough to accommodate the likely scale of any future mass army, forward progress was as much by stealth and suggestion as by practical experimentation and logical deduction. For in practice the War Office would indicate its requirements and the trade would translate these into practicality, as far as was possible, using components already available for commercial vehicle production.[2]

This compromise worked after a fashion, but compromise it was, since motor manufacturers produced what they could sell, and what this might be was limited by the normal rules of the road as they pertained at the time. Overall measurements, weights and axle loadings as prescribed by law for civilian vehicles therefore determined what was available to the military in terms of components. Much went unprocured on the basis that it could be secured by impressment in the event of emergency. Unsurprisingly, therefore, the Army landed up with what has been described as 'near civilian types' in the period up to September 1939. This familial connection was further emphasised by the fact that vehicles carried civilian registration plates front and rear, in addition to their service serial number, and were registered in the county of Middlesex wherever they happened to be. Never the less, the British Army was much smaller than that of Germany, and partly for this reason by 1939 had achieved a higher proportion of motor vehicles, and much less reliance upon the horse, only about 5,000 of which remained with the Army.

At the outbreak of war, the total number of vehicles in British Army service was about 85,000, and of these almost a third were impressed from civilian sources. In some instances the conversion to military use was as simple as an all-over coat of khaki paint to obscure chrome fittings as well as camouflage the body. Only after the war started would opportunity arise to cast aside convention and begin to produce types of vehicles that hitherto existed mainly on paper. Civilian registrations were now discarded, and service numbers were now painted larger. These numbers were prefixed by a letter code signifying the following types:

A	Ambulances
C	Motorcycles
F	Armoured Cars and Scout Cars
H	Tractors
L	Trucks (1 ton and over)
M	Cars and Light Utilities
P	Amphibious Vehicles
S	Self-Propelled Guns
T	Carriers and Tanks
V	Vans
X	Trailers
Z	Trucks (under 1 ton)

Interestingly general nomenclature evolved so that whilst the term 'truck' was used to describe load-carrying vehicles under 1 ton, 'lorry' was used to denote larger-load carriers. 'Vans' were effectively trucks with fixed tops, and tractors were vehicles for pulling or towing anything including artillery.

It is easy to forget quite how different, slow and temperamental military vehicles actually were early in the Second World War. Indeed, advances like windscreen wipers and hydraulic systems were comparatively recent departures. Partially or completely open cabs and general absence of vehicle heaters meant that the age of the driving coat was not dead. Moreover, unarmoured 'soft-skinned' vehicles were extremely vulnerable to battle or accidental damage: a handful of grenade splinters or a couple of pistol bullets could damage a radiator or other parts badly enough to put a vehicle out of action. Ordinary tyres were susceptible to puncture, and military motorcycles frequently written off in accidents, especially in the blackout or bad weather. Every different type of vehicle required an inventory of spares, training for mechanics, and a new list of hazards to avoid if a machine was to be kept moving and trouble-free.

Maintenance schedules were extensive and new vehicles required careful 'running in'. As the 1937 *Manual of Driving and Maintenance for Mechanical Vehicles (Wheeled)*, reprinted in 1940, explained:

Troop-laden British lorries passing through a French village, October 1939. (Fox photos / Getty Images)

Libya 1942: British troops load a recently captured German eight wheeler armoured car onto a flat bed transporter. The improvement and proliferation of tank and other transporters aided vehicle recovery and reduced traditional reliance on railways. (Planet News Archive/SSPL/ Getty Images).

'High-speed working parts of a vehicle, particularly of the engine, cannot be polished by the makers to rub together with as little friction as is the case with parts which have polished themselves in use. The process of running in consists of allowing this self-polishing of working parts to be carried out without risk of damage to the vehicle on account of extra friction. In addition, the assembly of many components when new differs slightly from the positions of assembly which they take up after running for some time; they are said to settle. Precautions must be taken that this settlement does not upset any important adjustments. Not only, therefore, is careful treatment required while the vehicle is passing through the running in stage, but a close watch must be kept on its performance in general.'

As a guideline to prevent overheating and seizure, drivers of new vehicles were instructed not to exceed half-engine speed, or 15mph (24kph), for the first 500 miles (800km), then 20mph (32kph) for the subsequent 250 miles (400km). 'Running in' periods were usually concluded with a service that included the checking of cylinder heads; steering alignment; tappet adjustment; and a cleaning of fuel and filter systems.

Road conditions also set limits: the UK had nothing like the *Autobahn*, and it was still expected that the majority of long-range movement would be by rail. Over much of the Empire, road conditions were appalling, and the Far East and other warm areas added the perils of frequent overheating and rapid deterioration of rubber and leather parts. In deserts, sand and dust led to severe wear to moving parts, obscured windscreens, and caused ditching on soft going. The cumulative effect of such parameters was frequently very slow speed of travel. Convoys took some planning, and according to the manual steady pace and correct spacing were vital: moreover, it was intended that the pace set by leaders should

be that which enabled 'the slowest vehicle' to keep position. Small convoy 'blocks' were commanded by NCOs during the movement. Verbal orders were possible when the convoy was at the halt, but once moving, leaders became dependent on a system of hand and whistle signals – prefaced by a loud 'cautionary' whistle blast to gain attention. Some of the hand signals, such as 'halt' or 'advance' were fairly self-explanatory, but others required learning. Waving both hands above the head was a warning that enemy aircraft were in sight: 'gas alarm' was given by a motorcyclist riding along the convoy with his mask on sounding his horn. 'Switch off engines' involved waving the hand across the body, palm downwards, parallel to the ground.[3]

By way of example, it is worth looking in greater detail at just one of many thousands of similar long-distance road journeys made during the war: that of 88th Field Regiment, Royal Artillery, Territorial Army (RA TA), from Preston in Lancashire to France, joining the BEF in the autumn of 1939. As Territorials, the regiment had to be 'embodied' and kitted out, and any last-minute alterations and training completed before departure. 'Calling Out' notices were therefore issued at the end of August, before the actual outbreak of war, and the men reported for duty on 1 September. Over two weeks were then spent on initial preparations. On 19 September an officer was sent ahead to the 'Road Convoy Regulating Post' at Southampton to ease the co-ordination of movement. A week later the road convoy itself set out, carrying with it about a third of the total personnel, driving via Warrington, Wellington and Worcester. Orders were for an average speed of 12mph (19kph), with a maximum of 20mph (32kph). Breaks of fifteen minutes every three hours were incorporated into the schedule. Column density was kept down to twenty-five vehicles per mile, with any one 'block' of trucks and cars not to exceed six. Newport in South Wales was reached without incident, and soon after the vehicles embarked for France. They finally arrived at Nantes on 1 October, but took two days to unload and reorganise. The rest of the troops got onto their rather faster train from Preston on 3 October, and, taking a more direct route across the Channel from Southampton, quickly gained a whole week on their road companions. The regiment was rejoined, and on 7 October began to move towards the front. Remarkably this was not unusually slow, and the mechanical performance of the motor vehicles was actually better than average, perhaps because the regiment contained a decent smattering of experienced drivers, fitters and garage mechanics amongst its Territorials.[4]

In the desert, techniques were different, but speeds even slower, as one contemporary account of the advance of an artillery field regiment from Egypt made clear:

'The long move from Eygpt into Cyrenaica was interesting at times, but it was conventional move along roads and tracks. From El Adem, south of Tobruk, the advance however became a desert movement in which the regiment learned a new technique. The brigade group to which it belonged for the time being advanced in close parallel columns, each about ten miles long including gaps between units. The infantry were lorry borne. The density was something rather less than 15 vehicles to the mile and the interval between vehicles varied with the ground from 50 yards to several hundred. Drivers were soon cured of the column of route complex and taught the spirit of the broad front. Officers were able to look back and see the whole of their troops or batteries winding their way in four columns between the bushes, rocks and hummocks. The ground varied from smooth gravel plain, where it would have been possible to move on a much broader front, to very bumpy, broken or rocky ground where good battery leading was needed to find four feasible routes. The tracks of the advanced guard were normally visible to tempt units to follow the same routes, but an experienced eye often saw something better to one flank or another. This all added to the interest and prevented the long day becoming monotonous. An officer in the advanced guard navigated by compass: unit navigators behind checked his course against gross error. This was the first time the regiment had made serious use of the sun compass, a far more convenient instrument when the course is maintained for many miles without change… The speed of the advance varied with the ground, and surprisingly it varied with different units. A few believed in keeping up 15mph at any cost to springs: most were content with about 10. Thus considerable gaps were apt to appear in some parts of the brigade groups, whilst in other parts rear units were fretting and pressing to increase pace and get in earlier at the end of the day.'[5]

During the 'advance to contact' in the desert there were other factors to worry about, particularly when confronted by defiles or minefields. For not only were these obstacles in themselves; convoy commanders had to decide whether to risk closing up their columns to press quickly through narrow gaps, or to halt parts of the unit to allow others to proceed at normal speed. Various solutions were applied, including advanced reconnaissance to examine checkpoints and possible ambush zones, and find other crossings and routes; 'digging parties' to create better going and establish new routes; and closing all, or parts, of columns up to forty vehicles per mile. When 'brigade groups' were on the move in four columns, and space allowed, density could be dropped to about ten vehicles per mile, but this meant that a typical column then extended to about 15 miles (24km) in length.

Long journeys, particularly in hot climates, were always bound to be something of a trial, and worse wherever supply dumps and dedicated refuelling vehicles were lacking. On most trucks a standard fitting was the 'POW' – or 'Petrol, Oil, Water' – carrier. This was a simple frame closed by a bar with a padlock. If kept full, this coped to some extent with engines that were prone to leak, and provided fuel for an emergency top-up. Yet poor consumption statistics often meant vehicles needing to carry additional supplies. Sometimes so much was needed that many vehicles had to be added to convoys simply to keep them moving, and these additional trucks needed more trucks in their turn to keep them mobile. Early in the war, the only way for non-specialist vehicles to carry fuel or water was in 'flimsies' – thin-walled oblong steel cans with little structural rigidity and poor ergonomics, usually containing 2 or 4 gallons apiece. As the *Driving and Maintenance* manual observed, all that could really be done to keep down leakage from rough

going and fragile containers was to check them during halts and use up quickly any that showed any sign of compromise. Later, however, following contact with *Wehrmacht* liquid containers, British soldiers became enthusiastic converts to the 'Jerry Can'. These had greater rigidity due to their stamped side panels, had better balance, and a simple but very useful triple-handle arrangement at the top. This allowed either one man, or two, to carry the can between them by grasping the outer handle on each side.

Arguably the worst baptism of fire for British Army vehicles was in Malaya and Burma at the end of 1941 and in early 1942. Here inexperienced Indian divisions and a smaller number of British formations confronted not only the awful conditions of unmetalled narrow jungle tracks, but also an enemy with air support and armour. The British units in question had not been intended to fight in rubber plantations, thick forest and swamps, but in the more open conditions of North India and Europe. Their relatively lavish provision of transport quickly turned from advantage to handicap as heavy lorries slithered off the trail or became bogged down and blocked convoys into helpless traffic jams. In many instances the best that could be achieved was a steady walking speed that left columns not only very vulnerable to air attack, but no swifter than Japanese cycle troops.

At the defeat of Singapore, many lorries fell into enemy hands, and whilst some of these were run by their captors for some time, many were broken up due to lack of spares or fuel, and some were even transformed into so-called 'Changi Chariots', engineless hulks that prisoners were forced to tow around by sheer dint of muscle power.

Though the evacuation from Dunkirk cost the British Army most of the vehicles it had taken to France, leaving a very serious shortfall in the summer of 1940, early loss was actually made up again surprisingly quickly. For by the end of the year, vehicle stocks were back to what they were, and, despite bombing, continued to climb from early 1941. Part of the reason this was possible was the dispersion of production. Garages and small producers who had largely lost their civilian market were now brought into war production.

North America also made a highly significant contribution as time went on, and it is notable that Canada in particular moved swiftly from a virtual standing start to the production of most major categories of military trucks and lorries by mid-1940. Pre-war Canadian production had focused on American-designed trucks of commercial patterns built by local subsidiaries of Ford, General Motors and Chrysler, but now new types were commenced direct from British blueprints, redrawn to fit North American thread gauges and machinery. Such standardised models for British Army use were dubbed 'Canadian Military Pattern' or 'CMP'. Eventually Canada made about 900,000 military vehicles of all descriptions, and more than 400,000 of these were CMP types. Canadian production included 8, 15 and 30cwt trucks as well as 3-tonners and artillery tractors. In some instances Canadian chassis were finished off with British bodies. Interestingly there was a two-way trade, as the Canadians produced mainly medium-sized vehicles, and purchased many large vehicles from Britain and the USA. At the other end of the scale, Jeeps were also bought from the Americans for Canadian forces.[6]

By the time of the Italian campaign, each infantry division in that theatre possessed 3,745 motor vehicles including 951 motorcycles. This conferred a very high degree of mobility, though it also absorbed large numbers of skilled men as drivers and mechanics and to handle stores such as fuel and spares. As of June 1944, 919,111 wheeled vehicles had been manufactured in the UK 'for the services', and whilst it has to be admitted that some of these went to the Royal Navy and Airforce, there were also many made in the USA and Canada that went to the Army. About half of the total British production was defined as 'heavy', being trucks and other large vehicles, approximately 40 per cent motorcycles, and the remainder divided roughly equally between 'light vans' and armoured cars and carriers.

By the end of the war the total number of 'soft-skinned' vehicles in use by British forces was about 1.25 million, a total that does not of course include armour, armoured cars or carriers. Arguably, and though the British Army had sought, and largely achieved, 'mechanisation' by 1939, vehicles were now even more important. For one thing, lifting whole battalions and brigades by means of the 'Troop Carrying Vehicles' of the Royal Army Service Corps had become commonplace, for another there were now more classes of specialist vehicles able to move more, across more difficult terrain. Tank transporters made spectacular progress; half-tracks and amphibians were acquired from the USA as well as the Jeep; and the idea of carrying infantry squads into battle in fully tracked carriers had been born.[7]

Motorcycles

A Grenadier Guardsman demonstrates one of the less practical motorcycle devices, a mounting for a Thompson sub-machine gun. Whilst carrying Bren guns in side cars was a well established practice, this idea never really caught on. (FPG/Hulton Archive/Getty Images)

The Norton 16H solo in the late 1930s, complete with rider clad in waterproofs and sheepskin gauntlets and carrying a map case. Evaluation of the 16H began in 1932, orders being placed in 1936. Significant numbers were made for the military until 1943 when production trailed off. (Author)

Motorcycles were used in numbers during the First World War when the firm of Douglas had been the leading Army supplier. Though the involvement of Douglas shrank to almost nothing by 1939, the military in general remained convinced that motorcycles retained an important role in war. Some of their key advantages were small size making for easy concealment; cheapness; ability to get around obstacles that would defeat other types of transport; relative ease of maintenance; and some off-road capacity dependent on model. These characteristics made motorcycles particularly useful for despatch riders, reconnaissance, general communications tasks and convenient run-arounds. They were much less practical as load carriers: but motorcycle combinations with relatively capacious sidecars were used, and were especially significant early in the war, though many of their tasks were progressively taken over by light cars and, from 1942, by the US Jeep.[8]

Many inter-war British motorcycles were 350cc models, a capacity then regarded as adequate; but from the mid-1930s experiments were made with more powerful types. As of 1939 an official specification was issued for bikes weighing up to 250lb (113kg) and a performance standard equating to that of a 500cc machine. Developmental work and selection remained incomplete at the outbreak of war with the result that quite a few older designs were still in service and continued to be supplied. By the middle of the conflict there were attempts to standardise on two main types, 350cc overhead valve models, and 500cc side valve types. This was at least partially successful, somewhat improving and simplifying training, servicing and supply of spares. It has been estimated that the total number of motorcycles used by British forces during the Second World War was approximately half a million, the majority of these going to the Army and Home Guard.

Eventually a bewildering range of bikes from many different manufacturers saw service. This was at least in part because loss of many machines at Dunkirk was followed by a crash programme of replacement sweeping up civilian machines by requisition, donation, or emergency contracts. A very motley selection of upwards of 8,000 motorcycles was rapidly taken into use, some going to the regulars as well as Local Defence Volunteer and Civil Defence organisations. It is recorded, for example, that a battalion of the Argyll and Sutherland Highlanders took onto its books a number of Automobile Association machines to mount its own coast patrols in Scotland during the worst of the invasion scares. Similar expedients occurred in many other parts of the UK. Lend Lease from the USA later added some American models to the inventory in the shape of Harley-Davidson and

Indian bikes, most of the former being combinations shipped on to South Africa. A number of British companies supplied only tiny numbers for defence contracts, as for example Francis-Barnett, recorded as delivering just twenty-five of its 150cc 'Plover' machines to the government in 1941, or AJS, whose name appeared on only a handful of motorcycles in 1940 before the AMC parent company supplied machines for large official orders under the Matchless name. Only one example of the extraordinary Swiss-origin Moto-Chenille 350cc *Mercier* is recorded in War Office data for 1939, and this heavy beast with a track unit at the front and wheel at the rear was quickly rejected since it was unable to corner safely at any speed. Later, as the war gradually turned in favour of the Allies, enough German machines were captured to make it worthwhile allotting them British serial numbers.

At the other end of the scale to such Lilliputian efforts, it was a relatively small group of firms that made the vast bulk of the Army's motorcycles produced during the war. The US *Handbook* of 1942 states that the BSA and the Norton are the 'standard' British Army solo motorcycles at that date:

> '*They will normally carry one rider, with his pack and blanket stored in pannier bags on either side of the rear wheel. A pillion seat is also provided for occasional use. Brakes are mechanically operated, internal expanding [drum brake]. A foot brake operates the rear wheel; a hand brake, the front wheel. Standing orders require that every British Army officer below the grade of colonel be a proficient motorcycle operator. Motorcycles are widely used by dispatch riders (messengers).*'

Handbook went on to explain that these were single-cylinder machines weighing a little over 300lb, (136kg) and had a top speed of about 60mph (97kph). With a fuel consumption of approximately 46mph (74kph) under good conditions, they covered anything up to about 150 miles (241km) before refuelling. The Norton combination was also used by infantry battalions and armoured regiments, and 'in a combination box body' with provost companies.

By the peak of wartime production, BSA was making 1,000 motorbikes per week for the government, total orders coming to over 125,000 machines by the end of the war. The company's main service model was the M20, a single-cylinder 496cc type evaluated by MEE in 1937. Though judged only 'fair' for purposes in mind, the M20, in various guises and slightly

modified models, went on to be the most widely used motorcycle in the Army. Some of the more obvious alterations included a less bulbous 3-gallon fuel tank on the W-M20 from October 1939; changes to fork dampening introduced after experiences in North Africa; the deletion of rubber fittings to save resources in late 1942; and further changes to suspension, crank case and air intake from 1943. Though less popular with troops than many military machines, the M20 achieved decent standards of reliability over time, and was used virtually everywhere the Army went. Two idiosyncrasies were difficulty of restarting if the bike was hot, and a tendency towards backfiring.

Norton was a major supplier to both British and Canadian armed services and roughly a quarter of all British military motorcycles, or over 100,000, came from this firm. The main Norton solo was the WD 16H. Tested in 1935, this model was accepted following a number of modifications, and continued to be an important type until 1941, when other manufacturers, producing newer models, took a larger share of orders. The 16H was then largely relegated to second line and training duties.

Corps of Military Police motorcyclists of the 'Traffic Control Branch', pictured en masse during training, March 1943. The Corps swelled massively during the war to encompass different areas including not only traffic control, but the Field Security Wing; Provost Wing; Vulnerable Points Wing and Special Investigation Branch. (Author)

Norton's other main Army product was the 'No. 1' combination, often known as the 'Big Four'. Accepted for service use in the late 1930s, this was a 633cc machine with improved shaft drive and sidecar capable of carrying a Bren gun. Having good cross-country performance and ability to shift three men and weapons, it was regarded as a useful reconnaissance machine and saw widespread deployment, with a few even being used by glider troops. However, this was but part of the story, for though BSA and Norton were indeed the leading and second-biggest suppliers of motorcycles respectively a number of other firms continued to make significant contributions.

Matchless, the third-largest contractor, was well known for its G3 types. The company supplied both the Army and the RAF, making over 40,000 motorcycles for government contracts. The very popular G3/L 347cc, with its 'teledraulic' front forks, was tested in 1940 and produced all the way through from 1941 to 1944, remaining in service long after the end of the war. Royal Enfield was also a big contractor for the Army, delivering, for example, the 1940 civilian model range finished in green, as well as lightweight types. Triumph promised great things, and did indeed deliver upwards of 20,000 machines for government service, but its efforts were hamstrung by the Blitz on Coventry that badly damaged its factory as well as much of the city centre. Never the less, limited production was continued there, with a temporary works operating in Warwick. The new Meridan factory opened in 1942, making a 350cc model.

Apart from conventional solos and combinations, a number of special-purpose machines saw Army service. One of the most interesting of these was the 'Welbike' designed by John Robert Vernon Dolphin. This was a folding miniature bike specially developed with Airborne forces in mind, capable of being packed away in small spaces and containers. Though only a tiny 98cc model, the Welbike proved useful where compact transport was in demand, and several thousand were made from 1942, use being eventually

expanded to Commandos, Marines and RAF. Innovative as the Welbike was, this was not the only time that lightweight machines were used or considered. Royal Enfields were examined at an early stage, and from 1942 their two-stroke 125cc WD RE type was fitted with a 'dropping cradle' for parachute landing. About 8,000 of this and similar models were delivered, primarily for Airborne and assault uses. The James 150cc 'Flying Flea' was likewise tested, and although deemed too heavy, a new K17 prototype 125cc type was worked up, eventually becoming the James 'ML' or 'Military Lightweight'. The ML saw significant use, though mainly with ground forces. In Normandy it acquired the reputation of being a 'mechanical sheep dog', rounding up troops and darting with messages from one unit to another. Though still a little heavier than its Royal Enfield competitor, the ML achieved a reputation for reliability and durability.

Initially Army motorcycles were supplied in a deep bronze-green finish, with casings and other components left dull, or black enamelled. After the outbreak of war, camouflage was improved with a change to light khaki, a colour that varied in practice from more green to more brown. Motorcycles could be repainted during their service life, both in dedicated workshops,

A Royal Army Medical Corps motorcyclist tows a patient on a Miller James wheeled stretcher from a Regimental Aid Post to a casualty collecting point. The Miller James had been used in the First World War, and featured a collapsible frame for transportation. Pneumatic types with a broad tread improved stability and movement on soft ground. (Keystone/Getty Images)

and in the field, where sprays and brushes were used fairly indiscriminately. Camouflage schemes of various types were also applied, as for example splodges of brown, and the distinctive 'stone' pattern extensively used on Malta.

From Cars and 'Tillies' to Heavy Lorries

Many of the cars and small utility vehicles used early in the war were either of civilian patterns or impressed, though subsequently a variety of specific War Department models came on stream. Austin, which manufactured two-seater 8hp tourers, and 10hp saloons and light utilities, was the largest producer. As the 1943 US manual *Handbook on the British Army* explained, the basic Austin 10hp was, 'a light two-seater open runabout with a baggage space behind the seat. It is a convenient vehicle for directing convoys because of its ability to cut through congested traffic where a larger vehicle would be held up.' The four-cylinder Austin had a top speed of 52mph (84kph), a then healthy 33 miles (53km) per gallon, and a radius of action of about 230 miles (370km). Useful as it might be, the Austin was essentially a road vehicle with just a 1,200cc engine and little cross-country capacity. Much the same could be said of the Hillman and Standard 10hp four-seater models. It was also the case that at first glance the Austin, Morris and Hillman light utilities were all of similar appearance with a cab open to the back, on top of which was perched the spare wheel, and a box-like body behind covered with a canvas tilt. In some versions light utilities also featured two seats in the back, though in practice more bodies or equipment could be crowded aboard if comfort was ignored and the seats folded flat.

The Ford WOA1 4x2, which became something of a standard four-seater type, was developed from the 1938 saloon, but was fitted with a more powerful V8 30hp engine. It also looked more businesslike, having cutaway wings to allow for larger tyres or special 'sand tyres'. Greater engine power gave the Ford an impressive maximum speed of 76mph (122kph), but made the car thirsty, dropping the miles per gallon to just 13 (20km). However, the ultimate in staff cars was the Humber Snipe, and in fact several distinctly different bodies were grafted onto the pre-war 4-litre 'Super Snipe' chassis. The saloon, tourer and light utility were reasonably close to their civilian

counterparts, but the Humber also provided the starting point for an 8cwt personnel truck, and the Humber Pullman, a six-seater limousine. Humber also produced the only British-made four-wheel drive military utility of the period.

One of the most important classes of British military vehicle was undoubtedly the 15cwt light truck. This was so much so that as it became possible to rationalise, 8cwt trucks were discontinued, and the number of 15cwt types rose from barely 15,000 at the outset to 250,000 during the course of the war. The 15cwt General Service-class was actually born as early as 1933, when the War Office invited tenders for this type, having a particular requirement for 'platoon trucks' with which to motorise the equipment of the infantry. Though the main intention was to move supplies and weapons, the vehicle could accommodate a section, with space for a driver and front-seat passenger, and eight troops in the back – arranged facing inwards four on each side. Later, the little 15cwt became something of a maid of all work.[9]

First to join the Army was the Morris Commercial CS8 in 1934, followed later by the Guy 'Ant', Bedford, Ford and Commer. A fair degree of standardisation for the General Service (GS) was achieved by the fitting of a universal War Department body, which at least allowed common calculations

The versatility of the army 30cwt knew few bounds. Here it is being used as an impromptu London bus, 581 Angel to Bloomsbury, during the civilian bus drivers' strike of April 1944. (Popperfoto/Getty Images)

to be made on loadings, and the number of vehicles and journeys required to complete a given task. Fordson joined the stable in 1940 with the WOT2 model. By now the 15cwt was to be seen in many guises, including radio truck, 'light machinery' carrier, mobile office, compressor vehicle, fire tender, and 200-gallon water tanker. These vehicles were modified according to task with van bodies, cylinders, and hoses and taps – or roofs instead of tilts – as required. One of the most novel transformations was as 'portee' for a light gun mounted in the back. Towards the end of the war, there was also a 4x4 version of the 15cwt that added significantly to the vehicle's cross-country performance.

Perhaps the most famous of the wartime 2-ton British 4x2 lorries was the Austin K2. This was completed in a number of configurations but was also the basis for a standard ambulance design, the K2/Y, known affectionately as the 'Katie'. About 13,000 ambulances were built at the Longbridge plant. Fitted with a Mann Egerton box body to accommodate four stretchers and adorned with huge red Geneva crosses, the 'Katie' ferried the wounded in many theatres of war, including the desert with 7th Armoured Division. Whilst four casualties were carried in reasonable comfort, ten or more 'walking wounded' could be transported if seated. With a six-cylinder 60hp engine, the K2/Y had a top speed of about 50mph (80kph).

In the class of medium lorries, the 'three tonner', as defined by its 3-ton carrying capacity, would become the most useful and adaptable type used by the Army during the war, and approximately 400,000 of various models were made by 1945. Well-known manufacturers of 4x2 types included Austin with their K3, Commer who made the Q4, Leyland with the 'Lynx', Thorneycroft, Albion, and Dodge. Never the less, pre-eminent amongst the basic 3-tonners was Bedford, who made the ubiquitous OYD 'General Service', and the OY series was actually developed from the commercial OL series of 1939. Though essentially a road vehicle, the 3-tonner Bedford was capable of some off-road movement. As the US manual of 1943 explained, it was:

> '...representative of the type adapted to take special low pressure tyres and to give adequate clearance for moderate cross-country work. This type is the main load carrier of the Army. The body is a general service body with a flat floor and a detachable canopy mounted on hoopsticks. The enclosed steel-panelled cab seats two. The dimensions are: internal length, 11 feet six inches; internal width six feet six inches.'

With a six-cylinder engine and a top speed of just over 40mph (64kph), the vehicle had a range of about 300 miles (480km) before requiring refuelling. The usual fuel tank

Manoeuvres in the North African desert. Small trucks with large tyres helped in rough or soft terrain, but had limited capacity. Gas masks are worn as a simple way to limit the effect of dust and sandstorms. (Fox Photos/Getty Images)

configuration was a tank either side below the forward end of the stowage deck. Fuel capacities for various Bedfords are quoted at anywhere between 32 and 45 gallons.

Some 3-tonners had solid cab roofs, others were fitted with a circular 'hip ring' opening, allowing the front-seat passenger to stand and view the sky, or road, ahead from an elevated position. As the US manual of the British Army observed, as of 1942:

> 'The present trend in all wheeled vehicles is to design or modify them so that an anti-aircraft sentry, with all-round field of vision, can be posted in the vehicle. British units in the Middle East have cut holes in the top of the passenger cars and closed cab trucks so that sentries can stand on the driver's [more usually the passenger's] seat and have their heads and shoulders protrude through the roof of the vehicle. On some of the closed cab trucks the tops have been removed. On large cargo trucks the sentry is seated on top of the cover.'

A number of companies also made 4x4 all-wheel drive 3-tonners from the middle period of the war onwards. These all had a basic similarity, having a ladder-frame chassis, mid-

Montgomery in his Humber staff car heading a column crossing the Seine at Vernon, 1 September 1944. (Sgt Morris/IWM via Getty Images)

Far right: In the back of a signals truck an operator wearing 'Bombay Bloomers' uses the No. 11 radio. Designed in 1938 this set weighed 43 lb and had a maximum range of about 20 miles with an aerial. It could be used with batteries or mains power. (Official/author)

mounted transfer box, semi-elliptic springs and servo-assisted hydraulic brakes, but again there were several distinctive models within the general class. The Fordson WOT6, in production from 1942 to 1945, featured a detachable cab roof to reduce shipping height, and the AEC Matador appeared in a General Service role and as an armoured ammunition carrier with low open body. Austin produced the K5 with a distinctive angular cab, also known popularly as the 'screamer' due to the noise of its transmission. Arguably the iconic 4x4 3-tonner was again a Bedford, the QL, of which about 50,000 were made from 1941 to the end of the war. The QL in particular had many different specialist variants, slab-sided wireless vehicles, Light AA tractors and gun portees being only some of the most obvious. The QLT was a purpose-built 'troop carrier'.

Trucks and 'utilities' undergoing maintenance at a desert camp near Cairo. Rolls-Royce armoured cars are visible in the background. (Margaret Bourke-White/The Life Picture Collection/Getty Images)

Retriever and Terrier, and various Crossley, AEC (Associated Equipment Company) and Fordson models. Six-wheelers were also converted to provide mobile offices, cranes, fuel carriers and fire tenders.

At the heaviest end of the transport lorry scale were vehicles in the 5- to 10-ton class. Many of these originated from civilian precursors, and continued to look very much like their non-military cousins. This may have been partly due to oversight and the pressing nature of other developmental demands, but given their size and the relative impracticality of using such beasts in any true battlefield role, much effort in this direction was probably viewed as wasted. The majority of 6-ton vehicles were finished with War Department-pattern wooden bodies and used as General Service load carriers, but there were at least a few specialist types such as the perennially malodorous 'Cesspool Emptier', which was usually based on a Dennis chassis. Many of the 10-ton lorries were likewise fitted with General Service bodies and used for longer-distance haulage work. Key manufacturers of these heavyweights included Albion, Foden and Leyland. Perhaps best known in the class was the Leyland Hippo. In its Mark I version the Hippo was essentially a civilian commercial vehicle with double rear wheels and fitted with a War Department open cab. However, as of 1944 the Hippo was considerably improved in a Mark II version. The 6x4 Mark II had an enclosed cab, single rear wheels, and its six-cylinder diesel engine gave 100hp. At 27 feet (8m) in length it required a turning circle of 63 feet (19m), and returned little more than 7 miles (11km) per gallon.

Next up in terms of scale were the 6x4 lorries – typically over 20 feet (6m) in overall length, and weighing in at about 6 tons unladen. These 'rigid six wheelers' were a general type specifically encouraged into production by the War Office as early as the 1920s. Yet whilst these vehicles had undoubted advantages in terms of extra wheels and traction, and could carry bulky loads such as pontoons and bridge sections, they were rather unwieldy, fuel-thirsty, and generally felt to be old-fashioned when measured against the performance of the latest 4x4 3-tonner types. Never the less, the niche requirement remained and so the 6x4s continued to be made. Representatives of the class included the Austin K3, Guy FBAX, Leyland

Artillery Tractors

The vehicles that pulled guns and other heavy equipment were a vital class, adding particularly significantly to the viability and flexibility of the artillery arm. The Victorians had experimented with the movement of even super heavy artillery during the fitting out of Palmerston's coastal forts, and subsequent exercises mounted to test their ability to resist siege, but arguably genuinely practical and systematic efforts at battlefield mechanical traction had been lacking until after the invention of the internal combustion engine – and the confrontation of the Army by the mud of Flanders during the First World War. After 1918, official efforts slackened, but interestingly in the straitened financial climate of the inter-war period, Territorial Artillery units had also done quite a bit of experimentation with tractors and other civilian machinery in efforts to get guns into position during camps in the wet British climate. By the 1930s, Scammell, Guy, Morris and FWD were all producing petrol-engined tractors for towing field guns, and until 1940 these regularly worked alongside fully tracked 'dragons'. For reasons of both economy, and the gradually increasing cross-country performance of wheeled vehicles, the fully tracked vehicles were then generally superseded by those with wheels.

Thereafter, the Morris C8 Tractor, a four-wheeled, four-wheel drive with a decent cross-country performance, emerged as the main towing vehicle of the field artillery and the angular 'Quad' tractor – pulling the 25pdr – became one of the ubiquitous images of war from the Far East to Europe and wherever the Royal Artillery was engaged. Though it had taken some years to replace its rivals, the project that had produced the Quad 'FAT' or 'Field Artillery Tractor' had in fact commenced as early as 1937, when the War Department had issued a new specification. This included carriage of a gun-traversing platform on the roof, a sloped metal body for ease of chemical decontamination, and the ability to carry twenty-four rounds of 25pdr ammunition, six men, and other stores. Guy Motors also submitted a new design, but it was the Morris that eventually won out. The new C8 had a new 70hp four-cylinder engine, numerous stowage lockers, a top speed of 50mph (80kph) and an operational range of 160 miles (257km). Small numbers of the 'Mark I' version rolled off the production line in 1939 and early 1940 before the introduction of the Mark II Quad with its simplified front axle. About 4,000 of these were made before the appearance of the improved

Mark III in 1941, of which about 6,000 were manufactured by the end of the war. Some of the later types featured a canvas roof, or canvas roof sections.

Early in the war, Morris Quads pulled 18pdrs, 18/25pdrs, 4.5-inch howitzers, and 75mm guns. Commonly a Field Artillery regiment was equipped with thirty-six Quads of which twenty-four towed a limber and a gun, and twelve pulled two limbers. Later, along with the Anti-Tank regiments, Quads were also deployed with 6pdr and 17pdr anti-tank guns. Useful as the Quad was, the larger weapons in particular stretched the capabilities of its engine rather too far, resulting in modest performance, particularly on hills in bad weather. Other vehicles used to pull the smaller species of artillery included the Bedford QL and Austin K5 lorries, which were adequate for the Bofors 40mm.

More powerful traction was needed for the bigger guns, and in fact some of the medium 'Dragons' were retained for some time, though by late 1941 they were regarded as essentially being obsolete in anything other than training scenarios. Much more widely seen were heavier wheeled tractors and lorries. Foremost amongst the medium artillery tractors was the 4x4 AEC Matador. The distinctive flat-fronted Matador had a cab made from ash coated with steel and was capable only of a fairly sedate 30mph (48kph), but was never the less a powerful towing unit with a fair off-road ability. The reason behind this

An AEC Matador leads a column of D-Day reinforcements through London, 14 June 1944. Further down the line are 3-ton Bedford lorries. (Popperfoto/Getty Images)

A stream of gun tractors and other vehicles heads through Malaya towards Singapore Island, 1941. There were units that lost their vehicles at Dunkirk, were requipped, then captured at Singapore. About a quarter of the British troops captured by the Japanese died in captivity. (Fox Photos/Getty Images)

performance was a 7.6-litre diesel engine giving 95hp, making it a practical motive unit for 3.7-, 4.5- and 5.5-inch guns. Over 9,000 Matadors were built by 1945, and they saw particularly extensive use in Europe after D-Day. Where even the Matador was not powerful enough, larger Scammell, Bedford OXC, and imported Canadian and US tractors were put to use.[10]

The Carriers

The idea that infantry could be mounted for cross-country movement in small tracked armoured vehicles went back as far as French proposals of 1915. British 'tankettes' were seriously considered in the early 1920s, when enthusiast and gifted amateur mechanic Lieutenant Colonel Giffard Martel, a former member of the Tank Corps, began to design a one-man machine using both car components and tracks. Perhaps overambitiously, or too farsightedly, Martel believed that it might one day be possible to carry entire units to battle in such machines. In this futuristic scenario, total numbers of troops might be reduced, whilst firepower and mobility were markedly increased by these machine-gun carrying vehicles. 'Foot' soldiers could then be relegated to the mountains and forests. In the event, Martel proved persuasive enough that some tankettes were indeed procured for experiments by the War Office; though these were mainly two-seat vehicles as it was thought, probably correctly, that a single individual would not be able to fight and drive at

the same time. Moreover, one person alone might well have suffered in terms of morale when attempting to confront an enemy deployed in numbers. The tankette concept was further developed by Sir John Carden, supported by military theoretician and pundit Basil Liddell Hart. Small 'Carden-Loyd' carriers continued to be produced under the auspices of Vickers when the large Vickers-Armstrong concern took over Carden-Loyd Tractors Limited. As of May 1928, experimental vehicles with a rather odd wheel and track arrangement were used by 2nd Battalion King's Royal Rifle Corps as transport for a machine gun company.[11]

This was not a great success but other versions, of simplified design, showed greater promise. In the Carden-Loyd Mark VI appeared a vehicle of recognisably similar layout to the carriers in use in the Second World War. This was essentially a lightly armoured two-seater open-topped box atop a small pair of tracks. Driven by a Ford Model T engine, it could be armed with a Vickers machine gun, and managed a healthy 30mph (48kph) road speed. It was quickly realised that such a vehicle might be made to perform many different tasks, and prototypes and small runs totalling about 300 units were made, including carriers mounted with mortars. One vehicle, christened the 'Infighter', was given a raised armoured screen. Its tactical purpose was described as being to push its way forwards in the fighting, and cover the advance of infantry using its machine gun. Another use for carrier type vehicles was also found in the development of 'Dragon' tracked gun tractors. Though the quaint-sounding 'tankette' fell by the wayside, the notion of small tracked multi-purpose carriers was continued into the 1930s.

So it was that from 1934 Vickers-Armstrong began the development of the 'D50', a replacement vehicle for the Carden-Loyds to be used as either a tractor or machine-gun carrier. Unlike its predecessors, this was intended to be able to carry both a support weapon and crew that could be dropped off to operate entirely independently from the vehicle as required. This 'Experimental Carrier, Machine Gun' set the tone for what followed. A few examples of a 'Carrier, Machine Gun, No. 1' were deployed in 1936, but it was 1937 by the time the 'No. 2 Mark I' version entered service. This seated three men, weighed just over 3 tons, had 10mm of armour and was powered by a 30hp engine. Further modifications, led by John I. Thornycroft & Company, enabled carriers to mount the new Bren gun, thus producing the true 'Bren carrier' in 1938. This was a particularly interesting development, as one might have thought that carriers were best devoted to carrying 'heavy' machine guns, but the logic appears to have been that Brens were likely to be used further

forwards, so might benefit from a lightly armoured carrier and greater speed of deployment. Soon vehicles were also fitted with the Boys Anti-Tank rifle, or produced to different specifications to perform a wide variety of different tasks. In the 'Scout' carrier, a No. 11 wireless set was transported with its batteries protected in a bullet-proof box. In the 'Cavalry' carrier, six men were seated on benches to the rear of the armoured forward compartment. Other very limited productions were armed with guns, notably the 2pdr, and the Home Guard 'Smith Gun'.[12]

In the 'motor battalions' of armoured brigades, each company had a 'scout platoon' of eleven carriers. The ten carriers supplied to infantry battalions were arranged as a 'Carrier Platoon', or fourth platoon of the headquarters company. Nine formed three sections of three carriers each, the tenth being that of platoon HQ. Each carrier section had nine men, the main armament of which was three Bren guns and an anti-tank rifle. Wherever possible, weapons teams were transported forwards, then dismounted to fight from a covered position. In *Notes on the Tactical Handling of the Carrier Platoon in Attack*, issued in 1939,

A Carrier, Machine Gun, No.2 with the Cheshire Regiment. Introduced in 1937 to carry a Vickers MG, this type was later reworked to Bren carrier standards. (Author)

commanders received a frank assessment of the likely value of the vehicle in action:

> 'It is bullet proof against rifle bullets fired on the same level, but the personnel are vulnerable to bullets fired from above, or when the carrier is on a forward slope. It is, therefore, a partially protected vehicle only… It can move fast across country, but will be stopped by trenches, by any obstacle which is a tank obstacle, and by many which are not. Its mobility in action, therefore, is considerably less than that of the tank, and often good ground scouting will be required if it is to get forward. There will be occasions when it is unable to get forward at all… The LMG [Bren] detachment, consisting of two men, cannot be expected to do more than keep the gun in action either in the vehicle or on the ground. Once in action the detachment has little or no power to protect itself by observation; it is, therefore, very vulnerable to quick attack by one or two determined infantrymen. They cannot be expected to hold an isolated position for long, unless each section works on a system whereby the LMG detachments protect each other, nor can they mop up.'

The moment of greatest vulnerability was while the team were dismounting, which was best achieved under cover and 'very quickly'. The Bren carrier itself was then concealed close by, or withdrawn. On the positive side, the firepower of the carrier platoon was considerable, being 'the equivalent of one rifle company plus one LMG'. For short periods the unit might be expected to hold a front from 500 to 1,000 yards (457 to 914m) in length. When taking part in a combined attack with tanks, the armour was to be used to surmount obstacles, deal with machine guns, and 'keep down the fire of the anti-tank localities'. However, the carriers could not be expected to follow the first wave too closely, but might be 'well forward in the second echelon', finding fire positions, and advancing from one to the next as the attack unfolded. In attacks where no tanks were available, a carrier was not itself to act as 'a light tank' but as 'an armoured machine for conveying the LMG from place to place, but also from which the LMG can be fired if necessary'.[13]

Experience in France taught other important lessons. Carriers were found useful for 'infiltration' or the rushing forwards of parties of 'bombers', and during night patrols might be mistaken for tanks by the enemy. Now there was 'a general demand for increased numbers by all arms and for many purposes'. Indeed, it was even accepted that carriers could be used in the 'assault role', even though they had never been designed for this. As the post-Dunkirk Bartholomew Committee observed, 'The Carrier Platoon provides the Battalion Commander with a reserve of firepower and the means with which to carry out a counter attack… Carriers proved of immense value in every role, mounted, dismounted or when driven across the front to frighten enemy infantry.'

So it was that the Committee recommended that the carrier platoons should be strengthened, and this suggestion was later carried out. Now there were thirteen carriers grouped in the 'carrier platoon'. Each of the four 'carrier sections' within the

The crew of a Bren carrier pause to examine a recently erected Italian monument at Sidi Barrani, 16 December 1940. The battle of Sidi Barrani, fought only a few days earlier, was a crushing defeat for the Italians in which about 40,000 men were lost, the vast majority of them taken prisoner. (Capt G Keating/IWM via Getty Images)

platoon was armed with three Bren guns, an anti-tank rifle, a 2-inch mortar, a submachine gun and nine rifles.

In the deserts of North Africa, expansion of the carrier arm was substantively justified by the amount of use that was squeezed out of them, in patrolling, reconnaissance, transporting men and stores, and as a mobile machine-gun platform. There were complaints about lack of armour and carriers wearing out, but they were now being used far beyond their original specification, and often on hard and unforgiving ground. There were also expedient battlefield modifications, such as covering the floors of the carrier with full sandbags as mine protection. In later campaigns, carriers found a niche in forming 'joint posts' as linking points within their brigade. Being mobile and well-armed, they could form a cement to hold together a front that might otherwise have dangerous gaps vulnerable to exploitation.[14]

Though the handy Bren carrier was a useful maid of all work, the plethora of different models was quickly recognised as uneconomic, and a significant handicap to smooth production and distribution. So it was that as early as 1939 a decision had been taken to change to making just one basic carrier, with special tasks being fulfilled by only minor modifications to the standard design. This 'Universal' carrier which began to reach the troops in 1940 would remain the standard combat model throughout the war. The hull took elements of both the Bren and Scout carriers. Its lightly armoured box was divided into three, with a forward compartment, and two rear compartments, one either side of the Ford V8 65hp engine. The front compartment contained the driver on the right and a gunner on the left to man the Bren, Boys, or other equipment. In the rear, one compartment was usually given over to a third crewman, whilst the other contained stores and weapons. An improved Mark II model Universal carrier was introduced in 1942. This was 12 feet (3.7m) long, had a combat weight of 4.5 tons, a maximum speed of 30mph (48kph), and a range of 140mph (225kph), consuming a gallon of fuel per 7 miles (11km). The Mark II was similar to its predecessor, but featured a slightly more powerful engine, and revised stowage arrangements. As the handbook of January 1943 explained:

> *'The Mark II has a crew of four, two in the front compartment and two seats in the hull, one either side. The front quarter of the top track run is totally enclosed by a valance. Four foot steps are provided, two on each side of the vehicle. A spare wheel and tow rope are fitted across the front of the vehicle. A large kit box fits transversely across the rear of the hull.'*

These basic configurations could be changed, for example, to allow for a mortar to be mounted on the engine cover, or for a Bren to be put up on an anti-aircraft mounting. In some versions, as those issued to the carrier platoons of infantry battalions, a 2-inch mortar mounting was affixed inside the front compartment beside the gunner. The Australians, who produced their own model and also supplied China, reprised the earlier history of the carrier by mounting a Vickers machine gun. British troops followed suit in the middle of the war when Motor Machine Gun battalions put a Vickers with a crew of four into the carrier. In other variations, carriers were used for the 3-inch mortar, or fitted with smoke dischargers. The Royal Artillery got their own type of Universal carrier in the form of the 'AOP' or Armoured Observation Post with radio, cable reel at the back, and three-man crew. In case of extremis, virtually anything could be crammed into a Universal carrier, including, in some remarkable instances, Browning machine guns up to .50-calibre, Besa or Vickers 'K' machine guns, and the German MG 34. Indeed, there were even cases of mounting the 20mm Solothurn anti-tank gun. Armoured units also used special Universal carriers as ambulances, arranged so as to allow a stretcher case to be carried either side of the engine casing. At

A typical interior layout of a Universal Carrier from the US *Handbook on the British Army, 1943*. There is accommodation for a Bren and magazines; up to three rifles; an anti-tank rifle; ammunition; a 'Verey' signal pistol; smoke canisters and four grenades, plus a variety of tools and other equipment. (Author)

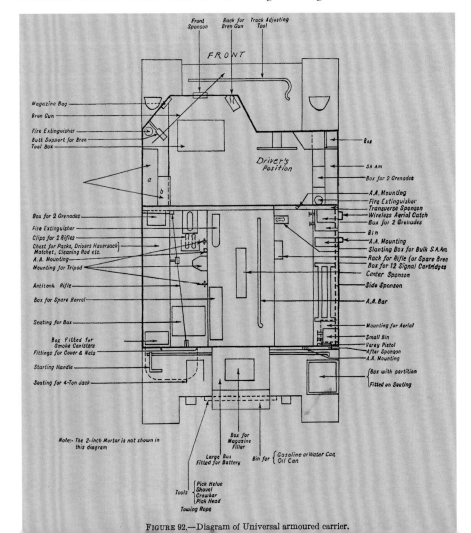

FIGURE 92.—Diagram of Universal armoured carrier.

a pinch, an ordinary carrier could also be used in this role with a stretcher laid across the top of the hull.

Other oddities developed for use with Universal carriers included a 'carpet' device which unwound hessian from a spool, enabling the carrier to cross wire obstacle zones and lay a pathway for infantry; 'Conger' for exploding mines; and 'Kid', a demolition device of 1944, consisting of 600lb (272kg) of high-explosive attached to a frame. The driver simply drove as near as he dared to the target and then jumped out. The carrier and its huge bomb exploded on impact. An ingenious Canadian idea that saw limited use in 1944 to 1945 was the carrier with 'PIAT Battery'. In this, two rows of seven PIAT projectors were mounted on a frame on the rear, and could be fired simultaneously by means of a system of steel rods and triggers. Whilst the original notion of universality had been a good one, it began to break down both with such diverse deployment and the further production of carriers in North America. In both the more powerful US T16, which saw British use, and the Canadian-manufactured 'Windsor', the whole vehicle actually became larger. Remarkably Captain Vivian Loyd, former partner of Sir John Carden, also continued in the carrier business, and his products saw use mainly as troop carriers and towing vehicles. Though similar to the Bren and Universal carriers, the Loyd types were distinguishable at a glance as they had a shorter, arched engine compartment, and a flatter, less complex front. Often the Loyd types were preferred by their drivers as the personnel-carrying model could accommodate eight troops, and steering was easier. Eventually the total of all carrier production comfortably exceeded 100,000 units.[15]

One of the most notable variations on the carrier theme was the development of flame-thrower carriers. Development of these 'Wasps' began early in the war, and in the Mark I version two pressurised fuel bottles totalling 100 gallons were contained within the rear compartments, with a crew of two in the front. The projector nozzle was a large tube pointing out over the crew compartment. The range of the flame jet was about 80 to 100 yards (73 to 91m). An order for 1,000 vehicles was placed in 1942, and completed just over a year later. In the Mark II there were a number of improvements, the projector being better designed and fitted lower down in the place where the Bren gun was normally mounted. In the 2C, or Canadian, version of the Wasp there was just one fuel container, mounted outside

A 'Carrier Tracked Towing' of an anti-tank platoon in a London street, 1944. This model, which could either tow a 6pdr, or carry a 4.2-inch mortar, and several similar, were Loyd designs. Some were built by Ford in Canada. (Popperfoto/Getty)

and to the rear of the carrier, allowing the carriage of an extra crewman. So useful was the Canadian design that in June 1944 all Wasp production was switched to the 2C type.

As the manual *Tactical Handling of Flame-Throwers* (1945) observed:

> *'The present operational carrier-borne flame-thrower is the Wasp Mark 2C. The flame gun is mounted in the forward light machine-gun mounting; its traverse therefore is restricted to 25 degrees on either side of the direction of movement. The fuel tank, holding 75 gallons, is mounted externally on the rear of the carrier, giving 20 to 30 one-second shots before refuelling. The pressure bottle is carried in the left rear well and will exhaust two fills of fuel when charged with carbon dioxide, but only one when using inert air. A crew of three can be carried – the carrier driver, the flame gunner and a third member who is available to use a light machine gun, throw grenades etc. The additional space in the other rear well of the carrier is utilised for carrying ammunition such as light machine gun and 2-inch mortar ammunition, high-explosive and smoke grenades. Maintenance of the carrier engine is possible without dismantling the flame equipment… The carrier has armour that is proof only against small arms fire and is vulnerable above to air burst high-explosives, grenades and snipers in trees. Plastic armour, fitted to the front and sides of the front compartment, is now provided for Wasps, and gives much greater protection as well as raising considerably the morale of the crew. The vulnerability to overhead fire means that the Wasp cannot be expected to find much employment in thick jungle, though in more open country in the Far East Wasps can be, and have been, used to advantage.'[16]*

Versatile as they were, what the little Bren and Universal carriers could never do was transport a full infantry section into combat under small arms fire. The M3 and M5 series US half-tracks might manage this, but were only slightly better protected, and were somewhat disadvantaged in combat by the presence of front wheels. Therefore, arguably the biggest breakthrough in the story of British carriers of the Second World War was the fully tracked carrier, based on tank chassis and running gear. That the idea was relatively slow to develop was at least partly due to a lack of tanks, and indeed tanks of a suitable size to make conversion to the new role viable. Early experiments with light tank chassis were limited in impact. Only in the last year of the war, with masses of medium tanks and self-propelled guns now available (many of them of US-manufacture), did it become practicable to convert some to troop carriers. Even so, first

operational use was claimed by the Canadians, who transported men forwards during the breakout from Caen in August 1944. In this battle, so-called 'unfrocked Priests', self-propelled guns with the main armament removed, were used as expedient carriers. This successful trial led on to further conversions in Italy, and similar use of turretless Shermans. At the end of 1944, the 'Ram Kangeroo' troop carrier, based on the Canadian Ram tank, made its first appearance.

Taking an exciting idea one stage further, a number of armoured units were reorganised to include both conventional tanks and armoured carriers. Each could now offer the other very close support in action, infantry 'debussing' to weedle out enemy anti-tank teams and guns, armour blasting machine-gun posts and other tanks during the advance. Never the less, as was apparent from the April 1945 document *Current Reports from Overseas*, combat doctrine for the new breed of fully tracked armoured carrier was still being worked out at the end of the war. In theory, once the tanks were impeded, Kangeroo drivers were to halt completely before entering battle, with one man crewing the vehicle-mounted Browning as the troops scrambled clear. The infantry would then go forwards and tackle whatever was holding up the tanks. That this was not always followed in practice was demonstrated at the Battle of Medicina in Northern Italy on 16 April 1945. Here the Shermans of the 14th/20th King's Hussars 'charged' into the town ahead of the unfrocked Priests of their 'A' Squadron, annihilation being narrowly avoided when the

A demonstration of the Wasp, spouting flame. In the Wasp 2 and 2C the flame-thrower was fitted in the bay where the machine gun was mounted in other carriers. In Normandy it was used in support of infantry operations where the enemy had taken up defensive positions. (Official/author)

latter caught up and 2nd/6th Gurkhas quickly spilled out of their carriers to outflank anti-tank teams.[17]

US Vehicles

American tanks in British service have attracted considerable attention: yet it should not be forgotten that these were just a small fraction of the US vehicles adopted by the British Army during the Second World War. Moreover, these not only swelled numbers, but in certain areas made possible types of movement or tactics that would otherwise have been impossible had the Army been limited to home-produced vehicles. Key contributions were made in terms of movement across rough terrain, amphibious capability, and the transport of troops not only to the battlefield, but across it in concert with armour and other arms. Of all the wide range supplied from the USA, it is therefore arguable that four types of vehicle stood head and shoulders above the others: the half-track, the DUKW, the LVT (known as 'Buffalo' in British service) and of course the ubiquitous Jeep.[18]

Partially tracked tractors had existed since about 1900, and were indeed used to pull heavy artillery at an early date, but the modern half-track is usually thought to be descended from the work of French engineer Adolphe Kégresse, who had applied his system to Russian military vehicles prior to the fall of the Czar. These were studied and improved by US engineers during the inter-war period, and by 1940 the M2 half-track had been devised. During the Second World War, White, Autocar, Diamond T and International Harvester all built military half-tracks, producing more than 50,000 units of various models. It was International Harvester that supplied Britain with the M5 model, most of which were made during 1943 and 1944. The M5 was very similar to the M3 that equipped the US-armoured infantry, and could carry a section of troops or light weapons. It was capable of a top speed of 42mph (68kph) on road. One of the main differences was that the M5 had slightly heavier welded homogenous plate armour, though in either instance it could not stop more than small arms fire.[19]

Designed by a combined USA and British team, the DUKW was sometimes nicknamed the 'Duck', but the letters were

A field of US army Jeeps await return to the States at Toddington England, August 1945. Defined by Ernie Pyle the war correspondent as 'a divine instrument of wartime locomotion', the Jeep went to most places, and did most things, with the British Army during the second half of the war. To name the obvious functions it served as command and reconnaissance vehicle; weapons carrier; lightweight towing tractor; front-line medical evacuation vehicle; ground transport for airborne troops, and as special forces runabout. (Keystone-France/ Gamma Keystone via Getty Images)

version supplied to the British Army, becoming known as the 'Buffalo', and many of these were armed with a 20mm Polsten cannon and two .30 machine guns. On land the Buffalo could reach about 25mph (40kph) and water propulsion was by means of grousers on the tracks, giving up to 5 knots in water. It was able to carry small guns or a Jeep. The vehicle saw particularly important service during the Scheldt operations and the Rhine crossing. Significantly, given a reasonably level landing area, the Buffalo could climb straight out of the water and move inland before discharging its passengers or cargo. This was an important tactical advantage when compared to landing craft that had to stop, lower a ramp, and disgorge troops onto an open beach.[20]

The Jeep, arguably one of the most important military vehicles of recent history, was designed in response to a US Army call for a new reconnaissance car. The vehicle was to be an all-wheel drive, four-wheeler, defined as a 'Truck $^1/_4$ Ton'. Many companies were contacted, though only three would have a significant input to the iconic machine that emerged. Most of the design work was done by Karl Probst of Bantam over a period of a few days in July 1940, and a prototype was ready for testing before the end of September. The Jeeps were then produced in two versions by Willys and Ford with full-scale production underway by mid-1941. The vast majority were therefore manufactured from 1942 to 1945. About 640,000 were made during the war at a unit cost of about $700, this being almost 20 per cent of all wheeled vehicles built in the USA at that time. The name 'Jeep' was filed as a trademark by Willys in 1943. Large numbers of Jeeps went to both the UK and the Soviet Union. It was used in a wide variety of roles in many theatres. It was able to tow small guns or trailers, could take a stretcher mounted on a frame, or a machine gun on a pintle, and

actually a General Motors Corporation code indicating that the vehicle was an all-wheel drive utility. First manufactured in 1942, with drive to all wheels, and a dual rear axle, the DUKW had six wheels, weighed 6.5 tons, and had a watertight hull and a propellor. On roads it could manage 50mph (80kph), or in water 5.5 knots. Some of the novel ideas incorporated included an ability to vary tyre pressure from inside the cab, and a bilge pump capable of dealing with water entering through a hole in the steel body anything up to 2 inches (5cm) in diameter. So it was that though the DUKW was not armoured, it could take modest damage and not sink. The variable tyre pressure feature was useful in transferring from soft going, such as a muddy river bank or beach, to a metalled road. About 2,000 were supplied to Britain, and the DUKW saw service in a number of operations including D-Day and the Scheldt.

The 'LVT', or 'Landing Vehicle Tracked', had its origins in the 'Alligator' – a tracked amphibious vehicle of the 1930s developed by Donald Roebling. The significance of the idea being recognised by the US Marine Corps, further work was carried out, leading to the creation of the LVT-1. This was capable of carrying eighteen troops or cargo, and two .30 machine guns, but lacked armoured protection. Later models added a rear ramp, armour and a variety of armaments, including other machine guns, or even a 75mm howitzer, greatly increasing operational flexibility. The LVT-4 of 1943 was the

Used by British and Canadian forces in the latter part of the war the LVT-4 Buffalo had a maximum armour of 14mm and a range of 75 miles (120km) in water or 250 miles (400km) on land. (Official/author)

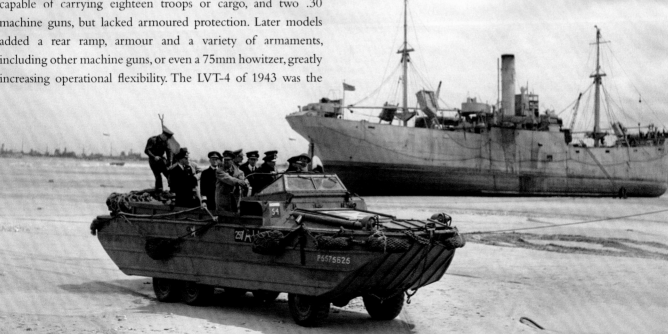

King George VI, accompanied by Admirals Ramsay and Cunningham, touring the Normandy beaches in a DUKW amphibian, June 1944. On land the range of operation of the DUKW on roads was a healthy 400 miles (644km) at 35 mph (56kph). (Lt CH Parnall/IWM via Getty Images)

was used as a support vehicle for Airborne forces. It had sufficient off-road capability to cope with a muddy field or jungle track, and was fast enough for any reconnaissance mission.[21]

Markings and Camouflage

The painting of British Army tanks and vehicles evolved considerably with the course of the war, mainly because different colour schemes were required for different environments, but also because serial numbers, vehicle types,

The M7 Priest self-propelled 105 mm howitzer. Both the US Priest and the British-made Sexton with a 25pdr served with the British Army. (Myron Davis/ The Life Picture Collection/Getty Images)

colour standards and terminology changed, and sometimes with surprising frequency. Up until 1939, the normal finish for all vehicles in Europe was a deep bronze green. Though usually dark, there were variations, as for example due to weathering or where paint was hastily applied over a civilian colour. With *Military Training Pamphlet No. 20* of June 1939, a new scheme was introduced whereby bold diagonal or horizontal patterns of two different greens created a more effective method of breaking up shape and blending with vegetation – usually these colours were khaki green and dark green. Tilts, originally a light canvas colour, were later painted over with bands of a darker hue. A further official alteration as of *Army Council Instructions 1559*, published in January 1941, was the colouring of canvas hoods and tilts in a dark tarmac grey.

Tank interiors, originally silver, were generally switched to white after 1940, though soft-skin vehicles were usually painted the same tone inside as the base colour used on the exterior. In August 1941, khaki green and dark tarmac were authorised as colours for the bodywork of soft-skin vehicles, with dark green and dark brown to be used on canvas surfaces. That November another contradictory instruction prescribed charcoal grey or black for the upper surfaces of soft-skinned vehicles, presumably with the intention that this would serve to hide them from above when parked in shadow, under trees or netting.

During 1942, the British Standards Institution issued further lists of camouflage colours intended to regularise the hues used. Now there was greater emphasis on browns, and according to some accounts this was to economise on the chemicals required to produce strong greens. A common scheme in the field was to apply patterns of charcoal grey over khaki. A copy of *War Emergency British Standard 987C* of September 1942, used by the Walpamur company of Darwen, Lancashire, makes it clear that more than fourteen shades were recognised in total, though at this date it would appear only eleven were actually in production.

These were:

1A	Charcoal Grey
2	Earth Brown
4	Khaki
5	Sage Green
7	Dark Green
10	Chocolate Brown
11A	Red Brown
11B	Pinkish Sand
12	Grey
13	Olive Green
14	Black[22]

Vehicles for UK and European theatres were now often painted earth brown prior to delivery, and the manufacture of hoods and tilts was altered to match. Some vehicles were operated just like this and without further embellishment. However, the current palette made possible a number of different schemes, some of which were aimed primarily at disguise against aerial observation. These included foliage and dapple patterns, either mimicking vegetation, or the effects of light through leaves. In the 'Mickey Mouse' variation, large rounded areas – not unlike the mouse's distinctive ears – were applied in a darker colour over a lighter base. As of October 1943, *Army Council Instruction*

other colours, were allowed to fade, or chemically bleached to a less obvious pale brown.

With entry into Tunisia, and then the invasions of Sicily and Italy, vehicles required new colour schemes to match new environments. So it was that of April 1943 a light mud colour with black or green bold disruptive patterns was instituted. Never the less, as was so often the case, things remained complicated. Some Shermans were to be seen in an unusual spotted colour scheme, and many US-supplied vehicles were seen with the light mud colour painted over a base of olive drab. Moreover, by the latter stages of the war, the Allies reached relatively verdant areas of Italy in which northern European type colour schemes were applicable. As in northern Europe and the UK, standard colour 15, olive drab, became the issue colour for new vehicles in British service in mid-1944. In the early, and often disastrous, phase of the war in the Far East, vehicles were usually painted in approximations of the European and Middle Eastern colour schemes. However, as of 1943 standard colour 13, olive green, was accepted as the base colour for India and Burma. Dark drab was also used, and often disruptive patterns were omitted in the latter part of the war.

Over the basic paint and camouflage schemes was applied the heraldry of war. Common to the vast majority of vehicles was a unique stencilled or painted War Department (WD) identifying number. This was prefixed with a code letter denoting the type of vehicle: for example, 'T' for tank and 'F' for armoured car, with 'S' for self-propelled gun, 'P' for amphibious cargo carriers, and

1496 authorised black as the main shade over earth brown. Finally in April 1944, 'olive drab', designated as standard colour 15, was authorised as the new basic colour. This brought Britain into line with her biggest ally, and meant that the many US vehicles supplied in olive drab did not need repainting. After August that year, disruptive patterns were generally abandoned on new vehicles, though they remained in use on many that retained the earth brown base colour.

The Middle East, with its bright sunlight and frequently dry terrains of rock, earth and sand, demanded radically different treatments. So it was that from late 1939 to 1940, a stone base colour with disruptive patterns of 'dark sand' was regarded as standard. However, new vehicles arriving in theatre from mid-1940 were painted a variety of subtly differing base shades, as for example pale cream, light stone, or Portland stone. Towards the end of the year, new camouflage schemes were promulgated in which angular disruptive stripes of slate, khaki, or silver grey were painted over base colour. For Greece in 1941 the stripes appear to have been slate, or even what has been described as a light 'purple brown'. In Malta, with its stone walls, buildings and rock patterns, an even more distinctive camouflage scheme was used in which stone shades were overpainted with thick lines of khaki green or other dark shades to create blocks or irregular patches. By early 1942, a variety of schemes were in use in the Middle East and North Africa and it was at the time of El Alamein that a serious, but not entirely successful, attempt was finally made to tidy up many anomalies with the introduction of a new directive. Now the base colour was to be desert pink, over which was applied disruptive patterns in dark green, dark brown or slate. Canvas tilts, that had originally been supplied in

Far left: April 1945: British infantry, supported by Achilles 17pdr self-propelled guns, on the road to Ferrara, Italy. (Hulton Archive via Getty Images)

A British Sherman landing in Sicily, October 1943. In addition to a camouflage pattern over a base of 'light mud', unit marks, vehicle registration number, and a British red, white, red, vertical stripe recognition mark are shown. The tank is named 'Churchill'. (Keystone/Getty Images)

'REC' for armoured recovery vehicles. Canadian-built vehicles added an initial 'C' before the designation. The variety of letters naturally increased with the introduction of new classes of vehicle.

Tactical markings existed for tanks before 1939, and at the outbreak of war included a diamond to denote a battalion headquarters, a red triangle for 'A' company, a yellow square for 'B' and a blue circle for 'C'. Company letters or section numbers were painted within the shape. As of 1940, the system was expanded and the colours altered to denote battalion rather than company, with red for the most senior, yellow the second, blue third, and green fourth. As a security measure, unit titles were either omitted from new vehicles, or painted out, and replaced with coded signs. Usually this took the form of a number in white on a coloured square, and was carried in addition to a divisional or similar sign. In theory, the unit code sign was front and rear on the right-hand side from the driver's point of view and the formation sign on the left. However, there were frequent errors of placement or compromises with vehicle shape, and sometimes one was even painted above the other.

Another marking seen on tanks was a general recognition sign, allowing friendly forces to identify them as British. In France in 1940, this took the form of a white square on all four sides of the hull, but later a white band was painted around the turret instead. As of 1942, bands were either replaced, or used in conjunction with a new painted rectangular recognition sign of red, white, red, or in the Middle East white, red, white, vertical stripes. This sign, supposed to be 10 inches (25cm) high by 18 inches (48cm) long, was seen painted on hulls, front and rear, or on one or more mud guards until late 1943 or early 1944. Thereafter, the UK fell into line with US practice, using a white five-pointed star, on its own or within an outer ring. This was eminently practical as it was immediately apparent to American troops what it meant, and Soviet forces were also using a star. As always, there was a delicate balance between making oneself known, and thereby avoiding friendly fire, and inconspicuousness, thereby avoiding enemy fire. As the Japanese were generally short of effective tanks and anti-tank guns, a more generous use of Allied stars was made on British vehicles in the Far East than in Europe, where the Germans had a more comprehensive range of anti-tank weaponry. In the middle of the war, a St Andrew's cross, or a roundel on the top deck, was sometimes used as an air-recognition sign. These were abandoned by the middle of 1943, being replaced by flags or triangles that had the advantage that they could be stowed away when not required, but put out when friendly craft were about.[23]

Interestingly the idea that tank types and models should have generic names – such as the 'Crusader' or the 'Cromwell' – was one pushed by Churchill himself. As he remarked to the Chief Imperial General Staff in June 1941:

'Some time ago I formed the opinion that it would be far better to give names to the various marks of tanks. These could be kept readily in mind, and would avoid the confusing titles by marks and numbers. This idea did not find favour at the time, but it is evident that a real need for it exists, because the "I" tank, Mark II, is widely known as Matilda, and one of the other Infantry tanks is called Valentine. Moreover, the existing denominations are changed and varied. A22 has an alias I think. Pray therefore set out a list of existing official titles of all the types and marks now existing or under construction or design in our service and in American service, together with suggested names for them, in order that these may be considered and discussed.'[24]

These general names did of course stick. Moreover – unlike other vehicles – most tanks, and many armoured cars, were also given individual names, either by their regiment or their crews, and in different periods and theatres these names were seen painted variously on hulls and turrets, in contrasting paint colours to the camouflage scheme. In some instances names followed a logic that allowed those in the know to make deductions about the formation. So it was, for example, that in the Royal Tank Regiment names were initially selected by taking the letter of the alphabet that coincided with the number of the battalion. The 1st Battalion names began with 'A', 4th Battalion with 'D', and so on. However, this apparently neat scheme broke down for a number of reasons, not least because new battalions were numbered over 40, and thus had no corresponding letter, and 7th Battalion RTR was destroyed at Tobruk in 1942, this leading to battalion renumbering, but no corresponding re-naming of vehicles. Later on, 42nd RTR took names beginning with 'P', but in 45th and 47th battalions, for example, the tank names followed the squadron letter. In some units, replacement tanks took entirely new names, or reused old names, perhaps with a Roman numeral suffix, and these did not necessarily follow pre-existing schemes. By June 1944, even 1st Battalion was in a situation where its 'A' Squadron mainly retained names beginning with that letter, as for example *Apache*, *Andrea* and *Achtung*, but 'B' and 'C' were entirely muddled, and included everything from *Little Audrey II*, through to *Lilli Marlene*, *Champ II*, *Venus*, *Farleesh*, *Slaphappy* and even *Donkey's Serenade*.

The Cavalry and Yeomanry who made up a large portion of the wartime Royal Armoured Corps were even less consistent from the start, with some regiments omitting names entirely and others following some scheme or tradition of their own. In the Household Cavalry Training Regiment, the armoured cars were named after racehorses; in 1st King's Dragoon Guards, vehicles were named after the drivers' home towns; in 4th/7th Royal Dragoon Guards an early scheme using the names of steeplechasers and hunts was superseded by one using towns and regimental battle honours. In 7th Queen's Own, and 8th King's Royal Irish Hussars, were schemes based on the squadron letter. The 3rd Carabiniers painted regimental feathers on their turrets in addition to names, whilst 14th/20th King's Hussars' tanks used the regimental black Prussian Eagle early in the war together with the names of British castles, though the intelligence officer named three of the Universal carriers *Cholmondeley*, *Marjoriebanks* and *Featherstonehaugh*. In 1942, the squadrons of the 22nd Dragoons were named respectively after towns, battles and aircraft, though the HQ tanks took the names of the patron saints of England, Scotland, Ireland and Wales. Some Yeomanry followed the idea of names matching the squadron letter, others were more imaginative or anarchic.

In 1943, the Inns of Court Yeomanry possessed a Humber titled *Rough Justice*, whilst 1st Lothians and Border Horse went for thoroughly Scottish names like *Rob Roy* and *William Wallace*. Similarly the North Irish Horse used the names of Irish towns for their Churchills and other tanks.

Similar considerations applied to converted Guards and infantry battalions. The 1st Coldstream Guards used the names of historic colonels, but also birds. The 4th Battalion Grenadier Guards went with English towns. In June 1944, 3rd Scots Guards were using Scottish towns, mountains and islands, with odd additions of things like *Macbeth*, *Robert the Bruce*, and *Blue Bonnets* for its scout cars. The former Border Regiment 110th Regiment chose suitably 'border' names like *John Peel* and the names of Cumbrian mountains. The 153rd, a former Essex Regiment formation, likewise used mainly Essex towns. Conversely the 111th, which had a Manchesters heritage, chose the names of British warships such as *Renown* and *Furious*, whilst the 150th (York and Lancaster), painted a Tiger taken from the cap badge on hulls and used names matching squadron letters. The 144th (East Lancashire) picked names beginning with 'EL', until D-Day, when large serial numbers were applied instead. Perhaps most extraordinarily the 145th (Duke of Wellington's) used the titles of dukes for Regimental HQ, individual names for tanks, but christened a captured Panther *Deserter*.[25]

Infantry of 78th Division passing a Daimler Dingo Mark II scout car during the advance in Italy, June 1944. The 'F' prefix to the War Department registration was general to armoured cars and scout cars. (Sgt Johnson/IWM via Getty Images)

CHAPTER NINE
Special Forces
The Commandos

It can be claimed with reasonable justification that the British Special Forces of the Second World War would not have existed without Winston Churchill. For whilst ad hoc 'special companies' for 'special service of a hazardous nature' were hurriedly drawn from the Territorial Army for the Norwegian campaign of 1940, they failed to function in anything like the conception of a modern 'special force'. It was only with Dunkirk that the new Prime Minister, thrown back on the now slender resources of the UK, standing alone against a victorious German Army, cast about for something, indeed anything, with which to strike back. So it was that Churchill wrote to General Hastings Ismay on 4 June, railing against the 'defensive habit of mind' that had been the downfall of the French, and calling for raiding forces to fall upon the coasts of the recently conquered nations: 'Such forces might be composed of self-contained, thoroughly equipped units of say one thousand up to not more than ten thousand when combined.' This would maintain the initiative; pin down the enemy on shores where the inhabitants were friendly to Britain; and last, but certainly not least, it would demonstrate

New Zealanders of the Long Range Desert Group with their vehicles. The LRDG was organised in 'Patrols' and 'Squadrons', and indeed 'Long Range Patrol' was used as a unit title at an early stage. Most of the initial personnel were from 2nd New Zealand division, soon expanded by volunteers from the Brigade of Guards, the Yeomanry, and Southern Rhodesians. (Popperfoto/Getty Images)

to both the political opposition at home and the free world at large that Britain had the will and determination to carry on the fight. In essence this was to become the distillation of the 'Churchillian' spirit, expressed in a new part of the British Army.

A couple of days later, Churchill was musing pugnaciously that a 'reign of terror' could be created by 'specially trained troops of the hunter class'. The main tactic of these 'striking companies' at this early stage would be to 'butcher and bolt'. Possibly the Australians could be used on their arrival in the UK to form 250-man detachments, armed with 'grenades, trench mortars, Tommy guns, armoured vehicles and the like'. At the same time, steps were to be taken to develop a parachute force, to match that so successfully used by the enemy, and to investigate better methods of landing tanks. On 18 June, Churchill thought the unthinkable when he enquired about the formation of British 'Storm Troops': something that the establishment had always set its face against but had been a 'leading cause' of the German victory. A counter strike force ought, he proposed, 'to be at least 20,000 Storm Troops or "Leopards" drawn from existing units, ready to spring at the throat of any small landing or descents. These officers and men should be armed with the latest equipment, Tommy guns, grenades, etc. and should be given great facilities in motorcycles and armoured cars.'

All this was admirable, but alas, far from practical in June 1940. Dunkirk had cost the Army not only most of its viable tanks and other heavy equipment, but had also left it disorganised and short of key personnel. Despite Churchill's striking of belligerent poses with a submachine gun, 'Tommy guns' in particular were close to non-existent. General Bernard Paget was particularly worried about the notion of British Storm Troops, something that seemed to suggest that the Army lacked its own ideas and that the enemy had had the best military concepts all along. So it was, probably correctly, that the main effort was focused on raising sixty new conventional battalions of conscripts, cap badged to existing regiments, some of which would later be converted to tanks. Industry directed all spare capacity into new aircraft, as well as replacing the most vital classes of Army weaponry and equipment, notably tanks, artillery and ammunition.[1]

However, as was so often the case, Churchill was not to be entirely deflected from a new hobby horse, and, seeing any opposition as obfuscation if not outright defeatism, seized upon the concept of 'Special Irregular Units' as something to be pushed at every opportunity. As early as a week after Dunkirk, the Chief of Staff responded to Churchill's urgent demands for action by means of a brief memorandum penned by his military assistant Lieutenant Colonel Dudley Clarke. It was this document that first coined, or rather revived, the word 'Commando' as a title for Churchill's new raiding force. Given the Prime Minister's own experiences in his youth, it was a well calculated move to strike the sort of resonance Churchill had in mind. On 9 June a fresh call went out for volunteers for 'special service', and soon men were being interviewed for enrolment, though as yet few had any idea what it was they would be doing.

As of 13 June Major General R.H. Dewing, director of operations at the War Office, summarised the object of forming 'a Commando' as being:

'to collect together a number of individuals trained to fight individually as an irregular and not as a formed military unit. For this reason a commando will have no unit equipment and need not necessarily have a fixed establishment. Any establishment that may be produced will be for the purposes of allotting appropriate ranks in the right proportions to each other. Irregular operations will be initiated by the War Office. Each one must necessarily require different arms, equipment and methods, and the purpose of the commandos will be to produce whatever number of irregulars are

required to carry out operations… As a rule the operation will not take more than a few days, after which the commando will be returned to its original "Home Town" where it will train and wait, probably for several weeks, before taking part in another operation.'

Given its raiding objective, a Commando need only be able to operate independently for twenty-four hours, but was required to have the ability to undertake individual actions over a dispersed area. Whilst it was expected to hit hard and by surprise, the Commando was not to stand and fight, being insufficiently strong to undertake a planned defence or overcome alert organised resistance. As the 13 June memorandum explained, the original Commando organisation was intended 'to provide no more than a pool of specialised soldiers from which irregular units of any size and type can very quickly be created to undertake any particular task'. Importantly the new force was to be made up from the fresh wave of volunteers, sifted by the keen and active leaders who were to command them in action. Any

Close-Quarter Fighting

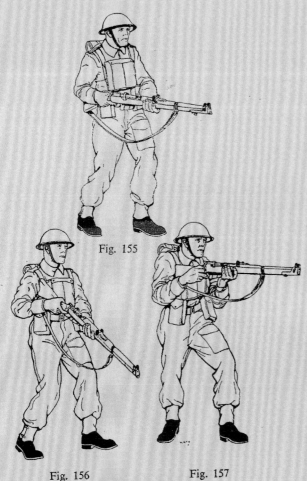

Fig. 155

Fig. 156   Fig. 157

that did not quickly make the grade could drop out voluntarily, or at any time be deselected for 'Return to Unit'. This principle turned out to be crucial to the notion of special forces in general, and arguably was the key to maintenance of not only discipline, but the self-discipline that was required of men who frequently operated in small groups, and were sometimes even expected to have the self-reliance to act alone out of sight of an officer.

Under their first establishment, ten Commandos of about 500 men each were planned, two each drawn from the resources of Southern, Eastern and Northern Commands, one each from Scottish and Northern Commands. One would come from mixed areas, and one from the reorganisation of the existing 'special companies' formed for Norway. Each of the Commandos comprised ten fighting 'Troops' led by a captain, and each Troop was subdivided into two large 'Sections' each led by a subaltern. These Commandos were to be a 'guerrilla' force by inspiration, trained to operate 'smash and grab' raids into enemy territory.

Such was the theory, but in the event the Commandos were not neatly and consecutively raised numbers '1' to '10'. Reorganising the existing special companies was accorded a relatively low priority against creating the new units, and 'No. 2' Commando was quickly hived off to undergo parachute training, thus becoming the earliest ancestor of the Parachute Regiment, with No. 10 Commando initially being stillborn due to a lack of volunteers. A fresh start would be made later with the creation of 'No. 10' Inter Allied Commando, using French, Dutch, Eastern European and Norwegian volunteers. 'No. 3' Commando was thus the first of the new breed of unit ready for service. A 'No. 11' and 'No. 12' Commando were also formed even though the lower numbered formations were incomplete. In the Middle East, Commandos were also raised in the following months. These were numbered '50', '51' and '52', clearly distinguishing them from the sequence created in the UK. According to the 'provisional establishment' of July 1940, a Middle East Commando initially comprised only 371 all ranks, being three fighting Troops of about a hundred each, with each Troop having four twenty-five-man sections led by an officer. The HQ included not only the command, medical personnel and an armourer, but also two very necessary interpreters.

To meet Churchill's demands for immediate action, it was 'No. 11' Special Company that was first thrown into rather ineffective cross-Channel action near Boulogne on 24 June, and it was that same unit – plus a portion of 'No. 3' Commando – that ventured

The 'close quarter fighting' method for rifle-armed troops devised by Captain P.N. Walbridge. The rifle may be fired from the hip (155), or from a wary advance (156), the rifle is raised swiftly to fire from the shoulder, pointing rather than taking slow aim. The hand may be arranged so that the bolt is still held between rounds. (Author) to Guernsey early in July. In truth next to nothing was achieved, but there was at least proof positive that there was still fight in Britain despite Dunkirk, and it provided something other than bad news to print in the newspapers. On 17 July the 'Directorate of Combined Operations' was formed, under the command of Admiral Sir Roger Keyes, hero of the Zeebrugge raid of 1918. However, by the late summer Churchill's initial enthusiasm was sated, with the prime author of the little raids now dismissing them as 'silly fiascos'. Yet this was not because Churchill wanted all attacks to cease, and still less that he was now against the notion of Commandos. For the time being he wanted Keyes to think more ambitiously, to consider 'medium raids' of five to ten thousand men, and to help create the wherewithal in terms of landing craft and tactics for invasions.

Whether Churchill was oblivious to the arguments his new force ignited, or deliberately sought to create competition and consternation in existing armed services that he saw as complacent and inflexible, is debatable. What is clear is that 'Combined Operations' and 'guerrilla' style Commandos operating outside the existing regimental structures opened debates that would barely be resolved by 1945. One issue was that creating a 'Combined Operations' organisation largely circumvented existing chains of command and threatened to give the Prime Minister his own little private army under a favoured subordinate. Another was that by deploying hit and run 'irregulars' behind enemy lines he skated on the margins of the rules of war and international conventions. Given the flouting of treaties, and their conduct, especially on the Eastern Front from 1941, the enemy certainly had no moral high ground – but the creation of an official 'guerrilla' arm would allow Hitler to rail against unfair tactics and to distract from far more serious matters elsewhere. All this would unravel in the tit for tat that

surrounded the Führer's infamous 'Commando Order' of 1942, and the executions and retaliations against Commandos that followed in its wake.

However, for the time being the internal struggle in the British Armed forces was more of a familiar one. The Navy sought to maintain its position as the 'Senior Service' and looked askance at soldiers who appeared to be usurping the traditional role of the Royal Marines, and the regiments of the Army who had released some of their best men for what they had thought was a limited period felt cheated. Tacticians and traditionalists alike argued that a few men with knives, rifles, Bren guns, and a very few Tommy guns, but no transport or barracks, were hardly a viable force. On this last point many of the Commando officers were inclined to agree, and themselves argued for better resources and equipment or different organisation. One sign of all this was another revision of structure in the autumn of 1940 under which the Commandos were paired together to create five 'Special Service battalions' of the Special Service Brigade. The result was units approximating in size to normal battalions of the Army, but was pretty impractical given that there were few if any transports suitable for raiding coasts with full battalions, and no immediate prospect of deploying thousand-man Commando formations. However, by luck or design, the notion of a 'five thousand' force met, just about, Churchill's latest ideas on the minimum size for a 'medium raid'.[2]

The awkwardness of the Special Service Battalion must have been apparent almost immediately, for seemingly inexorably one reorganisation followed hard on the heels of another. In early 1941 another shake-up created a new model for the force in which each Commando was now divided into six slightly larger Troops under a HQ along the following lines:

The landing ground at Juno Beach, Normandy, June 1944. Commandos came in along the British and Canadian landing grounds as a second wave, to pass through, knock out strong points and connect the conventional forces. The transition from light raider to elite assault infantry was complete and dramatic. (Official/author)

Commando HQ

Lieutenant colonel (commanding officer)

Major (second in command)

Two captains (adjutant and admin officer)

One lieutenant (intelligence officer)

Four NCOs (regimental sergeant major, quartermaster, pay and
orderly sergeants)

Six clerks

Six batmen/drivers

Seventeen drivers and motorcyclists

Attached medical services, one medical officer and six orderlies

Armourer and two assistants

Signal Platoon, one officer and twenty-one NCOs and men

Six Troops each comprising:

Troop HQ: one captain, one private

Two Section HQs: one lieutenant, one sergeant, one private

Two Sections: four corporals, four lance corporals, twenty
privates

The usefulness of this arrangement is apparent when one considers that two complete Commandos could now be fitted into a Glen type landing ship, and one Commando into a smaller one. Two Assault Landing Craft could carry a Troop. Moreover, with three officers and eighteen NCOs in each fighting Troop, there were plenty of junior leaders, allowing formations to be broken down into very small ad hoc subunits to fit almost any eventuality or movement scenario.

Armament also improved with time. As one American military intelligence bulletin was able to report:

> 'Every man who joins the commando brings his own rifle or pistol, and he is also provided with a fighting knife, which is used by the commandos with particular effectiveness. Each commando headquarters has a separate store of extra weapons so that extreme flexibility in armament is assured. A typical store contains: Bren guns; Thompson sub-machine guns; caliber .50 [sic. Boys .55] anti-tank rifles; 2-inch and 3-inch mortars with a supply of both smoke and high-explosive shells; defensive (fragmentation) Mills hand grenades; offensive (plastic body, concussion type) hand grenades; smoke pots; Very pistols; "knuckle dusters" (brass knuckles); "Limpets" (magnetic, acid, high-explosive mines), one type suitable for use against ships and another against tanks; and demolitions of all types. Each Troop is equipped with Bren guns, Thompson sub-machine guns, an anti-tank rifle, and a 2-inch

> mortar; normally each subsection is allocated one Bren gun and a sub-machine gun, the allocation of the anti-tank rifle and the mortar being left to the discretion of the Troop commander.'

As of March 1941, the history of the Commandos made a sharp divergence when Nos. 7, 8 and 11 Commandos, plus a Troop of 'No. 3' and a group soon to be christened the 'Special Boat Section', were sent out to the Middle East forming a small brigade under the command of Colonel Robert Laycock. Churchill himself had demanded this a couple of months previously, along with the building of the Commandos at home up to a strength of 5,000. The Middle East 'Layforce' was reorganised as four battalions, whilst the understrength 50 and 52 Middle East Commandos were amalgamated. Layforce did undertake raids, as for example at Bardia in April, but general shortages of troops meant that it was often used in a conventional role for which its relatively slender equipment rendered it unsuitable. 'No. 8' Commando was depleted to reinforce Tobruk, and in Crete the Commandos took heavy casualties. As of the late summer of 1941, and much to the chagrin of Churchill, Layforce had virtually ceased to exist.[3]

Never the less, Laycock survived to lead the famous raid on Rommel's headquarters in November, in which he led 'No. 11' Commando ashore in rubber dinghies, before Major Geoffrey

Commandos wearing green berets, Bergen rucksacks, Commando shoulder titles and combined operations shoulder flashes. Over time Commandos ceased to be a temporary phenomenon dressed in the distinctions of parent units and gained a distinctive identity of their own. (Official/author)

Keyes advanced to Sidi Rafa with a small party to attack Rommel's house. The result was a celebrated brave failure, for though Keyes gained access to the house and engaged the occupants in a firefight, Rommel was not at home, and Keyes was mortally wounded. The subsequent escape of Laycock and Sergeant Terry across the desert became a thing of legend, and the adventure appears to have added to, rather than detracted from, the laurels of Laycock – who would eventually be promoted to Chief of Combined Operations two years later. The death of Keyes did however have two other impacts. In becoming the first Commando to win the Victoria Cross, he became something of a totem for his comrades: but his demise created a double blow for his father Admiral Keyes, who had but recently stood down following Churchill's failure to back him in disputes with General Alan Brooke and other service chiefs.

However, nothing seemed to dampen Churchill's ardour for the attack, and in place of Keyes he installed Lord Louis Mountbatten at Combined Operations. As Churchill related in his own history of the war:

> '*In October 1941 Admiral Keyes was succeeded by Captain [sic] Lord Louis Mountbatten. We were still hard pressed, and our only ally, Russia, seemed near to defeat. Never the less, I had resolved to prepare for an invasion of the Continent when the tide should turn. First we had to increase the scope and intensity of our raids, and then translate all this experience into something more massive. To mount a successful invasion from the United Kingdom new engines of war must be contrived and developed, the three fighting Services must be trained to plan and fight as one team, supported by the industry of the nation… When Mountbatten visited me at Chequers before taking up his new duties I told him, according to his account, "You are to plan for the offensive. In your headquarters you will never think defensively." This governed his actions. To provide him with the necessary authority for his task he had been made a member of the Chiefs of Staff Committee, with the acting rank of Vice Admiral and equivalent honorary rank in the other Services. As Minister of Defence I retained personal responsibility for his headquarters, and thus he reported direct to me whenever necessary.'*[4]

Whilst 1941 and the Middle East proved the grave – or disappointment – of far too many Commandos, the other half of the raiding force, left behind in Western Europe, faired rather better, and amongst them it was arguably 'No. 2', 'No. 3' and 'No. 4' that garnered most approval from both the public and the Prime Minister. Though there were many small actions, the most significant were in Norway, long a subject of Churchill's fascination, and having a long and relatively poorly defended coast was a particularly tempting subject for special forces operations. In Operation Claymore in March, the Commandos struck at the Lofoten Islands inside the Arctic Circle. In December Vaagso was the target, and though most famous for its bloody little street battle, this operation also resulted in the destruction of nine enemy and enemy-controlled vessels. Perhaps most importantly these raids helped to persuade the Germans that the threat of Allied invasion was real in Norway, and resulted in the moving of additional troops to the area. Churchill was disappointed, but his more cautious advisors were pleased that this was so, since any Germans moved to Norway were unavailable either on the Eastern Front, or in France where the real invasion was actually most likely to fall.

A wounded Commando is helped back to a landing craft after street fighting at Vaagso, December 1941. The early Commando missions may have been limited in strategic impact but spoke volumes to Britain's allies and boosted home morale. They were also a particular obsession of Churchill. (Underwood Archives/Getty Images)

a pipe band. As numbers to be trained grew, volunteers were later allotted to a 'Holding Commando' to ensure they were fit, and newly qualified troops passed back into this formation for further advanced training. From here drafts were sent to the units in the field.

The year 1942 saw the biggest Commando raids on France: and in this instance Churchill was arguably the main stimulus, seeing such efforts as something to demonstrate that Britain and the Western Allies in general were attempting to make a contribution to the war in a year when the conflict on the Eastern Front was consuming hundreds of thousands – ultimately millions – of Russian lives. Such actions certainly answered the Prime Minister's demand for raids that were no longer of the 'pinprick' variety. The finest hour of 'No. 2' Commando came in March at the port of St Nazaire. Here, supported by smaller numbers of men from other Commandos, they fell on the docks, knocking them out of action in a way that would have been impossible by might of airpower alone without inflicting unacceptable casualties on the French population. The final *coup de grâce* was delivered by the old destroyer HMS *Campbeltown*, which had been packed with explosives and thus converted into a massive bomb for the purpose. Yet success came at a very serious price in the shape of the loss of over half of the 611 men deployed – killed, wounded and captured – as well as most of the small vessels used.

Dieppe in 1942 featured mainly 'No. 3' and 'No. 4' Commandos, as well as the new Royal Marine Commandos, and this was genuinely the sort of raid in strength that Churchill had called for. Yet planning was muddled and the execution disastrous, to an extent only fully revealed after the event. Men of 'No. 3' and 'No. 4' Commandos opened the way with partial success, but quite what tanks and Canadian infantry were supposed to achieve on a limited timescale against a well-defended port was never entirely clear. As war correspondent A.B. Austin put it, even at the time:

> '*We had all heard about the Commandos, the raiding shock troops of the British Army, the hand-picked, disciplined guerrillas of our war, volunteers from every famous regiment, trained together for jobs which needed fast movement on foot, physical endurance, and quick thinking by every man. We had heard of the Vaagso, Lofoten, St Nazaire and Boulogne raids, all of them carried out by comparatively small Commando forces and we supposed there would be more raids of the same sort, perhaps bigger ones. But*

Commando training with the F-S knife in Scotland. According to Fairbairn an accurate thrust to the carotid artery could render a man unconscious In five seconds. The 'victim' in this scenario also carries a Commando blade in the leg pocket of his Battle Dress. (Popperfoto/Getty)

Enhanced professionalisation plus better training of the Commando force, along with a better ability to replace losses, came with the opening of the Commando Depot, at Achnacarry in 1942. Later also known as the 'Commando Basic Training Centre', the camp was based around Achnacarry Castle, ancestral seat of the chiefs of Clan Cameron of Lochiel in the Western Highlands of Scotland. The intake of new volunteers was usually divided into three separate training Commandos, each with a dedicated officer instructor. The intensive training schedule included small boats and river crossings; sports; street fighting; climbing; fieldcraft; physical training and other specialisms, but as always the largest single element of the curriculum was weapons training, occupying almost a third of the time available. This included not just the standard British infantry small arms and hand-held anti-tank weapons, but mines and demolitions, American weapons such as the Garand and M1 Carbine, and enemy pieces. A vital adjunct to training efforts was the experienced 'Demonstration Troop', which not only showed trainees what to do but played the part of enemy troops in exercises and fired both live and blank rounds to add a frightening degree of realism. Its members doubled as

A soldier of 'No. 3' Commando, wearing non-standard balaclava and camouflage paint, armed with the M1 version of the Thompson at Largs Scotland, May 1943. 'No.3' gained widespread raiding experience, including Vaagso and Dieppe, and also fought in Sicily and Italy before landing on D-Day. Later they crossed the Rhine and advanced through Germany to Lübeck. (Lt WT Lockeyear/ IWM via Getty Images)

beyond that most of us had not, at that time, thought much about the practical problems of raiding on a scale large enough to amount to a second front diversion, or even of establishing a more permanent Second Front.'

The result was that whilst 'No. 4' Commando put in textbook service in their miniature set piece Operation Cauldron against one of the German batteries, pretty well everything else that could go wrong, did. About a third of the Commandos, and two-thirds of the Canadians, were lost.

From 1942 the Commando force would begin a complete overhaul in the face of a dramatically changing strategic situation. In addition to Royal Marine Commandos, a new 'No. 10' (Inter-Allied) Commando was added to the order of battle, and this would ultimately include Troops of French; Dutch; Belgians; Norwegians and Yugoslavs as well as a 'miscellaneous' Troop. This was notionally 'English' but in fact only the officers were British citizens whilst the men were anti-Nazi aliens and German-speaking Czechs; Danes; Hungarians; Russians and Rumanians. These would have special roles in scouting ahead of the Commandos and in spreading

confusion amongst the enemy. Another special force within the Commandos was the new 'No. 30' Commando, originally designated 'Special Engineering Unit'. In fact 'No. 30' Commando included both Naval and Army Troops, and their main task was to seize documents, new weapons and stores. 'No. 62' Commando was another oddity, existing essentially as a cover for the 'Special Raiding Force', run jointly by the Special Operations Executive (SOE) and Combined Operations headquarters.

Whilst it was not really the case that Dieppe was some sort of 'practice for D-Day' – a story that surfaced at the time, and has been oft-repeated since – it is certainly true that the Commandos as a whole pioneered many of the Combined Operations skills that would be crucial in the numerous landings required to liberate the many parts of the world occupied by Axis forces in the first three years of war. At the same time the strategic and tactical purposes of the Commandos themselves would change from lightly equipped raiders designed to strike and bolt, to highly trained spearhead assault infantry intended to land and seize crucial points and fortifications ahead of main bodies. Tactics advanced gradually, and sometimes painfully, by means of the now familiar process of 'lessons learned'. An operation was planned and then executed, a 'debrief' undertaken, and reports written. Importantly the 'debrief' was not just for the benefit of those who had directed the operation

or taken part, but a detailed analysis by means of which specific techniques could be improved in the future. A summation of these ideas had appeared as a chapter in the US intelligence publication *British Commandos* (1942), and in much more detail in the British series of *Combined Operations* pamphlets leading up to the invasions of Italy and France. With some justification the role of Commando forces in the Mediterranean in 1943 has therefore been described as that of 'shock troops', and in a growing number of instances Commandos had to remain in the field, sometimes fighting alongside the infantry – as for example had 'No. 1' and 'No. 6' Commandos in Tunisia. 'No. 2' Commando raided in Sicily, and led the force ashore at Marina Cove in Italy in September. Commandos also formed part of the Allied effort to support partisan operations in Yugoslavia.

By this time the 'Special Service' had expanded to the size of a large brigade under Brigadier Robert Laycock. This was partly at the behest of Churchill – who had agitated for the reformation of those Commando units lost or dispersed from 1940 to 1943 – but this was not generally done, with the obvious exception of the rebuilding of 'No. 2' Commando after St Nazaire. Instead the Commando force was mainly topped up by the formation of new Royal Marine Commandos, and the creation of the new specialist units as noted. As a result the special force now comprised the following major elements:

No. 1 Commando
No. 2 Commando
No. 3 Commando
No. 4 Commando
No. 5 Commando
No. 6 Commando
No. 9 Commando
No. 10 (Inter-Allied) Commando
No. 12 Commando
No. 14 Commando
No. 30 Commando
No. 40 Royal Marines (RM) Commando
No. 41 (RM) Commando
No. 62 Commando
Special Boat Service
Depots and camps including Achnacarry, Snow Warfare, etc.

In accordance with the possibility that Commandos might take part in set-piece attacks requiring support fire integral to the unit, or an organised defence, 3-inch mortars and Vickers medium machine guns were added to the regular establishment. As of the summer of 1943, the basic order of battle of a Commando therefore comprised 458 all ranks, in a headquarters, and five ordinary Troops, plus a heavy weapons Troop for the mortar and machine gun detachments. The headquarters included attached signallers and other Corps personnel, and was home to the commanding officer, a lieutenant colonel, a second in command ranking as major, adjutant, admin officer, and the regimental sergeant major. The Troops were led by captains, and divided into two sections each led by a subaltern and numbering thirty-one all ranks. The smallest unit on the books was the subsection, two of which comprised the section. The subsection was led by a lance sergeant assisted by a corporal and two lance corporals, and had ten private soldiers. Never the less, on operations Commandos were often used more flexibly, with the precise composition of subunits adjusted to fit operational requirements. Bren guns were now issued on a scale of at least forty-three per Commando, with some of these held in the HQ reserve, and PIAT anti-tank weapons and 2-inch mortars were carried as a matter of course. Transport was improved with Jeeps to carry the heavy weapons, and with eight 30cwt trucks.[8]

In late 1943 and early 1944, in the run-up to D-Day, the Commandos were finally expanded into a 'Special Service Group' under command of Major General Robert Sturges of the Royal Marines. Gradually Royal Marine Commandos numbers 42, 43, 44, 45, 46, 47 and 48 were added to the order of battle, so the force finally equated to a large division. Interestingly early plans were that the formation should have a 'Royal Marine Brigade' and an 'Army Brigade', but this was dropped on the grounds that this would tend to foster inter-service rivalry – the Royal Marines being part of the Admiralty and the Army Commandos part of the Army. Never the less, this final major expansion did alter the character of the Commandos to some extent, as up until this time Army Commandos had been in a clear majority and the force commander was an Army brigadier. After the completion of the group in March 1944, Navy men marginally outnumbered the Army component. As of this date the group was organised in four brigades as follows:[9]

1st Special Service: 3, 4 and 6 Army, 45 (RM) Commando
2nd Special Service: 2 and 9 Army, 40 and 43 (RM) Commando
3rd Special Service: 1 and 5 Army, 42 and 44 (RM) Commando
4th Special Service: 41, 46, 47 (RM) and 10 (Inter-Allied) Commando

Additionally each brigade had a signal troop and a Light Aid Detachment, and the group had its own police, postal and other support formations.

Interestingly the Commandos were not first ashore in Normandy on 6 June, their landings being timed to put them on the beaches just after the first wave. From here they would leapfrog and infiltrate around specific enemy strongpoints, unhinging the defences and connecting the landing grounds. This worked, but at a price, as on the beaches and at difficult objectives such as St Aubin; Langrune; Merville Battery and Le Plein heavy casualties were taken and Commandos were expected to hang on in front-line positions for protracted periods. Indeed, 6 June to 30 September 1944 proved expensive on all fronts to which Commandos were committed on active operations, with thirty-nine officers and 371 other ranks reported killed; 114 officers and 1,324 other ranks wounded; and seven officers and 162 other ranks missing – a number equal to the strength of several complete Commandos.

In the latter part of the war two brigades of Commandos were left to serve in northwest Europe, one in the Mediterranean, and one in South East Asia. Army 'No. 4' Commando, together with three Royal Marine Commandos and two attached Troops from the 'No. 10' (Inter-Allied) Commando, formed the 4th Special Service Brigade, committed to Operation Infatuate, the bloody but successful action at Walcheren in November 1944 under Brigadier B. W. 'Jumbo' Leicester. Army Commandos Nos 1 and 5 were part of the 3rd Commando Brigade, together with two Royal Marine Commandos and a Troop of 'No. 10' under Brigadier Campbell Hardy. This formation sailed to South East Asia soon after its creation, and was trained for jungle warfare in India. Towards the end of 1944 it was used in the offensive down the Arakan coast, fighting its way towards Rangoon, and took Akyab Island unopposed, then spearheaded the attack on the Myebon peninsula.

Thereafter 3rd Commando Brigade was landed near Kangaw, and 'No. 1' Commando occupied the soon to become infamous Hill 170. Shelling and Japanese counterattacks quickly escalated into a full-scale battle in which the Commandos were supported by tanks and an Indian infantry brigade. In furious fighting Lieutenant George Knowland added a Victoria Cross to the now impressive Commando total. By the end of the war, the Commandos had won no less than ten Victoria Crosses; thirty-two Distinguished Service Orders and seven bars; 135 Military

Crosses with ten bars; forty-six Distinguished Conduct Medals, and 289 Military Medals with ten bars. This was all the more remarkable since peak strength was approximately 10,000 and the Commandos had not existed at all until the summer of 1940. Yet their accumulated orders, decorations and gallantry medals exceeded the numbers awarded to many old, distinguished and much larger units, and stood as mute testimony to the number of dangerous assignments to which they were committed.[10]

Though the Army Commandos were disbanded in 1946, the Royal Marine Commandos would remain, and the importance of the idea was arguably out of all proportion to simple statistics. The Commandos had been a valuable boost to national morale at a time of dire danger, demonstrated to Allied powers that Britain had the will to continue to fight, and gave the Soviets at least a token towards a new land front in the West whilst Russian sacrifices carried the main burden in the East. Moreover, the Commandos showed that new and more flexible formations and tactics could be used to fight new sorts of war, not least in closely co-ordinated Combined Operations, raids and spearhead assaults. The Commandos also gave birth to, or inspired, several of the other British and foreign special forces of the war.[11]

The Airborne[12]

A parachutist poised to jump through a hole in the floor of a converted bomber. He watches for the signal light to change to green, his dismantled Sten gun poked through his straps. Floor exit proved less satisfactory for parachuting than side doors. (Haywood Magee/ Picture Post/Getty Images)

In Montgomery's considered opinion, parachute troops were 'men apart'; every man, in his own small way, 'an Emperor' – who as the author of his own fortune had 'conquered fear'. Though the Russians had dropped a whole battalion – complete with machine and field guns – from the sky as early as in 1936, Britain had no parachute force until long after the outbreak of war. It was Churchill, speaking in the shock of Dunkirk and in the face of the successful use of German paratroops, who himself proposed that a similarly powerful force should be formed in mid-1940: 'We ought to have a corps of at least 5,000 paratroops… I hear that something is already being done to form such a corps but only, I believe, on a very small scale. Advantage must be taken of the summer to train these forces, who can none the less play their part meanwhile as shock troops in home defence.' So it was that the original 'No. 2' Commando found themselves transposed to Ringway airport near Manchester. Here the first, but now quaint-looking, essays in full-sized unit British Army parachute training began.

Yet as the Parachute Regiment's own history observed, 'Not all those in authority at Ringway were amateurs. There were from the start a number of Royal Air Force instructors from the establishment at Henlow where for some years before the war pilots had been put through a course of parachuting.' These instructors formed the nucleus of the school of the 'Central Landing Establishment', staying ahead of their trainees at least in part by repeated jumping and learning by experience. Under their charge the four Troops of 'No. 2' Commando mastered their new craft in secret, at first with no additional inducement whatever, but later with the benefit of a two shillings a day extra

duty bonus. Medical advice was that mainly men under the age of thirty should be chosen for training, and it was soon discovered that some well under that age were unable to complete the course. This was not just due to the parachuting itself, but also some particularly rigorous soldiering and physical training, as it was reasonably calculated that to be worth all the trouble and expense of getting parachutists to the battlefield by air, when they reached the ground they should be fit enough to march immediately. Moreover, they would not expect transport on the ground, might have to cover ground simply to fall in, and would fight against heavy weapons with only what they could carry.

Early jump training was conducted using a 'pull off method'. The trainee squatted on a small platform created by removing part of the rear gun turret of a Whitley bomber and simply pulled his ripcord. The drag from the opening chute jerked him into the sky. This sounds dangerous, and it was. The first fatality, suffered on 25 July, was Driver Evans, formerly of the Royal Army Service Corps. Following more accidents, jumps from Whitleys were abandoned, only being resumed on the direct intervention of the Prime Minister. Next a hole through the fuselage floor through which men could drop was used. This was slightly better, but the narrowness of the aperture was such that a careless exit resulted in men 'ringing the bell' – or banging their heads on the rim. Some use was made of Bombay troop carrier aircraft, which were more suitable as they were slow and had seats and a door, but such opportunities were few and far between.

Despite the perils, by August 1940 all those who had stayed the course and completed three jumps were thereby deemed 'qualified' parachutists. Only later, as better facilities became available, could the standard of qualifications be raised, first to six jumps, and finally to ten, with one at night. Fresh calls for volunteers were put out. Yet by November 1940 Britain could boast not the 5,000 parachute troops Churchill had asked for, but barely 500. The force was now designated 11th 'Special Air Service' Battalion, a short-lived name in this context, but one that would also give the inspiration for another 'special force'. Indeed, at this time it was imagined that – given the strategic situation and the modest number of Airborne troops available – they would all be used essentially as raiders to be extracted either by sea or air upon completion of the mission, and indeed this is exactly what would be done in 1941 and early 1942.

As might be expected, Churchill reacted extremely badly to the slow expansion of the Airborne: but to be fair when he

Paratroopers watch an equipment demonstration. The man centre right wears an oversmock over both his equipment and the Denison camouflaged smock. Officially known as the 'Jacket, Parachutists, 1942 Pattern', the zip-fronted sleeveless oversmock was of hard-wearing green denim. Its pockets could be used for grenades. (Author) examined the files, he came to the conclusion that he himself should have pushed even harder than he did for the growth of this new arm. As he put it to the Chiefs of Staff Committee in May 1941:

> 'This is a sad story, and I feel myself greatly to blame for allowing myself to be overborne by the resistances which were offered. One can see how wrongly based these resistances were when we read the Air Staff paper in the light of what is happening in Crete, and may soon be happening in Cyprus and Syria… The gliders have been produced on the smallest possible scale, and so we have practically now neither the parachutists nor the gliders, except these 500. Thus we are always found behind hand by the enemy. We ought to have 5,000 parachutists and an Airborne Division on the German model, with any improvements which might suggest themselves from experience. We ought also to have a number of carrier aircraft. These will be necessary in the Mediterranean fighting of 1942, or earlier if possible… A whole year has been lost.' [13]

To expand the Airborne further in the face of a lack of suitable aircraft, more had to be done to give basic training on the ground, so increasing throughput of troops. So it was that various devices were introduced to mimic air drops. These included jumping from the tailboard of a moving lorry; a 'gallows' rigged like a seesaw with a weight at one end and the trainee at the other; and an ingenious machine known as the 'fan'. This was a large cable-wound drum to which the trainee was attached.

Men of 1st Parachute Regiment occupy a modified shell hole during the battle for Arnhem, 1944. The nine-man parachute sections usually included a Sergeant as well as a Corporal or Lance Corporal, and were armed with a Bren gun, two Sten guns and six rifles. (Author)

When he jumped from a platform the cable unwound, but was slowed by two vanes acting as air brakes. The speed to which descent was reduced approximately replicated the force with which a parachutist hit the ground. To add realism the fuselages of various planes were mocked up inside huts and hangars, and troops practised going out through holes and doors. Balloon drops were introduced in April 1941, with the trainee exiting through a hole in the floor of a cage intended to represent the floor of the Whitley, and were not generally popular.

That same month Churchill, his wife, General Ismay and other dignitaries gathered to witness a demonstration drop by five Whitleys, and a number of paratroops were injured. As of August 1941, the capacity of a training squadron was still only forty men a week, but this rose to a hundred in September. The 2nd Parachute Battalion was formed in September under Lieutenant Colonel Alan Flavell. As of November, training of a small brigade was under way. Only by the end of the year were courses of over 200 men at a time being put through, with 4,000 drops being performed each month, a figure at last calculated to be able to fill, then maintain, whole parachute divisions in the coming year. In March 1942, the new 1st Parachute Brigade, consisting of the first three battalions, was moved to Bulford on Salisbury Plain. At this time the men were still wearing the head dress, cap badges, and various other distinctions of their old regiments. So it was that the 'Parachute battalions', as they were now known, were recognised by coloured lanyards: green for the 1st; yellow for the 2nd; red for the 3rd and soon black for the 4th. The name and status of 'Parachute Regiment' was granted that summer with Army Order 128, of 1 August 1942.

However, problems with recruiting 4th Battalion led to new methods for raising the later higher numbered units, and thereafter an existing infantry battalion was taken as a nucleus around which to build. The 5th Parachute started from 7th Cameron Highlanders; the 6th from 10th Royal Welch Fusiliers; 7th from 10th Somerset Light Infantry; 8th from 13th Royal Warwickshires; and 9th from 10th Essex. Some glib statements have been made about the 'conversion' of existing infantry units to parachute troops, but in fact it was never so simple. According to the history of the Somersets, for example, 10th Battalion was called upon to volunteer for parachute service, and as a result 450 men stepped forwards, but in the event just 200 were accepted. In the case of 10th Battalion of the Parachute Regiment, volunteers from 2nd, 4th and 5th battalions of the Royal Sussex were called together in Kabrit, India. The 11th was created around another Indian-based cadre, temporarily numbered as 20th Queen's Regiment. The 12th and 13th Parachute battalions were respectively given a Yorkshire and Lancashire flavour, by building around Yorkshire Yeomanry, and a Territorial battalion of the South Lancashires. The 15th and 16th battalions of the Parachute Regiment were again started in India, this time taking a nucleus from 1st King's and 1st South Staffordshires respectively, but were not complete until March 1945.

The standard military 'statichute', devised by Raymond Quilter and Leslie Irvin as a result of early experiences and

some dreadful accidents with inferior types, was described in the official publication *By Air to Battle* in the following terms:

'To the parachute harness is attached a bag carried on the back. In it is housed the parachute in an internal bag divided into two compartments. The outside bag remains attached to the harness: the inside is pulled violently from it by a static line, which is a length of webbing, of which one end is attached strongly to the inner bag. At the other end is a metal "D" ring, which engages a hook attached to the end of a strop. The strop is also made of webbing and its top end is secured to a "strong point" in the aircraft. The length of the static line is twelve feet six inches. The strop has to be long enough to ensure that the parachute will be well below the aircraft before it opens, and short enough so the chute is not caught in the slipstream and twisted round the rear plane or the tail wheel. In a Dakota the strop is attached to a steel cable running along the side of the aircraft. The strop attachment is clipped to this cable and moves with the jumpers

as they shuffle one by one towards the exit. The canopy of the parachute is usually made of nylon, though sometimes of cotton [or silk in early versions], and has a diameter of twenty eight feet. In the middle of it is a circular hole, the vent, twenty-two inches in diameter. This vent prevents undue strain on the canopy when it begins to open, and is said to reduce oscillation. The rigging lines attached to the canopy are twenty-two feet long.'[14]

It is worth noting the Type X Mark II parachute, in use in 1944, was 26 feet (8m) in diameter, and that this was still rather larger than aircrew chutes, being intended thereby to give a softer landing. The twenty-eight rigging lines of the Mark II were 25 feet (7.6m) in length with a minimum breaking strength of 400lb (181kg). The canopy was silk initially, but later of a special 'Ramex' cotton. The harness was fastened on the lower chest by a quick-release box. Though jumping remained dangerous and British paratroops carried only one chute, the packing of parachutes was remarkably consistent and mishap free. Indeed, of half a million drops, and quite a few accidents, at Ringway only one could be traced back to an error by WAAF parachute packers, who laboured under a large sign reading, 'Remember a man's life depends on every parachute you pack.'[15]

In 1945 the wearing of the jump kit was described as follows:

'His clothes, though seemingly complicated, are simple to

Heavily armed glider troops in Normandy. Both the Bren gunner, left, and the Lance Corporal, right, carry pistols in holsters. The man in the centre has both a Sten Mk V, complete with bayonet, and a captured enemy pistol, the muzzle of which projects from his Denison smock. Two of the team have toggle ropes around the waist. (Author)

Far left: 'Angels with Dirty Faces' glider troops en route for France in a Horsa glider. (Getty Images)

Right hand pulls quick release after jumping & pays out rope until valise is suspended 20ft below man

A Parachutist equipped with the 'drop bag' or valise. The bag was secured during exit from the plane, but lowered below the parachutist once the canopy had deployed. (Author)

Right: The parachute troops' cylindrical equipment container, designed for arms, ammunition, and supplies. (Author)

wear and designed to give him maximum warmth in the air and the maximum of mobility on the ground. He wears a parachute harness over his jumping jacket [Oversmock, Parachutist]. Beneath that is the equipment that he will carry into battle. This in turn is worn over his parachute smock [Smock, Denison], a garment of windproof material with large pockets. Beneath the smock is the ordinary battle dress, but the trousers have very wide exterior pockets. At first his boots were provided with very thick crêpe rubber soles, but lately this has been found unnecessary, and now ordinary Army boots are worn. The all-important parachute knife, with which the parachute soldier can cut himself free if necessary, is strapped to his right leg. On his head is a special form of helmet like a flat, circular cheese. This is used for practice jumps. On operations a steel helmet, not unlike a bowler hat, but without a brim is worn.'

Basic jump drill was as follows: the navigator determined that the aircraft was in the right place, and the pilot set as straight and level a course as possible for the run. Ideally the airspeed was slow, at less than 100 mph (140kph) but frequently tactical requirements or enemy intervention demanded faster speeds. A red light indicated that the paratroops should get set, and green commenced jumping. In the Douglas Dakota C-47 that became the standard troop carrier later in the war, the first man crouched in the doorway, before pushing himself out. The paratroops went out in order starting with number one of the stick, and followed in quick succession. Where equipment containers were included in a stick of ten, a short interval was allowed between jumpers five and six for these to be released from under the plane. Though some veterans recalled being physically shoved out by keen dispatchers, there was little point to

this in training as those who refused to jump could be returned to their original unit. After qualification a refusal to jump became a disciplinary offence.

Out in the air of the slipstream, the parachutist was quickly blown virtually horizontal, but fell only for about a second and a half before the line began to pull out the chute. This the soldier might feel as a 'nibbling' at the shoulders, before the much stronger jerk of the canopy deployment. As aircrew were taught to drop paratroops low to avoid flak and danger to vulnerable troops in the air, jumpers usually had but little time to check any oscillation of the parachute, attempting to avoid their fellows and any obvious obstacles. Then it was preparation for landing, the object of which was to distribute the shock of impact, being roughly equivalent to a jump from a 6- or 8-foot (1.8 or 2.4m) wall. Knees together, ankles, knees and hips flexed, usually with the man rolling in as controlled a fashion as possible to the ground. Parachutes were gathered again in training but usually jettisoned in action, the paratrooper concentrating on his quick release, readying his arms and locating his companions.

Air-dropped equipment containers were always problematic. In the first experiments they tended to smash to the ground, or split, damaging or scattering their contents. However, soon some standard models were devised that proved more reliable. The yard-long oblong wicker pannier was not suitable for much equipment,

being limited to relatively short items weighing up to 347lb (157kg), but was better than its antiquated appearance might suggest, as it weighed barely 50lb (23kg) complete with straps, and had a certain amount of natural give and flexibility. Though the weight that the Mark I metallic container could hold was similar, it was very different in appearance, being a cylinder 5.5 feet (1.68m) in length, dangling nose downwards from its parachute and allowing a domed end with perforated shock absorber to take first impact. Recommended loadings for the Mark I included five haversacks, a bandolier of Sten ammunition and two rifles; or four haversacks and four rifles. The Mark I container was used for supplying all types of ground troops and was dropped with paratroops. Other drop containers included the types 'E' and

'F', which held a 'No. 18' and 'No. 21' radio respectively; and the 'Type H'. This last was interesting in that whilst similar in general appearance to the Mark I, it consisted of five adjoining units held together with two threaded rods and screws.

Yet all containers, however well designed, had the same basic disadvantages. For to prevent damage they had to be well packed and protected, and packing took time to remove. Moreover, to empty a container a paratroop had to be aware where it landed and to reach it, and containers did not steer themselves to the ideal spot. All too often containers fell out of sight in the dark, or into enemy hands, or could not be opened quickly enough. One expedient used on the Bruneval Raid was to attach coloured identification lights, powered by dry cell batteries, to containers, with for example red signifying arms, and purple engineer stores. However, this still did not mean that the enemy might not see them first. For this reason many paratroops jumped with a Sten gun pushed through and secured in their harness, or made use of a 'drop bag'. This device, invented in 1942, was the brainchild of Major J. Lander. Capable of holding as much as 100lb (45kg) of additional equipment, commonly including a Bren gun or ammunition, it consisted of a canvas bag and 20 feet (6m) of rope, the end of which was secured to a harness at the jumper's waist. The parachutist exited the aircraft with the bag strapped to his leg, but after his chute deployed operated a quick release leaving the bag dangling below himself. The bag hit the ground first, and therefore did not increase the shock of landing for the parachutist, but the load always remained within a few yards.[16]

As of September 1944, a full-strength parachute battalion comprised thirty-six officers and 696 other ranks, though for Arnhem the actual strength of the battalions as dropped averaged 548 all ranks. There were three rifle companies per battalion and three sections to each platoon, and a high proportion of sergeants who usually commanded sections. Support weapons included the Vickers and 3-inch mortar, with the basic platoons depending on Bren guns, Sten guns, No. 4 rifles, grenades and pistols. Anti-tank weaponry was limited to Gammon bombs and PIATs. The relatively slender size of parachute battalions was recognised as something of a handicap, as was pointed out in the planning for D-Day, when it was necessary for parachutists to attack entrenched or fortified targets:

'A parachute battalion at War Establishment has three rifle companies. One of these together with the Anti-Tank platoon is required to breach [fortified positions] with bangalore torpedoes.

Therefore only 208 other ranks are available for the assault. Approximately forty-eight of these are required to support the assault with Light machine Guns and 2-inch mortars leaving approximately 160 "bayonets" for the actual assault if no casualties have occurred by then.'

The idea that no casualties would happen prior to a close assault was also highly questionable, for almost inevitably a few aircraft would either be shot down, or simply miss their drop zone. A few men would become *hors de combat* by dint of bad landings, of being hit, or becoming lost on their way to the forming-up point. The chance of assembling even 160 men from each battalion at the point of a final assault against a fortified position was therefore small.[17]

Parachutists were in fact only a part of the Airborne force, for as early as August 1940 the Air Staff was already becoming gloomy concerning the future of the parachute and considering other options:

'We are beginning to incline to the view that dropping troops from the air by parachute is a clumsy and obsolescent method and that there are far more important possibilities in gliders. The Germans made excellent use of their parachute troops in the Low Countries by exploiting surprise, and by virtue of the fact that they had practically no opposition. But it seems to us at least possible that this may be the last time that parachute troops are used on a serious scale in major operations.'

Whilst this paper was entirely wrong about the future of parachute operations, it was one spur towards the development

The interior of a Horsa glider, 1943. The troops face each other seated down either side, seen here holding their No.4 rifles. (Keystone-France/ Gamma-Keystone via Getty Images)

of troop-carrying gliders. So it was that the Hotspur first flew in November of that year, but was not operational until early 1941. A design based on the premise that it would carry a single squad of eight men to the heart of the action, the original Mark I Hotspur had a wingspan of 62 feet (19m) and weighed about 3,600lb (1,633kg). It was not a great success, and was quickly modified to a more compact Mark II form with a reduced wingspan of 45 feet (13.7m). Given its limited load-carrying capacity, the Hotspur was used mainly in training, but never the less continued in production until as late as 1943, and about 1,000 were made.

With the Hotspur effectively sidelined, attention turned to the Horsa. Initially designated the AS 51, an order for the new glider was placed in early 1941 with the first prototype flying that September, though full production was not achieved until early 1942. Interestingly the Horsa was designed from the outset to be constructed from sub-assemblies, with a high use of wood in order to save materials for powered aircraft. A high-winged monoplane design, with a tricycle undercarriage that could be jettisoned, the glider had a wingspan of 88 feet (26.8m). A key feature of the Horsa was an increased seating capacity of twenty-five, or thirty, in the final configuration. The flight crew sat side by side in front with the 'first pilot' on the left, working similar controls to those found in powered craft of the period, though with the absence of throttles and the addition of a tow rope release and a 'Cable Angle Indicator'. The latter was crucial, as the glider had to be kept either slightly above or below its tug, out of its slipstream. Large wing flaps allowed the glider to descend quickly, taking advantage of confined landing zones.

The Horsa could be towed into action by a variety of aircraft including the Stirling, Halifax and Whitley bombers, and also the Dakota, though the latter was not used often due to the weight of the Horsa. For its time the Horsa was a good glider, arguably its greatest weakness being that much of the equipment it was eventually called upon to carry was not even invented at the time it was designed. The result was that some delicate and time-consuming manoeuvring was required to unload items such as Jeeps and guns. Amongst the ordnance carried by the Horsa was the 6pdr anti-tank gun, and the American-made 75mm gun. The latter was light and compact enough to be transported in one piece, and a glider could take the gun, a Jeep and a trailer of ammunition. About 4,000 Horsas were manufactured, a quarter of them being used at Arnhem alone.

The main passenger compartment of the Horsa was described as follows:

> *'Inside, the Horsa looks not unlike a section of the London Tube railway in miniature, the fuselage being circular and made of a skin of plywood attached to numerous circular ribs of stouter wood. The seats run down the length of each side and are also of light wood, each being provided with a safety harness fitting over the shoulders of the wearer, while a belt encircles his waist. The floor of the glider is corrugated to prevent slipping. There are two entrances, one to port near the nose, the other to starboard near the stern. The doors slide vertically upwards, but the whole tail is detachable to enable the quick unloading of Jeeps, anti-tank guns and other heavy material. In an emergency the tail can be blown off by means of a dynamite cartridge, but this method involves a risk of fire. Escape hatches are*

About 350 massive Hamilcar gliders were produced by General Aircraft Limited. A Hamilcar is seen here disgorging a US M22 Locust light tank: the Locust had a crew of three, a 37mm main armament, and a machine gun. Its maximum armour was 25mm. A handful of Locusts were used in the Rhine crossing operation of 1945. (Planet News Archive/SSPL/Getty Images)

An Airspeed Horsa glider after combat landing on D-Day. Swift exit of men and weapons was of paramount importance, but bulky kit precluded niceties. (Author)

fitted so that, if the glider falls in the sea, the occupants can leave it quickly. One great advantage possessed by gliders is that their wooden construction gives them buoyancy. Some of them have been known to float for twenty-four hours.'

The Hamilcar was the largest of the Airborne forces' gliders, a craft with a 110-foot (33.5m) wingspan intended essentially as a cargo carrier. It was made of birch and spruce with metal reinforcement, and a fabric-covered plywood outer skin. Its specification allowed for the carrying of either two Bren carriers, or a light tank. The two pilots sat in a narrow cockpit perched atop the high fuselage. Given its size and weight, its tug was usually the Halifax bomber. Despite its size and apparent ungainliness, the Hamilcar was not difficult to fly. Though work began in 1941, it would be 1943 before general manufacture started owing to production problems. Numbers actually built were modest, with barely eighty in service by mid-1944. Production ended in 1946 with less than 350 completed. Never the less, Hamilcars saw active service in the invasion of Normandy and Arnhem, as well as in the Rhine crossing operations. Loads carried included mortars, Tetrarch light tanks and other equipment. Perhaps most importantly the Hamilcars proved capable of transporting 17pdr anti-tank guns, towing vehicles and crews, thus providing the Airborne with their most potent anti-armour weapon.[18]

Glider pilots were something of a conundrum, since unlike RAF pilots who were expected to return to base at the end of a sortie, they would perforce land up on the ground with their passengers, probably in contact with the enemy. So it was soon decided that glider pilots could never be but passive spectators in battle and were accordingly made a regiment of their own in December 1941. Shortly afterwards the regiment was designated part of the Army Air Corps, which also included air observation units, and, for various periods, both the Parachute Regiment and the SAS. As 'complete' soldiers, glider pilots were expected first to fly the craft, then to man a weapon or perform other tasks on the ground. At Arnhem alone, 1,262 men of the Glider Pilot Regiment were deployed and after landing, some were allotted to the infantry and artillery units they had transported into action, with others forming a reserve under divisional control.

Interestingly the troops carried in gliders were not all volunteers, and neither were they in 'Parachute brigades' but formed 'Air Landing brigades' within the Airborne divisions. At the start, many of the glider troops were either Regulars or Territorials, and battalions were converted wholesale from battalions of line regiments. So it was that the first 'Air Landing' battalion in the British Army was actually 1st Battalion the Border Regiment, converted in 1940: no less than 15 per cent of this unit would die at Arnhem. Their comrades in 1st Air Landing Brigade were 2nd Battalion South Staffordshires and 7th King's Own Scottish Borderers, plus an HQ and 1 Landing Field Ambulance. Glider battalions were usually stronger than their parachute equivalents. At Arnhem they averaged 773 all ranks, transported by sixty-two Horsas and a Hamilcar. Support companies were also larger, and anti-tank platoons with 6pdr guns were included. However, the basic infantry platoon was just twenty-six men, this being what could be fitted with all its attendant equipment into the Horsa. There were four rifle companies per battalion, and four platoons per company. The glider troops shared the privilege of the red beret, and in battle the men were dressed and equipped similarly to their parachutist comrades.

Whilst most regiments of the Army deployed battalions to different divisions in disparate theatres of war, often for long-term commitments, the battalions of the Airborne units were usually used in discrete, and relatively brief, operations. It is therefore possible to give a shortlist of key missions. The first was Operation Colossus, the attack on the Tragino Aqueduct in Southern Italy on 10 February 1941. Ordered personally by the Prime Minister, this involved but thirty-eight all ranks. With them went no less than 160 boxes of gun cotton, other explosives and stores packed in thirty-three containers. The target was badly damaged, but promptly repaired. The Bruneval Raid on the French coast just over a year later was also small but arguably much more significant, with the seizure of important German radar equipment. In November 1942, 1st, 2nd and 3rd Parachute battalions were all used successfully in North Africa, now with Dakota aircraft. Never the less, much of the force landed up fighting from behind enemy lines, and heavy casualties were taken as parachutists were left fighting for long periods as infantry on the ground. In the same month came the disaster of Operation Freshman in which two glider teams, sent to destroy heavy water facilities at Vermork in Norway, crashed. The survivors were executed by the enemy. In 1943 there were major operations in Italy and Sicily using the whole of 1st Airborne Division. These included the attack on the Primosole Bridge, glider assault on the Ponte Grande, and seaborne invasion at Taranto. In September 1943 a small force managed to seize, but ultimately not to hold, the Greek island of Kos.

In June 1944, in the largest and most important mission to date, the recently formed 6th Airborne Division played a crucial role in D-Day, seizing vital bridges and securing the entire left flank of the invasion force. It also had to contend with subsequent German counterattacks. Key actions included the taking of Pegasus Bridge, the struggle for the Merville Battery and the Battle of Bréville. Besides such climactic events, it is sometimes overlooked that British Airborne troops were also used a month later when 2nd Independent Parachute Brigade Group took part in Operation Dragoon, the very successful invasion of the South of France.[19]

Thought was given to other parachute drops in Normandy after the D-Day landings, but with the speed of the land campaign after the August breakout, the Allies had reached the Dutch border before the next operation could be mounted in northwest Europe. Arnhem in September that year was an attempt to create an 'Airborne corridor' through the Netherlands using not just British 1st Airborne, but US and Polish Airborne forces. Over 30,000 men were therefore used in this Airborne offensive, roughly two-thirds being parachutists and one-third glider troops. The bridge at Arnhem was just one of several attacked, and has been justly dubbed the 'bridge too far'. The British Airborne seized the bridge but were trapped and not relieved, most being finally confined to a cauldron around Oosterbeek from which only a minority managed to escape across the Rhine. What turned out to be a serious miscalculation led to the loss of 7,000 British Airborne troops, killed, wounded and captured. The 1st, 2nd, 3rd, 10th and 11th battalions of the Parachute Regiment were all but destroyed, and the latter two were not reconstructed after the campaign. In Operation Varsity it was the turn of 6th Airborne to be used alongside US and Canadian troops in the crossing of the Rhine. Hugely successful, but far from bloodless, this mission in March 1945 was the last major deployment of the Airborne.[20]

The Special Air Service and Long Range Desert Group

In 1940 the hostile environment of the 'sand sea' of the vast Libyan Desert was both threat and opportunity to the British Army. A threat because it was difficult to know who or what might be probing around its fringes to menace the British power base of Egypt and the Suez Canal. Opportunity because he who mastered the desert might ultimately outflank, out-reconnoitre, and ultimately raid, harass and destroy his enemy's lines of communication. Most conventional actions of the war in North Africa happened close to the coast: opening up the furthest reaches of the desert granted space and depth for manoeuvre. Yet none of this was entirely new, for cavalry and 'Light Car Patrols' had been mounted against hostile tribesmen here in the First World War.

So it was that Major R.A. Bagnold of the Royal Corps of Signals volunteered his services to General Wavell. Bagnold was an intrepid adventurer who first succeeded in traversing the sand sea in the inter-war years, and had pioneered the use of steel 'sand channels' to unditch vehicles in the desert. Bagnold outlined a plan for a motorised 'ground scouting force' and Wavell accepted the idea. Three patrols were soon formed – 'R', 'T' and 'W' – each consisting of two officers and about thirty men. Whilst most of the originals were New Zealanders, Captain Patrick Clayton had been one of Bagnold's companions on earlier desert forays. The heavily armed patrols were mounted in a generous allocation of Chevrolet 30cwt trucks with a 15cwt car to lead. Early weaponry was Lewis guns, Boys Anti-Tank rifles, a 37mm Bofors gun, and a selection of pistols and rifles. Other vital equipment included radios and a selection of spares with which fitters continually strived to keep vehicles running. Ordinary navigation aids were supplemented by sun compasses, primitive in design, but which gave true bearings rather than the magnetic bearings provided by the normal compass.

In the first small-scale experiment, using just two cars, Clayton ventured out to check Italian supply lines from Benghazi. He succeeded in coming and going undetected, and the route he pioneered would soon be used by other patrols. The rest of the LRDG left Cairo for the front in early September. In October 1940, 'R' Patrol under Captain Donald Steele laid mines across a supply route, and destroyed a munitions dump. In November, the LRDG mounted small attacks on Italian outposts. These and other successes secured, the formation was reorganised and expanded, and 'G' Patrol formed from Coldstream and Scots Guards, which commenced its first operation on Boxing Day. Together, 'G' and 'T' patrols drove 1,440 miles (2,317km) to attack the airfield and forts at Murzuk. In the resulting battle, the LRDG destroyed three aircraft, burnt a hangar, and killed or captured dozens of enemy troops. One fort was temporarily

A radio-equipped Long Range Desert Group Canadian-built Chevrolet crossing desert. Armaments include a Lewis gun, a 3inch mortar, and a Boys Anti-Tank rifle. Sand channels are carried for unditching the vehicle. (Popperfoto/Getty Images)

taken. Though one man was killed and the patrols had to escape into a sandstorm, the LRDG eventually made safety at the Free French fort at Zouar in Chad. Though the Italians were now thoroughly alerted, the patrols continued their mission in concert with French troops, with the result that Clayton was captured after an air attack and several men were lost. Eventually, after an operation that covered 4,300 miles (6,920km), the patrols returned to Cairo on 9 February 1941.[21]

Again the LRDG was expanded: this time by the formation of 'Y' or Yeomanry Patrol and the 'S' Southern Rhodesian Patrol, and the small units were grouped together in 'A' and 'B'

Lieutenant E. MacDonald, foreground, and his SAS jeep patrol, January 1943. Note the twin Lewis guns. (Hulton Archive/ Getty Images)

squadrons each of three patrols, one to operate in the outlying oases, the other to act under command of what would soon become the 8th Army. In August, Bagnold was promoted to the rank of colonel. At about the same time it was decided that large patrols were unwieldy and were now reduced to under twenty all ranks in half a dozen vehicles. This was accomplished by splitting the large patrols into two, the parts becoming, for example, 'T1' and 'T2'. Weapons were progressively updated through 1940 to 1942 and eventually included the 20mm Breda, Browning machine guns in .30- and .5-calibre, twin Vickers 'K' guns, and even mortars.

Interestingly the LRDG did not generally fear enemy ground troops, as these could usually be seen miles off, and outrun by the patrols. Far more of a threat were enemy aircraft, for unless camouflage was good, vehicles were easy to spot in open desert and chances of escape were few. In addition to observation and raiding, the LRDG was used to insert agents behind enemy lines and to transport stores. Other passengers included a group of Senussi Arab fighters under the command of the Belgian-Russian Vladimir Peniakoff, now better known to the world as 'Popski'. Towards the end of the year the LRDG would make acquaintance with another body of raiders, in their way every bid as extraordinary as 'Popski's private army'.

As we have seen, the title 'Special Air Service' was first used as early as 1940 as a general name for a parachute force. Its reuse, in the Middle East in October 1941, was initially intended to mislead the Germans that a sizeable British Airborne element had reached North Africa, poised for action. In fact there was no such threat at this date. Never the less, the decoy name stuck, and in its own way brought terror to the enemy. The key raw material for what would eventually become an entirely new special forces regiment was the remnants of Layforce, the Commando Brigade led to the Eastern Mediterranean by Colonel Robert Laycock, but arguably squandered in the attempt to cover the retreat from Crete in the face of the parachute attack in April 1941. Father of the new unit was the then Lieutenant David Stirling, Scots Guards.

Stirling's idea for a new type of raiding force came to him during a stay in hospital after a parachute accident in training. It was very daring, but really quite simple. A small parachute force would be dropped behind enemy lines, form up and attack a vital target, then be met by a ground element with transport who whisked them away before superior forces could catch and crush them. Stirling took his idea direct to General Sir Neil Ritchie, who passed it with his endorsement to General Claude Auchinleck. It now seems incredible that no lesser figure than Auchinleck should have listened to Stirling, a very junior officer in his mid-twenties, who had been sent down from Cambridge, and whose early life appeared to be a riotous mix of adventure and irresponsibility and included a spell as a cowboy and a trip to Paris with the intention of becoming an artist: but listen he did. It may be speculated that one of the reasons that he was inclined to do so was the element of bluff it entailed, and the potential surprise it might bring to the enemy. For, after all, desert supply lines were long, and so stretched that the Germans could not possibly protect everything everywhere. An additional attraction was the notion perhaps that in this little venture, at least the desert army could be seen to be fulfilling two of Churchill's key demands: to strike using raiders, and to make early and aggressive use of parachute forces. Another colder calculation was that Auchinleck had but little to lose. Stirling was given

permission to put together a team of just five officers and sixty men who would become 'L Detachment' of the imaginary '1st Special Air Service Brigade'. If they were lost, the enemy might yet be deceived, and Churchill to some modest extent be placated. If they succeeded against the odds a coup might be claimed at minimum cost.

So it was that Stirling was promoted and, with his key lieutenants, including R.B. 'Paddy' Maine and 'Jock' Lewes, set about preparing for the first SAS raid on enemy airfields at Timini and Gazala. The object was in part destruction, but also diversion of attention from the major offensive, Operation Crusader. The conditions on 16 November 1941 were gusty and unsuitable for parachuting, but the raid was ordered to proceed and took place the following day, and since that day 17 November has been celebrated as the birthday of the SAS. The result was little short of disaster, as of fifty-five men sent into action just under half returned, Stirling and Maine being picked up by the LRDG, and no damage being inflicted on the enemy.

Never the less, the idea did not die, and moreover it was now decided that if the LRDG could successfully locate and extricate raiders, there was little point in risking the SAS by parachute in the first place. Thus it was that the LRDG were now accepted as return-fare taxi drivers to the SAS. Somewhat quaintly, LRDG reports of the period still referred to 'dropping' parachutists even though the SAS were delivered by truck. Missions were now mounted to Sirte, Tamet, Aphelia and Agedabia and enemy aircraft were destroyed just as Stirling had planned. However, the intrepid Lewes, who also invented the incendiary 'Lewes bomb', was killed on 31 December 1941.[22]

During 1942, and perhaps under the influence of the Prime Minister's personal interest, the SAS was significantly expanded. As of September the SAS assumed battalion status, and with this Stirling – the 'Phantom Major' – attained the rank of lieutenant colonel. The Special Boat Section (SBS) was absorbed by the SAS, and also included in the order of battle was a detachment of Free French parachutists. During this period the SAS also sprouted its own transport, usually in the form of US Jeeps, with a variety of weapons. Key amongst these were pairs of Vickers 'K' guns of the type formerly fitted in the now obsolete Gloster Gladiator biplane, but a variety of other guns were also carried. Photographs of SAS Jeeps of the period show up to four machine guns mounted on a single machine: a forward-firing .50-calibre Browning manned by the front-seat passenger; a Vickers 'K' ready for the use of the driver when halted, and a pair of similar guns atop the rear compartment. Such firepower was ideal for shooting up aircraft on the ground, so much so that raids were sometimes conducted without actually leaving the Jeep when in the target zone. The Jeep had great manoeuvrability, was relatively easy to hide, and less difficult to drive cross-country than larger vehicles. It was also easy to maintain. On the downside it had a shorter range as it was less able to carry its own fuel supplies, and as a result fuel was either carried in 3-ton lorries used as support vehicles, or pre-dumped for the Jeep teams to pick up en route. Added strength made the SAS a potent force, but perhaps paradoxically Stirling was uneasy about the use of 'thundering herds' that might easily compromise the element of surprise.

The marriage of Randolph Churchill (1911–1968), 4th Hussars, to Pamela Digby, October 1939. Winston's son joined his father's regiment, was elected to Parliament, became a journalist, and was attached to the SAS going behind enemy lines in North Africa with Fitzroy Maclean in May 1942. Despite all this he never lived up to expectations. The marriage ended in 1945, the same year Randolph lost his seat in Parliament. (Bettmann/Getty Images)

Hit and run operations continued under Stirling's direction during the Alamein campaign and, as Rommel withdrew, the SAS was tasked with harassing the enemy. A reinforced LRDG, acting as guides to conventional forces, also had frequent contacts and early in the new year was called upon to reconnoitre into southern Tunisia. However, in January 1943 Stirling himself was captured. The story was later related by Rommel:

> 'During January, a number of our AA gunners succeeded in surprising a British column of the Long Range Desert Group in Tunisia and captured the commander of the 1st SAS Regiment Lieutenant Colonel David Stirling. Insufficiently guarded, he managed to escape and made his way to some Arabs, to whom he offered a reward if they would get him back to British lines. But his bid must have been too small, for the Arabs, with their usual eye to business, offered him to us for 5kg of tea – a bargain which we soon clinched. Thus the British lost the very able and adaptable commander of the desert group which had caused us more damage than any other British unit of equal strength.'

Stirling would make other escape attempts, unsurprisingly ending up at Colditz Castle in 1944.

With its founder out of action and fighting about to move on to Sicily and Italy, the SAS was again reorganised. The 1st SAS now operated under the new title 'Special Raiding Squadron' commanded by Paddy Mayne, and a 2nd SAS was formally incorporated in May 1943 under David Stirling's brother Bill. In July 1943, 300 men of the SRS took ship for Sicily, coming ashore from landing craft at Cape Murro di Porco to capture three Italian batteries. Thereafter, in Italy both the SRS and 2nd SAS were again employed in Jeep-mounted operations. At Termoli the SRS took sixty-eight casualties, which was extremely serious given the relatively small size of this special force. Missions were also launched in small boats in attempts to outflank the front lines. However, both the SRS and SAS were withdrawn by the end of the year, first to North Africa, and then back to the UK in readiness for the invasion of northwest Europe.[23]

In preparation for the 'Great Crusade', the SAS units were reformed into a brigade as part of 1st Airborne, and duly adopted the Red Beret, albeit with SAS insignia. Including French and Belgian elements, and the GHQ Liaison squadrons, the formation now numbered about 2,500. In Scotland Troopers learned, or relearned, the art of parachuting, using drop bags, cutting communications, attacking railway stations, and entering submarine bases, sometimes using the Home Guard to play the enemy.

During the initial period of preparation and training for D-Day it was proposed that the SAS should be dropped as

Men of 2nd SAS supporting partisan operations, Castino, Northern Italy, 1945. The men carry a Vickers machine gun: the load is split with one man carrying the tripod, one the barrel, and one the water container. All three are festooned with ammunition belts. (Author)

another species of parachutist, between the enemy front and his reserves, in order to cut communications between the two. This was controversial to say the least. According to Roy Farran:

'Bill Sterling was bitterly opposed to this idea, saying we were strategic troops who should be used against communications far from the main battle area. Eventually the authorities compromised by allowing the major part of the brigade to be dropped deep into France, while only a small number of parties operated in the coastal area.'[24]

In any event Bill Stirling still resigned and was replaced by Lieutenant Colonel B.M.F. Franks. So it was that some SAS were dropped into Brittany to co-operate with the Maquis. 'Phantom' groups with GHQ liaison troops were dropped to transmit information back to the RAF, and in Operation Titanic a few attempted to create diversions behind the lines. However, it was not until 21 June that a whole squadron was inserted, and thereafter operations came thick and fast. A base was established south of Dijon complete with 6pdr anti-tank gun, another near Auxerre, and in the Vosges a ninety-man team from 2nd SAS conducted a ten-week campaign of harassment, but suffered heavily in the process. According to one authority, no less than forty-three places in France were eventually used as jumping-off points for operations. By mid-August, as the Allied breakout from Normandy gathered pace, SAS activities changed gear in step. In Operation Wallace, a Jeep-mounted squadron of 2nd SAS pushed through the Forêt d'Orléans, passed north of Dijon, and mounted an attack at Châtillon, then passed deeper behind the enemy lines as the Germans began to abandon France. Later missions were continued into Belgium, with particular reliance on the Belgian SAS, and even into Germany during Operation Archway.[24]

In December an SAS squadron was again deployed to Italy. Here they engaged in a number of ambushes and other operations, sometimes against the Germans, sometimes against Italian fascists. The biggest of these missions was Operation Tombola, which commenced in March 1945, involving not only SAS personnel but Italian partisans and escaped Russian prisoners of war. An attack was mounted on a German Corps HQ, and the enemy struck back against the SAS hideouts. However, by early April four small mixed 'columns' were formed of about 250 British, Italian and Russian personnel, equipped not only with some air-dropped Jeeps, but heavy weapons in the shape of mortars, Vickers machine guns, a couple of Browning .5-inch machine guns, and even a 75mm howitzer. These were

able to mount offensive operations on Highway 12 before the end of hostilities.[25]

The Chindits

It could be argued that the Chindits were the least 'special' of the special forces, but though they neither sprang from the original 'special service' idea of 1940, nor dropped by parachute, they were in their own way just as revolutionary. Interestingly the Chindits never were one unit, nor did they ever become a regiment in their own right. For they were, in effect, a brigade, later a division, brought into being for a specific strategic purpose in the war against Japan. The Chindit idea began, and arguably ended, with Orde Wingate, hard on the heels of the somewhat ignominious retreat from Burma in front of the triumphant Japanese in 1942. Wingate met with General Wavell and convinced him that the enemy, having extended their supply lines so far so quickly, were now vulnerable to counter strikes against their communications. Accordingly Wingate was authorised to take his 77th Indian Brigade into Burma in February 1943. His aim was the cutting of the railway between Shwebo and Myitkyina, and if this was successful to cross the Irrawaddy. By doing so he would both weaken enemy forces threatening India, and aid the Chinese.[26]

Wingate certainly gave his men the impression they were special, and subjected them to hitherto alien and rigorous methods of training and operation. For a start, he organised them into independent 'columns'. In 1943 there were eight in total, each the size of a reinforced company, and four were essentially British and four Gurkha. Each column had three infantry platoons, a support platoon of Vickers machine guns and mortars, a reconnaissance platoon drawn from the Burma Rifles, and a 'Commando' platoon comprised of sappers and infantry. Total column strength was about 400 all ranks. The troops had no transport, but equipment was carried on mules, and the whole could thus pick its way through jungle in single-file 'column snake' formation without needing to hold and maintain regular roads. Importantly Wingate intended that the columns should be re-supplied by air, and accordingly an RAF section was attached to each. The bulk of the British troops comprised 13th Battalion King's Liverpool Regiment, on the face of it hardly special forces material, as the unit had been raised as a Home Forces battalion of the line infantry as recently as the summer of 1940, and the men had an average age of over

our operations on the Indian front, his force and achievements stand out, and no mere question of seniority must obstruct the advance of real personalities to their proper stations in war.'

There was indeed little doubting that the first Chindit mission was a significant boost to the morale of an Army that had hitherto been beaten by the Japanese. It was now considered that a bigger operation in early 1944 would pay dividends: accordingly Wingate was called home to meet with Alan Brooke, Chief of the General Staff, and also with Churchill, who took him on to the 'Quadrant' conference in Canada. Wingate's plans were well received, and a larger force was built up for 1944, though there was much disagreement between Wavell, Wingate and others as to what troops might be suitable as Chindit fighters. In the event a whole division, 3rd Indian Infantry, or 'Special Force', was assembled. This comprised five complete brigades as well as divisional Troops and some detachments, and each brigade formed from seven to eleven columns. The new Chindit force included not only British and Gurkha troops, but men of the Nigeria Regiment, a Hong Kong volunteer unit, some Burmese and others. Air support was provided by the US Army Air Force. [28]

The British infantry were provided by 2nd Black Watch; 1st Bedford and Hertfordshire; 2nd York and Lancaster; 2nd and 7th Royal Leicestershire; 2nd Queen's Royal West Surrey; 1st Essex; 2nd Duke of Wellington's; 4th Border; 1st King's Liverpools; 1st Lancashire Fusiliers; 1st Staffordshire; 1st Cameronians; and 2nd King's Own. These were mainly well-trained battalions, and split to form two columns each. The columns were numbered, but in a non-consecutive (and to the enemy confusing) manner. For the most part, these numbers were chosen using the pre-1881 regimental system. So it was, for example, that the first column of the Lancashire Fusiliers was numbered '20', that of the Black Watch '42', and that of the Duke of Wellington's '33'. The columns were supported by artillery, 25pdrs, 40mm Bofors, and .5inch Hispano Light Anti-Aircraft guns. These were used to defend 'strongholds' and 'blocks' from positions difficult for the enemy to find and engage with their main forces. The objectives of Operation Thursday would be to stem the flow of supplies and reinforcements to the Japanese facing US General Joseph Stilwell's Army in the north, create a situation suitable for a Chinese advance, and inflict the 'maximum confusion, damage and loss on the Japanese in North Burma'. [29]

Part of a typical Chindit column. Slouch hats are worn and mules transport supplies and ammunition moving in single file. Wingate ordered the men to grow beards sparing water, time, and shaving kit. (Hulton Archive/ Getty Images)

thirty. The 'Chinthe' formation badge of the Chindits depicted the mythical beast statues of which guarded Burmese temples. [27]

In truth the 1943 Operation Longcloth was expensive in lives, and limited in its strategic impact, almost 900 men being lost of the 3,000 that participated, and Wingate returned feeling that he had failed. Yet the idea of independent columns of jungle fighting troops supplied by air – able to maraud at will behind enemy lines – was vitally important, at the time, and subsequently. Raiding would become fully developed 'Deep Penetration'. As Wingate himself explained, 'Deep Penetration means the operation of regular columns of high calibre in the heart of the enemy's war machine, engaging targets he is unable adequately to protect, and thus compelling him to alter his plans, thus causing a situation of which our own main forces can take advantage.' The aggressive nature of Wingate's methods appealed hugely to the Prime Minister, whose minute of 24 July 1943 waxed lyrical on the general's character and potential:

'I consider Wingate should command the Army against Burma. He is a man of genius and audacity, and rightly has been discerned by all eyes as a figure quite above the ordinary level. The expression "Clive of Burma" has already gained currency. There is no doubt that in the welter of inefficiency and lassitude which has characterised

An important aspect of the operation was deployment by glider: a risky option but one which put 9,000 men, 1,350 mules, 250 tons of stores and a couple of batteries into the heart of enemy-occupied Burma in early March. The Chindits then marched and established their strongholds and blocking positions: rail bridges and lines were blown and cut. As expected the surprised Japanese attempted counter-attacks in order to maintain their supply lines and oust the intruders, but most of these attacks suffered far more than the Chindits. So the many small battles continued, until eventually the commanders of the strongholds were forced to decide to abandon their positions before they could be overwhelmed. Weakened by sickness as well as battle casualties, they withdrew to the north, but continued to fight. After this they were reorganised. Wingate, killed in an air crash early in the operation, did not live to see much of this, and the Chindits would cease to exist as such in February 1945.[30]

Remarkable as the Chindit operations had been, they remained controversial. For, according to some commentators, they were both revolutionary, and the vital blows which began the rot of the Japanese occupation of Burma. Yet critics give them less credit, pointing out the greater significance of the major defensive battles at Imphal and Kohima. As Shelford Bidwell put it:

'The arguments revolve around rival theories of warfare. Orthodox strategists take the view that resources squandered

Lord Mountbatten, Supreme Commander South East Asia, and a favourite of Churchill, examines M1 carbines issued to 36th Division in Burma, 1944. (Keystone-France/ Gamma-Keystone via Getty Images

could have been better used elsewhere. Had for instance, the 70th Division not been plundered to make up the Special Force it would have been available to reinforce Imphal, which was momentarily in jeopardy while a division was flown up from the Arakan. Others, while recognising Operation Thursday as the prototype of air mobile warfare, argue that it would have been better to use it concentrated on one decisive spot. In complete contrast some of Wingate's followers see Long Range Penetration as an extreme variant of the "indirect approach", which would infallibly have succeeded had not Wingate's original plans been abandoned and perverted by Lentaigne and Stilwell.'[31]

Chindits river crossing in Burma. Other than mule transport, Chindits had to rely on modified 1937 Pattern webbing to carry their equipment. (Popperfoto/Getty Images)

CHAPTER TEN
Auxilliary Forces
Home Guard[1]

Churchill is reported to have said that the Home Guard was 'as much a part of the Army as the Coldstream Guards'. This was no mere rhetorical flourish, for not only did the Prime Minister regard the Home Guard as vital to the country in its hour of need, and a vital bolster to morale, he both named and nurtured this auxiliary force, taking it to his heart in a manner not enjoyed by many regiments or corps. Indeed, even before he was Prime Minister, he had agitated for such an organisation to be brought into existence. On 8 October 1939 he wrote to the Lord Privy Seal asking:

> *'Why do we not form a Home Guard of half a million men over forty (if they like to volunteer) and put all our elder stars at the head and in the structure of these new formations. Let these five hundred thousand men come along and push the young and active out of their home billets. If uniforms are lacking a brassard would suffice, and I am assured there are plenty of rifles at any rate.'*

Clothes maketh the man (Proverb).
A Battalion H.Q. Mannequin Parade.

This was by no means as extraordinary as it might now seem, bodies of volunteers having been raised to defend Britain's shores on a number of previous occasions — most notably in answer to French threats in the late eighteenth century, against Napoleon I, and in the middle of the nineteenth century. In any event, what might have seemed Churchillian eccentricity in 1939 became widespread desire in 1940. Scares about enemy 'fifth columns' were multiplied in May when German parachutists were in the forefront of the attack at Eben-Emael in Belgium. Suggestions regarding various sorts of levy to guard places

Winston Churchill inspects the House of Commons Home Guard in Spencer's Yard, London. Between them the two houses of Parliament found a half company, originally part of the 1st County of London (Westminster). This was transferred to 25th County of London Battallion in October 1940. (Topical Press Agency/Getty Images)

Far left: Shortages and Home Guard humour with 10th Torbay Battalion. (Author) of importance or repel potential invasions were made in both Houses of Parliament. In the press there were both solid arguments for the enlistment of new types of volunteers, and more bizarre calls – such as the idea that golfers should be trained in rifle shooting so as to pick off any enemy who came down near the links. For some time, and with good reason, the Home Office remained unconvinced, reminding the public that gentlemen in civilian attire taking casual pot shots at enemy troops were prone to be shot out of hand if captured.

Never the less, even before the campaign in the Low Countries began, there were local and spontaneous attempts to begin the unofficial recruiting of special volunteers, and in Essex, for example, these involved the existing Territorial Association. In the Welsh borders, Lady Helena Gleichen started what was effectively a private army in the shape of the 'Much Marcle Watchers' with about eighty of her staff and tenants. In response to such popular pressure, GHQ Home Forces devised a plan for small forces to be raised in the localities, organised at county level under the Lords Lieutenant in a manner that harked back to the medieval militia. In a rival scheme, the Adjutant General proposed attaching groups of British Legion volunteers to searchlight companies. None the less, by 13 May many of the details were settled, and it was expected that General Walter Kirke, Commander-in-Chief Home Forces, would now put out the call for volunteers.

However, at the eleventh hour, the new Secretary of State for War decided that it was his personal duty to address the nation. So it was that on 14 May Anthony Eden made his famous broadcast, appealing for 'large numbers' of British subjects, aged between seventeen and sixty-five, to give their names offering their services for the 'Local Defence Volunteers'. They would not be paid, but would be uniformed and armed as being part of the forces of the Crown and subject to military law. It was expected that volunteers would have knowledge of firearms and be of 'reasonable' physical fitness. The next morning, lines of men formed up outside police stations. Bearing in mind the threat from the air, the popular press dubbed the new organisation the 'parashots'. Under initial organisation it was intended that ten volunteers made up a section, with three sections to a platoon and four platoons to a company.[2]

At first there were no 'officers' in the sense of commissions and normal Army rank structure, nor any complex record keeping: but there were company commanders and enrolment forms with a question about previous military service. There was a stationery and postage allowance of 2s 6d per rifle issued with £10 to go to 'zone organisers' whose areas approximated to police districts. Many of these senior organisers were retired generals or other officers. In most areas men were keen to lead, but this was not universally the case. The history of the 10th Devonshire, for example, records that at first in Torbay the humble 'section leaders' in particular were in short supply. Men were apparently discouraged to volunteer for this post at least in part because of fear of being left out of pocket and the possibility that once in post there would be variations to the conditions of service. It was also thought that the very idea of equality, much trumpeted in some quarters, might undermine nascent leaders.[3]

The one benefit universally open to Local Defence Volunteers from July 1940 was not a particularly welcome one, for as of this date they became eligible for a disablement allowance. Assuming that such disability was both 'total' and caused by 'wound, injury or disease' attributable to volunteer service, the man would be

The 7th Lancashire (Blackpool) Home Guard in their denim uniform with rifles but no anklets or equipment. (Author)

granted 35s per week 'basic rate'. Wife and children increased this figure, though if the man was in hospital then a deduction of 10s 6d applied. Payments were normally expected to cease after six months or discharge from the force. Partial disability payments could also be made similar to those available to an ordinary Army private.[4]

Any expectation of immediate arms and uniforms was certainly wildly over-optimistic. Such was the demand that the War Office was at first only able to offer arm bands stencilled 'LDV', and many volunteers used whatever sporting rifles and shotguns they could get supplemented by farm implements and edged weapons. Even Lieutenant General Sir Henry Pownall, the 'Inspector General' of the new force, admitted, at least to his diary, that it had been formed without sufficient forethought. In an interesting echo of the 'Pals' of the First World War, many men joined up in groups from businesses, clubs or areas. Some factories organised their own LDV defence guards. Eventually there were some whole battalions based around the post offices and railways. The BBC had its own Home Guards to protect its London premises, and as of September 1940 these were formalised as the 4th Company of the 2nd Battalion City of London Home Guard. The Glasgow BBC also raised a platoon, initially against the wishes of its management. Parliament boasted its own 'Palace of Westminster' unit containing no less than ninety-five MPs and seventeen peers. This was something of a gift to Churchill, who mentioned it in a speech, thereby stressing the nature of a war in which everybody was 'in it together'.

It is a record of fact that the Home Guard contained some remarkably old men. The 1st Caernarvonshire had an officer who had first joined the Volunteers in 1889, and there were some in most battalions who lied about being under sixty-five in order to join. Famously Thomas Walton, a veteran of the Sudan, was eighty-four years old when he managed to talk his way into the LDV. The area organisers were retired generals, mostly over sixty. Yet the idea that the bulk of the Home Guard were septuagenarians, or at least veterans of the First World War, is folklore born of humour, fuelled by ill-informed newspaper pieces – but still perpetuated through ignorance. Complete figures have not been published, but the elderly were definitely not in a majority. War Office estimates of 1941 suggested that 40 per cent of the force were veterans of 1914–1918: but in the early 1940s many veterans of the First World War were still under the age of fifty. On the basis of the surviving evidence it has reasonably been suggested that the mean age of the Home Guard

in 1940 was about thirty-five. The reasons for this sort of yardstick include the large number of teenagers, not yet wanted by the forces, but keen to do their bit alongside the thirty- to sixty-year-olds, and the fact that the regular forces had not as yet mopped up maximum available manpower from other age groups. In the unusual instance of the 7th and 8th Cambridgeshire battalions, the former was partly, and the latter entirely, composed of students. The 7th was designated as a 'Mobile' battalion, but the 8th was a 'University Senior Training Corps' battalion rebranded as Home Guard – at one point boasting a light tank and four armoured cars on its strength. The average age of a ranker in the 8th was about eighteen, though the officers were drawn mainly from university dons. Since many of the students were only present for part of the year, the commanders became adept at swift changes to rolls, and in transferring men back and forth between the 7th and 8th battalions as strengths fluctuated. An estimate from the middle period of the war suggests that by that time 'over 100,000 youths under 18' were in the Home Guard, this position being regularised when sixteen-year-olds were formally accepted with the proviso that those so young were only permitted to perform 'communication duties'.[5]

Though a few fortunate units managed to tack themselves onto existing military facilities, the vast majority had no such luck, making do with whatever they could get – including rooms lent to them by police and Civil Defence, church halls, public houses and even private homes. In just one example of improvisation, 'B' company of the 3rd Isle of Ely Battalion began life in 'small rooms' lent to them by other organisations, and fell in for drill and parades – usually by platoons – opposite the police station or in a private yard behind another building. Later the headquarters was set up in the Crown Theatre, but in the winter of 1940 this had to be given up in exchange for a

A veteran of the First World War now serving as a Lance Corporal in 11th City of Edinburgh (11 GPO) Battalion, Home Guard, wearing Battle Dress and gas mask bag. Publicists were keen to point out that the Home Guard was inclusive and from every part of Britain. (Author)

A London Home Guard armed with a Thompson M1 demonstrating innovative urban camouflage. To blend with a built-up environment required a breaking up of outlines and the colours of brick, concrete, asphalt, and urban rubbish. Many home Guard defence plans depended on delaying the enemy at road junctions and in towns and villages. (Keystone/ Getty Images)

at parachutists and reporting 'suspicious' matters to the police soon gave way to the holding of 'defensive localities', road blocks and ambush points. Later, Home Guards would replace regular troops in defensive positions, provide the opposition on exercises, and begin to man anti-aircraft rocket batteries. Finally they would be expected to take a far more active and mobile role.

From a very poor start, armament came on in leaps and bounds. The East Kent LDV, being in the eye of any possible invasion storm, were amongst the first to get a proper distribution of service rifles, receiving 497 weapons together with ten rounds apiece as early as the afternoon of 17 May. Weekly returns showed that about 56,000 private rifles and shotguns formed the bulk of the first LDV arsenal, but by the second week of July 1940 almost 83,000 rifles of reasonably modern type had been added from official sources. By early August there were half a million firearms held by volunteers all over the UK, and the majority of these were proper rifles of military calibre, albeit of several different types. Indeed, it was the poor supplies of ammunition, and almost total lack of heavy weapons, which were much more of a limiting factor than the sheer number of rifles at this early stage. Moreover, the ammunition question was not just one of quantity but of type, as diverse types of weapon required different sorts of cartridge. Perhaps most significantly the British rifles left over from the First World War were in .303-calibre, while those supplied from America came in .300-calibre. Whilst having a superficial similarity, rounds for one were useless in the other. This problem was roughly, if incompletely, solved by marking American-calibre weapons with an obvious red band.

small Salvation Army hut. Some of the observation posts had a modicum of cover, but road blocks and the post on top of Mr Seward's private house were pretty much open air until some of the more inventive borrowed sheds in which they installed beds for periods that they were not actually on watch. By late 1941, lack of accommodation reached crisis point and at last the company was moved into the church rooms at Chatteris.

The first tactical instruction as to what the new recruits were actually intended to do came in June, when the War Office observed that the LDV 'are neither trained nor equipped to offer strong prolonged resistance to highly trained German troops, and they will therefore best fulfill their role by observation, by the rapid transmission of information, and by confining the enemy's activities. They will also act as guards at places of tactical or industrial importance.' Never the less, not all accepted this essentially passive role, and some immediately began to prepare for offensive action. Moreover, the official role of the LDV, soon to be the Home Guard, would evolve very significantly with the passage of time and improvement of training and weapons. Firing

Though some of the first attempts at improvised armament have become the stuff of legend, many outlandish devices did in fact exist. The 55th County of Lancaster Battalion armed each man on duty with a 6-foot (1.8m) spear and a weighted truncheon made by Manchester Collieries. Several battalions made use of obsolete arms, including Martini–Henry rifles and weapons borrowed from cadets or museum collections. Within one London unit was formed a 'Cutlass Platoon' led by an old naval rating. Many units drilled with crude dummy rifles or broomsticks. A number of units also came up with the same idea with the production of simple 'drain pipe' mortars – a form of weapon that had actually, if briefly, seen front-line service in the First World War. Bolsover Collieries made their own anti-tank gun consisting of a boiler tube with an electric firing system and a projectile that consisted of a broomstick with an anti-tank mine secured at the fore end. For similar work, the 1st

Cambridgeshire Battalion obtained a 1-inch-calibre breech-loading punt gun and manufactured solid-steel rounds. Crow bars, lengths of railway line and pickaxes also featured in official training literature for anti-tank work and street fighting. Sadly there were tragic accidents with homemade weapons, such that at times orders were issued that no more were to be produced. [6]

Many volunteers were not shy about using their arms either. There were alarms, and serious accidents, when overzealous – even trigger-happy – volunteers shot motorists who failed to halt when challenged, or fired on friendly aircraft. On at least one occasion, an RAF officer who had successfully bailed out after air combat was shot and killed. Conversely at least one Home Guard history points out that there were quite a number of motorists out at night under the influence of drink, and that drivers could be erratic, dangerous or simply rude to patrols and Guards on road blocks. 'A' Company 10th Torbay Home Guard recorded an Army major who was inebriated enough to require preventing getting back into his car, a pilot 'roaring drunk', and an admiral with outriders who produced his identity card

enquiring whether the Guard thought he was a 'handsome-looking bastard'.

Various sorts of 'Molotov Cocktail' incendiary were an early staple of the Home Guard arsenal, and instructions were issued as to the best types of combustant and bottle as well as an approved throwing technique, which was usually underarm or involved dropping out of windows onto vehicles below. Some of the most enthusiastic early exponents of the Molotov were the Bexley company of the Kent LDV. The Group Commander ordered bottles to be filled with tar and petrol, and – none being issued – Captain Baker toured the village on a farm cart:

'Collecting any old used whiskey and soft drink bottles (beer bottles being too hard for easy breakage). Several hundred potential missiles were thus collected. The making of the mixture was carried out in a wood with the aid of a twig fire for boiling the tar, which was necessary in order to make it mix well… Wooden bottles were made for use in practice throwing, and, as a target, a tank was drawn in chalk on the wall of a disused

Typical Home Guard technique covering a road or track from a camouflaged weapons pit. One man fires a P17 Enfield, the Lance Corporal throws a Molotov cocktail made from a spirit bottle full of flammable liquid fused with a length of camera film. (Author)

house, points being given for the best hits registered at vulnerable parts. Later, an old car was bought (fitted and covered in sheet iron) and towed along a quiet road, Molotov throwers hiding either side ready to throw as the tank-like vehicle passed along. Incidentally the tank was called the "Hitler bus", and had many slogans painted thereon, such as "don't you miss it", "The road to Berlin", and so on. During many of these practices actual air raids were taking place, thereby giving an excellent touch of realism. The ladies came to our help splendidly, and one of their efforts was to make canvas carriers for the bottles so that they could be carried on both arms (six Molotovs in each bag). These carriers were made out of old mattress covers, sackcloth and any suitable material that could be collected.' [7]

Famously some of the auxiliary force were issued with pikes, and remarkably this move seems directly attributable to Churchill's own impatience. However, it did not happen in the first flush of desperation, as many now believe, but in late 1941 and early 1942. During 1941, Home Guard weapon shortages had persisted, mainly because the organisation had expanded to such a prodigious size so quickly. Home forces were now lower in the pecking order, and the government came in for criticism. That June, Churchill was stung into action, writing to the War Office that it was intolerable that any man should have nothing at all and that even 'a mace or pike' might suffice until enough modern weapons were available. The War Office duly began to issue truncheons, and now placed an order for 250,000 metal tubes with bayonet blades welded to the ends. Understandably the pikes unleashed a wave of derision, and in places anger. In the interesting instance of Torbay, the *Torquay Times* prepared an article gently lampooning the pike as an 'improvised medieval weapon' that might in future be used like a lance on horseback and promptly fell foul of the regional censor. Some unit commanders regarded the pikes as so counterproductive and damaging to morale that they simply hid them away in store, praying that no emergency would be so dire as to need their reappearance. Churchill quietly forgot his involvement, leaving Lord Henry Page Croft, the Under-Secretary of State for War, to carry the can and defend the pike as being better than nothing.

One of the Loyal North Lancashire Regiment cap badged Home Guard units on the march, 1944. They wear greatcoats, steel helmets and leather equipment, and carry P17 Enfield rifles. They are older than the average soldier, but not geriatric in appearance. (Author)

Whilst many LDV wore civilian dress with armband, there was also early improvisation in the question of uniform. Perhaps the most fortunate unit was in Harrogate, home to Sir Montague Burton of the tailoring family. Sir Montague took his patriotic duty seriously enough to immediately order 1,500 battledress uniforms of Barathea, thus ensuring that his neighbours were as well attired as any front-line officer. In some places boiler suits were worn, steel helmets were borrowed from Air Raid Precautions (ARP), and raincoats added a semblance of uniformity on parade. The Cambridgeshire history makes specific reference to the 'rape of a hundred helmets from the Civil Defence' as well as a church collection of suitable boots and shoes.[8] Sir Edward Grigg claimed in Hansard that, as early as 22 May, no less than 90,000 'overalls' had 'been issued' and that 250,000 field caps were 'available' – the latter probably being parliamentary speak for no headgear actually having been distributed yet. Though the official parliament record notes the overalls as 'linen', it would seem probable that these are the type now referred to as 'denim' overalls, cut to the same pattern as battledress. Issues of a serge battledress identical to that of the regulars began as early as the late summer of 1940, and before the end of the year volunteers had also begun to receive knee-length capes of the same material.

The change of title from LDV to Home Guard was personally pushed through by Churchill during July 1940, when he brushed aside complaints about cost and confusion telling the Minister for Information that he intended to get the new name adopted forthwith and expected that it be suitably publicised. Churchill himself used the title in speeches whenever possible. On 21 July Lieutenant General Henry Pownall suggested formalising NCO ranks within the organisation, and so it was that soon afterwards one-, two- and three-stripe Home Guards were officially known as lance corporal, corporal and sergeant, like their regular equivalents. Regularisation took a further step forwards on 3 August when Home Guards were authorised to wear the cap badge of the county regiments to which they were affiliated. At or above the rank of full colonel, a Home Guard officer was to wear the Royal Crest as his cap badge. By early 1941, Home Guard officers had been brought approximately into line with the full-time Army, with zone or group commanders authorised as colonels; battalion commanders as lieutenant colonels; majors or captains commanding companies and a lieutenant assisted by a subaltern for the platoons. Even so, Home Guard units remained numerically much larger than line infantry equivalents and battalions of 1,500, and sometimes many more, were quite typical. In some cases, individual companies grew to such sizes that they had to be divided into two and more officers introduced to make them practical.

Despite continuing accretion of the traditional trappings of the military as unpaid part-time citizen volunteers, who usually knew each other in civilian life, the Home Guard remained much more democratic than the regular Army. In the first few days units had even selected their own leaders, and there were brief 'strikes' when popular figures were dismissed or overlooked. There was also jealousy between the Home Guard and ARP as the latter had been formed first and already had official assistance with stores, whereas, initially at least, Home Guards often found their own camp beds, transport and other items. Egalitarianism and self-help did not always go down well, either with regular officers, or with Parliament, and officialdom looked askance at left-wing enthusiasts like Tom Wintringham, who saw the Home Guard more as popular militia than auxiliaries to an established armed force. On the other side of the coin, it is of course dubious whether the Home Guard would have got off the ground at all were it not for a cheerful willingness to 'make do' and improvise. The difference between Home Guard and regular was gradually eroded but would never disappear, and acceptance by the public of the force as real soldiers was never complete.

In truth, what the Home Guard was actually for changed with time, and surprisingly briskly. The initial and limited concept of small and very local sections watching for – and hopefully shooting at – parachutists lasted only a few weeks before a more formal company and battalion organisation was superimposed. These larger units were soon focused on the 'defended localities' and 'nodal points' that were supposed to hinder enemy mobility on the ground. During 1941, Home Guard tacticians not only thought more seriously about street fighting, but also of the potential of mobile 'fighting patrols' capable of intercepting the enemy before he could concentrate. Any notion that the Home Guard was a 'guerrilla' force was now firmly quashed.

However, there were still many local variations. Some units kept cap badges different to the local infantry regiment, or oddities of organisation. The 5th (Worthing) Battalion of the Sussex Home Guard was unusual in that it chose to lump together all of its heavy weapons into a 'Machine Gun Company', though this was essentially a matter of training, the weapons being distributed tactically as required over the whole battalion area for action. The London BBC Home Guard, having

difficulties keeping up regular numbers and parades when many of its men lived a distance away and were employed in shift work, was actually reorganised in 1941 to create that contradiction in terms – a full-time Home Guard. There was thus one platoon permanently on hand upon which the other three of the company would attempt to join in case of emergency. The following year, it was shifted into the ambit of a different battalion, becoming 'E' (BBC) Company of the 5th County of London, wearing the badge of the King's Royal Rifle Corps.

In several areas, the hobby of pigeon racing and fancying became an official part of Home Guard communications – in Yorkshire there were several lofts forming the 'West Riding Home Guard Carrier Pigeon Service'. Waterway patrols were mounted on major rivers and canals, as well as on Lake Windermere. One of the first of these was the LDV 'River Company' that patrolled the Thames from London Bridge to Teddington, later becoming the 34th County of London (London River South) Battalion. Though some water patrols were scrapped in 1941, they remained in a number of places, notably the Thames, the Trent, the Fal in Cornwall, and on Windermere. As of May 1942, almost 200 vessels were still operating, the largest flotillas being those of the upper Thames and Trent. In Scotland, the Home Guard took over the manning of three armoured trains, from Polish troops in 1942. The trains were armed with 6pdrs and Bren guns and remained patrolling until September 1944.

A number of units possessed various unofficial forms of land motor transport from the outset. Some of these formations were soon recognised as different in type, as for example the 12th Sussex Battalion, which drew its personnel from Southdown Motor Transport and became an 'MT' battalion in January 1941. The 59th County of London was a taxi battalion, whilst the 51st London and 26th Kent were bus units. The 31st and 32nd Warwickshire battalions (formerly 11th and 12th Birmingham 'Public Utility') were also based on bus garages, and other transport facilities and initial recruitment was from employees of Birmingham City Transport. One of their first duties was to

'The Home Guard can Fight', a message from Tom Wintringham in the *Picture Post*. Wintringham was a key figure in the Home Guard movement and modern tactics, but was suspect due to his left-wing credentials. Some viewed the force as popular militia, others as a branch of the Army: some thought of the Home Guard more as a bolster to national morale and the will to resist. Its capacities and strategic purpose changed over time. (Zoltan Glass/ Picture Post/Hulton Archive/Getty)

protect their own depots and buses from sabotage and bomb damage, and in some places guards were mounted right through until late 1944. [9]

The 7th Cambridgeshire (Mobile) was exceptional in being originally raised in July 1940 by a colonel serving with the Canadian forces. The initial pool of volunteers was medical students and the staffs of the larger Cambridge businesses including Eaden Lilley's, Joshua Taylor's, Matthews and Sainsbury's. Unusually twenty-five of the original 145 recruits were car owners, so the bulk of the unit was motorised from its inception and was thus able to race to the scene of suspicious incidents surprisingly quickly. Later the battalion grew and fielded two companies of cyclists as well as motor vehicles. The Oxford and Warwick University battalions followed a similar 'mobile' trajectory, if more slowly. Oxford later created what was described as a 'mobile column of all arms', and Warwick's cadet undergraduates are finally recorded as being equipped with thoroughly modern Bren guns and 25pdr field guns. Sussex also formed what it called a 'Recovery Company', bringing together Home Guards who ran garages and breakdown vehicles so that eventually there were five platoons acting with an ordnance workshop.

More surprisingly, Home Guard units in twenty-four counties maintained horse patrols totalling almost 900 beasts for use on moorland and in other rough country. Like the motorised transport, these were mainly retrospectively recognised, and in May 1942 a 15s monthly allowance per horse was approved. This shrank to 10s where saddlery was supplied by the War Office. Use of horses had dwindled somewhat by late 1943, but even then there were 772 horses with forty-four battalions. The largest number were maintained in Western Command where

A machine-gun-armed Home Guard Sunbeam armoured car. The force never managed to field modern armour, and much of what it did was improvised. This vehicle is little more than a saloon car with weapons and thin plates. The 'Beaverette', or Car Armoured Light Standard, was slightly more sturdy with wood-backed 11mm armour, produced in numbers from 1940–1942, but was still less than truly battle-worthy. (Central Press/Getty Images)

there were 286, and four Glamorgan battalions alone fielded nearly ninety. At the other end of the scale, the London District had just a dozen horses, all with the 59th Surrey.

All training methods became steadily more regular in character with the progress of time, and many units gained permanent staff instructors during 1941. In December that year Churchill signalled that the new auxiliary Army would cease to be either amateur, or voluntary. Speaking of the new National Service bill, he remarked that the Home Guard had become, 'a most powerful, trained, uniform body, which plays a vital part in our national defence. We must make sure that this great bulwark of our safety does not deteriorate during the inevitably prolonged and indefinite waiting period through which we have to pass or may have to pass. Power must now be taken by statute to direct men into the Home Guard in areas where it is necessary and to require them to attend drills and musters indispensable to the maintenance of efficiency.' In a similar vein, Home Guard *Instruction* 38 'winter training 1941–1942' looked forward to a new era, in which though, 'the possibility of invasion must never be allowed to slip into the background, the time has come when commanding officers will do well to begin thinking about their plans for a second winter of training and preparation for battle'.

Home Guard units were now encouraged to divide their men into two categories: those who had undergone individual training elsewhere and those who had not. New intakes might well include men with no prior knowledge whatever, and novices were to be kept separate from old hands who had already mastered the basics. The new men would start with drill, weapons training, gas, sentry duty, elementary tactics and map reading. By this means, newcomers learned at their own speed whilst the experienced moved on to more advanced training and new subjects, not getting bored by repetition. Advanced men were now to concentrate on 'training in more mobile forms of defence as applied to their operational role'. Specific subjects to be taught included night operations; battlecraft; patrols, 'mobile' and local; anti-tank mines; enemy equipment and tactics as well as the specialisms of signallers, intelligence, mortars and 'sub-artillery', and first aid.

A 'skeleton training programme' recommended in September 1941 actually showed a tripartite division of Home Guard trainees into 'recruits', 'semi-trained' and 'specialists'. The recruits were to devote 40 per cent of their time to weapons training, and 20 per cent to tactical instruction aided by sand tables and cloth models. A total of 10 per cent each were to go to movement with and without the rifle; compass and map reading; anti-gas work; and films, lectures and competitions. The semi-trained men followed a similar schedule but included bombs, grenades and mines in the weapons work, spent a greater proportion of their time on tactics, and made deductive efforts regarding the ground from their map observations. The specialists were to spend a full 80 per cent of their time on specialist subjects and half of this on crew-served weapons and their tactics. The remaining 20 per cent might be spent on 'refreshers'. A number of games were suggested to enliven the more pedestrian aspects of learning. Some were very practical, such as identifying locations shown in photographs on a map, or writing messages based on actual field observations. Others were less serious, intentionally or otherwise. These included throwing darts at drawings of enemy vehicles, and efforts at memory and concentration that were deliberately interrupted by spoof events.

Interestingly, whilst it appears that the majority of Home Guard training, excluding bigger exercises, was mounted

within individual Home Guard units, quite a few men attended courses elsewhere. In the case of the two Birmingham transport battalions, for example, it is recorded that no fewer than 333 men went on external courses. These were divided into broad categories: those mounted by the Birmingham Zone of the Home Guard, and courses elsewhere. The more distant training was divided into sessions defined as long or short depending on whether or not they exceeded five days. Perhaps surprisingly, seventy-three of the Birmingham men travelled as far as Altcar in Lancashire for wireless training, with smaller parties going to Prestatyn in Wales, and Catterick in North Yorkshire. The biggest of the Birmingham Zone courses was 'physical training, bayonet fighting and unarmed combat', attended by sixty-two men. All this was in addition to the camp at Bewdley through which many men passed during the summer of 1943 in batches of up to 100 at a time. This entirely 'self-supported' venture 'gave the men an insight into camp life and provided excellent opportunities for special training and recreation not readily available in Birmingham'. [10]

There had been unofficial or semi-official manuals for the LDV and Home Guard from the start, and John Brophy's *Home*

A mounted patrol of the Cumberland Home Guard, July 1943. Though in existence earlier two Cumberland mounted patrols were formally authorised in 1942, one each for the Cockermouth and Penrith battalions totalling thirty-one horses. The men wear riding breeches and Pattern 1903 bandoliers and use US-manufactured Enfields. (Popperfoto/Getty Images)

Guard: A Handbook for the LDV was a hit as early as September 1940. Another popular publication was A.F.U. Green's *Home Guard Pocket Book*, which quickly ran to 8,000 copies promoted by Kent Messenger Newspapers. John Langdon-Davies's *Home Guard Training Manual* of December 1940 was already billed as based on 'War Office instruction books', and the worthy and seriously practical were sold alongside such splendidly eccentric titles as the cartoon-illustrated *Art of Prowling*, and the well-endorsed *Imaginary Battle of Handley Cross*. However, the Home Guard progressively became the subject of a burgeoning official War Office literature for both training and general bureaucratic purposes. *Home Guard Instruction* booklets were issued as a series that had reached its forty-third edition by January 1942, and these ran alongside brief *Information Circulars* that reached issue 20 by the end of the year. Interestingly Home Guards were specifically encouraged to make use of the pamphlets issued for the regulars, and also to watch selected training films. These included titles on aircraft and AFV recognition, patrolling,

weapons, camouflage, prisoners of war, defence of small towns, and unarmed combat. The last of these posed some problems, for whilst it was recognised that Home Guards needed some knowledge, it was desirable to allot only the fittest to roles where they were likely to require the contact skills of close and unarmed combat. Fit men were therefore to be chosen for 'active' roles such as patrolling. Candidates sufficiently well trained were put forward for the general Home Guard test announced in 1941, which allowed the man to wear a proficiency badge. [11]

The proficiency test as described in 1943 updated the existing tests and introduced graded badges, a simple red diamond for qualification under the old system and bars for the latest qualification and renewals. The badge was worn on the lower left sleeve. It was accompanied by a certificate that was supposed to be used by any who subsequently passed on into the regular forces as evidence of previous attainment. What was actually examined depended on the type of Home Guard unit. For the majority of

Men of 22nd Kent (Tunbridge Wells) Battalion, Home Guard, with a US .30 Browning machine gun. First introduced to American service in 1917, this weapon was supplied to the Home Guard from 1940. Coastal units were equipped first, but by the end of 1942 there were over 6,000 in use around the country. Its performance was similar to the Vickers machine gun. (Author)

'General Service' formations, the compulsory tests were general knowledge; rifle; No. 36 Mills bomb and battlecraft. On top of this, each man would be examined on one of the crew-served weapons or signalling, and either map reading or first aid, making a total of six subjects. The artillerists of Heavy AA units and rocket batteries studied only five subjects, including their own ordnance; the rifle; Sten gun; general knowledge; and a choice of map reading, field works, or first aid. The coast gunners had four subjects: their own guns; general knowledge; rifle or Sten gun; and the choice between map reading, field works, or first aid. The River Patrols, Auxiliary Bomb Disposal, and Motor Transport units likewise included their own specialism as a subject of examination, but dropped some of the other options. 'Examining Boards' were composed of both Home Guard and ordinary officers, each board requiring an officer 'not below field rank' as 'president'. Boards set the tests and also had a duty not to allow those who had just taken a test to come into contact with those about to take the examination.

A set of sample questions was included with the pamphlet *Qualifications for, and Conditions Governing the Award*. This made clear that much of the examination was to be practical rather than written or theoretical. Rifle tests involved firing, achieving a 2-inch (5cm) group at 25 yards (22.8m) as well as correct aiming and firing technique, including rapid fire. Machine gunners responded to orders, loaded weapons, aimed and worked the mechanisms – though calculation of 'indirect fire' was not required at this level. Sten gunners demonstrated correct handling and answered three of four questions correctly to pass. Signallers who operated telephones had to handle a set number of calls with 85 per cent accuracy in a given period. [12]

In battlecraft tests the candidates were asked questions on movement, cover, night movement and crossing obstacles. In the Cheshire Home Guard, it is also recorded that 'tactical and battlecraft tests' were run in the form of competitions, with platoons put through their paces in 'strange country' and with as

Home Guard instruction on the rifle discharger. The men are now equipped with capes, uniform, webbing and steel helmets. When using the discharger the rifle is held magazine upwards, and in the trench behind the firer are boxes of Mills bombs ready for use. (Author)

much realism as possible. In October 1943, a Chester subdistrict final was held, pitting the best platoons from five sectors against each other at Wrexham. Live ammunition and rifle grenades were used, with the enemy represented by figure targets, and incoming fire simulated by electrically initiated detonations. Additional verisimilitude was created by manoeuvring the competing platoons to their starting points independently and briefing them via a runner and their scouts as to the tactical situation to which they were expected to react. The number four platoon of 14th Tarporley emerged victorious. Chester sub-district also did similar work with weapons competitions that year, matching the leading rifle shots; Sten teams; rifle bombers and heavy weapons crews against each other. In these competitions, not only accuracy but also speed of bringing different weapons into action – and time getting rounds on target – were taken into account. Many similar activities took place in other counties.

By now, Home Guard manuals looked very much like those of the regular Army and contained information that was pretty much up to date technically and tactically, though often adapted to a previous generation of weapons. In accordance with the *Regulations for the Home Guard, 1942*, formal printed 'hours of attendance' registers were issued all the way down to section level and these created a formal record of time completed by each man on either training or operational duties. The books were supposed to be inspected monthly with the section commander signing them off.

So it was that as matters progressed, the Home Guard became less of a local defence against invasion and more a pool of semi-trained manpower, to replace regular troops in their own areas, or to provide an opposition during exercises. By 1942, conscripting men into the Home Guard had proved a cheap way to bolster home defence, without at the same time denuding war production too seriously. In May of that year, home anti-aircraft units were combed out to find a further 50,000 men for more active duties, whilst their places were progressively filled by Home Guards and the ATS. Compulsion to serve in the Home Guard was backed by force of law so that courts were enabled to impose up to a one-month prison sentence and a fine of £10. In practice these were rarely needed and different magistrates took different views of what penalties should be in specific cases. An unexpected bonus of compulsion was that the influx of new blood, much of it younger than existing manpower, gave opportunity for some of the old to retire more or less gracefully. The 1st County of London Home Guard shed seventeen men over sixty-six at this point, including two lords and a clergyman. Six were holders of a DSO, and one had a Military Cross. All zone, group and battalion commanders were now also compelled to retire at sixty-five. Something of a mark of pride for many Home Guard battalions was that as their professionalism increased, they were regarded as fit to provide ceremonial guards to visiting dignitaries. In the Birmingham instance, notables given Home Guard 'guards of honour' included Charles de Gaulle; King Haakon VII of Norway; British and US generals including Field Marshal Bernard Montgomery; the Duke of Gloucester; Viscount Robert Bridgeman; the Director General of the Home Guard; the Chinese Ambassador and Churchill himself. [13]

Two areas which had initially hamstrung the Home Guard's ability to become 'proper soldiers', transport and heavy weapons, were gradually eased with the passage of time. Many

Southern Railway Home Guard firing 75mm guns on the range at Lydd under instruction of Royal Artillery personnel, 1943. The 75mm 'QF' was another US import, being a 1916 model fitted with pneumatic tyres. Once loaded and aimed the gun is discharged by a pull on the lanyard. (Planet News Archive/SSPL/Getty Images)

Home Guards never did obtain modern vehicles, but mobile units were upgraded and reorganised, and most formations trained with regulars who had transport. The official authority for the formation of Home Guard motor coach and transport companies was granted in May 1941, and in quite a number of instances this was retrospective recognition of what local commanders had already achieved. In September 1942, Home Guard transport was improved by the institution of a measure allowing the designation of civilian vehicles for requisition. Some degree of standardisation was achieved by basing organisation on that of Royal Army Service Corps companies and platoons with a 90-ton lift capacity, and a requirement that transport units be able to operate anywhere in the UK. Eventually a total of 127 Home Guard Motor Transport Units were formed countrywide. As of February 1943, the transport units were numbered in a '2,000' series, allowing instant identification in an order of battle. The Eastern Command numbers ran from 2,000 to 2,029; London from 2,030 to 2,059; Northern from 2,060 to 2,089; Southeastern from 2,090 to 2,159; Southern from 2,130 to 2,159; Scottish from 2,160 to 2,199; and Western

from 2,200 to 2,249. Though theoretically they were all 'MT' or 'Motor Transport', some hung on to their traditional 'General Transport' or 'Motor Coach' titles. In January 1944, transport was organised into twenty-six 'Home Guard Transport Columns' with headquarters in each command area. Though a few of these were merged, shuffled, or disbanded in the coming months, it simplified the task of creating and commanding large columns for the lift of big formations. [14]

Permanent armament in a reasonably effective form was eventually achieved. A stock take at the beginning of 1943 showed that the Home Guard then possessed almost 19,000 Northover projectors and a similar number of Spigot mortars as well as 3,000 Smith guns and almost 900 flame-throwers. Most of this was short-range weaponry, initially improvised in a hurry, but cast-offs from the regulars provided a more serious backbone. About 100,000 Boys Anti-Tank rifles went to the Home Guard in 1943, as well as some 75mm hybrid anti-tank guns on old howitzer carriages. Some 18pdr field guns and 2pdr anti-tank guns were also taken on when these were no longer needed in

General Sir Frederick Pile inspects Home Guards manning a 40mm Bofors gun at a Southern Railways works. Later in the war Home Guards took over many anti-aircraft batteries, freeing up regular full-time troops for the front. The barrel is raised and traversed by the gunners on the cranks and could manage more than one round per second for short periods. (Fred Morley/Fox Photos/Getty Images)

Children watch a demonstration of the Northover projector. Imaginative, but of limited use on a modern battlefield, the Northover was an 'ambush weapon' throwing small incendiary bombs and grenades 200 yards (183m). By mid-1941 there were about 7,000 in the hands of the Home Guard, rising later to almost 19,000. (Official/Author)

the front line where better weapons were now beginning to arrive. Whilst most of this old artillery and anti-tank equipment would have been utterly useless on the Continent against a well-equipped enemy, it was adequate enough for ambushes mounted against light opposition on home territory.

If ground artillery remained sketchy, the same was not true of Home Guard anti-aircraft armament, and eventually the Home Guard produced over 140,000 men for AA duties, manning almost half the equipment in the UK. It provided twenty-eight Anti-Aircraft regiments, and more than 200 smaller Light Anti-Aircraft Troops. Though the Light Troops were originally mainly equipped with machine guns like the Lewis, these were gradually supplanted by 20mm and 40mm guns. These were clustered around vulnerable targets, as for example Cardiff, Newport and Port Talbot docks, Royal Ordnance Factory installations, aircraft factories like A.V. Roe, Bristol, and de Havilland, steel and chemical works, oil and rail facilities. As well as manning ordinary anti-aircraft artillery, Home Guards also gained anti-aircraft rocket batteries known as 'Z batteries'. These were first brought into service with the Royal Artillery in 1941. Originally twin mountings, there were later versions that fired four, nine and even twenty rocket projectiles. By March 1944, there were ninety-three rocket batteries in service. Since anti-aircraft weapons had to be manned for long periods and sometimes all night, guns and rockets were given several crews who turned out as reliefs for different nights in a rota. [15]

Many of the anti-aircraft Home Guards played a role in actual combat, particularly where they lay in the path of important bombing targets. In the case of Kent, for example, the Home

Guard provided two whole battalions (Nos. 101 and 102) for anti-aircraft duties. Each provided a rocket battery, which may not sound like very much until one considers that by the end of 1942 the strength of a single battery was 1,444 all ranks equipped with sixty-four rocket projectors. As of 1944, these batteries became the 5th Home Guard Anti-Aircraft Regiment. Additionally part of the 30th Sheppey Battalion was affiliated to the Royal Artillery manning coastal defence guns, whilst the 14th Hoo Battalion incorporated the light anti-aircraft guns protecting the important oil storage facilities nearby. In 1943, the 28th and 33rd Kent battalions also formed light anti-aircraft Troops armed with 20mm Hispano guns to defend the Southern Railway works at Ashford, and Rochester airport.

The picture regarding small arms and machine weapons was also much improved. Persistent rifle shortages were effectively ended when massive Sten gun production allowed these to be issued to the Home Guard in numbers, giving the force a fairly high proportion of submachine guns. Many new Stens also went as secondary arms to artillery crews. By the beginning of 1943, the inventory included 900,000 rifles; 248,000 Sten guns and 13,000 Thompsons; 26,000 Browning Automatic Rifles; 20,000 assorted machine guns of Lewis, Vickers and Browning types plus 30,000 shotguns. Weaponry of all types was made all the more viable by an increasing availability of ammunition over time. For example, in the case of Kent, by September 1942 each medium machine gun had a stock of 10,000 rounds, every light machine gun 4,000 rounds, and, depending on the exact model, each rifle between 200 and 2,000 rounds. Spigot mortars had from twenty to thirty bombs, and each platoon had a stock of forty-eight Mills grenades of the same type used by the regulars. This last must have been welcome since no less than eighteen varieties, including seven drill and instructional types, had been in circulation. As of late 1942, a quarter of a million Home Guards had fired three million rounds of ammunition on the ranges at Bisley alone.

Since as early as the summer of 1940, a vocal group of women had agitated for female inclusion in first the LDV, then the Home Guard. One of these women was Marjorie Foster, who had won the King's Prize on the shooting range at Bisley in 1930, and in fact a number of small female groups did form themselves into so called 'Amazons' at an early stage. This intrigued and excited the popular press more than having any practical impact, but in December 1941 Labour MP Dr Edith Summerskill went a step further – founding an organisation she called the 'Women's Home Defence', uniformed in converted brown service overalls and with its own badge. In 1942, the 'WHD' played their part as scouts and signallers in a London battle exercise, and in many Home Guard units female assistants were actually accepted, where they mainly adopted ancillary roles, but were as yet not formally recognised outside their own unit.

Officialdom was extremely slow to accept such notions, and never did endorse an actual fighting role for women. However, eventually the government was forced to admit that they existed, and to include them within official statistics. Thus it was that the employment of 'Nominated Women' was sanctioned by an announcement in the House of Commons on 20 April 1943. These helpers were to be aged between eighteen and sixty-five and to perform such non-combat tasks as cooking, driving and clerical work. The original ungainly title was changed to the slightly more catchy-sounding 'Home Guard Auxiliary' in the summer of 1944. Auxiliaries lacked uniform, at least officially, but did wear a special brooch-style badge on their civilian clothing. A certificate issued to each woman stated that she was 'authorised to follow the Armed Forces of the Crown', was of equivalent status to a private soldier, and entitled to be treated as a prisoner of war in the event of capture. On the subject of minorities, it is similarly interesting to note that Graves' history of 1943 was keen to point out that outside Britain twelve colonies had formed their own Home Guards 'irrespective of colour', and that the Home Guard in the UK operated 'no colour bar; though of course the number of coloured men available for Home Guard duties was very small'. [16]

Every Home Guard unit had its own unique character, but as the force went through common stages of development at approximately the same point in time, it is worth giving the complete history of at least one, as example of the many. The 4th Guildford Battalion of the Surrey Home Guard was raised by Colonel G.W. Geddes, with its first 300 volunteers reporting at the police headquarters on 18 May 1940. The battalion territory was Guildford, having a 25-mile (40km) circumference divided into twelve platoon areas, and these soon swelled to a hundred men each. The platoon commanders were 'selected' from a police-approved list. Work started, as its commander remembered, 'from zero' – there being at that time no outside help, no arms, equipment or uniforms. Given the lack of suitable accommodation, many platoons had to be based in private houses, but Surrey County Council soon provided Henley Fort for use as a headquarters, and the Borough Police allowed its North Street headquarters to be used as an arsenal.

A manual for the US-made .300 Lewis gun. This model was at first issued without a support and was rested on cover when firing. The American .300 calibre became something of a Home Guard standard so guns taking this ammunition were marked with a red band to remind troops not to attempt to load the British .303 inch. (Author)

The military experience of the first officers was extensive, and the eleven platoon commanders mentioned in the published 'first list of officers' included a number already identified by previous officer ranks. Company organisation was adopted in early July, and was achieved partly by platoon commanders being promoted to company command, and section commanders to platoon command. The four company commanders now included a retired Territorial colonel with a Military Cross, a lieutenant colonel with a DSO, and Captain C.H. Frisby, who held the Victoria Cross. The four second in commands of companies included at least two more very experienced officers, one of whom was Captain E.H. Shepard, decorated war veteran and illustrator of Winnie the Pooh. Colonel A.D. Geddes himself held a DSO and was supported in his headquarters at Borough Hall by two other experienced officers.

Just one day after the first enrolments, 150 Canadian Ross rifles were issued together with twenty rounds each, and these were supplemented with privately owned shotguns. That same evening, 19 May 1940, saw the holding of the first 'battalion conference', as a result of which areas of platoon responsibility were allotted. The first and only directive issued that night was to defend these areas. Railway lines, major roads and reservoirs were identified as particularly important tactical points. It being realised that there were neither resources nor time for regular Army training, at the outset the battalion was expected to immediately model itself on other 'citizen forces' such as the Boers, 'tribesmen of the North West Frontier', or partisans. A motto of the 'Four Is' was adopted, being 'Invisibility, Inaudibility, Individuality and Initiative': teaching would focus on the rifle, fieldcraft and camouflage. Following the first 'conference', a regular Monday night officer's conference was instituted that would run every week for the next four-and-a-half years. 'LDV' armlets were issued on 14 June, and denim uniform and field service caps followed on 6 July.

Guildford also housed the initial training centre of the Queen's Regiment, and to this fell the official duty of the defence of

Guildford town, which the LDV now supported by defending road blocks on the approaches and covering and observing roads. As of the beginning of June, the LDV also mounted guards on the various waterworks, and a month later a standard company 'piquet' was fixed at thirty men, and these stood to guard duty nightly from sunset to sunrise until the end of 1942. Traffic control duties, patrols and exercises were all added progressively during the summer. By the end of July 1940, the Ross rifles had been exchanged for P14 Enfields, and the battalion consisted of 850 uniformed men with 450 firearms of which 90 per cent were reasonably up to date military rifles. In August, weaponry was improved again with the substitution of 700 American P17 rifles with forty rounds each for the existing personal arms, and the introduction of twelve Browning Automatic Rifles. The Home Guards also purchased 10,000 rounds of ammunition privately, and used this to practise on the ranges at Bisley. By October the battalion had swollen again to 1,800 and, with the approach of winter, greatcoats were added to the uniform. [17]

By 1941 Geddes was describing his command as 'highly efficient', carrying out exercises of up to eighteen hours' duration. On the second day of the new year, the battalion got not only a permanent staff instructor in the shape of Company Sergeant Major Flower of the East Surreys, but the first serge battledress, steel helmets, haversacks, and another issue of greatcoats. In February came service-type respirators to replace the civilian ones already in use, and six medium machine guns, two Vickers and four Brownings. By March everybody had the serge battledress and the denims were returned to store, and Northover projectors were issued as stopgap anti-tank weapons. In April came twelve Thompson submachine guns, though the battalion was not allowed to retain these permanently.

In the summer, the very large battalion was reorganised into six 'general duty' companies, and one 'factory guard' company. An extensive weapons training course at Bisley saw 92 per cent of the battalion shoot on the ranges, and now the Home Guard was ready to take on a new level of responsibility. In mid-August, the Queen's Royal Regiment moved out of Guildford, and the defence of the town was left to Geddes and his battalion. Soon afterwards the men were preparing the perimeter of this 'Nodal Point' with new anti-tank ditches, wire and other works, and the area was divided into five smaller company areas with 'E' Company held back as general reserve. Apart from weekday and evening parades, two Sundays per month were devoted to exercises, one of the main points of which was to

Merseyside Home Guards manning a 'Z' rocket battery. The 3-inch (7.5cm) rockets were designed in the late 1930s: characteristically Churchill demanded 'large supplies' of rocket projectors for home defence in 1940. They were not very accurate and best fired in salvos. (Official/author)

The 29mm Spigot Mortar in an emplacement mounted on a concrete pillar. The mortar's 20lb (9kg) high explosive bomb wreacked considerable havoc, but was short range and best placed to cover roads. Supplied from 1941 the 'Blacker Bombard' Spigot Mortar was used in large numbers by the Home Guard with an official scale of two per company. (Author)

test communications and the ability of the battalion to turn out to 'action stations': it was determined that most of the battalion would be in place within two hours of an alarm.[18]

Similar activity continued into 1942, and an issue of Spigot mortars began in March with twenty-four eventually available. Teams were trained and carefully sited emplacements were constructed for the static defence of the 'nodal point'. As the spring wore on, training focused on street fighting, and the stock of automatic weapons was gradually built up so that eventually the battalion had sixteen Vickers and two Browning machine guns. These – together with the Smith guns issued later – were worked into the defensive fire plan, and further emplacements were prepared. Sten machine carbines began to arrive a few months later. May heralded the beginning of a new wave of exercises, in which the Home Guard worked with the ATS and a young soldier battalion of the East Surreys. In one large exercise, 93 per cent of the battalion participated, giving a good showing against the young soldiers, Geddes taking pride in the fact that his men showed 'a considerable knowledge of

unarmed combat'. In June the Home Guard worked with the machine-gun battalion of the Toronto Scottish, who played the part of enemy parachutists in a new exercise scenario. Training included 'battle inoculation' with live firing from the machine guns. Troops were also worked from 'Tactical Camps of Training' where 'the men lived hard'.

Arguably the Guildford Battalion reached its peak in late 1942 and 1943. The compulsory 'direction' of men into the Home Guard, and the formation of a 'Transport Section' using the vehicles of local tradesmen, gave some tactical mobility at the same time as pushing numbers first to 2,700, and in 1943 to a remarkable 3,200 men. Conscription and the increasing unlikelihood of invasion did not as yet greatly dull participation, with well over 80 per cent taking part in the biggest exercise. The unit was by now well-enough trained and armed to find many of its own instructors, and individual proficiency tests were mounted. Nissen storage huts were built at Lea Pale Lane barracks and teams were trained in rescue work. A ceremonial parade marking the anniversary of the foundation of the Home

Guard was followed by an anti-tank demonstration. In one of many exercises, 'E' Company furnished a thirty-four-man party to represent a German parachute raid on Chilworth Station. Exercise 'Dash' was a great success for the Guildford men, who 'destroyed' the bridge, sidings and signal box before the opposition could react. Instruction courses and range firing were executed on a plethora of weapons including Sten guns, Spigot mortars and Smith guns. At some point, half a dozen Boys Anti-Tank rifles were also acquired. By now, the battalion also had its own 'bombing range' on which Mills bombs were thrown, and there was short-range practice with small arms.

Orders of battle from 1943 show the Guildford Home Guard organised on a company sector basis to cover the 'Guildford Nodal Point' with five companies lettered 'A', 'B', 'C', 'D' and 'F' in established positions. The 'E' Company was held as a 'general reserve', and 'G' Company was the 'Factory Unit' for Dennis Brothers Ltd and the Borough Electricity facilities. Within each company sector were located from half a dozen to a dozen numbered 'garrison' localities. As a general rule, and unless redeployed as part of an exercise or to cover other duties, many of the personal and heavy weapons were allotted to each of these localities. More mobile 'Battle Sections' backed up the web of defence created by the heavy weapons. For example, in 'A' Company there were eight garrison localities with strengths varying from ten to thirty-two men. Machine guns, Smith guns and Spigot mortars were allotted according to tactical need rather than evenly distributed, so that locality '6' had thirty-two men but only one machine gun and one Spigot mortar, while locality '7' had a garrison of twenty but boasted a total of four heavy weapons. Of the company strength, sixty men were held

back in 'Battle Sections' and seventy-two in two reserves, one each at the football ground and Stoke Mansion. The effective strength of these deployments was calculated as being the total 'paper strength' minus a notional 20 per cent, presumably because civilians — having other jobs, needs to travel, and being just as prone to sickness as anybody else — might not gain their posts quickly enough to be counted. Almost inevitably there would also be at least a few novices who had just joined and might lack training or equipment. 'A' Company was thus over 340 strong on the enrolment books, but allowed for 288 effectives in planning.

In 1944, the battalion carried out many 'action stations' drills in which defensive positions were manned as quickly as possible. In April, during a special exercise, the battalion was called out without notice. In June they demonstrated various skills at the 'miniature Aldershot Tattoo' on Shelford Flats. These included bringing machine guns into action at speed, rescue drills, and using live shells from the Smith guns against dummy tanks moved by a system of rails and pulleys. In what was arguably the highlight, a mock battle saw one body 'disguised in the uniform of German airborne troops' attack a perimeter held by their comrades. The 'Germans' did well until a counterattack by 'battle sections' drove them off. In a more serious vein, the Guildford Battalion exercised with US paratroops, and mounted guards at the Chalk and Sand tunnels, relieving regular troops for other duties. The defences laid out included a 'large and ambitious' wiring scheme erected under the direction of Major Cyril Frisby VC. Less successful was Major Bevan, who injured himself with a booby trap a few days later, but soon recovered. The battalion's final parade was on 3 December 1944: the

Scottish Home Guards on patrol along Loch Stack, February 1941. The weaponry includes a Vickers machine gun, two P17 rifles, and something which may be a sporting rifle or shot gun in a carrying slip. Sparsely populated areas and vast coastlines had to be watched by somebody, and using Home Guards with local knowledge saved the use of full-time soldiers. (Lt WT Lockeyear/IWM via Getty Images)

number of men inspected was 1,200, after which arms and equipment were handed in. At official disbandment at the end of the month, total strength was calculated as 1,887. However, paperwork continued well into the new year, when it was noted that the battalion had put in 308 days service since its formation, of which seventy-eight were 'operational' in the sense of piquet duties and patrols, and a further fifteen on static guard duty.

One facet of the Home Guard that is frequently overlooked is that although it sprang from impromptu local defence, and later became an important auxiliary army, it also served as cover to another force within. Interestingly the possibility that the UK might one day be invaded had been considered as early as 1938. What could be done to counter the enemy in occupied areas became subject of study for Military Intelligence Section D and the War Office department known as General Staff Research. Models considered included the IRA, Boer farmers, Chinese and Spanish irregulars, and civil war fighters and their weapons and tactics. Major Colin Gubbins produced some brief manuals of partisan and guerrilla fighting. Some early work was put in on shaped charges and sticky bombs, and contacts were made with certain sympathetic civilians who had skills likely to be of use to a possible future resistance force. In the first few months of the war, Section D began the task of creating secret caches of stores, based on the premise that 'stay behind' parties of troops might be able to continue the fight behind enemy lines. In the summer of 1940, the idea was revisited as a matter of urgency, with Churchill in particular keen to promote the idea of a 'British

Resistance'. As a Cabinet paper of 2 July put it, 'The regular defences require supplementing with guerilla type troops, who will allow themselves to be overrun and who thereafter will be responsible for hitting the enemy in the comparatively soft spots behind zones of concentrated attack.' [19]

Colin Gubbins, now a colonel, had founded the 'Independent Companies' intended to operate as guerrilla forces in Norway, but following the debacle there, now returned to the UK and was appointed to raise the undercover force. Work started on the southeast coast, this being identified as at most immediate risk of invasion. He began by recruiting Army officers to act on his behalf in different localities. The primary task of these was to find about thirty reliable men, who would each supervise a dump of munitions and supplies and create local cells of half a dozen men. Gubbins' deputies included a remarkable range of characters, but for Kent – likely to be in the eye of any invasion storm – the organiser was Guards officer Captain Peter Fleming, brother of Ian, and later one of the most probable models for the character James Bond. Kent would be taken as something of a model for development, with for example, the commanders of East Anglia and Devon and Cornwall coming to Fleming to study his methods for use elsewhere.

General Andrew Thorne, whose XII Corps' area of responsibility extended from the Thames to Hampshire, had already suggested that this vital sector required a 'stay behind'

force for emergencies, and so it was that Fleming formed one of the most important resistance organisations with the active co-operation of the local command. Fleming's resisters existed under the double cover of 'XII Corps Observation Unit', with most of its members unaware that there were like bodies forming elsewhere. Indeed, this ignorance was a general characteristic of the Auxiliaries so that the cell structure meant that outside his own cell the resistance operative was unlikely to be aware of other cells or members. Communication was usually by various blind or 'dead letter boxes', and it was hoped that, in the event of discovery, compromise might thereby be limited to a single cell at a time.

Recruitment to the secret ranks had to be done discreetly, quickly, and as far as possible from men with good knowledge of a specific local area who were likely to prove reliable. The shortcut was to go directly through the Army corps and divisions to the Home Guard, using a blanket authority to choose whoever was wanted from those that were willing to take part. The resistance men came from every profession and walk of life, and were aged from their teens to those in their seventies. They ranged from vicars to publicans and shopkeepers: yet some classes were more favoured than others. Particular value was found in poachers and gamekeepers, fishermen, hunters and miners – men who might already be adept at camouflage, stalking, explosives, shooting, digging and other relevant skills. Some additional bodies were picked up through the early contacts made by Section D. Initially no women were recruited, at least in part because there were none as yet in the Home Guard. Personnel were further vetted by means of a police check, though the constabulary were not informed why a man's background required investigation. For the most part, the recruits already had Home Guard uniform and a valid story to tell families and friends about any suspicious night-time absences

and weaponry. They were now also given the cover of the most anodyne unit designation that could be imagined. So it was that they became 'Auxiliary Units' of the Home Guard with the camouflage titles 201 (Scotland), 202 (Northern England) and 203 (Southern England) battalions.[20]

However, none of this would have given them any protection under the Geneva Convention as it was probable that they would operate behind enemy lines, often in civilian attire, and methods of engagement would include planting bombs, intelligence gathering, execution of prominent collaborators and general acts of sabotage. Moreover, the limited amount of paperwork that existed was kept out of the mainstream Home Guard and official registers, and the resistance was entirely deniable in the event of any unfortunate incidents. Until an area was overrun, it was expected that the Auxiliary men would continue their daily lives as usual, including any voluntary duty with ARP and the like, but it was expected that the majority would simply disappear with the arrival of the enemy. They would probably be assumed lost in battle or to have fled from the region, and no attempt would be made to contact families for reasons of security and the safety of loved ones. Initial expectation was that the resisters would not remain undercover very long, but would emerge fairly quickly to attack enemy lines of communication in concert with counterattacks by the regular forces. Later, with the examples of Europe in mind, this general vision was revised and updated perhaps to include some very long periods undercover, or men in 'sleeper' occupations who would in effect become part-time freedom fighters – doubtless what the Germans would have called 'terrorists'.

Eventually the dumps became very significant stockpiles of explosives and ammunition. One of them, looked after by a Mr Reginald Sennitt in the Essex marshes, remained undisturbed at the end of the war until finally announced and handed in by its caretaker in 1964. It then comprised 1,205lb (547kg) of gelignite; almost 15,000 rounds of small arms ammunition; about 4,000 time pencils, delay switches and detonators; almost 500 assorted thunder flashes, grenades and smoke bombs; and a collection of various booby trapping devices and fuses. By way of yardstick, it is worth noting that most grenades contain barely 2 ounces (50g) of explosive, and that a car can be completely destroyed, with damage to the surrounding area, by 2lb (900g). It is also worth noting that some of the newest devices, including plastic explosives, found their way quickly to the Auxiliaries. Patrols were eventually armed with not only ordinary military

Elderly Home Guards existed but were only part of the force. There were also recently retired Army officers and other ranks, men in reserved occupations, and many patriotic youngsters. Notable Home Guards included George Formby; C.S. Lewis; Tony Benn; Patrick Moore; John Laurie; George Orwell and Jimmy Perry. (Popperfoto/Getty Images)

small arms, but also a range of special weapons. These included a lightweight .22 sound-moderated sniping rifle, Commando daggers, rubber coshes, the PIAT, and different sorts of mine.

The basic hideout of the Auxiliary patrol was the 'Operational Base', in reality almost always a proactive euphemism for a well-concealed hole in the ground in which, during times of emergency, a patrol of half a dozen men might have to exist for an extended period. When the invasion warning 'Cromwell' was sent in September 1940, the Scottish units did actually go to ground. Many of them remained hidden for five days. Never the less, some hides were constructed with an active defence in mind, incorporating loops, booby traps or outlying early warning posts, and others had observation points. Many relied simply on being located far from habitation, difficult to find and well camouflaged. Sketches of the post at Charing in Kent show an underground box, entered down a ladder through what appeared to be a sheep trough on top. Rabbit holes into the contour of the hill were converted into spy holes. The hide at Challock near Faversham was an enlarged badger sett, another at Evington was in the cellars of a manor house long since destroyed by fire. Some hideouts were simple holes with log roofs, or tunnels into rock: but others were well planned, even brick-lined, with two or more exits giving the occupants different avenues of escape. At Lydden the base was hidden

under a brick works, and could be entered through a machinery house or a concealed entrance at the bottom of a clay pit. Many of the entrances were variations on a trap door, enhanced by counterweights and concealed catches, often hidden in woods or under vegetation. On coasts, caves were occupied, and in Wales some of the bases were in mines. Ruined Scottish castles hid more than one lair. The best bases were prepared using the Royal Engineers or civilian labour, though it was wise to use personnel from a different area and send them away again with no hint of what it was they had worked upon.

The secret HQ of the 'Aux units' was Coleshill House near Swindon. Naturally those visiting or attending training courses were not simply given the address but were told to report to Highworth Post Office and observed. If nothing was found to be amiss then a car would be sent to collect them. Whilst operational units did most of their training in their own localities, special equipment like plastic explosives or different time pencils were often first demonstrated at Coleshill, or other regional centres such as Melville House in Fife. Larger exhibitions were also mounted in which, for example, anti-tank methods were shown. For at least some of the period of its existence, Coleshill had a small staff of demonstrators drawn from the Lovat Scouts and others picked for their fieldcraft skills. Unarmed combat sessions were also arranged by the Army Physical Training Corps.

Churchill displays satisfaction at an enthusiastic, if dangerous, simulation of a road ambush using Molotov cocktails. If Winston had any doubts about Auxiliary Forces and primitive methods he never showed them, and maximum capital was made of mass engagement and solidarity in adversity. (Official/ author)

As of 1941, the Auxiliary Units were well armed, organised, and present in numbers over much of the country. By this date, Gubbins had gone on to the challenge of SOE – the 'Special Operations Executive' – and the Auxiliaries were now commanded by Brigadier W. Major, though few in the organisation would have known this. The organisation was in four regions divided into a little over twenty areas. Each region had several officers, and each area its own intelligence officer ranking as a Home Guard captain. Under Major's leadership, the system was for several patrols to be under one leader who ranked as a Home Guard sergeant, up the chain of command group leaders ranked as captains.

Some areas were huge with very few operatives, as for example that covering the Hebrides, most of the north of Scotland, and Aberdeenshire, making do with twenty-six patrols of 138 men; or the North Riding of Yorkshire, Northumberland and Durham, counting just fifteen patrols totalling sixty-six personnel. Other areas, particularly the coasts and some other parts of the south of England, were much smaller with more concentrated presence. Kent boasted no less than thirty-three patrols with 208 men, Suffolk twenty-eight patrols and 180 men. Hampshire and Somerset had the greatest number of trained resistance men with forty-seven patrols and 301 men, and forty-four patrols and 287 men, respectively. Secret area headquarters were essentially accommodation addresses, mainly in private homes, and none of them within military bases. Amongst them were the local post office, a few country manors, and some inconspicuous addresses in villages and towns such as '68 Monmouth Street Bridgewater'. Total strength of the organisation was a little over 3,500, and the vast majority of the 576 patrols already had its own hideout, while more hideouts and patrols were in the process of formation.

As of late 1942, female signallers – recruited and trained by the Royal Corps of Signals – were added to the Auxiliary organisation. Many were already members of the ATS, and now formed what was known as the 'Special Duties Section'. Together with male operatives, they worked from stations completely separate from the hides and gathered intelligence using a range of operatives including health workers, bus drivers, farmers, and indeed anybody who might be able to move around without suspicion. The basic resistance radio was short-range and contained in a box 15 inches (38cm) long, tiny by the technological standards of the day. They were assembled in secret from parts by signallers at Coleshill, with the result that few people would have been able to identify them. Commonly signallers had more than one set of equipment, and operated from huts or elsewhere above ground: the spare set was hidden in reserve, perhaps in an underground 'Zero' station. Information was sent using a system in which the most used phrases were replaced by a single word, and the entire message was itself encoded relatively simply, but using a key that changed every day. The enemy might thus be able to break the system, but not every day and not quickly enough. Whilst the work of 'Special Duties' personnel directly aided the men of the operational teams, they were not usually told anything about field units or the identities of individuals, thus reducing the risk of compromise.

In their daily work, 'Auxiliary Units' obviously used very little paperwork that would be vulnerable to falling into enemy hands, but they did have a limited amount of training literature

A typical Home Guard Platoon. Weaponry includes a Browning machine gun, three Browning Automatic rifles and US Enfield rifles. Long service good-conduct stripes and First World War medal ribbons are worn by the older men. A civilian nurse and chaplain are included. (Author)

for ready reference, disguised as other things. A doctored *1937 Calendar*, probably actually produced in 1940, concealed sabotage notes, and a new version, disguised as a *1938 Calendar*, expanded the original document with updates and specific designs for booby traps. However, the most complete manual was the forty-two page *Countryman's Diary 1939*, probably issued in late 1942 or 1943. This omitted some obsolete advice, as for example on the old 'Sticky Bomb', but did include new material on smoke grenades and incendiaries including the 'Fire Pot' and 'Pocket Time Incendiary'. Regarding improvised mines, it was recommended that a highly effective type could be fabricated from an old motorcycle engine cylinder, these being tough but breaking into lethal splinters on detonation. The *Countryman's Diary* had a humorous touch in that it was endorsed as with the compliments of 'Highworth and Company', a producer of fertiliser that did its stuff unseen – 'until you see the results'. [21]

By early 1944, it was very unlikely that a British resistance would be required in its original form. Its scope was reduced by amalgamating various groups. The 'Special Duties' personnel were stood down and the ATS returned to other work. Arguably the last real use of the Auxiliary Units was at the time of D-Day when parts of the network were alerted to possible retaliatory action by the enemy on British soil, and thought was given to turning the poachers into gamekeepers, tracking down enemy parachutists or infiltrating forces. Many of the secret facilities were shut down and others blown up. It was also during the course of 1944 that some of the most enthusiastic of the

resistance army left the Auxiliaries to seek more active roles, with at least a few joining the SAS in Europe, or supporting SOE. Auxiliary intelligence officer G.R. McNicholl found a specific niche when he was employed to help hunt out 'Werewolves', Germans whose job it was to continue resistance after the Allied invasion of the Reich. Once it had ceased to exist, the resistance army also ceased to be secret, and in April 1945 *The Times* published an article that simultaneously announced both its foundation and demise.

The Home Guard lasted a little longer than most of the 'Aux' units, but by the summer of 1944 the Allies were in Europe. That winter, the British and US armies entered Germany and the Russians were well on their way through Poland to Berlin. Over the months of the Allied advance, Home Guard morale followed an inverse path as men increasingly perceived themselves as wasting time and energy under a now rather pointless regime of compulsion. Evidence is as yet patchy and often anecdotal, but it would seem that many began to put in a minimum of time rather than responding with the genuine enthusiasm of 1940. The No. 2 'Battle Squad' of 9 Platoon, C Company, 12th Middlesex may not have been typical, but it was one good example of how many such units may have operated in the summer and autumn of 1944. Of its thirteen men, there was a sergeant in charge supported by two lance corporals, and ten privates. Sergeant Hingerton was a generally good attendance role model, yet between the last week of July and the first week of September there were a couple of short periods when he performed no Home Guard duty whatsoever – indeed nobody at all turned up on either 6 or 13 August. On 15 August, Hingerton attended duty alone, declaring himself 'operational' for nine hours. Lance Corporal Marsh made only two brief appearances in the five weeks in question, putting in a grand total of four-and-a-half hours. Privates Sandler, Fountain and Mowbray were absent for the entire period, though the register does not explain why. Private Spiro managed a total of three hours, and whilst Private Chidgey did turn up for one full day, he missed every other parade for more than a month. In some ways the lack of activity was surprising, as by this time the London area was under attack from V1 'Doodlebugs'. However, something important must have happened on 4 September, as five members of the section did a full day of operational duty: but whatever it was, Sergeant Hingerton and Lance Corporal Newman were attended by only three of their comrades.

Manufacturing and replacements for the front line, as well as preparing for final efforts against Japan, were now the priorities. Indeed, as early as the end of 1942, the War Office had found it necessary to point out that 'Home Guard duty is carried out in a man's spare time', and that where men were engaged in war work, spare-time activity should not impinge on his efficiency to do that work. Conversely it reminded employers that the Home Guard was there very much to protect them and their livelihoods, and should be supported accordingly:

> 'As a rule, any difficulties which arise can be settled between Home Guard commanders and the management, calling in the regional representative of the supply department concerned if necessary. But if the difficulty cannot be settled in this way, it may be referred to the factory liaison officer. The War Office has appointed one of these in each military command, and it will be their duty to give advice and assistance in such matter. They will maintain close touch with the regional boards.'

By the latter part of 1944, to keep such a large part-time Army under arms in Britain now appeared more of a luxury than it was worth. So it was that the government prepared a message, personally overseen and corrected by Churchill, to be put out by the King on 14 November. In this, the Home Guard were thanked for their services, and told that their 'long tour of duty under arms' was coming to an end. On 3 December, the King broadcast another message of similar sentiment and in various parts of the country final parades were mounted to mark the 'stand down'. In the biggest of these events, 7,000 Home Guards drawn from all over the country marched through the West End of London to be formally reviewed. Despite putting away its weapons, the force continued to exist for a few weeks longer until its disbandment on New Year's Eve.[22]

Given that the Home Guard never faced the ultimate test of invasion, it is extremely difficult to say how effective it was as a fighting force. However, it is very clear that its viability passed through stages, starting from the position of a mere propagandistic statement of intent, going right through to become what would have been a very serious military headache for any enemy. Unless very small, it is dubious that the Home Guard could have stopped a serious German ground incursion entirely by itself: but that was never the point. The force was 'Auxiliary' to the Army, and tactically it was to locate, report, disorientate and slow the enemy advance. Quite possibly they would have suffered a terrible price in doing so, especially if an invasion had come before the issue of uniforms, which would have made legal the mass shooting of them as *francs-tireurs* – a fate that the German government promised in May 1940. Eighteen months later and things were very different. The enemy was weaker, the RAF and Navy stronger, and the Home Guard had 1.5 million men with at least basic arms and ammunition and a tolerable level of training. It was certainly a backstop that would have severely depleted and harassed any seaborne invasion, and would probably have only had to face a modest enemy force given that much could have been stopped by other means.

The German *Volkssturm*, formed as a 'people's militia' just as the decision to stand down the Home Guard was being made,

makes an interesting comparison. Under invasion of home territory it did fight, sometimes desperately, particularly against the Soviets. It inflicted and took casualties. Though it had some good close-range anti-tank weapons, its small arms and uniforms were arguably inferior to those of the Home Guard. The human material in its ranks was also arguably poorer, since by late 1944 a great proportion of young, fit, committed German males had

already been enlisted or killed. When unsupported by any regular force, or caught entirely without weapons and ammunition, the tendency of the *Volkssturm* was to melt away. It would therefore appear reasonable to suggest that the performance of the Home Guard would have been at least as good in late 1940, and probably rather better in subsequent years.

The history of the Cheshire force refers to the Home Guard as 'the cheapest and most surprising army in the world'. That it was genuinely inexpensive in relation to its size is difficult to contradict: its total monetary cost has been reckoned at less than one million pounds per month, and whilst there were some expenses, its recruits were not paid. Moreover, whilst men were uniformed, many of the weapons were recycled or handed down from the full-time Army. The 5th Berkshire Battalion was proud enough of its cost effectiveness to publish a sample account. Its average annual cost, not counting the stores, uniform and

equipment, was £10,206 3s 4d. Of this, about a third went on subsistence allowances, and a little less to the pay of storemen and clerks. After this, the next largest costs were transport; building hire; postage, stationery and telephones; minor works and repairs; and heating, lighting and cleaning. Some measure of just how much marching and training actually went on can be gleaned from the fact that boot repairs ran at just over £73 per annum. For this relatively modest sum, 5th Berkshire put under arms 1,850 men in the Wantage area. Apart from its physical capabilities, great size and slight cost, one has to acknowledge that the Home Guard was also important as an expression of national will, a confirmation from the darkest hour that many, maybe most, Britons were ready and willing to continue the fight. In this it was a masterstroke and very much the important ally of Churchill's vision for final victory. [23]

It should also not be forgotten that sometimes the Home Guard did actually fight, and took casualties, albeit mainly in combat with the *Luftwaffe* or the aftermath of their attacks. Deaths on duty due to all causes eventually numbered 1,206, though some of these were natural or accidental, and included those killed in bomb disposal and training. Some units under the Blitz faced death on a regular basis. The 33rd Surrey (County Borough of Croydon) Battalion won one George Cross – awarded to Captain R.T. Harris for bomb disposal work – as well as four George Medals and three British Empire Medals. Two of its men had died due to enemy action before 1943 was out. At Coventry, on the fateful night of 14 November 1940, most of the Home Guard turned out, many of them without orders to do so, in support of the Civil Defence. They dug survivors from the rubble, ran a despatch rider service, dealt with bodies and repaired damage. By

1943, Coventry Zone Home Guard had nine dead as a direct result of enemy action, and a George Medal.

Statistical evidence on Home Guard losses appears very incomplete. Never the less, some formations kept, and later published, detailed rolls recording the reasons for which men left the ranks. In the 31st Warwickshire battalion, for example, 266 men passed out of the ranks before the official 'stand down' of their comrades. Of these, 132 were 'discharged on medical grounds', and six were discharged on attaining the age limit, but no fewer than ninety-nine of the younger men left 'on joining His Majesty's Forces'. Of those that actually died, twenty-four passed away of natural causes, four were 'killed by enemy action' and just one was 'killed whilst on Home Guard Duty'. In the sister 32nd Warwickshire, the general picture was similar, with nineteen natural deaths, two 'killed by enemy action' and again just one 'killed whilst on Home Guard Duty'. Very probably, if it ever is possible to provide a national picture, there will be close correlation found between amounts of bombing and the number of Home Guard casualties in a given area. Interestingly it has been suggested that when one takes into account natural mortality and the fact that a Home Guard was only usually 'on duty' for a few hours a week and 'operational' even less often, his proportionate chance of death was actually similar to that of a regular.[24]

Auxiliary Territorial and Other Female Services [25]

The various women's military services of the First World War were formally wound up and disembodied by the end of 1921. Never the less, several active voluntary associations remained and some women's organisations did come out to assist the government during the General Strike of 1926. The First Aid Nursing Yeomanry in particular now allied itself to the Royal Army Service Corps. The 'FANY' would remain a particularly influential lobby as it drew on the educated middle and upper echelons of society, and encouraged its members to learn the new skills of communications, driving and mechanics. With the increasing threat of war, from 1934 onwards a campaign grew to restore and formalise female military service, pushed forwards by such luminaries as Lady Londonderry and Dame Helen Gwynne-Vaughan, veteran of the Women's Auxiliary Corps in

the First World War. Various options were now considered, but as late as 1937 the Cabinet considered women would not be required as part of the Army, but only recruited as needed, like civilians, through the Ministry of Labour.

However, the threat of conflict was soon so serious that the government finally relented to the extent that it was proposed that the voluntary groups be united within the framework of the Territorial Army. On 9 September 1938, the 'Auxiliary Territorial Service' was finally brought into existence by a Royal Warrant declaring that it was now deemed 'expedient' for women to be recruited to perform 'certain non-combatant duties' with the 'military and air forces'. To provide a cadre of female officers, women were drawn from the existing voluntary services and passed through a selection process at the Duke of York's Headquarters, Chelsea. More women were soon raised to fill the ranks, but in relatively modest numbers, with an early ceiling being set at 17,000. Women were officially accepted in the age range of seventeen to forty-three, though in the case of veterans of the Women's Auxiliary Army Corps of the First World War, they were accepted up to fifty. Some of the new companies formed were dedicated to driving or clerical work, while others were 'General Duties'. These 'GD' outfits contained clerks, store women and cooks, but also those with no defined specialism. Interestingly 'FANY' was not fully integrated into the organisation, and retained a separate identity, though later it also raised driver companies.[26]

Whilst matters were at first poorly organised, the ATS quickly gained significant patronage. This included the support of the Princess Royal, who initially accepted an honorary appointment

The ATS cipher and switchboard operators of First Allied Airborne headquarters. All four wear the light blue shoulder flash of 1st Allied Airborne, which was established in August 1944 as a co-ordinating body for all allied airborne operations. Three have the ATS cap badge in metal: Private Percival, second left, wears the plastic version. (J Wilds/Keystone/Getty Images) and eventually became Chief Controller, and Queen Elizabeth, later the Queen Mother, who was created Commander-in-Chief soon after the outbreak of war. Finally Princess Elizabeth joined the ATS when she came of age, the training programme being discussed in advance by George VI with Commandant Maud McLellan. According to later press reports, the future Queen underwent individual driving instruction in Windsor Great Park, later progressing to the Camberley training centre for which she was picked up every morning from Windsor Castle, swapping places with the car driver so as to gain experience. At Camberley she took courses in maintenance, map reading and ATS administration. When her parents paid the centre an official visit, the Princess took part in preparations, remarking with some surprise, 'I never knew how much trouble we give people when we go to inspect anything.' Being fully trained as a driver, she was commissioned in March 1945.[27]

A more typical experience of induction was related by volunteer, later Corporal, Mary Blades, who was inducted through what had once been a teacher training establishment in Durham. As with many male soldiers, this began with basic training, including being issued with uniform and being taught to wear and care for it. Marching and physical training took place every day, and recruits were taught Army ranks and how to salute. Pay was small, but as food and accommodation were included it was described as 'adequate'. Once the basics were mastered, the new ATS volunteer moved on to a specialism, and in Blades' case this was cookery. Thereafter the volunteer became operational, and in the case of cooks might well be placed on Army bases to provide food around the clock, often working shifts. Some holes in provision for personnel were filled by the Duchess of Northumberland ATS comforts fund.

Initially the ATS had an entirely separate rank structure in which NCOs and other ranks were described as 'volunteers' and 'leaders', under officers who were 'commanders', 'commandants' and 'controllers'. This was changed in June 1941 when the other rank titles were brought directly into line with male equivalents. At the same time the 'junior commanders' and 'company assistants' were also converted to subalterns and second subalterns, though the more senior officers were left with their existing titles. To produce additional leaders, Officer Cadet Training Units began to be opened. The ATS would have three chief controllers over the period of hostilities: Helen Gwynne-Vaughan from 1939 to 1941; Jean Knox from 1941 to 1943; and Leslie Whateley from then until 1946.

One of the first and biggest tasks taken on by the ATS and FANY was the collection and delivery of vehicles and parts from manufacturers, and their delivery to units. This effort revolved around the Central Ordnance Depot at Chilwell, and was by no means as simple as it might seem at first sight. Quite apart from the fact that vehicles of the time required a considerable amount of 'running in' and maintenance, delivery could pose serious problems. Where the receiving unit was abroad, for example, vehicles recently put together might have to be stripped down again and various fittings packed into cases. Paperwork was needed from units and headquarters outlining what was to be collected and delivered, and would also be required as a trail to sign for equipment as it passed down the line. Another vehicle-associated trade that the ATS adopted at an early stage was that of motorcycle despatch rider. Never risk free, this could be particularly problematic under the blackout conditions of the UK.

Though non-combatant, the ATS also served abroad from early in the war, with the first contribution being a platoon of bilingual telephonists deployed to Paris. The FANY were likewise used as ambulance drivers in France. By December 1940, the ATS were serving as far away as Egypt, and overall numbers had reached about 34,000. With the passage of the National Service Act, women became liable to call-up, though in fact the number put into the ATS against their will was negligible. Women were allowed to object to service on moral grounds as conscientious objectors, which some did, but more importantly options existed to join the Women's Voluntary Service (WVS) or the Women's Land Army.

Georgy Masson on the cover of *Picture Post*, December 1943. According to the article Masson was one of thirty girls from the West Indies who had volunteered for the ATS. (Leonard McCombe/IPC Magazines/Getty Images)

With the ATS becoming fully subject to military law in 1941, this suddenly gave rise to the problem of how this new level of discipline could be enforced without some form of female military police service. Accordingly volunteers were sent to the Corps of Military Police Depot at Mytchett for training, and the ATS Provost Wing was formed early in 1942. Other jobs tackled by women were as diverse as the running of the Army

The Archbishop of Canterbury visits women the ATS at Richmond, 1943. The women wear cold weather 'Smocks AA (Wool Pile) ATS', the 'teddy bear coat' and helmets with artillery flashes. (Author)

Military and fashionable: London ATS aircraft spotter 'Miss Parker'. (Reg Speller/Fox Photos/ Getty Images)

Blood Depot and provision of draughtswomen and secretarial staff to many of the corps. In the arena of film and photography, ATS personnel took a role in photography and projection, for which there was a specialist eight-week course. The Army postal services alone absorbed 1,500 women, many of whom worked sorting letters on regular eight-hour shifts. The Royal Army Ordnance Corps eventually employed another 22,000 and the Royal Army Service Corps took over 17,000 female drivers, mechanics and storekeepers. As of December 1943, there were over 207,000 ATS serving in over eighty different trades, and in virtually every theatre where the Army was to be found. [28]

In addition, it should be noted that the separate Queen Alexandra's Imperial Military Nursing Service was also vastly expanded. This had fewer than 700 regular female nurses before the war, but was quickly augmented by its reserve and the mobilisation of the Territorial Army Nursing Service. Like the ATS, female Army nurses served in most theatres of operations.

Interestingly QAIMNS nurses had enjoyed officer status since as early as 1904, partly in recognition of skills needed but doubtless also to encourage respect from other rank male patients. So it was that the 'matron in chief' ranked as a brigadier; a 'chief principal matron' as a colonel, and 'principal matrons' as lieutenant colonels. An ordinary 'matron' was the equivalent of a major, and 'senior sisters' and 'sisters' as captains and lieutenants respectively. Though the traditional colours of the QAIMNS uniform were scarlet and grey, khaki Service Dress and Battle Dress in a style very similar to that of the ATS was increasingly worn. An order that all Army nurses should adopt the uniform of an ATS officer but with appropriate badges was issued on 1 January 1944.

Even before the war, a role was also envisaged for women with the anti-aircraft artillery, and some of the earliest volunteers were given non-combatant jobs supporting the Royal Artillery. Major General Frederick Alfred Pile even brought in a female consultant to ascertain what jobs might profitably be done by female personnel with the gun batteries, and it was concluded that, short of moving the heaviest shells and equipment, most tasks could be tackled by women. By the late summer of 1940, there was a call for female volunteers to join Anti-Aircraft Command. Though there was some public disquiet that this would bring them

into combat, the Defence Regulations of 1941 accorded women military status under the Army Act, and soon fully integrated mixed batteries were operating with the Heavy branch of Anti-Aircraft Command.

In action, ATS women crewed fire-control instruments, whilst men actually fired the guns, and the Royal Artillery gun position officer remained in charge. Women were also deployed to searchlight units and performed most of the tasks, though again they were not allowed to use the light machine gun with which such units were equipped for close defence. An all-female experimental searchlight troop was also created in 1941, and the following year the female 93rd Searchlight Regiment was formed. Only the commanding officer was male, and he was assisted by a female adjutant. Also in 1942, women were introduced to the rocket batteries, where they provided four officers and 170 other ranks to support the main body of the units which was provided by the Home Guard.

At first at least, female officers had no part in the commanding of any battery in action, a stricture that rankled especially as it appeared to reduce them to the role of administrator and chaperone at the most important moment. The rule was gradually relaxed as the presence of women became less of a novelty, and female officers were later allowed to direct the guns, at least during exercises. Female officers were then also permitted onto the gun positions during action to supervise, and sometimes even perform, duties already undertaken by the ATS other ranks. The increasing role of women may have been speeded up by the fact that whether combatant or not, ATS personnel of AA Command were liable to be killed or injured. Private Nora Caveney of 148th Regiment was the first to be killed in action in the UK, hit by an enemy bomb splinter whilst working the predictor, but others soon followed.

In the ideal mixed AA Brigade structure, the brigadier was assisted by a deputy director ATS who ranked as a chief commander (lieutenant colonel). The ATS were then grouped together for administrative purposes into a company under a senior commander (major). The possible shock of the integration of women was lessened by the forming of entirely new units, not suddenly introducing female personnel to an existing unit. Actual integration took place at an early stage, just after the completion of basic training, when a mixed Heavy Anti-Aircraft

training regiment was formed. Interestingly it was observed that the ATS were not as good spotters as the men, something put down to early male interest in aircraft types and aviation, but that women were better at height finding. Interestingly Churchill spoke up for the increasing role of women in anti-aircraft defence, following a thought-provoking visit to a unit in October 1941:

'During my visit to Richmond Anti-Aircraft mixed battery, I learned, with much surprise, that the present policy of the Auxiliary Territorial Service is that ATS personnel in mixed batteries should not consider themselves part of the battery, and that no "battery esprit de corps" was to be allowed. This is very wounding to the ATS personnel, who have been deprived of badges, lanyards etc., of which they were proud. Considering they share the risks and the work of the battery in fact, there can be no justification for denying them incorporation in form... I found a universal desire among all ranks that the women who serve their country by manning guns should be called "Gunners" and Members of the Royal Regiment of Artillery. There would be no objection to the letters "ATS" being retained.' [29]

An ATS Bombardier height finder with an anti-aircraft battery. Purpose-made ATS Battle Dress was introduced in 1941. (Author)

In 1942, the fruits of experience were gathered together in the document *Formation, Training and Command of Mixed Heavy Anti-Aircraft Batteries, Royal Artillery*. Churchill continued to take direct personal interest in the progress of women in Anti-Aircraft Command, and Mary – his youngest daughter – was one of the many who worked with the artillery, ranking as a junior commander. When her unit, 481 Battery, was in Hyde Park, Churchill also paid it an impromptu visit. The request of the Prime Minister that women on the gun sites, and on the gun sites only, would be allowed to be called 'bombardiers' and 'gunners' was accepted.

By late 1943, a total of 56,000 women were involved in AA Command. It has been argued that this mainly worked well because the Command was largely Territorial, and many of the

Winston with
General Sir
Frederick Pile and
Mary Churchill at
an anti-aircraft site,
June 1944. The
Churchill family
were no hypocrites
when it came to
calls for military
service, all of
Winston's surviving
children being in the
military during the
Second World War.
Randolph was in
the Army; Diana in
the Women's Royal
Naval Service;
Sarah, in the
Women's Auxiliary
Air Force, and Mary
(1922–2014) in the
ATS. Mary, who
learned a cigar-
smoking habit from
her father, was
posted to Belgium
in the latter part of
the war. (IWM/Getty
Images)

men serving with it were already used to working with women in their civilian employment. However, it was a rule that married couples could not serve together, so if any relationship reached this stage one or other party had to be posted away from the unit. It has been calculated that the addition of women to AA Command thereby enabled the formation of a total of approximately seventy more regiments than would have been possible without their participation, and consequently this also freed up men for other formations. There was a distinct feeling within the Royal Artillery that the ATS attached to its units should be absorbed completely into the gunner structure, but this was never done. The notion was strongly resisted by the chief controller, at least partly on grounds that keeping the ATS separate allowed maximum flexibility for them to be reposted wherever they were needed. There may have been something in this argument, as later in the war the number of home AA regiments was reduced, and some women were indeed posted elsewhere.

Though the contribution of the ATS to the defence of British cities against conventional bombing was highly significant, it was not the only important deployment. In Operation Diver – against the V1 or 'Doodlebug' – the ATS played their role, with formations redeployed as screens to stop the missiles getting through. In the first phase, the guns and detection equipments were ranged as a belt along the South Coast. Next, as the campaign in Normandy gradually advanced, the threat from the South receded and the biggest threat now came from the East. Accordingly the main defensive screen was now moved to the coast from Clacton to Yarmouth. Finally, with the land battle advancing towards the German border in the winter of 1944, anti-V1 units were deployed to Belgium where they could protect ground installations. As the batteries became more practised in the art of shooting at unmanned craft, equipment also improved, with better prediction, more automation and radar. The result was a significant improvement in hit rates, increasing in many instances from a small minority of the targets, up to a distinct majority in some cases.[30]

Churchill's own attitude to the employment of women in the Army was interesting: for on the one hand he was very much the Victorian, and on the other sought to make as pragmatic use of everything and everyone to the common goal

The total ATS casualties of 1939 to 1945, counting all types of service and unit, was at least 389 killed and wounded, some estimates being rather higher. In the biggest single loss of life, an ATS billet in Great Yarmouth was hit by a bomb on 11 May 1943, leading to twenty-six fatalities. The period from June to September 1944, when the enemy 'V' weapons came into play, was also particularly difficult. In that time, twelve ATS were killed and 131 were wounded.

A less obvious female contribution was that the 'FANY', which still existed as a separate entity, and was often used as a conduit to, or a cover for, women to be recruited to the SOE. Interestingly, and despite Churchill's reservations, the ATS did not face the same sort of arbitrary dissolution in 1945 that the Women's Army Auxiliary Corps had faced after the First World War. Instead, it was decided that a scaled-back version should become a voluntary, regular component of the armed forces. The detail of how this was to be done, and what the women's force should now be called, took a long time to determine and for legislation to be put into place. Never the less, the Women's Royal Army Corps (WRAC) came into existence in 1949.

Ceaselessly new vehicles roll off the production lines. Army units await them, the ATS deliver them

Far left: 'ATS at the wheel', war poster by artist Beverly Pick, 1941. (Buyenlarge/Getty Images)

of defeating the enemy as possible. This of course extended to the service of his own daughter. In 1944, he cajoled for the use of more ATS personnel to support HQs abroad, but in 1945 he was very much of the opinion that they should be brought home and demobilised first. Part of the reason was that he considered that they might have less of an unsettling impact on the labour market:

'Women ought not to be treated the same as men… They do not mutiny or cause disturbances, and the sooner they are back at their homes the better. The idea of keeping masses of highly paid young women hanging around at RAF stations and in Army and Navy work, with a redundant staff finding them a job in teaching them to lead a better life, is one which should be completely cut out of our system. All women should be free to retire as soon as possible from the Services, and those who like to stay will be found sufficient to do the necessary jobs. A regular ramp is growing up to hold on to these women. No one who is not absolutely necessary to the war effort can in any circumstances be retained.' [31]

With an expanding female service its own police force was formed in 1942. These ATS 'Provosts', were pictured in 1943. (Official/author)

Appendix I

Growth of the British Army 1939–1945

(From Service Department Statistics)

It is very apparent that expansion of the Army, from a base level of less than a million at the outbreak of war, was initially relatively sluggish. Even in the immediate aftermath of Dunkirk the sudden appearance of large numbers of the LDV, soon to be the Home Guard, can only have added modestly to overall strength, as now much equipment was lost and the Auxiliary force was not yet trained. Matters certainly improved during the course of the following year. In 1941 the Home Guard had a recruitment maximum set at 1.8 million. This was raised to 2.5 million in May 1942, when compulsory enrolment was introduced, though this number – then equal to the rest of the Army – was never reached. Female Home Guard Auxiliaries existed before mid-1943, but formal acceptance and enrolment lagged. Total Army strength – including Home Guard and female recruits – peaked at almost 4.7 million, and remained about its zenith from late 1943 and through 1944. Though the full-time Army had reached nearly three million by victory in Europe, and was at a similar level in the final months before victory over Japan in August 1945, 'Stand Down' of the Home Guard was announced in November 1944, and carried out on 3 December 1944. The Home Guard was formally disbanded at the end of 1945, and many of the units raised during the war were likewise disbanded, amalgamated, or put into 'suspended animation' in 1945–1947.

Year	Month	Army (male)	Auxiliary Territorial Service (female)	Home Guard (male)	Home Guard (female)
1939	September	897,000			
	December	1,128,000	23,900		
1940	March	1,361,000			
	June	1,650,000	31,500	1,456,000	
	September	1,888,000	36,100	1,472,000	
	December	2,075,000	36,400		
1941	March	2,166,000	37,500		
	June	2,221,000	42,800	1,603,000	
	September	2,292,000	65,000		
	December	2,340,000	85,100	1,530,000	
1942	March	2,387,000	111,100		
	June	2,453,000	140,200	1,565,000	
	September	2,494,000	162,200		
	December	2,566,000	180,700	1,741,000	
1943	March	2,628,000	195,300	1,793,000	
	June	2,673,000	210,300	1,784,000	4,000
	September	2,679,000	212,500	1,769,000	16,000
	December	2,680,000	207,500	1,754,000	22,000
1944	March	2,680,000	206,200	1,739,000	28,000
	June	2,720,000	199,000	1,727,000	31,000
	September	2,741,000	198,200	1,698,000	32,000
	December	2,760,000	196,400	1,685,000	
1945	March	2,802,000	195,300	(Stood down)	
	June	2,920,000	190,800		

Appendix II

Typical Unit Equipments

INFANTRY BATTALIONS

INFANTRY BATTALION FRANCE 1939–1940

HQ Company: Admin; Pioneer; Signals; Anti-Aircraft, Mortar and Carrier platoons (14 Bren Carriers). Armament includes 4 twin Bren guns; 7 anti-tank rifles; 6 3-inch and 4 2-inch mortars.

Battalion Transport: 6 cars; 34 x 15cwt trucks; and 13 x 3-ton lorries.

Four Rifle Companies: Each with a Company HQ, and 3 platoons. Each platoon contains 33 rifles; 3 Bren guns; 1 x 2-inch mortar and 1 AT rifle.

MOTOR BATTALION 1942

Battalion HQ

Anti-Tank Company: HQ carrier and 15cwt truck, plus 4 AT platoons each with 4 x 6pdr guns and 6 Carriers.

Three Motor Companies: Each with Company HQ in 2 x 15cwt trucks, and 3 motor platoons, each with 3 x 15cwt trucks and 3 Bren LMG.

Scout Platoon: 9 Carriers.

Machine Gun Platoon: 4 x 15cwt trucks, 4 Vickers MMG.

Mortar Section: 4 x 15cwt trucks, 2 x 3-inch mortars.

INFANTRY BATTALION 1943

Battalion HQ: 1 Carrier; 1 Scout Car.

HQ Company: 1 Jeep; 5 x 15cwt trucks; 13 x 3-ton lorries (often with attached Royal Army Service Corps Platoon with 36 x 3-ton lorries).

Support Company: Carrier Platoon (13 Carriers, 2 x 15cwt trucks); Anti-Tank Platoon (6 x 6pdrs; 12 Carriers and 1 Observation Post Carrier); Mortar Platoon (6 x 3-inch mortars; 7 Carriers; 3 x 15cwt trucks); Pioneer Platoon (3 Jeeps, 1 Half-track)

Four Rifle Companies: Each with a Company HQ (1 Jeep; 3 x 15cwt trucks; 1 Carrier); three Rifle platoons (each 21 rifles; 3 Bren guns; 1 x 2-inch mortar; 1 PIAT)

ARMOURED REGIMENTS

ARMOURED REGIMENT, FRANCE 1939–1940

Regimental HQ: 4 Crusier Tanks (A9, A10, or A13 types).

HQ Squadron: (Regimental transport).

Two Light Squadrons: Each, 1 Squadron HQ (3 Vickers Light Tanks) and 5 Troops (each 3 Vickers Light Tanks).

One Heavy Squadron: Squadron HQ (2 Cruiser Tanks; 1 x 3-inch Howitzer Cruiser); 5 Troops (each 3 Cruiser Tanks).

ARMOURED REGIMENT, EGYPT 1941

Regimental HQ: 4 Crusaders or Stuarts.

HQ Squadron: 4 Crusaders or Stuarts, plus Regimental transport.

Three Squadrons: Each, 1 Squadron HQ (2 Crusaders or Stuarts; 2 x 3-inch Howitzer Cruisers); 4 Troops (3 Crusaders or Stuarts).

ARMOURED REGIMENT NORTH AFRICA, OCTOBER 1942

Regimental HQ: (Regimental transport).

HQ Squadron: 4 Shermans, 4 Crusader AA tanks.

Three Squadrons: Each, 1 Squadron HQ (4 Shermans); 4 Troops (3 Shermans).

ARMOURED REGIMENT 1944

Regimental HQ: (4 Shermans or Cromwells, plus Regimental transport).

HQ Squadron: Squadron HQ; 11 Stuarts; 6 Crusader AA tanks.

Three Squadrons: Each, 1 Squadron HQ (4 Shermans or Cromwells); 4 Troops (3 Shermans or Cromwells); 1 Heavy Troop (3 Firefly or Challenger 17pdr).

ARMOURED REGIMENT 1944 (FLAIL TANKS)

Regimental HQ: 3 Command Tanks; 2 Half-tracks; 2 Armoured 15cwt trucks; 2 x 15cwt trucks; 6 x 3-ton lorries.

Three Squadrons: Each, 1 Squadron HQ (3 Scout Cars; 3 Command Tanks; 1 Armoured Recovery Vehicle); 1 Admin Troop (2 x 15cwt trucks; 17 x 3-ton lorries; 1 Half-track; 1 Carrier); 3 Flail Troops (each 5 Sherman Crab Flail Tanks).

ARMOURED CAR REGIMENTS

Corps Armoured Car Regiment, France 1939–1940

Regimental HQ: Regimental Transport.

HQ Squadron: Squadron HQ; 11 Stuarts; 6 Crusader AA tanks.

Three Squadrons: Each, 1 Squadron HQ (1 Morris C9 Light Armoured Car; 3 x 15cwt trucks); 4 Troops (each 3 Morris C9 Light Armoured Cars; 1 x 15cwt truck).

Notes

INTRODUCTION

1. The single most useful, and certainly most extensive, work on Winston Churchill is the official biography by Randolph S. Churchill and Martin Gilbert, published during the latter part of the twentieth century. Randolph Churchill authored the first two volumes, *Youth* and *Young Statesman*, covering the period up to 1914. After Randolph Churchill's death in 1968, Martin Gilbert continued the story in a further six volumes. Volumes VI and VII, *Finest Hour* and *Road to Victory*, cover the period of the Second World War. Winston Churchill's own account of 1939 to 1945 is the similarly massive, *The Second World War*. In recent years Churchill's impressive reputation has been increasingly brought into question by a number of works. Perhaps the apogee of this revisionism is Nigel Knight's uncompromising contradiction of Winston's own version of history, *Churchill: The Greatest Briton Unmasked* (Newton Abbot, 2008).

2. Martin Gilbert, *The Challenge of War* (Volume III of the official biography, place: Houghton Mifflin Company, 1973), pp. 324–571.

3. *Ibid.*, pp. 572–589, citing letters by Grigg and Churchill.

4. *Ibid.*, pp. 648–826.

5. Carlo D'Este, *Warlord: A Life of Churchill at War*, p. 345.

6. *Ibid.*, pp. 358–368.

7. Winston S. Churchill, *The Second World War*, Volume 1, pp. 356–360.

8. Winston S. Churchill, *The Second World War*, Volume 1, p. 511; Francois Kersaudy, *Norway 1940*, passim.

9. Winston S. Churchill, *The Second World War*, Volume 3, pp. 693–694.

10. John Keegan (ed.), *Churchill's Generals*, p. 4.

11. Brooke cited in John Keegan (ed.), *Churchill's Generals*, p. 11.

12. Winston S. Churchill, *The Second World War*, Volume 3, p. 668.

13. John Keegan (ed.), *Churchill's Generals*, London, 1991, p. 15.

GENERALS

1) The main sources for these biographies are the *Dictionary of National Biography*; *Who's Who*; T.A. Heathcote, *The British Field Marshals 1736–1997*, London, 1999; Richard Mead, *Churchill's Lions*, Stroud, 2007; Alex Danchev and Dan Todman (ed), *Alanbrooke War Diaries 1939–1945*, London, 2001; Brian Horrocks, *A Full Life*, 1960; Nigel Hamilton, *Monty*, London, 1981–1986; John Keegan (ed), *Churchill's Generals*, London, 1991; Nick Smart, *Biographical Dictionary of British Generals of the Second World War*, Barnsley, 2005; National Army Museum summaries, official *Army Lists* and *London Gazette*.

2) Correlli Barnett, *Britain and Her Army 1509–1970*, London, 1970, p. 411.

REGIMENTS AND CORPS

1) Major sources for this section are: *The Monthly Army List*, August 1939; J.B.M. Frederick, *Lineage Book of British Land Forces*, Wakefield, 1984; Correlli Barnett, *Britain and Her Army 1509–1970*, London, 1970; Arthur Swinson, *A Register of the Regiments and Corps of the British Army*, London, 1972, and George Forty, *British Army Handbook 1939–1945*, Stroud, 1998.

2) Many of the regiments and corps of 1939–1945 still have their own museums. Details of these are listed in Colin Sibun's Army Museums Ogilby Trust publication *Military Museums in the UK* and on the website at www.armymuseums.org.uk.

3) G.F. Ellenberger, *The History of the King's Own Yorkshire Light Infantry*, Volume VI, Aldershot, 1961, p. xiii–xiv.

4) See Charles Graham Troughton Dean, *The Loyal Regiment (North Lancashire) 1919–1953*, Preston, 1958.

5) Col D. McCorquodale, *History of the King's Dragoon Guards 1938–1945*, Glasgow, 1950, pp. 374–375.

6) See J.B.M. Frederick, *Lineage Book of British Land Forces*, Wakefield, 1984, Volume 2, passim.

7) *National Service*, HMSO, 1939, passim.

8) Winston S. Churchill, *The Second World War*, Volume 3, 1950, p. 706.

9) *Ibid.*, p. 738.

10) *The Daily Telegraph*, London, 3 December 1941.

11) Winston S. Churchill, *The Second World War*, Volume 6, 1954, p. 853.

12) *Ibid.*, pp. 594, 599.

13) *Ibid.*, pp. 614–615.

14) See David French, *Raising Churchill's Army*, Oxford, 2000, pp. 243–246; Carlo D'Este, *Decision in Normandy*, London, 1983, pp. 252–270; Winston S. Churchill, *The Second World War*, Volume 6, 1954, pp. 617–618, 624.

UNIFORM

1) *Dress Regulations for the Army*, 1934, passim.

2) Brian L. Davis, *British Army Uniforms and Insignia*, London, 1983, pp. 120–179; Martin Brayley and Richard Ingram, *The World War II Tommy: British Army Uniforms European Theatre 1939–1945*, Marlborough, new edition 2007, pp. 9–24.

3) See Howard Ripley, *Buttons of the British Army 1855–1970*, London, 1971, passim.

A Daimler armoured car opens fire during the start of the battle for Tripoli, January 1943. Powered by a 95hp engine with four-wheel drive, a crew of three and a tank type turret, the Daimler was one of the more successful armoured cars. Its armament was both machine guns, and a 2pdr gun. (Capt G Keating/IWM via Getty Images)

4) Martin Brayley and Richard Ingram, *World War II British Women's Uniforms*, London, 1995, pp. 3, 22–56.

5) Brian L. Davis, *British Army Uniforms and Insignia*, London, 1983, pp. 181–196; Martin Brayley and Richard Ingram, *The World War II Tommy: British Army Uniforms European Theatre 1939–1945*, Marlborough, new edition 2007, pp. 15, 22–24, 64.

6) Brian Jewell and Mike Chappell, *British Battledress 1937–1961*, London, 1981, passim.

7) Brian L. Davis, *British Army Uniforms and Insignia*, London, 1983, pp. 134–138; Jean Bouchery, *The British Soldier From D–Day to VE–Day*, Volume 1, Paris, 1998, pp. 16–20.

8) David Erskine, *The Scots Guards 1919–1945*, London, 1956, p. 594.

9) Brian L. Davis, *British Army Uniforms and Insignia*, London, 1983, pp. 129–142.

10) Bashford Dean, *Helmets and Body Armour in Modern Warfare*, new edition, New York, 1977, pp. 128–130, 193–222; Stephen Bull, *Encyclopedia of Military Technology and Innovation*, Westport, 2004, pp. 125–126.

11) M. Cotton, 'British Steel Helmets' in *Militaria*, English edition, number 9, October 1994, pp. 43–49.

12) Martin Brayley and Richard Ingram, *The World War II Tommy: British Army Uniforms European Theatre 1939–1945*, Marlborough, new edition 2007, p. 135; Brian L. Davis, *British Army Uniforms and Insignia*, London, 1983, pp. 220–224.

13) See Marcus Cotton, 'The British MRC Body Armour' in *Militaria*, English edition, Volume 20, London, 1995 pp. 30–35, and French editions 122 and 132, 1995–1996; also Brian L. Davis, *British Army Uniforms and Insignia*, London, 1983, pp. 246–247.

14) See Martin Brayley and Richard Ingram, *Khaki Drill and Jungle Green: British Tropical Uniforms 1939–45 in Colour Photographs*, Marlborough, 2000, passim, and Brian L. Davis, *British Army Uniforms and Insignia*, London, 1983, pp. 174–177.

15) Edmund Tytler Burke, *Tropical Tips for Troops*, London, 1941, pp. 5–6.

16) See Stephen Bull, *World War II Winter and Mountain Warfare Tactics*, Oxford, 2013, passim.

17) Martin Brayley and Richard Ingram, *The World War II Tommy: British Army Uniforms European Theatre 1939–1945*, Marlborough, new edition, 2007, pp. 98–103.

18) Martin Brayley, *British Web Equipment of the Two World Wars*, Marlborough, 2005, pp. 3–21; Mike Chappell, *British Infantry Equipments 1908–1980*, London, 1980, pp. 3–14.

19) War Office, *The Pattern 1937 Web Equipment*, 1939, pp. 3–14.

20) War Office, *Light Machine Gun*, 1942, pp. 36–37. The author is indebted to the late Colonel A. Moore of the King's Liverpool Regiment for observations on these points.

21) War Office, *The Pattern 1944 Web Equipment*, 1946, pp. 3–12.

22) *Field Service Pocket Book*, Pamphlet No. 11, 1939, Discipline, Office Work and Burial Parties, 1939, pp. 17–20.

23) Jean Bouchery, *The British Soldier: From D–Day to VE Day*, Paris, 1998, pp. 51–53.

24) See J. Mills, 'British Anti-Gas Equipment 1939–1943' in *Militaria*, English edition, volumes 8 and 13, London, 1994–1995; and Brian L. Davis, *British Army Uniforms and Insignia*, London, 1983, pp. 238–245.

25) See William Reid, 'Binoculars in the Army', parts II and III, in *Army Museum 82*, pp. 15–30, and 83, pp. 39–51 (London 1983–1984).

BADGES AND MEDALS

1) See Arthur L. Kipling and Hugh L. King, *Headdress Badges of the British Army 1800–1918*, Volume 2, London, 1979, passim.

2) Marcus Cotton, 'British Plastic Cap Badges' in *Militaria* 10, November 1994, pp. 18–22.

3) David Erskine, *The Scots Guards 1919–1955*, London, 1956, p. 594.

4) See Nicholas Payan Dawnay, *The Distinction of Rank of Regimental Officers 1684 to 1855*, Society for Army Historical Research, London, 1960, passim.

5) Brian L. Davies, *British Army Uniforms and Insignia of World War II*, London, 1983, pp. 16–30; Nicholas Payan Dawnay, *The Badges of Warrant and Non-Commissioned Rank in the British Army*, Society for Army Historical Research, London, 1949, pp. 42–62.

6) See David Linaker and Gordon Dine, *Cavalry Warrant Officer and Non-Commissioned Officers' Arm Badges*, London, 1997, passim.

7) See Ray A. Westlake, *Collecting Metal Shoulder Titles*, London, 1980, passim; and Brian L. Davis, *British Army Uniforms and Insignia*, London, 1983 pp. 36–40; J.G. Short, *Special Forces Insignia, British and Commonwealth Units*, London, 1988, pp. 20–30.

8) David Erskine, *The Scots Guards 1919–1955*, London, 1956, p. 592.

9) Winston S. Churchill, *The Second World War*, Volume 3, 1950, p. 745.

10) Denis Edwards and David Langley, *British Army Proficiency Badges*, Nottingham, 1984, pp. 1–6, 76–99.

11) See Howard N. Cole, *Formation Badges of World War II*, new

edition, London, 1985; and Mike Chappell, *British Battle Insignia, 1939–1945*, London, 1987, passim.

12) Howard N. Cole, *Formation Badges of World War II*, new edition, London, 1985, passim; Brian L. Davies, *British Army Uniforms and Insignia of World War II*, London, 1983, pp. 92–102.

13) See Brian L. Davies, *British Army Uniforms and Insignia of World War II*, London, 1983, pp. 45–50.

14) Winston S. Churchill, *The Second World War*, Volume 5, London, 1952, p. 567; Brian L. Davies, *British Army Uniforms and Insignia of World War II*, London, 1983, pp. 51, 113–114.

15) M.J. Crook, *The Evolution of the Victoria Cross*, Speldhurst, 1975, pp. 5–68.

16) See Nora Buzzell, *The Register of the Victoria Cross*, Cheltenham, 1988, passim, Crook pp. 210, 222.

17) See A.R. Litherland and B.T. Simpkin, *Standard Catalogue of British and Associated Orders, Decorations and Medals*, London, 1990, passim.

18) See Edward C. Joslin (et al), *British Battles and Medals*, London, 1988.

SMALL ARMS

1) Ian D. Skennerton, *The British Service Lee*, Margate, 1982, pp. 59–123; Herbert Woodend, *British Rifles: Catalogue of the Enfield Pattern Room*, London, 1981, pp. 48–51.

2) War Office, *Rifle*, 1937, passim.

3) War Office, *Bayonet*, Small Arms Training Volume I, Pamphlet No. 12, 1937, pp. 1–18.

4) Anonymous, *The Bayonet: Bayonet Fighting*, Aldershot, undated, passim.

5) Ian D. Skennerton, *British and Commonwealth Bayonets*, Margate, 1986, pp. 186–229; War Office, *Bayonet*, Small Arms Training Volume I, Pamphlet No. 12, 1942, reprinted with amendments 1945, passim.

6) *Notes on the Training of Snipers*, MTP 44, 1940 reprinted with amendments, 1941, pp. 1–12, 30–31.

7) Ian D. Skennerton, *The British Sniper*, Margate, 1984, pp. 104–167.

8) Clifford Shore, *With British Snipers to the Reich*, new edition, London, 1997, pp. 163–169; Martin Pegler, *Sniper Rifles*, Oxford, 2010, pp. 39–52.

9) Bruce N. Canfield, *The M1 Garand and the M1 Carbine*, Lincoln, 1988, passim; Ian V. Hogg and John Weeks, *Military Small Arms of the Twentieth Century*, London, 1977, pp. 118–128, 180–185.

10) *Ibid.*, pp. 98–101; Anonymous, *The Thompson Machine Carbine Made Easy*, Aldershot, undated, pp. 5–32; War Office, *The Machine Carbine*, SAT, Volume I, No. 21, 1944, pp. 2–11.

11) H.W. Bodman (et al), *Sten Machine Carbine*, fourth edition, Bradford on Avon, 1942; Anonymous, *The Sten Machine Carbine*, Aldershot, undated; War Office, *Sten Machine Carbine*, SAT, Volume I, No. 22; War Office, SAT, No. 21, 1944, *Amendments*, No. 3, 1946.

12) War Office, *Sten Machine Carbine*, SAT, Volume I, No. 22, pp. 1–3.

13) Ian V. Hogg and John Weeks, *Military Small Arms of the Twentieth Century*, London, 1977, pp. 76–79; Clifford Shore, *With British Snipers to the Reich*, new edition, London, 1997, pp. 208–209, 316–317.

14) J.D. Truby, *The Lewis Gun*, Boulder, 1976, pp. 35–125; Ian Skennerton, *British Small Arms of World War II*, Margate, 1988, pp. 58–60.

15) *Small Arms Training*, Volume II, 1931, pp. 1–2.

16) Ian V. Hogg and John Weeks, *Military Small Arms of the Twentieth Century*, London, 1977, pp. 222–227.

17) *Small Arms Training*, Volume I, Pamphlet 20, pp. 5–6

18) 'T.J.', The *Complete Lewis Gunner*, Aldershot, 1941; G. Jacklin and Derek Whipp, *The Lewis Gun*, London, 1941; H.W. Bodman, *.300 Lewis Machine Gun for the Home Guard*, Bradford on Avon, 1940.

19) *Small Arms Training*, Volume I, Pamphlet 4, *Light Machine Gun*, 1939, pp. 4–35; F.W.A. Hobart, *The Bren Gun*, Small Arms Profile 13, 1972, passim.

20) Clifford Shore, *With British Snipers to the Reich*, new edition, London, 1997, pp. 209–211; David French, *Raising Churchill's Army*, Oxford, 2000, pp. 86–87.

21) Ian V. Hogg, *Encyclopedia of Infantry Weapons of World War II*, London, 1977, pp. 72–74.

22) A.C. Bell, *History of the Manchester Regiment*, 1922–1948, pp. 22–23.

23) See also Ian V. Hogg and John Weeks, *Military Small Arms of the Twentieth Century*, London, 1977, pp. 220–224.

24) Stephen Bull, *Encyclopedia of Military Technology and Innovation*, Westport, 2004, pp. 49–51; *Instructional Notes on the .300-inch Browning Automatic Rifle*, 1940, passim.

Princess Elizabeth changing the tyre of a vehicle as she trains as an ATS Officer during the Second World War, at the ATS training centre, 18 April, 1945. The vehicle in the background is an Austin K2 ambulance. (Central Press/Hulton Archive/Getty Images)

25) SAT, Volume I, Pamphlet 8, *Mortar (2–inch)*, 1939, p. 4; see also John Norris, *Infantry Mortars of World War II*, Oxford, 2002, pp. 3–14, 25–29.

26) *Handbook for the Ordnance, ML 2–Inch Mortar, Mark II*, 1939, passim. See also George Forty, *British Army Handbook 1939–1945*, Stroud, 1998, pp. 206–210.

27) Ian V. Hogg and John Weeks, *Military Small Arms of the Twentieth Century*, London, 1977, pp. 8–15, 37–42.

28) SAT, Volume I, Pamphlet No. 11, *Pistol (.38 inch)*, 1941, p. 16.

29) Ian D. Skennerton, *British Small Arms of World War II*, Margate, 1988, pp. 22–32.

30) W.C. Dowell, *The Webley Story*, Leeds, 1962, passim; John Walter, *Dictionary of Guns and Gunmakers*, London, 2001, pp. 547–548.

31) SAT, Volume I, Pamphlet 14, *Annual (1939) Range Courses*, 1938, pp. 48–54; SAT, Volume I, Pamphlet 5, *Anti–Tank Rifle*, 1937, passim; SAT, Volume I, Pamphlet 18, Supplement: *Anti-Tank Rifle Course*, 1940, pp. 3–14.

32) *Projector Infantry Anti-Tank*, 1943, provisional, passim; Ian D. Skennerton, *British Small Arms*, Margate, 1988, pp. 63–64.

33) Small Arms Training, *Grenade* (editions of 1937 and 1942), passim; Small Arms Training, *Supplement*, No. 2, 1941, pp. 2–8; D. Whipp, *Anti-Tank Weapons*, London, 1942, pp. 42–44.

34) Winston S. Churchill, *The Second World War*, Volume 3, 1950, p. 732.

35) See also Rick Landers, *Identification Handbook of British Grenades, 1900–1960*, Dural, 2002, pp. 3–4, 8–9, 24, 30–43; and Ian D. Skennerton, *Introduction to British Grenades*, Margate, 1988, pp. 39–49.

36) *Tank Hunting and Destruction*, MTP 42, 1940, pp. 8–11, 18–19, 23–38.

37) *Tactical Handling of Flame–Throwers*, 1945, pp. 7–13; *Handbook for the Flame-Thrower, Portable, No. 2, Mark 2*, passim.

38) See Brian Robson, *Swords of the British Army*, new edition, London, 1996.

39) R.A. Buerlein, *Allied Military Fighting Knives*, Boulder, 2001, passim; Stephen Bull, *Commando Tactics*, Barnsley, 2010, pp. 109–110, 111–120.

ARTILLERY

1) David French, *Raising Churchill's Army*, Oxford, 2000, pp. 255–259.

2) *Operations*, MTP No. 23, 'General Principles', March 1942, pp. 17–20; see also George Forty, *British Army Handbook 1939–1945*, Stroud, 1998, pp. 71–80.

3) Ian V. Hogg, *British and American Artillery of World War Two*, London, 1978, pp. 18–42; S. Bidwell and D. Graham *Fire–Power*, London, 1982, pp. 221–281.

4) *Construction of Gun Emplacements*, MTP 43, 1940, pp. 1–5.

5) C. Ellis and P. Chamberlain (eds), *Handbook on the British Army 1943*, revised edition, London 1975, pp. 153–154.

6) C.H.T. MacFetridge and J.P. Warren, *Tales of the Mountain Gunners*, Edinburgh, 1973, pp. 142–174.

7) *Home Guard Instruction* No. 51, Part IV, November 1943, pp. 80–96; S.P. Mackenzie, *The Home Guard*, Oxford, 1995, pp. 120–121.

8) Ian V. Hogg, *British and American Artillery of World War Two*, London, 1978, pp. 42–49.

9) *Ibid.*, pp. 134–136.

10) *Ibid.*, pp. 138–140, 146–151; P. Chamberlain and T. Gander, *Heavy Artillery*, London, 1975, pp. 39–54.

11) Ian V. Hogg, *British and American Artillery of World War Two*, London, 1978, pp. 143–174.

12) *Ibid.*, pp. 195–202.

13) Winston S. Churchill, *The Second World War*, Volume 6, 1954, pp. 610–611.

14) Ian V. Hogg, *British and American Artillery of World War Two*, London, 1978, pp. 107–115.

15) *Ibid.*, pp. 94–133.

16) Winston S. Churchill, *The Second World War*, Volume 6, 1954, pp. 622; Volume 3, p. 753.

17) *Preliminary Report No. 10. German Pz.Kw.I (Model B)*, School of Tank Technology, Egham, April 1943, STT 8/2/8.

18) Winston S. Churchill, *The Second World War*, Volume 2, p. 785.

19) David French, *Raising Churchill's Army*, Oxford, 2000, pp. 93–96; see also *Gun Drill for 2pdr Anti-Tank Gun*, 1940, reprinted with amendments 1942, pp. 1–62.

20) *Gun Drill for QF 6pdr*, 1944, passim; Artillery Training.

21) Ian V. Hogg, *British and American Artillery of World War Two*, London, 1978, pp. 75–78.

22) Chris Henry, *British Anti–tank Artillery 1939–1945*, Oxford, 2004 pp. 12–20.

23) *Artillery Training: Field Gunnery*, Pamphlet 9, Anti-tank Gunnery, 1943, passim.

TANKS

1) See Peter Beale, *Death by Design: British Tank Development in the Second World War*, Stroud, 2009, passim; Anonymous, *Fire and Movement*, RAC Tank Museum, Bovington, 1975, pp. 10–14; Peter Gudgin, *Armoured Firepower: The Development of Tank Armament 1939–1945*, Stroud, 1997, passim; David French, *Raising Churchill's Army*, Oxford, 2000 pp. 96–103.

2) David French, 'Doctrine and Organisation in the British Army, 1919–1932', in *The Historical Journal*, Cambridge 2001, pp. 497–515.

3) Colonel D. McCorquodale, *History of the King's Dragoon Guards, 1938–1945*, Glasgow, 1950, p. 1.

4) Details of these changes may be followed in Frederick, J.B.M., *Lineage Book of British Land Forces*, two volumes, revised edition, Wakefield, 1984.

5) Richard Brett-Smith, *The 11th Hussars*, London, 1969, p. 206–247.

6) Winston S. Churchill, *The Second World War*, Volume 2, pp. 850–851; Volume 3, p. 675.

7) Useful explanations of contemporary tank terminology are given in *Tank Terms: A Glossary of Expressions Commonly Used in Connection with Fighting Vehicles*, Military College of Science, Chertsey, 1944.

8) David Fletcher, *Mechanised Force*, HMSO, 1991, pp. 48–60.

9) George Forty, *United States Tanks of World War II*, Poole, 1983 pp. 42–56; P. Chamberlain and C. Ellis, *British and American Tanks*, London, 1969, pp. 88–92.

10) See Bryan Perrett, *The Matilda*, London, 1973, passim.

11) David Fletcher, *Mechanised Force*, HMSO, 1991, pp. 124–126; Bryan Perrett, *Matilda*, London, 1973, passim.

12) P. Chamberlain and C. Ellis, *British and American Tanks*, London, 1969, pp. 30–39.

13) Anonymous, *British War Production*, London, 1945, p. 64.

14) David Fletcher, *Mr Churchill's Tank*, Atglen, 1999, pp. 8–25.

15) *Ibid.*, pp. 73–115; Winston S. Churchill, *The Second World War*, Volume 2, p. 850.

16) Anonymous, *Churchill Tank: Vehicle History and Specification*, London, 1983, passim.

17) George Forty, *United States Tanks*, Poole, 1983, pp. 78–96.

18) David Fletcher, *The Universal Tank*, HMSO, 1993, pp. 60–63.

19) Stephen Bull, *Encyclopedia of Military Technology and Innovation*, Westport, 2004, pp. 231–233.

20) David Fletcher, *Sherman Firefly*, Oxford, 2008, pp. 5–12.

21) David Fletcher, *Swimming Shermans*, Oxford, 2006, pp. 3–14.

22) *Ibid.*, pp. 20–39.

23) P. Chamberlain and C. Ellis, *British and American Tanks*, pp. 41–42.

24) Anonymous, *Cromwell Tank, Vehicle History and Specification*, HMSO, London, 1983, passim.

25) *Ibid.* pp. vi–xiv.

26) See also David French, *Raising Churchill's Army*, Oxford, 2000, pp. 103–109.

Vehicles

1) Times Newspapers, *British War Production 1939–1945*, London, 1945, p. 101.

2) David E. Jane, *British Military Transport*, second edition, Retford, 1994, pp. 2–4.

3) Many of the general observations in this section are drawn from *Manual of Driving Maintenance for Mechanical Vehicles (Wheeled) 1937*, reprinted 1940.

4) Stephen Bull, *Lancashire Gunners at War: the 88th Field Regiment, 1939–1945*, Lancaster, 1999, pp. 13–16; *War Diary*, National Archives 167/499; 166/1511.

5) 'A Field Regiment in the Middle East' in, *The Journal of the Royal Artillery*, Volume LXX, No. 4, Woolwich, October 1943, pp. 233–247.

6) A detailed listing of Canadian vehicles and specifications on the eve of D–Day was given in the *Vehicle Data Book: Canadian Army Overseas*, March 1944.

7) George Forty, *British Army Handbook 1939–1945*, Stroud, 1998, pp. 252–280; David French, *Raising Churchill's Army*, Oxford, 2000, pp. 110–115.

8) See C.J. Orchard and S.J. Madden, *British Forces Motorcycles, 1925–1945*, Stroud, 1995, passim.

9) David E. Jane, *British Military Transport*, second edition, Retford, 1994, passim.

10) *Ibid.*

11) David Fletcher, *Mechanised Force*, HMSO, 1991, pp. 36–47.

12) P. Chamberlain and C. Ellis, *Making Tracks*, Windsor, 1973, pp. 14–43.

13) *Tactical Handling of the Carrier Platoon in Attack*, 1939, pp. 1–3.

14) *Army Training Memorandum*, June 1940.

15) David Fletcher, *Universal Carrier*, Oxford, 2005, pp. 9–39.

16) *Tactical Handling of Flame –Throwers*, 1945, pp. 6–7.

17) Colonel L.B. Oatts, *Emperor's Chambermaids*, London, 1973. pp. 448–455.

18) See J.M. Boniface and J.G. Jeudy, *US Army Vehicles of World War II*, Newbury Park, 1991, passim.

19) P. Chamberlain and C. Ellis, *British and American Tanks*, London, 1969, pp. 186–194; Stephen Bull, *Encyclopedia of Military Technology and Innovation*, Westport, 2004, pp. 117–118.

20) Henry Haven Windsor, 'Water Buffalo Can Fight on Land and Sea' in *Popular Mechanics*, June 1944.

21) Herbert R. Rifkind, *The Jeep: Its Developement and Procurement*, London, 1988, passim; William Munro, *Jeep: From Bantam to Wrangler*, Marlborough, 2000, passim.

22) *War Emergency British Standard* 987C, September 1942, reproduction supplied by Crown Paints to Lancashire Museums.

23) B.T. White, *British Tank Markings and Names*, London, 1978, pp. 68–86.

24) Winston S. Churchill, *The Second World War*, Volume 3, p. 692.

25) B.T. White, *British Tank Markings and Names*, London, 1978 pp. 13–63.

Special Forces

1) David Fraser, *And We Shall Shock Them*, London, 1983, pp. 93–96; Stephen Bull, *Commando Tactics*, Barnsley, 2010, pp. 1–28; James D. Ladd, *Commandos and Rangers of World War II*, London, 1978, pp. 12–55.

2) Tim Moreman, *British Commandos 1940–46*, Oxford, 2006, pp. 4–16.

3) Winston S. Churchill, *The Second World War*, Volume 3, p. 700; see also William Seymour, *British Special Forces*, London, 1985, pp. 37–160.

4) Winston S. Churchill, *The Second World War*, Volume 5, pp. 64–65.

5) US War Department, *Tactical and Technical Trends*, No. 28, 1 July 1943; 'Commando Raid on Varengeville, France', US War Department Special Series, No. 1; *British Commandos*, 1942, passim; James Dunning, *The Fighting Fourth*, Stroud, 2003, pp. 43–87.

6) Robin Neillands, *The Raiders: Army Commandos 1940–1946*, London, 1989, pp. 162–263, and James D. Ladd, *Commandos and Rangers of World War II*, London, 1978, pp. 114–163.

7) US War Department, Special Series No. 1, *British Commandos*, 1942, pp. 119–138.

8) Stephen Bull, *Commando Tactics*, Barnsley, 2010, pp. 133–162; Tim Moreman, *British Commandos*, Oxford, 2006, pp. 21–52.

9) Tim Moreman, *British Commandos*, Oxford, 2006, pp. 71–85.

10) George A. Brown, *Commando Gallantry Awards of World War II*, Loughborough, 1991, pp. 11, 263, 325–327.

11) Stephen Bull, *Commando Tactics*, Barnsley, 2010, pp. 163–206.

12) Major sources for this section on the Airborne are H.S.G. Saunders, *The Red Beret*, London, 1950; T.B.H. Otway (ed), *Airborne Forces*, London, 1951; and *By Air to Battle*, HMSO, London, 1945.

13) Winston S. Churchill, *The Second World War*, Volume 3, p. 683.

14) HMSO, London, 1945, *By Air to Battle*, p. 12.

15) National Army Museum data for parachute (NAM 1983–06–37–3).

16) Much of the equipment mentioned is illustrated in Jean Bouchery, *The British Tommy*, Volume 1, Paris, 1998, pp. 92–103.

17) See also Martin Middlebrook, *Arnhem 1944*, London, 1994, pp. 20–89, 455–477.

18) *By Air to Battle*, HMSO, London, 1945, passim.

19) Stephen E. Ambrose, *Pegasus Bridge*, London, 1984, pp. 30–121.

20) Martin Middlebrook, *Arnhem 1944*, London, 1994, passim; Robert J. Kershaw, *It Never Snows in September*, Marlborough, 1990, passim.

21) William Seymour, *British Special Forces*, London, 1985, pp. 206–293.

22) Julian Thompson, *War Behind Enemy Lines*, London, 1998, 12–110.

23) *Ibid.*, pp. 257–292.

24) Roy Farran, *Winged Dagger*, new edition, London, 1998, p. 222.

25) William Seymour, *British Special Forces*, London, 1985, pp. 385–390.

26) Julian Thompson, *War Behind Enemy Lines*, London, 1998, pp. 297–380.

27) *Ibid.*, pp. 130–171.

28) Bernard Fergusson, *Beyond the Chindwin*, London, 1945, passim.

29) R.R. James, *Chindit*, London, 1980, pp. 93–204.

Poster for the Red Cross Prisoner 'penny a week fund' depicting RAF and Army prisoners. The 'Red Cross' parcel made a very significant difference to prisoners in Europe, and often the only thing that kept men alive in the Far East. (Author)

Give an **EXTRA** penny-a-week to the **RED CROSS PENNY-A-WEEK FUND**

30) Shelford Bidwell, *The Chindit War*, London, 1979, passim.

31) See also Julian Thompson, *War in Burma 1942–1945*, London, 2002, pp. 229–270.

AUXILIARY FORCES

1) Key sources for the Home Guard include, Charles Graves, *The Home Guard of Britain*, London, 1943; L.B. Whittaker, *Stand Down*, Newport, 1990; Simon P. MacKenzie, *The Home Guard: A Military and Political History*, Oxford, 1995.

2) Simon P. MacKenzie, *The Home Guard: A Military and Political History*, Oxford, 1995, pp. 18–37.

3) G.H. Lidstone, *On Guard! 10th (Torbay) Battalion Devonshire Home Guard*, Torquay, 1945, pp. 11–14.

4) *Special Army Order*, 19 July 1940.

5) Charles Graves, *The Home Guard of Britain*, London, 1943, p. 150.

6) Simon P. MacKenzie, *The Home Guard: A Military and Political History*, Oxford, 1995, pp. 37–86.

7) Charles Graves, *The Home Guard of Britain*, London, 1943 p. 228.

8) Cambridgeshire Territorial Association, *We Also Served*, Cambridge, 1944, p. 32.

9) Anonymous, *Record of the Birmingham City Transport Home Guard*, 1945, pp. 13–14.

10) *Ibid.*, pp. 12–24.

11) *Home Guard Instruction*, No. 38, September 1941, passim.

12) *Qualifications for, and Conditions Governing the Award of the Home Guard Proficiency Badges and Certificates,* May 1943, pp. 2–13, and *Amendment* number 3, June 1944.

13) Simon P. MacKenzie, *The Home Guard: A Military and Political History*, Oxford, 1995, pp. 87–129; Charles Graves, *The Home Guard of Britain*, London, 1943, pp. 123–168.

14) L.B. Whittaker, *Stand Down*, Newport, 1990, pp. 16–18.

15) Simon P. MacKenzie, *The Home Guard: A Military and Political History*, Oxford, 1995, p. 122.

16) Charles Graves, *The Home Guard of Britain*, London, 1943, p. 160.

17) Colonel G.W. Geddes, *The Guildford Home Guard*, Aldershot, undated, pp. 1–5.

18) *Ibid.*, pp. 6–33.

19) David Lampe, *The Last Ditch*, London, 1968, pp. 1–9, 58–150.

20) A small museum to the 'Aux' units was opened at Parham Airfield in 1997: a replica operational base was added in 2004.

21) *The Countryman's Diary*, 1939, passim.

22) K.R. Gulvin, *The Kent Home Guard*, Rochester, 1980, pp. 34–42.

23) Anonymous, *History of the Cheshire Home Guard*, Aldershot, 1950, p. 1; Anonymous, *5th Berkshire Battalion Home Guard*, Wantage, 1945, p. 37.

24) MacKenzie, pp. 122–125.

25) The section on women's services draws particularly on Shelford Bidwell, *The Women's Royal Army Corps*, London, 1977, pp. 1–133; Eileen Bigland, *Britain's Other Army: The Story of the ATS*, London, 1946; and J.M. Cowper, *The Auxiliary Territorial Service*, London, 1949.

26) See also Hugh Popham, *FANY: The Story of the Women's Transport Service, 1907–1984*, London, 1984, passim.

27) *People's Journal*, 23 February 1952, lead article.

28) Shelford Bidwell, *The Women's Royal Army Corps*, London, 1977, pp. 74–92.

29) Winston S. Churchill, *The Second World War*, Volume 3, 1950, p. 743.

30) Shelford Bidwell, *The Women's Royal Army Corps*, London, 1977, pp. 117–128.

31) Winston S. Churchill, *The Second World War*, Volume 6, 1954, pp. 653–654.

Allied servicemen in France: British troops meet Americans and French. (Author)

Bibliography

GENERAL

Ambrose, Stephen E., *Pegasus Bridge: D-day: The Daring British Airborne Raid*, London, 1984

Anon, *BBC War Report: 6 June 1944 to 5 May 1945*, Oxford, 1945

Atkinson, Rick, *An Army at Dawn: The War in Africa, 1942–1943*, London, 2003

Baker, Anthony, *Battle Honours of the British and Commonwealth Armies*, London, 1986

Bellis, M.A., *British Regiments 1939–45: Armour and Infantry*, Crewe, 2003

Bidwell, Shelford, *The Chindit War: Stilwell, Wingate, and the Campaign in Burma, 1944*, London, 1979

Bidwell, Shelford and Graham, Dominick, *Fire-Power: The British Army – Weapons and Theories of War, 1904–1945*, Winchester, 1982

Bierman, John and Smith, Colin, *Alamein: War Without Hate*, London, 2002

Cherry, Niall, *Striking Back: Britain's Airborne and Commando Raids 1940–42*, Solihull, 2009

Churchill, Randolph S. and Gilbert, Martin, *The Official Biography of Winston S. Churchill*, in eight volumes

Churchill, Winston S., *The Second World War*, London, 1948

Dear, I.C.B. (ed), *The Oxford Companion to World War II*, Oxford, 1995

D'Este, Carlo, *Decision in Normandy: The Real Story of Montgomery and the Allied Campaign*, London, 1983

Eisenhower, Dwight D., *Crusade in Europe*, London, 1948

Elliot, Andrew G., *The Home Guard Encyclopedia*, London, 1942

Ellis, Chris and Chamberlain, Peter (eds), *Handbook of the British Army 1943*, London, 1975

Ellis, John, *The Sharp End: The Fighting Man in World War II*, London, 1980

Forty, George, *The British Army Handbook 1939–1945*, Stroud, 1998

Fraser, David, *And We Shall Shock Them: The British Army in the Second World War*, London, 1983

Frederick, J.B.M., *Lineage Book of British Land Forces 1660–1978* (2 volumes, revised edition), Wakefield, 1984

French, David, *Raising Churchill's Army: The British Army and the War Against Germany 1919–1945*, Oxford, 2000

Gorman, J.T., *The British Army of Today*, London, 1939

Heathcote, T.A., *The British Field Marshalls 1736–1997: A Biographical Dictionary*, London, 1999

Holmes, Richard, *Churchill's Bunker: The Secret Headquarters at the Heart of Britain's Victory*, London, 2009

Howlett, Peter, *Fighting with Figures: A Statistical Digest of the Second World War*, London, 1995

Imperial War Museum, *Review* (12 volumes), London, 1986–1999

Joslen, H.F., *Orders of Battle: Second World War 1939–45*, London, 1960

Kersaudy, Francois, *Norway 1940*, London, 1990

Kershaw, Robert, *Tank Men: The Human Story of Tanks at War*, London, 2008

Knight, Nigel, *Churchill: The Greatest Briton Unmasked*, Newton Abbot, 2008

Lampe, David, *The Last Ditch: Britain's Resistance Plans Against the Nazis* (1968, new edition), London, 2007

MacDonald, Callum, *The Lost Battle: Crete 1941*, London, 1993

MacRae, Stuart, *Winston Churchill's Toyshop: The Inside Story of Military Intelligence (Research)*, new edition, Stroud, 2010

Mead, Peter, *Orde Wingate and the Historians*, Braunton, 1987

Middlebrook, Martin, *Arnhem 1944: The Airborne Battle*, London, 1994

Place, Timothy Harrison, *Military Training in the British Army, 1940–1944: From Dunkirk to D-Day*, London, 2000

Seymour, William, *British Special Forces*, London, 1986

Smart, Nick, *Biographical Dictionary of British Generals of the Second World War*, Barnsley, 2005

Swinson, Arthur, *A Register of the Regiments and Corps of the British Army*, London, 1972

Thompson, Julian, *The Imperial War Museum Book of the War in Burma 1942–1945*, London, 2002

Thompson, Julian, *The Imperial War Museum Book of War Behind Enemy Lines: Special Forces in Action, 1940–45*, London, 1998

Van Meel, Rob, *War Establishments British Airborne Forces*, Netherlands, undated

War Office, *Index to Army Orders, 1940*, London, 1941

White, Arthur S., *A Bibliography of Regimental Histories of the British Army* (new edition), Dallington, 1992

Whittaker, L.B., *Stand Down: Orders of Battle for Units of the Home Guard of the United Kingdom, November 1944*, Newport, 1990

Wills, Henry, *Pillboxes: A Study of the UK Defences 1940*, London, 1985

SMALL ARMS

Auto-Ordnance Corporation, *Handbook of the Thompson Submachine Gun: Model of 1928: Model M1: Edition of 1940*, Bridgeport, 1940

Buerlein, Robert A., *Allied Military Fighting Knives: And the Men Who Made Them Famous*, Boulder, 2001

Dugelby, T.B., *The Bren Gun Saga*, Toronto, 1986

Easterly, William M., *The Belgian Rattlesnake: The Lewis Automatic*, Ontario, 1998

Goldsmith, Dolf L., *The Grand Old lady of No Man's Land*, Ontario, 1994

Hill, Tracie L., *Thompson: The American Legend: The First Submachine Gun*, Ontario, 1996

Hobart, F.W.A., *Pictorial History of the Sub-Machine Gun*, London, 1973

Hogg, Ian V., *Encyclopedia of Infantry Weapons of World War II*, London, 1977

Iannamico, Frank, *The British Sten Manual for Shooters and Collectors*, Harmony, 1997

Landers, Rick, *Identification Handbook of British Grenades 1900–1960*, Dural, 2002

Marshall, T.C., *British Grenades*, Novato, 1982

Norris, John, *Infantry Mortars of World War II*, Oxford, 2002

Putnam, T. and Weinbren, D., *A Short History of the Royal Small Arms Factory Enfield*, Middlesex University, 1995

Robson, Brian, *Swords of the British Army: The Regulation Patterns 1788 to 1914*, London, 1975

Skennerton, Ian D., *An Introduction to British Grenades*, Margate, 1988

Skennerton, Ian D., *British Small Arms of World War 2*, Margate, 1988

Skennerton, Ian D., *The British Service Lee: The Lee-Metford and Lee-Enfield Rifles and Carbines 1880–1980*, Margate, 1982

Skennerton, Ian D., *The British Sniper: British and Commonwealth Sniping and Equipment*, Margate, 1983

Truby, J.D., *The Lewis Gun*, Boulder, 1986

UNIFORMS, BADGES, AND MEDALS

Bouchery, Jean, *The British Soldier: From D-Day to VE Day*, Paris, 1998

Brayley, Martin J., *British Web Equipment of the Two World Wars*, Marlborough, 2005

Brayley, Martin and Ingram, Richard, *Khaki Drill and Jungle Green: British Tropical Uniforms 1939–45 in Colour Photographs*, Marlborough, 2000

Brayley, Martin and Ingram, Richard, *The World War II Tommy: British Army Uniforms, European Theatre 1939–45*, Marlborough, 1998

Brayley, Martin and Ingram, Richard, *World War II British Women's Uniforms*, London, 1995

Buzzell, Nora, *The Register of the Victoria Cross*, Cheltenham, 1988

Chappell, Mike, *British Battle Insignia 1939–1945*, London, 1987

Chappell, Mike, *British Cavalry Equipments 1800–1941*, London, 1983

Chappell, Mike, *British Infantry Equipments 1908–1980*, London, 1980.

Chappell, Mike, *The Guards Divisions 1914–1945*, London, 1995

Churchill, Colin and Westlake, Ray A., *British Army Collar Badges*, London, 1986

Cole, Howard N., *Formation Badges of World War Two: Britain, Commonwealth and Empire*, London, 1985

Cole, Howard N., *Coronation and Royal Commemorative Medals 1887–1977*, London, 1977

Crook, M.J., *The Evolution of the Victoria Cross*, Speldhurst, 1975

Davis, Brian L., *British Army Cloth Insignia: 1940 to the Present*, London, 1985

Davis, Brian L., *British Army Uniforms and Insignia of World War Two*, London, 1983

Dawnay, N.P., *The Badges of Warrant and Non-Commissioned Rank in the British Army, Society for Army Historical Research*, London, 1949

Edwards, Denis and Langley, David, *British Army Proficiency Badges*, Prestatyn, 1984

Fisch, Robert W., *Field Equipment of the Infantry, 1914–1945*, Sykesville, 1989

Hanham, Andrew, *A Manual for the Wearing of Orders, Decorations and Medals*, London, 2005

Harfield, Alan G., *Headdress, Badges and Embellishments of the Royal Corps of Signals*, Chippenham, 1982

Jewell, Brian and Chappell, Mike, *British Battledress, 1937–1961*, London, 1981

Joslin, E.C. (et al), *British Battles and Medals*, London, 1988

Kipling, Arthur L. and King, Hugh L., *Head Dress Badges of the British Army* (volume 2), London, 1979

Linaker, David and Dine, Gordon, *Cavalry Warrant Officer and Non Commissioned Officers' Arm Badges*, London, 1997

Litherland, A.R. and Simpkin, B.T., *Standard Catalogue of British and Associated Orders, Decorations and Medals*, London, 1990

Ripley, Howard, *Buttons of the British Army 1855–1970*, London, 1971

Rosignoli, Guido, *Army Badges and Insignia of World War II* (volume 1), London, 1972

Spencer, William, *Medals: The Researcher's Guide*, London, 2006

Tylden, Major G., *Horses and Saddlery*, London, 1965

War Office, *Dress Regulations for the Army*, London, 1934

Weeks, John *Airborne Equipment*, Newton Abbot, 1976

Westlake, Ray A., *Collecting Metal Shoulder Titles*, London, 1980

TANKS, VEHICLES AND ARTILLERY

Anon, *Churchill Tank: Vehicle History and Specification*, London, 1983

Anon, *Cromwell Tank: Vehicle History and Specification*, London, 1983

Baker, A.D. (ed), *Allied Landing Craft of World War II*, London, 1985

Beale, Peter, *Death by Design: British Tank Development in the Second World War*, Stroud, 1998

Boniface, J.M. and Jeudy, J.G. *US Army Vehicles of World War II*, Newbury Park, 1991

Chamberlain, Peter and Ellis, Chris, *Making Tracks: British Carrier Story 1914–1972*, Windsor, 1973

Crow, Duncan, *British and Commonwealth Armoured Formations 1919–1946*, Windsor, 1971

Fletcher, David, *Mechanised Force: British Tanks Between the Wars*, HMSO, 1991

Fletcher, David, *Mr Churchill's Tank: The British Infantry Tank Mark IV*, Atglen, 1999

Fletcher, David, *Sherman Firefly*, Oxford, 2008

Fletcher, David, *The Universal Carrier 1936–48*, Oxford, 2005

Fletcher, David, *The Universal Tank: British Armour in the Second World War*, HMSO, 1993

Forty, George, *United States Tanks of World War II*, Poole, 1983

Foss, Christopher F. and McKenzie Peter, *The Vickers Tanks*, Wellingborough, 1988

Gregg, W.A., *Canada's Fighting Vehicles: Europe 1943–1945*, Oakville, 1980

Gudgin, Peter, *Armoured Firepower: The Development of Tank Armament 1939–1945*, Stroud, 1997

Hogg, Ian V., *British and American Artillery of World War Two*, London, 1978

Hunnicutt, R.P., *Half-Track: A History of American Semi-Tracked Vehicles*, Novato, 2001

Orchard, C.J. and Madden, S.J., *British Forces Motorcycles, 1925–1945*, Stroud, 1995

Perrett, Bryan, *The Matilda*, London, 1973

Turner, John T., *'Nellie': The History of Churchill's Lincoln Built Trenching Machine*, Gainsborough, 1988

White, Brian Terence, *British Tanks and Fighting Vehicles 1914–1945*, London, 1970

White, B.T., *British Tank Markings and Names*, London, 1978

MANUALS

Anon, *The Sten Machine Carbine*, Aldershot, undated

Anon, *The Countryman's Diary 1939 (Home Guard Auxiliary)*, c.1942

Barlow, J.A. and Johnson, R.E.W., *Small Arms Manual* (revised edition), 1943

Bodman, H.W., *Sten Machine Carbine*, Bradford-on-Avon, 1942

Burke, Edmund Tytler, *Tropical Tips for Troops*, London, 1941

Fairbairn, W.E. and Sykes, E.A., *All in Fighting*, 1942

Green, A.F.U., *Home Guard Pocket Book*, Worthing, 1940

Commander-in-Chief, Home Forces, *The Instructor's Handbook on Fieldcraft and Battle Drill*, 1942

Commander-in-Chief, Home Forces, *Home Guard Instructions, 43; 51; 64*, 1942–1944

HMSO, *National Service*, London, 1939

Levy, A., *Guerrilla Warfare*, London, 1941

Military Intelligence (US), *British Commandos*, Washington, 1942

War Office, *Aids to Visual Deception, MTP No. 57*, 1943

War Office, *AFV Recognition: British and Allied Turreted AFVs*, 1942

War Office, *Annual Range Courses, Small Arms Training* (volume 1, No. 14), 1938

War Office, *AFV Recognition: British and Allied Turreted AFVs*, 1942

War Office, *Army Equipment News Bulletin, No. 9*, 1943

War Office, *Bayonet, Small Arms Training* (volume 1, No. 12), 1942

War Office, *Combined Operations: RA*, 1943

War Office, *Dannert Concertina Wire Obstacles, MTP No. 21*, 1939

War Office, *Handbook on Clothing and Equipment Required in Cold Climates*, 1941

War Office, *Individual Battle Practices, Small Arms Training* (volume 1, No. 18, Supplement 1), 1943

War Office, *Infantry Training*, 1937

War Office, *Infantry Training*, 1944

War Office, *Light Machine Gun, Small Arms Training* (volume 1, No. 4), 1942

War Office, *Manual of Driving and Maintenance for Mechanical Vehicles (Wheeled)*, 1937

War Office, *Manual of Field Engineering*, 1936

War Office, *Notes From Theatres of War, No. 13, North Africa – Algeria and Tunisia*, 1943

War Office, *Notes on Concealment and Camouflage*, 1938

War Office, *Notes on the Tactical Handling of the Carrier Platoon in the Attack, MTP No. 13*, 1939

War Office, *Projector Infantry Anti-Tank, Small Arms Training* (volume 1, No. 24), 1943

War Office, *Small Arms Training*, 1931

War Office, *Tactical Handling of Flame-Throwers, MTP No. 68*, 1945

War Office, *The Soldier's Welfare: Notes For Officers*, 1941

UNIT HISTORIES

Anon, *5th Berkshire Battalion Home Guard*, Wantage, 1945

Anon, *History of the 359 (4th West Lancashire) Medium Regiment RA (TA)*, Liverpool, 1959

Anon, *History of the Cheshire Home Guard*, Aldershot, 1950

Anon, *Record of the Birmingham City Transport Home Guard*, Birmingham, 1945

Anon, *Royal Devon Yeomanry*, Eastbourne, 1947

Anon, *The Royal Artillery Commemoration Book 1939–1945*, London, 1950

Bailey, Harry, *Playboys: 'B' Squadron 141st Regiment RAC*, Leeds, undated

Barclay, C.N., *The History of the Cameronians, volume 3, 1933–1946*, London, 1949

Barclay, C.N., *The History of the Duke of Wellington's Regiment, 1919–1952*, London, 1953

Barclay, C.N., *The History of the Sherwood Foresters, 1919–1957*, London, 1959

Barnes, B.S., *The Sign of the Double 'T'*, Hull, 1999

Beddington, W.R., *A History of the Queen's Bays 1929–1945*, Winchester, 1954

Bidwell, Shelford, *The Women's Royal Army Corps*, London, 1977

Blacker, Cecil and Woods, H.G., *5th Royal Inniskilling Dragoon Guards: Change and Challenge 1928–1978*, London, 1978

Blight, Gordon, *The History of the Royal Berkshire Regiment*, London, 1953

Bright, Joan (ed), *The Ninth Queen's Royal Lancers, 1936–1945*, Aldershot, 1951

Borthwick, Alastair, *Battalion*, London, 1994

Brett, G.A. (et al), *The History of the South Wales Borderers and The Monmouthshire Regiment 1937–1952*, 5 vols, Pontypool, 1953–1956

Brett-Smith, Richard, *The 11th Hussars*, London, 1969

Brophy, John, *Britain's Home Guard*, London, 1945

Bull, Stephen, *Lancashire Gunners at War: The 88th Field Regiment*, Lancaster, 1999

Cambridgeshire, T.A. Association, *We Also Served: The Story of the Home Guard in Cambridgeshire and the Isle of Ely*, Cambridge, 1944

Chaplin, H.D., *The Queen's Own Royal West Kent Regiment, 1920–1950*, London, 1954

Cocks, A.E., *Churchill's Secret Army 1939–45*, Lewes, 1992

Courage, G., *The History of the 15th/19th The King's Royal Hussars*, Aldershot, 1949

Crookenden, Arthur, *The History of the Cheshire Regiment in the Second World War*, Chester, 1949

Crozier, S.F., *The History of the Corps of Royal Military Police*, Aldershot, 1951

Cunliffe, Marcus, *History of the Royal Warwickshire Regiment 1919–1955*, London, 1956

Cunliffe, Marcus, *The Royal Irish Fusiliers*, London, 1952

Daniell, David Scott, *4th Hussar: The Story of the 4th Queen's Own Hussars*, Aldershot, 1959

Delaforce, Patrick, *Churchill's Desert Rats*, Stroud, 1994

Delaforce, Patrick, *Monty's Highlanders*, Stroud, 2000

Delaforce, Patrick, *Monty's Iron Sides*, Stroud, 1995

Delaforce, Patrick, *The Fighting Wessex Wyverns*, Stroud, 1994

Delaforce, Patrick, *The Polar Bears*, Stroud, 1995

Dean, C.G.T., *The Loyal Regiment (North Lancashire) 1919–1953*, Preston, 1958

Dunning, James, *The British Commandos*, Boulder, 2000

Dunning, James, *The Fighting Fourth: No. 4 Commando at War 1940–45*, Stroud, 2003

Durnford-Slater, John, *Commando*, London, 1953

Ellenberger, G.F., *History of the King's Own Yorkshire Light Infantry, volume 6, 1939–1948*, Aldershot, 1961

Ellis, L.F., *Welsh Guards at War*, Aldershot, 1946

Erskine, David, *The Scots Guards 1919–1945*, London, 1956

Ferguson, Gregor, *The Paras: British Airborne Forces 1940–1984*, London, 1984

Fitzgerald, D.J.L., *The Irish Guards in the Second World War*, Aldershot, 1949

Forbes, Patrick, *6th Guards Tank Brigade*, London, 1946

Foster, R.C.G., *History of the Queen's Royal Regiment, volume 8, 1924–1948*, Aldershot, 1953

Fox, Frank, *The Royal Inniskilling Fusiliers in the Second World War*, Aldershot, 1951

Graves, Charles, *The Home Guard of Britain*, London, 1943

Gulvin, K.R., *Kent Home Guard*, Rochester, 1980

Gunning, H., *Borderers in Battle*, Berwick, 1948

Hart, Peter, *The Heat of Battle: 16th Battalion Durham Light Infantry, 1943–1945*, Barnsley, 1999

Hastings, R.H.W.S., *The Rifle Brigade in the Second World War*, Aldershot, 1950

Holman, Gordon, *Commando Attack*, London, 1942

Hornby, Robin Montague (et al), *5th Berkshire Battalion Home Guard*, Wantage, 1945

Jervois, Wilfred John, *The History of the Northamptonshire Regiment, 1934–1948*, Northampton, 1953

Jocelyne, R.A., *'A' Squadron War Diary, 7th Royal Tank Regiment*,

Krefeld, 1946

Knight, R., *The 59th Division*, Worcester, 1954

Ladd, James D., *Commandos and Rangers of World War II*, London, 1979

Langley, Michael, *The Loyal Regiment*, London, 1976

Lidstone, G.H. (ed), *On Guard! A History of 10th (Torbay) Battalion Devonshire Home Guard*, Torquay, 1945

Lomax, C.E.N. (et al), *The History of the Welch Regiment, 1919–1951*, Cardiff, 1952

Longmate, Norman, *The Real Dad's Army*, London, 1974

Mackenzie, Simon P., *The Home Guard*, Oxford, 1995

Martin, T.A., *The Essex Regiment, 1929–1950*, Brentwood, 1952

McCorquodale, D., *History of the King's Dragoon Guards, 1938–1945*, Glasgow, 1950

Meredith, J.L.J., *From Normandy to Hannover: The Story of the Seventh Battalion The Somerset light Infantry*, Germany, 1945

Miles, Wilfrid, *The Gordon Highlanders 1919–1945*, Aberdeen, 1961

Miller, C.H., *History of the 13th/18th Royal Hussars*, London, 1949

Mortimer, Gavin, *Stirling's Men*, London, 2004

Mullaly, B.R., *The South Lancashire Regiment*, Bristol, 1952

Murland, J.R.W., *The Royal Armoured Corps*, London, 1943

Nalder, R.F.H., *The History of the Royal Army Signals in the Second World War*, London, 1953

Neillands, Robin, *The Raiders: The Army Commandos*, London, 1989

Nicholson, Nigel and Forbes, Patrick, *The Grenadier Guards in the War of 1939–1945*, Aldershot, 1945

Nicholson, Nigel, *The Suffolk Regiment, 1928–1946*, Ipswich, 1948

Parkinson, C. Northcote, *Always a Fusilier: The War History of the Royal Fusiliers*, London, 1949

Pitman, Stuart, *Second Royal Gloucestershire Hussars*, London, 1952

Orde, R., *The Household Cavalry at War*, Aldershot, 1953

Otway, T.B.H. (ed), *Airborne Forces*, London, 1951

Owen, F. and Atkins, H.W., *The Royal Armoured Corps*, London, 1945

Popham, Hugh, *FANY: The Story of the Women's Transport Service, 1907–1984*, London, 1984

Popham, Hugh, *The Somerset Light Infantry*, London, 1968

Reeves, Dennis, *Special Service of a Hazardous Nature: The Story of Liverpool Scottish Involvement in Special Forces Operations*, Liverpool, 2007

Rhodes-James, Richard, *Chindit*, London, 1980

Rhodes-Wood, Edward Harold, *A War History of the Royal Pioneer Corps*, Aldershot, 1960

Robertson, G.W., *The Rose and Arrow: A Life Story of 136th (1st West Lancashire) Field Regiment Royal Artillery*, Dorset, undated

Saunders, Hilary St George, *The Red Beret*, London, 1950

Scarfe, Norman, *Assault Division: A History of 3rd Division*, London, 1947

Shears, Philip J., *The Story of the Border Regiment, 1939–1945*, London, 1948

Stringer, L.E., *The History of the 16th Battalion Durham Light Infantry, 1940–1946*, Graz, 1946

Synge, W.A.T., *The Story of the Green Howards, 1939–1945*, Richmond, 1952

Underhill, W.E. (ed), *The Royal Leicestershire Regiment*, Plymouth, 1958

Watson, D.Y., *The First Battalion the Worcestershire Regiment in North West Europe*, Worcester, 1948

White, O.G.W., *Straight on For Tokyo: The War History of the 2nd Battalion The Dorsetshire Regiment*, Aldershot, 1948

Wilson, H.M. (et al), *The History of the 1st Battalion The Royal Norfolk Regiment during the World War, 1939–1945*, Norwich, 1947

MEMOIRS

Churchill, Thomas, *Commando Crusade*, London, 1987

Cochrane, Peter, *Charlie Company: In Service with C Company the 2nd Queen's Own Cameron Highlanders*, London, 1977

Farran, Roy, *Winged Dagger*, London, 1948

Fergusson, Bernard, *Beyond the Chindwin*, London, 1945

Horrocks, Brian, *A Full Life*, London, 1960

Merewood, Jack, *To War with The Bays*, Cardiff, 1996

Montgomery, Viscount B.L., *Normandy to the Baltic*, London, 1947

Shaw Frank and Joan, *We Remember the Home Guard*, Hinckley, 1990

Shore, Clifford, *With British Snipers to the Reich* (new edition), London, 1997

Swaab, Jack, *Field of Fire: Diary of a Gunner Officer*, Stroud, 2005

Wavell, Archibald Percival, *The Good Soldier*, London, 1948

White, Peter, *With the Jocks*, Stroud, 2001

Young, Peter, *Storm from the Sea* (new edition), London, 1989

Index